Europe by Rail

The Definitive Guide

Nicky Gardner and Susanne Kries

Fully updated 16th edition

hidden europe publications

EUROPE BY RAIL: THE DEFINITIVE GUIDE

Sixteenth edition. Published October 2019.

ISBN 978-3-945225-02-8

Published by
hidden europe publications
Gardner u. Kries GbR, Geraer Str. 14-c, D-12209 Berlin, Germany
www.hiddeneurope.co.uk

Design and layout by hidden europe editorial bureau of Berlin, Germany
Printed and bound by GraphyCems of Villatuerta (Navarra), Spain
Distribution by SaltWay Global Ltd of Cirencester, England

Colour maps on inside covers by David McCutcheon FBCart.S., www.dvdmaps.co.uk.

Our front cover image shows a train departing Blair Atholl station in Scotland. Blair Atholl is on Route 2 in this book (photo © lucentius / istockphoto.com).

This book has a dedicated website at www.europebyrail.eu
There is an associated twitter account at www.twitter.com/europebyrail
Follow us on facebook at www.facebook.com/europebyrailguide and find us on Instagram at www.instagram.com/europebyrailguide

The authors can be contacted by e-mail at editors@europebyrail.eu

Disclaimer
The authors have done their level best to make sure that the information published in this book is accurate. But things can change. A hotel remembered with affection may have turned into a dive, and of course public transport timetables change. Entire rail routes may close. So always check details before setting out, and bear in mind that savvy local advice may be worth much more than what you read in a guidebook. If you feel that we have made a mistake somewhere, please do let us know. But do note that neither the authors nor the publisher can accept any responsibility for loss, damage, injury or inconvenience occasioned by material included, or anything not mentioned, in this book or on any websites maintained by the authors or publisher.

GAZETTEER   446

A country-by-country guide to exploring Europe by rail in alphabetical order: major countries listed here, for others see the gazetteer

REFERENCE SECTION

A word of welcome

For well over two decades, successive editions of *Europe by Rail* have shaped travellers' plans, encouraging readers to be more adventurous. With **tips on ticketing, fares and accommodation**, *Europe by Rail* has become the definitive guide to exploring Europe by train. This 16th edition of the book highlights the rich and intriguing possibilities that await, whether it be for a handful of short trips or for a more extended tour.

Rail travel is convivial in a way that is nowadays rarely encountered on planes and has never been a feature of car travel. We have swapped stories with strangers on trains in Ukraine, we have been on trains marooned in deep midwinter snow in Scandinavia and we have shared meals on night trains that slipped in the dark past silent factories in unnamed towns.

In preparing this new edition, we have criss-crossed Europe by train, from fast journeys on **sleek expresses** to memorably **slow meanderings** on remote branch lines. We have taken slow trains through Belarus and even slower trains through Bohemia. We've also introduced five entirely new routes covering Britain and Ireland. We also reworked our Balkan routes, responding to many reader requests that we include the spectacular journey from Belgrade to the port of Bar on the Adriatic coast. Throughout the book, we have included many new accommodation options, favouring hotels which are close to railway stations and have a touch of character.

Forces of nationalism threaten to split Europe at the moment. But rail travel is a great unifier. Trains bring places and people closer. Is it not a matter of wonder that one can board a night train in the Rhineland and alight next morning in the Austrian Tyrol? Or travel from Nice or Paris directly to Russia?

The **Interrail pass programme** has since 1972 been a potent force in fostering mutual understanding between Europeans. We know that many readers of this book, be they young or old, will be using Interrail passes. Interrail (along with a sister scheme called **Eurail** – for those not resident in Europe) remains in our view the best choice for those intent on following some of the longer journeys in this book. We take a look at how Interrail has evolved on pp11–13. In North America, **Rail Europe** (which sold the very first Eurail passes way back in 1959) has since the early 1930s played a seminal role in shaping Americans' perceptions of Europe as a potential travel destination. It was organisations like Rail Europe, along with the Interrail and Eurail schemes, which in their early advertising gave prominence to the journey rather than merely the destination.

THE JOURNEY OR THE DESTINATION?

With the development of Europe's first railways, people were suddenly on the move, with the restless English often leading the way. The guidebook market blossomed as travellers packed a **Baedeker** or a **Murray** before embarking on a new journey. Today's traveller is more likely to turn to the Internet, just before departure hurriedly downloading a few pages on their chosen destination. More people than ever are travelling, but many just dash to their destination – and the range of favoured destinations tends to narrow rather than widen.

In travelling by train around Europe, it is possible to rediscover the sheer joy of the journey itself. Trains are fun. So in *Europe by Rail* we put the journey at the centre. We present **52 rail routes** that between them cover the full gamut of European rail travel. There are routes where trains speed across great plains, routes where slow trains dawdle from one village to another and there are routes where trains traverse harsh tundra and great mountain ranges. In addition to our 52 routes, we offer **25 mini-features** (called Sidetracks); these are bite-size teasers which invite you to reflect on rail-related themes or venture into regions not covered by our 52 routes.

Travel by train across Europe and you will inevitably be struck by the sheer variety of our continent. Our 52 routes reflect that mix. We include some high-speed hops, where you can cover a lot of ground fast. But we also highlight slow trains that follow less-frequented rail routes. It is on such journeys that the **texture and detail of European life** is most easily appreciated, whether it be in the changing landscapes beyond the carriage window, the architecture of villages you pass through along the way or in the faces and accents of fellow travellers with whom you share a railway carriage.

The opening of new rail routes has slashed journey times. Today's traveller can take an early morning **Eurostar from London** and by mid-afternoon be standing on the shores of the Mediterranean. A judicious combination of daytime high-speed services and overnight trains allows longer journeys across the continent to be undertaken very comfortably by train. Few experiences compare with opening the blinds of the night sleeper in the morning to find a fragile blanket of morning mist over a foreign landscape. You can read more about **night trains** on pp520–22.

The imaginations of travellers today are unfettered. Classic destinations like the Rhine, Switzerland and the northern shores of the Mediterranean no longer command attention to the exclusion of other parts of Europe. The routes in this book will take you far **beyond the Arctic Circle** and on

A WORD OF THANKS

We offer our sincere thanks to the many writers who contributed to earlier editions of the book, so **helping shape a volume** which has evolved over nearly a quarter of a century. Thanks are due to David McCutcheon of DVD maps for producing the colour overview maps which appear on the inside front and back covers of this edition. We also wish to thank Murray Mahon and Chris McLaren of SaltWay Global Ltd for handling the worldwide distribution of *Europe by Rail*.

mountain railways across the Pyrenees and the Alps. We shall lead you from **great cities** in eastern Europe to the **Irish hills**, from Balkan byways to the Baltic and the Bay of Biscay.

Taking time

Some readers might try and undertake a dozen or more of these routes within a month. We would just sound a note of caution. That way madness lies. Better to focus a little, and take time to **stop off here and there** along the way. Branch out from main rail routes and choose slower trains on at least some parts of your journey to discover the **joys of Slow Travel**. You can get some inspiration by reading our *Manifesto for Slow Travel* at www. slowtraveleurope.eu. Exploring Europe by rail is a great way to put Slow Travel principles into practice.

Rethinking our relationship with travel is no mere luxury. It's now an absolutely necessity to save our home planet. Across much of Europe, people are **switching from air to rail**. Train travel is often modestly priced, generally very comfortable and appeals to the pieties of a new generation of environmentally aware travellers. It was surely not by chance that the very first public Eurostar train to leave London's magnificently refurbished St Pancras International station (12 years ago in November 2007) was powered by two engines with the names *Tread Lightly* and *Voyage Vert*. The train comes with green credentials.

Practicalities

Travel light if you possibly can. Heavy luggage and trains do not make good companions. Take this book along of course, and don't forget to take a print copy of the **European Rail Timetable**, frequently referred to as 'ERT' in this book. This veritable masterpiece of compression is published six times each year (see www.europeanrailtimetable.eu). An up-to-date copy of that timetable, and the *Rail Map Europe* (also published by European Rail Timetable Ltd), are natural partners to this volume. Guidebook, map, timetable – these three remain the indispensable assets in the traveller's armamentarium.

So are you game to join us on this journey? The best way to get started is to read 'How to use this book' (p14). You will find **useful maps** on the inside front cover and inside back cover showing the routes in this volume (numbered 1 to 52). And you may like to know that we have a website to accompany this book at www.europebyrail.eu.

Enjoy the ride.

Nicky Gardner and Susanne Kries
October 2019

Rail passes in perspective

Feedback from readers of earlier editions of *Europe by Rail* often prompts us to reflect on how **rail travel is changing**. A common thought among older readers of previous editions was: "Interrail isn't the same as in the early days." Several correspondents have contacted us with stories of how Interrail and Eurail have lost their gloss. Yet we think that both schemes can offer tremendous value, all the more so since they were revamped in 2019.

"Too many supplements nowadays," moaned a Danish reader, who explained how, although Greta Thunberg wouldn't approve, she will take the plane next summer for the journey from Stockholm to Sorrento rather than having to pay "all sorts of extras on top of the cost of a rail pass."

"It's not like it was forty years ago," said another reader, "when you could just hop on any train and travel where you wanted."

MYTHS OF LONG-LOST HALYCON DAYS

We agree that supplements and reservation fees really undermine the benefits of a pass. But we should put the record straight. There never was a time, not even back in the **early days of Interrail**, when travellers with a pass could just hop on any train without having to bother with reservations. It has become part of the mythology of Interrail that there was a great moment in history when the pass cost hardly anything and one could travel across Europe without having to worry about reservations and supplements. Memories of holidays in our youth invariably become rose-tinted with the passage of time.

Let's take a closer look. **Interrail has certainly changed** in the nearly half-century since it was launched, and in our view it is a better value and more flexible product today than it was back in 1972. Read more about what's on offer in our rail pass briefing on pp525–28. We have investigated how the cost of the classic global youth pass has increased in price over the years and it is clear that incomes have increased far more rapidly than have pass prices. Today's Interrail pass allows completely free travel in more countries and on many more trains than did the earliest Interrail passes. The **rules for the Global Pass** were recently amended to allow two journeys in the pass holder's home country. This is a considerable bonus.

True, there have been some **big changes in the night train market**, and some overnight services have been withdrawn. Day trains have sped up so much that there is simply less need to travel overnight. The night trains that remain, generally on longer-distance routes, have moved upmarket with sleeping cars and couchette coaches replacing long rakes of carriages with regular seated accommodation. Travellers today evidently like their creature comforts, and superior accommodation requires a supplement – just as it did in the earliest days of Interrail.

No-go zones for the pioneers of Interrail

Turn to the day train market, and Interrail always came laced with all sorts of restrictions. The entire *Trans-Europe Express* (TEE) network was simply out-of-bounds to pass holders. This was not a question of having to pay a supplement. **TEE was a complete no-go area** for Interrail travellers. Prime-time departures from Zurich to Munich (on the *Bavaria*), Hamburg (the *Helvetia*) and Paris (*L'Arbalète*) were barred to pass holders. The same applied to sensibly timed morning trains from Milan to Geneva (the *Lemano*), Nice (the *Ligure*), Lyon (the *Mont Cenis*) and Munich (the *Mediolanum*).

France was as difficult for the Interrail pioneers as it can still be today. The fastest trains on key routes from Paris to the provinces (eg. on the lines to Toulouse and Clermont-Ferrand as well as on services to Alsace and the Rhône Valley) were all first-class only and thus not available to Interrail pass holders. Even more annoyingly, Interrail was **barred on some regional services** where alternatives were slow or circuitous. For example on the only Rapide of the day from Nantes and Tours to Lyon Interrail was not valid. Perversely, or so it seemed to pass holders, SNCF would not accept Interrail on the sole daily direct train from Bordeaux to Grenoble.

Many trains on prime routes to the **Adriatic resorts** of what was then Yugoslavia were barred to holders of Interrail passes. This meant that pass holders could not use the *Marjan Express* from Zagreb to Split, the *Arena* from Zagreb to Pula or the fastest trains from Zagreb to Rijeka. Similarly, the *Sarajevo Express* from Belgrade to Sarajevo was a no-go zone for holders of an Interrail pass.

The secret of rail pass success: taking the slow train

The early users of Interrail passes worked around the complicated web of restrictions. They eschewed the premium services and took slower options. And they did not complain. Free was free and they rejoiced at being able to travel from northern Norway to the toe of Italy without having to pay a cent beyond that initial outlay for an Interrail pass.

That is still perfectly possible today. Nothing has changed except the **horizons of a new generation of travellers** that values high-speed and long-distance as virtues in their own right. Very few early Interrail pass holders set off to conquer huge swathes of Europe in a single trip. How times have changed. Today folk set out with the notion that Poland and Portugal must be clocked within the compass of a fortnight.

Those who have used Interrail a few times know the **secret of success**. Less is more. Slower trains offer a far better perspective on European land-scapes. And the local service allows a better engagement with the communities through which you pass. Nowadays, supplement-free slower trains criss-crossing Europe are generally very much faster than they were in the 1970s. The fastest daytime service on the Barcelona-Zaragoza-Madrid route in the early 1970s took 13 hours for the 680-km journey. To use that premium service, holders of Interrail passes had to pay a special high-speed supplement. Yes, there was a time when fifty kilometres per hour counted as high speed. Today the slow train dashes from Barcelona to Madrid in just over nine hours. No supplement. No need to book. Just hop on and ride. Yet if you are in a rush, you can pay a supplement to ride the fast AVE train.

ALTERNATIVES TO HIGH-SPEED TRAINS

Slow trains have become very much faster over the years, and in our view they are the **best way to use Interrail**. If you want to speed across France on a TGV, the option is there, but you'll need to book a seat and pay a supplement. That means committing yourself to a particular itinerary. So easy is it nowadays to buy cheap tickets on premium trains across Europe, that Interrail hardly makes sense on those fastest trains. If you must make haste on certain legs of your itinerary, book high-speed services well in advance and your point-to-point ticket may work out cheaper than a rail pass.

Where the **pass really comes into its own** is on slower journeys and rural routes where there are few cheap deals on offer. Dynamic pricing means great offers on busy routes, but shift to lesser routes and you may find that old-style distance-based tariffs are the only option. Interrail is superb for such slower journeys. It preserves total flexibility, you can stop off on a whim, and you can savour the serendipitous delays and diversions that come with slow travel. One of our favourite writers, an early exponent of slow travel, is **Théophile Gautier**. "What charm can there be in a journey when one is always sure to arrive," queried Gautier in 1843.

SLOWNESS AS A PRIVILEGE OF WEALTH

Interrail allows us to escape the rush of modernity and to **rediscover a slower Europe**. True, you might well still move faster than the snail's pace that characterised the itineraries of the Interrail pioneers.

How often have we heard the mantra: "But I need to cover a lot of distance and stick to fast trains. If I don't I'll not be getting the best value out of my Interrail pass." This tragic chorus has become a convention. Travellers opt for a Global Pass and become enslaved to speed.

But best value does not mean trying to beat distance records. It might be measured by the **level of spontaneity** that surrounds a journey. It may be judged by the level of engagement with local communities that your journey affords. And if you really want to bring it down to euros and cents, best value is certainly a journey that uses slow trains to the utmost. Tickets for slow trains rarely have the discounts available for faster services. Odd, is it not, how slowness is nowadays a privilege reserved only for the most wealthy – and for those who appreciate the **real value of an Interrail pass**.

How to use this book

The best guidebooks, and we really hope this is one of the best, both **inspire and inform** in equal measure. At the heart of this volume are 52 rail routes that criss-cross Europe. The **full-colour map** on the inside front cover shows most routes. On the inside back cover you'll find our Scandinavia map and an enlargement of the wider Alpine region showing our routes there in more detail. These maps allow you to plot longer itineraries across the continent (eg. Lisbon to Stockholm or Dublin to Belgrade).

OVER FIFTY ROUTES

The main part of this book (between p49 and p445) describes the 52 routes featured in *Europe by Rail*. A **full list** of these routes appears in the table of contents and, in another format, on pages pp16–17. In the latter version, we give the length of each route in kilometres and the travel time.

Each route kicks off with our personal appraisal using a **star rating** (one to three stars with three being the best), and a note of the countries through which the route passes. We also give the **length of the route** (in kilometres) and the rough amount of time that you'll be spending on trains if you follow each leg, as we describe it, right through to the end of the route. Bear in mind that there will often be faster ways of getting from the start to the end of the route – and we usually highlight such options where they are available. But our aim in this book is to showcase the most interesting and scenic options – and those are not necessarily the fastest. You'll find a URL to an online map for each route next to the length of each journey.

Every **route description** includes a simple **sketch map**, showing principal places along the way, with an adjacent table giving route details and the general pattern of rail services along that route. Those route details also list the respective table numbers in the *European Rail Timetable* (ERT) where you will find the timings for any particular leg. In some cases we may indicate a higher **frequency of service** than shown in the ERT. This is merely because the ERT does not always show the full range of local trains.

A route may very occasionally depend on a leg being undertaken by **bus or boat**. On the route sketch map we indicate that by the use of a 🚌 symbol or a ⛴ symbol. Although the route sketches are schematic, they are all aligned with north at the top of the page. The red numbers found on many sketch maps show where the route in question intersects with other routes described in this book. Of course no one dictates that you must follow our routes in their entirety. You can pick and choose, switching from one to another where they intersect, and sometimes branching out on your own to explore territory beyond our recommended routes. Indeed, we very much hope that following a few routes in this book will give you the confidence to **start creating your own itineraries**.

SIDETRACKS, CITY LINKS AND MORE

Our **Sidetracks** mini-features, 25 of them in all, might also encourage you to strike out independently. These are not strictly routes, but rather bold leaps. Some will lead to offshore islands (such as Sardinia or Mallorca), others will take you well beyond the regular tourist trails, even to countries like Albania and Kosovo which often get completely overlooked in many travel guides to Europe. Sidetracks also cover topics such as railways and world heritage, carriage design and grand stations.

So 52 routes, all with a number and a name, and 25 Sidetracks, each with an identifying letter (from A to Y). Cast an eye again at those **full-colour maps** of the routes (on the inside covers at either end of the book) and you'll see that letters appear on those maps too, giving an indication of the area to which particular Sidetracks relate. Some Sidetracks are less geographical in character, exploring a rail-related theme rather than a place, so for those there's no corresponding pin on the full-colour maps.

If you want to get an overview of rail travel in Europe on a country-by-country basis, turn to our **gazetteer** on pp446–511. That country gazetteer also includes key facts on each country such as the currency and languages used, time zone, etc.

Following the overview table of our 52 routes (on pp16–17), we give a wealth of advice on how best to **plan your itinerary** (pp18–20), on **ticket deals** (pp21–28) and on key shipping links (pp29–31), concluding with our thoughts on 25 years of Eurostar (p32). Tucked away towards the back of the book, after the country gazetteer, you'll find some real nuggets of information. Our list of **city links** (pp513–17) shows travel times on direct trains between principal European places. And we also have sections on **night trains** (pp520–22) and **cruise trains** (p523), a **rail pass directory** (pp525–28) and an A-Z of **travel facts** (pp529–33).

Throughout the book we use the **abbreviation ERT** to refer to the **European Rail Timetable**. It is printed six times each year; the most important timetable changes feature in the seasonal editions published in June and December respectively. You may find it worthwhile to buy a copy to assist in journey planning and to have with you as you travel. The **Rail Map Europe** (also published by European Rail Timetable Limited) will of course help keep you on the right track as you travel around the continent by train. You can find out more about the timetables and map at www.europeanrailtimetable.eu. At some places in this book, we use **short links** (eg. www.ebrweb.eu/1) to represent a URL. Some of these lead to **online maps** of the 52 routes (read more on p544). The use of these short links is purely a convenience. We use them merely to abbreviate an otherwise cumbersome URL. It does not necessarily imply that we have any connection with the businesses associated with those URLs.

Overview: The 52 routes

Our **52 journeys** include some which are short and sweet and others that are long-haul adventures. **Route 8** and **37** are both less than 300 kilometres long while **Route 29, 32, 33** and **51** each extend to more than 1,500 kilometres. Our table (below and opposite) shows the countries covered, the overall travel time and the length of each route. Note that the **travel time** quoted below does not make any allowance for breaking a journey or any overnight stops along the way. It's just an indication of how long you'll spend on trains if you follow the route, as we describe it, from end to end.

No.	From–to	countries	distance in km	travel time
1	London – Penzance	England	491	5h30
2	London – Kyle	England, Scotland	1,047	12h
3	Rotterdam – Mallaig	Netherlands, England, Scotland	1,210	27h30
4	Rotterdam – Killarney	Netherlands, England, Wales, Ireland	1,194	26h30
5	London – Galway	England, Wales, Ireland	1,006	18h
6	London – Nîmes	England, France	1,220	12h
7	Paris – Marseille	France	863	9h
8	Marseille – Nice	France	229	3h
9	Paris – Cherbourg	France	434	4h15
10	Paris – San Sebastián	France, Spain	1,030	16h
11	Paris – Barcelona	France, Spain	1,039	13h
12	Geneva – Barcelona	Switzerland, France, Spain	856	12h
13	Barcelona – Cádiz	Spain	1,324	13h20
14	Barcelona – Málaga	Spain	1,136	6h
15	San Sebastián – Santiago de Compostela	Spain	825	10h30
16	Santiago de Compostela – Lisbon	Spain, Portugal	616	6h
17	Lille – Amsterdam	France, Belgium, Netherlands	368	6h
18	Lille – Cologne	France, Belgium, Germany	357	3h
19	Amsterdam – Lausanne	Netherlands, Belgium, Luxembourg, France, Switzerland	1,020	12h30
20	Cologne – Zurich	Germany, Switzerland	611	7h30
21	Cologne – Berlin	Germany	612	6h
22	Hannover – Magdeburg	Germany	302	9h

No.	From–to	countries	distance in km	travel time
23	Berlin – Salzburg	Germany, Austria	943	10h
24	Nuremberg – Prague	Germany, Czech Republic	560	9h30
25	Hamburg – Budapest	Germany, Czech Republic, Slovakia, Hungary	1,291	13h45
26	Budapest – Lviv	Hungary, Ukraine	607	14h
27	Venice – Zagreb	Italy, Slovenia, Croatia	430	11h
28	Hamburg – Stockholm	Germany, Denmark, Sweden	997	12h
29	Amsterdam – Oslo	Netherlands, Germany, Denmark, Norway	1,611	24h
30	Copenhagen – Bergen	Denmark, Sweden, Norway	1,192	14h30
31	Oslo – Svolvær	Norway	1,450	20h
32	Stockholm – Svolvær	Sweden, Norway	1,735	21h
33	Boden – St Petersburg	Sweden, Finland, Russia	1,598	18h30
34	Vienna – Venice	Austria, Italy	620	7h40
35	Zurich – Bratislava	Switzerland, Liechtenstein, Austria, Slovakia	911	11h
36	Zurich – Milan	Switzerland, Italy	415	8h30
37	St Moritz – Zermatt	Switzerland	290	8h15
38	Zurich – Geneva	Switzerland	338	7h30
39	Munich – Verona	Germany, Austria, Italy	434	6h20
40	Nice – Pisa	France, Monaco, Italy	370	6h
41	Pisa – Rome	Italy	474	8h
42	Verona – Rome	Italy	562	6h45
43	Genoa – Venice	Italy	461	5h30
44	Rome – Siracusa	Italy	858	11h
45	Budapest – Bar	Hungary, Serbia, Bosnia & Herzegovina, Montenegro	874	21h
46	Budapest – Dubrovnik	Hungary, Croatia	1,037	17h30
47	Zagreb – Thessaloniki	Croatia, Serbia, Bulgaria, Greece	1,166	25h
48	Berlin – Lviv	Germany, Poland, Ukraine	1,207	15h
49	Dresden – Zakopane	Germany, Poland	685	11h30
50	Warsaw – St Petersburg	Poland, Belarus, Russia	1,425	27h
51	Helsinki – Oslo	Finland, Estonia, Latvia, Sweden, Norway	1,592	25h
52	Debrecen – Lviv	Hungary, Romania, Ukraine	938	22h

Planning your itinerary

There is an untold pleasure in just breezing off without having given any real thought as to where you are bound. Some of the finest journeys are those which are least planned. Spontaneity brings its own rewards. But, as you'll quickly appreciate when you read our thoughts on train ticket deals (see pp21–28), spontaneity is often a very expensive luxury. You can save a packet if you book at least some aspects of your journey in advance.

Even if money is no object, a modicum of **advance planning** still makes good sense. Missing the weekly train from Menton to Minsk may not trouble you at all. Menton is, after all, a splendid spot to hole up for a week if you have ample funds. But miss the only Saturday departure from a dreary small town in the Balkans, and finding that the next train out is not till Monday, may not be quite so much fun.

How much planning *you* need to do for *your* explorations of Europe by train has a lot to do with your **budget** and your **personal psyche**. Do you relish uncertainty? Will you be unduly troubled if you cannot easily find a place to stay overnight? Only you can answer such questions.

Two key planning tools are the *European Rail Timetable* (ERT) and the celebrated *Man in Seat Sixty-One* website (www.seat61.com) which is a gold-mine of great advice. A good website for **checking train times** across much of Europe is http://bahn.hafas.de. But bear in mind that the database upon which this website draws is very incomplete when it comes to Spain, parts of the Balkans, Finland and eastern Europe. Even in Italy, entire rail routes in the south of the country are missing.

Solo travel

The question of whether you travel alone is one that is ultimately a matter of personal choice. Solo travel can be immensely rewarding. The lone traveller is far more likely to strike up conversation with locals and fellow travellers. But an extended solo journey takes a certain grit and resilience, especially when all does not go quite as you might hope. There are times when being able to **share experiences** with a friend or partner can help make a journey take on new meaning. Bear in mind, too, that accommodation costs are heavily stacked against the single traveller.

Beware the packed itinerary

By far the biggest mistake made by first timers embarking on a vacation exploring Europe by train is to bite off far more than is feasible. With so much on offer, it is all too tempting to say "Let's just throw in Venice. And Florence. Perhaps we have an afternoon in Paris too."

Sketch out your **first tentative itinerary** and then halve the number of places you intend to visit. A two-night stop is hugely more rewarding than

SEVEN STEPS TO PERFECT PLANNING

Prepare a budget that includes estimates of accommodation, food and travel costs, including seat reservation fees and travel supplements for rail pass holders. Now add on a good allowance for incidentals. Entrance fees to galleries and museums and left-luggage charges may be hefty, not to mention coffees and cocktails.

Tune your expectations to match your budget. A gondola ride across the Grand Canal in Venice costs just a couple of euros. But if you wish to be serenaded while drifting through Venice on your own private gondola, expect to pay upwards of €100. The grandest French clarets will not cost any less in a fine Bordeaux restaurant than at home. Even modest fare may test the depth of your wallet in some of Europe's more expensive countries such as Norway.

Review visa requirements earlier rather than later. If any country on your provisional itinerary might demand a visa, remember to make provision in your budget. For holders of EU passports, the sole journeys in this book that require visas to be procured prior to setting out are **Route 33** and **50**. The Republic of Belarus and the Russian Federation still insist on a visa for EU citizens.

Consider money matters early. Do you have cash point (ATM) and credit cards to support your journey? Remember that even the most popular **credit cards** (VISA and Mastercard) may not be widely accepted in some European countries. Do you have a card that allows you to draw cash in local currency from your bank account? Know in advance what currencies you'll need at each stop on your itinerary. Give early thought as to where you'll pack cash to minimise the risk of loss or theft.

Think about luggage at the outset for how much you lug around will dramatically influence how manageable your itinerary is. A small amount of luggage, never more than you can comfortably carry without assistance, can be a wonderful asset. More just becomes a terrible burden. We know travellers who have survived long tours around Europe without a portable ice-bucket and a miner's lamp. But we judge a small torch, a corkscrew and appropriate plug adaptors to be essentials. There is no such thing as a universal packing list to suit all, but http://upl.codeq.info is a good start. And it's fun to play with.

Buy insurance early for, while it is a sound principle never to travel with something that you would be desperately sorry to lose, things do go astray. And medical cover is essential. If you are resident in any of the 30 or so European countries participating in the **EHIC scheme**, you should obtain a European Health Insurance Card before leaving home. The EHIC card is free. You should review whether it provides adequate cover, and you may consider top-up medical insurance.

Weather watching makes sense. Find out what sort of weather you can expect along the way. Bear in mind that an itinerary which includes both Arctic Norway and the Greek islands will traverse several climate zones. Explore the excellent graphics in the climate section of www.weatheronline.co.uk. And remember that places blessed with a wonderful climate may still turn out to have terrible weather on the week you visit.

having just one night in a new city. Three nights is even better. If you opt for a fortnight of one-night stays, each morning setting off for a new city, Europe will collapse in a mishmash of blurred memories. Similarly, **long travel days** take their toll as do several consecutive nights of overnight travel. There will be times when a ten-hour haul by day will allow you to cover a lot of ground. And it may be good fun, especially if you follow a route that takes in some great scenery. But if you have several such long days on the trot, the appeal of train travel will surely wane.

Careful planning can make a long travel day much more enjoyable. If you must make a ten-hour journey in a single day, then why not break it up into two legs of five hours each, and schedule **a decent-length break** at a midway point. A brisk walk or a relaxed lunch (or both) will leave you refreshed for the second stretch of the journey.

THE PLANE QUESTION

This book is all about exploring Europe by rail. It's not about flying. If you don't worry about the environmental impact of flying, there are many itineraries where a **leg by plane** may make sense, whether at the start or end of your itinerary, or to shift quickly from one part of Europe to another in the middle of a long trip.

Before you start booking many sectors by plane, just consider what **alternatives** might be available. A long overnight journey by train or by boat may usefully bridge a gap. For example we've combined a week exploring Italy with a subsequent week in Spain by taking a ship between the two countries. If you must fly, bear in mind that **early bookers** bag the cheapest fares. Don't just focus on the discount airlines. Close to the travel date, you may find that so-called budget carriers are even more expensive that the traditional full-cost airlines.

URBAN OR RURAL?

What kind of Europe are you eager to discover? A Europe full of **cosmopolitan flair**, such as you might encounter in Paris, Dublin and Milan, or a quieter, more rural Europe where the locals may even still have time for and interest in the visitors who come their way?

If you stick to premier-league tourist destinations, you'll probably have a ball, but you'll see places that are not always typical of the countries in which they are located. The wonderful thing about travelling by train is the European rail network can take you to backwaters frequented by few tourists. So make time for some of the small towns and branch lines that we mention in this book and you will be handsomely rewarded. And allow time for slow trains that dawdle through the countryside, stopping off here and there along the way.

Getting the best deals on tickets

For almost any traveller exploring Europe by rail, train tickets will be one of the two principal categories of expenditure, the other of course being accommodation. How much you spend on tickets will be determined by your itinerary, whether you opt for second or first class and – in many countries – whether you can **book well in advance**. Across large parts of Europe, this last factor will dramatically influence how much you pay.

THE RAIL FARES JUNGLE

Wouldn't it be a wonderful world if you could walk down to your local station in suburban London (or Oslo or Madrid) and buy a through train ticket to the other side of Europe? Sadly, Europe's railway administrations don't quite see it that way and travellers embarking on a **complicated international itinerary** must generally obtain a number of separate tickets to cover their entire journey. Matters have improved over the last year or two, with tickets for many multi-sector itineraries now available online, particularly through agencies like **Loco2**, now part of Rail Europe (www.raileurope.co.uk), and **Trainline** (www.trainline.eu).

For those with the patience to check out a variety of different websites and agents, there are some fabulous deals there for the taking, especially for early bookers. It is still possible to travel from Schaffhausen in Switzerland to southern Sweden for less than €60. Or from Amsterdam to Salzburg for under €40. These are exceptionally good offers and sometimes one might have to pay much more for the same trips. On p23, we list some of the **principal websites and agencies** that we have found useful in researching and buying rail tickets and passes for travel around Europe.

HOW FAR IN ADVANCE CAN I BOOK?

The key to securing the best fares is usually to book your tickets the moment they become available. One small caveat is that, in a few countries, premium fares aimed at the business market may become available slightly prior to discounted tariffs. The **forward booking horizon** for rail operators across continental Europe generally varies from two to six months.

Some operators (like Deutsche Bahn and Thalys) open bookings on a **day by day basis** with the booking period advancing by one day in the early hours of each morning. Others (like Renfe in Spain) **release tickets in waves**, with each new wave covering up to a month. So you may search in vain for tickets for a journey just six weeks hence, but then bookings open all at once for the entire summer. Yet others, like SNCF in France, generally follow a fixed booking horizon (three months for SNCF) but may release tickets for mid-summer travel in a single wave. Bookings for most Russian trains open only 60 days in advance (and that applies equally to journeys on Russian trains within the European Union). In Croatia and Denmark, tickets for domestic journeys go on sale just two months in advance. At the other extreme is *Caledonian Sleeper*, operator of Anglo-Scottish overnight trains, where you can book your ticket a full year in advance.

Whenever there are major timetable changes, generally on the **second weekend in December** each year across much of western and central Europe, ticket sales for the new timetable period will not open until the new schedules have been confirmed, and that may mean that, for a spell each autumn, the forward booking horizon is shorter than normal.

BIG REWARDS FOR EARLY BOOKERS

Across much of continental Europe, though less so in eastern Europe and the Balkans, there has been a **revolution in rail tariffs** over the last ten years. Fares were traditionally based on the length of your proposed journey. While these kilometre-based tariffs still often apply to passengers who purchase their tickets on the day of travel, many countries now offer a vast range of cheaper options.

Let's take two routes of similar length. The regular **distance-based fares** from both Paris to Leipzig and Amsterdam to Salzburg (each journeys of about 1,000 km) are similar: in each case about €170. The precise amount payable varies by the route you elect to follow.

But canny travellers on a budget always book well ahead. Commit yourself in the few days after ticket sales open and you will almost certainly pay just €39.90 for either of our two sample journeys above. Even if you book just a week in advance, there is still a very good chance of bagging a good deal – no longer €39.90 but maybe €99.90.

Most rail operators in western Europe have fallen in love with **market pricing**, where the fare on offer is carefully tuned to reflect anticipated demand, and where the customer prepared to book well in advance and – most importantly – **commit to a particular itinerary** and specific trains can travel for a fraction of the regular fare. The best deals are always on off-peak services.

Of course, our Paris to Leipzig and Amsterdam to Salzburg examples both come from an area of Europe where rail tariffs are pricier than elsewhere across the continent. Move east a little and the same outlay of €170 will buy you a **fully flexible ticket** for a journey of over 2,000 km from Prague to Turkey. No need to book in advance and you can even stop off as often as you wish along the way within the period your ticket is valid.

Our general rule of thumb is that, in those areas where market pricing gives **advantages to early bookers**, you can normally expect to pay about one quarter of the regular fare if you book within a week or two of tickets being released for sale. The names given to these early deals vary confusingly by country and rail operator. But whether it be *prems* (on French TGV

Booking tips

One thing that's clear from our review of rail tickets is that fares and ticketing are complicated matters, the high theology of which is understood by only a handful of people on the entire planet. The average travel agent will not be able to help you a lot, so if you need help, it is best to turn to specialists. A good source of online advice is **Mark Smith**, the much-quoted **Man in Seat Sixty-One**, whose comprehensive website at www.seat61.com gives information on the best fares and where to book.

Most of the main national rail websites have online **booking systems** for booking domestic and some international tickets. Some of these booking systems are ferociously complicated, others are relatively easy to use but still demand a good appreciation of railway geography and service patterns. **Websites of national rail operators** we use a lot are those from Germany (www.bahn.de), the Czech Republic (www.cd.cz), Austria (www.oebb.at) and Switzerland (www.sbb.ch). Other good national websites are those from France (www.oui.sncf), Italy (www.trenitalia.com) and Spain (www.renfe.com). We book journeys on Russian trains, even where those journeys are entirely within the European Union (eg. the overnight train from Paris to Berlin or the daytime service from Nice to Verona), on the main RZD website (www.ebrweb.eu/rzd).

None of these sites charge **booking fees**. It's worth bearing in mind that well over 99% of European train tickets are purchased without the addition of any booking fees. A very small number of sales channels may levy an administrative charge or booking fee. If it's an unusual ticket not available elsewhere, or if there's some real added value (such as first-class customer service), then paying a fee may be money well spent. We leave you to decide.

It is worth bearing in mind that **e-tickets** are now very much the norm. In some countries, an electronic train ticket is tagged to a specific identity document. Where this is the case, you are given the chance to say what that document will be at the time of purchase. A credit card is a common choice. When you present your ticket for inspection on the train, you will need to have to hand the credit card (or other form of identification) that you specified when making your booking. **Mobile tickets** are also on the rise with many operators. These have a matrix barcode (usually a QR or Aztec code) and are presented to the conductor on board straight from your mobile device.

With such a fragmented market, the Holy Grail in European rail ticketing has been to create a platform that integrates fares data from a variety of vendors to create through itineraries. The pioneering London-based start-up Loco2 did just this. Everyone one is now keenly watching to see how Loco2 will fare following its late 2019 merger with **Rail Europe**. Check www.raileurope.co.uk where you should still be able to access Loco2's impressive inventory (albeit now with a booking fee on many routes).

We recommend the following UK-based agents for their considerable expertise in European ticketing. They are also able to handle enquiries and bookings for clients based outside Britain: **Trainseurope** (www.trainseurope.co.uk, ☎ +44 871 700 7722), **Ffestiniog Travel** (www.ffestiniogtravel.com, ☎ +44 1766 512 400), **International Rail** (www.internationalrail.com, ☎ +44 871 231 0790) and **Rail Canterbury** (www.rail-canterbury.co.uk, ☎ +44 1227 450 088). For booking **Interrail or Eurail passes**, we suggest that you first take a look at those schemes' official websites: www.interrail.eu and www.eurail.com respectively. In late 2019, a new website at www.trainplanet.com launched a service for pass holders to reserve seats on many European trains. We've tried it out and were impressed.

services), *mini* (on Thalys trains), *minipris* (in Norway), or *Sparpreis Europa* (on international journeys to or from Germany), the underlying message is that a very good deal is on offer.

YOUTH AND SENIOR DISCOUNTS

While every country offers child discounts, there are few **across-the-board discounts** for young people, students or seniors. Where such discounts do exist, they are usually calculated as a percentage reduction on the regular full fare, and are rarely as cheap as the bargain-basement fares available to anyone who books well in advance.

Eurostar is a happy exception and offers discounts to young people and seniors even on many discounted standard-class fares. And **Hungary** is a wonderful oddity and offers free rail travel (on all but a small number of express services) to all EU citizens aged 65 or older. There are also railcards geared to specific market segments (eg. youth or senior travellers). Read more about those below.

RAILCARDS

Many European rail operators offer **reductions on their regular tariffs**, and sometimes also on their discounted early-booking fares, to holders of selected railcards. Most of these cards are actively marketed only within the countries where they are valid. These railcards are usually **valid for one year** and can be purchased by anyone, so you do not need to be a local resident.

Examples are the Swiss *Halbtax* card, the Czech *In Karta*, the Slovakian *Klasik Railplus*, the French *Carte Avantage Week-end*, the German *BahnCard* and the Dutch *Voordeelurenkaart*. Many countries also have specific railcards aimed at the youth and senior-citizen markets. In **France**, for example, there is the *Carte Avantage Jeune* and *Carte Senior+*. Other countries sell their national railcards to youths and seniors at a reduced price. The Austrian *Vorteilscard*, for example, normally costs €99 for a year, but young travellers (under 26) pay just €19 and seniors (over 62) pay €29.

The *Vorteilscard* is affiliated to the **Railplus scheme** and thus gives discounts on some international journeys too. Indeed, most national railcards mentioned above confer *Railplus* benefits. Note however that this privilege does not extend to holders of railcards issued in the United Kingdom. As this new edition of *Europe by Rail* goes to press in October 2019, there are rumours that the Railplus scheme may be substantially amended or even scrapped.

You have to be doing a **lot of travelling** over an extended period to make the purchase of such railcards worthwhile. They are however an attractive option for residents or for those who frequently visit one particular country. For example, many British residents who are regular Channel-hoppers have realised that a French railcard can be a very sensible investment.

FIRST CLASS COMFORT

First-class carriages may offer **better leg-room, extra space for luggage** and a higher level of service. That may include snacks and drinks served at your seat (often at a price), complimentary newspapers, power sockets and free wi-fi access. Quite what you actually get for the extra outlay **varies greatly by country and category of train**. Generally if a train has air conditioning, then it is available in every carriage. But there is a dwindling minority of trains across Europe where only first-class carriages have air conditioning.

On a very small number of trains, passengers in first or premium classes may receive a complimentary snack or meal. Examples of where you can enjoy such perks include TGV Lyria trains between France and Switzerland in their new business premier class (introduced in December 2017) and Eurostar trains, where passengers in standard premier are offered complimentary snacks and drinks while business premier **travellers enjoy substantial meals** complemented by fine wines.

Whether you think it worth splashing out for first class is really a matter of personal choice. Bear in mind that first class affords much **less opportunity for contact with locals**. The availability of first-class seating may be very limited on some routes. On certain long-distance daytime trains in central Europe and the Balkans, for example, just a small part of a single carriage is designated as first class – Munich to Zagreb and Belgrade to Budapest are examples.

The extra you pay for first class varies greatly. As a general rule, expect to pay about 50% more than for a second-class fare. In some countries you just pay a flat fare supplement on top of the regular price. Norway is an instance of this, where the upgrade to the higher class (called *NSB Komfort*) costs 90 NOK (€10), whatever the length of journey.

The question of class is **more complex on night trains**, where the basic distinction is between seats, couchettes and sleeping compartments. The highest sleeping compartment category will usually only be available to holders of first-class tickets (plus the sleeper supplement). For more on night trains see pp520–22.

SECOND CLASS OR FIRST CLASS?

Most European local trains are one class only. Many regional trains and most express or long-distance services offer **two classes of service**, often called second and first. The names vary. On many Finnish trains for example, the two classes are called *Eco* and *Extra* respectively. In many countries, second class may be marketed as economy or standard.

If you are buying tickets at a railway station, and you don't specify to the contrary, the booking clerk will generally assume that you wish to travel second class. Most booking websites also take second (or standard) class as the default or norm.

A small number of trains offer **three levels of services**. On such trains, the middle of the three classes is usually roughly equivalent to first class, and the highest class is a premium product. **Eurostar's services** from London to Paris and Brussels have standard, standard premier and business premier. **Thalys** services have standard, comfort and premium classes.

Some **Italian high-speed services** have no less than four different classes of travel. **NTV Italo** pretentiously asserts (at www.italotreno.it): "We do not have classes, but four journey *ambiences*: smart, comfort, prima and club executive." The last of these is clearly designed for travellers who only very reluctantly leave their private jet at home. On Trenitalia's Frecciarossa trains the four classes are marketed as standard, premium, business and executive.

Unless you really value creature comforts, the regular second-class (or standard-class) carriages are more than adequate on most day trains (see the box on p25 to find out more about what to expect in first class). The question of **comfort levels on night trains** is more complicated, and the simple distinction between first and second class no longer applies. See our feature on night trains (pp520–22).

FIRST CLASS BARGAINS

The real surprise for many travellers is that there are times when first-class **tickets may be cheaper** than second class. Early bookers can sometimes take advantage of special offers, usually only available online, for heavily discounted first-class tickets. We have noted many instances of journeys in western Europe where the cheapest available ticket is in first class.

You are most likely to encounter this oddity some time after bookings first open, when **budget-conscious travellers** have already snapped up all the cheap second-class seats, but bookings in first class are still very light. This is most likely at weekends and during summer holidays – so when budget leisure travel is in high demand but there are fewer business travellers on the move.

RAIL PASSES OR REGULAR TICKETS

The question that many travellers ponder endlessly before, during and even after exploring Europe by rail is whether **investing in a rail pass** makes good financial sense.

Cast back 30 or 40 years and an earlier generation of Interrail pass holders explored Europe's principal cities by day and slept by night on trains making long nocturnal hops across Europe. Others partied by night and slept on trains by day. Either way, the Interrail pass was a fine investment. Young backpackers with stamina could criss-cross Europe for a month and hardly pay a cent for accommodation.

Times have changed. Many European railway administrations have introduced **supplementary charges for pass holders** wishing to use even the most basic category of accommodation on overnight services. Some countries also levy a supplement for pass holders using premium daytime express trains. These supplements must usually be paid in local currency prior to boarding. The growing number of supplements may undermine the

RAIL PASS SUPPLEMENTS

A rail pass does not necessarily entitle you to totally free travel. **Many trains require that you pay a supplement.** If you are keen to avoid supplements, always check at the ticket office before boarding. And be aware that on selected trains (eg. on TGV and Thalys services), there may be only a limited contingent of seats available for pass holders. Travellers who hop aboard without pre-checking availability, and without having paid for the necessary supplement, may be in for a big surprise as they are charged the full fare for their journey.

A supplement of €10 or €20 is payable on **TGV services** within France. Whether you pay the lower or higher fee depends on how busy the train is in your preferred class of travel. Stick to off-peak trains to be assured of only having to pay €10 for each journey. For international journeys on TGVs, the supplements may be very much more, even around €50 for first-class journeys from **Paris to Barcelona**, Geneva or Zurich. From Paris or Lyon to Turin or Milan, on the **direct TGV trains**, the supplement for holders of an Interrail pass is €31 second class or €45 first class. For domestic journeys on **Trenitalia high-speed trains** or Eurocity services in Italy, €10 is the norm. Not bad for a long-distance leap across Italy, but pricey if you are just making a short hop. The fastest trains in Sweden charge €7 or €17 for second and first class reservations respectively – and you have no choice but to get a reservation. For **AVE trains in Spain**, where reservation is also compulsory, the fees are €10 and €23.50 for second and first class. The Brenner route Eurocity trains (on **Route 39**) have supplements of €13 and €9 in first and second class respectively.

All that sounds like bad news. But choose your trains and routes carefully and it is possible to roam around Europe for a month or more **without having to pay a single supplement**. Britain, Ireland, Denmark, Germany, Switzerland and Austria are all very Interrail-friendly with few daytime trains where pass holders must pay a supplement. And, across much of central Europe (including the Czech Republic, Slovakia and Hungary), supplements – where they exist at all – are no more than a couple of euros.

Interrail and Eurail passes are now accepted on most **Eurostar trains**. This is a very welcome innovation, even though a supplement is still payable. But the supplement isn't outrageous: €30 for travel in standard class and, for holders of first-class passes, €38 for a seat in standard premier. These fares are valid on Eurostar trains to Brussels and Paris (both the city centre and Marne-la-Vallée–Chessy). Prices are €5 more on journeys to Amsterdam. Passes are not accepted on Eurostar trains to the French Alps, Lyon, Avignon or Marseille.

Most **night trains** require advance reservation and some sort of extra payment, even if you are willing to spend the entire night in a seat. Trade up to a couchette or sleeping berth and even pass holders will face a substantial supplement. In Italy, for example, pass holders might typically pay €48 for a berth in a shared sleeper or €122 for sole occupancy of that sleeper compartment. We have been struck by how variable these supplements are. On the *Alpine Pearls* night train from Zurich to Zagreb, pass holders may pay as little as €19 for a couchette or €39 for a sleeping berth. Read more about night trains on pp520–22 and see our **list of pass supplements** at www.ebrweb.eu/rps.

value of a pass, as the holder can no longer breeze through the station and avoid the queues at the ticket office. You can read **more about supplements** in the box on p27.

A pass may make very good sense if you really intend to **travel very intensively** and cover long distances in those countries where rail tariffs are generally high. Bear in mind that Europe-wide passes (often referred to as global passes) are priced at a level that reflects the high prices of flexible walk-up tickets in countries such as Scandinavia, the Netherlands, France, Germany and Switzerland.

If your travel horizons lead you further east to areas where even flexible tickets are cheap, then a rail pass may be a poor investment. Even in Italy, they are not such a good deal – in part because the regular fares are very modestly priced, and also due to the **hefty supplements** demanded of pass holders using express services in Italy.

In those areas of Europe where **market pricing** offers potentially great deals for early bookers, travellers prepared to commit two or three months in advance will almost certainly pay less than pass holders. And yet every year, thousands of travellers do buy rail passes and never regret that decision.

The nub of the argument is that with a rail pass you **purchase enormous flexibility**. The freedom to roam at will does not come cheap, but can be incredibly liberating. Yet for those committed to keeping costs to a minimum, provided they are prepared to book well in advance and not change their itinerary, a rail pass may seem an expensive luxury.

Our comments on the **relative merits of rail passes** versus regular tickets relate mainly to global passes that cover a large part of Europe. If your geographical horizons are more limited, restricted to one country or even just one part of a country, you may well find a more restricted pass that meets your needs perfectly. In the **reference section** at the end of this book we give the low-down on the most commonly used rail passes (see pp525–28). You'll find lots of nitty-gritty detail there.

At this stage, you may want to note just the bare facts. **Interrail** is designed for residents of Europe, while **Eurail** is designed for those who live outside Europe. Both Interrail and Eurail Global Passes now have identical geographical validity. They both cover all of Europe (plus Turkey) bar for eight countries, all of these exceptions are in eastern Europe or the southern Balkans. There are **some passes that are valid** for a single country or just part of a country. You will find mention of these under the relevant country entry in the **gazetteer section** of this book (see pp446–511).

Ultimately, the key decision – one which should be made before buying *any* tickets or passes – is about the style and manner of travel which best suits you. Do you value the security of having everything booked in advance or do you prefer to **retain a measure of spontaneity**? If the latter is important, then a rail pass may well be the best option.

Key shipping links

At many points in this book, we refer to ferries or other shipping services. Some of these sea journeys are an integral part of the routes we describe. Examples are **Route 3** and **4**, which both cross the North Sea, or **Route 29** which includes a short hop on a ferry from Denmark to Norway. We have always found during our travels that a journey on a comfortable ship offers a welcome change of pace. It's a chance to relax and recharge your batteries.

In our listings below, we highlight just a small selection of Europe's rich network of coastal and inshore shipping services, focusing on those with better rail links at ports. Most of the routes listed do offer some concession for travellers using Eurail or Interrail – just check the operator's website.

Apart from the key markets mentioned in the tables below, there are of course a wealth of other ferries, covering the Irish Sea, the Norwegian coast, the Scottish islands and the Black Sea. There are even year-round scheduled shipping services between the European mainland and Iceland. Perhaps one day we'll write a book called *Europe by Boat*.

Key to ferry companies

Adria Ferries	www.adriaferries.com
Anek Lines	www.anek.gr
Brittany Ferries	www.brittany-ferries.co.uk
Corsica Ferries	www.corsica-ferries.fr
DFDS	www.dfds.com
Finnlines	www.finnlines.com
Grandi Navi Veloci	www.gnv.it
Grimaldi Lines	www.grimaldi-lines.com
Irish Ferries	www.irishferries.com
P&O Ferries	www.poferries.com
Superfast Ferries	www.superfast.com
St Peter Line	www.stpeterline.com
Stena Line	www.stenaline.com
Tallink Silja Line	www.tallinksilja.com
Tirrenia	www.tirrenia.it

ADRIATIC CRUISES

Train services are so slow in some parts of the Balkans that for journeys to Albania and Greece it sometimes makes perfect sense to take a ship.

From	To	Operator	Time
Venice (IT)	Pátras (GR)	Anek Lines	32–33 hrs
Bari (IT)	Pátras (GR)	Superfast Ferries	16–18 hrs
Trieste (IT)	Durrës (AL)	Adria Ferries	23 hrs

CROSS-MED SAILINGS

On any longer tour of southern Europe, especially on itineraries which combine Spain and Italy, it may make sense to take one of the many Mediterranean shipping services. Don't always think of these journeys as being merely one long leg. There are some good island-hopping opportunities. For example, many of the Grimaldi Lines sailings from Barcelona to Italy stop en route at Porto Torres in Sardinia. Some sample routes are below.

From	To	Operator	Time
Barcelona (ES)	Civitavecchia (IT)	Grimaldi Lines	20–22 hrs
Barcelona (ES)	Genoa (IT)	Grandi Navi Veloci	20–22 hrs
Barcelona (ES)	Savona (IT)	Grimaldi Lines	20 hrs
Mallorca (ES)	Toulon (FR)	Corsica Ferries	11–13 hrs X

SICILIAN ESCAPES

Route 44 is the long-haul south by train to Sicily. You might consider returning to the mainland by boat. Here's a small selection of the many options available.

From	To	Operator	Time
Catania (IT)	Salerno (IT)	Grimaldi Lines	13 hrs
Palermo (IT)	Genoa (IT)	Grandi Navi Veloci	21 hrs
Palermo (IT)	Naples (IT)	Tirrenia	11 hrs
Trapani (IT)	Toulon (FR)	Corsica Ferries	21 hrs X

NORTH SEA CROSSINGS

Here's a handful of really useful routes for travellers heading to Britain who fancy arriving on a boat – as indeed befits an island – rather than taking the Eurostar train to London. These routes are especially good if you are keen to avoid the busy London region.

From	To	Operator	Time
Amsterdam (NL)	Newcastle (ENG)	DFDS	17 hrs
Rotterdam (NL)	Hull (ENG)	P&O Ferries	11–12 hrs
Hoek (NL)	Harwich (ENG)	Stena Line	7–10 hrs
Zeebrugge (BE)	Hull (ENG)	P&O Ferries	14–15 hrs

Notes

A – Travelling from Stockholm to St Petersburg, there is usually a 7-hr stop in Helsinki. On journeys from Russia back to Stockholm, there is generally a 6 to 9-hr stop in Tallinn.
P – Foot passengers not accepted on every sailing.
X – Route may not operate year-round.

BISCAY AND WESTERN CHANNEL

There are some excellent longer routes which take travellers directly from Spain and France to south-west England and the Republic of Ireland. Here are some key routes.

From	To	Operator	Time
Santander (ES)	Cork (IE)	Brittany Ferries	25–27 hrs
Santander (ES)	Portsmouth (ENG)	Brittany Ferries	24–29 hrs
Bilbao (ES)	Portsmouth (ENG)	Brittany Ferries	24–29 hrs
Roscoff (FR)	Cork (IE)	Brittany Ferries	10 hrs **X**
Roscoff (FR)	Plymouth (ENG)	Brittany Ferries	6–9 hrs
Cherbourg (FR)	Rosslare (IE)	Stena Line	17–20 hrs
Cherbourg (FR)	Dublin (IE)	Irish Ferries	19 hrs **P**

SHORT SEA SPRINTS

There is a good range of ferry links across La Manche (known as the English Channel in Britain).

From	To	Operator	Time
Calais (FR)	Dover (ENG)	P&O Ferries	90 mins **P**
Dieppe (FR)	Newhaven (ENG)	DFDS	4–5 hrs
Le Havre (FR)	Portsmouth (ENG)	Brittany Ferries	6–10 hrs
Cherbourg (FR)	Portsmouth (ENG)	Brittany Ferries	3 hrs **X**

BALTIC BREEZES

Baltic cruise-ferries are some of the finest vessels in European waters. These cross-Baltic routes are among some of our favourites. They are at their best in the early spring when, following a cold winter, the Baltic may still be a great white expanse of ice. The Riga to Stockholm route mentioned below forms part of **Route 51** in this book.

From	To	Operator	Time
Copenhagen (DK)	Oslo (NO)	DFDS	17–18 hrs
Travemünde (DE)	Malmö (SE)	Finnlines	9–10 hrs
Helsinki (FI)	Travemünde (DE)	Finnlines	30 hrs
Kiel (DE)	Klaipėda (LT)	DFDS	20 hrs
Riga (LV)	Stockholm (SE)	Tallink Silja Line	18 hrs
Stockholm (SE)	St Petersburg (RU)	St Peter Line	38 hrs **A**

25 years of Eurostar

The 52 routes in this book focus firmly on the landscapes, cultures and sights of the countries through which they pass. Although we generally say little about the actual trains, Eurostar really deserves a mention in its own right. Many readers of this book will **start or end their journeys in Britain**; others will add on a short side trip to London as part of a longer tour of the European mainland. Since it was **launched in November 1994**, the Eurostar train service has transformed Britain's relationship with its near neighbours on the continent. The move of Eurostar to its distinguished new London terminus at **St Pancras** in 2007, coinciding with the opening of the new high-speed rail link from London to the Channel coast, reinforced the train's iconic status and its standing in the public imagination – on both sides of the Channel – as a very sensible way to travel between London and the continent. St Pancras was further enhanced by the reopening in 2011 of the station hotel – now called the St Pancras Renaissance.

It seems a miracle that you can scan the train departures board at St Pancras and, amid the lists of domestic services, continental destinations now feature. Brussels rubs shoulders with Bedford. There's Lyon jostling for position with Leicester. The geography of England has been reshaped by the country's **first high-speed railway** as the fast line linking London with the Channel Tunnel has brought benefits to domestic travellers too. An older generation of Londoners could never have imagined that St Pancras might become the natural departure point for Chatham or Margate.

25 years after its launch, Eurostar still exhilarates by diminishing distance. Speed soaks up detail as poppies in the fields of Flanders become a red haze. It is quite simply a magnificent way to travel. **Route 6** in this edition starts with a fast run on Eurostar. The company now offers **year-round direct services** to Brussels, Paris, Lille, Calais, Marne-la-Vallée, Rotterdam and Amsterdam. Those two Dutch destinations were added in 2018. There are also summer services to Lyon, Avignon and Marseille and winter ski trains to three stations in the Tarentaise Valley in the French Alps.

For many Londoners, the Eurostar fast rail service to the continent has been a journey of discovery. London is now closer to Brussels than it is to Leeds or Liverpool. And this book is full of such **journeys of discovery**, with 52 carefully crafted routes that invite you to experience and rethink Europe. Get a taste of what is to come with our 16-page colour feature starting on the opposite page.

Note on colour feature

Every place included in our colour feature is on or close to one or more of the routes in this book. When a photo is credited to 'hidden europe', it comes from the collection of the authors of this book. All other images, each duly credited to the original photographer, were sourced through www.dreamstime.com.

Europe in colour:
Journeys of discovery

VENICE For John Ruskin, Venice was "a golden city melting into its lagoon." It's more a place for boats than trains, but Venice is on **Routes 27, 34** and **43** (photo © Grafner).

Steaming through Scotland! This elegantly curved viaduct at Glenfinnan on the West Highland Railway features on **Route 3**. The route is served by regular diesel trains as well as *The Jacobite* steam special (photo © Miroslav Liska). GLENFINNAN

RIBBLEHEAD   Ribblehead is a delightful rural station on the Settle and Carlisle
Railway in northern England. This is a line which is included
for the first time in this edition of *Europe by Rail*. Read more in
Route 3 (photo © Georgesixth).

Mock Gothic and neo-Romanesque styles collide on
the Fisherman's Bastion in Buda. The Hungarian capital
features on four different journeys described in this book:
Routes 25, 26, 45 and **46** (photo © Mdorottya).   BUDAPEST

MANAROLA

SUBOTICA

ABOVE: Pastel shades aplenty on the jumble of houses which make up Manarola, one of the Cinque Terre villages on **Route 40**. A pedestrian tunnel links the railway station with the village (photo © Augustin Florian).

RIGHT: The town of Subotica (Суботица) in northern Serbia is an unlikely outpost of art nouveau architecture. After spells under Ottoman, Habsburg and Hungarian administration, Subotica is these days the second largest city (after Novi Sad) in the autonomous Vojvodina region. That strikingly multicultural area is part of **Route 45** (photo © hidden europe).

This forest of arches in the Mezquita at Córdoba captures the visual drama of a city which, in the 10th century, became the prosperous capital of an important caliphate. But the architectural reference to oriental aesthetics glosses over the fact that this one-time grand mosque was later converted into a Roman Catholic cathedral. Visit Córdoba as part of **Routes 13** or **14** (photo © Bjeayes).   CÓRDOBA

SOFIA   The Bulgarian capital features on **Route 47** in this book. Riding the 14 tram routes which criss-cross the city is a fine way of taking the pulse of Sofia life (photo © Tupungato).

Lviv has been under Habsburg, Polish and Soviet control. Today it is part of Ukraine and the end point of **Routes 26, 48** and **52**. This is the eastern side of the main market square, with a fine mix of Rococo and Renaissance architecture. In 1998, the square was inscribed on UNESCO's World Heritage List (photo © Tainar).

LVIV

The *Speicherstadt* (warehouse district) in Hamburg, its brick Gothic style redolent of the heyday of the Hanseatic League, dates from the end of the 19th century. This great port city on the River Elbe features on **Routes 25, 28** and **29** (photo ©minnystock).

HAMBURG

ST PETERSBURG

LEFT: Russian imitation of French style in the Grand Cascade at Peterhof Palace in St Petersburg. You can visit this Russian Versailles at the end of **Route 33** from Finland and **Route 50**, which runs from Warsaw to St Petersburg (photo © Javarman).

BELOW: A tinted mosaic of purple-black bog, heather-clad hillocks and the glint of sun on distant lochs: the only real way to see the remotest part of Rannoch Moor is on foot or by train. Join us as we ride over the moor in **Route 3** (photo © Photos1st).

RANNOCH MOOR

ZURICH

The Swiss city of Zurich is not as tame as some would have you believe. It's a place with radical traditions, whether in religion (Zwingli), art (Dadaism) or politics (Bolsheviks and anarchists). But this homely city is also a key European rail hub. It is on **Routes 20, 35, 36** and **38** (photo © Sborisov).

BARCELONA

Relax and catch the pulse of street life in the Catalan capital. Barcelona is on **Routes 11, 12, 13** and **14**. The Plaça Reial in the Barri Gòtic (Gothic Quarter) of the city is the hub of Barcelona nightlife (photo © Valentin Armianu).

CHERNIVTSI
The UNESCO-listed former episcopal residence and seminary in the Ukrainian city of Chernivtsi (Чернівці) is today part of the university. The buildings themselves attest to the twin pillars of Chernivtsi life in the late 19th century, viz. Habsburg civil authority and the Orthodox Church. Chernivtsi is on **Route 52** (photo © Mariana Ianovska).

This is the first edition of *Europe by Rail* in which we have included routes in Ireland. **Route 5** in this book runs west to the shores of Galway Bay (photo © James Byard).

GALWAY

HARZ MOUNTAINS   Steam-hauled trains are still seen every day in the Harz Mountains in eastern Germany. Explore the region by following **Route 22**. This image shows a train taking water at Eisfelder Talmühle (photo © hidden europe).

Visit Mariánské Lázně (once known as Marienbad) by stopping off on **Route 24**. The Bohemian spa town has attracted poets and potentates, among them Goethe and King Edward VII (photo © hidden europe).   MARIÁNSKÉ LÁZNĚ

SUCEAVA

ABOVE: Voroneț Monastery is one of the UNESCO-listed painted monasteries of the southern Bukovina. It's easily visited as a short excursion from Suceava, the Romanian town which features on **Route 52** in this book (photo © Andrei Stancu).

LEFT: The German city of Görlitz found itself uncomfortably split by a new international frontier in 1945. The Neisse River divides Germany from Poland. Make time for Görlitz which is on **Route 49** (photo © AliTu).

GÖRLITZ

AMSTERDAM

Amsterdam can be formidably busy with tourists, but cut off the main streets to discover the city's peaceful charm. This shot shows the Lekkeresluis Bridge at the point where the Prinsengracht intersects the Brouwersgracht. Amsterdam is on **Routes 17, 19** and **29** (photo © Dennis van de Water).

In 1816, the English poets Byron and Shelley visited Château de Chillon, the lakeshore castle by Lake Geneva. Two centuries on, the castle is a still a mainstay on the literary tourism circuit. Travel there by boat from Montreux, which is on **Route 38** (photo © Eva Bocek).

LAKE GENEVA

The Sicilian town of Taormina may be a premier league
tourist destination, but it can be mercifully quiet off-season.
It's a great place to stop off when following **Route 44** which
runs down Sicily's east coast to Siracusa (photo © Milosk50).

TAORMINA

PARIS

The Gare du Nord in Paris is the busiest railway station on the
European mainland. It's a place for comings and goings. For
travellers arriving on Eurostar from London (on **Route 6**), it is a
first taste of the continent (photo © Viorel Dudau).

Few railway stations can match São Bento in the Portuguese city of Porto when it comes to interior design. This fabulous *azulejo* tile work is in the station's main reception hall. Porto is an obvious place for an overnight stop when following **Route 16** from Santiago de Compostela to Lisbon (photo © Saiko3p).

PORTO

STARI BAR

The port city of Bar is the Adriatic terminus for **Route 45**. Just a few kilometres from the modern port, the old village of Stari Bar (Old Bar) captures the feel of the Montenegro of yesteryear (photo © Fotokon).

KRAKÓW

LEFT: When art appears in the marketplace, it's usually a sure sign that a city cuts a dash on the tourist circuit. Kraków certainly does that. It is Poland's most-visited destination. It features on **Routes 48** and **49**. It may be packed mid-summer, but off season this Polish city is very much quieter (photo © Deymos).

BELOW: Prepare to be overwhelmed by a surfeit of Renaissance crucifixions as you explore the Galleria degli Uffizi in Florence. This Italian city is on **Routes 41** and **42** (photo © Gordon Bell).

FLORENCE

The UNESCO-listed harmonious cityscape of Nancy has several showpiece squares. This city in eastern France has a feast of fine baroque, neoclassical and art nouveau architecture. Stop off in Nancy while following **Route 19** (photo © Mikeltrako).

NANCY

STOCKHOLM

Sweden's watery capital is built on a series of islands. Stockholm is a fine place to stop off for a day or two when exploring **Routes 28, 32** or **51** (photo © Sergiyn).

VITEBSK

Enthusiasm for Soviet-style memorials has not waned in Belarus. These stone heroes are enjoying Belarusian sunshine in Vitebsk, the city where artist Marc Chagall was born. Vitebsk is a good overnight stop when following **Route 50** (photo © hidden europe).

A university city noted for eccentric dons, dreaming spires and cutting-edge science, Oxford has been laser-focused on academic excellence for centuries. The neoclassical domed building is the Radcliffe Camera, part of the university's rich library network. Visit Oxford on **Route 5** (photo © Shao-chun Wang).

OXFORD

Routes

52 key rail routes which together capture the very best that Europe has to offer. Our routes cover cities and landscapes from the Arctic to Andalucía, from the Baltic to the Bay of Biscay, from the Atlantic coast of Ireland to the Carpathians. Use our route overview list on pp16–17 to see the specific countries which feature on each of our 52 routes. Or use our index (pp534–44) to identify communities across Europe which feature in our 52 routes or elsewhere in this book.

DISCOVER BRITAIN AND IRELAND
An introduction

Britain created the railway. And the **railway created modern Britain**. There was 19th-century apprehension about newly emerging industrial landscapes, and the developing rail network had many vocal critics. John Ruskin was one of them. Yet very quickly the railway embedded itself in the national psyche. For writers like **Hilaire Belloc** and **Edward Thomas** the rural railway was the very embodiment of Englishness. In Wales, Scotland and Ireland, the **Age of Steam** transformed cities and the countryside; developments in those countries occasionally even outpaced those in England. Dublin had its first suburban railway before London did.

New routes in this edition

It's an enormous pleasure for us as travellers and writers to be able to introduce new routes in **Great Britain and Ireland** in this 16th edition of *Europe by Rail*. Over the last year we have travelled both islands by train, taking the pulse of railway life, stopping off here and there in country towns or rural halts. From London to Limerick, Tralee to Tyndrum, we've been there.

Beyond the routes presented in this section, you might like to try the railway that runs west from Shrewsbury to Machynlleth then up the coast to Harlech and beyond (ERT 147/148). It's stunning. In Ireland, there are **many fine journeys** to which we've only been able to allude *en passant*. The line from Coleraine to Derry is unforgettable (ERT 231) and might, in a future edition, be a fitting finale to a new route from Dublin to Derry. We also had our sights on a classic Irish rural journey, that from Waterford to Galway via Cahir and Limerick (ERT 239/242), but in the end there wasn't space.

Train travel in Britain and Ireland is **perfect for visitors** who want to make use of rail passes. Very few trains require advance reservation and you'll not run across those painful supplements which limit pass use in France and Spain. **Eurail and Interrail passes** are valid throughout Britain and Ireland. There were rumours in late-summer 2019 that Britain – sadly now more isolationist than for many decades – might no longer accept the two above-mentioned passes. But it now seems clear that both will continue to be valid at least for 2020. Great Britain also has its own home-grown pass. It's called **BritRail**. There's also an excellent range of regional rover tickets in Britain which allow one or more days travel within a clearly defined area.

Two of the routes that follow in this section cross the North Sea to reach England from the continent. And there are two routes which cross the Irish Sea. For such journeys, there are tremendous bargains with **rail-sea tickets**, both between Holland and England (or vice versa) or from any station in Britain to destinations in Ireland (and back again). ∎

LONDON

While some great European cities – think Vienna, Berlin, Copenhagen or Milan – have a grand central station, London has **a dozen different railway termini**. All date back to the Victorian era. For generations of travellers, these railway stations have been the gateways to a city that has fuelled imperial ambition. Multiracial and multicultural London is a **vibrant world city**, a place which has attracted entrepreneurs and eccentrics, revolutionaries and reactionaries. With a week to spare, one might take in some of the planet's best art collections, exploring bustling local markets and relax in the city's legendary green spaces.

With just a day or two, it's best to focus on the cluster of main sights on the north side of the Thames, broadly between Westminster and the Tower. From Green Park and St James's Park, it's a pleasant wander on past **Trafalgar Square** (for the National Gallery) to **Covent Garden** and Lincoln's Inn, continuing east to the heart of London's business district – known, a little confusingly, as 'the City'.

From there it is but a short hop on to up-and-coming Whitechapel or, closer to the river, the Tower. You may want to venture south of the river into Southwark to visit the **Tate Modern** (www.tate.org.uk) or tickle your taste buds in **Borough Market** (www.boroughmarket.org.uk).

London is a city shaped by its river, so make use of the regular boat services, branded as MBNA **Thames Clippers** (www.thamesclippers.com), which run downriver from Westminster Millennium Pier (near Big Ben) to Greenwich and beyond. With half a dozen intermediate stops between Westminster and the Tower alone, you're never far from a landing stage.

ARRIVAL, INFORMATION, ACCOMMODATION

⇌ There are direct **Eurostar** trains to London from ten stations on the continent (although services from five of these are just seasonal). These trains all arrive at **St Pancras International**, a glorious architectural extravaganza of a station (see p97). The Greater London area is divided into six fare zones. Information on travel in London is available at www.tfl.gov.uk. The integrated ticketing scheme accepts **Oyster** and contactless cards. Just remember to touch-in at the start of each journey and touch-out (not necessary on buses) at the end. It's possible to buy tickets at machines for tube and train journeys (not possible for buses), but that's rather expensive. Apart from using the Thames Clippers, the top deck of one of the iconic, red London buses is a great way to see the city. **⌘** Tourist office: there's a travel information centre at St Pancras station and visitor centres at Liverpool Street station and Paddington station (www.visitlondon.com).

⨳ Located in Spitalfields, not far from Liverpool Street station, **Batty Langley's**, 12 Folgate St, ☎ 020 737 743 90 (www.battylangleys.com) is an elegant and highly regarded hotel in Georgian style. Well west of the main tourist attractions, but conveniently located for both Paddington station and Kensington Gardens, is the friendly **Westbourne Hyde Park**, 51 Gloucester Terrace, ☎ 020 740 250 77 (www.thewestbournelondon.co.uk). If you don't mind the institutional feel of a large chain hotel, then the **Premier Inn London King's Cross**, 26–30 York Way King's Cross, ☎ 0333 322 1272 (www.premierinn.com) is good value for money and close to King's Cross and St Pancras stations.

Route 1: Following Brunel to Cornwall

Cities: ★ Culture: ★★ History: ★ Scenery: ★★
Countries covered: England (ENG)
Journey time: 5 hrs 30 mins | Distance: 491 km | Map: www.ebrweb.eu/map1

In the beginning there were the graceful classical baths of the Roman Empire. Then came fine cathedrals. But by the late 19th century, **great railway termini** were acclaimed as the representative buildings of the Steam Age. Stations quickly became the unashamed status symbols of any city with ambition. Some echoed the showcase buildings of earlier eras. In New York, Penn Central was inspired by the great Roman baths at Caracalla. While in London, **St Pancras** took a cue from Europe's soaring Gothic cathedrals.

Whichever of the routes you follow in this book, make time for Europe's great railway stations. While some are sadly neglected and others have been the victims of wilful architectural vandalism, such cases are the exception. Many are beautiful places which lift the spirits.

Our very first journey in *Europe by Rail* starts at London's **Paddington station**; it is the unsung star of London's railway termini (for more on the capital of the UK see p51). St Pancras is the most grandiose and architecturally ambitious. Following recent renovations, **King's Cross** may now claim to be the most stately. But Paddington has a light elegance which is utterly charming. Despite its Moorish accents, there is something quintessentially English about Paddington. There are echoes of Paxton's magnificent great glasshouse, built for the Great Exhibition held in London in 1851. Paddington is a fine London home for a railway associated with one great name in 19th-century engineering: **Isambard Kingdom Brunel**. He was the driving force behind the **Great Western Railway**, the legendary GWR. In Victorian England, it was often suggested that the initials GWR stood for God's Wonderful Railway.

Paddington is the perfect place to embark on a journey which takes in some of the finest countryside in southern England. And this is a **London** station which has forever been associated with pleasure. Some termini were always, and still are, stations for commuters. Others suggested trade and commerce. But Paddington was for holidays. So, join us as we climb aboard one of the Great Western Railway trains **bound for Cornwall**.

Suggested Itinerary

It's a shade under 500 km from **London to Penzance** and the fastest GWR trains take just over five hours for the journey. It's the quick and easy way to get from the capital to Cornwall. There is also the *Night Riviera* sleeper service from London to Penzance.

This is a route which serves some of the most delightful towns in south-west England, including a bevy of fine coastal resorts – some of them not actually on the main line, but reached by minor rail routes which branch off from our route to serve ports and villages on the coasts of **Devon and Cornwall**. So in the description that follows, we highlight points

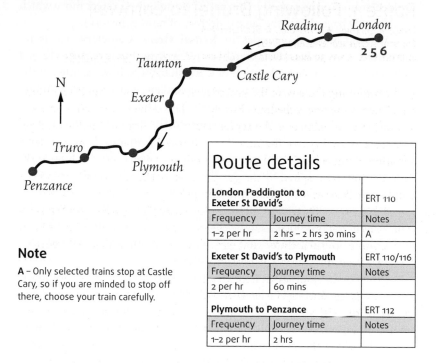

Route details		
London Paddington to Exeter St David's		ERT 110
Frequency	Journey time	Notes
1–2 per hr	2 hrs – 2 hrs 30 mins	A
Exeter St David's to Plymouth		ERT 110/116
Frequency	Journey time	Notes
2 per hr	60 mins	
Plymouth to Penzance		ERT 112
Frequency	Journey time	Notes
1–2 per hr	2 hrs	

Note

A – Only selected trains stop at Castle Cary, so if you are minded to stop off there, choose your train carefully.

in the journey where you may want to branch off and explore, stopping off perhaps for a night or two on the coast before returning to the main route.

Our top choices for overnight stops are **Castle Cary**, **Looe** and **St Mawes**. The likeable Somerset market town of Castle Cary has the advantage of being on the main GWR route. It's a good option if you are only able to leave London in the afternoon and want an early antidote to the noise and bustle of the capital. Both Looe and St Mawes are in Cornwall and require a diversion from the main line (see our Sidetracks feature on p58).

Penzance is the end of the line. But those who have followed Brunel's wonderful railway the whole way can venture further by boat on the daily sailing to the **Isles of Scilly**. If you opt to turn round and head back towards London, note that there is alternative, more southerly, route from Exeter to London Waterloo (ERT 108). It is every bit as beautiful as the GWR route to Paddington, taking in fine Dorset scenery and the cathedral city of Salisbury – always a good choice for an overnight stop, making time for a visit to nearby **Stonehenge**, served by regular bus services from Salisbury station (www.thestonehengetour.info).

West to Reading

This is a journey packed with interest. Hardly has the train left Paddington than there is an excellent view to the right, looking over the **Grand Union Canal**, towards Kensal Green Cemetery. There lie interred the remains of half a dozen members of the Brunel family, including Isambard Kingdom himself. Brunel was the son of a French cabinetmaker who only narrowly avoided ordination as a priest in his native Normandy (a career move which would surely have altered the later trajectory of railway history).

Wilkie Collins also resides in **Kensal Green Cemetery**. He is remembered more for his novels than his travel writing, but his *Rambles beyond Railways* is a perceptive exploration of Cornish byways. It was written at the time when Brunel's Great Western was colonising Cornwall by building branch lines to the remotest corners of the Royal Duchy.

There's a distant view of lofty **Harrow-on-the-Hill**, then comes the old asylum at Hanwell. The latter was built in 1831 for what in those days were then called 'the pauper insane'. The editor of *The Gentleman's Magazine*, one Edward Cave (who wrote under the pen name Sylvanus Urban) drew attention in 1858 to this landmark on the line out of Paddington. "A plain but handsome structure, which stands cheerily in open country," he wrote. No longer is this open country. London has crept west, a tangled web of streets and housing invading old villages and depriving them of their identity.

Speeding west through **Southall**, our train now crosses the Grand Union Canal. We have a guidebook from 1924 which describes a rural scene "with bridges, barges and ducks all doing their best to make it picturesque." Southall has subtly changed. The ducks are gone and just south of the railway is a spectacular Sikh temple. Signs on the railway platforms at Southall are in both English and Punjabi.

Leaving Southall there is little by way of green landscapes. But it is fascinating. Look out for art-deco style in the EMI factory at **Hayes**, planes closing in on Heathrow and the spiral swirls of motorways to nowhere. Beyond West Drayton lorry parks and container dumps go head-to-head with crazy golf and garden centres. This is magnificent stuff, a social roller coaster of a ride through modern England. But there are touches of antiquity too. **Windsor Castle** is visible away to the south.

Away to the right is **Stoke Poges**, where Thomas Gray penned his *Elegy Written in a Country Churchyard*. Nowadays modern **Slough** obscures what was presumably once a glorious vista over open countryside towards Stoke Poges. But, despite the poet John Betjeman's plea ("Come, friendly bombs, and fall on Slough"), the town looks remarkably spick and span as the GWR train speeds past Slough's elegant railway station. Burnham station is next on the line. It was once called Burnham Beeches, but the word 'Beeches' was suppressed in 1930. Happily the beech woods are still there, though you'll be hard pushed to see them from the train.

Beyond Brunel's famous brick bridge, captured in JMW Turner's painting *Rain, Steam and Speed – The Great Western Railway* (first exhibited in 1844), which escorts our train over the Thames at **Maidenhead**, the train sweeps through a swathe of cuttings with fleeting glimpses of Berkshire villages at points where the embankments are happily lower. To our right there's Ruscombe. That's the village where **William Penn** died in poverty in

1718. The infirm Quaker would most surely have preferred to meet his maker in Pennsylvania.

And so we slow for a first stop in Reading where another famous Quaker, George Palmer, saw the potential of the railway in helping distribute his company's biscuits. Reading gave us the custard cream. **Oscar Wilde** helped seal Reading's fate in his *Ballad of Reading Gaol*. These days this town on the Thames, just where the southernmost ripples of the Chiltern Hills slip down to the river, is part of London's busy commuter belt.

From Thames to Tamar

Leaving the Thames Valley at **Reading**, the GWR takes about three hours to reach Brunel's celebrated Royal Albert Bridge which spans the River Tamar at Plymouth, marking the point where the railway crosses from Devon into Cornwall. We rate this ride from Reading to Plymouth as perhaps the finest three-hour main-line train ride anywhere in England.

West from Reading, the train slips through **Aldermaston**, a Berkshire village which for 60 years has been the focus of Britain's pacifist lobby on account of an atomic weapons research centre located here. Just beyond Aldermaston, **Newbury** marks the end of the electrified route – just extended here in early 2019 – from Paddington. With Newbury behind us, the landscape becomes more assertively rural as the railway follows the Kennet Valley upstream through gentle chalk hills, paralleling the picturesque **Kennet and Avon Canal** for long stretches.

Until 1906, GWR trains from London to Devon took a much longer route via Swindon and Bristol. This new line via the Kennet Valley and Castle Cary trimmed the travel time; it's called the **Berks & Hants Line**, taking that name from two English counties, although oddly the railway line never actually touches Hampshire. Instead it takes in a fine swathe of North Wessex landscapes, seen at their best in the low sun angles of a spring morning or summer evening. Watch out for moorhens by the canal and the bold shapes of huge white horses carved into the **chalk hillsides** (there are three of them on the stretch between Newbury and Castle Cary, none of them anywhere near as ancient as locals would have one believe).

This GWR route to south-west England became an **economic lifeline** for the distant counties of Somerset, Devon and Cornwall. Before the coming of the railway, Cornish labourers emigrated to the Americas; only when Brunel's first trains arrived did those Cornish workers seriously think of looking for jobs in London. And the **GWR**, ever alert to the power of a good marketing campaign, filled its trains by promoting Devon and Cornwall as desirable destinations. For over 100 years, until cheap flights on jet aircraft tempted the sun-starved English to the Mediterranean, 'Glorious Devon' and the 'Cornish Riviera' were brands which lured **millions of holidaymakers** onto GWR trains. With a benign climate and lush vegetation, especially on the south coast of those two counties, there was something deliciously exotic about this far-flung part of England. Sandy coves, seagulls, Devon clotted cream and Cornish pasties sealed the holiday imagination for generations of English families.

It wasn't all one-way trade. New potatoes and early spring flowers from the Isles of Scilly were shipped from Penzance to London by train. Teasel from the Mendips and willow from the Somerset Levels, strawberries from the Tamar Valley and fresh fish from Looe and Brixham all helped fill the freight wagons which brought goods to London.

But we are distracting you. We've slipped by Savernake Forest and the Vale of Pewsey, and already we are in **Somerset**, speeding past Frome and Bruton to reach the market town of **Castle Cary**.

CASTLE CARY HINTS

Castle Cary is one of those solid, handsome country towns where there's nothing exception-al to see, but it's a fine choice for an overnight stay. It's a 20-minute walk into town, gently uphill but very pleasant, on a well-signed footpath. Or take the bus or taxi from the station up to the town centre.

Descriptions of several fine walks around the town are online at www.castle-cary. co.uk or visit the tourist office in the Market House. The thatched-roofed **George Hotel**, Market Place, ☎ 01963 350 761 (www.thegeorgehotelcastlecary.co.uk) is a good choice for an overnight stop. From Castle Cary, there's a pretty branch line which tracks south through **Hardy's Wessex** to Dorchester and the coast at Weymouth.

Just beyond Castle Cary, you'll see in the distance (to the right) the distinctive profile of **Glastonbury Tor**, a place so overburdened with myth and legend – the Holy Grail, King Arthur and more – that it attracts more visitors than it can possibly cope with. The flat terrain traversed by the railway was once marshy country, but now drained and known as the Somerset Levels.

Beyond Taunton, the line skirts a busy motorway south to reach the Devon county town of **Exeter**. The train stops at St David's station, and the city centre is about a 20-minute walk to the south-east. Exeter Central, easily reached by trains from St David's via a line which climbs very steeply, is better placed for the centre. If you wish to stop overnight try the Rougemont Hotel, ☎ 01392 410 237 (www.accorhotels.com) right by Exeter Central.

EXETER CONNECTIONS

Take the train to the coast at Exmouth on the **Avocet Line** (ERT 113) or explore Devon's beautiful interior by riding the **Tarka Line** (also ERT 113) up to Barnstaple. If you don't have time to venture further along Route 1, then you can return to London via Dorset and Salisbury – a one-time main-line now reduced to secondary status, but with plenty of gorgeous scenery along the way (ERT 108).

In a route that brims with superlatives, it might raise eyebrows to suggest that the stretch beyond Exeter is the very best section of the line to Cornwall.

Sit on the left for gorgeous sea views as the railway runs south beside the Exe Estuary, and then along the coast at Dawlish. It's all too brief, as the railway forsakes the coast at Teignmouth, running inland and skirting the southern edge of Dartmoor to reach **Plymouth**, the last stop in Devon before the train slips over the River Tamar into Cornwall.

Kernow a'gas dynergh: Welcome to Cornwall

Saltash, just west of the **Royal Albert Bridge** and the first station in Cornwall, has multilingual signs welcoming travellers to the county. It's likely that you'll want to stop off here and there on the journey through Cornwall and our Sidetracks feature on the next page gives tips on how to make the most of the branch lines which run down to the coast.

Staying on the train towards Penzance, it's easy to discern the main features of the Cornish landscape. There are deeply incised, wooded valleys with occasional distant views of the coast. At one point (near Par), our route touches the south coast, and then at Hayle it briefly skirts the north coast before flitting over to the south coast again, skirting the half-moon shaped Mount's Bay on the final approach into Penzance.

Penzance

Penzance is an unassuming working town, a place where one senses that the business of everyday life continues in spite of the seasonal crowds of visitors. Wander down the waterfront through Wherrytown to **Newlyn** to discover that fishing is still big business in Cornwall. A little further is the pretty coastal village of Mousehole. 🚌 M6 runs every 20–30 mins between Penzance and Mousehole via Newlyn.

ARRIVAL, INFORMATION, ACCOMMODATION
🚆 Just a short walk east of the city centre. 🛈 Tourist office: just outside the station entrance (www.purelypenzance.co.uk).

🛏 Located in two Edwardian merchants' houses, a short walk from the station, the **Hotel Penzance**, Britons Hill, ☎ 01736 363 117 (www.hotelpenzance.com), has rooms with great views over the bay. Or try the friendly **Bay Lodge** B&B, 5 Chyandour Square, ☎ 01736 351 090 (www.baylodgepenzance.com), also in the vicinity. Further away from the station, between Newlyn and the terminal for ferries to the Isles of Scilly, is the welcoming **Beachfield** B&B, The Promenad, ☎ 01736 331 100 (www.beachfield.co.uk).

CONNECTIONS FROM PENZANCE
Land's End is the obvious excursion from Penzance and 🚌 A1 will whisk you there in an hour. Contrary to popular belief, it's not the westernmost point on the British mainland. That honour goes to Corrachadh Mòr, a rocky headland on Scotland's Ardnamurchan Peninsula.

But Land's End is fun and worth the bus ride. Ignore the commercial tack and tourist traps and just savour the fresh sea air and awesome views. It's a magnificent counterpoint to Paddington station in London where we started this very first route in *Europe by Rail*.

SIDETRACKS: CORNISH BRANCH LINES

West from Plymouth, there are still no less than six minor railway lines branching off from the main **Great Western Railway** (GWR) route to Penzance. The first runs up the Tamar Valley to terminate well inland at Gunnislake in east Cornwall, a one-time mining town in a region with rich deposits of tin, copper, silver and arsenic. Of the other five branch lines, one is a **seasonal heritage railway** linking Bodmin Parkway with Bodmin town centre (www.bodminrailway.co.uk).

That leaves four other routes, all of them connecting the main line with a coastal community. Each of these is a gem. Dedicated baggers of unusual railways could feasibly cover all four in a day, and it needn't be expensive. There's a **Cornwall Rover ticket** valid from Plymouth to all points west which allows one day's travel for just £12.50 (discounts for GB railcard holders). But these four branch railways give access to such interesting places that one could easily spent a whole week exploring Cornwall, relying in the main on rail transport, augmented here and there by ferries and bus services. Moving west from Tamar, the lines that run to the coast are Liskeard to Looe, Par to Newquay, Truro to Falmouth, and St Erth to St Ives. The times in parentheses below give the journey time to each destination from the main-line junction.

If you cover just one of these lines, make it the branch railway to **Looe** (30 mins), which is short but very sweet, dropping down steeping from Liskeard and then following the East Looe River down to the coast. The fishing port of Looe is the perfect place for a first night's stop in Cornwall. If you'd like to stay overnight, **Little Mainstone Guest House**, The Quay, ☎ 01503 262983 (www. littlemainstone-looe.com), on the west side of the river, is a welcoming B&B with great views over the harbour.

Next up, as we move west on the main line, is the branch to **Newquay** (50 mins), which diverges from the Penzance route at Par, a tiny south-coast port which makes a living through exports of china clay. Of the four branch lines to the coast, this one wins hands down for giving views of the sometimes bleak landscapes of the Cornish interior. It's an interesting run, but not entirely pretty.

The next diversion is the short hop from Truro down to **Falmouth** (20 mins), which competes with Penzance as the major urban centre on Cornwall's south coast. It's a pleasant ride and, though Falmouth hardly rates as quaint, it has a lively arts scene and **Pendennis Castle** is not to be missed. The real draw, though, are the villages easily reached by regular ferries from Falmouth. We recommend **St Mawes**, perfectly positioned on the east side of the Carrick Roads with grand views of the coast. A friendly B&B to stay overnight is **Nearwater**, Polvarth Rd, ☎ 01326 279278 (www.nearwaterstmawes.co.uk).

St Mawes is one of those spots you may never want to leave. If you really must leave, add a dash of romance to the moment by taking the boat back to Truro to rejoin the main GWR rail route to the west.

Last, but by no means least of the four branches to the coast, is the short line from **St Erth to St Ives** (10 mins), which gives fine views of some of the best beaches on the north coast before skirting Carbis Bay to reach St Ives. This pretty coastal town can be impossibly crowded in summer, but it's a fine spot to while away a few wet winter days.

Route 2: Cathedrals, castles and glens

CITIES: ★★★ CULTURE: ★★ HISTORY: ★★ SCENERY: ★★
COUNTRIES COVERED: ENGLAND (ENG), SCOTLAND (SCT)
JOURNEY TIME: 12 HRS | DISTANCE: 1,047 KM | MAP: WWW.EBRWEB.EU/MAP2

If there is one rail journey which has consistently fired the English imagination, it is the ride from **London to the Scottish Highlands**. There are two celebrated paintings by the English artist George Earl, dating from 1876 and 1893 respectively, which both capture the excitement of wealthy Victorians leaving from King's Cross for the grouse-shooting season in the Scottish hills. The platform is packed with well-dressed travellers, surrounded by fishing tackle, hunting dogs – the latter a George Earl trademark – and all the paraphernalia necessary for a few weeks of 'sporting fun' in the Highlands. The poor grouse surely never saw anything very sporting in the escapade.

The hounds are long gone, but there's still a hint of magic about **King's Cross station**. In the *Harry Potter* books, the Hogwarts Express departs from Platform 9¾ at King's Cross, so there's usually a line of Ravenclaws and Gryffindors waiting to pay homage at the spot immortalised in JK Rowling's novels. Predictably, in this commercial age, there's a *Harry Potter* shop there too, so it's a handy opportunity to pick up a new wand or a time turner which might always come in useful on your trip to Scotland. Even the most adept wizard cannot magic away the Scottish midges though, so consider packing some midge cream before heading north.

We'll cover over a thousand kilometres by train, travelling **via York, Edinburgh and Inverness** to reach Kyle of Lochalsh on the west coast of Scotland. The journey doesn't end there, for from Kyle it is but a short hop by bus over the bridge to Skye, from where more adventurous travellers may wish to continue by boat to the Outer Hebrides. Along the way, we'll take in several great cathedrals, the Scottish capital and some very fine mountain landscapes including the **Cairngorms National Park**.

RECOMMENDED ITINERARY

This is a route replete with possibilities. With an early start from King's Cross and two changes of train – in Edinburgh and Inverness – it's perfectly possible to travel from King's Cross to Kyle of Lochalsh in a day. But you could do better by stopping off here and there along the way. York and Edinburgh are both good options.

If you are less inclined to linger, then why not book a first-class seat on the **Highland Chieftain** which leaves King's Cross for Inverness at midday? On weekdays, first-class passengers are served complimentary meals and drinks. The *Highland Chieftain* follows the route described here, bar for the stretch between Edinburgh and Perth where it routes via Stirling rather than the Forth Bridge and Fife. On a summer evening, the final two hours of the journey, from Perth to Inverness, really are hard to beat. Stay overnight at the Royal Highland Hotel (www.royalhighlandhotel.co.uk), which adjoins the railway station in Inverness, and then you'll be fresh as a fiddle in the morning for the stunning ride west to **Kyle of Lochalsh**.

Another possibility, if time is tight, is to travel by the overnight **Caledonian Sleeper** service from London to Edinburgh or Inverness. Note that all overnight services to Scotland depart from London Euston and follow the West Coast route. The Caledonian Sleeper is an experience in itself. Our feeling is that the night train to Edinburgh departs too late in the evening and gives an uncomfortably early arrival in the Scottish capital. The Inverness train is here the better option – and bacon rolls with fresh coffee at the crack of dawn as the train cruises down the Spey Valley, with great views of the **Cairngorms**, are hard to beat. Note that the Caledonian Sleeper services do not run in either direction on Saturday nights.

North to York

The main **East Coast route** might better have been called the Cathedrals Line. Sit on the right side of the train and you should be able to spot three historic ecclesiastical gems on the ride north – they are at Peterborough, York and Durham. This line from **King's Cross** is the most uncompromising of the main-line rail routes running north from London. It runs in a pretty straight line to York and beyond. Being a late addition to England's railway geography, tempting off-route cities like Nottingham and Leeds had already been 'claimed' by rival companies. The **Great Northern Railway (GNR)** had its eyes set on the North and nothing less. Branch lines to growing industrial cities were all well and good, but the GNR didn't want to risk the great prize of capturing the traffic from London to York and beyond.

Curiously, one of the biggest challenges for the GNR's talented engineers was getting out of London. The capital's leafy northern heights and the easternmost ripples of the **Chiltern Hills** in Hertfordshire were tackled in a series of dramatic viaducts, dark tunnels and deep cuttings which still today add a touch of drama to the first half hour of the run out of King's Cross.

The train north dashes over Welwyn Viaduct, which bridges the Mimram Valley, in an ambitious streak of 40 fine arches, styled in the manner of a Roman aqueduct. Then the railway uses the gentle vales created by two chalkland streams, the Hiz and the Ivel, to reach the River Ouse which it follows north towards **Peterborough**. There's a touch of the Fenlands in the sedge and mere terrain around Peterborough, although the town itself, bar for its remarkable but oddly asymmetric cathedral, is nothing special.

CONNECTIONS FROM PETERBOROUGH

For better views of the **watery Fenlands**, take the trains which run east from Peterborough to Ely (ERT 205, 206 & 208), where there's another fine cathedral. These trains continue beyond Ely to Cambridge (ERT 208) or Norwich (ERT 206). Connect at Peterborough onto **Route 4** in this book, which runs west via Birmingham (ERT 208) to North Wales and Ireland. Or follow Route 4 in reverse to the Essex port of Harwich for ferries to the Netherlands. If you are not in any rush to head north, there is an appealing rural route from Peterborough via Spalding and Lincoln which rejoins the main East Coast line at Doncaster (ERT 186).

From Peterborough, our route north rises very gently to **Stoke Summit**. It was on this stretch of track that in 1938 a London-bound train hauled by

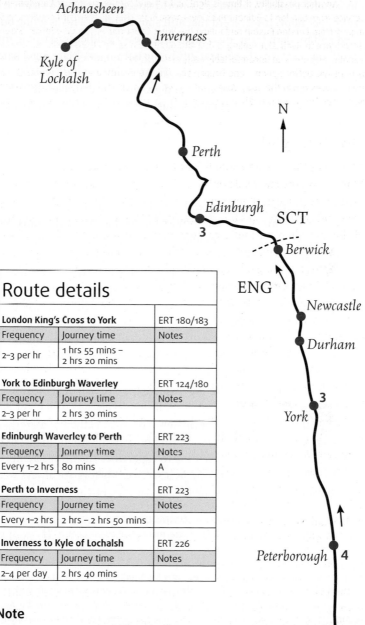

Route details

London King's Cross to York		ERT 180/183
Frequency	Journey time	Notes
2–3 per hr	1 hrs 55 mins – 2 hrs 20 mins	
York to Edinburgh Waverley		ERT 124/180
Frequency	Journey time	Notes
2–3 per hr	2 hrs 30 mins	
Edinburgh Waverley to Perth		ERT 223
Frequency	Journey time	Notes
Every 1–2 hrs	80 mins	A
Perth to Inverness		ERT 223
Frequency	Journey time	Notes
Every 1–2 hrs	2 hrs – 2 hrs 50 mins	
Inverness to Kyle of Lochalsh		ERT 226
Frequency	Journey time	Notes
2–4 per day	2 hrs 40 mins	

Note

A – There is an alternative route from Edinburgh to Perth via Stirling – normally requiring a change in Stirling. Trains on this route run at least hourly. Travel time is 80–90 mins.

a locomotive called *Mallard* set a **world speed record** for a steam train of 203 km per hour. It's a record that still stands today. This is a line built for speed and modern trains make light of the easy gradients, dashing through Grantham – a town whose great gift to the nation was Margaret Thatcher – and on past the power stations in the Trent Valley around Newark.

Retford and **Doncaster** come and go, with the countryside beyond the carriage window assuming a more industrial demeanour. If you've opted for one of the fast trains, just short of two hours after leaving London the train is already slowing for York.

York (suggested stopover)

York's elegant railway station with its striking curved platforms is a fine introduction to one of England's most interesting cities. **Romans, Vikings and Quakers** have all helped mould York; today it rates as an appealing place to stop off for a night or longer. The **Jorvik Viking centre** gives a splendid introduction to life in York under Scandinavian rule (when York was known as Jórvík; www.jorvikwikingcentre.co.uk). It's not all sepia-tinged romance, so you'll learn a lot about fleas, lice and Viking rubbish. It's fun, educational and not to be missed. In similar vein, make time for the **National Railway Museum** (free entry, check details on www.railwaymuseum.org.uk), which is nowhere near as geeky as it sounds. It's a brilliant romp through the world of trains with as much social history as engineering.

York was made for wandering. Explore the city walls, cobbled streets and intriguing pedestrian alleys (locally called snickelways) which cut between buildings, then head for **York Minster**. The great cathedral at York, whose bishop rates second only to that of Canterbury in the Anglican hierarchy, has magnificent stained glass. Take time to experience the calm serenity of this great sanctuary, ideally by taking in a service. Visitors are always welcome. A good choice is choral evensong (usually at 17.15, but at 16.00 on Sundays).

Arrival, Information and Accommodation
⇄ Very centrally located, just west of the mediaeval town centre. **ℹ** Tourist office: 1 Museum Street (www.visityork.org).

🛏 The **Parisi**, 51 St Denys Road, ☎ 01904 658 815 (www.theparisi.com) is a cosy and friendly hotel in the medieval part of town, a short walk from all major attractions. Or try **Dean Court Hotel**, Duncombe Place, ☎ 01904 625 082 (www.deancourt-york.co.uk); its location close to York Minster is hard to beat. Located in a Victorian town house, the **No 21 York**, 21 St Mary's, ☎ 01904 629 494 (www.no21york.co.uk) is a very hospitable B&B within easy reach of the station and just a short stroll from the town centre.

Connections from York
For a great railway centre, it's no surprise that there's a feast of onward connections from York. For a very fine day out from York, consider taking the 🚌 840 or X40 to Pickering (about 80 mins from York) to pick up the **North Yorkshire Moors Railway** heritage steam line to the picturesque port of Whitby (ERT 211, see also www.nymr.co.uk). From Whitby,

it is a beautiful journey through moorland wilderness to Middlesbrough (ERT 211), whence there are hourly direct trains back to York (ERT 188).

Join **Route 3**, the next journey in this book, for an alternative itinerary to Scotland, crossing the Pennines on the famous **Settle & Carlisle railway**. Or follow Route 3 in reverse to Hull (ERT 179) for overnight shipping services to Belgium (ERT 2230) or Holland (ERT 2220). From York, trains head west to Harrogate (ERT 175), over the **Pennines** to Manchester and Liverpool (ERT 188) or east to the coast at Scarborough (also ERT 188).

York to Edinburgh

From York, our route continues north through the Vale of York in an un-compromising straight line, but now – on a clear day – the broad contours of Yorkshire geography become more evident. The high terrain of the **North York Moors National Park** rises up away to the east, while well west of the vale one can see the Yorkshire Dales, which form part of the Pennine chain, running up the spine of northern England.

There are three great rivers in north-east England – the Tees, Wear and Tyne – and we cross all three of them. Shortly after crossing the River Tees, the route passes through Darlington, home in 1825 to the world's very first public **steam-operated railway**. Just 15 minutes further north, there is (to

THE RACE TO THE NORTH

Cast back 250 years, and those who wanted to get from **London to Edinburgh** would travel by ship or by stagecoach – those who opted for the latter could easily spend a fortnight on the journey. In 1847, the first railway across the Anglo-Scottish border opened for traffic – that was the line running north from Carlisle which is followed by Route 3 in this book.

Fifteen years later, the main East Coast line from London to Edinburgh opened, ushering in an era of fierce competition between the **West Coast** (from Euston via Carlisle) and the **East Coast** (from King's Cross via York) routes. Each company sought to provide the best service and the shortest journey times – even to the extent that they compromised on safety in the early days of the competition. If you are making a return journey from London to Scotland, you might consider travelling out from King's Cross following the journey described here, and then using the West Coast line through Carlisle for the southbound run. The latter includes an exceptionally fine stretch skirting the eastern edge of the **Lake District** in north-west England.

With the debut of the East Coast line in 1862, the *Special Scotch Express* – a precursor of the famous **Flying Scotsman** – left both London and Edinburgh at 10 each morning, with the 632-km run taking ten hours. Today the fastest train of the day on the East Coast route is the southbound *Flying Scotsman* which leaves Edinburgh at the crack of dawn on weekday mornings and dashes to London in just four hours.

Referring to these key routes to Scotland as the East Coast and West Coast lines is desperately misleading as neither of them hugs the coast. On the East Coast line, described in **Route 2**, you'll not get a first glimpse of the sea until well north of Newcastle-upon-Tyne. On the West Coast line, there's no real coastal scenery, but you do skirt the shores of Morecambe Bay just beyond Lancaster and eagle-eyed observers may get a fleeting glimpse of the Solway Firth as the train crosses the Scottish border.

the right) one the finest urban panoramas of the entire run as the train skirts the cathedral city of **Durham**. It's matched by two others in the following hour, one at Newcastle as the train approaches the main station with a dramatic bridging of the River Tyne, and then at Berwick-upon-Tweed, where the crossing of the Royal Border Bridge is pure theatre.

Our feeling is that the journey from **York to Edinburgh** is best done in one go. There's a real symphonic quality to the route, and in some ways it's sad to interrupt that. But we don't want to diminish the charms of Durham, where it's easy to idle away a day or two, or write off the more edgy appeal of Newcastle, which is a major rail hub.

NEWCASTLE LINKS

There is an especially fine railway which runs west from Newcastle-upon-Tyne, initially following the Tyne Valley up to Hexham and beyond and then broadly following Hadrian's Wall west to Carlisle (ERT 210), where one can join **Route 3** in this book. Newcastle is also a good jumping-off point for the continent, with a daily late afternoon sailing from North Shields to IJmuiden on the Dutch coast not far from Amsterdam (ERT 2255).

Dashing north from Newcastle towards **Berwick**, we get our first hint of the sea, with especially fine views of the coastal community of Alnmouth and later Holy Island. Heading over the Scottish border, just beyond Berwick, the railway plays cat and mouse with the coast, with tantalising glimpses of cliffs, sandy coves and occasional fishing villages. Approaching Edinburgh, there are good views over the Firth of Forth to Fife while on the left side of the train the great volcanic plug known as Arthur's Seat hoves into view.

Few capital city stations are so centrally positioned as Waverley, the main railway hub in **Edinburgh**. It is set in a valley with the mediaeval Old Town just to the south (ie. your left as you arrive from York) and the neoclassical and Georgian New Town equally close at hand to the north. Alighting from the train at Waverley station is always special; it is as if the city is rising around you on all sides.

For our account of Edinburgh with onward connections see **Route 3** (pp74–75). You can follow Route 3 to Scotland's west coast at Mallaig (ERT 218), or return to England by following Route 3 in reverse, taking the old Caledonian main line to Carlisle and beyond (ERT 154).

Highland adventure

In a route which has already had its fair share of superlatives, the best is yet to come. There are two routes from **Edinburgh to Perth**. The more westerly option follows the Forth Valley to Stirling and then north through Strathallan to Perth. It's a fine ride, but we think the eastern route has the edge, if only because it crosses the Forth Rail Bridge – a real *Europe by Rail* magic moment.

Heading west from Waverley, all Perth-bound trains pause at Haymarket (at the western end of the city centre), from where it is about a dozen minutes to the **Forth Bridge**. From the right side of the train, you get a fine view of the bridge on the approach. Once on the bridge, you can see the two road bridges away to your left. The more distant of the two is the new Queensferry Crossing, which opened to traffic in 2017.

Gaining the north bank, the railway skirts the Fife coast before turning inland and then leaving the main line to Aberdeen at Ladybank. This is a more rural route, and the first stretch of single track railway on our journey from London. But not the last for henceforth most of **Route 2** is on single track lines. Almost immediately there's a taste of the hills, as the train cuts through the easternmost outliers of the Ochils. The railway runs through Collessie Den and skirts **Lindores Loch** to reach the shore of the Firth of Tay at the port of Newburgh, where the locals are still very miffed that their railway station was closed in 1955 and trains have never stopped since. From here it's just a few minutes to **Perth**, a handsome station with a complicated layout of platforms.

Perth Conections

There are hourly trains running south-west to Stirling and Glasgow (ERT 222 & 223) or east through the Carse of Gowrie to Dundee and on up the coast to **Aberdeen** (ERT 223), from where those prepared to venture to rail-free islands can sail north to Orkney and Shetland (ERT 2200).

Leaving Perth, the railway traverses pastoral Tayside landscapes, with views of the river to the right. Cutting through a short tunnel (the first since Perth), we traverse **Birnam Wood**. No ordinary wood this, for much is made of Birnam in Shakespeare's *Macbeth*. Now the landscape assumes a real Highland demeanour. First stop, but not for express trains which just speed through, is Dunkeld & Birnam, twin towns on either side of the **River Tay**, linked by a striking iron bridge designed by Thomas Telford. The hills close in as the railway climbs up through the valleys of the Tay and the Tummel to reach Glen Garry, along the way stopping at solid, handsome townships like Pitlochry and Blair Atholl (the latter's station is pictured on the front cover of this book).

Cresting the summit of the line at Drumochter, we are now in the heart of the **Grampian Mountains**, amid some of Scotland's remotest terrain. Sit back and relax as the train drops gently down towards Glen Truim and the Spey Valley. The whisky distillery at Dalwhinnie (to the right of the railway) is a reminder that this is the land of *uisge beatha* – the water of life.

All trains stop at the two main **Spey Valley** communities – the first, Kingussie, is as nice a wee town as one could wish. Nothing ever happens here, but it's a pleasant base for tame walks and adventurous hikes. The second stop is at Aviemore, an extraordinary eyesore and a reminder of just how bad town planning was in the 1960s. The town is an ill-conceived attempt to create an Alpine style resort in the Highlands. Avert your eyes or, better still, let them be drawn to the fine range of hills away to the east. These are the **Cairngorms**, whose summits are – bar for Ben Nevis well away to the west – the loftiest in Britain. This is wild country which in winter has a real hint of the Arctic. Even when spring has come to the Spey Valley, it may still be wild winter on the Cairngorm tops, the late snows sintering into ice and lingering on till summer on shady north slopes. Make time for the Scottish hills and perhaps read Nan Shepherd's *The Living Mountain*, a wonderful piece of nature writing about the author's Cairngorm encounters.

From **Aviemore**, the railway tracks north-west, paralleling the main A9 road towards Inverness, climbing up to Slochd Summit, from where it's downhill all the way to Inverness, with two especially fine viaducts on that descent. The first is at Tomatin where the railway crosses Strathdearn, high above the River Findhorn, and the second is a gracious, gently curved 29-arch viaduct at **Culloden**, close to the spot where in 1745 government forces loyal to England's Hanoverian monarchs brutally snuffed out the Jacobite rebellion, inflicting a blow on Scottish life and culture which is still a sore point in Anglo-Scottish relations. These are thoughts to ponder as, with fine views of Moray Firth to the north, the train drops down into Inverness.

INVERNESS CONNECTIONS

Hourly trains run east on a pleasantly rural railway to **Aberdeen** (ERT 225), a route which never really cuts into the hills, but nonetheless affords great views along almost its entire length. Inverness is also the jumping-off point for the slow but utterly beautiful ride north to Caithness. Four trains a day (fewer on Sundays) leave Inverness for **Thurso and Wick** (ERT 226), along the way taking in a colourful medley of coastal and moorland landscapes. A highlight is the half-hour stretch between Kinbrace and Scotscalder where the railway traverses an eerily desolate expanse of blanket bog. Tales are told of trains being stranded here for days in winter snowstorms.

By mountain, moors and lochs

Over the past 50 years, timetable improvements have trimmed almost an hour off the travel time from **Inverness to Kyle**, but the journey is as beautiful as ever. This is the only rail route in Great Britain which affords fine views of both the east and west coasts. The train skirts Beauly Firth on leaving Inverness, and then on leaving Dingwall there is a great panorama of **Cromarty Firth** away to the north-east. But those east coast tasters are merely the prelude to a journey which takes in mountains and moorland, forest and glens before a glorious, almost operatic finale as the line skirts west-coast sea lochs on the approach to Kyle of Lochalsh.

The first part of the route out of Inverness has the feel of a very local railway. Three stations between Inverness and **Dingwall**, all closed in 1960, have reopened to passenger traffic in recent years. Beyond Dingwall, the railway swings west and climbs slowly into the mountains. Once past Garve, the hills close in and our train glides past mossy cliffs on the north side of the tracks. In winter, the green moss is eclipsed by cascades of icicles.

The coffee trolley – usually hoisted on board the train at Dingwall – doesn't come a moment too soon. Okay, it's not quite the same as the restaurant car which used to feature on the morning Kyle train as far as Achnasheen, where it was detached and sent back to Inverness with lunchtime duties on the homeward run.

Achnasheen is a place in the wilderness, as indeed are many stations on this rural railway. Two deer look idly on as the train slips by. The station names trip alliteratively off the tongue: Achnashellach, Achnasheen, Achanalt. And soon we are dropping down into Strathcarron, the great glen which drains west to the sea. We speed through **Attadale**, a remote halt where trains stop only on request. The gardens right by the station are an excellent place to break your journey (open daily April–October). From this little fragment of Paradise there are wonderful views of Skye. Not far beyond Attadale is Stromeferry, a delightfully misleading station name for there is no ferry. A three-minute stop is a chance to gulp fresh Highland air, but we are quickly on our way again.

The last twenty minutes down to Kyle are offer a tantalising mix of coast, headlands and islands. The sun sparkles on **Loch Carron** and later catches the Crowlin Islands – while all the while there are glorious views north to the rugged Applecross Peninsula. Seals scuttle for safety as we approach Duncraig and all too soon we are pulling into **Kyle of Lochalsh**.

"For those of you who liked it so much that you want to ride back with us to Inverness, we'll be leaving Kyle just after midday," the guard announces. It seems that most of those on board plan to do just that. But for others, Kyle is merely a way station on a longer journey so they alight from the train and head for a waiting bus to take them further into the hills.

ONWARD FROM KYLE

Bus connections are well signed at Kyle station. On summer weekdays, buses leave about hourly from the harbour slipway (4 mins walk from the station) to cross the bridge to Broadford in **Skye** (services are less frequent on Sundays and in the winter). Most of these buses continue to Portree, about 70 mins by bus from Kyle, a pleasant small town which is the hub of Skye life. Just beyond Portree, on Skye's north-west coast, is the port of Uig (regular buses from Portree), whence there are ferries to Tarbert (Harris) and Lochmaddy (North Uist), both in the **Outer Hebrides**.

Broadford is an unlovely introduction to Skye, so there's no reason to stop here other than to change buses if you are heading for the island's beautiful Sleat Peninsula. Occasional buses run from Broadford to Armadale, from where you can take the CalMac ferry to Mallaig to connect into **Route 3**. Check bus and ferry times carefully, and bear in mind that the ferry service over the Sound of Sleat to Mallaig may be disrupted by high winds. By using this bus and ferry connection from Kyle to **Mallaig**, it is possible to combine **Route 2** and **3** in this book to create a marvellous round trip from Edinburgh through the Highlands to Syke, returning to the Scottish capital by an entirely different route.

SIDETRACKS: THE HEBRIDES

Few parts of Europe possess such wild beauty as the **Hebrides**, the complex archipelago off Scotland's west coast. There are about three dozen inhabited islands in the Inner Hebrides, which lie close to the Scottish mainland. And there are around 15 islands in the more distant Outer Hebrides which host a permanent population. The ferry services to the islands are operated by **Caledonian MacBrayne** (CalMac; details on www.calmac.co.uk). These services run from four mainland ports, namely Ullapool, Mallaig, Oban and Kennacraig. In addition, CalMac operates ferries to the islands of Harris and North Uist (both in the Outer Hebrides) from the small port of Uig on the Isle of Skye.

CalMac's comprehensive network of ferry services to, from and between the Hebridean islands offers some of the finest inshore shipping routes in Europe, with superb opportunities for island hopping by scheduled ferry services. Rail travellers often head for **Mallaig**, at the very end of the **West Highland Line** (on **Route 3** in this book), whence there are year-round CalMac services to six different Hebridean islands (five in the Inner Hebrides, plus South Uist in the Outer Isles). The destination list from Oban also runs to half-a-dozen islands ranging from serene Colonsay (in the Inner Hebrides) to beautiful Barra (at the southern end of the Outer Hebrides).

Direct trains from **Glasgow** run to both Oban and Mallaig and at each port it is just a short walk from train to ship. The boats are of different sizes, but on the bigger vessels, travellers will find every creature comfort with a good choice of Scottish fare on offer in the restaurants. All ferries convey cars, but it's also very easy to devised creative itineraries through the Hebrides relying entirely on public transport.

These ferries provide **lifeline links** to some of Scotland's remotest communities; they are essential to the economic and social fabric of the region. And, in a region noted for its wild Atlantic weather, that means being flexible. On a breezy day in November, for example, CalMac advised that gusting winds might cause disruption to the **MS Clansman** as she set off on her scheduled sailing from Oban to Coll and Tiree. A footnote in that CalMac advisory, indicated that "the captain is fine with taking livestock" – it was a nice reminder that the company's vessels are part and parcel of Hebridean life. During the late summer and autumn, the company lays on extra sailings to accommodate livestock sales in Tiree and the Uists.

For a first taste of the Hebrides, and with a full week to spare, we recommend sailing out from **Oban to Barra**, then tracking north through the Outer Hebrides to Tarbert on Harris, from where it's just a short hop across to Uig on Skye. One might then enjoy a day or two on Skye before crossing the **Sound of Sleat** on the ferry from Armadale to Mallaig, where one can rejoin the mainland rail network.

This itinerary requires five ferries in all, with an all-inclusive fare for those five boats of about £32 per person – using CalMac's **Hopscotch ticket** no. 23. It's a chance to discover island communities with their own distinctive culture, language and stories. **Route 2** and **3** in this book make fine preludes to Hebridean adventures.

Route 3: The rural route to the West Highlands

CITIES: ★★ CULTURE: ★ HISTORY: ★★ SCENERY: ★★★
COUNTRIES COVERED: NETHERLANDS (NL), ENGLAND (ENG), SCOTLAND (SCT)
JOURNEY TIME: 27 HRS 30 MINS | DISTANCE: 1,210 KM | MAP: WWW.EBRWEB.EU/MAP3

In the history of *Europe by Rail*, which now spans a quarter of a century, we've never before had a route which started on the European mainland and ended in Scotland. So this really is a first, and we hope it might act as encouragement for continental Europeans to take advantage of sterling's declining value (which has made Britain more affordable) to explore the **hill country** of northern England and Scotland.

But equally this route can be followed in reverse, perhaps by urbanites from Glasgow, Edinburgh and Leeds who might be tempted to forsake the plane and travel instead by train and ferry to the continent.

The highlights of this journey **from Rotterdam to the West Highlands of Scotland** are two railways which are both in the premier league of Europe's most celebrated lines: the first is the **Settle and Carlisle railway**, a line which really engages with Pennine landscapes, and the second is the **West Highland Line** from Glasgow to the fishing port of Mallaig by the Sound of Sleat on Scotland's west coast. Along the way we travel through such fine cities as York and Edinburgh.

ITINERARY THOUGHTS

We recommend splitting this route into three legs. Travelling **overnight on the ship** to Hull is always fun, but you may not want to then spend the whole of the following day on trains. Better we think to travel from Hull to York by train, spend a few hours there, and then overnight in either Knaresborough or Harrogate. Then start afresh in the morning for the ride via Settle and Carlisle to Edinburgh. After a night or two in **Edinburgh**, continue into the Highlands following the route right through to its conclusion in Mallaig.

A Voyage with the Peninsular & Oriental

Route 3 is the only journey in this book which **starts with a bus**. It's only a short hop, but you will need to take the special coach service which links central Rotterdam with dock number 5805 at Europoort, from where the overnight ship to Hull departs. Not any ship but a **P&O vessel**. Yes, the Peninsular and Oriental Steam Navigation Company wouldn't be out of place running ships to Sumatra or Suriname, but these days it shuttles across the North Sea to Hull.

The ferry needs to be pre-booked (www.poferries.com). The bus is operated by De Jong Tours and leaves from Conradstraat right by **Rotterdam** Centraal railway station (south side). Look for the clearly marked bus stop for international departures on stance HH in the area where buses come and go. Be at the bus stop by 16.50 for a prompt 17.00 departure (the one-way

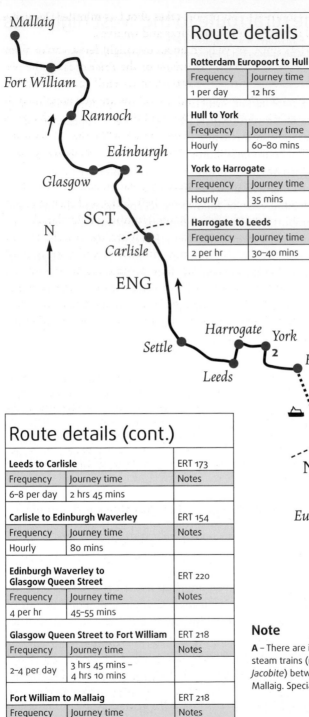

Route details

Rotterdam Europoort to Hull		ERT 2220
Frequency	Journey time	Notes
1 per day	12 hrs	
Hull to York		ERT 179
Frequency	Journey time	Notes
Hourly	60–80 mins	
York to Harrogate		ERT 175
Frequency	Journey time	Notes
Hourly	35 mins	
Harrogate to Leeds		ERT 175
Frequency	Journey time	Notes
2 per hr	30–40 mins	

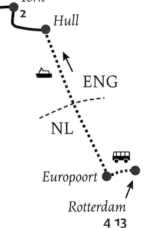

Route details (cont.)

Leeds to Carlisle		ERT 173
Frequency	Journey time	Notes
6–8 per day	2 hrs 45 mins	
Carlisle to Edinburgh Waverley		ERT 154
Frequency	Journey time	Notes
Hourly	80 mins	
Edinburgh Waverley to Glasgow Queen Street		ERT 220
Frequency	Journey time	Notes
4 per hr	45–55 mins	
Glasgow Queen Street to Fort William		ERT 218
Frequency	Journey time	Notes
2–4 per day	3 hrs 45 mins – 4 hrs 10 mins	
Fort William to Mallaig		ERT 218
Frequency	Journey time	Notes
3–4 per day	85 mins	A

Note

A – There are in addition seasonal steam trains (marketed as *The Jacobite*) between Fort William and Mallaig. Special fares apply.

fare is €9). The bus journey to Europoort takes about 45 minutes through a netherworld of oil refineries, container parks and wharves.

If it's a few years since you've been on an overnight ferry, you're in for a surprise as you board the *Pride of Rotterdam* or the *Pride of Hull*, the two P&O vessels which alternate on the **Rotterdam to Hull** route. There's a real touch of luxury about these ships and the cabins are well appointed. If your budget stretches to it, definitely book one of the premier or club cabins (both categories have windows, but the club ones are just a wee bit classier). We tend to go prepared with a supper picnic, but there is of course a good choice of on-board eateries.

Slipping out of Europoort, you'll surely see great oil tankers, complicated lines of coloured pipework dancing along their decks, and then it's open water all the way to the mouth of the **River Humber** on England's east coast. Expect to disembark just after eight in the morning, or a shade later on weekend days. Bus number 70 runs into **Hull**, on a working day most likely riding bumper to bumber with impatient commuters, to deposit you at the oddly named Paragon Interchange — which is the main transport hub where trains and buses from all parts gather. The tourist office is there too, so if you are minded to linger in one of England's most underrated cities, that's the place to head for.

Hull connections

If you are tempted to forsake Route 3 already, then Hull is replete with opportunity. There are direct trains to London (ERT 181) or over the Pennines to Manchester (ERT 188a). If you've a bit of time on your hands and want to take a **rural route to York**, hop on the next train to Scarborough (ERT 177), from where it is a but a short ride to York (ERT 188). There's some decent countryside along the way and beyond Beverley, the train skirts the **Yorkshire Wolds**. On the ride from Scarborough to York, there is an especially fine stretch as the railway follows the River Derwent downstream from Malton, at Kirkham passing the striking ruins of a former Augustinian priory.

If you follow the route we describe here, then the entire journey from Hull to Carlisle, just short of the Scottish border, will be with **Northern**, a train company which operates a maze of secondary routes right across northern England. It's a no-frills service, relying on trains that are designed for short and medium-length journeys, usually carrying only standard-class seating.

Across Yorkshire by train

Our first intermediate destination out of Hull is **York**. Rattling west with the Humber on our left, there's a good view of the gracious suspension bridge which spans the river. Then the line is dead-straight to Selby, entering the town on a swing bridge over the River Ouse. It's a pleasant enough spot to wander for an hour, the highlight being **Selby Abbey** (which can be seen to the right of the train).

From Selby the train tracks north over Ouse flatlands to the great city of York (described in **Route 2** in this book, see p62). If you've just arrived in England via this overnight route from Holland, then York is a good place to pause and take stock.

York Connections

You can connect in York onto **Route 2**, which offers an **alternative route north to Scotland** via Berwick-upon-Tweed. There are fast trains from York to both Newcastle and Edinburgh (ERT 124 & 180). You can follow Route 2 in reverse too, heading south to London, which is just two hours away (ERT 180 & 183). York also has regular direct trains to Birmingham, Oxford, Bristol and south-west England (ERT 124). For more York connections see p62.

Avoid the main line from **York to Leeds** – merely because the slow route via Knaresborough is just so much nicer. The latter takes longer but it's a fun detour – though Northern do pretend at York station that these trains, which normally leave from Platform 8, don't actually go to Leeds at all. They are signed as going to Harrogate or Burley Park. They leave York station in entirely the wrong direction for a train that eventually goes to Leeds, initially running north (as if bound for Scotland), then turning west to trundle over the charming meadows surrounding the River Nidd. Look back to see **York Minster** slipping away and to the left of the train is Marston Moor, where in 1644 of one of the set-piece battles of the Civil War took place.

The two towns on this back route to Leeds are Knaresborough and Harrogate. Both are delightful places, **Knaresborough** a pleasant tumble of characterful buildings around the River Nidd with a gracious market square, while **Harrogate** has some of the elegance of the spa towns of central Europe. Either would make a fine first night in England. Opt for homely Knaresborough if you prefer to stay in a typical smallish Yorkshire town, or stay on the train to Harrogate, reached eight minutes later, for a very much bigger community with handsome buildings and parks.

Arrival, information, accommodation

≼ Centrally located in both Harrogate and Knaresborough. 🛈 Tourist offices: in the library on Market Place (Knaresborough); Royal Baths, Crescent Road (Harrogate); for both places see www.visitharrogate.co.uk.

🛏 Just a short walk north-west of Harrogate city centre is the boutique B&B **The Bijou**, 17 Ripon Road, ☎ 07897 576 476 (www.thebijou.co.uk), located in a Victorian villa. Closer to Harrogate station in a terrace of Georgian houses is the stylish, wine-themed **Hotel du Vin**, Prospect Place, ☎ 01423 608 121 (www.hotelduvin.com). A great place to stay in Knaresborough is **Teardrop Cottage**, Waterside, ☎ 01423 797 275 (www.teardropcottage. com), right on the river, with good views of the Victorian viaduct and close to the station.

The railway crosses the **River Nidd** in Knaresborough on a fine old bridge then just beyond Harrogate two remarkable viaducts escort the railway over the Crimple Valley and the Wharfe Valley. The train then plunges through **Bramhope Tunnel** to emerge on the northern fringes of Leeds.

In the 19th century there were four stations serving the city centre – today just one remains. If the new high-speed from London to Leeds is ever completed, residents of Leeds will be able to dash to the capital in just 88 minutes. That's a dream for the future, but the route we are following is a celebration of slow travel, so let's make our way to the local train to Carlisle.

The Settle & Carlisle Railway

Leeds is the natural jumping-off point for the **Settle and Carlisle line (S&C)**. This is quite simply the finest rail route in the Pennines. That it has survived at all is a miracle. In the early 1980s, when the entire route from Settle to Carlisle was slated for closure, community activism did not merely save the line but really propelled it to prominence. Long abandoned stations were reopened, and today this railway plays a central role in both local life and tourism in the remote villages which it serves in the Yorkshire Dales and Cumbria's Eden Valley.

We don't join the actual Settle and Carlisle line until about an hour out of Leeds. So first there's a pleasant run up **Airedale to Skipton** and beyond. Along the way, we pass Saltaire, a UNESCO World Heritage industrial village which oozes architectural ambition and is a fine legacy of philanthropic paternalism. Saltaire's key industry was textiles and, as we travel further up Airedale we pass towns like Bingley and Keithley which were once big players in the global woollen trade.

Skipton marks the end of the overhead wires, so it's diesel only from this point with the landscape becoming decidedly more rural with good views of distant moors. Swinging off to the right beyond Long Preston to join the S&C, the train climbs up through **Ribbledale**. Settle is a handsome small town, again a good place to pause for a coffee or lunch, its station a characterful reminder of a bygone age of rail travel.

The entire S&C route is an ever-changing treat. The first stretch is real **limestone country**, with distinctive white stone walls defining the fields, giving way at high levels to barren moorland. There is a magnificent, **curved viaduct at Ribblehead**, beyond which is Blea Moor tunnel. Dent is perhaps the loneliest railway station in all of England, perched on a shelf high above the scattered Dentdale dwellings which it serves. After Dent, the railway skirts Baugh Fell (to the left), cresting the summit of the line at Ais Gill, and dropping down into the **Eden Valley**, which it follows all the way down to **Carlisle**. The station has a fine neo-Tudor frontage, but the real star is the traditional station bar, called *301 Miles from London*, on Platform 4.

CARLISLE CONNECTIONS

From Carlisle, there's a fast train to London every hour (ERT 154). It's also the starting point for two north of England **branch line adventures**. The first runs east through verdant countryside to Hexham and Newcastle (ERT 210), where you can connect with **Route 2** in this book. If you yearn for the sea, then hop on the slow train around the Cumbrian coast (ERT 159) to **Whitehaven and Barrow**. If you are Scotland bound, there's plenty of choice with usually at least three trains an hour heading north over the border. Of the two routes to Glasgow, the one via Dumfries (ERT 214) is slower but has a better mix of scenery.

Over the Border

There used to be two rail routes from **Carlisle to Edinburgh.** The classic Waverley route through the borders to Edinburgh is long gone, although the section from Tweedbank and Galashiels to Edinburgh reopened in 2015 (ERT 222a). For a dose of lovely **Borders scenery**, the 🚌 X95 bus leaves from outside the court building on English Street in Carlisle and takes two hours for the run to Galashiels, where you can transfer onto the train to Edinburgh.

Alternatively, stick with us here on Route 3 and take the train on the surviving rail route to Edinburgh (ERT 154), which runs through pastoral Annandale scenery and on over Beattock Summit. The route descends into the uppermost part of the **Clyde Valley** and then veers off to the east, skirting the **Pentland Hills** to reach the Scottish capital where the trains stop first at Haymarket and then at Waverley station. The latter is better placed for the city centre.

Edinburgh (suggested stopover)

Edinburgh is Scotland's major hub of **political and cultural life**, though Glaswegians often assert that their city has the edge over Edinburgh when it comes to the arts and creative industries. Few cities so elegantly undulate over gentle hills as Edinburgh, and walking the city streets is enlivened by occasional views of more significant hills such as **Arthur's Seat** and the Salisbury Crags or, especially in the **New Town** (ie. the area on the low ridge north of Princes Street, the city's main shopping street), glimpses of the Firth of Forth.

Edinburgh has its fair share of annual cultural events, of which the best known is the **Edinburgh Fringe** which takes place in in August and started as an antidote to the high-culture Edinburgh Festival: enjoy music, theatre, comedy and performance art. A walk down the **Royal Mile** gets you from the **Castle** down to the **Scottish Parliament** (open to the public Mon–Sat; www.parliament.scot) by Holyrood Park. You'll pass on the way an array of shops, cafés and the 12th-century **St Giles's Cathedral** – the latter is regarded as the Mother Church of Presbyterianism.

ARRIVAL, INFORMATION, ACCOMMODATION

🚊 Edinburgh has two railway stations, of which **Waverley** is the more central (and right on Pricess Street). **Haymarket**, in the city's West End area, is connected to the ✈ airport (www.edinburghairport.com) by frequent trams which take 25 mins for the ride (buy a ticket before boarding). 🛈 Tourist office: 249 High Street (www.edinburgh.org).

⛴ Be aware that staying in Edinburgh is pretty pricey. The city gets booked up during the Fringe, so plan ahead if you're staying in the summer. An affordable, friendly B&B about 20 minutes on foot south of Waverley is the **Southside Guest House**, 8 Newington Road, ☎ 0131 466 6573 (www.southsideguesthouse.co.uk), well placed for climbing Arthur's Seat. Or stay at **Millers64**, 64 Pilrig Street , ☎ 0131 454 3666 (www.millers64.com), a B&B in a modernised Victorian town house off Leith Walk. **Six Brunton Place**, 6 Brunton Place, ☎ 0131 623 6405 (www.sixbruntonplace.com), is a cosy B&B in a Georgian town house.

✗ If you want to treat yourself to something special, visit **Valvona & Crolla**, 19 Elm Row. It's an Edinburgh institution. Pick up some Italian deli treats or have a snack in the café. Enjoy fish suppers in the city's trendy **Leith harbour** district.

CONNECTIONS FROM EDINBURGH

You can connect in Edinburgh onto **Route 2**, following it north into the Highlands. With a short hop over the island of Skye, it's easy to combine Route 2 and 3 into a **perfect round trip** through some of Scotland's finest scenery. Equally, Route 2 can be used to return south from Edinburgh. You can follow it back via the **East Coast line** to York and London. There are departures from Edinburgh at least hourly on that route (ERT 180).

Now it's time for us to head for the hills. There's a vast choice of trains from Edinburgh for the **short hop to Glasgow** (ERT 220 shows the three main routes linking Scotland's two premier cities). The fastest route is that via Falkirk High. Running west out of Edinburgh, the railway broadly follows two canals (first the **Union Canal** and later the Forth and Clyde) all the way to Glasgow, with good views to the right of the Campsie Fells during the latter part of the journey. It's just a first taste of the hills.

There's a notably steep descent down into the Queen Street terminus in **Glasgow**. One 19th-century guidebook describes it thus: "The immediate approach to the city, dull enough in an artistic sense, is rendered interesting by the famous Cowlairs Incline, the train being lowered by wire ropes along a steep tunnel... which brings us to Queen Street Station."

GLASGOW CONNECTIONS

Queen Street is one of two major rail termini in Glasgow. The other is **Glasgow Central**, about a ten-minute walk south from Queen Street, but still on the north bank of the Clyde. Both stations also have low-level (ie. underground) platforms used in the main by suburban services.

Of the two stations, Glasgow Central is by far the more striking with its elegant iron columns, decorated with classical capitals and a remarkable **Edwardian-era booking hall**. It's from here that all trains to England depart, with direct trains to Manchester, Birmingham and London (ERT154). There are also trains to the Ayrshire coast (ERT 215) and Dumfries (ERT 216). Queen Street station serves all trains bound for the **Highlands**.

Loch Lomond, Rannoch and more

There's often a real sense of anticipation surrounding the departure of the **West Highland Line** trains from Glasgow Queen Street. Those in the know grab seats on the left side of the train for the first part of the journey. Modern trains make light of **Cowlairs Incline**, swinging off to the left at the top of the hill and skimming Glasgow suburbs to reach the Clyde near the Erskine Bridge. The first great landmark is **Dumbarton Castle** (on the left), perched on a double-humped rock just by the spot where the waters of the Leven decant into the Clyde.

There are fine views of the Clyde at Cardross, and then the train swings off to the right, climbing up beyond Helensburgh to reach the shores of **Gare Loch**, where the train passes the military base at Faslane which is home to the Trident submarine fleet which carries nuclear weapons. Since 1982, there has been a permanent peace camp here, with protesters highlighting the unwanted presence of a nuclear arsenal in the Scottish hills.

Passing a gentle watershed at the top end of Loch Long, the train drops down towards **Loch Lomond** (on the right), and this is the moment to switch seats, if space permits, to the right side of the carriage. Now there's a real sense of being in the Highlands, with dramatic views across Loch Lomond to the hills beyond.

At **Crianlarich**, the line to Oban branchees off to the left, and carriages for that coastal port are usually detached from the Fort William train at Crianlarich. After that, the railway runs up Strath Fillan and then climbs up onto **Rannoch Moor**, a bleakly evocative landscape of **peat bogs**. "A wearier-looking desert man never saw," in Robert Louis Stevenson's words. We see it more positively: a tinted mosaic of purple-black bog, heather-clad hillocks and the glint of sun on distant lochs.

Like many stations along the line, that at Rannoch has a Swiss-chalet style with Arts and Crafts affectations. Then comes the most remote part of the route. It is not for nothing that just outside **Corrour station**, the railway line runs through snow sheds that prevent drifting snow from blocking the line in winter. They are not always successful, and many are the times when blizzards prevent the trains from crossing the moor to Corrour where, quite improbably, there is a really **cosy café** on the station platform. Do check in advance that it's open (usually from mid-March till the end of October) before alighting from the train (www.corrour.co.uk; ☎ 01397 732 236) as this is not a spot you'd want to be left stranded. North from Corrour, the line gently descends, slipping by Loch Treig to reach Glen Spean and then skirting the north flank of Ben Nevis to reach **Fort William**.

FORT WILLIAM CONNECTIONS

If you are on a tight schedule and with time only for the briefest glimpse of the Highlands, Fort William might be as far as you'll get. It's worth remembering that Fort William has a **night train** (daily except Sat) direct to London.

If you are eager to see **Loch Ness** (with or without its monster), then hop on Scottish Citylink 🚌 919 to Inverness, a two-hour journey which runs along the shores of Loch Ness (sit on the right side of the bus for loch views). 🚌 918 runs twice daily (not Sun) down to **Oban**, offering brilliant coastal views along the way. Again, take a seat on the right side of the bus. In Oban you can connect onto trains back to Glasgow (ERT 218) or CalMac ferries to the **Inner and Outer Hebrides**.

Jacobite Country

No one forgets the ride on the final stretch of the West Highland Line from **Fort William to Mallaig**. This is a railway which has been propelled to prominence by the *Harry Potter* films and the steam train, called *The Jacobite*, which plies the route from late April to October (details on www. westcoastrailways.co.uk). The steam train is very pricey (over £30 for a single journey from Fort William to Mallaig), but the scenery is just the same if you stick to the regular Scotrail train. The best scenery is on the left side.

Leaving Fort William, the train swings west to cross the **River Lochy**. Shortly thereafter, just after the halt at Banavie (where trains stop only on request), there's a fine view to the right up **Neptune's Staircase** – that's the name of the great series of locks, constructed by Thomas Telford and opened in 1820, which allows boats to gain elevation and follow the Caledonian Canal north to Loch Ness.

The railway runs along the north shore of Loch Eil then, just after a short tunnel, there's a moment of real drama as the line crosses **Glenfinnan Viaduct**, with a tremendous vista south down towards Loch Shiel. A memorial, visible from the train, recalls the historic importance of Glenfinnan; it was here that in 1745 the Jacobites gathered to launch their campaign to reclaim the British crown for the Stuarts. Slipping on through Lochailort, the railway makes real contact with the coast, with gorgeous views over the **Sound of Arisaig**, before running north to Mallaig.

Mallaig

Mallaig is a pleasant wee port which can be busy when the **steam train** is in town. Most of the visitors on *The Jacobite* stay just a couple of hours. Mallaig deserves more. It's a place for fish & chips, seagulls, and just enjoying a pint or two by the quayside, watching the fishing boats come and go.

ARRIVAL, INFORMATION, ACCOMMODATION

≥ The station is well placed for the harbour and the western part of Mallaig. Walk down Station Road to get to the 🚹 tourist information (www.road-to-the-isles.org.uk).

🛏 The **Springbank Guest House**, Eastbay, ☎ 01687 462459 (www.springbank-mallaig.co.uk) is a comfortable B&B, located on the bay and with good views across to harbour. ✗ For a good fish supper, head for the **Terrace Restaurant** (in the West Highland Hotel, ☎ 1687 462 210) or the **Cornerstone Restaurant** on Main Street (☎ 01687 462 306).

ONWARD CONNECTIONS

There's a fine range of waterborne adventures from Mallaig. There are year-round ferries to **Eigg, Muck, Canna and Rum** – collectively known as the Small Isles – and also to Inverie on the Knoydart Peninsula. The car ferry shuttles over to Armadale on **Skye**, from where you can travel on by bus via Broadford to Kyle (on **Route 2**). The *Lord of the Isles* sails from Mallaig to Lochboisdale in the **Outer Hebrides** (weather permitting, daily in summer and irregularly in winter; www.calmac.co.uk).

Route 4: Across England and Wales to Ireland

CITIES: ★★ CULTURE: ★★ HISTORY: ★★ SCENERY: ★★
COUNTRIES COVERED: NETHERLANDS (NL), ENGLAND (ENG), WALES (WLS), IRELAND (IE)
JOURNEY TIME: 26 HRS 30 MINS | DISTANCE: 1,194 KM | MAP: WWW.EBRWEB.EU/MAP4

Beurs metro station in the busy heart of **Rotterdam** is the improbable starting point for this journey which takes in four countries and ends in south-west Ireland on the edge of the country's first national park. The contrasts between start and end points couldn't be sharper. Along the way, we take in ferries across the **North Sea** and the **Irish Sea** and some nicely rural rail routes through England, Wales and Ireland.

ITINERARY OPTIONS

It's a route that is best spread over four days, with the first night on the **boat to Harwich**, and then overnight stops in **Chester** and **Dublin**. The journey from Harwich to Chester, as described here, takes about seven hours. Assuming you use the overnight boat from Holland, you'll have an early arrival in Harwich, so you may want to stop off here and there on the journey to Chester. Bury St Edmunds, Cambridge and Stamford are all good options.

You'll need the yellow-themed Route B from **Rotterdam Beurs metro station** for the 14-stop ride to Hoek van Holland. This line to Hoek opened in autumn 2019, replacing the erstwhile rail route to the port. Happily, most of the journey is above ground, and it's a ride to make you think. It's odd to depart on such an ambitious journey on a local metro tram. There's a melancholy born of leaving the continent without having properly said one's farewells. There is no such thing as a grand exit via **Hoek van Holland**.

Along the way, the metro slips past the shadows of quiet villages gobbled up by the city. There are echoes of the last psalms recited in the synagogue at Maassluis. And there are the voices of Jewish children. Thousands upon thousands of them who, in the months prior to the outbreak of the Second World War, travelled by special *Kindertransport* trains to Hoek van Holland, there to board the ship for the crossing to Harwich and new lives in England.

The Stena Line **ship to Harwich** is extremely comfortable. We favour the overnight boat, which doesn't leave till late evening, but foot passengers can normally board from about 18.45 – and we're the ones there at the front

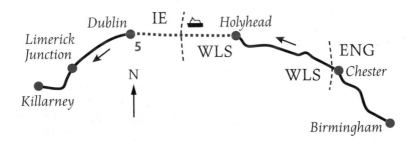

of the line when they open the gate. It's worth boarding early. Take a picnic supper, or for onboard dining choose between the very reasonably priced self-service cafeteria or the more upmarket Metropolitan restaurant.

It's often so placid that one barely notices the short hours as the ship slips over to England. Indeed there were occasions when we awoke to find that we were already quayside in **Harwich** without having even realised that we'd left Hoek van Holland. Foot passengers disembark about 06.45 for a bleary eyed encounter with the uniformed representatives of *Border Force* – men and women with padded shoulders, lots of gear, working on the front line of defence in the war against outsiders. It is a depressing mark of what Britain has become, not helped by the fact that Harwich is not pretty.

Route details

Rotterdam Beurs to Hoek van Holland		
Frequency	Journey time	Notes
3 per hr	40 mins	

Hoek van Holland to Harwich	ERT 2210	
Frequency	Journey time	Notes
2 per day	6 hrs 30 mins – 9 hrs 30 mins	

Harwich to Cambridge	ERT 200/205	
Frequency	Journey time	Notes
Every 1–2 hrs	1 hrs 50 mins – 2 hrs 30 mins	A

Cambridge to Birmingham New Street	ERT 208	
Frequency	Journey time	Notes
Hourly	2 hrs 40 mins	

Route details (cont.)

Birmingham New Street to Chester	ERT 145	
Frequency	Journey time	Notes
Hourly	2 hrs	B

Chester to Holyhead	ERT 160	
Frequency	Journey time	Notes
Hourly	1 hr 20 mins – 2 hrs	

Holyhead to Dublin Port	ERT 2040	
Frequency	Journey time	Notes
6–8 per day	2 hrs 15 mins – 3 hrs 15 mins	

Dublin Heuston to Killarney	ERT 245/246	
Frequency	Journey time	Notes
Every 2 hrs	3 hrs 20 mins	C

Notes

A – There are only occasional direct trains. It is usually necessary to change at Manningtree and Ipswich.

B – Alternate trains require a change at Shrewsbury.
C – Most journeys from Dublin to Killarney require a change of train in Mallow.

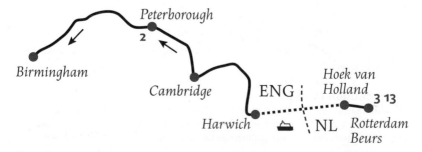

Emerging from that brush with bureaucracy into the soulless terminal building, you may want to grab a coffee at the Quayside Café which is anything but quayside, but one level up an escalator from the railway platforms. It's also a chance for a first encounter with the **bacon roll**, a cholesterol-laden morning fix upon which the English rely to supercharge their arteries. Yet, despite all this, there's something really nice about being up bright and early with a fine train journey ahead.

Westward across England

There's a direct train to Cambridge which connects nicely with the overnight boat. At other times you may need to change at Manningtree and Ipswich. Sit on the right of the train from **Harwich** for pleasing views of the River Stour, with the moorings and maltings at Mistley. Then, skirting lowland landscapes which so inspired the English artist **John Constable**, the train heads north into Suffolk.

It's an excellent run across Suffolk towards Cambridge with frothy meadowsweet, wild roses and willowherb aplenty by the tracks. Along the way, all trains stop in **Bury St Edmunds** where the magnificent St Edmundsbury Cathedral is good enough cause to pause for an hour or two. Bury has some appealing Georgian architecture and some decent cafés.

If this is your first time in England, Bury St Edmunds is a place which can easily win your heart over. The town centre is about ten minutes on foot south of the station. Some trains run directly from Bury St Edmunds to Ely and Peterborough, but sometimes it's faster to route via Newmarket and Cambridge.

Beyond Bury St Edmunds, the landscape becomes less intimate, with large, **rolling fields**, which give way to grassland and paddocks at Newmarket, where the local economy is driven by horse breeding and racing. **Cambridge** station is inconveniently placed for the city centre, but fortunately there are buses aplenty into town from the station forecourt. Look out for 🚌 Citi 3 which leaves every ten minutes from bus stop 6 (single fare £1).

The journey north from Cambridge runs through **marshy Fenland** countryside to Ely (where the direct line from Bury rejoins from the right). The cathedral town of Ely takes its name from the local eels which were once common; major drainage projects in the Fens have tamed a landscape which was once a reedy wilderness of meres and tidal creeks. From Ely, you'll see a great swathe of Fenland landscape as the train continues to March and **Peterborough**.

PETERBOROUGH LINKS

This major railway centre on the East Coast main line – that's the principal line from London to Edinburgh – is the place to connect into **Route 2** in this book (see p59). It's under four hours from Peterborough to the Scottish capital (ERT 180).

Our westward journey continues, skirting a tip of Lincolnshire, with all trains pausing in the market town of **Stamford** where the handsome mock-Tudor style railway station is just a taste of what this lovely market town has to offer. It's a ten-minute walk from the station to the town centre, which is on rising ground north of the River Welland. West of Stamford, the railway enters hillier terrain and England's smallest county, Rutland, from where it's an easy ride on through less interesting scenery to Leicester and **Birmingham**, where all trains from the east terminate at New Street station.

England's second city was born early in the railway age, and grew rapidly through a preoccupation with profit and industry. Entrepreneurial spirit was more important than civic beauty, and it's said that Queen Victoria would ask for the window blinds to be lowered as the royal train passed through Birmingham. These days Birmingham has spruced itself up, and the city has enviable drive and energy. Imposing squares and canals dominate the modern cityscape, but you can still feel the pulse of a more industrial Birmingham in the **Jewellery Quarter**, just north of the city centre.

BIRMINGHAM STATIONS AND CONNECTIONS

From the railway platforms at **Birmingham New Street** station, head upstairs to the newly refurbished concourse for a dash of contemporary style. The city centre's second station is **Moor Street**, much more intimate than New Street, and magnificently refurbished in Edwardian style. It is the starting point for the excellent Chiltern route to London Marylebone (ERT 128) and Stratford-upon-Avon (ERT 127). All other long-distance trains from Birmingham leave from New Street with regular departures to Bristol and Devon (ERT 116), Carlisle, Edinburgh and Glasgow (ERT 154), Oxford and the south coast (ERT 114).

From Birmingham New Street there are two rail routes to Chester – one via Crewe and the other via Shrewsbury. We strongly recommend the latter; it's far more scenic. Edging out of Birmingham, the train parallels a canal through urban terrain, eventually reaching more open country beyond Wolverhampton with views south to the Wrekin and other **Shropshire hills**. Soon we are rolling into **Shrewsbury** where, if you have an hour to kill, the ornate station facade is worth a look, and it's an easy walk into the town centre which has a feast of Georgian and timber-framed buildings.

Sit on the right for the one-hour ride from Shrewsbury to Chester. The railway dips into Wales north of Gobowen, crossing the River Ceiriog to reach Welsh territory. Just to the right of the railway there's a fine view of **Chirk Aqueduct** which carries the Llangollen Canal over the Ceiriog Valley. Beyond Wrexham, the railway crosses back into England, running north across the River Dee, passing Chester racecourse to reach the town's station.

Chester

The handsome walled city of Chester, so proud of its **Roman origins**, is located on the north side of the River Dee. With Merseyside just a stone's throw away the north, and much of city's hinterland in Wales, Chester often struggles to assert a regional identity. But with its largely traffic-free central area it's a great place for an overnight stop. Explore the curious **Chester Rows** (a shopping area with elevated walkways in a row of late-mediaeval buildings), check out the Gothic cathedral and explore the city walls. If you are spending a couple of nights in Chester, you might consider a visit to vibrant **Liverpool**, just 45 minutes away on frequent local trains.

ARRIVAL, INFORMATION, ACCOMMODATION

≥ Just a 10-minute walk, north-east of the city centre. 🛈 Tourist office: at the Town Hall (www.visitcheshire.com).

🛏 **Oddfellows**, 20 Lower Bridge Street, ☎ 01244 345 454 (www.oddfellowschester. com), is a comfortable option with quirky interiors, a beer garden and lively bar. Or try the **Coach House Inn**, 39 Northgate St, ☎ 01244 351 900 (www.coachhousechester.co.uk), a highly regarded gastro pub with rooms, located close to the cathedral. More upmarket is the elegant **Chester Grosvenor**, Eastgate, ☎ 01244 324 024 (www.chestergrosvenor.com), a listed building with a black-and-white timbered facade in the heart of the city.

To the Celtic world

If you stay overnight in Chester, you'll not need an early start to reach the afternoon boat from Holyhead to Ireland. Even the slowest trains take only two hours. If you are inclined to stop off along the way, the small town of Conwy is a nice spot to spend a couple of hours.

Leaving Chester, the train slips into **Wales** in the most unromantic manner amid a maze of power lines and factories. But it gets better with the good views to the right across the salt marshes that rim the Dee Estuary.

WELSH WALES

Crossing the **Vale of Conwy**, there is a sense of entering a more **elemental Wales** – a country whose very nature is shaped by rock. Route 4 merely skims the north coast, and you need to cut inland to really get a sense of Welsh Wales. That's the part of the country where, mainly in more rural areas, the Welsh language is still spoken. It extends west from Snowdonia into the Llŷn Peninsula, and south through Merioneth into Ceredigion.

Llandudno Junction is a spot to embark on a journey into the Welsh hills. There's a branch railway which runs south up the Vale of Conwy to reach the slate-strewn town of Blaenau Ffestiniog, where you can join the narrow-gauge **Ffestiniog Railway** (www.festrail.co.uk) down to the coast at Porthmadog (ERT 160). From there, it's a fine run south along the Cambrian coast line (ERT 148), crossing the **Mawddach Estuary** at Barmouth. If you don't mind some longish bus journeys, you can work your way south through deeply rural countryside to join **Route 5** at Llandovery, Carmarthen or Fishguard. It's a chance to see Methodist chapels and remote villages in the hills and a chance to touch the life and spirit of a distinctive culture which has always been undervalued by the English. But beware: one dose of Welsh Wales might be enough to have you hooked for ever. If you are tempted, the book to read in preparation for this cultural expedition is **Jan Morris**' *Wales: Epic Views of a Small Country*.

Then, if you avert your eyes from the dreary ribbon development along the coast, we slowly reach the hills. Approaching **Llandudno Junction**, the great limestone headland of Great Orme rears up to the right, and beyond Conwy there are fine vistas of the hills of Snowdonia to the left, with the island of Anglesey visible across the Menai Strait.

The finest part of the journey from **Chester to Holyhead** is the section from Conwy to just beyond Bangor where the train crosses the Britannia Bridge to reach Anglesey (Ynys Môn). The first station on the island, served only by local trains, is a 58-letters long, tongue-twisting Welsh place name often shortened to Llanfair PG – an enigmatic abbreviation hinting at the linguistic challenges which lie ahead. From here, it's an easy cruise over rough pasture and gorse heath until on the right you'll spot the abandoned aluminium smelter which announces arrival in **Holyhead**.

The railway station has been rudely separated from the town by the security paraphernalia that surround the port. By way of mild recompense, there's a dramatic new footbridge leading from the station into town, nicely embellished with a Welsh inscription which translates as "Pass this way with a pure heart." You'll need it to discern any beauty in run-down Holyhead.

Stena Line and Irish Ferries compete on the **shipping route to Dublin**, the latter offering a choice of a traditional cruise ferry or a catamaran. You'll most likely find that the early afternoon Irish Ferries sailing works well. It's usually operated by the *MS Ulysses*, a traditional vessel with an excellent club-class lounge. It's worth paying the modest supplement for the upgrade. From that lounge, you'll have grand views on a clear day, initially of the Welsh hills slipping away to the east and later, as you approach Ireland, of the **Wicklow Mountains**. Whichever crossing you opt for, buses meet the ferries to carry foot passengers into town.

Dublin (suggested stopover)

The Irish capital is quite simply phenomenal. Few other European cities have quite the buzz and flair of Dublin (which is known as Baile Átha Cliath in Irish). The **River Liffey** flows from west to east through the centre of town, decanting into Dublin Bay, with the city itself split predictably into **Northside** and **Southside**. The latter is stylish and arty, all the more so following the smartening up of the **Temple Bar** cultural quarter, while life on the north bank of the Liffey is that little bit more edgy. But we mustn't generalise, for the Irish President's offical residence (Áras an Uachtaráin) is in Northside – set in **Phoenix Park**, a wonderful open space just west of the central area and open to the public. This huge park – plenty of monuments, meadows and deer – is a great place to relax.

In Southside, to the east of Temple Bar, is the main **Trinity College** campus, extending from College Green east to Pearse station. You can wander freely through the grounds of Trinity, and the *Book of Kells* exhibition is definitely worth a visit. From the campus, it's a short walk to the **National Gallery** (www.nationalgallery.ie), from where it's easy to explore Merrion Square, the grandest of the city's Georgian squares. The entire area from **Merrion Square** down to Fitzwilliam Square is delightful. But by now you'll have walked your socks off so make for St Stephen's Green, a Victorian-style park which is a great spot to just watch Dubliners come and go.

ARRIVAL, INFORMATION, ACCOMMODATION

≥ **Dublin Connolly**, on the north bank of the River Liffey, is the departure point for the cross-border *Enterprise* train service to Newry and Belfast (ERT 230), as well as commuter and DART suburban trains – the latter stop at two Southside stations, Tara Street and Pearse, both of which are more convenient for many Dublin districts south of the Liffey (eg. Trinity College and the Georgian quarter around Merrion Square and the Temple Bar area). The other main station, **Dublin Heuston**, is well west of the city centre, just on the south bank of the Liffey: main-line trains to the County Mayo outposts of Ballina and Westport (ERT 240), Kilkenny and Waterford (ERT 241), Cork (ERT 245) and Galway (ERT 240). Heuston and Connolly stations are connected by the red **Luas tram line** (www.luas.ie). Buy tickets from the machine at each stop (valid for 90 mins; zonal tariff). Tickets for the bus can be purchased on board (cash allowed, but exact fare only; see www.dublinbus.ie). 🛈 Tourist office: 17 Lower O'Connell Street and 26 Bachelors Walk (www.visitdublin.com).

📨 Brace yourself for Dublin hotel and B&B prices! Booking ahead will help you save on your accommodation costs. Some more affordable options can be found south-east of the city centre – try for example **Pembroke Hall**, 76 Pembroke Rd, ☎ 01668 99 93 (www.pembroke-hall.ie), a welcoming guesthouse in a quiet neighbourhood. Or opt for **Mespil Hotel**, 50–60 Mespil Road, ☎ 01488 46 00 (www.mespilhotel.com), right on the Grand Canal. Convenient for both Heuston station and Phoenix Park is the highly regarded **Ashling Hotel**, 10–13 Parkgate Street, ☎ 01677 23 24 (www.ashlinghotel.ie).

DUBLIN CONNECTIONS

The **Irish border** (with or without its backstop) is 100 km north of Dublin. Trains from Dublin Connolly leave for Belfast (ERT 230), Sligo (ERT 236) and the east coast route to Wexford and Rosslare (ERT 237), which we'll follow in **Route 5**. For great seafood and coastal walks, take the half-hour ride on the DART out to Howth. It's a splendid spot to spend a summer evening. For a good **full day out by train** from Dublin see the box on p94.

🚢 **Dublin Port** has, apart from the direct ferry links to Wales, a year-round shipping link with Cherbourg in France (where you can connect onto **Route 9**). However, Irish Ferries only accept foot passengers on this service when it is operated by the company's new cruise ferry *MV WB Yeats* (which entered service in 2019). We understand that this new ship will serve the route from April to October each year. During the winter months, when the *MS Epsilon* plies the route, foot passengers are not carried.

Kerry Bound

The Irish county most conspicuously associated with **Romantic ideas** about the picturesque and the sublime is Kerry. And if there is one spot in Kerry which has above all fired the Romantic imagination it is Killarney. Every tour of Ireland must perforce take in Killarney (ideally with a big pinch of salt these days). The town itself is very pleasant, a little too dominated by shamrock tack perhaps, but the real draw are the gorgeous landscapes of County Kerry which are all around Killarney.

These are thoughts to ponder as you wait at **Dublin Heuston**, a handsome station in Corinthian style, for the train to the far south-west of Ireland. Originally known as Dublin Kingsbridge, the station was renamed in 1966 to recall Seán Heuston, one the of republican rebels who was executed by the British after the **Easter Rising**. Heuston was himself a railway clerk. As the train slips out of Dublin to the west, it passes through Kilmainham where Heuston was shot on Sunday 7 May 1916.

Picking up speed, the train passes through unassuming suburbs to reach open country with good views of the **Wicklow Hills** well away to the left. The grassy heathlands around Kildare are premier-league territory for Irish horse breeders. Curragh is the name of the heath and also of the racecourse which you'll see to the left of the train.

Beyond **Kildare**, the landscape becomes slightly hillier, with a fine view of the Barrow Valley at Monasterevin. Passing through Port Laoise, the forested Slieve Bloom Mountains edge closer and then, just a little later, the Galtee Mountains hove into view on the left. Most trains stop at **Limerick Junction**, one of those strange spots which is never a destination in its own right, but a place where all travellers in Ireland end up eventually.

LIMERICK JUNCTION

This station in the middle of an area often known as West Tipp – the nearest town is Tipperary away to the south-east – is really a curiosity, and one celebrated by train enthusiasts for the oddity of its railway operations. **Two main lines cross here**, and transferring trains from one line to the other requires some shunting to and fro. It was made more complex by the fact that until late 2019, the station had only one main platform.

It is a place for changing trains. There are frequent connections to **Limerick City** (ERT 243), where the station is called Limerick Colbert, being named after Cornelius Colbert, another of the Easter Rising leaders shot by a firing squad at Kilmainham gaol in May 1916. From Limerick Colbert, five trains a day (four on Sun) run north through County Clare to Galway (ERT 242), where you can connect onto **Route 5** in this book.

Limerick Junction is also the starting point for the rural route to Waterford, which follows the **Suir Valley** for much of the way. We rate this as the finest rural rail ride in Ireland, but it requires careful planning, as there are only two trains a day (not Sun) in each direction (ERT 239). This line features in the itinerary described in the boxed text on p94.

From Limerick Junction, it's just 30 minutes through rich dairy-farming country, often colloquially known as the **Golden Vale** (or Golden Vein), to Mallow in County Cork. There our route turns to the west, following the Blackwater Valley up to Rathmore. Sit on the left for gorgeous views both on the approach to Rathmore and then on to Killarney. This is one of the most famous vistas in Ireland with Mangerton Mountain to the left, grading westward into the great ridge of **MacGillycuddy's Reeks**. The train rolls slowly down to **Killarney**, which marks the end of Route 4. We have come a long way from that metro station in Rotterdam where our journey started.

Killarney

Nowhere is Irish culture more packaged and sold than in Killarney. This is not new. In the late 18th century, Killarney had already claimed status as the gateway to the exquisite mountain landscapes of County Kerry, and tourism was given a further boost by the **arrival of the railway** and Queen Victoria. The contours of the Killarney experience have hardly changed in 150 years: waterside walks, high tea, and excursions by pony traps (locally called jaunting cars) into the hills. The hucksters and heather-toting colleens, who attracted the opprobrium of late Victorian writers, are still there. But cut through the shamrock haze and Killarney is very special. You just have to ignore the commerce.

Make time to wander through town of course, but the real draw is **Killarney National Park**, the nearest parts of which are within walking distance of the city centre. If you can stay a day or two, perhaps renting bicycles or venturing out on local buses, you begin to get a feel for a landscape shaped by glaciation and a big dose of Irish mythology. During the season, there's a very useful and moderately priced shuttle bus service (www.killarneyshuttlebus.com) which ferries visitors from the centre of Killarney to **Ross Castle**, Torc Waterfall, the Gap of Dunloe and other local beauty spots. There are also year-round one-day bus trips around the Iveragh peninsula – this is famous **Ring of Kerry** route (www.ringofkerrytourism.com).

ARRIVAL, INFORMATION, ACCOMMODATION

≈ Right on the eastern edge of the city centre. 🛈 Tourist office: Beech Road (www.killarney.ie).

🛏 The Victorian-era **Great Southern Killarney**, East Avenue Road, ☎ 064 663 80 00 (www.greatsouthernkillarney.com), right by the railway station, is a great place to stay in Killarney. We certainly enjoyed it (and the good news is that they do a lot of discounting). Just a 5-minute walk south of the city centre is the very friendly **Algret House B&B**, Countess Grove, ☎ 064 663 23 37 (www.algrethouse.com), in a quiet neighbourhood. An equally good option in the same direction is **Killarney Lodge** guesthouse, Countess Rd, ☎ 064 663 64 99 (www.killarneylodge.ie).

KILLARNEY CONNECTIONS

When the train pulls up at Killarney station, the buffer stops ahead seem to make it clear that this is the end of the line. But Irish trains are cunning. The train in fact reverses out of the station, then branches off to the north, running on to **Tralee**. The latter is a pleasant wee town, dominated by the Slieve Mish Mountains to the south, and the natural jumping-off point for excursions to the Dingle Peninsula.

There are buses aplenty from Killarney. Bus Éireann Expressway service 🚌 40 runs east to Cork, Waterford and Rosslare (on **Route 5**), connecting in all three places with trains back to Dublin. During July and August only, there's a really adventurous afternoon bus connection from **Killarney to Cork**, which takes in some of the best landscapes of County Kerry and West Cork. Take 🚌 270 from Killarney to Kenmare, connecting there onto 🚌 252 to Cork. The latter bus runs via Glengarriff, Skibbereen and Clonakilty, along the way skirting many coastal inlets. Sit on the right of the bus for the best views.

SIDETRACKS: IRISH QUESTIONS

Dún Laoghaire, on the south shore of Dublin Bay, was the traditional port for the city of Dublin. In the heyday of **Ireland's Railway Age**, Dún Laoghaire went by the English name of Kingstown, a colonial imposition recalling King George IV's visit to Ireland in 1821.

Kingstown was more than merely a port through which thousands of travellers passed en route to and from Dublin. It thrived on sea trade and became one of the most desirable of Dublin suburbs. The "gaiety of life around the jetty" and "the rippling of the sleepless tide" – as the writer GW Powell remarked – combined to make the port a charmed spot.

So it's no surprise that, when it came to building **Ireland's first passenger railway**, the route selected was between Dublin and Kingstown. The line opened in December 1834. Dublin thus had a working suburban railway even before London – the first passenger service in the English capital, a line to Deptford, did not open until 1836.

In Ireland, as across the water in Britain, there was uncertainty about the preferred track gauge for the emerging rail network. How wide apart should the lines be placed? The initial **Dublin to Kingstown line** was built to 1,435 mm gauge – that is the measure used for most railways in Britain and much of western and central Europe today. Yet it was an Irish one-off. Elsewhere around the island, railways were being built to much wider or much narrower gauges. By the start of the 20th century, Ireland had Europe's most extensive **network of three-foot-gauge railways** (914 mm). From the Glens of Antrim and remote valleys in Donegal to the rugged Dingle Peninsula, Ireland's three-foot network criss-crossed the land. Just imagine what fine tourism assets these could be today had they survived. The last to close was the West Clare Railway; that was in 1961.

Ireland eventually settled on one rail gauge, and it was a peculiarly Irish solution. No other country in Europe uses the 1,600 mm gauge which is now the norm for all railways in Ireland, both north and south of the border. That's even wider than the Russian gauge, where tracks are spaced further apart than further west in Europe.

The tussle over track gauge was as nothing compared to the friction caused by the **partition of Ireland** in 1921. A new frontier cut rudely across the landscape, placing new bureaucratic burdens on hard-pressed rail operators. In the ensuing years, most cross-border routes closed. Only that between Dundalk and Newry survived; it is still used today by the *Enterprise* trains from Dublin to Belfast.

You can ride the route of Ireland's very first railway, which has long since been changed to the Irish 1,600 mm gauge. That line from Dublin to Kingstown – now happily renamed Dún Laoghaire – is one of the busiest in the country. It's used by **DART commuter services** running south from Dublin and also forms part of the next route in this book. And these days Dún Laoghaire station is called Dún Laoghaire Mallin, a quiet homage to Michael Mallin. He was a quiet man – a silk weaver, devout Catholic and committed socialist. Mallin was executed by the British for his involvement in the 1916 **Easter Rising**.

Route 5: West to Europe's Celtic fringe

Cities: ★★ Culture: ★ History: ★ Scenery: ★★
Countries covered: England (ENG), Wales (WLS), Ireland (IE)
Journey time: 18 hrs | Distance: 1,006 km | Map: www.ebrweb.eu/map5

One of the great things about Galway, we were told when we visited in 2019, is that the Irish city doesn't have a working airport. It closed in 2011, and since then visitors have been forced to travel to Galway by road or rail. Most Galway-bound travellers fly in via Dublin or Shannon; this route shows that you could do better. It's perfectly possible to travel from **London to Galway** in a day by the rail-sea route via Holyhead. But Route 5 is the way to do it if you want to see some of the finest scenery in England, Wales and Ireland along the way. It's a chance to **savour a journey** for its own sake.

ITINERARY SUGGESTIONS

Route 5 is best spread over three travel days, with overnight stops in **Llandovery** and **Wexford**. If you are minded to take longer, the possibilities are endless. How about extra stops in Oxford, Hereford and Dublin? Or make time for one of the small Shropshire towns on this route. Ludlow is a good choice. If you are pushed for time and simply cannot follow our meandering route, then leave London Paddington at 07.45 (daily except Sun) and, with a change of train in Swansea, reach Fishguard in time to join the afternoon **boat to Ireland**.

Chilterns and Cotswolds

Our route kicks off with the short hop from **London to Oxford**. Choose between the Thames Valley route from Paddington (which follows **Route 1** to Reading) or the Chiltern line from Marylebone. We think the latter has the edge, and diminutive Marylebone – the London terminus from which all Chiltern trains depart – is a characterful starting point. Look out for the white lattice arch of the new **Wembley Stadium** as the train speeds out

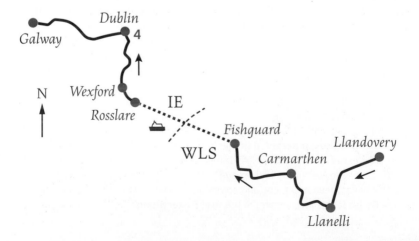

toward leafy London suburbs and the beech woods of the Chiltern Hills. There's a brilliant stretch just beyond High Wycombe where the railway cuts through fine chalk downland, dropping down to reach the Vale of Aylesbury at Princes Risborough. All trains to Oxford stop at **Bicester Village**, which has become a popular shopping Mecca for overseas visitors to Britain. Yep, you read that right. People make day trips from London to go shopping in Bicester where all the top brands have staked a claim to retail space. Announcements at Bicester Village station are made in English, Mandarin and Arabic.

Beyond Bicester, the railway skirts damp Otmoor to reach **Oxford**, stopping first at Oxford Parkway and then at the city-centre station (simply

Route details

London Marylebone to Oxford		ERT 128a
Frequency	Journey time	Notes
2 per hr	65 mins	A

Oxford to Hereford		ERT 130
Frequency	Journey time	Notes
Every 1–2 hrs	2 hrs 10 mins – 3 hrs	B

Hereford to Craven Arms		ERT 149
Frequency	Journey time	Notes
Every 1–2 hrs	30 mins	

Craven Arms to Llanelli		FRT 146
Frequency	Journey time	Notes
2–4 per day	3 hrs – 3 hrs 15 mins	

Route details (cont.)

Llanelli to Fishguard Harbour		ERT 136
Frequency	Journey time	Notes
4 per day	75–95 mins	C

Fishguard Harbour to Rosslare Harbour		ERT 2040
Frequency	Journey time	Notes
2 per day	3 hrs 15 mins	

Rosslare Harbour to Dublin Connolly		ERT 237
Frequency	Journey time	Notes
3–4 per day	3 hrs	

Dublin Heuston to Galway		ERT 240
Frequency	Journey time	Notes
6–9 per day	2 hrs 30 mins	

Notes

A – Additional trains, also 2 per hr, run from London Paddington to Oxford.
B – There are 4 or 5 direct trains per day on this route. Where there's no direct train, change at Worcester Foregate St or Great Malvern.
C – Some journeys require a change of train at Carmarthen.

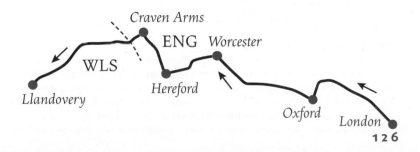

126

called Oxford). The station belies the grace of the city it serves. The city centre, with the main colleges, is just an eight-minute walk to the east. Make for St Giles, Broad Street, Radcliffe Square, the High Street and Christ Church Meadow (in that order) and you'll begin to see what makes Oxford so special.

Our route then tracks broadly north-west from Oxford following a deeply rural railway which winds through **gentle Cotswold landscapes**. There are neat fields, limestone cottages roofed with local slates and in spring and summer a feast of lineside wild flowers. The railway follows the Evenlode Valley upstream, just beyond Kingham passing though the now abandoned station at Adlestrop where one hot June afternoon in 1914 a train from London, carrying the then unknown poet **Edward Thomas**, stopped. Thomas recalled the moment in a poem (called *Adlestrop*) which touches some very English sensibilities about rural life. There's an added poignancy that Thomas was killed in the First World War (at the Battle of Arras in 1917).

Tunnelling through the Cotswold ridge by Chipping Campden, the railway drops down into the **Vale of Evesham**, so swapping the pastoral scenes of the Cotswolds for one of England's most productive horticultural region. From soft fruits to summer cherries, from asparagus to Brussels sprouts, this really is a premier-league region for market gardening.

Evesham occupies a plum spot within the neck of a meander on the River Avon, and there's an especially good view of the river as the train leaves Evesham, bridging the river with houseboats bobbing below. Then it's just a few minutes across the vale to **Worcester** on the River Severn, where there are two stations: Shrub Hill and Foregate Street, the latter much better placed for the centre.

Sit on the right beyond Worcester for great views of the Malvern Hills as the train approaches the sedate town of **Great Malvern** where, if you've an hour to spare, there's a pleasant café on the London-bound platform. Cutting through the hills in a tunnel, the train then rolls west into Herefordshire with its distinctive black-and-white timber-framed houses set harmoniously amid the hills and woods. **Hereford's** compact town centre is a delight, and remembered most notably for its fine cathedral, where the star treasure is a mediaeval map of the world (called the *mappa mundi*). The town also has much pleasing Georgian and Victorian architecture.

Connections from Hereford

All trains from the east terminate at Hereford. Even though this is still England, train services on the north-south main line through Hereford are all run by Transport for Wales (TfW or *Trafnidiaeth Cymru*). Hourly trains run north to Manchester, flying the Welsh flag all the way (ERT 149). There are also direct services to Chester and **Holyhead** (also ERT 149), thus giving a convenient connection onto **Route 4**. The early evening TfW train from Hereford to Holyhead offers (Mon-Fri only) a really excellent business-class service where the real perk is complimentary dinner served along the way. The accent is very much on locally sourced food. TfW also run south from Hereford to Cardiff (ERT 149) with many services continuing to Swansea and beyond.

The Heart of Wales

From Hereford, it is just a short hop north through beautiful Marches countryside to **Craven Arms**. The agreeable market town of Ludlow is an appealing intermediate stop with a good choice of accommodation. For a treat, try Dinham Hall, ☎ 01584 876 464 (www.dinhamhall.com) just by the castle. At Craven Arms, we turn decisively west and make for Wales. If you find yourself with a long connection time at Craven Arms, consider changing instead at Church Stretton (which is just nine minutes north of Craven Arms). It does of course mean backtracking, but Church Stretton, enviably set among the **Shropshire Hills**, is much the nicer place to while away an hour or two.

There are few better ways of approaching Wales than on the **Heart of Wales line** (*Rheilffordd Calon Cymru*) which we rate as one of Europe's finest rural rail rambles. Just four trains a day (less on Sundays) run the full 146 km from Craven Arms to Llanelli. These trains start their run in Shrewsbury and then pause in Church Stretton before turning off onto the Heart of Wales railway at Craven Arms.

Like the Settle and Carlisle line (which forms part of **Route 3** in this book), the Heart of Wales railway is a good example of a rural rail route which not merely survives, but really thrives, because of local community involvement in the venture.

It's a brilliant ride in any weather. We've done it on a clear summer day but also in less clement weather, with mist shrouding the hills and sheep fading into the fog. We start by tracking south-west towards the Teme Valley which we follow upstream to **Knighton**. The village is on the south bank of the river in Wales, but here the railway and Knighton station are still on English soil. Bridging the river just after Knighton, the train enters Wales, skirting the northern edge of Radnor Forest to reach the Victorian spa town of Llandrindod Wells.

Travel on this line is always fun. Usually it's just a single railcar on the route, and the train guard, who also sells tickets, is often on first-name terms with the regular passengers. Many of the stations are served only on request. "I've never once had anyone ask us to stop at Sugar Loaf," says the guard as we slip through that tiny wayside station, which is on the most dramatic section of the line as the railway cuts through the hills between the Irfon and Tywi valleys. **Llandovery** is the first place of any size, and it's a good choice for an overnight stop. It has the feel of a traditional Welsh market town, with painted stucco buildings with slate roofs and deep eaves. We can recommend the Castle Hotel, Kings Rd, ☎ 01550 720 343 (www.castle-hotel-llandovery.co.uk) or the New White Lion, Stone St, ☎ 01550 720 685 (www.newwhitelion.com).

Leaving Llandovery, it's a pleasant run down the **Tywi Valley**, with fine views up towards Black Mountain to the left. You'll see Llandeilo's bright colour-washed cottages to the right, and then the train cuts through the hills to reach a more industrial landscape and a tidal estuary which escorts us down to **Llanelli**. It's here that one must change trains for Fishguard, but if there's no good onward connection you may prefer to stay on the Heart of Wales train till Swansea, which is just 20 minutes down the line. It'll mean backtracking of course, but that's never an issue if you are using a rail pass.

It's just 90 minutes from Llanelli to **Fishguard**, but what a ride. Sit on the left for the best views. We pass Pembrey Burrows – a huge area of sand dunes now largely afforested – beyond which are the long, silky sands of Cefn Sidan beach. We then follow the **Tywi Estuary** upstream through salt meadows towards Carmarthen. The train now heads decisively west, traversing good farming country to reach Pembrokeshire. Only on the final approach to Fishguard is there any great change in the landscape, and it's quite a dramatic one, with barren, rock-strewn hillocks as the train follows the fast-flowing Western Cleddau upstream, cutting between hills to reveal a fine view of Fishguard Bay ahead.

At Fishguard Harbour, the second of the two stations in Fishguard, the train pulls up alongside the quay from where the Stena Line ships leave for Ireland.

The Fishguard to Rosslare **ferry service** relies on the MS *Stena Europe* being used for most sailings. Although almost 40 years old, she's a comfort-

FISHGUARD FACTS

The west side of the bay, where the ferries come and go, is Goodwick. Fishguard (Abergwaun in Welsh) itself is the small town which sits on a distinct hill away to the east (you'll see it to the right from the train). If you want the boat to Ireland, then stay on the train until **Fishguard Harbour**. For anywhere else, alight at Fishguard & Goodwick, which is in Goodwick village. It's a 15-minute walk east to Fishguard, but there are also buses. If staying overnight, make for Fishguard itself, where Manor Townhouse, Main St, ☎ 0348 873 260 (www.manortownhouse.com) offers stylish rooms, the best of them with stunning sea views.

Fishguard is the end of the railway, but there are excellent bus connections. Venture to the very tip of **Pembrokeshire** by taking the bus to St Davids. 🚌 T11 follows the main road, but the less-frequent 🚌 404 is a better choice, as it detours via Strumble Head with better views of the coast. 🚌 T5 runs hourly up the coast to Aberystwyth, where there are good connections onto the 🚌 T2 for **Bangor** (where you can connect onto **Route 2**). This is really only a journey for dedicated bus travellers. Fishguard to Bangor takes seven hours. The one-way fare is £11 on weekdays, but travel on this route is free at weekends – an amazing concession in a small country which takes public transport seriously.

able vessel. For a small premium, upgrade to the Stena Plus lounge which is often a haven of quiet on an otherwise busy ship.

It's worth noting that there is an alternative ferry link from south-west Wales to **Rosslare**, with Irish Ferries sailing from Pembroke Dock (ERT 2055). This alternative Welsh departure point is served by direct trains from Swansea, Llanelli and Carmarthen (ERT 136). The train to ship transfer is not as slick at Pembroke Dock, which is why we favour the Fishguard route.

Céad Míle Fáilte: Welcome to Ireland

A notice inside the **ferry terminal** at Rosslare welcomes new arrivals to Ireland. "Céad Míle Fáilte" – a hundred thousand welcomes. It's an odd precursor to the soul-destroying walk between fierce metal barriers to the railway station. Worry not! Ireland does get better than this. The station was moved from the quayside to its new less convenient location in 2008 – a mark of how undervalued foot passengers are on the ferries.

ROSSLARE CONNECTIONS

If you are heading west, bear in mind that the Expressway 🚌 40 (operated by Bus Éireann; www.buseireann.ie) runs from just outside the ferry terminal to Waterford and Cork, with good connections onto the Irish rail network in both those cities. The bus that connects with the early morning boat arrival in Rosslare runs right through to **Killarney** to connect onto **Route 4** in this book. Rosslare to Killarney costs €28 and takes just over six hours.

The train from Rosslare Europort station runs to Dublin. It's far too fine a route to travel in darkness. So, unless it's a long summer evening, if you arrive off the afternoon boat from Fishguard, you may want to stay overnight close to Rosslare and then continue next morning. **Wexford**, just 20 mins around the bay by bus or train from Rosslare Harbour, is the obvious choice. It's an amiable small town, just perfect for a first night in Ireland. Clayton Whites, Alley St, ☎ 091 22 311 (www.claytonwhiteshotel.com) is a decent hotel with a good, contemporary feel and a convenient location, less than 10 minutes on foot from the station

The railway through the centre of Wexford is one of the most extra-ordinary we know. The trains run at walking pace along the streets that mark the waterfront. Arriving from Rosslare, you'll have **Wexford Harbour** on your right and a row of shops to your left as the train inches past parked cars to reach O'Hanrahan station at the far end of Wexford's busy central area. The station is named after Michael O'Hanrahan, executed by the British for his role in the **Easter Rising** in 1916.

Ireland's East Coast

Many things may strike you on your first journey on any Iarnród Éireann (Irish Rail) train. **Irish Gaelic** is still very much used in the on-board

DUBLIN DAY OUT

Any trip to Ireland should venture beyond Dublin. If you are not staying with Route 5 on to **Galway**, then here's a thought. For those who enjoy seeing something of the countryside by train, we think that the Dublin – Limerick Junction – Waterford – Kilkenny – Dublin circuit (ERT 245 then 239 then 241) makes a very fine first taste of Ireland beyond the capital. With a 08.00 start from Dublin Heuston, follow **Route 4** to Limerick Junction (see p85), changing there onto the beautiful Suir Valley line to reach **Waterford** by late morning. That city is worth a stop, but also plan to spend three or four hours in Kilkenny, which is by far the most atmospheric of Ireland's mediaeval cities. **Kilkenny** lies just 35 mins north of Waterford on the main line back to Dublin. This entire circuit requires five-and-a-half hours on trains; that's a lot, but it takes in some glorious scenery, and you get to spend some time in two fine cities: Waterford and Kilkenny. It's a perfect trip for a midsummer day, when you can expect fine views along the **Barrow Valley** on the evening journey back to Dublin.

announcements and on many trains there's a very sociable, even communal, feel. Travelling by train in Ireland is invariably fun and on most trains they even manage to have the tables perfectly aligned with the windows, so allowing unimpeded views of the passing scenery. And on the run from Wexford up to Dublin, the best of that scenery is all to the east, so grab a seat on the right side of the train.

It's a grand ride north from Wexford, following the tidal lower reaches of the **River Slaney** upstream to Enniscorthy with a panorama to the distant Blackstairs Mountains away to the north-west. Continuing on through Gorey to Arklow, where that Irish word Fáilte is rendered in patterned tile work on a wall by the station platform, the railway then turns inland, plunging deep into the **Wicklow Hills**. This is the most beautiful part of the journey, as the railway follows the wooded Vale of Avoca.

Returning to the coast at Wicklow, the train then hugs the coast as it runs north through small coastal communities which these days are among the most desirable places to live in the Dublin commuter belt. The section of the railway through the cliffs at Bray Head, originally engineered by **Isambard Kingdom Brunel**, really rates as one of Europe's finest sections of coastal railway. Then it's an easy run on through Dún Laoghaire into Dublin. The train from Rosslare and Wexford stops first at Pearse station in Dublin and then continues over the River Liffey to terminate at Dublin Connolly. For more on **Dublin**, and on connecting trains, see p83.

To the wild Atlantic coast

It's a short ride on the Luas Tram red route (single fare €2.10) from Connolly to **Heuston station** for the onward train to Galway. For the first 70 km out of Dublin, the Galway train follows the main rail route to Cork and Killarney (also part of **Route 4**), swinging off right at Portarlington to cross the River

Barrow and enter County Offaly. Much of the single-track route to Galway has a very rural feel. Timetabling has to be slick with many heavy timber trains using the route. We slip over the **Grand Canal** at Tullamore and then, approaching Clara, a town with strong Quaker connections, lush pasture land gives way to rougher terrain. **Athlone** has a nice enough position by the Shannon at the southern end of Lough Ree but it is perhaps a shade pretentious for the locals to refer to Athlone as the Irish Athens. However, there's a great view of the classical, if rather bland, green-domed parish church to the left as the train crosses the Shannon.

Then it's pancake-flat to **Ballinasloe** and then gorse hedges and limestone walls as the railway crosses slightly higher land to reach Athenry, beyond which the grass gets ever greener as we speed west to Galway. The last stretch into Galway is very memorable with fine views to the left over **Galway Bay** to the wild hills of County Clare beyond.

Galway

Galway is one of our favourite Irish cities. Chilled and laid-back, it is the perfect place to spend a few days. The town itself is appealing, and it's a good base for day trips to **Clifden** or the **Aran Islands**. The station is right by **Eyre Square** where the petite statue of Galway-born writer Pádraic Ó Conaire is a natural focal point.

Amble west though the pedestrianised city centre, where traditional Irish music is a staple, to the banks of the turbulent River Corrib. Take time to let the Guinness settle and, when you've had your fill of city flair, walk out along the windy causeway to **Mutton Island**.

ARRIVAL, INFORMATION, ACCOMMODATION

🚆 Just off the southern end of Eyre Square (it's also where all buses depart). 🛈 Tourist office: Forster St. (www.galwaytourism.ie).

🛏 The **Park House Hotel**, Forster Street, ☎ 091 564 924 (www.parkhousehotel.ie) close to Eyre Square is an excellent place to stay in Galway, with discounted rates if you stay for a few days. Equally well located is the **Skeffington Arms Hotel**, Eyre Square, ☎ 091 563 173 (www.skeffington.ie) which is a Galway institution next to the lively Skeff Bar. The friendly **St Jude's Lodge** B&B, 24 College Road, ☎ 091 569 100 (www.galwayguesthouses. ie) is handy for the station and just a few minutes away from the city centre.

✖ Fresh fish is available everywhere. We especially enjoyed The Seafood Bar @ Kirwan's, Kirwan's Lane, ☎ 091 568 266 (www.kirwanslane.ie) in Galway's Old Town, which has a good selection of wines by the glass.

GALWAY CONNECTIONS

There's a very useful local rail route which runs south through County Clare to **Limerick** and Limerick Junction (ERT 242), where you can connect into **Route 4** to **Killarney** and onto the fast trains to Cork (ERT 245).

Galway is the gateway to the beautiful Connemara region, easily reached by taking the 🚌 419 to Clifden. Bus Éireann service 🚌 64 runs north via Sligo and Donegal to **Derry**, the latter more than five hours away to the north.

A TASTE OF FRANCE
An introduction

How might one best get a taste of France by train? There is, to be sure, a real thrill in being on a high-speed train as it storms out of a rail tunnel for a **first encounter with France**. Perhaps you are emerging from the Channel Tunnel to find the grey skies of Calais. Or possibly you are on a sleek Spanish train which has dived under the Pyrenees through the Perthus Tunnel and dashes out into sharp southern sunshine after a subterranean crossing of the border **from Spain to France**. You might be slipping quietly over the French frontier on a local train through the Jura hills or on one trundling through vineyards on the west side of the Rhine.

Whatever way you arrive in France, and particularly if you arrive by train or boat rather than by plane, there is **a sense of occasion**. To get the most out of your rail travels around France, it is important to cut off the high-speed lines and explore lesser rail routes.

The first French high-speed railway was opened in 1981 – that was between Paris and Lyon. Four decades on, the country has almost 3,000 km of high-speed lines, known in France as *lignes à grande vitesse* (LGV). That's a magnificent achievement, one which has enhanced regional connectivity and reshaped the geography of France. But, let's face it, those **LGV routes** were certainly not designed for sightseeing.

Life beyond the high-speed routes

Happily, France still has a very extensive web of traditional railways, quite apart from the modern LGV network. Several routes in this book all rely on these non-high-speed lines which criss-cross the country. We have included **some of our favourites**, but there were many potential candidates. Would that there had been space to include the 277-km long *ligne des Causses* from Béziers to Neussargues (ERT 332) or the 'old' line from Paris to Mulhouse via Troyes and Belfort (ERT 380 and 378a). Whenever we have the time, that's still our preferred route for journeys from the French capital to Basel (Bâle) and the northernmost cantons of Switzerland.

Whereas, almost without exception, seats must be reserved in advance for trains using high-speed routes, you can travel with much more spontaneity if you stay off LGV routes. Some, but by no means all, Intercités trains require seat reservations. And the entire **TER network** of regional trains is there for you to roam at will. None of these trains need advance reservation.

When you are planning longer-distance journeys through **rural France**, it is worth bearing in mind that services may be thin. The idea of easily memorised regular-interval departure times, has never quite caught on in France. So check those schedules carefully! ■

Route 6: From London to the Mediterranean

CITIES: ★★ CULTURE: ★★ HISTORY: ★ SCENERY: ★★
COUNTRIES COVERED: ENGLAND (ENG), FRANCE (FR)
JOURNEY TIME: 12 HRS | DISTANCE: 1,220 KM | MAP: WWW.EBRWEB.EU/MAP6

This first journey to France in *Europe by Rail* kicks off with an exquisite piece of theatre. It starts at **London's St Pancras station**, as inspiring a space as any cathedral. Great train stations have their own energy, each with its own shades and shadows. At St Pancras there is a bluish tinge to the light which picks up the blue of the soaring ironwork in William Barlow's dramatic train shed. Take time to linger at St Pancras, a station rescued from dereliction through a superb restoration. Then join us for a **fast run to Paris** on Eurostar. We continue south from the French capital on a route which takes us almost to the shores of the Mediterranean. For lovers of rural landscapes, that journey from Paris to southern France is much superior to the more usual route along high-speed lines. We follow an old main line for the entire route from **Paris to the Mediterranean**, cutting through the mountainous Massif Central region which lies well west of the Rhône Valley. From the French capital to Clermont-Ferrand we follow the *ligne du Bourbonnais*, then from Clermont-Ferrand to Nîmes we ride the *ligne des Cévennes*. The latter is one of Europe's finest stretches of railway.

ITINERARY OPTIONS

Paris, of course, demands a stop. It is then perfectly possible to complete this journey in a day, leaving Paris after breakfast and arriving in **Nîmes** by 18.00 – in time to continue if you wish beyond Nîmes to Avignon, Marseille or Montpellier. But there's such a feast of scenery on this route that we recommend also breaking the journey at **Vichy**.

With time on your hands you might consider taking one of the slightly slower trains for the first leg from Paris to Nevers. This route takes in one of the nicest stretches of the Loire Valley, and it's a pity to dash through on a fast express which does not stop between Paris and Nevers. After a leisurely lunch in Nevers, you could then continue to Vichy for an overnight stay. Next day, the journey continues via **Clermont-Ferrand** to Nîmes. Should you only leave Paris in the afternoon, Nevers is also a good choice for an overnight stop.

The commuter crowds are long gone, and St Pancras has settled into the quiet rhythm of a spring day when all the trains are running perfectly to time. The first corks have been popped at the station's pretentiously long champagne bar, and oysters and quail eggs are being served to those who know a *blanc de blancs* from a *blanc de noirs*. The area just north of the station, once a maze of sheds and sidings, coal dumps and grain stores, has been reclaimed, but happily not entirely tamed. **Camley Street Park**, tucked into a strip of land between the railway and Regent's Canal, is a sanctuary just a stone's throw from the platforms at St Pancras. It is a place to listen to reed warblers and watch a lively siskin searching for seeds. There is hazel, willow and silver birch.

Route details

London St Pancras to Paris Nord		ERT 10
Frequency	Journey time	Notes
1–2 per hr	2 hrs 15 mins – 2 hrs 40 mins	

Paris Bercy to Nevers		ERT 330
Frequency	Journey time	Notes
Every 1–2 hrs	2 hrs 10 mins – 2 hrs 40 mins	

Nevers to Vichy		ERT 330
Frequency	Journey time	Notes
Every 2–3 hrs	60 mins	

Vichy to Clermont-Ferrand		ERT 328/330
Frequency	Journey time	Notes
Hourly	30–35 mins	A

Clermont-Ferrand to Nîmes		ERT 333
Frequency	Journey time	Notes
2–3 per day	5 hrs – 5 hrs 10 mins	B

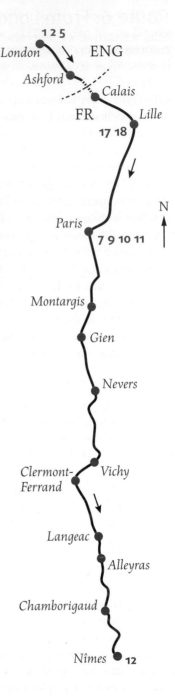

Notes

A – Frequent trains run between Vichy and Clermont-Ferrand in the morning and late afternoon rush hours on Mondays to Fridays.
B – Services on the *ligne des Cévennes* from Clermont-Ferrand to Nîmes are very prone to alterations due to engineering work on the line. It is wise to check times in the latest issue of the *European Rail Timetable* (ERT).

The **numbers in red** adjacent to some cities on our route maps refer to other routes in this book which also include that particular city.

The ERT numbers in our route details refer to the table numbers in the *European Rail Timetable* (ERT) where you will find train schedules for that particular section of the route.

On the other side of the railway tracks, headstones are stacked neatly around an old oak tree. They were placed there when graves were moved in Victorian times to allow the **Midland Railway** to build its line into St Pancras. A young trainee architect named **Thomas Hardy** helped clear part of the cemetery; he of course changed profession and become a celebrated writer. Just as St Pancras station, after a long period of decline, changed course and reinvented itself as London's gateway to the continent.

From the Thames to the Seine

"I have little doubt that British Railways will do away with St Pancras altogether," said the poet **John Betjeman** in 1952. "It is too beautiful and too romantic to survive. It is not of this age." But, despite decades of corporate neglect and vandalism, St Pancras has indeed survived and a huge statue of the poet, hand on hat, now stands on the station concourse. The rejuvenation of St Pancras station and the surrounding area is indeed a wondrous thing.

The journey on **Eurostar** from London to Paris is one of many moods and changing landscapes. Within a minute or two of departure, London is eclipsed by darkness. Watch for tantalising shadows at Stratford, then a burst of sunshine as our train, picking up speed now, storms out of the London tunnels onto the Thames marshes. This is a busy, fractured world of overhead pylons, silt lagoons and container parks: the melancholic edgelands where the capital blurs with Essex.

Eurostar dives under the **River Thames**, emerging in moments into industrial north Kent, which quickly transforms into a green and pleasant land. The **Medway Viaduct** is a gem, one that sadly goes unnoticed and unremarked by most travellers. The train speeds over the river where once the Dutch tried to attack the English fleet. The view up the Medway Valley (to the right of the train) is one of delicate beauty.

The rail route dances with the ancient Pilgrim's Way, coasting past orchards and oast houses, and within half an hour of leaving London we are approaching the **Channel Tunnel**. Emerging from the tunnel after 25 minutes, the first glimpses of France at Calais do the country no favours. But industry quickly gives way to an expansive rural landscape. Brick villages sit squat in Flanders fields.

Speeding south-east towards Lille, the town of **Cassel** stands bold and clear on a rare hill away to the left. Just beyond **Lille**, our Paris-bound train turns sharply to the right, now heading decisively south towards Picardy. We dash through a landscape once full of sandbags and barbed wire, now scattered with war cemeteries that burst with poppies. The ashen face of death, drenched by hopeless rain and shrapnel scarred, has been replaced by a quiet beauty, broken only by the whoosh of the fast trains that speed by on their way to Paris.

This is territory defined by its rivers. We cross the Scarpe, the Somme and the Oise. The first clear hint of approaching Paris is the line of planes away to our left descending into Charles de Gaulle airport. Suddenly, to the right, there is a tantalising glimpse of the River Seine.

The Gare du Nord

Our journey on Eurostar ends at the Gare du Nord. Each of the principal railway stations in Paris has its own character. Saint-Lazare is for artists (think Manet and Monet) while the Gare de Lyon has the lure of the sunny south of France. The Gare de l'Est is the place where there are meetings and greetings as the train from Russia arrives. But the Gare du Nord is a place apart, a station where the routine comings and goings are unexceptional. It is in a part of Paris full of moral and sexual hazards – hardly changed from the days of *L'Assommoir* except that the downtrodden working-class French residents of **Émile Zola's day** have been replaced by migrants from across the world.

If, like us, you need to pause after such a fast train journey, then make for the courtyard of **Lariboisière Hospital**, as close to the Gare du Nord as the canalside wilderness at Camley Street is to St Pancras. No wilderness or warblers here, but an elegant and quiet space surrounded by neoclassical colonnades. It's a good spot to ponder your onward journey, for Paris is just the beginning, as the French capital is the starting point for five journeys described in this book.

Paris (suggested stopover)

Paris has always held great allure – it's been a byword for **style, glamour and romance** since railway tourism began and the English started to go there for weekends in the 19th century. **Baron Haussmann** transformed the city for Napoleon III, sweeping away many of its crowded slum quarters and replacing them with tree-lined boulevards too wide to barricade. Today, these stately avenues of elegantly matching, shuttered buildings and imposing monuments form the framework of much of modern Paris.

The Île de la Cité in the River Seine, scarred by the fire which so terribly damaged **Notre-Dame** Cathedral in April 2019, is still the heart of the city. Students traditionally hang out in the Latin Quarter on the Left Bank, so-called because studies at the Sorbonne were originally in Latin. The once seedy area around the Bastille has shaken off its revolutionary past to become one of the city's trendiest nightspots with a multitude of bars and restaurants.

Older quarters such as **Le Marais and Montmartre** remain warrens of picturesque old streets. The Palais Galliera – the city's museum devoted to fashion – will open its doors again in 2020 after major refurbishments that will double the exhibition space.

Rail history buffs might be interested in the fact that the home of one of Paris' most famous museums – **Musée d'Orsay** – is a grand structure that was built as a train station for the World's Fair in 1900.

ARRIVAL, INFORMATION, ACCOMMODATION

➹ There are seven main rail stations in Paris, each has its own métro stop; all except Montparnasse and Gare de l'Est are also served by express RER trains. ✈ **Roissy-Charles de Gaulle** (CDG) is 27 km north-east of the city, linked by RER line B to Gare du Nord and on to Châtelet-Les Halles, 04.50–00.05, every 10 or 20 mins, taking about 30 mins to/from Châtelet-Les Halles. ✈ **Orly** is 14 km south; the automated métro links the airport with Antony, where you can join RER line B for the city centre. Take advantage of the efficient and well coordinated public transport system, made up of the métro and buses of RATP (Régie Autonome des Transports Parisiens) and RER (Réseau Express Régional) trains. RER trains run about 06.00–00.30, consisting of five rail lines (A, B, C, D and E), which are basically express services between the city and the suburbs. 🛈 Tourist office: Hôtel de Ville, 29 r. de Rivoli (www.parisinfo.com) and at Gare du Nord. The **Batobus** (www.batobus. com), is a water-bus (without commentary) and a good way of seeing Paris from the Seine. The Batobus stops at the Eiffel Tower, Musée d'Orsay, St-Germain-des-Prés, Notre-Dame, Jardin des Plantes, Hôtel de Ville, the Louvre, Champs-Élysées and Beaugrenelle.

➹ Cheaper accommodation is getting harder to find anywhere near the city centre, and if you're on a tight budget, you may have to stay out of the centre. We can very much recommend the comfortable **Hôtel du Jeu de Paume**, 54 r. Saint-Louis-en-l'île, ☎ 01 43 26 14 18 (www.jeudepaumehotel.com), which is on the Île Saint-Louis in the middle of the Seine, just a few minutes' walk away from Notre-Dame. The location could not be better – but it has its price. The **Hôtel Langlois**, 63 r. St-Lazare, ☎ 01 48 74 78 24 (www.hotel-langlois.com), is a lovely place full of character and well worth the price-tag. A good option in Montmartre in a quiet street is the boutique **Hôtel des Arts**, 5 r. Tholoze, ☎ 01 46 06 30 52 (www.arts-hotel-paris.com).

The ligne du Bourbonnais

Our onward journey south from the French capital starts at **Paris Bercy** station, which sadly wins no marks for grace and charm. If you opt for one of the Intercités trains which runs non-stop to Nevers, you'll need to reserve a seat in advance. These fast trains all continue beyond Nevers to Vichy and Clermont-Ferrand. The slower Intercités trains to Nevers make nine intermediate stops; they do not require advance reservation.

The main *ligne du Bourbonnais* runs south from Paris; it was promoted in the mid-19th century by the PLM; that's the same company which ran the line from Paris to Lyon and Marseille (featured in **Route 7** in this book). We rate the *ligne du Bourbonnais* as the most interesting of the great arterial routes radiating from Paris. It has been much improved and was electrified right through to Clermont-Ferrand in 1990.

The train dashes south through the forests of **Fontainebleau**, then cruises up the Loing Valley through Montargis, cresting a gentle watershed and dropping down to reach the Loire Valley at Gien. For the next 75 km, the railway hugs the east bank of the river – sit on the right for the best views. Watch out for the great **aqueduct at Briare**, parts of which were designed by Gustave Eiffel. It carries a canal over the Loire. A little later you'll see the celebrated wine village of Sancerre perched on a hill on the far bank of the river, and shortly thereafter the train cuts through the chalky vineyards where flinty Pouilly Fumé is produced.

The first city of any size on the run south from Paris is **Nevers**. It's a fine provincial centre, with a strong porcelain tradition. It's one of those unsung towns which are instantly appealing. Look out for the cathedral and the ducal palace. If you are tempted to stay overnight, and are not looking for anything fancy, the Hôtel de Clèves, ☎ 03 86 61 15 87 (www.hoteldecleves.fr) at 8 r. Saint Didier is perfectly adequate; it's just a 5-min walk from the station. From Nevers, it is just under an hour on the train south to Vichy.

Vichy (suggested stopover)

If you want to break your journey to the south, Vichy is a good choice. This sedate spa town is best known for its role from 1940 to 1944 as the de facto capital of that part of France not under German occupation. If you are looking for a place with a buzzing nightlife, Vichy probably isn't for you. But it's **quirky and interesting** and, with a wide choice of hotels and some fine parks and promenades, it makes a great overnight stop.

ARRIVAL, INFORMATION, ACCOMMODATION

⇌ Pl. de la Gare, a 10-min walk east of the city centre. ⓘ Tourist office: 19 r. du parc (www.vichy-destinations.fr). ⊨ A good-value option is the centrally located **Arverna Citotel Vichy**, 12 r. Desbrest, ☎ 04 70 31 31 19 (www.arverna-hotels-vichy.com). Budget options include the **Biarritz**, 3 r. Grangier, ☎ 04 70 97 81 20 (www.hoteldebiarritz-vichy.com), just 5-min from the town centre, and the **Hôtel DeGrignan**, 7 pl. Sévigné, ☎ 04 70 32 08 11 (www.hoteldegrignan.fr), with its central and quiet location.

CONNECTIONS FROM VICHY

There are direct trains running east from Vichy to Lyon (ERT 328) to connect into **Route 7**.

Through the Auvergne

Already in Vichy you have a sense of the hills closing in. Our route now tracks south through **Clermont-Ferrand**, where a change of train is always necessary. The city is the centre of the French rubber industry and birthplace of Michelin tyres; it's built of a dark volcanic stone, and wins no prizes for beauty. But the centre has an absorbing maze of little lanes and alleys, dominated by the hilltop Gothic cathedral. The building to seek out is the 11th-century church of Notre-Dame-du-Port, place du Port, one of France's greatest examples of the local Romanesque style.

Connections from Clermont-Ferrand

Our recommended route south from Clermont-Ferrand follows the *ligne des Cévennes* south-east via the Allier gorges to Nîmes. But there are alternatives. There is a once-daily connection south via **Millau to Béziers** (ERT 332). It follows the *ligne des Causses*, a single-track railway which cuts through very wild terrain. After closure for track renewal for part of 2019, the future of this line now looks more secure.

Running south from Clermont, the scenery becomes ever better. There are glimpses of magnificent **Romanesque churches** and mediaeval red-roofed villages – some of the latter with that haunting run-down look which makes one wonder if they have been purposefully placed as follies for the benefit of artists and passing train travellers.

Beyond **Langeac** you travel through the spectacular Allier gorges amid the wild, volcanic scenery. You'll glimpse fierce chasms and chaotic rock-strewn slopes as the train cuts through sparsely populated territory which lies well beyond the usual tourist trails. If you are tempted to stop off, consider an overnight stay in **Alleyras** where the Hôtel Le Haut-Allier (www.hotel-lehautallier.com; just 2 mins on foot from the station) has reasonably priced rooms and a much acclaimed restaurant.

Further south, after a stop at La Bastide-Saint-Laurent, the train skirts the eastern flank of Mount Lozère, running for long stretches through tunnels. After that comes the highlight of the journey: the magnificent **viaduct at Chamborigaud**. Then it is mainly downhill all the way to Nîmes. Since 2018, all trains on this line from Clermont-Ferrand to Nîmes have been classed as regional (ie. TER) services.

Nîmes

Nîmes boasts several superb Roman buildings. Les Arènes, seating 23,000 in 34 elliptical tiers, is said to be the best preserved Roman amphitheatre in the world. It still stages concerts, theatrical events and bullfights (open daily). **Maison Carrée**, a well-preserved 1st-century temple, is now an exhibition centre (open daily). Next door is the futuristic Carré d'Art, a contemporary art gallery designed by Norman Foster (closed Mon). To the west, reached by a bridge from Quai de la Fontaine, is the 18th-century Jardins de la Fontaine which features a romantic Temple of Diana. The **Musée de la Romanité** opened in June 2018.

Arrival, information, accommodation

⇝ Blvd. Talabot, a 10-min walk south-east of the centre. 🅱 Tourist office: 6 blvd. des Arènes (www.nimes-tourisme.com). ⋈ A good mid-range option opposite the station is the Ibis Styles **Nimes Gare Centre**, 19 Al. Boissy d'Anglas, ☎ 04 66 05 54 30 (www.accorhotels.com). Or try the very comfortable **Hotel des Tuileries**, 22 r. Roussy, ☎ 04 66 21 31 15 (www.hoteldestuileries.com). Centrally located, the **Hôtel de L'Amphithéâtre**, 4 r. des Arènes, ☎ 04 66 67 28 51 (www.hoteldelamphitheatre.com), is close to the main sights.

Route 7: Burgundy and the Rhône Valley

CITIES: ★★★ CULTURE: ★★ HISTORY: ★★ SCENERY: ★★
COUNTRIES COVERED: FRANCE (FR)
JOURNEY TIME: 9 HRS | DISTANCE: 863 KM | MAP: www.ebrweb.eu/MAP7

The Mediterranean has long held special appeal for northern Europeans. For the sun-starved English heading south, the natural route to Provence was always to cross the English Channel and travel south via **Paris** to the Rhône Valley. Fifty years ago, travellers from London to Provence might have chosen to start their journey by climbing aboard one of the blue-and-gold Wagons-Lits sleeping cars that every evening left London Victoria station for Paris. The entire train was shipped on a ferry across the Channel. Eleven hours to Paris, changing stations there, and with time for a late breakfast at the stylish **Train Bleu**, a belle époque restaurant at the Gare de Lyon, before boarding a lunchtime train which arrived in Marseille in the evening.

That journey from London to Marseille, which in summer 1966 took 22 hours, can today be accomplished in under seven hours, using the Eurostar service which since 2015 has run from London right through to Marseille. It is a superb way of reaching the south of France from London.

But might we suggest an alternative? **Eurostar** is definitely worth taking, for the run out of London is a fine piece of travel theatre (see **Route 6**). But having sped to Paris, why not then dawdle through France? True, there are plenty of TGVs which speed **south from Paris**, reaching Marseille in just over three hours, but we often take slower trains instead. Nowadays relegated to the status of a secondary route, the classic line south from Paris (via Sens and Dijon), which we describe here, is dubbed the **Paris-Lyon-Méditerreanée (PLM) route**. PLM was the company which introduced to the route such celebrated luxury trains as the *Côte d'Azur Rapide* and *Le Train Bleu*.

Back in 1966, the crack daytime express on the PLM route from Paris to Marseille was called *Le Mistral*; its train number, TEE 1, signalled its status as the flagship of the then newly created *Trans-Europe Express* network. With first-class only seating, two restaurant cars and air-conditioned carriages (a rarity in those days), *Le Mistral* was a train of real distinction, attracting the rich and famous. By the 1970s, the amenities on board had expanded to include a bookstall and a hairdressing salon.

RECOMMENDED ITINERARY

You'll not be able to get your hair styled on the trains which today follow the route once taken by *Le Mistral*. But there are compensations. As you move south along the PLM line, the scenery on this route becomes ever more compelling, and the journey culminates in a magnificent ride south through the **Rhône Valley to the Mediterranean**.

You can easily complete this journey in a single day. It requires just one change of train at Lyon Part Dieu station. The trains upon which this journey relies are TER services:

these are regional trains where there's no need to pre-book and there are no supplements for holders of rail passes.

This is a journey which might profitably be split into several legs with overnight stops along the way. If pressed to nominate our favourite spots for **stopovers** on this route, we would opt for Beaune and Valence. As an alternative to Valence, or in addition to Valence if you are minded to spread the journey over more days, you might consider Avignon (which features in this book as a recommended overnight stop on **Route 12** — see p141). If you prefer to stop at places with more of a big-city feel, then Dijon and Lyon are your best bets.

South from Paris

For the journey south from Paris, you'll depart from Paris Bercy, an unlovely concrete station which accommodates trains not grand enough to deserve space at the platforms of the nearby Gare du Lyon. If you are keen to push on south at speed, make for the Gare de Lyon from where a TGV will whisk you non-stop to Dijon in just 100 minutes. But far better, if you can possibly afford the time, to take the TER train from **Paris Bercy to Dijon** — a three-hour journey that gets more interesting with every mile that passes. Since December 2011, five trains per day on the classic Paris to Dijon route have been extended to Lyon, a move by SNCF that surely pleased PLM purists.

If you shun the TGV and take the slower TER from Paris Bercy to Dijon, you will quickly discover why artists like Millet were so taken by the landscapes south-east of Paris. The train runs through the **forests of Fontainebleau**, following the Seine and then the Yonne Valley upstream to Sens. The train may be slow in comparison with the TGV, but it still sets a cracking pace on this first part of the journey south from Paris. Beyond Sens, the pace slows with the train making more frequent stops and the hills around becoming ever more emphatic.

The area through which the train passes just beyond Montbard is the heartland of ancient Gaul. To the right of the train you'll see Mont Auxois, where Julius Caesar defeated the Gallic tribes in the Battle of Alésia. 20 minutes later the train cuts through a long tunnel and drops down steeply into the Saône Valley to reach Dijon.

Dijon is an excellent introduction to **Bourgogne** (Burgundy), the region of France that is so intimately associated with the fine wines of the same name. The city's grandest building is the strikingly elegant Palais des Ducs et des États de Bourgogne, best viewed from the pl. de la Libération. The building reflects the great wealth of the Dukes of Burgundy and now serves as the town hall, also housing the Musée des Beaux-Arts (closed Tues, free entry). This is a superb collection of paintings, sculptures and tapestries.

CONNECTIONS FROM DIJON

TER trains run north to Nancy (ERT 379), and there are TGVs heading east to Strasbourg (also ERT 379) to join **Route 19**. There is a regional rail route to **Troyes**, an engaging market

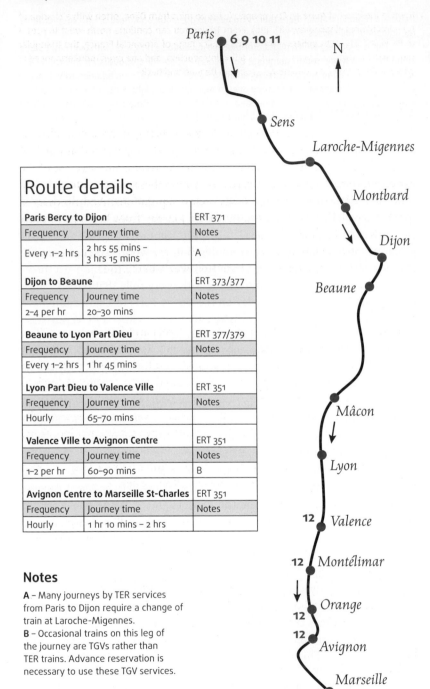

Route details

Paris Bercy to Dijon		ERT 371
Frequency	**Journey time**	**Notes**
Every 1–2 hrs	2 hrs 55 mins – 3 hrs 15 mins	A

Dijon to Beaune		ERT 373/377
Frequency	**Journey time**	**Notes**
2–4 per hr	20–30 mins	

Beaune to Lyon Part Dieu		ERT 377/379
Frequency	**Journey time**	**Notes**
Every 1–2 hrs	1 hr 45 mins	

Lyon Part Dieu to Valence Ville		ERT 351
Frequency	**Journey time**	**Notes**
Hourly	65–70 mins	

Valence Ville to Avignon Centre		ERT 351
Frequency	**Journey time**	**Notes**
1–2 per hr	60–90 mins	B

Avignon Centre to Marseille St-Charles		ERT 351
Frequency	**Journey time**	**Notes**
Hourly	1 hr 10 mins – 2 hrs	

Notes

A – Many journeys by TER services from Paris to Dijon require a change of train at Laroche-Migennes.
B – Occasional trains on this leg of the journey are TGVs rather than TER trains. Advance reservation is necessary to use these TGV services.

town in the heart of Aube en Champagne (2 hrs 20 mins from Dijon, often with a change of train in Culmont-Chalindrey, ERT 380). From Troyes you can continue north-west to return to Paris. In fact, for travellers wanting just a quick taste of provincial France, the triangular route Paris – Dijon – Troyes – Paris is a fine introduction, and one even more enhanced if, while in Dijon, you take time to ride south to Beaune and back.

Wine country

The entire route south from Dijon to Avignon takes you through or close to some of France's **most celebrated vineyards**, producing wines that north of Lyon are generally classified as Burgundy and south of Lyon carry one of the various Rhône appellations. Tucked away within these general categories are some small properties that have world-class reputations. And nowhere is that more true than on the 20-minute train journey from Dijon to Beaune, which skirts the **Côte de Nuits**. The vineyards to the right of the train produce some of the most expensive wines in the world, among them the grands crus from Chambertin, Vosne-Romanée and Corton.

Beaune (suggested stopover)

Beaune is a charming old town of cobbled streets and fine mansions. The magnificent Hôtel-Dieu, r. de l'Hôtel-Dieu, with its flamboyant patterned roof of colourful geometric tiles, was originally built in the 15th century as a hospital for the sick and needy. Inside, don't miss the 15th-century **Polyptych of the Last Judgement**, its nine oak panels showing sinners tumbling to an unpleasant fate. This building, with its lovely courtyard, is the centre of the prestigious Côte de Beaune and Côte de Nuits wine trade; many local *caves* (wine cellars) offer *dégustations* (tastings). The old ducal palace houses a fine museum dedicated to wine: Musée du Vin, r. d'Enfer (closed Tues and also Dec–early Apr; also closed Mon during Oct, Nov; €5.80).

ARRIVAL, INFORMATION, ACCOMMODATION

⇝ Av. du 8 Septembre, east of town, just outside the old walls. 🛈 Tourist office: Porte Marie de Bourgogne, 6 blvd. Perpreuil (www.beaune-tourism.com). ⊨ Located in a historic building, the **Hôtel de la Paix**, 45 r. du faubourg Madeleine, ☎ 03 80 24 78 08 (www.hotelpaix.com), is an affordable option. Nearby is the **Hôtel de la Cloche**, 40–42 r. du faubourg Madeleine, ☎ 03 80 24 66 33 (www.hotel-lacloche-beaune.com). Slightly more upmarket is the stylish **Les Chambres de l'imprimerie** B&B set in a former printer's house at 12 r. Colbert, ☎ 06 52 41 03 21 (www.chambres-de-limprimerie.fr). All three places are only a 10-min walk from the train station.

Lyon (population approx. 1.5 million), at the junction of the Saône and the Rhône, has a lovely old centre, with a hive of charming streets and some truly amazing restaurants; it's rated as one of France's gastronomic high points, and as you might expect from a major university city, there's a lively buzz about the place.

The two rivers divide the city into three parts. On the west bank of the Saône is **Vieux Lyon**, the Renaissance quarter, while on the east bank of the Rhône is the modern business sector, with its high-rise offices and apartment blocks. Lyon's Part-Dieu station, where you change trains when following the old PLM route from Paris to Marseille, is in this modern quarter. The station is part of a major urban redevelopment project dating from the 1980s. It's functional, but nothing more. You'll not get a sense of 'old' Lyon if your sole encounter with the city is a quick change of trains at Part-Dieu. Well west of Part-Dieu, between the Rhône and the Saône, lies the partly pedestrianised city centre, dating largely from the 17th and 18th centuries. It runs from pl. Bellecour, where the tourist office stands, north to the old silk quarter of La Croix-Rousse.

Lyon is famous for its *traboules* – covered passageways between streets – that once served as shortcuts for the silk traders, protecting their precious cargoes from the weather. Most *traboules* are in Vieux Lyon and La Croix-Rousse. Just across Pont Galliéni over the Rhône from Perrache station is the poignant **Centre d'Histoire de la Résistance et de la Déportation**, 14 av. Berthelot (closed Mon & Tues).

CONNECTIONS FROM LYON

Lyon is handily placed for heading east to explore the Alps by rail. For a superb route east **into the Alps**, go via Culoz, Aix-les-Bains, Annecy (all in ERT 345) and La Roche-sur-Foron, where you can either continue to Geneva (p339) or take the **narrow-gauge mountain railway** from Chamonix-Mont-Blanc to Martigny (ERT 572). There is also a much less interesting direct line from Lyon to Geneva (takes 2 hrs, ERT 346). Culoz is a gateway for the Marais de Lavours, a national park noted for its marshland habitats, while beyond the well-heeled lakeside spa of **Aix-les-Bains** (where excursion boats cross Lac du Bourget to the mystical monastery of L'Abbaye d'Hautecombe) is Annecy, an upmarket, but still very beautiful, resort town in the heart of the Savoy Alps.

If you continue to Martigny, you switch to a metre-gauge line and climb into the mountains, with the option of a side trip on the **Tramway du Mont-Blanc** (ERT 397) from St-Gervais-le-Fayet to (summer only) the Nid d'Aigle (2,386 m — and a 15-min stroll from the Bionnassay Glacier). Chamonix is placed beneath Mont Blanc, the highest peak in the Alps; the Montenvers rack railway (ERT 397) climbs 5 km to a height of 1,913 m, looking over the **Mer de Glace**, France's biggest glacier, which you can actually enter by way of a tunnel to visit the ice grotto. You can also travel east from Lyon into Italy; the TGV to Turin and Milan runs via Chambéry, Modane and through the 12.8 km Fréjus tunnel and past the Italian ski resort of Bardonecchia.

South from Lyon

Lyon marks your first encounter with the **River Rhône**, and Route 7 beyond this point hugs the river for the journey south to Avignon. This is an oddly mixed landscape. Just south of Lyon huge oil refineries tower over historic villages. Nuclear power stations sit cheek by jowl with vineyards producing some of the Rhône's finest wines. The latter include the parched slopes of the Côte Rôtie which you'll see high above the far bank of the river. A little further south the railway snakes between the tiered terraces of the Hermitage vineyards, the names of the principal growers highlighted in huge signs beside the tracks.

Valence (suggested stopover)

We like Valence for its mood and its feel. It's one of those smaller cities which make for a perfect stopover. In truth, there is not really a huge amount to see, but Valence is the first town on the PLM route which really gives a sense of being in the south of France. **Valence Ville railway station** lies a short walk south-east of the city centre. The current main station building marked in 2016 its 150th anniversary. It opened in 1866 (though the PLM line reached Valence in 1854); the station's broad design was inspired by the north facade of the Petit Trianon, a small palace in the grounds of the gardens at Versailles.

An overnight stop in Valence gives time to see the town's oddly squat cathedral, dedicated to Saint Apollinaris, and wander through the narrow alleys and streets to the north. Don't miss the flamboyant **Maison des Têtes** at 57 Grande Rue, an extraordinary Renaissance building which is the city's pride and joy.

The nearby place des Clercs is a good spot to relax over a glass of local wine and reflect on the fate of evildoers. A plaque marks the spot where Louis Mandrin was executed in 1755 to the general approbation of watching crowds. Mandrin was a notorious smuggler and brigand who is nowadays celebrated as a sort of French Robin Hood.

Arrival, information, accommodation
⇌ R. Denis Papin, just a 10-min walk south-east of the city centre. 🛈 Tourist office: 11 blvd. Bancel (www.valence-romans-tourisme.com).
⊨ The **Hôtel de France**, 16 blvd. du G de Gaulle, ☎ 04 75 43 00 87 (www.hotel-valence.com) is a modern and comfortable hotel just a few minutes from the railway station towards the city centre. Just east of the centre, **Hôtel Atrium**, 20 r. Jean Louis Barrault, ☎ 04 75 55 53 62 (www.atrium-hotel.fr) is a more functional option, stylish in a very modern way. A budget option in a good location is **Les Négociants**, 27 av. Pierre Semard, ☎ 04 75 44 01 86 (www.hotelvalence.com).

Connections from Valence
An important regional rail route follows the **Isère Valley** upsteam from Valence, giving useful connections to Savoie and beyond (see **Route 12**). TER trains leave Valence Ville every two hours for Grenoble, Chambéry and Annecy (ERT 364). There are also thrice-daily direct trains to Geneva (3 hrs 15 mins, ERT 364).
Valence also has a **TGV railway station**, 10 km north-east of the city centre. Local trains and SNCF buses shuttle between Valence Ville station and the out-of-town TGV station, giving good connections with high-speed trains to Barcelona (4 hrs 15 mins, ERT 13), Marseille (70 mins, ERT 350), Paris (2 hrs 10 mins, ERT 355) and Nice (4 hrs, ERT 350).

Leaving Valence, there are fine views across the River Rhône, with peach and apricot orchards giving way to the volcanic hills of the Ardèche region. The railway follows the east bank of the river south through **Montélimar**, once famed for its nougat, but now sadly bypassed by most travellers making for the south. The next major city is **Orange**, which had a population of some 80,000 in Roman times and several sites from the period are still in existence. The **Arc de Triomphe** is the third largest Roman arch to have survived, and was originally in fact a gate to the ancient walled city. Dating from about 25 BC, it is a majestic three-arched structure lavishly decorated with reliefs depicting battles, naval and military trophies, and prisoners, honouring the victories of Augustus and the setting up of Arausio (Orange) as a colony. Orange's most famous sight is its Roman theatre, dating from the 1st century AD.

To the coast

South of Avignon (see p141 on **Route 12**) you are spoilt for choice with three routes south to Marseille. None wins any prizes for outstanding beauty, but whichever one you take, you will be struck by how the landscape opens out and becomes much more southern in demeanour. There are distant views of the arid limestone peaks of the Alpilles and on the route via Arles glimpses of flat delta landscapes that merge into the **Camargue**. Whichever route you opt for, our journey from London to the Mediterranean ends with an eyeful of the northern suburbs of Marseille – not always pretty but a reminder that the city of *pastis* and *bouillabaisse* is also a major industrial centre.

Arriving in Marseille

Marseille is an **earthy Mediterranean city** and hectically vibrant, with a great music scene and superb fish-based cuisine. The busiest port in France, it's a melting pot of French and North African cultures. Marseille's grubby, rough-and-ready character appeals to some, while others will want to move on swiftly – though watch this space, because big regeneration schemes are changing the city, especially in the northern dock areas. There's a good métro and bus system, and three tram lines.

Full of small restaurants and street cafés, the **Vieux Port** (Old Port) is the hub of Marseille life and is guarded by the forts of St-Jean and St-Nicholas on either side of its entrance. From the quai des Belges, the main boulevard of La Canebière extends back into the city. Across the port from the steep narrow streets of **Le Panier** – the oldest part of Marseille – rises Notre-Dame de la Garde, an impressive 19th-century basilica that is Marseille's most distinctive landmark (take 🚌 60 – it's a steep uphill climb otherwise). The golden Virgin atop the church watches over all sailors and travellers; the interior is full of paintings and mementos of the disasters the Virgin is supposed to have protected people from. In Dumas' novel of the same name the Count of Monte Cristo was imprisoned in Château d'If on one of the little Îles de Frioul just outside the harbour; it can be visited by boat on the **Frioul-If-Express** (www.lebateau-frioul-if.fr). The **Musée des civilisations de l'Europe et de la Méditerranée** (www.mucem.org; closed Tues) right on the seafront by Fort Saint-Jean is a highlight on Marseille's cultural circuit.

The central (Vieux Port) area is walkable. Elsewhere, use the métro and buses, both run by RTM (Régie des Transports de Marseille; www.rtm.fr). *Plan du Réseau* (from the tourist office and RTM kiosks) covers the routes: the map looks complicated but the system is easy to use. After 21.00 the normal bus routes are replaced by a 12-route evening network called Fluobus, centred on Canebière (Bourse).

ARRIVAL, INFORMATION, ACCOMMODATION

≽ Gare St-Charles, pl. Victor Hugo, is the main station, a 20-min walk north-east of the Vieux Port (Old Port): head down the steps and straight along blvd. d'Athènes and blvd. Dugommier to La Canebière, then turn right; or take the métro, direction La Timone, station Vieux Port/Hôtel de Ville. Facilities include left luggage, open daily 08.15–23.00.

⛴ Ferries connecting Marseille with Corsica (ERT 2565), Sardinia (ERT 2675) and North Africa (ERT 2558, 2602 & 2615) all berth at the Gare Maritime ferry terminal, just north of the Old Port; follow r. de la République. ✈ Marseille–Provence Aéroport (www.marseille-airport.com); at Marignane, 25 km north-west of the city. An airport bus runs between the airport and St-Charles railway station at least every 20 mins, taking 25 mins.

🛈 Tourist office: 11 La Canebière (www.marseille-tourisme.com). ⊨ Small and cosy, the **Pension Edelweiss**, 6 r. Lafayette, ☎ 09 51 23 35 11 (www.pension-edelweiss.fr), is a 2-min walk from the station. Also close by St-Charles is the retro-style B&B **Casa Ortega**, 46 r. des Petites Maries, ☎ 06 80 62 53 21 (www.casa-ortega.com). If you want great views of the Vieux Port and and are willing to pay for it consider the **Hotel La Résidence**, 18 quai du port, ☎ 04 91 91 91 22 (www.hotel-residence-marseille.com).

✗ The harbour and the streets leading from it are lined with Mediterranean and fish restaurants: Cours Julien is good for trendier, international fare, and more elegant restaurants are found along corniche Président J F Kennedy.

CONNECTIONS FROM MARSEILLE

Marseille is a major rail junction and the starting point for some of the most scenic lines in France. In addition to exploring **Route 8**, east along the Riviera to Nice and further on to Genoa and the Cinque Terre villages (**Route 40**), you can take the slow route to Paris via the Allier Gorge (**Route 6**). Or make an excursion to Aix-en-Provence (ERT 362). Beyond Aix, the line continues round the hills of the Lubéron (the subject of Peter Mayle's book *A Year in Provence*), and then through increasingly dramatic limestone scenery as you enter the foothills of the Alps. Beyond **Gap**, you're really into the Alps proper; you can continue on to Briançon (ERT 362), a major centre for the mountains.

Alternatively, stop at Montdauphin-Guillestre (between Gap and Briançon); from here there are connecting minibuses to the Parc Naturel Régional du Queyras, one of the most rural parts of the French Alps. Good bases are Saint-Véran (one of Europe's highest permanently inhabited villages) and Ceillac.

SIDETRACKS: THROUGH THE JURA

Route 7 in this book is a fine example of a longish journey which can be accomplished without having to use trains that require advance reservation. We know from feedback from readers of earlier editions of *Europe by Rail* that the fiddly business of **procuring seat reservations** undermines the ability to travel on a whim – though spontaneity is often lauded as one of the principal advantages of having a **rail pass** such as Interrail or Eurail.

Pass holders often incur **substantial supplements** for travel on high-speed trains. The direct TGV Lyria trains between Paris and destinations in Switzerland are comfortable and reliable. But pass holders must pay a hefty fee to secure a seat reservation on these trains. Second-class supplements for journeys from **Paris to destinations in Switzerland** start at €21; in first class, the fee is a minimum of €54. Interestingly, canny souls without rail passes who book bargain basement fares on TGV Lyria off-peak services may pay as little as €29 standard class and €49 standard première for travel from Paris to Switzerland.

But experienced travellers know better than always to hop on the fastest trains. There are very **appealing slower routes** from Paris to Switzerland which sidestep trains on which you might have to pay a pass holder's supplement or splash out for a compulsory seat reservation. And what's more, those alternative routes, using slower trains along secondary rail routes, often afford a **far better view of the country** than you would ever secure from a high-speed service.

On journeys from Paris to western Switzerland, we especially recommend the sublimely beautiful cross-border railway from **Besançon** (France) to **La Chaux-de-Fonds** (Switzerland). It has just three trains a day, the timings of which are shown in ERT 376a. With a little ingenuity, you can use this line to create credible itineraries from Paris to a great range of Swiss cities. Most of these will start by following **Route 7** in this book from **Paris to Dijon**. We did just that two or three years ago, travelling from Paris to Dijon and then on by regional train (ERT 374) to Besançon, where the beautiful town centre is contained within a great loop of the River Doubs. There we stopped for lunch before taking the early afternoon train across the Swiss border. Our train was almost empty, bar for a dozen soldiers who all alighted at the military camp at Valdahon, which has its own dedicated railway station.

The line to La Chaux-de-Fonds climbs gradually to a summit at **Avoudrey**, then dips down to cross the **River Doubs** in Morteau, before climbing again to the Swiss border at Col-des-Roches. There is a real sense of entering Switzerland by stealth on this remarkable railway which cuts across the grain of the Jura landscape. The country on the Swiss side of the border is more tame. But tame landscapes sometimes breed radical ideas, for it was to these hills that many political thinkers, among them **Bakunin, Kropotkin and later Lenin**, came to study and understand the attitudes and beliefs of Swiss watchmakers – a group of workers who profoundly influenced the development of European anarchism and socialism.

The French train from Besançon terminates at La Chaux-de-Fonds, but it connects perfectly there with Swiss trains to **Neuchâtel** and beyond (ERT 512). Within an hour or two you can be in Berne, Lausanne or Geneva.

Route 8: Exploring the French Riviera

CITIES: ★★ CULTURE: ★★ HISTORY: ★ SCENERY: ★★
COUNTRIES COVERED: FRANCE (FR)
JOURNEY TIME: 3 HRS | DISTANCE: 229 KM | MAP: WWW.EBRWEB.EU/MAP8

The train journey east from **Marseille** towards the Italian border is superb, a trip that rates alongside the Rhine Valley (**Route 20**) or some of our Swiss mountain routes as a true European classic. We have travelled this route a dozen times or more, and the most memorable journeys have all been at low sun angles. So this is an ideal journey for a summer morning before the crowds are up and about. The route has a grand, almost **cinematic appeal** when seen from the comfort of a TGV, but suddenly becomes more intimate when you experience it from one of the slower TER services which stop off at lesser stations en route. If you want to use TER trains throughout, you'll need to make a couple of changes of train along the way. Many trains on this route are **double-deckers**, so grab a place upstairs and on the seaward side (ie. on the right as you leave Marseille), sit back and enjoy the view.

The stretch of coast east of **Toulon** became the haunt of British aristocrats in the 19th century, heralding its new status as a sophisticated playground for the famous, beautiful or just plain rich. Grand hotels and casinos sprang up to cater for the incomers' tastes. Although parts of the **Côte d'Azur** have declined into untidy sprawls, there's still an engaging mix of ostentatious villas, pretty waterside towns and fine beaches. **Cannes** and Juan-les-Pins are hot spots for nightlife, while **Nice** is large, cosmopolitan and still pulls the crowds from far and wide. Behind the coast the land rises abruptly and you're in a different world, with rugged mountains and ancient perched villages. Much of that mountainous hinterland is difficult to reach without a car.

SUGGESTED ITINERARY

This route is so short that it's by no means necessary to make an overnight stop. Indeed, part of the appeal of this route is the visual drama of the journey as it unfolds. That said, there are a number of very appealing places along the way, so if you are inclined to break your journey, take your pick from the various communities mentioned below.

The **TER services** on this route do not require advance reservation; nor do the slightly faster trains which are branded Intervilles. The TGV trains and the once-daily Thello Eurocity service do require seat reservations. Note that rail passes are not accepted on the Thello train (which continues beyond Nice to Genoa and Milan).

From Marseille to Toulon

The initial part of this route, running out from **Marseille** (p110), is dismal. The views are dominated by motorways and the low-slung aluminium sheds which seem to have become the favoured architecture for the periphery of French cities. But suddenly the train emerges from a long tunnel near Cassis

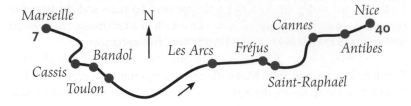

Notes

A – Local trains from Marseille to Toulon all stop at both Cassis and Bandol. Those local trains generally run every half hour from Mondays to Fridays and hourly at weekends.
B – Occasional trains on this leg of the journey are TGVs rather than TER trains. Advance reservation is necessary to use these TGV services.
C – Only occasional trains stop at minor stations mentioned in the text (viz. Agay and Le Trayas).

Route details

Marseille St-Charles to Toulon		ERT 360
Frequency	Journey time	Notes
2–3 per hr	45–65 mins	A, B

Toulon to Les Arcs-Draguignan		ERT 360
Frequency	Journey time	Notes
Hourly	35–65 mins	B

Les Arcs-Draguignan to Cannes		ERT 361
Frequency	Journey time	Notes
Hourly	40–60 mins	B, C

Cannes to Nice-Ville		ERT 361
Frequency	Journey time	Notes
2–3 per hr	25–45 mins	B

to give a tantalising glimpse of the Mediterranean – a hint of what is to come.

Centred around a pretty fishing harbour ringed with restaurants and an easy day trip from Marseille by train, **Cassis** makes a handy base for seeing the spectacular *calanques*, rocky inlets that cut into the limestone cliffs just west of the town. The station is 4 km out of Cassis, but a small shuttle bus (called *La Marcouline*) runs into town at least hourly. Cassis is a lovely spot in the winter, when the crowds stay away. And winter is the season for the local delicacy of sea urchins, which go down a treat with the dry white wine of the region. Cassis was a one-time haunt of the **Bloomsbury set**, so you could stop off for a few weeks and follow Virginia Woolf's example, quaffing white wine and smoking cigars.

East of Cassis the railway drops down to the coast and skirts the **vineyards of Bandol** – which produce some stunning rosé wines. Bandol was once very popular with the literary crowd – the New Zealand writer Katherine Mansfield wrote some of her best work here – but nowadays the writers have been replaced by the yachting set. Bandol is very much larger than Cassis and lacks the appeal of the latter. But it does offer an oddball excursion by boat to the **Île de Bendor**. This small island has been owned by the Ricard family (makers of pastis) for over 60 years and the island is nowadays a tribute to alcohol. There's an excellent small museum on wines and spirits (summer only, closed Tues & Sun, free entrance).

The busy **port of Toulon** is the largest town on this stretch of coast. If you have travelled from Marseille on the stopping train, you'll need to change here for the onward journey to Nice. There's not a lot to detain you in Toulon but, if you have an hour or two to spare, wander down to the traffic-free quayside (curiously named **quai Cronstadt** after the Russian naval base near St Petersburg) where there are fine views over the port and several good seafood restaurants.

CONNECTIONS FROM TOULON

There are local trains from Toulon which follow a branch line to **Hyères** (see lower panels in ERT 360), one of the most venerable resorts on the Riviera coast. It caught the attention of English travellers long before the railway from Toulon to Nice was built. Ease of access and a benign climate swept Hyères to popularity, and the roll call of distinguished visitors includes Queen Victoria, Tolstoy, Turgenev and Robert Louis Stevenson.

From Hyères, there are ferries (year round, but not daily in winter) to the islands in Hyères Bay; this small archipelago is known as the **Îles d'Hyères** or the Îles d'Or. Three of the islands have permanent settlements. Head for Port-Cros, reached in an hour by ferry from Hyères port, for wonderful woodland walks.

Skirting the Maures

It is one of the surprises of this journey from Marseille to Nice that the railway doesn't hug the coast beyond Toulon. And that makes the route all the more interesting. When railway engineers planned the railway east of Toulon, the prospect of following the rugged coast of the **Massif de Maures** was just too daunting. So the railway follows a more northerly course, passing *behind* the mountains and only regaining the coast at Fréjus. A modern motorway parallels the railway.

This **diversion inland** offers the chance to see a very different side of Provence, in winter often very green and lush, but parched in the summer months. Sit on the right side of the train for fine views of the forested Maures hills. The highest point, **La Sauvette** (779 m), is visible from the train.

The TER trains on this route serve a number of appealing villages. If you are in no hurry, think of stopping off. But check onward train times carefully, as there are some mighty gaps between trains at the smaller stations. A good choice for a stop in this area is the small town of **Les Arcs** in the Argens Valley because all TER, Intervilles and Intercités trains stop there, plus a handful of TGVs each day. It's a 20-minute walk from the station up into the centre of the village which is very pretty. If you're ready for the hike, we can recommend Le Logis du Guetteur, ☎ 04 94 99 51 10 (www.logisduguetteur.com) as a good choice for lunch or an overnight stay.

CONNECTIONS FROM LES ARCS

The full name of the station is Les Arcs-Draguignan, which misleadingly suggests that Draguignan is close to hand. Passengers bound for Draguignan travel by bus (TED bus ligne 5), which departs at least hourly from the station forecourt. It's a 25-min journey.

The Esterel Coast

Beyond Les Arcs, the railway follows the Argens Valley down to the coast at **Fréjus**. The ancient Roman port of Fréjus and the modern beach resort of Saint-Raphaël fuse to form one urban area, though each has its own identity and its own station. **Saint-Raphaël** is the upmarket end and the main transport hub, with spacious beaches and a tiny Old Quarter. Fréjus-Plage is a strip of bars, restaurants and a giant marina lying between the sea and Fréjus town.

The high point of the entire journey comes after Saint-Raphaël when, for 20 minutes, the train cruises around the coast of the **Esterel Massif**. The red volcanic hills tumble down to the sea, and the terrain is so rugged that the creeping urbanisation so prevalent elsewhere on the Côte d'Azur has been kept at bay. Apart from the frequent fast trains which use this railway, there are half a dozen local services each day which serve eight intermediate stations between Saint-Raphaël and Cannes (not all shown in the ERT). If you take one of these stopping trains, you'll get more chance to appreciate this marvellous stretch of coast.

As the train runs through **Le Dramont** (east of Saint-Raphaël), you'll see a small island dominated by a Saracen-style tower. The island is called the **Île d'Or** (not to be confused with the Îles d'Or in Hyères Bay mentioned earlier). The name is misleading, as the island is not gold but tawny-red in colour. A local doctor, Auguste Lutaud, won the island in a bet in 1909, and promptly set about creating his own micro-nation, issuing stamps and coins with inscriptions in Latin and Arabic (but not French). Lutaud styled himself *Roi de l'Île d'Or* (King of the Golden Isle). The French state soon reasserted its authority over the island as an integral part of France.

If you'd like to break your journey along the Esterel coast, we suggest a stop at either Agay or Le Trayas. **Agay** is much the larger of the two but, by Riviera standards, it's still a small resort. The town clusters around a lovely horseshoe-shaped bay. The Villa Matuzia, ☎ 04 94 82 79 95 (www.matuzia. com), just a 5-min walk from the station via r. Agathonis, offers excellent Provençale cuisine and has a couple of fairly basic rooms (closed Mon).

While Agay is sheltered and serene, the station at **Le Trayas** is in an altogether wilder location. It's a great spot to watch the waves crash on the rocks on a stormy day. You can always take refuge in Les Calanques, ☎ 04 94 44 14 06 (www.relaisdescalanques.fr), a restaurant and hotel near the station with a fabulous view of the coast. Beyond Le Trayas, the landscape becomes tamer as the railway skirts the **Golfe de Napoule** to reach Cannes.

Cannes

Cannes is more than merely the world's glitziest **film festival** (see box below). Surprisingly, perhaps, it's perfectly possible to enjoy Cannes without spending a fortune. Make for **Le Suquet** (also called Vieux Suquet or the Vielle Ville), the compact but charming hilly Old Town, where the daily market, cafés and castle panorama sum up the good life on the Riviera. Look out for **cinematic murals** around town tracing the history of the silver screen from Buster Keaton to Charlie Chaplin and Marilyn Monroe. In summer, relax at the beach cafés along **La Croisette**.

ESCAPE FROM CANNES

Off Cannes, the **Îles de Lérins** are an antidote to chic. Île Sainte-Marguerite is the larger of the two, and boasts the better beaches. At the north end, Fort Sainte-Marguerite was commissioned by Richelieu and enlarged by Vauban in 1712. It is the legendary home of the mythical **Man in the Iron Mask**, made famous by the author Alexandre Dumas. There are daily ferry departures from the quai Laubeuf (close to r. du Port). It's worth venturing further beyond Sainte-Marguerite to the Île Saint-Honorat, home to a large community of Cistercian monks. After the worldly pleasures of Cannes, it is the perfect place to enjoy some sacred solitude.

SPRINGTIME IN CANNES

Travel writer Lisa Gerard-Sharp, who contributed to several early editions of Europe by Rail, lives in the hills above Cannes. Here she reflects on the appeal of the Riviera community she calls home. Find out more about Lisa at www.lisagerardsharp.com.

May is when the Mediterranean scene wakes up. The *beau monde* dons dinner jackets and descends on Cannes for the **film festival**. Woody Allen dusts down his old jokes: "Eternity is a long experience, especially towards the end." The wrong film always wins but posing Cannes still looks the part. And the Med works its magic – even when the super-yachts exhaust their supplies of smoked salmon and starlets. After the motley crew decamps to Monaco for the Grand Prix, the Riviera is yours once more, from the art trails to the **Michelin-starred restaurants**. Life has moved on since Queen Victoria visited on the royal train, bringing down her own Irish stew to be sure of decent food in France.

The Cote d'Azur is full of Cezanne scenery and Picasso panoramas. But in Provence the food can be as painterly as the art, especially in the hands of master-chefs. Somewhat surreally, Cezanne's peaches can look juicier than the real thing. But when the tastes of *pistou*, *ratatouille* and *bouillabaisse* trump the art, that's when you really love the Cote d'Azur.

"Cannes is for living, Monte Carlo for gambling and Menton for dying" was the Victorian mantra – and Cannes is still living it up. Boosted by the gleaming **Palais des Festivals**, the city is promoting its cuisine as well as its cultural side. On both fronts, style tends to triumph over substance. Still, with its art deco dining room, La Palme d'Or's movie star looks are matched by Michelin-starred Mediterranean cuisine. But once the season starts, fine dining loses out to the beachside bars. On **La Croisette**, Le Baoli Beach is made for posing. More welcoming are the brasseries in the steep and sinuous Old Town. L'Enoteca is typical; it's a cosy haunt with live jazz and good for local staples such as rabbit in red wine sauce.

The branch railway running inland from Cannes to **Grasse** (ERT 361), newly reopened after a major upgrade, offers an inviting excursion possibility from the coast. Grasse is an appealing inland resort town, famous for its many parfumeries. The penultimate station on the line, just south of Grasse, is **Mouans-Sartoux** (not shown in ERT, but all trains to and from Grasse stop there). It's a handsome small town (pop. 10,000) with a strong commitment to the arts.

Along the Côte d'Azur

The railway follows the coast for much of the way from Cannes to Nice, veering inland only to avoid the great headland which juts south from Antibes. Just before **Cap d'Antibes**, the TER trains pause at **Juan-les-Pins** where the Côte d'Azur's summer season was invented in 1921. Until then, the Riviera had been primarily a winter destination. Juan has sandy beaches (many are private, but there is still some public space), bars, discos and, in July, the Riviera's most renowned jazz festival, **Jazz à Juan**. It is worth exploring the footpath around the coast of Cap d'Antibes.

The biggest boats in the northern Med may moor in **Antibes**, but the likeable old town is a pretty unpretentious place, with a relaxed atmosphere and a lively bar and restaurant scene. Take a walk along the port, and don't miss the **Musée Picasso**, looking over the sea from its home in the Château Grimaldi. Picasso worked here in 1946 and this excellent museum displays some of his most entertaining creations from that period (closed Mon).

Nice

Nice has been the undisputed queen of the Riviera ever since the 19th-century British elite began to grace the elegant seafront **Promenade des Anglais**. In those days Nice was Nizza and part of the Kingdom of Sardinia. The city was ceded to France in 1860. Hotels such as the **Negresco** capture the old Riviera style and are still as luxurious and imposing as ever, and not excessively expensive for a snack or a drink to sample how the other half lives. Nowadays you are more likely to hear Russian voices around the salons and promenades once so favoured by English visitors. Standing apart from the belle époque hotels and villas, **Vieux Nice** (the Old Town) is the true heart of the city and, with its green Ligurian-style shutters, seems more Italian than French. There are wonderful outdoor markets, countless cafés and restaurants, and many of Nice's liveliest bars.

Nice boasts some of the best museums in France. Most open 10.00–18.00, are closed on Tuesdays and are easily accessible by local bus. Best of the bunch is the **Musée Matisse**, 164 av. des Arènes de Cimiez (www.musee-matisse-nice.org), wonderfully set in a 17th-century villa amongst the Roman ruins of Cimiez. It houses Matisse's personal collection of paintings (🚌 15/17/20/25 from pl. Masséna). Next door **Musée et Site Archéologiques de**

Nice Cimiez, 160 av. des Arènes de Cimiez (closed Tues), exhibits the copious finds dug up while excavating the Roman arenas in Cimiez (🚌 15/17/20/25 to Arènes). Matisse and fellow artist Raoul Dufy are buried in the nearby Couvent des Frères Mineurs. Also in Cimiez, the **Musée National Marc Chagall**, 36 av. Dr Ménard, is a graceful temple to Chagall's genius – beautifully lit to display his huge biblical canvases (🚌 15; closed Tues).

In the centre of town, the **Musée d'Art Moderne et d'Art Contemporain**, Place Yves Klein (www.mamac-nice.org), is a white marble cliff rising above the street and filled with striking pop art (🚌 3/7/9/10; closed Mon). On summer nights, Nice parties till long after midnight, thanks to its many Irish-style pubs and live music venues, though younger visitors often gravitate to the beach.

ARRIVAL, INFORMATION, ACCOMMODATION

🚆 Nice-Ville, av. Thiers. Frequent services to all resorts along the Côte d'Azur. A 15-min walk to the town centre. ⛴ Corsica Ferries (www.corsica-ferries.co.uk) offer crossings to Corsica and Sardinia. ✈ Nice-Côte d'Azur, 7 km west of the city (www.nice.aeroport.fr). Airport 🚌 98 runs along Promenade des Anglais to the Promenade des Arts bus station every 20 mins (05.40–23.45) and 🚌 99 from T1 and T2 to the Gare SNCF every 30 mins (07.50–20.50). 🚺 Tourist offices: 5 Promenade des Anglais (www.nicetourisme.com) and at the railway station. See Lignes d'Azur (www.lignesdazur.com) for bus and tram information.

🛏 Try the highly rated **Villa Les Cygnes**, 6 av. du Château de la Tour, ☎ 04 97 03 23 35 (www.villalescygnes.com). A good value option is the centrally located **Le Grimaldi**, 15 r. Grimaldi, ☎ 04 93 16 00 24 (www.le-grimaldi.com), which is only a 10-min walk from the railway station. Set slightly above the town in Cimiez, the belle époque **Hôtel du Petit Palais**, 17 av. Émile Bieckert, ☎ 04 93 62 19 11 (www.petitpalaisnice.fr), offers great views of Nice. It is also very convenient for the Matisse and Chagall museums.

🍴 Something of a culinary paradise, Nice is influenced by its neighbour, Italy, and by the Mediterranean. Specialities are *pissaladière*, a Niçois onion tart garnished with anchovies and olives, *socca*, a traditional lunchtime snack of flat bread made from crushed chickpeas, and of course *salade niçoise*.

The Old Town is best for eating out – particularly the warren of streets running north from Cours Saleya and the cathedral. North of the Old Town, pl. Garibaldi boasts the best shellfish. **Le Transsibérien**, 1 r. Bottero, ☎ 04 93 96 49 05 (closed Sun & Mon), is a rail-themed restaurant which offers good Russian food.

NICE CONNECTIONS

There are excellent onward connections beyond Nice. There are thrice-daily Eurocity services to Genoa and Milan operated by Thello (ERT 90). **Russian Railways** (RZD) offer a weekly service from Nice to Vienna, Warsaw, Minsk and Moscow (ERT 25). It leaves Nice on Sunday mornings. French TER trains shuttle east along the coast at least hourly to Monaco and Menton, most of these services continuing over the Italian frontier to Ventimiglia (ERT 361). This latter journey is described as **Route 40** in this book.

For lovers of great scenery, there is a superb route through the hills to **Digne-les-Bains** (ERT 359). This narrow-gauge rail line is privately operated and holders of Interrail and Eurail passes cannot travel for free but receive a 50% discount on the regular fare. From Digne, you can travel south-west by fast bus to the TGV railway station at Aix-en-Provence, or take the local bus to Veynes (both bus routes are in ERT 359). From Veynes there are local TER trains to Valence in the Rhône Valley (ERT 362).

Route 9: The Seine Valley and Normandy

CITIES: ★★ CULTURE: ★★ HISTORY: ★★★ SCENERY: ★★
COUNTRIES COVERED: FRANCE (FR)
JOURNEY TIME: 4 HRS 15 MINS | DISTANCE: 434 KM | MAP: WWW.EBRWEB.EU/MAP9

This route takes in some of the finest townscapes and countryside in **Normandy**. It is one of the shorter adventures in this book. If you are in a hurry, you can get a fast train from Paris to Cherbourg in just over three hours – though the direct trains by-pass the city of **Rouen**, which is one of the high points of the route. The route via Rouen, which follows the River Seine downstream from Paris, is much prettier than the direct line.

The entire journey as described below can be completed using just TER trains; these are regional services where no advance reservation is necessary and there are no supplements for holders of Eurail and Interrail passes. This is therefore a journey well suited to those who prefer to travel spontaneously, stopping off here and there along the way. Intercités trains augment the TER services on some parts of the route; these trains are also now free of supplements for pass holders. From **Cherbourg** you can continue by ferry (see p29), so this journey offers an unusual routing from Paris to southern England or the Republic of Ireland. Check onward ferry times carefully as off-season services are sparse.

If time is tight, and you can allow yourself just a single overnight stop along this route, make it at **Bayeux**. It's a smallish town, but Bayeux has an intimacy which makes it easy to catch the spirit of Normandy – a part of France where regional identity finds full expression in the countryside and small towns much more than in the big cities.

The Seine Valley

The Paris departure point for trains to Normandy is the **Gare Saint-Lazare**. This is the Paris railway station which more than any other attracted the attention of French artists in the 1870s. In 1877, Monet made 11 paintings of his favourite Paris station. Saint-Lazare had already featured four years earlier in Édouard Manet's celebrated painting *The Railway*. The smoke and steam which so inspired both Manet and Monet are gone, but the Gare Saint-Lazare still has shifting patterns of colour and light.

The ride to Rouen is defined by the valley of the **River Seine**, with the train crossing the river on a number of occasions during the 140-km journey. For the best views, sit on the right of the train. At one point, there is a glorious panorama across the River Seine to the village of **Giverny** on the far bank of the river. Monet was so taken with that perspective from the train that he returned to Giverny and rented a house there. His one-time home, studio and gardens now pull the crowds from far and wide (open

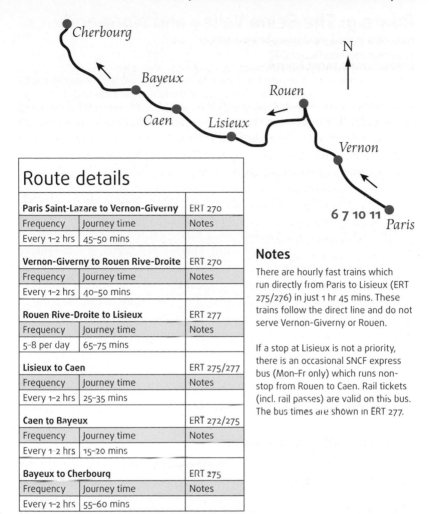

Route details

Paris Saint-Lazare to Vernon-Giverny	ERT 270	
Frequency	Journey time	Notes
Every 1–2 hrs	45–50 mins	

Vernon-Giverny to Rouen Rive-Droite	ERT 270	
Frequency	Journey time	Notes
Every 1–2 hrs	40–50 mins	

Rouen Rive-Droite to Lisieux	ERT 277	
Frequency	Journey time	Notes
5–8 per day	65–75 mins	

Lisieux to Caen	ERT 275/277	
Frequency	Journey time	Notes
Every 1–2 hrs	25–35 mins	

Caen to Bayeux	ERT 272/275	
Frequency	Journey time	Notes
Every 1–2 hrs	15–20 mins	

Bayeux to Cherbourg	ERT 275	
Frequency	Journey time	Notes
Every 1–2 hrs	55–60 mins	

Notes

There are hourly fast trains which run directly from Paris to Lisieux (ERT 275/276) in just 1 hr 45 mins. These trains follow the direct line and do not serve Vernon-Giverny or Rouen.

If a stop at Lisieux is not a priority, there is an occasional SNCF express bus (Mon–Fr only) which runs non-stop from Rouen to Caen. Rail tickets (incl. rail passes) are valid on this bus. The bus times are shown in ERT 277.

daily April to October, www.ebrweb.eu/giv). There is a useful bus link to Giverny from the station at Vernon on the south bank of the river.

From Vernon-Giverny, it is a short hop downstream to **Rouen**, the principal city in Upper Normandy. You'll arrive at Rouen Rive-Droite station, from where it is a 15-minute walk south to the city centre where the star turn is the famous **Cathédrale Notre-Dame**, the subject of another series of Monet paintings. An example of his work showing the western facade can be seen at the attractively restored **Musée des Beaux Arts**, pl. Verdrel (closed Tues). The old city centre, restored after war damage, has many colourful half-timbered buildings. At the end of the main street, in pl. du Vieux Marché, a 20-m cross by the church marks the spot where **Joan of Arc** was burned at the stake in 1431. La Tour Jeanne d'Arc, r. Bouvreuil (closed Tues), is the only remaining tower of the castle where Joan of Arc was imprisoned just before her execution.

CONNECTIONS FROM ROUEN
Dieppe, reached in about an hour from Rouen by train (ERT 270a) is an attractive coastal town. Its flint and sandstone château is perched on the lofty white cliffs rising high above the shingle beach. The harbour is a lively area, lined with seafood restaurants. In the streets behind, a busy Saturday market draws crowds from far and wide. From Dieppe, there is still a useful direct DFDS ferry to **Newhaven** (ERT 2125).

To Lisieux and beyond

The TER train from Rouen to Caen crosses pretty Normandy countryside (with fruit orchards and flowers aplenty in season). The most notable community along the way is **Lisieux**, a place that would barely feature on the tourist map were it not for Saint Thérèse of Lisieux, a 19th-century mystic and nun whose life and work has had an extraordinary influence well beyond Roman Catholicism. Thérèse spent the last nine years of her life in the **Carmelite convent** at Lisieux, so sealing the future fate of the town as a destination for pilgrimages. Make of it what you will, but it's definitely worth a stop. The devotional industry surrounding Thérèse of Lisieux was given a further boost in late 2015 with the canonisation of both her parents and few families can claim such an abundance of sanctity (www.ebrweb.eu/lis). Beyond Lisieux the railway passes through Caen, but there is no good reason to linger. It's best to press on to Bayeux.

Bayeux (suggested stopover)

The first town liberated by the Allies at the end of Second World War, Bayeux escaped any damage to its fine mediaeval centre, dominated by the spires of the magnificent Cathédrale Notre-Dame. The world-famous **Bayeux tapestry** is a 70-m long embroidered linen illustrating the Norman Conquest of England. It is thought to have been commissioned soon after the Battle of Hastings by the Bishop of Bayeux from an Anglo-Saxon workshop run by monks. The historical explanations, film shows and displays in the Centre Guillaume-le-Conquérant in rue Nesmond, where it is housed, interpret the scenes very thoroughly, but it is worth hiring a multilingual audio-guide as you walk round. The **Musée Mémorial de la Bataille de Normandie**, blvd. Fabian Ware, is one of the best museums in the area covering the Normandy campaign of the Second World War.

ARRIVAL, INFORMATION, ACCOMMODATION
≥ Pl. de la Gare, a 10- to 15-min walk south-east of the centre. ⓘ Tourist office: Pont Saint-Jean (www.bayeux-bessin-tourisme.com). ⋈ The **Reine Mathilde**, 23 r. Larcher, ☎ 02 31 92 08 13 (www.hotel-bayeux-reinemathilde.fr), has recently been refurbished and is located over a popular brasserie in the Old Town while the **Hôtel d'Argouges**, 21 r.

Saint-Patrice, ☎ 02 31 92 88 86 (www.hotel-dargouges.com), is an upmarket option in an 18th-century building. The centrally located **Le Bayeux**, 9 r. Tardif, ☎ 02 31 92 70 08 (www.hotellebayeux.com), is a former coaching inn.

Connections from Bayeux

TER trains run direct from Bayeux to Coutances and the port of **Granville** (ERT 272), in our view one of the finest spots on the coast of Normandy. The upper part of the town is a fortified citadel. From Granville there are year-round ferries to the Archipel de Chausey, the only part of the Channel Islands under French jurisdiction. From mid-April to December, there are also direct ferries (but not always daily) from Granville to **Jersey**.

From Bayeux, it is a pleasant one-hour journey by train north through the **Cotentin Peninsula** to Cherbourg. The landscape is unchallenging, a mix of coppice woodland and pasture known locally as *bocage*. Although you are never far from the sea, the coast is curiously invisible from the train.

Arriving in Cherbourg

Essentially a commercial and military port, **Cherbourg** played a key role in the Battle of Normandy. It was liberated by American troops three weeks after the landings on Utah Beach and used as a deep-water port. Hilltop **Fort du Roule**, overlooking the town and port, has a museum commemorating the Allied liberation of Cherbourg and the Cotentin Peninsula. A worthwhile recent attraction is the **Cité de la Mer**, housed in the former transatlantic ferry terminal, a grand art deco building. Its exhibits cover the theme of underwater exploration, and include Europe's largest aquarium plus a decommissioned nuclear submarine (www.citedelamer.com).

Arrival, information, accommodation

⇛ Pl. Jean Jaurès, at the south end of Bassin du Commerce (harbour). ⛴ The Gare-Maritime ferry port is north-east of the town centre; a shuttle bus runs between the two. 🅸 Tourist office: 14 quai Alexandre III (www.cherbourgtourisme.com).

⛴ The area north of the tourist office offers some cheap lodging options. Try the **Hôtel de la Renaissance**, 4 r. de l'Église, ☎ 02 33 43 23 90 (www.hotel-renaissance-cherbourg.com), with views of the sea; or the **Hôtel Ambassadeur**, 22 quai de Caligny, ☎ 02 33 43 10 00 (www.ambassadeurhotel.com), old-fashioned but comfortable, with views of the harbour. Just off the main square, the **Croix de Malte** is a modernised option, 5 r. des Halles, ☎ 02 33 43 19 16 (www.hotelcroixmalte.com).

✗ Lots of glass-fronted restaurants line the quayside road; there are cheaper options in the streets behind, where vestiges of the Old Town survive around pl. Centrale.

Connections from Cherbourg

There are useful **cross-channel ferries** to the south coast of England, with a year-round service to Poole (ERT 2145) and a seasonal link to Portsmouth (ERT 2160); the latter route features a high-speed catamaran called *Normandie Express* which takes just 3 hrs for the crossing. There are also thrice-weekly direct ferries to **Rosslare** in Ireland (ERT 2010).

Happily the Irish Ferries sailings to Dublin (ERT 2027), which were in the past reserved for car travellers, are now available to foot passengers – at least for the spring and summer seasons.

THROUGH FRANCE TO SPAIN
An introduction

Rail travellers bound for the Iberian Peninsula must inevitably cross France to reach Spain. For decades Spain was in some measure detached from France when it came to railways. As Spain developed its rail network in the 1850s, engineers opted for a wider track gauge than that favoured north of the Pyrenees. The result was that running trains from France into Spain was impossible without adjusting the width of carriage bogies at the border.

Over the last 30 years, Spain has undergone the most **comprehensive modernisation of its rail network** of any country in Europe. Many new rail routes have been constructed, and these have normally been at the standard gauge of 1,435 mm (rather than the wider Iberian gauge of 1,668 mm). The first major standard-gauge cross-border route was the new line from Perpignan (in south-west France) to Barcelona. It dives under the Pyrenees in the **Perthus Tunnel**, which opened in 2013, so allowing through running of high-speed trains from **Paris to Barcelona** or from Marseille to Madrid.

If you are in a rush to get to Spain, you can dash through France on a high-speed train in just a few hours. Paris to Barcelona on a direct train takes under seven hours. For those heading from Paris to Spain's Basque region, the opening in July 2017 of the **new L'Océane high-speed line** from Tours to Bordeaux has trimmed journey times. The extension of the standard-gauge tracks beyond the border at Irun to the Basque city of Donostia (San Sebastián in Spanish) will further enhance cross-border connectivity.

Pyrenean diversions

In this section of *Europe by Rail*, we describe three journeys which take very different routes across France to Spain. As ever in this volume, there are alternatives which merit attention. If you have time to spare, there is a much more creative way of engaging with the Pyrenees than merely entering Spain on one of the TGVs or AVEs which speed through the Perthus Tunnel. From Perpignan, you can take the **mountain route** via Villefranche–Vernet-les-Bains and Latour-de-Carol to Barcelona (timings in ERT 354 and 656). Instead of 80 minutes on a high-speed train, you'll have eight hours on local trains and some glorious mountain scenery. This route includes a ride on the famous **Petit Train Jaune** (Little Yellow Train; see p135).

Another **engaging alternative** is to take the newly reopened railway from Pau (in France) to Bedous, whence there is a connecting bus service to Canfranc in Spain (timings for both trains and buses are in ERT 324). The bus takes 40 minutes for the 35-km run over the border, taking in some great scenery. From **Canfranc**, where the extraordinary station building is worth a peek, there are onward trains to Zaragoza (ERT 670). ∎

Route 10: The Loire Valley and Atlantic coast

CITIES: ★★★ CULTURE: ★★★ HISTORY: ★★ SCENERY: ★★
COUNTRIES COVERED: FRANCE (FR), SPAIN (ES)
JOURNEY TIME: 16 HRS | DISTANCE: 1,030 KM | MAP: WWW.EBRWEB.EU/MAP10

The 19th-century English lawyer and explorer **Charles Packe** knew western France like the back of his hand, criss-crossing the region on journeys to and from his beloved Pyrenees. But he bemoaned how slow the trains were. Over 12 hours in 1862 by the fastest express from Paris to Bordeaux, and 20 hours with the slower trains. Today's traveller can speed from **Paris to Bordeaux** in little more than two hours, thanks to a new high-speed line from Tours to Bordeaux which opened in mid-2017.

Route 10 is for those less inclined to hurry. It is a leisurely amble through some of Atlantic Europe's most **striking cultural landscapes**: the Loire Valley, Aquitaine and the Basque region. The entire journey can be completed without once resorting to a high-speed service. That's a great advantage for travellers who share our affection for travelling more spontaneously. You can follow this entire route without needing to make a single advance reservation. This route takes in **several superb cities**, notably Chartres, Angers and Bordeaux. It also features several important **coastal resorts**, among them La Rochelle, Biarritz and San Sebastián.

SUGGESTED ITINERARY

If you are in a rush to get to the **Basque region** and beyond, you can always hop on a fast TGV from Paris to Bordeaux, and join the latter part of this route for the journey beyond Bordeaux. Or you can skip the first part of journey by speeding from Paris to Angers on a high-speed TGV. In an ideal world, if time is no object, you could spin this journey out to a full week, with stops along the way in Chartres, Angers, La Rochelle, Bordeaux and Biarritz. Angers and Bordeaux have more than enough to justify a two-night stay. If you can afford just a couple of **overnight stops**, we recommend you make them at Angers and Bordeaux.

Bear in mind that during 2020, engineering work on the railway between Hendaye and San Sebastián means that only a limited number of trains are running across the French-Spanish border. Your best bet for this leg is the **Metro Donostialdea tram**.

From Paris to the Loire

The regional rail route from Paris to Angers in the **Loire Valley** always requires a change of train in Le Mans. The TER services to Le Mans leave from Montparnasse station in the French capital. The fast TGV trains which run direct to Angers leave from the same station. The TER route tracks west past Versailles and the forests of Rambouillet, then follows the gentle Eure Valley upstream to **Chartres**, where it is definitely worth stopping for a couple of hours to see the superb Gothic cathedral. It is an easy 10-min walk east of the railway station. The **Cathédrale Notre-Dame** is especially known for the quality and brilliance of its 13th-century stained

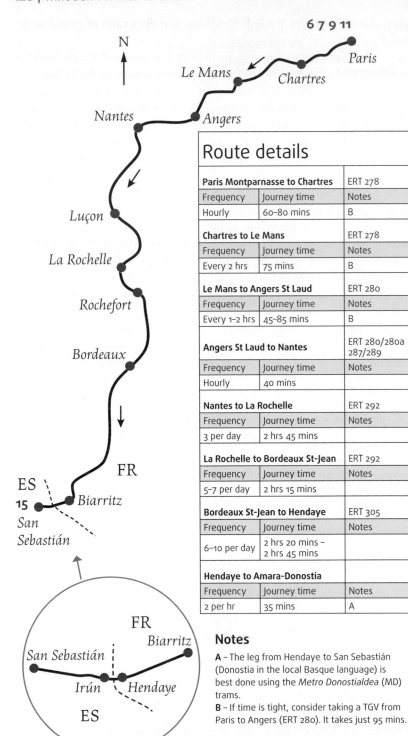

6 7 9 11

Paris

Le Mans

Chartres

Nantes

Angers

Luçon

La Rochelle

Rochefort

Bordeaux

FR

ES

15

Biarritz

San Sebastián

Route details

Paris Montparnasse to Chartres		ERT 278
Frequency	Journey time	Notes
Hourly	60–80 mins	B

Chartres to Le Mans		ERT 278
Frequency	Journey time	Notes
Every 2 hrs	75 mins	B

Le Mans to Angers St Laud		ERT 280
Frequency	Journey time	Notes
Every 1–2 hrs	45–85 mins	B

Angers St Laud to Nantes		ERT 280/280a 287/289
Frequency	Journey time	Notes
Hourly	40 mins	

Nantes to La Rochelle		ERT 292
Frequency	Journey time	Notes
3 per day	2 hrs 45 mins	

La Rochelle to Bordeaux St-Jean		ERT 292
Frequency	Journey time	Notes
5–7 per day	2 hrs 15 mins	

Bordeaux St-Jean to Hendaye		ERT 305
Frequency	Journey time	Notes
6–10 per day	2 hrs 20 mins – 2 hrs 45 mins	

Hendaye to Amara-Donostia		
Frequency	Journey time	Notes
2 per hr	35 mins	A

FR

Biarritz

San Sebastián

Irún

Hendaye

ES

Notes

A – The leg from Hendaye to San Sebastián (Donostia in the local Basque language) is best done using the *Metro Donostialdea* (MD) trams.

B – If time is tight, consider taking a TGV from Paris to Angers (ERT 280). It takes just 95 mins.

glass, dazzling even on the dullest of days, and the wealth of carved stone, notably around the west doorways.

From Chartres the TER rail route continues west, cutting through the southernmost corner of Normandy. This area, known as **La Perche**, has idyllic rural landscapes; the area's quiet beauty is best appreciated in the low sun angles of a summer evening. Sit back and enjoy the view; before long you'll be rolling into the station at **Le Mans** where you change trains. The railway from Le Mans follows the Sarthe Valley downstream all the way to Angers. There are some very pleasant **riverine landscapes** as the railway skirts the Fôret de Pincé just beyond the small town of Sablé-sur-Sarthe.

Angers

Angers is an attractive wine-producing town dominated by the massive striped walls of the 13th-century **Château d'Angers**, whose 17 towers now reach only half of their original height. The moat has been converted into formal gardens. Inside is a series of great 14th-century tapestries known as the *Tenture de l'Apocalypse* (the Apocalypse of St John). As well as wine, Angers produces the liqueur Cointreau (visits to the distillery museum on blvd. des Bretonnières, 🚌 7, are by appointment only, ☎ 02 41 31 50 50).

The principal railway station in the town is called Angers-Saint-Laud. From the station it is just a 7-min walk north along r. Marceau to the château. The cathedral is just a few steps beyond the château.

ARRIVAL, INFORMATION, ACCOMMODATION

🚆 About a 10-min walk south of the centre, or take 🚌 1. ℹ Tourist office: 7 pl. Kennedy (www.tourisme.destination-angers.com). 🛏 The **Hôtel de l'Europe**, 3 r. de Châteaugontier, ☎ 02 41 88 67 45 (www.hoteldeleurope-angers.com), is reasonably priced and well located. A functional, good-value hotel close to the station is **Le Progrès**, 26 av. Denis Papin, ☎ 02 41 88 10 14 (www.hotelleprogres.com). For a treat, try the stylish **21 Foch**, 21 blv. Foch, ☎ 02 30 31 41 00 (www.21foch.fr).

CONNECTIONS FROM ANGERS

Occasional TER trains run from Angers (taking 20–30 mins, ERT 289) to the town of **Saumur**, with its famous cavalry riding school (the Cadre Noir). The 14th-century château was originally a fortress for Louis I. It later became a country residence for the Dukes of Anjou, then a state prison, and now houses two museums. There are tours in English in summer. **Vineyards** surround the town, and mushrooms are grown in the caves that riddle the local hills, making good use of by-products from the riding school.

The Atlantic Coast of France

From Saint-Laud station at Angers it is just a short hop down the Loire Valley to **Nantes**. Regular TER trains ply the route, and there are occasional trains branded InterLoire (IL). Neither TER or IL services require advance reservation. Sit on the left for good views of the **River Loire**.

Nantes is a place first and foremost to change trains, but if you have an hour or two to spare, you may want to walk west from the station to the nearby Château des Ducs, where you can wander without charge through the moated gardens and climb the ramparts.

CONNECTIONS FROM NANTES

Nantes was historically part of Brittany and that's reflected in the rail timetables. There are direct trains to Lorient and Quimper (ERT 285), with connections in Quimper for Brest (ERT 286). Travellers heading to the north **coast of Brittany** can use the regular services from Nantes to Rennes (ERT 287), where there are good connections to Saint Malo (ERT 281).

Closer to hand there are local services from Nantes to nearby places on the coast. One excursion we especially like is to **La Baule-Escoublac** (ERT 288), a resort town which deftly manages to combine Breton charm with Riviera style.

The leg from Nantes to La Rochelle is the trickiest part of this entire route. Several trains each day run south from Nantes as far as **Luçon**, but there are just three trains which run beyond Luçon to La Rochelle.

La Rochelle is a popular sailing centre. The town is elegant and striking, built in bright limestone, with gracious old squares, a fine town hall and arcaded Renaissance houses. Life focuses on the old harbour, which has some excellent fish restaurants. Two mediaeval towers preside over the harbour entrance, once linked by a protective chain. La Rochelle is a spring-board for boat trips and island visits, notably to the **Île de Ré**, connected to the town by a 3-km toll bridge, offering beaches (some are naturist ones) and quiet picnic spots. It's reachable by bus, but best explored by bike.

From La Rochelle you have a choice of TER and Intercités trains, none requiring advance reservation, for the ride south to Bordeaux. Sit on the right for good views of the coast on the initial stretch from La Rochelle. Leaving the coast at **Rochefort**, the railway follows the River Charente upstream before tracking south through increasingly forested country to reach Bordeaux. You cross the two great rivers which have shaped the region on the approach to Bordeaux: first the Dordogne and then the Garonne.

Bordeaux (suggested stopover)

Set on the **Garonne River** just before it joins the Dordogne, Bordeaux is a busy, working city with an 18th-century core of monumental splendour surrounded by industrial gloom. A massive recent revitalisation programme has restored the handsome old centre and made it more pedestrian-friendly.

Above all, the city is the commercial heart of one of the world's greatest wine-growing areas, surrounded by revered appellations such as Saint-Émilion, Graves, Médoc and Sauternes. The **Maison du Vin de Bordeaux**, opposite the main tourist office, arranges courses, tours and tastings. Most of Bordeaux's main sights lie within easy walking distance, but a high-tech tram network is also in place.

Best of the city's historic buildings include the neoclassical Grand Théâtre, on pl. de la Comédie, the **Musée National des Douanes**, housed in the 18th-century Customs House, and the elegant place de la Bourse. The **Musée Mer Marine** (www.mmmbordeaux.com), located in the historic port area, opened its doors to visitors in June 2019 (closed Mon).

ARRIVAL, INFORMATION, ACCOMMODATION

⇌ Gare St-Jean, r. Charles Domercq, about 2 km south-east of the centre (tram line C runs from Quinconces to the station). ✈ Bordeaux-Mérignac, 12 km from the city (www. bordeaux.aeroport.fr). There are buses at least every 20 mins to Gare St-Jean. ❸ Tourist office: 12 cours du XXX Juillet (www.bordeaux-tourisme.com) with an outpost at the station.

⊨ Near the centre, r. Huguerie is a good place to look for budget accommodation. Good mid-range options are the friendly and central **Majestic**, 2 r. de Condé, ☎ 05 56 52 60 44 (www.hotel-majestic.com) or the cosy **Chez Dupont** guesthouse, 2 r. Cornac, ☎ 06 95 15 77 37 (www.chez-dupont.com). If you want to splash out, try the stylish **Le Boutique Hôtel**, 3 r. Lafaurie de Monbadon, ☎ 05 56 48 80 40 (www.hotelbordeauxcentre.com), set in an 18th-century town house in the heart of the city. ✗ The quartier St-Pierre is a bustling district filled with boutiques and cafés, and pl. du Parlement is a good place to look for restaurants. Take in the *guingettes* (waterfront seafood stalls) along quai des Chartrons.

CONNECTIONS FROM BORDEAUX

One very good reason for coming to Bordeaux is to visit the great wineries in the surrounding countryside. There are bus tours (ask at the tourist office), but also a local rail line to Lesparre and Le Verdon (ERT 307), with en route stops at places with names suggestive of great claret (Margaux, Pauillac, Ludon, Moulis-Listrac, etc.).

Bordeaux is a **major rail interchange**. There are regular services to Toulouse (ERT 320), some of which continue to Marseille (ERT 321). There are excellent connections to Angoulême (ERT 300), Périgueux and Limoges (both ERT 302). A very scenic branch line runs from Bordeaux up the Dordogne Valley to Bergerac and **Sarlat** (ERT 318). The ride to Sarlat and back, a round trip of 336 km, makes an excellent one-day excursion from Bordeaux. Allow time for a leisurely lunch in Sarlat, which has an appealing Old Town. On hot summer days, join the Bordeaux crowds who escape to the beach by taking the local train to Arcachon on the Côte d'Argent (ERT 306).

The two-hour train journey from Bordeaux to **Biarritz** reveals a landscape not usually associated with France – a seemingly endless sandy pine forest. The smart set have been coming to Biarritz since the splendid beaches and mild climate were 'discovered' in the mid-19th century by such visitors as Napoleon III and Queen Victoria. Although less grand now, it is still a fairly upmarket coastal resort with nice beaches, great surfing and a casino.

The route south from Biarritz hugs the coast. The little town of **Saint-Jean-de-Luz**, halfway between Biarritz and the Spanish border, deserves a look. All trains stop at Saint-Jean. If you can avoid the high-season crowds, this bustling fishing port is a fine place to linger.

The train journey across the border to San Sebastián requires a change of train at **Hendaye**. It was at this station that Hitler met Franco in October 1940. It is the only remarkable thing about an otherwise rather unlovely place.

The onward journey to San Sebastián is with the frequent **Metro Donostialdea** (MD) tram service, which is often referred to by the name of the service operator Euskotren (schedules at foot of ERT 689). MD does not accept rail passes, but the fare from Hendaye to San Sebastián costs €2.65. An alternative is to take one of the few French trains that continue from Hendaye over the bridge to **Irún** in Spain, where you can change onto a regular Renfe train to San Sebastián (less frequent than MD but rail passes are accepted). If you opt for the tram, you'll find the tram stop in the forecourt of Hendaye station. Bear in mind that the Basque language is the norm here, so note that the Basque name for San Sebastián is Donostia. For the city centre, buy a 2-zone ticket to Amara-Donostia.

San Sebastián (Donostia)

San Sebastián is an **elegant resort**, with tamarisks gracing the promenade which runs along a crescent-shaped bay. Formerly a whaling and deep-sea fishing port doubling as a stopover for pilgrims en route to Santiago de Compostela, San Sebastián really came into its own in the mid-19th century as a fashionable health resort. Take time to wander the streets of the Old Town, or *parte vieja*, which lies at the foot of **Monte Urgull**. Although mainly rebuilt in the 19th century, it retains a characterful maze of small streets, tiny darkened shops and bars, arcaded plazas like the **Plaza de la Constitución**, which used to serve as a bullring, and churches such as the beautiful baroque Basílica de Santa María del Coro. Fishing is still much in evidence, with the daily catch on show on stalls in the **fish market**.

The **Museum of San Telmo**, 1 Plaza Zubaga (closed Mon), occupies a former Dominican monastery and includes a striking new pavilion which blends neatly into the cityscape. At the far end of the quay you'll find the **Naval Museum** (closed Mon) and the renovated Aquarium. For superb views, climb Monte Urgull itself, topped by a much rebuilt fort (the Castillo de la Mota). Standing proudly near the top of the hill is the statue of the Sagrado Corazón (Sacred Heart), which watches over the city.

ARRIVAL, INFORMATION, ACCOMMODATION

⇌ **Renfe**: Estación del Norte, Paseo de Francia. Cross the ornate María-Cristina Bridge, turn right, and it is a short walk through the 19th-century area to the Old Town. **Euskotren**: Estación de Amara, Plaza Easo. 🛈 Tourist office: Alameda del Boulevard, 8 (www.sansebastianturismoa.eus). 🛏 Head for the Old Town: hidden amongst the narrow streets are many *pensiones*. Try **Pensión Amaiur**, C. 31 de Agosto 44, ☎ 09 43 42 96 54 (www.pensionamaiur.com), which offers spotless, comfortable rooms, or **Casa Nicolasa**, C. Aldamar 4, ☎ 09 43 43 01 43 (www.pensioncasanicolasa.com). A friendly place in a quiet location is **Pensión Iturriza**, Campanario 10, 2, ☎ 09 43 56 29 59 (www.pensioniturriza.com). ✗ There are many good backstreet tapas bars — try monkfish kebabs, stuffed peppers and wild mushroom vol-au-vents. Two excellent markets: La Bretxa, on Alameda del Boulevard, and San Martin, near the cathedral on C. Loiola. For the best small restaurants, try the Old Town and the fishing harbour at the north end of Playa de la Concha.

Route 11: To the Pyrenees

CITIES: ★★ CULTURE: ★ HISTORY: ★ SCENERY: ★★
COUNTRIES COVERED: FRANCE (FR), SPAIN (ES)
JOURNEY TIME: 13 HRS | DISTANCE: 1,039 KM | MAP: WWW.EBRWEB.EU/MAP11

With the opening in 2013 of the Perthus Tunnel through the eastern Pyrenees, two great cities, Paris and Barcelona, moved closer together. You can now board a train in Paris and be in the Catalan capital less than seven hours later. The route taken by those fast TGV trains is actually far from direct; they dash south through Burgundy and the Rhône Valley, skirting Avignon and then broadly follow the coast west through Languedoc and Roussillon towards the Pyrenees.

The journey we describe here is a more direct, but very much slower, route from **Paris to Barcelona**. It runs south-west from Paris, crossing the Loire at Orléans and cutting through the Dordogne to reach **Toulouse**. We then follow the Ariège Valley up into the Pyrenees, crossing into Spain just east of Andorra, and then dropping down to the coast at Barcelona.

The highpoint of the journey is of course the **Pyrenees**; our route follows the only railway still in use which really crosses the mountains – as opposed to tunnelling under them (as the new Perthus Tunnel does) or hugging the coast and skirting around either edge of the mountains (as **Route 10** and **Route 12** in this book do).

The route we follow is a more traditional approach to the Pyrenees and northern Spain, one much favoured by travellers of yesteryear. Prior to the French Revolution this was the *route royale* from the capital to south-west France. With the coming of the motor car, the old royal road morphed into **Route Nationale 20**, the principal road artery from the French capital to Spain. The rail journey described here criss-crosses that highway more than a dozen times.

ITINERARY AND TICKETS

On those days when there is an early train from **Paris Austerlitz to Toulouse Matabiau** (currently 06.37, not Sundays, but check times in ERT 310), it is possible to cover this route in its entirety in a long day. It would be better, we think, to break the journey. Cahors is a good choice for an **overnight stop**. If you want to spread the journey over three days, then Cahors and Foix are good places for stopovers.

On some evenings, not daily, there is a direct **overnight train** from Paris to Latour-de-Carol. It follows the route described here. This is one of France's few surviving night trains with couchettes and reclining seats. Although the train offers no great luxury, the delight of awakening on a bright spring morning as the train heads up the **Ariège Valley** into the mountains more than compensates for any modest overnight discomfort. On those nights when this train runs, it is a sensible way of travelling from Paris to northern Spain. Arriving in **Latour-de-Carol** just after nine in the morning, there's time to savour clear Pyrenean air before joining the onward train to Barcelona.

In our experience, it is simply impossible to buy a through ticket to Barcelona (or anywhere else in Spain) via Latour-de-Carol. This is because the line on the Spanish side

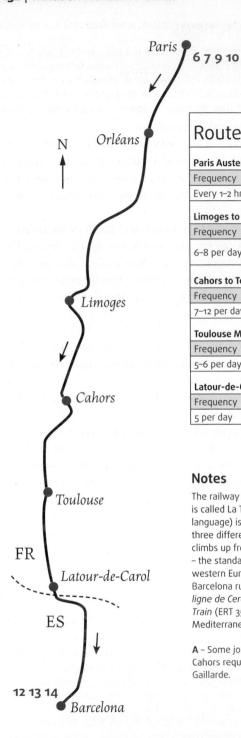

Route details

Paris Austerlitz to Limoges		ERT 310
Frequency	Journey time	Notes
Every 1–2 hrs	3 hrs – 3 hrs 30 mins	

Limoges to Cahors		ERT 310
Frequency	Journey time	Notes
6–8 per day	1 hr 15 mins – 2 hrs 30 mins	A

Cahors to Toulouse Matabiau		ERT 310
Frequency	Journey time	Notes
7–12 per day	65–85 mins	

Toulouse Matabiau to Latour-de-Carol		ERT 312
Frequency	Journey time	Notes
5–6 per day	3 hrs	

Latour-de-Carol to Barcelona Sants		ERT 656
Frequency	Journey time	Notes
5 per day	3 hrs – 3 hrs 10 mins	

Notes

The railway station at Latour-de-Carol (which is called La Tor de Querol-Enveig in the Catalan language) is unusual in hosting tracks of three different gauges. The French line which climbs up from Toulouse is 1,437-mm gauge – the standard width of railways in most of western Europe. The onward Spanish train to Barcelona runs on 1,668-mm gauge tracks. The *ligne de Cerdagne*, used by the *Little Yellow Train* (ERT 354), which runs east towards the Mediterranean coast is a metre-gauge railway.

A – Some journeys between Limoges and Cahors require a change of train at Brive-la-Gaillarde.

of the frontier, part of the **Rodalies de Catalunya** network, is not integrated into the wider European rail ticketing system.

So if you are following this route, just buy a ticket to Latour-de-Carol, which is the last station in France before the border. Oui.sncf (www.oui.sncf) sells a full range of French tickets (including the night train from Paris to Latour-de-Carol). However, the ticket for the final hop from **Latour-de-Carol** (the station is called La Tor de Querol–Enveig in Catalan) to Barcelona can only be purchased at Latour-de-Carol. The one-way fare is €12 (in late 2019).

The railway from Paris to Toulouse was one of France's first *grandes lignes*; the section from Paris to Orléans opened in 1840. Until the advent of dedicated high-speed railways in France (the Paris–Lyon line opened in 1981), the railway we follow south from Paris on Route 11 was one of the most advanced in the country.

In 1967, the **premium trains** between Paris and Toulouse (branded *Le Capitole*) became the first in Europe to be timetabled to run at 200 kilometres per hour – albeit only for a 100-km long stretch near Vierzon. The fastest trains sped from Paris to Toulouse in just six hours. Half a century later, no train on this line comes close to matching the performance of *Le Capitole*.

From Paris to the Dordogne

From **Paris** (see p100) to Orléans, the railway traverses unremarkable agricultural country, though on the final approach to the Loire city, the line cuts through the edge of the Forêt d'Orléans, the former royal domain which is now the largest national forest in metropolitan France.

In **Orléans**, the train stops at Les Aubrais, a station north-east of the city centre, from where a local train shuttles into the central station. Orléans predictably makes much of its associations with **Jeanne d'Arc** (Joan of Arc, the Maid of Orléans), who saved the town from the English in 1429. Her statue takes pride of place in the spacious pl. du Martroi, and the nearby Maison de Jeanne d'Arc, pl. du Général de Gaulle, is a reconstruction of her lodgings with a museum recounting her life and the events of 1429.

From Orléans, the railway tracks due south to **Vierzon**, where it crosses the River Cher, and then continues on through slightly hillier terrain to Limoges, where the grandiose railway station is a feast of fine interior design. It certainly showcases Limoges' position in the French porcelain industry. Administrative capital of the Limousin region, **Limoges** is a large industrial city. Its delightful mediaeval centre is a web of dark, narrow streets filled with half-timbered houses, small boutiques, and antique and china shops.

Surrounded by well-maintained botanic gardens – and overlooking the River Vienne – is the Gothic **Cathédrale de St-Étienne** (St Stephen's). Limoges was a centre of the Resistance during the Second World War. The **Musée de la Résistance et de la Déportation** at r. Neuve Saint-Etienne traces some of the Resistance operations.

The scenery really picks up south of Limoges as the railway weaves through the valleys of the **Dordogne**, with superb views of crags, lush valleys and perched villages. The route crosses the **River Lot** at Cahors, a town tucked into a bend of the river.

Cahors (suggested stopover)

An important Roman base in a tortuously winding valley, Cahors is famed for its **red wine**, which at its best rivals some of the Bordeaux *crus*. Its major monument, frequently depicted on wine labels, is the 14th-century Pont Valentré, a six-arched fortified bridge with three towers, west of the centre (reached via r. du Président Wilson). **Gallo-Roman remains** dot the town, and well restored 15th-century houses cluster around the cathedral. Cahors may be short on big sights, but we rate this small town for its uncomplicated charm. It's a lovely place to spend a night on a long rail journey.

ARRIVAL, INFORMATION, ACCOMMODATION

≋ A 6-min walk west of the centre. 🚹 Tourist office: pl. François-Mitterrand (www. tourisme-cahors.fr). 🍽 For a special treat, the **Hôtel Terminus**, 5 av. Charles de Freycinet, ☎ 05 65 53 32 00 (www.balandre.com), is a beautifully restored station hotel dating from the 1920s. Also recommended for its great value for money is **Hôtel Jean XXII**, 2 r. Edmond Albe, ☎ 05 65 35 07 66 (www.hotel-jeanxxii.com). Convenient for both the station and the Old Town is the hotel **Le France**, 252 av. Jean Jaurès, ☎ 05 65 35 16 76 (https://cahors-france.brithotel.fr). ✗ At night, head out to one of the cafés and restaurants on blvd. Léon Gambetta or r. Nationale.

Beyond Cahors the railway, still loyally following Route Nationale 20, skirts the edge of the dry **Causse de Limogne** and then runs down the Garonne Valley to Toulouse.

Now a lively university city and cultural centre, **Toulouse** is one of France's largest cities, not consistently attractive, but lively, assertive and with economic muscle based on high-tech industries, space research and aviation. The pinky-red brick of many of the grandiose town houses has earned the city the epithet of the **Ville Rose**. Many of the main attractions are in the Old Town, centred on pl. du Capitole, dominated by the 18th-century **Le Capitole** (town hall). The superb St Sernin Basilica is the sole survivor of an 11th-century Benedictine monastery established to assist pilgrims en route to Santiago de Compostela.

The main railway station in Toulouse is named after the Toulouse district in which it is located: Matabiau. It is a splendid early 20th-century building by the Canal du Midi, about a ten-minute walk north-east of the city centre.

CONNECTIONS FROM TOULOUSE

Toulouse Matabiau station is an important hub for rail services in south-west France. Local trains shuttle west through the hills to Lourdes and Pau (ERT 325) or down to the

Mediterranean coast at Narbonne (ERT 321) which is on **Route 12** in this book. Bordeaux (on **Route 10**) is just a couple of hours away (ERT 320). There are occasional direct services to Marseille (ERT 321) with onward connections there to the French Riviera (**Route 8**).

There are direct TGV trains to Paris (ERT 320) as well as three-daily direct TGVs to Lyon which route south via the coast to Montpellier and Nîmes before running north via Valence to Lyon (ERT 321). Toulouse to Lyon takes four hours. By contrast, Spain seems remarkably close. The seasonal AVE to Barcelona (ERT 13) takes just over three hours.

Through the mountains

The first part of the run south from Toulouse is unexceptional, but suddenly the railway cuts through a distinct ridge of hills called the **Montagnes du Plantaurel** to reach **Foix**, a town well deserving of an overnight stop. It's one of those unsung but perfect-looking French towns. If you would like to stay, try the Hôtel Lons, 6 pl. Georges Dutilh, ☎ 05 34 09 28 00 (www.hotel-lons-foix.com).

The hillsides tilt ever sharper as the railway climbs the **Ariège Valley**, especially beyond the spa town of Ax-les-Thermes. Tight curves and tunnels are the prelude to arrival at Andorre-L'Hospitalet station. Despite the promise in the station name, there is no bus to Andorra! But see the gazetteer (p447) on how best to get to Andorra.

The train continues south through the Puymorens Tunnel to reach **Latour-de-Carol**, from where the narrow-gauge *Petit Train Jaune* (Little Yellow Train) runs east to Villefranche-de-Conflent (ERT 354). This is a very scenic diversion along a mountain railway which has been threatened with closure. Facilities are sparse at Latour-de-Carol, but the station is in a wonderful mountain location at 1,230 m above sea level. The village of **Enveitg** (Enveig in Catalan) is a seven-minute walk from the station; just follow the grandly named Avenue de la Gare Internationale.

Latour-de-Carol is in a sunny oasis of fertile soils in an otherwise rather wild region. This great depression is known as **Cerdanya** on the Spanish

TRAVELLERS IN THE PYRENEES

The Pyrenees mountain chain is one of the world's most emphatic national boundaries, a great wall of snow-capped peaks separating France from Spain. Yet the Pyrenees have never quite sparked the **collective travel imagination** in quite the same way as the Alps. Swinburne and de Carbonnière, respectively English and French 18th-century travel writers, both played up the dark and forbidding aspects of Pyrenean landscapes. Swinburne climbed the **Pic du Midi**, mistakenly thinking it was the highest mountain in the Pyrenees, though it is 500 metres less lofty than **Aneto**, which at 3,404 metres really is the highest summit. He wrote of the "horrible view" and "rude and barren mountains". Early accounts of Pyrenean journeys always had a dark, almost Gothic, character. It is no surprise therefore that, even with the coming of the railways, the wider travelling public never engaged with the Pyrenees, generally preferring to linger in the foothills, seeking out the sedate pleasures of towns like Pau and Ax-les-Thermes.

side and Cerdagne on the French side of the frontier. Not a lot of folk head for Cerdanya as a primary destination, but many pass through en route to ski slopes, mountain resorts and of course Andorra.

The entire Cerdanya region is one of Europe's deliciously ambiguous **border zones**. The area juggles three languages with dexterity: Catalan, French and Spanish, not to mention a handful of dialects. And the international frontier meanders across the region without reference to natural features. The very permeability of the border drains energy from communities on the French side. The French village of **Bourg-Madame** is notably down at heel, while neighbouring **Puigcerdà** on the Spanish side of the border is a hive of activity. Easily the most curious of the villages in Cerdanya is **Llívia**, a place which is Spanish through and through and yet is located in a little parcel of Spanish territory entirely surrounded by France.

From Latour-de-Carol, the R3 regional train service runs down through beautiful Catalonian countryside, increasingly more Mediterranean in demeanour, to Barcelona.

Barcelona

This may be 'officially' Spain's second city after Madrid, but Barcelona is the **capital of Catalonia**, and its real sense of regional pride, energy and style make it a capital city to rival any in Europe. Over the past two decades it has become one of Europe's most visited destinations, and every year millions of travellers and tourists descend on Barcelona to marvel at the modernist architecture of Antoni Gaudí, explore the museums and galleries devoted to the likes of **Picasso** on C. Montcada 15–23 (www.museupicasso.bcn.cat) and **Miró** in Parc de Montjuïc (www.fmirobcn.org), promenade along the wide boulevards of the Eixample, or get lost in the narrow streets and alleyways of the old Gothic Quarter (Barri Gòtic). **La Rambla** is the most famous boulevard in Spain and the hub of city life for locals and visitors.

Beyond the art and the architecture, Barcelona has plenty more to divert you. There are few better places in Europe to eat out, whether you find your dinner in tiny backstreet tapas bars and the food stalls of the **Boqueria market**, or restaurants helmed by award-winning chefs.

The summer months can be very crowded, especially around famous landmarks such as **Gaudí's Sagrada Família** (see box on the next page), and those crowds are a tempting target for the city's pickpockets and bag-snatchers, who have given Barcelona a sadly justified reputation for petty crime. None of this should put you off, however, as Barcelona would be a highlight on any tour, and a perfectly wonderful destination in its own right. Cosmopolitan, prosperous and confident, Barcelona has been forward-looking ever since it hosted the Olympic Games back in 1992 and is firmly established as one of Europe's truly great cities.

ANTONI GAUDÍ

For many people, Gaudí alone is sufficient reason to visit Barcelona. He designed many of its most characteristic buildings; throughout the city mansions, parks, schools, gateways, lamp posts and sculptures provide a constant reminder of his genius. Particularly striking are **Casa Milà**, with its extraordinary rippling facade devoid of straight lines and right-angled corners, and **Casa Batlló**, an imaginative example of the fusion of architecture with the decorative arts of the époque.

Gaudí's most emblematic structure is the still unfinished **Temple Expiatori de la Sagrada Família**, the city's iconic church that he spent over 40 years creating, personally going out into the street to raise funds among the passers-by to facilitate its construction.

ARRIVAL, INFORMATION, ACCOMMODATION

≋ There are two main stations: the central **Estació de França** (metro: Barceloneta), for most regional trains and certain long-distance national and international services; and **Estació de Sants**, Plaça dels Països Catalans, about 3.5 km from the Old Town (metro: Sants-Estació), for suburban, regional and international trains as well as those to the airport. 🚌 Estació d'Autobusos Barcelona Nord, Carrer d'Alí Bei 80 (www.barcelonanord.cat; metro: Arc de Triomf) and next to Sants station (www.eurolines.es).

✈ Aeroport del Prat is 12 km south-west of the city (www.aena.es). RENFE trains run every 30 mins to and from Estació de Sants, taking 19 mins, and Estació Passeig de Gràcia (26 mins). The Aerobús bus service runs every 5–10 minutes from Plaça de Catalunya to the airport. Metro line 9 connects the airport with Zona Universitària.

🄸 Tourist office: Plaça de Catalunya 17-S and at Estació de Sants (www.barcelonaturisme.com). Once in town, the metro service will get you around quickly and easily (www.tmb.cat). It has ten colour-coded lines, and trains are designated by the name of the last stop. There are single tickets valid for just one journey on a bus or metro and an integrated zonal travel card. Validate your ticket before travel and, in the case of the integrated travel card, for every transfer (except when changing between two metro lines).

🛏 Barcelona has as wide a range of hotels as any major European city, but be aware that prices are fairly high compared to the rest of Spain. In the summer it is worth reserving in advance, or at the very least, arriving early in the day. There are many reasonably priced *pensiones*, particularly in the areas just off La Rambla in the Raval neighbourhood. Chic and surprisingly affordable, the **Banys Orientals**, C. Argenteria 37, ☎ 932 688 460 (www.hotelbanysorientals.com), can be found in the heart of trendy El Born. Boutique-style at boutique prices, the **Casa Camper**, C. Elisabets 11, ☎ 933 426 280 (www.casacamper.com), is worth treating yourself to. The **Olivia Balmes Hotel**, C. Balmes 117, ☎ 932 144 163 (www.oliviabalmeshotel.com), is a good option in the Eixample district.

CONNECTIONS FROM BARCELONA

Barcelona is the perfect jumping-off point for explorations deeper into Spain. Choose between **Route 13** and **Route 14** for itineraries which lead south to Andalucía. There are **direct high-speed trains** from Barcelona to Madrid, Seville, Málaga and Granada (all ERT 650). A slower route cuts through the hills to Bilbao (ERT 654). There is a choice of daytime and overnight services to Vigo and other cities in Galicia in north-west Spain.

Barcelona's port offers a good range of shipping connections with sailings to Tangier (ERT 2508), Sardinia (ERT 2675) and several Italian mainland ports, among them Genoa (ERT 2537), Savona (ERT 2585) and Civitavecchia (ERT 2520). The latter is of course very convenient for Rome. **Overnight ferry journeys** like these are, like night trains, a creative way of covering a long distance while sleeping.

Route 12: From the Alps to Catalonia

CITIES: ★★★ CULTURE: ★★ HISTORY: ★★ SCENERY: ★★★
COUNTRIES COVERED: SWITZERLAND (CH), FRANCE (FR), SPAIN (ES)
JOURNEY TIME: 12 HRS | DISTANCE: 856 KM | MAP: WWW.EBRWEB.EU/MAP12

The train journey from **Geneva to Barcelona** is one of the finest excursions in this volume. It is a good practical way of covering a lot of ground, but it also takes in a wonderful medley of landscapes. This journey could reasonably form the basis for a multi-day trip, stopping off here and there along the way. It relies entirely on local or regional trains.

If time is of the essence, you can dash from Geneva to Barcelona by high-speed train in under eight hours, with just one change of train along the way (the fastest connection each day requires a change at Valence TGV). That high-speed alternative follows the route described here only between Nîmes and Perpignan, so although you'll still get good views of the **Languedoc coast**, you'll miss out on most of the scenery which makes this journey so interesting.

The cities at either end of the route are, at first sight, as different as chalk and cheese. The lakeshore city of Geneva is Switzerland's most **liberal and cosmopolitan city**; when it comes to culture and design, Barcelona would always claim to be more cutting-edge. But there are similarities between the two cities; neither is a capital, yet both punch well above their weight on the world stage. Both Geneva and Barcelona are semi-detached from the countries to which they belong. Geneva only became part of Switzerland in 1815; almost entirely surrounded by French territory, the **République et Canton de Genève** is still proudly independent, and the disposition of political power in Switzerland tolerates (or humours) Geneva's free-spirited approach to the Swiss national project.

In Barcelona, notions of secession are altogether more serious. The Spanish region of **Catalonia** (Calalunya in the local Catalan language) has spawned its own energetic brand of nationalism and Barcelona had led the rallying cry for complete independence from Spain. Madrid's mean-spirited clampdown on Catalan protesters has quelled that movement.

Recalling the Catalan Talgo

It is no surprise that, throughout the 20th century, other than in times of war, there were direct trains linking Geneva with Barcelona. Until 1969, that always meant a quick change of train at Portbou on the French-Spanish border. Until the 1990s, most rail routes in Spain were built to the wider **Iberian-track gauge** and passengers had to switch from a French to a Spanish-gauge train. From June 1969, a little technological magic made it possible for passengers to board the Catalan Talgo train in Geneva and ride

Route details

Geneva Cornavin to Aix-les-Bains		ERT 364
Frequency	Journey time	Notes
6 per day	65–85 mins	

Aix-les-Bains to Valence Ville		ERT 364
Frequency	Journey time	Notes
Hourly	2 hrs 10 mins – 2 hrs 20 mins	

Valence Ville to Avignon Centre		ERT 351
Frequency	Journey time	Notes
Hourly	70–85 mins	R

Avignon Centre to Perpignan		ERT 355
Frequency	Journey time	Notes
Hourly	3 hrs	

Perpignan to Collioure		ERT 355
Frequency	Journey time	Notes
Every 1–2 hrs	25 mins	

Collioure to Figueres		ERT 355/657
Frequency	Journey time	Notes
Every 2 hrs	70 mins	C

Figueres to Barcelona Sants		ERT 657
Frequency	Journey time	Notes
Hourly	1 hr 50 mins	

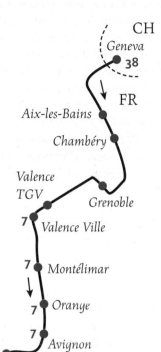

Notes

If you don't have time to follow this route in its entirety, you can make fast headway at the start by taking the TGV at 08.41 (timing in Oct 2019) from Geneva to Avignon TGV station, changing there onto the shuttle train to Avignon Centre to pick up Route 12. Arrival in Avignon Centre is at midday.

C – This leg requires a change of train at Portbou.
R – The journey time refers to the regional trains serving this route. There are some additional TGV services between these stations which are faster. These TGV trains require advance reservation.

right through to Barcelona. Axles that shifted in width allowed the train to slip easily from French to Spanish-gauge tracks at the border. By 1971, the Catalan Talgo took under ten hours for the journey from the shores of Lake Geneva to the heart of Catalonia.

The route taken by the Catalan Talgo in those days was a superb transect across France, taking in the **Savoy Alps** and then following the **Isère Valley** down to the Rhône. Later the train was rerouted via Lyon but in this journey for *Europe by Rail* we follow the **classic Catalan Talgo route**. Back in 1971, the through train from Geneva to Barcelona was one of Europe's premium services. It carried only first-class carriages and a special supplement was required to use the train. Lunch was served in the air-conditioned restaurant car between Chambéry and Avignon; passengers could enjoy early evening tapas and a glass of wine as the train crossed the French-Spanish border.

The style of yesteryear has gone. The notion of trains which only carry first-class passengers is almost unknown in Europe these days. But the same scenery is still there for the taking and today's travellers with time on their hands can follow the precise route taken by the Catalan Talgo 45 years ago. This journey now relies entirely on trains where there's **no need to book in advance**. The journey from Geneva to Barcelona by this route requires three changes of train along the way. Those changes are at Valence Ville, Avignon Centre and Portbou. And it's a mark of how rail travel has changed that these days all four trains carry only second-class seating.

RECOMMENDED ITINERARY

It is perfectly possible to follow this route in a day. It'll take about 12 hours. But this journey is too good to hurry. Make at least **one overnight stop** along the way. Ideally two. When it comes to places for those stopovers, our top choices would be Avignon and Collioure. As an alternative to Avignon, you may consider the Rhône Valley town of Valence (see p109) which gives a slightly shorter journey on the first day.

Two other cities on the journey feature on our must-see list, and for very different reasons. For a dash of **belle époque style**, the spa town of Aix-les-Bains is something quite special. Even if you are not into steamy, sulphurous spa treatments, Aix is a beautiful spot to relax. Another very worthwhile distraction is in the Catalan town of **Figueres** where the egg-topped Salvador Dalí Museum is a piece of theatre in itself.

Through the Alps

From **Geneva** (more on which on p339), the TER train (a French regional express) to Aix-les-Bains and Valence cuts through the western suburbs of the city and follows the right bank of the Rhône downstream to the French border. Within a dozen minutes of leaving Geneva, you are already in France. At **Culoz**, the train crosses the Rhône and takes to the hills.

Almost immediately, there is one of the highlights of the entire journey as the train runs along the east shore of the **Lac du Bourget**. This lakeshore railway line has long been a favourite for posters and advertisements proclaiming the merits of rail travel in France. The winning combination of lake and mountains is enhanced by the way in which the railway line hugs the very shore of the lake. At one point, as the route cuts around the **Baie de Grésine**, there is the brief but tantalising illusion of the train even crossing the lake with water on both sides.

After stops in **Aix** and **Chambéry**, the railway crests a low col to reach the Isère Valley, which it follows for almost 140 km downstream through Grenoble to Valence.

CONNECTIONS FROM AIX, CHAMBÉRY AND GRENOBLE

At Aix-les-Bains or Chambéry for TGVs to Paris (ERT 341). At Aix for Annecy (ERT 341 & 345). At Chambéry for the cross-border TGV services to Turin and Milan (ERT 44). At Grenoble for regional trains to Lyon (ERT 343) and Gap (ERT 362), and for TGVs to Paris (ERT 342).

A few minutes short of **Valence**, the train stops at a new station located at the point where the Grenoble to Valence railway crosses the high-speed rail route from Paris to the Mediterranean. The station itself is a striking glass structure with platforms on two levels.

From the TGV station, it is just another ten minutes on the regional train to the city centre station which is called Valence Ville. In Valence, there is a palpable sense of having reached the south of France – a region known in French as the **Midi**. You can read more about the town and the remarkable Valence Ville railway station on p109. It marks the end of the line for the regional express train from Geneva and you need to change trains here for the onward journey south.

From Valence Ville, our route to Barcelona follows the **Rhône Valley** south to Avignon. This 125-km stretch is also on **Route 7** in this book, and you'll find a brief account of the journey on p110.

CONNECTIONS FROM VALENCE

At Valence TGV for fast TGVs to Barcelona (ERT 13), Marseille (ERT 350), Nice (ERT 350) and Paris (ERT 13 & 350). At Valence Ville for occasional TGVs to Paris (ERT 351), and for regional train services to Lyon, Avignon and Marseille (all ERT 351).

Avignon (suggested stopover)

In 1305, troubles in Rome caused the Pope to move his power base to Avignon. Wealth flowed into the town – and remained after the papacy moved back to Rome 70 years later. The city walls, built to protect the papal assets, still surround the city and enclose just about everything worth seeing here. Jutting from the north-western section is **Pont Saint-Bénezet**, the unfinished bridge famed in song ("Sur le pont d'Avignon"). It is inevitably a tourist trap (€5), but it does have a museum and a restored rampart walk leading up to the **Rocher des Doms** garden, with great views over both the bridge and the nearby district of Villeneuve-lès-Avignon. Take the steps from the gardens down to the Romanesque cathedral, **Notre-Dame des Doms**, dating from the 12th century and containing the tombs of Pope John XXII and Pope Benedict XII.

Adjacent is the most photographed sight in the city, the huge **Palais des Papes** (Papal Palace), boasting a 45-metre-long banqueting hall where cardinals would meet to elect a new Pope. In appearance it's more like a fortress than a palace and is still the most prominent landmark in the city. It houses a collection of Renaissance treasures that has now made the building into an art museum (€12).

Contemporary art is to be found at the Collection Lambert, 5 r. Violette (closed Mon). In the middle of the Rhône lies **Île de la Barthelasse**, a favourite picnic island, with its own summer swimming pool. Place de l'Horloge is popular for its street entertainment and outdoor cafés.

ARRIVAL, INFORMATION, ACCOMMODATION

➤ Avignon-Centre, just outside Porte de la République gateway in the city walls. Local trains (ERT 351a) connect Avignon Centre with Avignon-TGV station, 4 km south of the city on the bank of the River Durance.

🛈 Tourist office: 41 cours J. Jaurès (www.avignon-tourisme.com). ⊨ Head into the Old Town, where you'll find a large number of reasonably priced pensions and hotels in the backstreets a few minutes away: try the **Garlande**, 20 r. Garlande, ☎ 04 90 80 08 85 (www.hoteldegarlande.com), which is central and comfortable. For a real treat, though it's pricey, take a look at the 4-star hotel **Cloître Saint Louis**, 20 r. du Portail Boquier, ☎ 04 90 27 55 55 (www.cloitre-saint-louis.com). An oasis of calm just off Avignon's main street, it combines tradition and modernity; the old part is housed in original 16th-century cloisters and the new wing was designed by Jean Nouvel. For something more modest, try **Hôtel Boquier**, a friendly, good-value option and centrally located, 6 r. du Portail Boquier, ☎ 04 90 82 34 43 (www.hotel-boquier.com).

CONNECTIONS FROM AVIGNON

Note that Avignon has two main railway stations. The **direct Eurostar** service to London (ERT 17) which used to run from Avignon Centre has since 2015 served Avignon TGV. The latter station also has **high-speed trains** to Perpignan, Barcelona and Madrid (all ERT 13), as well as services to Paris, Geneva and Nice (all ERT 350), Mulhouse and Strasbourg (ERT 379) and Frankfurt-am-Main (ERT 48).

Avignon Centre also has direct TGVs to Paris (ERT 351), which are slower than the fast trains from Avignon TGV station but via a more interesting route, with the Paris-bound TGVs following the Rhône Valley north all the way to Lyon. Avignon Centre has regular local trains to Marseille (ERT 351) and, since 2015, the newly-reopened line to Carpentras (ERT 351a) gives easy access to the Vaucluse region.

Into Languedoc

Moving on from Avignon, too many travellers head out to the TGV station on the southern outskirts of the city, from where a sleek Renfe **AVE train** whisks passengers with breathless speed and considerable comfort to Spain. The Madrid-bound AVEs dash from Avignon TGV to their first stop on Spanish territory in less than three hours. These fast trains (ERT 13) make just four intermediate stops in France before diving under the **Pyrenees** through the Perthus Tunnel, which opened to passenger trains in late 2013.

For this journey, we'll pass on the express and instead take the local train which runs all the way from Avignon Centre to **Portbou** in Spanish Catalonia with 22 stops along the way. It is a train used mainly by travellers making short hops between local stations. When we used this service, we were joined by shoppers on their way to Nîmes, students heading off later than they intended to lectures at the university in Montpellier, a small group of Catholic priests bound for a diocesan function in Perpignan and a young artist following in the footsteps of Matisse to Collioure.

Crossing the River Rhône at **Tarascon**, the train heads west across flat terrain to **Nîmes** (see p103), the city which invented denim and now courts controversy for its devotion to bullfights.

Connections from Nîmes

From Nîmes, a handful of local trains each day trundle south towards the **Rhône delta**; the line skirts salt pans, serving the fortress town of Aigues-Mortes on the way to the fishing port of Le Grau-du-Roi (55 mins from Nîmes). Both communities are interesting in their own way. The line gives glimpses of Camargue landscapes and some memorably ugly suburban sprawl. Note that timings for this branch line are not shown in ERT.

Several trains each day run north from Nîmes into the **Cévennes**, with three of these services running the full length of the beautiful *ligne des Cévennes* to Clermont-Ferrand (ERT 333). This line is described (from north to south) as **Route 6** in this book.

From Nîmes, it is just a short hop on to **Montpellier**, a university city which is assertively high-tech, young and trendy. The main attraction is that it's simply a fun place to be. It styles itself as a *cité intelligente*, though Montpellier is not as relentlessly modern as the promotional blurbs might suggest. In June 2019, **MoCo Montpellier Contemporain** (www.moco.art) – a multi-site project and exhibition centre dedicated to contemporary art – opened near Saint Roch railway station. The **Vieille Ville** (Old Town) mixes cobbled streets with many 17th- and 18th-century mansions. Northwards lies the **Jardin des Plantes**, France's oldest botanical garden.

Beyond Montpellier, the railway dances between the hills and the sea, skirting salty lagoons and serving Sète and Agde. There are solid towns like **Béziers**, with its cathedral perched on a low ridge above the River Orb. At certain times of the year, advertisements for upcoming bullfights on station platforms are a reminder that the cultural border between **Languedoc and Catalonia** is more a matter of the mind than a line on any map. At the Gare de Perpignan, the station which so inspired **Salvador Dalí** (see box on next page), there are bilingual station signs, Perpinyà in linguistic alliance with Perpignan.

Perpignan is the principal city of French Catalonia. Catalonia's national circle dance, the sardana, is performed to music a couple of times a week in summer in the mediaeval place de la Loge, Perpignan's main square

GOD, DALÍ AND PERPIGNAN

In 1965, Salvador Dalí completed his celebrated painting *La Gare de Perpignan*, which now hangs in the Museum Ludwig in Cologne. Dalí's artistic homage to Perpignan is a surrealist adventure, but it was not Dalí's first brush with the railway station at Perpignan. Two years earlier he had a powerful vision that marked out Perpignan station as a **pivot of the cosmos** which offered a unique perspective on the universe.

"On 19 September 1963, standing on the railway platform at Perpignan," he wrote in his diary, "I had a precise vision of the constitution of the universe." Clairvoyance slips easily into paranoia in the world of Salvador Dalí, but his vision has certainly helped place Perpignan on the map. Dalí regularly paced the platforms of the station, taking photographs and measurements; in 1966 he concluded that the measurements of the earth (and indeed the **weight of God**) are mirrored in the structure of Perpignan station.

Just as Shakespeare did his bit to promote Verona, so Dalí has turned out to be a great commercial asset in promoting Perpignan. Perhaps there are many travellers who, like us, make wholly unnecessary changes of train in the city merely to savour the surreal moment of being at one with the cosmos.

In appreciation of Dalí's enthusiasm for Perpignan railway station, the city council renamed the square in front of the station. **Place Salvador Dalí** is a good spot to reflect on the railway station's cosmic claim to fame. The building itself is a handsome example of a style of station that was often built in southern France, but no other station in the region has a statue of Salvador Dalí balanced on the roof. There are Dalíesque references aplenty in the colour scheme, which evokes something of the spirit of Catalonia.

A sign inside the station welcomes travellers to the "Gare de Perpignan: Centre du Monde." It might more properly claim, à la Dalí, that it is the "centre cosmique de l'univers."

From the Gare de Perpignan it is just 22 minutes on a high-speed train to Figueres, the Catalan town where Salvador Dalí was born in 1904 and died in 1989. But the slow route around the coast was the one used in Dalí's day, and that is the onward journey to Spain described in this section of this book.

and still the hub of the city's life. The imposing Citadelle, to the south, guards the 13th-century **Palais des Rois de Majorque** (Palace of the Kings of Mallorca). It's a reminder that the Kingdom of Mallorca once included extensive mainland territories north of the Pyrenees.

Rattling south from Perpignan, the train returns to the sea and hugs the Côte Vermeille on the run south to the Spanish border. This is a remarkable stretch of railway, once used by many main-line services, but since the opening of the Perthus Tunnel relegated to lesser status.

CONNECTIONS FROM PERPIGNAN: LE PETIT TRAIN JAUNE

Perpignan is the starting point for a remarkable rail adventure which leads high into the Pyrenees (ERT 354). A number of TER trains (or substitute buses) each day run west from Perpignan into the hills. At Villefranche-Vernet-les-Bains, passengers change onto the narrow-gauge *Petit Train Jaune (Little Yellow Train)* which negotiates the steep gradients and sharp curves of the 63-km long *ligne de Cerdagne*. In good summer weather, open carriages are used on this mountainous route. The line terminates at Latour-de-Carol-Enveitg, which is on **Route 11** in this book. It is possible to connect there with SNCF trains running north to Toulouse (ERT 312) and Catalan local trains down to Barcelona (ERT 656).

Collioure (suggested stopover)

Collioure on the **Côte Vermeille** makes an excellent overnight stop. This one-time fishing village – now an important centre for summer tourism – lies on a knob of land between two bays, overlooked by a 13th-century château. Matisse, Braque, Dufy and Picasso all discovered Collioure, and artists still set up their easels here. The domed church steeple looks distinctly Arabic.

ARRIVAL, INFORMATION, ACCOMMODATION

⇝ 400 m west of the centre. 🚺 Tourist office: pl. du 18 Juin (www.collioure.com). ⊨ **Hôtel Madeloc**, 24 r. Romain Rolland, ☎ 04 68 82 07 56 (www.madeloc.com), has a pool in a garden setting, but is pricey (as are other options); open Feb–Nov. Better value, and right on the water, is the **Hôtel Boramar**, 19 r. Jean Bart, ☎ 04 68 82 07 06 (www.hotel-boramar.fr). Only a few minutes walk from the centre is the very welcoming B&B **Villa Miranda**, 15 r. du Pla de les Forques, ☎ 04 68 98 03 79 (www.villamiranda.fr).

Across the Border

Beyond Collioure, the railway slips past a dozen capes and bays, each one a little more tantalising than its predecessor. The line runs through neat vineyards at Banyuls and just after **Cerbère** crosses the border into Spain.

The first station on Spanish territory is **Portbou**. It is a world apart from the mass tourism which defines most of the Costa Brava. Portbou has a real sense of isolation, and it's a pleasant spot to stop for an hour or two. You will in any case always need to change trains at Portbou. Continuing south, the railway all too soon cuts inland to Figueres, where the much-visited **Teatre-Museu Dalí** (www.salvador-dali.org, closed Mon except in summer) is the main attraction, honouring the town's most famous son. Whether you consider Dalí a genius or a madman, the museum is likely to confirm your views of the Surrealist artist. Appropriately enough, it's a bizarre building, parts of which Dalí designed himself (including his own grave), a terracotta edifice sporting giant sculpted eggs. The artist was back in the news in July 2017, when his body was exhumed in a legal tussle over a paternity suit.

The principal town between Figueres and Barcelona is **Girona** with a mediaeval Old Town on the east side of the River Onyar, connected by the **Pont de Pedra** to a prosperous new city in the west. From the bridge you can see the **Cases de l'Onyar** – a line of picturesque houses overhanging the river. In the heart of the labyrinthine Old Town is the Gothic cathedral. Check out the Banys Àrabs (Arab Baths), Romanesque with Moorish touches and dating from the 13th century. In the narrow streets of El Call (the old Jewish quarter) is the Bonastruc ça Porta Centre, which contains the **Museum of Jewish Culture** (entrance from C. de la Força 8).

From Girona, it's an easy run south to **Barcelona**. The railway enters the Catalan city through its unexciting northern suburbs and terminates in subterranean gloom at the Estació de Sants.

SIDETRACKS: NIGHT TRAIN PERSPECTIVE

Whatever's happening with Europe's night trains? After our block of three routes across the French-Spanish border, now is a good moment to pause and reflect on what's ado with Europe's sleeper services. "Can Europe's night trains survive?" asked a London newspaper in 2015. In February 2016, the French daily *Le Monde* gave the answer: "Le train de nuit. C'est fini." Yet now they are back in the news with new routes being planned, and in mid-2019 both Sweden and Switzerland committing to opening new international routes in the coming years.

Old issues of the *European Rail Timetable* (ERT) reveal a litany of lost overnight links. Just 20 years ago, it was still possible to travel in the **comfort of a sleeping car** from Brussels to Berne or from Calais to Cannes. Not so very long ago Bremen to Brussels, Nantes to Nice and Paris to Zurich were still on the overnight menu – again, all routes with proper sleeping cars. Today, travellers speed from Paris to Zurich on **high-speed trains** in just four hours. Faster daytime journey times dampened the market for premium overnight services. Travellers who explore the time versus money equation often concluded that top-quality sleeping cars are expensive and slow compared with **fast daytime services**.

The night train is of course imbued with a certain romance (for more on the topic of **travelling by night train** see our notes on pp520–22). But many passengers prefer the comfort of their own beds or a decent hotel, even accepting the burden of an early start in the morning to join the fast train (or perhaps even a short-haul flight) to their destination.

Nowhere is this better illustrated than across **France**. Until the opening of the new high-speed service between Paris and Barcelona, **Elipsos** night trains connected Paris with both Barcelona and Madrid. A lead-in fare of just over €100 could get you a seat on the Paris-Madrid overnight train on an off-peak day. Most passengers paid very much more. The one-way fare for a traveller wanting sole occupancy of a sleeper cabin with en suite facilities was over €500. The launch of high-speed trains across the French-Spanish border in late 2013 put paid to Elipsos. Both the budget-conscious leisure traveller and the expense account business executive have shown a preference for fast daytime services.

But greater awareness of the adverse environmental effects of flying prompted a real **swing in public opinion** in 2018 and 2019. ÖBB's *Nightjet* network has proved a major success. It's core network already covers six countries and more destinations are planned. Entirely new routes have been pioneered. The Polish city of Wrocław now finds itself happily reconnected to the international rail network with new overnight trains.

It's not just **ÖBB**. Over the last 12 months, our home city of Berlin has seen sleeper services reinstated to Austria, Poland, Slovakia and Hungary. The Berlin to Vienna train is a *Nightjet* service. The other destinations are run by other operators. Capacity has been increased on the Vienna to Ukraine route. Chic new carriages have started to run on the *Caledonian Sleeper* services from Scotland to London. With the Swedish environmental activist Greta Thunberg now tugging at the conscience of every European citizen, the night sleeper is making **an irresistible comeback**. *Le train de nuit. Ce n'est pas fini!*

IBERIAN CONNECTIONS
An introduction

It is almost 30 years since Spain's first high-speed rail route opened. That 1992 line from Madrid to Seville marked the start of the transformation of the Spanish rail network. Just a generation later, Spain now has Europe's most extensive network of **high-speed railways** with well over 3,000 route kilometres now in use. The experience of travelling on a high-speed train in Spain is quite special so it's appropriate that we include one long high-speed hop in this book. That features as **Route 14** (Barcelona to Málaga).

Sadly, rail links between Spain and Portugal have taken a dive. The closure of the route from Salamanca to northern Portugal in 1985 was a tragedy, though much of the route on the Portuguese side of the border survives (ERT 694). It makes a fine **excursion up the Douro Valley** from Porto (see p173). The more recent closure of other cross-border rail routes, running west from Cáceres and Badajoz respectively, were further blows. But one train a day from Badajoz into Portugal was recently reinstated (ERT 677 & 691). Improvements in services on the route from Vigo to Porto are of course very welcome and that cross-border link features in **Route 16** (which runs south from Santiago de Compostela through Porto to Lisbon).

Traditional rail routes

The **legacy rail network in Spain**, which existed well before the recent spate of high-speed lines, much of it dating back to the second half of the 19th century, offers many fine opportunities for explorations by rail and **Route 13** and **15** both rely entirely on those traditional lines. If you have time to follow just one route in this section, we recommend **Route 13** which cuts right across Spain from Barcelona to Cádiz, taking in an extraordinary variety of landscapes along the way.

There are of course many other routes which were candidates for inclusion. If you can find time to explore the line from **Zaragoza to València**, you're in for a treat (ERT 670). All the more so if you make an overnight stop at Teruel where you'll find some of the finest *mudéjar* architecture anywhere in Aragon. Another wonderful Spanish diversion is the long rail route which runs west from Santander all the way along the north coast to Ferrol (ERT 687). This 12-hour journey follows one of Europe's finest coastal rail routes.

It is possible to connect **Route 16** and **13** and thus create an Iberian circuit. Direct buses from Lisbon to Seville take about seven hours for the journey. But **more adventurous travellers** might prefer to travel by train through southern Portugal from Lisbon to Vila Real de Santo António (ERT 697 & 697a) from where it's just 10 minutes on a ferry to Ayamonte in Spain, where you can pick up a bus for the short hop on to Seville (ERT 676). ■

Route 13: Historic Spain

CITIES: ★★★ CULTURE: ★★ HISTORY: ★★ SCENERY: ★★
COUNTRIES COVERED: SPAIN (ES)
JOURNEY TIME: 13 HRS 20 MINS | DISTANCE: 1,324 KM | MAP: WWW.EBRWEB.EU/MAP13

Spain's high-speed rail network was inaugurated in 1992 with the opening of a fast link from Madrid to Seville. Since then, the network served by super-fast trains (known as Alta Velocidad Española or AVE services) has been progressively extended. With a little planning you can enjoy a Catalan breakfast in Barcelona, stop off for a leisurely lunch in Madrid and still be in Málaga in time for tapas. Route 14 in this book describes that fast route south from Catalonia to Andalucía.

Not everyone favours such speed, and Route 13 is a **real slow travel experience**. When the early Scottish traveller **Henry David Inglis** headed south from Madrid to Andalucía in 1830, he bemoaned the fact that the regular stage carriage took merely a week – too fast, he felt, to really do justice to the landscapes along the way. The old roads to Andalucía all converge on a single natural defile that strikes a huge gash through the mountains. The **Sierra Morena** may not tower to great heights, but the rugged demeanour of these mountains creates a formidable barrier to travellers bound for the south.

Despeñaperros is the name given to the great gorge that was, for travellers of yesteryear, the pre-eminent gateway to Andalucía. For men like Henry Inglis and others who ventured to Andalucía in the first half of the 19th century, the seductive beauty of the gypsies of Andalucía was presaged in the cruel beauty of Despeñaperros. This was, and still is, a place with fierce relief, great black rocky walls and wild torrents – everything that was needed in fact to appeal to the **Romantic imagination**.

If you take the modern high-speed line south to Andalucía described in **Route 14**, you'll find it slices through the Sierra Morena like butter. You'll hardly notice the hills. But if you have a few hours to spare why not take the old rail route that runs through the gorge at Despeñaperros. It's the route we describe here. This is truly one of **Europe's finest rail journeys**, and it's a creative way of linking Barcelona with southern Spain.

SUGGESTED ITINERARY

There is a once-daily direct Talgo train from Barcelona to Andalucía which follows precisely the route described here – so following the coast down to **València**, and later using the **Despeñaperros gorge** to reach Andalucía. It runs right through to Seville via Córdoba. In Seville, you can change onto a connecting train to Cádiz. If that seems too much of a long haul for one day – it takes just over 13 hours – try splitting the journey up into bite-size chunks. València, Córdoba and Seville all make rewarding stopovers. Along the early and closing sections of the route, there is a wide choice of trains. It is only between **Alcázar de San Juan and Córdoba** that you are restricted to just one train each day.

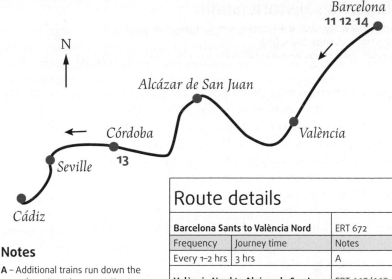

Route details

Barcelona Sants to València Nord		ERT 672
Frequency	Journey time	Notes
Every 1–2 hrs	3 hrs	A

València Nord to Alcázar de San Juan		ERT 668/668a
Frequency	Journey time	Notes
3–4 per day	3–4 hrs	B

Alcázar de San Juan to Córdoba		ERT 661
Frequency	Journey time	Notes
1 per day	3 hrs 30 mins	C

Córdoba to Seville Santa Justa		ERT 660/671
Frequency	Journey time	Notes
1–2 per hr	45–85 mins	

Seville Santa Justa to Cádiz		ERT 671
Frequency	Journey time	Notes
Every 1–2 hrs	1 hr 30 mins – 1 hr 45 mins	

Notes

A – Additional trains run down the coast from Barcelona to València, stopping in València at Joaquín Sorolla station instead of Nord. These trains, branded as *Euromed* services, take about 3 hrs 10 mins.
B – Some journeys between València and Alcázar require a change of train at Albacete.
C – The sole direct train is the *Torre del Oro*. There is also a morning option requiring a change of train in Jaén. It takes 5 hrs 10 mins (Jaén, not mentioned in the main text, is on a branch line to the south of this route).

Leaving Barcelona

The Catalan coast south-west of Barcelona (p136) is known as the **Costa Daurada**. It is not beautiful, yet tucked away in the ugly urban sprawl are some interesting spots. **Sitges** has quite a buzz as a hub of Catalonian counterculture and as one of the most gay-friendly resorts in Europe. But the real star of this stretch of coast is **Tarragona**, where the ancient walled town (above the modern settlement) enjoys a glorious clifftop position.

Continuing down the coast from Tarragona, the rail route skirts mile after mile of golden beaches – and some fabulously tacky resorts. A highlight is crossing the watery flatlands that blend into the **delta of the Ebro** (Spain's largest river). Despite one or two fine sights, such as the fortified coastal city of Peñíscola, there is no real reason to linger en route to València.

València (suggested stopover)

València is Spain's third city and the **home of paella**. It is a large, modern metropolis, with an enviable capacity for reinvention. València is in the forefront of style and fashion, and sees itself as the natural capital of the entire Levante region. At its heart there's a bustling **atmospheric Old Town** with two mediaeval gateways (Torres de Serranos and Torres de Quart), pleasant squares, characterful run-down backstreets, crumbling baroque mansions and a handful of other historic landmarks. The sizeable student population ensures that there's no shortage of nightlife.

Santiago Calatrava's stunning **City of Arts and Sciences** (www.cac. es), is the city's top attraction and a symbol of the 'new' València. It's a gleaming, white, futuristic entertainment complex which encompasses an excellent hands-on science museum, a vast aquarium, an arts centre and a planetarium. The port and beach area were dramatically revamped for the 2007 America's Cup and València is fast becoming one of the Med's most fashionable hot spots.

The Old Town, which contains the main sights, is easily covered on foot. Two towers preside over the **Plaça de la Reina**: the baroque spire of Santa Catalina and the Miguelete, which is the bell tower of the cathedral; climb the spiral staircase to the top for a good view. València's key building is its cathedral, a mixture of styles ranging from Romanesque to baroque. The city's finest building is the Gothic **Llotja de la Seda**, Plaça del Mercat (closed Mon, free entry), a legacy of the heady days of the 15th-century silk trade, while the nearby **Mercat Central** is a vast art nouveau market hall.

In summer, many cafés and bars in València offer *orxata*, a sweet milky drink made from *chufas*, or earth almonds, traditionally eaten with bread sticks (either chewy, sweet *fartons*, or more brittle *rosquilletas*).

TORRE DEL ORO OR GARCÍA LORCA

The **daily Talgo train** from Barcelona to Seville has an illustrious history. For 70 years, there has been a morning departure from Barcelona which follows this route to Andalucía. Fifty years ago, the journey from Barcelona to Seville took 25 hours. Now it takes just half that time. These days the train is called the *Torre del Oro*, taking its name from the watchtower and prison in Seville built by the **Almohad Caliphate** in the early 13th century. That's the same name as the train bore in the late 1980s. But for many years from late 1989 the train was named in honour of the radical Andalusian poet and playwright García Lorca.

Ten years ago the *García Lorca* was Spain's most interesting train; apart from the main portion bound for Seville, it carried through carriages to Málaga, Granada, Almería and even Badajoz, close to the Portuguese border in the Extremadura region. It still makes sense to use the *Torre del Oro* from Barcelona to reach all these destinations, but nowadays a change of train is necessary. The recent **reversion of the train name** from *García Lorca* to *Torre del Oro* is interesting. Metaphors of surveillance and detention are perhaps more in keeping with modern pieties than theatre and poetry.

ARRIVAL, INFORMATION, ACCOMMODATION

⇌ València is slightly complicated when it comes to train stations. The *Torre del Oro* train which forms the backbone of Route 13 stops at **Estació del Nord**, which has a magnificent tiled entrance hall – it's definitely worth a look. Most other fast trains from Barcelona, as well as the swift AVE service from Madrid, serve **Joaquín Sorolla** station (linked to Nord by a free bus service). Trains to Cuenca and Aranjuez leave from Nord. As a rule of thumb, most 'interesting' trains run to and from Nord. **i** Tourist office: Pl. del Ayuntamiento 1 (www.visitvalencia.com) and a branch at Joaquín Sorolla station.

🛏 Good budget areas are around Pl. del Ayuntamiento and Pl. del Mercado. The **Hostal Venecia**, Pl. del Ayuntamiento 3, ☎ 96 352 42 67 (www.hotelvenecia.com), is an excellent value 2-star hotel. The **Antigua Morellana**, C. d'En Bou 2, ☎ 96 391 57 73 (www.hostalam.com), is friendly and well located close to the central market. Well located on the edge of the Old Town and just a 5-min walk from Nord station is the modern and comfortable **Sorolla Centro**, Convento Santa Clara 5, ☎ 96 352 33 92 (www.hotelsorollacentro.com).

CONNECTIONS FROM VALÈNCIA

Trains run **down the coast** to Alicante, with some continuing to Murcia and Cartagena (all shown in ERT 672). Preliminary work has just started on a new rail link from Murcia to Almería, which will provide a new connection from the Spanish Levante into eastern Andalucía. Until, then you can bridge the gap in the rail network by taking a bus. ALSA (www.alsa.es) serve the Murcia to Almería route. The journey takes about three hours.

There are two very fine **rural rail routes** running inland from València, one to Zaragoza via Teruel (ERT 670) and the other via Cuenca and Aranjuez to Madrid (ERT 669). Fast trains to Madrid via the new high-speed line (ERT 668) take less than two hours to reach the capital. València has excellent ferry links with the Balearic Islands (ERT 2510). Our pick of the many routings available is the Saturday night sailing from València to Maó (Mahón) on the island of Menorca. It's a 15-hour crossing. In fine weather, this is a wonderful route. For more on Mallorca and the other Balearic Islands, see our **Sidetracks** feature on p162.

La Mancha

The three-hour stretch of the journey beyond València takes in a region of Spain well off the beaten track. You trade the lush landscapes of the coast for the arid interior. The first place of any size is **Xàtiva**, which looks uninspiring from the train but in fact has a delightful Old Town. The railway then turns decisively west, passing the distinctive Moorish castle at Almansa perched on its limestone crag. Olive groves and red soils are the keynote themes, as the train skirts the southern edge of the **Cordillera de Montearagón** and comes to rest in the ultra-modern station at Albacete-Los Llanos – where you can connect onto the high-speed network with the fastest AVEs running to Madrid in just 82 minutes (ERT 668).

After **Albacete**, the train runs through dusty small towns and crosses the Záncara Valley to reach Alcázar de San Juan. This is Don Quixote country; you'll spot several clusters of windmills from the train.

ALCÁZAR CONNECTIONS

The *Torre del Oro* train from Barcelona to Andalucía reverses direction at Alcázar de San Juan. This is an important railway junction. **Aranjuez**, a verdant oasis of green, is just an hour away to the north (ERT 661 & 668a). The *Torre del Oro* connects in Alcázar with a direct train to Merida and Badajoz (ERT 678). The run to Badajoz takes over six hours. There is also a connection at Alcázar into the Talgo train to **Almería** which, like the *Torre del Oro*, follows the Despeñaperros route. You can identify trains via Despeñaperros from the timetable as services that stop at both Alcázar de San Juan and Linares-Baeza (ERT 661; half a dozen daily services in each direction).

The finest part of the entire journey is the two-hour stretch beyond Alcázar de San Juan. The train lopes south through great vineyards towards the Sierra Morena. Cast back to before the construction of the railway and **Despeñaperros** was the haunt of *banditti* who would waylay innocent travellers as they ventured south to Andalucía. It is tamer nowadays, but still by far the most interesting rail route for those heading for Andalucía. South of Despeñaperros, you emerge into a land of dense olive groves and huge oleanders on the platforms of railway stations. Suddenly there are lush colours and Moorish architecture, and scenes outside the carriage window that seem to be taken directly from paintings by Murillo and Velázquez.

The first stop in Andalucía is **Vilches**, its neat blue-and-white station building a cool antidote to summer sun. The railway then follows the Guadalquivir Valley down to Córdoba – a city which, with its striking mosque-cum-cathedral, is simply not to be missed (read more on p160).

CONNECTIONS FROM CÓRDOBA

You can connect in Córdoba into **Route 14**, following it south to Antequera and Málaga (ERT 660) or north to Madrid and Barcelona (also ERT 660). A new four-times daily fast train from **Córdoba to Granada** started in summer 2019, bringing the travel time between the two cities down to about 95 minutes. It is thus now very easy to make a day trip from Córdoba to Granada to visit the Alhambra.

From Córdoba the *Torre del Oro* continues down the **Guadalquivir Valley** to Seville, through a landscape increasingly dominated by orange groves. The train terminates at Santa Justa station, a dramatic piece of architecture which opened just before Seville hosted the 1992 World's Fair.

Seville (Sevilla) – (suggested stopover)

Of all the Andalusian cities, Seville has the most to see. The **capital of Andalucía**, it's a romantic, theatrical place, with a captivating park, a gigantic cathedral and two very important fiestas: the Feria de Abril and the processions of Holy Week. **Columbus** set out from Seville to discover the New World, and *Don Giovanni, Carmen, The Barber of Seville* and *The Marriage of Figaro* were all set here.

Most places of interest are in the **Barrio de Santa Cruz**. A pleasant place for a stroll, it lives up to the idealised image of Spain; white-and-yellow houses with flower-bedecked balconies and romantic patios. The focal point is the Giralda, a minaret that has towered over the Old City since the 12th century and which now serves as a belfry to the cathedral. Built by the Almohad rulers 50 years before Ferdinand and Isabella's Christian Reconquest, it consists of a series of gentle ramps designed for horsemen to ride up; it's in excellent condition and worth climbing for the views.

The cathedral is the largest Gothic structure in the world, simply groaning with gold leaf. The **Sacristía Mayor** houses the treasury and Sacristía de los Cálices contains Murillos and a Goya. A huge memorial honours Christopher Columbus (who may or may not be buried here!).

The **Alcázar** (www.alcazarsevilla.org) was inspired by the Alhambra of Granada, but has been marred by later additions. Within is the Salón de Embajadores, where Columbus was received by Ferdinand and Isabella on his return from the Americas, and there are also shady, interconnected gardens separated by arched Moorish walls. The neighbouring **Casa Lonja** contains a collection of documents relating to the discovery of the Americas.

The **Museo de Bellas Artes** (closed Mon, free for EU nationals), Pl. del Museo 9, has a collection of 13th–20th-century Spanish paintings, second only to that of the Prado in Madrid.

ARRIVAL, INFORMATION, ACCOMMODATION

≈ Estación Santa Justa, Av. Kansas City; 15-min walk from the centre. 🚌 32 goes from the station to Plaza de la Encarnación; City buses: 🚌 C1 and C2 are circular routes around the town. Many buses pass through Plaza de la Encarnación, Plaza Nueva and Av. de la Constitución (for information see www.tussam.es). ✈ San Pablo Airport, 12 km east of town. Express buses (EA) take 35 mins to the centre. 🛈 Tourist office: Av. de las Delicias 9 (www.visitasevilla.es).

🛏 During Holy Week and the April Fair accommodation is very difficult to obtain and must be pre-booked. On the whole, staying in Seville tends to be expensive. A good budget option in a quiet location just by Gran Plaza metro station (so not in the Old Town) is **Hostal San Vicente II**, C. Beatriz de Suabia 104, ☎ 954 636 864 (www.hostalsanvicentesevilla. com). A nice and comfortable hotel in a quiet area, a 20-min walk from the town centre across the bridge at Av. Cristo de la Expiración, is the **Monte Triana**, Clara de Jesús Montero 24, ☎ 954 343 111 (www.ebrweb.eu/9). Or try the upmarket **Amadeus**, C. Farnesio 6 & C. San José 10, ☎ 954 501 443 (www.hotelamadeussevilla.com), right in the Old Town with wonderfully decorated public spaces that fit with the hotel's name.

✖ Seville is probably the best place to sample such typical Andalucían dishes as *gazpacho* (chilled tomato and pepper soup) and *pescaíto frito* (deep-fried fish). The liveliest bars and restaurants, frequented by students, are in Barrio de Santa Cruz.

CONNECTIONS FROM SEVILLE

There's a useful international bus service to **Faro in Portugal** (two to four times daily according to season; times in ERT 676), where you can connect onto the Portuguese rail network. The fastest trains from Faro to Lisbon take just over three hours (ERT 697).

A rural rail route runs north from Seville to the **Extremadura** region. Services are sparse (ERT 677), but you can take a direct train from Seville to both Merida and Cáceres. There is also a local train service from Seville to Huelva on the coast (ERT 671). The only reason you would want to go there is to catch one of the regular ferries to the Canary Islands (ERT 2512) – read more on shipping links from Huelva in the **Sidetracks** on p155.

JEREZ DE LA FRONTERA

Just before you reach Cádiz on the train from Seville you pass through the station for Jerez. This town has given its name to **sherry** and the bodegas are the town's main attraction; it's also home to Spanish brandy. Here you will find such familiar names as Harvey, González Byass and Domecq. Most **bodegas** offer tours (varying prices, reservations necessary for some; many close in Aug) that finish with a tasting. Sherry also appears in the local cuisine; try *riñones al Jerez* (kidneys in sherry sauce).

From Seville, it is just another 100 minutes down to the coast at Cádiz. It's an interesting run, passing **Jerez de la Frontera** and approaching Cádiz through a strange landscape of salt lagoons. For a more romantic approach alight from the train at El Puerto de Santa María and take the ferry across to Cádiz.

Cádiz

Like Venice, that other once-great naval city, Cádiz is approached by a **causeway** and all but surrounded by water. Its tight grid of streets, squares and crumbly ochre buildings exudes an atmosphere of gentle decay. It's all the better for that, and really comes into its own during the carnival in February and in the evening, when the promenaders come out and the bars open. Colourful tiling is a feature of the pavements, parks and even the **Catedral Nueva** (New Cathedral), which was rebuilt, like much of the rest, in the city's 18th-century heyday. However its origins go back to 1100 BC when the city was founded by the Phoenicians; the port was of vital importance at the time of the conquest of the Americas (which was why Sir Francis Drake attacked it). You can get a panoramic view of it all from **Torre Tavira**, both from the top of the tower and in the camera obscura below, via a mirror and lens on the roof.

There's always been fish aplenty on the Cádiz table and the residents of Cádiz are quick to remind British visitors that fried fish was a Cádiz staple centuries before it was even dreamt of in Britain. It was Sephardic Jews who took the idea from Spain to Britain.

ARRIVAL, INFORMATION, ACCOMMODATION

≈ The main station is at Pl. de Sevilla. 🅱 Tourist office: Pl. de Madrid (www.cadizturismo. com). ⊨ A friendly, small hotel in the Old Town not far from the station is **Hotel Argantonio**, C. Argantonio 3, ☎ 956 211 640 (www.hotelargantonio.es). The stylish El Armador Casa Palacio, C. Ancha 7, ☎ 654 383 851 (www.elarmadorcasapalacio.com), is well located near Pl. San Antonio in a lively street. A peaceful option in a refurbished convent located in the Old Town is **Convento Cadiz**, C. Santo Domingo 2, ☎ 856 924 826 (www.hotelconventocadiz.net).

CONNECTIONS FROM CÁDIZ

Cádiz is, quite literally, the **end of the line**. You can go no further by train. But our **Sidetracks** feature on the next page has a few words about boat connections from Cádiz.

SIDETRACKS: SOUTH FROM SPAIN

Route **13** and **14** end in a region deeply influenced by **settlers from North Africa**. In its heyday (in the 8th and 9th centuries AD), the Muslim caliphates and emirates collectively known as **al-Andalus** covered a much larger area than modern Andalucía, extending beyond the Iberian peninsula and the Pyrenees to Septimania, the region of south-west France around Narbonne. This veil of Moorish settlement gave Arab mariners control of much of the western Mediterranean and the Strait of Gibraltar.

Historically the links between **Andalucía** and North Africa have been forged by seafarers, but that may change in the years ahead as Morocco and Spain debate the possibility of a **rail tunnel linking Europe to Africa**. Don't hold your breath. If it comes to pass, the first trains from Madrid to Marrakech won't be running before 2030. So meanwhile it's the boat, and you are spoilt for choice. From **Málaga** (on **Route 14**), there are excellent links to Melilla (ERT 2595), one of two autonomous Spanish cities on the coast of North Africa which, along with some other tiny fragments of Spanish territory on the Moroccan coast and some inshore islands, are all that is left of **África Española**.

Melilla wins no prizes for beauty, but it is a curious political oddity (as indeed is Gibraltar on the European side of the water). From Melilla you can walk across the Moroccan border to the railway station at **Beni Nzar**. You'll find train times at the website of Moroccan rail operator ONCF (www.oncf.ma – website in Arabic, French and English).

More common jumping-off points for Africa, each with shorter crossings than from Málaga, are **Algeciras** and **Tarifa**. If you are bound for Tangier, Tarifa is the best bet, for services from there go to Tangier city rather than the out-of-town port (shown in timetables as Tangier Med). The crossing from Tarifa takes one hour (see www.frs.es for the timetable). From Algeciras, there are frequent crossings to Ceuta (the second Spanish city in North Africa). As in Melilla, you can walk into **Morocco**, along the way seeing the fierce fences that surround this little outpost of Europe in Africa to deter migrants who judge that Ceuta or Melilla might be an easy route into the European Union.

There is one port that, in terms of its historic status as a great mercantile centre, quite eclipses anywhere we have yet mentioned in this Sidetracks feature. And that is **Cádiz** (on **Route 13**). During more than 500 years under Moorish rule, Cádiz was very bound into Mediterranean and North African trade, but since the Spanish settlement of the Americas, Cádiz has set its sights on the Atlantic. That is reflected in modern shipping schedules, for Cádiz has no scheduled service to the African mainland. But the town has something special for those with a dose of sea fever, viz. a **ferry to the Canary Islands**. It takes 31 hrs to Lanzarote, 40 hrs to Las Palmas de Gran Canaria, 48 hrs to Santa Cruz de Tenerife, and 64 hours to Santa Cruz de La Palma (ERT 2512).

It used to be possible to continue beyond the Canary Islands to either Madeira or to El-Aaiún on the African mainland, but these routes were axed in 2012. You can however return by a completely different route to the European mainland, using the weekly Naviera Armas sailing back to **Huelva** (www.navieraarmas.com; not shown in ERT).

Route 14: High-speed Spain

CITIES: ★★ CULTURE: ★★ HISTORY: ★★ SCENERY: ★★
COUNTRIES COVERED: SPAIN (ES)
JOURNEY TIME: 6 HRS | DISTANCE: 1,136 KM | MAP: WWW.EBRWEB.EU/MAP14

The preceding route in the book, from Barcelona to Andalucía via the Despeñaperros gorge, is a very fine journey if you have plenty of time. Now, in Route 14, we present an alternative which relies entirely on **high-speed lines**. Our journey as presented here was made possible with the completion of the new fast line from Barcelona to Madrid in 2008. While our natural inclination is to avoid high-speed lines, this route for *Europe by Rail* really plugs a gap – and it's an enjoyable run, **full of quiet drama**, with some fine views across expansive Spanish landscapes.

No other country in Europe, not even France, has used high-speed rail to transform the relationship between regions as effectively as Spain. Twenty years ago, there were six daytime trains from **Barcelona to Madrid**. A journey time of seven to eight hours was normal. Today, there are 30 trains from Barcalona to Madrid on a typical weekday, the fastest taking just two-and-a-half hours to reach the capital. The geography of Spain has been reshaped by the railway.

SUGGESTED ITINERARY

You can dash from Barcelona to Málaga on an sleek high-speed train in less than six hours. But **Madrid** and **Córdoba** are too good to miss. Why not spend at least a night in each? Even if you are very pushed for time, you should at least stop for a few hours in Córdoba to view the Mezquita, which ranks alongside Granada's Alhambra as one of the grandest Moorish designs in Spain.

Slip on board the AVE in **Barcelona** (more on the city on p136) – having booked a window seat in advance – and relax as Spain slips by beyond the window. This is pure cinema. At one level this is a route which transcends geography, but it is also one constrained by the landscape. Having thought you were heading inland, there is suddenly a fleeting glimpse of the sea from above **Tarragona**. The railway then sneaks round the edge of the hills above Montblanc. By now the AVE is at full speed, sweeping east to the Ebro Valley. Some trains stop at **Zaragoza**, a city with a brace of fine cathedrals and a stunning Moorish fortress-palace called the Aljafería. The railway then follows the **River Jalón** upstream, cutting through the hills beyond Calatayud and coasting down to Madrid.

Madrid (suggested stopover)

Madrid occupies a location at the very centre of Spain, and deliberately so. In 1561 **Philip II** chose the city as his capital to avoid inflaming regional

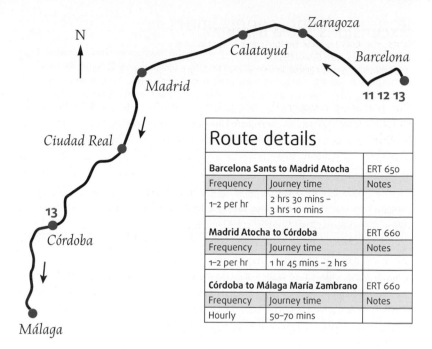

Route details

Barcelona Sants to Madrid Atocha		ERT 650
Frequency	Journey time	Notes
1–2 per hr	2 hrs 30 mins – 3 hrs 10 mins	
Madrid Atocha to Córdoba		ERT 660
Frequency	Journey time	Notes
1–2 per hr	1 hr 45 mins – 2 hrs	
Córdoba to Málaga María Zambrano		ERT 660
Frequency	Journey time	Notes
Hourly	50–70 mins	

Notes

Twice-daily AVEs (3 on certain peak-season days) run directly from Barcelona to Córdoba and Málaga without stopping in Madrid (although their route does take them through the suburbs of the Spanish capital). The fastest journey time from Barcelona to Málaga on a direct train is 5 hrs 45 mins (ERT 660).

There are some non-stop trains from Madrid to Málaga which dash between the two cities in just 2 hrs 25 mins (ERT 660).

jealousies. Beyond the mediaeval **Old Quarter**, the majority of Madrid was built from the 19th century on, and much of the city is given over to relentless, drab high-rise buildings. But its charm is not necessarily its architecture. What Madrid is good at is its street- and nightlife, with the smart, fun-loving Madrileños taking their evening *paseo* along **Calle del Carmen** and **Calle de Preciados**; thereafter the city keeps going late into the night.

The other main attraction of the city is the fine collection of museums. The **Prado** (www.museodelprado.es) is one of the world's great art galleries, and you could spend days exploring the collection in order to feel that you have done it justice. It celebrated the bicentenary of its opening in 2019. Elsewhere, the **Centro de Arte Reina Sofía** (www.museoreinasofia.es; closed

EXCURSIONS FROM MADRID

Few European capitals offer such a feast of wonderful days out by train as Madrid. Top of many visitors' lists is the palace-cum-monastery complex at **El Escorial**. As Europe's largest Renaissance building, the sheer scale of the place is daunting, to an extent that makes the gardens seem no more than a weak sideshow. A number of late 16th-century buildings arranged around a vast quadrangle are open to visitors (not Mondays). A visit to El Escorial is a great reminder of **Spain's fabulous wealth** in its heyday as an imperial power. Part of the appeal of El Escorial is its setting on the edge of the Sierra de Guadarrama. El Escorial is easily reached on *Cercanías* line C3, which runs hourly from Madrid Atocha (journey time 60 mins) or from Chamartín (taking 45 minutes). Reservations are not necessary on this rail route.

The same C3 suburban rail route runs in the opposite direction all the way to **Aranjuez**, normally every half hour, taking 45 minutes from Atocha and slightly more from Chamartín. Aranjuez is another wonderful palace and garden complex, but here the gardens definitely have the edge. As at El Escorial, the palace is closed Mondays, but the gardens are open daily.

Our third suggestion for a day trip from Madrid is to take the train to **Toledo**. Avant trains leave hourly from the main-line platforms at Atocha station, taking just 33 minutes for the 75-kilometre journey to Toledo (ERT 679). This is a rail route where you always need to reserve seats in advance. A palpable **sense of history** pervades every street and alley in the UNESCO-listed walled city of Toledo, which is perched on a hill with the Rio Tajo forming a natural moat on three sides. Even the railway station communicates a strong sense of **Toledo style**: look out for the colourful tiles and Moorish design. The heavily buttressed cathedral is renowned for its stained glass, delicate carvings and fine art collection: El Greco, van Dyck, Goya, Caravaggio and more. In Toledo's Jewish quarter, there are two spectacular synagogues.

Few other European cities can quite match Toledo in so brilliantly juxtaposing Muslim, Jewish and Christian heritage. It is an **incomparable cityscape**. No surprise, perhaps, that it can be busy. You might want to consider staying overnight for in the evening, once the day trippers have gone, Toledo is very special. A good, central hotel is the Santa Isabel, C. Santa Isabel 24, ☎ 925 25 31 20 (www.hotelsantaisabeltoledo.es).

Tues) houses a superb collection of modern art, including a masterpiece of anti-war painting: Picasso's *Guernica*. The **Royal Palace** and its gardens are worth exploring, as is the lovely green space of the Retiro, Madrid's biggest park just a short walk from the city's art museums. For train buffs, there is the **Railway Museum** (www.museodelferrocarril.org), located in the city's former Delicias station. More than anything though Madrid is a place where you can simply enjoy the atmosphere – on the city streets, in its many squares, or at the counter of a tapas bar.

There's a maze of quaint old streets to explore heading south and west from the city's principal square of the **Puerta del Sol**. Particularly picturesque is the Plaza de la Villa halfway down the Calle Mayor. The arcaded rectangle of **Plaza Mayor** is at the heart of the Old Town, a place to stroll around or have a coffee in the sunshine. The Plaza Mayor is close to the Puerta del Sol, and therefore is not only in the heart of the city, but a few steps away from Point Zero, from where all distances in Spain are measured.

ARRIVAL, INFORMATION, ACCOMMODATION

🚄 **Puerta de Atocha** Station (metro: Atocha Renfe), just south of the city centre, is Madrid's terminal for high-speed trains to the south (Córdoba, Málaga, Seville and Valencia) and north-east (Zaragoza and Barcelona). The magnificent original 19th-century building now shelters tropical gardens. However, most trains to the north-west and north of Spain and those to France via Irún/Hendaye and the overnight train to Lisbon, depart from Madrid's other main station, **Chamartín**, C. de Agustín de Foxá (metro: Chamartín), in the suburbs, 8 km north of the centre.

✈ Madrid Barajas Airport (www.ebrweb.eu/a), 12 km north-east of town, is served by suburban trains (Cercanías line C1), running every 30 mins (06.00–23.30) from terminal T4 to Chamartín (11 minutes), Atocha Cercanías (25 minutes) and Príncipe Pío (38 minutes), serving all stations en route. Metro line 8 runs into central Madrid in 12–15 mins.

Public transport: With services every 5 mins (06.00–01.30) and colour-coded lines the metro, which marked the centenary of its creation in 2019, is easy to use. Tickets are loaded onto a contatless, reloadable Public Transport Card (TTP), which you can purchase at ticket machines (www.metromadrid.es). The EMT city bus system is comprehensive, efficient and the same price as the metro. 🚹 Tourist office: Alcalá 31 and at Atocha station (www.esmadrid.com).

🛏 If you'd like to stay close to Atocha station, then the **Only You Hotel Atocha**, Paseo Infanta Isabel 13, ☎ 914 09 78 76 (www.ebrweb.eu/d) is a stylish and comfortable option. A wonderful place to rest your head is the **Palacio San Martín**, Pl. San Martín 5, ☎ 91 701 50 00 (www.ebrweb.eu/c), a 19th-century palace converted into a hotel with stunning views from the rooftop restaurant. Just a short walk from the Plaza Mayor and the Puerta del Sol, the **Mayerling**, Conde de Romanones 6, ☎ 91 420 15 80 (www.mayerlinghotel.com) is a good, comfortable option.

CONNECTIONS FROM MADRID

As the country's major rail hub, Madrid has direct trains to all major cities in Spain. Yet international offerings are limited to an **overnight service** to Lisbon (ERT 45), a fast AVE service to Marseille each afternoon (ERT 13). Direct trains to San Sebastián (four times daily) give onward connections to Hendaye in France (ERT 689).

South to Andalucía

Remember when leaving Madrid for the south that **Atocha** station is more like an airport than a railway station. Passengers boarding high-speed trains need to be at the station well in advance. Luggage is routinely scanned and only passengers with valid tickets can go to the platforms. The stretch of this route from **Madrid to Córdoba** was opened in 1992 as Spain's first high-speed railway. It's interesting to see how, a quarter of a century later, the railway has settled into the landscape.

Running south from Madrid, there is a glorious view of **Toledo's honey-hued townscape** in the distance. Just south of **Ciudad Real** (where some trains stop), you'll see one of Europe's most extraordinary architectural follies: a disused airport, complete with its own abandoned railway station. Beyond Puertollano, the landscape changes dramatically as the railway cuts through the **Sierra Morena**. This 100-kilometre stretch is nothing short of superb – perhaps Europe's best new-build railway.

All too son, the train pulls into **Córdoba**, where the star attraction is undoubtedly the Mezquita, the grandest and most beautiful mosque ever built in Spain. Córdoba is laden with history; the city boasts one of the largest mediaeval townscapes in Europe, and certainly the biggest in Spain, offering a harmonious blend of Christian, Jewish and Moorish architecture.

The huge **Mezquita** was founded in the 8th century by Caliph Abd al-Rahman I and was enlarged over the next 200 years. At the foot of the bell tower, the delicately carved Puerta del Perdón leads through the massive outer walls to the **Patio de los Naranjos** (Courtyard of the Orange Trees), a courtyard with fountains for ritual cleansing. Inside the mosque, the fantastic forest of 850 pillars, joined by two-tiered Moorish arches in stripes of red brick and white stone, extends over a vast area. After the Moors departed, the Christians added the cathedral within the complex, incongruous but stunning, and blocking out the light that was an integral part of the design.

If you are minded to stay overnight in Córdoba, you can try the style-conscious Viento 10, C. Ronquillo Briceño 10, ☎ 957 764 960 (www.hotelviento10.es) in a quiet area, a 15-min walk to the Old Town. A good central budget option is the Carpe Diem, C. Barroso 4, ☎ 957 476 221 (www.hotelcordobacarpediem.com), not far from the Mezquita.

Málaga had to wait until 2007 for the high-speed line from Madrid to Córdoba to be extended to the coast. The railway crosses the **River Guadalquivir** west of Córdoba and then gradually climbs into the hills which form a western extension of the **Sierra Nevada** range. Reaching 400 metres near Antequera (where there is a new station for high-speed trains), the line then drops down steeply through several tunnels to reach the coast at Málaga.

In the Andalusian city, all trains terminate at the stylish modern María Zambrano station, named in honour of the distinguished Andalusian-born philosopher who suffered greatly under the Franco regime.

Málaga

The sixth largest city in Spain and a **busy working port**, Málaga at first sight isn't pretty, with high-rise modern apartment blocks built up within close range of a dismal-looking canalised river. But the centre is a hundred times more cheerful and resolutely Spanish in character, with a tree-lined main boulevard, dark back alleys, an atmospheric covered market and traditional shops and bars where Spanish (not holidaymakers' English!) is very much the first language.

Málaga's past is most evident in the area near the port. The long, shady walks of the **Paseo del Parque** are overlooked by the **Alcazaba**, a fort built by the Moors on Roman foundations; it has the character of the Alhambra in Granada, albeit on a smaller scale, and the views extend over the city to the coast. Its neighbour, the **Gibralfaro castle**, is of Phoenician origin, reconstructed later by the Moors, and offers even better views.

Just off the Paseo is the **cathedral**, set in a secluded square and built between the 16th and 18th centuries. Close by, in Calle San Agustín, is the city's star attraction, the **Museo Picasso** (www.museopicassomalaga.org), where you can admire over 150 of the master's works in a 16th-century palace. Picasso was born in Málaga in 1881 and you can visit his birthplace, now the **Museo Casa Natal**, on the Plaza de la Merced 15, with works of art and personal effects. Plaza de la Merced is the city's liveliest and most attractive square with several good bars and restaurants. Fans of contemporary art might also like to visit the **Centro de Arte Contemporáneo** on Calle Alemania (www.cacmalaga.eu). It has a small permanent collection of art and is highly regarded for the quality of its temporary exhibitions.

Arrival, information, accommodation

≽ María Zambrano station, Explanada de la Estación, a 20- to 30-min walk from the centre of town. 🚋 3 goes to Alameda Principal and Paseo del Parque near the centre. Local trains for the coastal resorts leave from here as well (at a different level). Note this coastal rail route is also served by another more centrally located station, Centro Alameda. ✈ 8 km from the city. There is a tourist office in the main hall. Trains to Málaga run every 20 mins, taking about 15 mins. 🚺 Tourist office: Pl. de la Marina 11 (www.malagaturismo.com).

🛏 There is a good choice of hotels, including a small parador set in the gardens of the Gibralfaro castle (🚋 35 from Paseo del Parque) above the town. In high season, central Málaga is lively at night (all night); the only solution is to ask for a room away from the street, or buy earplugs. Well located for the Alcazaba, the port and the Paseo del Parque is the **Hotel MS Maestranza**, Avda. Cánovas del Castillo 1, ☎ 952 213 610 (www.hotelmsmaestranza.com). Or try the friendly, family-run **Monte Victoria**, C. Conde de Ureña 58, ☎ 952 656 525 (www.hotelmontevictoria.es), located on Mont Victoria with great views over the town. A good central option in the Old Town is the **Hotel del Pintor**, C. Álamos 27, ☎ 952 060 980 (www.hoteldelpintor.com).

✗ There are several good restaurants around the cathedral, especially along C. Cañón. Seafood and gazpacho are good bets. Paseo Marítimo and the seafront in Pedregalejo are the best areas for seafood restaurants.

Connections from Málaga

A frequent train service runs west from Málaga (Centro–Alameda and RENFE stations) along the **Costa del Sol**, connecting the city with its airport and the busy resorts of Torremolinos, Benalmádena and Fuengirola (ERT 662).

There is a not-to-be-missed regional rail route which runs north-west from Málaga, more or less paralleling the new high-speed line from Málaga to Córdoba, but hugely more exciting as it takes in the **El Chorro Gorge** – this stretch of railway is where the dramatic final scene of the film *Von Ryan's Express* was filmed. You can ride the El Chorro line by taking any Media Distancia (MD) train from Málaga bound for Seville or Ronda (all shown in ERT 673). There is also a high-speed service from Málaga to Seville (see the lower panels in ERT 660), but these Avant trains do not use the El Chorro route.

Finally, there is a daily ferry, usually departing late evening from Málaga to **Melilla** (ERT 2595), one of the fragments of Spanish territory on the north coast of Africa. It's a useful link from Málaga if you are making for Morocco.

SIDETRACKS: BALEARIC ISLANDS

Reached by ferry from Barcelona or València (both routes in ERT 2510), the perennially popular island of **Mallorca** is the largest and most varied in the Balearic group. While Mallorca is massively touristy, it has some surprisingly **beautiful scenery** and unspoilt villages, particularly in the rugged northern mountains. The island capital, Palma, is at the hub of a gentle bay that has been densely developed, but the compact **Old Town of Palma** is a gem and includes a splendid Gothic cathedral, the Moorish palace and Arab baths. There's no shortage of excellent sandy beaches around Palma and the other resorts, though in summer many get impossibly crowded. The big resorts around Palma Bay are the best places for raucous nightlife, though Palma itself has much classier nightspots.

    Narrow-gauge railway lines link Palma to Sa Pobla (46 mins), Manacor (57–62 mins) and Sóller (55 mins). Outline schedules for all these services are in ERT 674. Trains leave from the transport interchange on Plaça d'Espanya in Palma. Eurail and Interrail passes are not recognised on any of the island's railways. The train trip to the old fishing village of **Port de Sóller** is by far the most scenic of the three options. The *Ferrocarril de Sóller* (Sóller Railway) marked its centenary in 2011. The railway, funded through profits from the citrus trade, was built through difficult terrain and quite transformed access to remoter parts of Mallorca. The one-way fare from **Palma to Sóller** is €18 and the return €25. Sóller station is improbably grand for somewhere in the outback, and the town itself a happy maze of little lanes where you can still just imagine what life on this beautiful island might have been like before it was engulfed by tourists.

    If you do head out by train to Sóller, it is worth taking the **local tram** that connects with the train and runs out to Port de Sóller with its jetties, beaches and laid-back cafés and bars. You have to pay extra for the tram, but you can buy a combined train & tram ticket for the return trip from Palma to Port de Sóller for €32.

    Buses serve all the main towns and many villages across Mallorca and schedules are available from the Palma tourist office at Plaça de la Reina 2. **Boat trips** offer one of the most pleasant ways of seeing Mallorca. A popular cruise heads around the north-west coast from Port de Sóller to Sa Calobra. There's plenty of sightseeing elsewhere on the island, including some fine caves on the east coast. A must-see is the beautiful 14th-century **Monastery of Valldemossa** where Chopin and George Sand spent a winter.

    The majority of accommodation is in the form of large hotels built for the package tour industry, although Palma does have a number of inexpensive *hostales*, a growing number of characterful converted properties (most of which are relatively expensive), and two youth hostels – near Palma and outside Alcudia.

    Ferries also serve the other Balearic islands. **Ibiza** is a brash nightlife haunt. **Menorca** is much more low-key, and popular with families and older tourists; seek out the island's intriguing Bronze Age sites. Tiny **Formentera** is comparatively undeveloped, with hostel accommodation in La Savina; Playa Illetas and Playa Levante are among the best beaches.

Route 15: Pilgrim route to Santiago

CITIES: ★★ CULTURE: ★★ HISTORY: ★★ SCENERY: ★★
COUNTRIES COVERED: SPAIN (ES)
JOURNEY TIME: 10 HRS 30 MINS | DISTANCE: 825 KM | MAP: WWW.EBRWEB.EU/MAP15

If it were ever possible to make a **pilgrimage by rail**, this is it. Santiago de Compostela (or just plain Santiago to most) has been the goal for millions of pilgrims over many centuries, walking the various routes from France and across northern Spain that have come to be collectively known as the **Camino de Santiago** or the Route of St James. Even for those of no or little faith, this transect across northern Spain is a very fine journey, much enlivened by some splendid scenery and some of Spain's most historic cities along the way.

San Sebastián (Donostia in Basque) stands on the coast below the green, rainy foothills of the Pyrenees in the **Basque province**, the region of Spain known to the assertively independent Basque people as Euskal Herria. Conquered by neither the Romans nor the Moors, the Basques suffered appalling repression during the Franco period and their language was banned. Several decades of agitation by the *abertzale* followed up by ETA action have secured for the Basque people a measure of autonomy.

From the Basque region, we cut through the hills, reaching **Burgos** and **León**, both with superlative cathedrals, which lie in the great *meseta* (high plain) of Castilla y León (formerly known as Old Castile). To the north rise the **Picos de Europa**, not that well served by public transport, but offering some of the best mountain scenery in the country. By contrast, **Galicia**, comprising Spain's north-west corner, is lushly verdant and intricately hilly, with a complicated coastline buffeted by Atlantic gusts and characterised by fjord-like scenery.

ITINERARY THOUGHTS

This is a route which is well suited to being done end-to-end in a day. There is something about the way in which the landscape changes – from hills to plains and then hills again – which is rather like a sonata.

The **once-daily direct train** from San Sebastián to Santiago de Compostela recalls the name of the traditional pilgrim trail: it's called the *Camino de Santiago*. Perhaps realising that pilgrims shun creature comforts, the premium carriages on this Intercity train (*preferente* class) were withdrawn in early 2016, along with the on-board cafeteria. So pack your sandwiches and prepare for a day of simple pleasures. If you ride the *Camino de Santiago*, there are no complicated tariffs. From San Sebastián to Santiago there's **just one flexible fare**: it's €45.50. You can buy your ticket just prior to departure, but if you wish to be sure of getting a seat then it's wise to book in advance through an online sales channel like www.renfe.com.

Although the nature of the journey suggests covering the route in a long day, don't forget that there are many fine cities along the route. Should you be minded to **stop overnight**, we suggest the city of Burgos. That need not undermine the ascetic mood of the journey. While Burgos certainly has its worldly diversions, the city's main railway

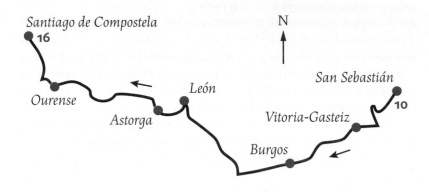

Route details

San Sebastián/Donostia to Burgos Rosa de Lima		ERT 689
Frequency	Journey time	Notes
7 per day	3 hrs	R

Burgos Rosa de Lima to León		ERT 681
Frequency	Journey time	Notes
4 per day	2 hrs	R

León to Santiago de Compostela		ERT 682/680
Frequency	Journey time	Notes
2 per day	4 hrs 30 mins – 5 hrs 20 mins	A, R

Notes

The once-daily direct train from San Sebastián/Donostia to Santiago de Compostela leaves San Sebastián at 09.33 and reaches Santiago at 19.59. These timings are correct as of October 2019.

A – Additional connections are available with a change of train in Ourense.
R – It is necessary to obtain a seat reservation prior to travel for all direct trains on this route.

The **numbers in red** adjacent to some cities on our route maps refer to other routes in this book which also include that particular city.

station is named in honour of **Saint Rose of Lima**, whose commitment to fasting and penance earned her the distinction of the first person from the New World ever to be canonised by the Roman Catholic Church.

Across the hills to Castile

Heading south from **San Sebastián** (see p130), our route cuts through the green hills of Gipuzkoa, a province where the Basque language and culture still thrive, especially in remoter communities away from main roads. After skirting the **Sierra de Aralar**, the railway cuts south with great views of the Basque region's highest peak, Aizkorri, away to the right of the train. This great limestone massif rises to 1,551 metres.

The next community of any size is the unofficial Basque capital: **Vitoria-Gasteiz**, though Basque speakers tend to refer to it simply as Gasteiz. The almost perfectly preserved centre of this mediaeval hill town has handsomely arcaded squares; at the centre of Plaza de la Virgen Blanca, a monument commemorates a nearby battle of 1813 in which Napoleon's army was defeated by the Duke of Wellington.

Beyond Vitoria-Gasteiz, the railway traverses easier terrain, crossing the **River Ebro** at Miranda and tracking south-west to Burgos.

Burgos (suggested stopover)

In mediaeval times Burgos grew rich on the wool trade, and in the 11th century the city became the **capital of Christian Spain** as well as the home of Rodrigo Díaz de Vivar, better known as **El Cid**, the romantic mercenary. During the Civil War in the 1930s, the town again rose to fame as the **Nationalist headquarters**. It was here that Franco formed his Falangist government. Burgos has now grown into a large and busy modern city, but its heart is the atmospheric Old Town around the ruined castle (itself of little interest apart from the views from it).

The grand entrance to old Burgos is formed by the **Arco de Santa María**, a fortified 14th-century gateway, altered and decorated in 1536 to pacify Charles V, depicting his figure and those of the founder (Diego Porcelos) and El Cid (whose equestrian statue stands near the Puente de San Pablo). From here, it's a short walk to the bulk of the main attractions, eating places and hotels.

Foremost is the **cathedral**, consecrated in 1260 but not completed until the 18th century, making it the third largest cathedral in Spain (after Toledo and Seville), and also probably the richest. Amidst the splendour of the 19 chapels and 38 altars, positively dripping in gold leaf, is El Cid's unobtrusive tomb and a grotesque crucifix, made in the 13th century with human hair, fingernails and a body of buffalo hide. Evening sees everyone promenade along the **Paseo del Espolón**, graced with fountains and statues, streched out along the river, with cafés and restaurants making the most of the atmosphere.

ARRIVAL, INFORMATION, ACCOMMODATION

⇌ The railway station is called Burgos Rosa de Lima; it's an assertively modern design in the Villímar district on the very edge of town, about 5 km north-east of the centre. Buses 25 and 43 shuttle into the centre. 🛈 Tourist office: C. Nuño Rasura 7 (www.turismoburgos. org). ⊨ Located in a former convent a short walk to the cathedral is the **Palacio de Burgos**, C. de la Merced 13, ☎ 94 747 99 00 (www.ebrweb.eu/nhburgos). A simple but comfortable hotel in the Old Town is the **Cordon**, C. la Puebla 6, ☎ 94 726 50 00 (www.hotelcordon.com). The **Mesón del Cid**, Pl. de Santa Maria 8, ☎ 94 720 87 15 (www.mesondelcid.es) has nice views of the cathedral and square.

CONNECTIONS FROM BURGOS

Burgos is a **major rail hub**. International departures are limited to an excellent overnight train to Lisbon (ERT 45) and four daily direct trains to San Sebastián with connections to Hendaye in France (ERT 689), where you can connect onto the French TGV network and **Route 10**. There are regular direct trains to Madrid (ERT 689), some using the **new high-speed line** and others taking the mountainous old route via Ávila which skirts the southern edge of the Sierra de Guadarrama and then drops down past El Escorial to reach the Spanish capital. Other cities in northern Spain with direct trains from Burgos include Salamanca, Bilbao and Barcelona (all ERT 689).

On the journey west of Burgos, the train initially follows the **Arlanzón Valley**, then branches off the Madrid line to run north-west across the plains towards León, on the way stopping at **Sahagún**. It is nowadays hardly a city of note, but in the past it played an immensely important role as a

SPAIN'S NORTH COAST BY TRAIN

Route 15 follows the main line taken by the daily Intercity train from San Sebastián to Santiago de Compostela. But there is an **entirely different rail route** between the two cities, one that takes very much longer and for much of the journey follows the north coast of Spain. If you follow Route 15 in its entirety, you may feel inclined to use this alternative coastal line for the return journey.

The railway along the north coast is sometimes referred to as the **FEVE line**, recalling the days when a separate company called FEVE ran the metre-gauge railways in northern Spain. FEVE stands for *Ferrocarriles Españoles de Vía Estrecha* (effectively Spanish narrow-gauge railways). Nowadays FEVE is merely an operating division of Spain's national rail operator Renfe.

This excursion is one of Europe's great narrow-gauge rail journeys. It extends from San Sebastián along the coast to Ferrol, from where it is a short hop (about 100 minutes) on a direct Alvia train to Santiago de Compostela. The **narrow-gauge coastal route** splits naturally into four stages, viz. San Sebastián – Bilbao – Santander – Oviedo – Ferrol. The one-way fare for the entire run from San Sebastián to Ferrol is about €60.

Our favourite stretch of this magnificent route is the section between Santander and Oviedo, where the railway cuts a narrow trail between the rugged **Picos de Europa** (to the south) and the dramatic coastline to the north. The small resort town of Llanes in the very middle of this stretch is an immensely tempting spot to alight and linger for a few days.

As well as regular services, a **very smart tourist train** called *El Transcantábrico* plies the narrow-gauge coastal line. Passengers are accommodated in deluxe suites on the train, and the package includes all meals with an emphasis on high quality local fare.

The eight-day journey from San Sebastián to Santiago de Compostela makes some use of road transport too, allowing participants in this rail cruise to see key sights across northern Asturias and Galicia. Naturally, **packages** like this are not cheap. The fare in summer 2020 for a couple sharing a cabin is €11,000. For a single traveller requiring sole occupancy of a cabin, the fare is €8,000. We leave you to judge whether that's a wonderful bargain or a downright waste of money.

way station on the pilgrim path to Santiago. Some fine *mudéjar* architecture gives a hint of Sahagún's erstwhile wealth and influence.

León was founded by the Romans, and over the years was ruled by Visigoths, Moors and Christians. In 1188, Alfonso IX summoned his first *Cortes* (parliament) here – one of the earliest democratic governments in Europe – but the court moved away permanently in the 13th century and León became little more than a trading centre until 1978, when it was made the capital of the province that shares its name. Today it's thriving once again. The major monuments are within easy walking distance of each other in the **Old Town**.

Of all the city's buildings, the most spectacular from the outside is the 16th-century, Plateresque-style **Monasterio de San Marcos** (now an upmarket parador, or state-run hotel, on Plaza de San Marcos), which was founded by Ferdinand and Isabella, the Catholic monarchs, as a pilgrim hostel and later rebuilt as the headquarters for the Knights of Santiago.

Beyond León, the scenery becomes more interesting, as we encounter the first ripples of the **Montes de León**. The train stops at **Astorga**, which the Roman historian Pliny lauded as a "magnificent city". Today it is a small, gracefully decaying country town, capital of the bleak moorland region of **La Maragatería**. Continuing west, the train cuts through increasingly dramatic hills, with a particularly fine stretch as the railway follows the Sil Valley west through O Barco and A Rúa. After flirting briefly with the **River Miño**, the train then cuts through a final ridge of low hills to reach Santiago de Compostela.

Santiago de Compostela

A magnet for millions of pilgrims for the last thousand years, Santiago de Compostela hit the big time when the **tomb of St James** (Sant' Iago, Spain's patron saint) was discovered in 813, supposedly by a shepherd who was guided to the site by a star.

Destroyed in 997 by the Moors, the town was rebuilt during the 11th century and began its Golden Age. In the 12th century, the Pope declared it a **Holy City**: for Catholics, only Jerusalem and Rome share this honour. The Old Town (contained within the mediaeval walls) is one of the most beautiful urban landscapes in Europe. It's not entirely given over to pilgrims, endowed as it is with a theatre, a concert hall and plenty of bars and clubs offering dancing and late-night drinking.

The **Old Town** contains a host of fine churches and monasteries as well as notable secular buildings tucked down the narrow side streets. The **cathedral** (started in 1075) is the obvious centre of attention. Its existing 18th-century baroque facade covers the original 12th-century facade, the Pórtico de la Gloria by Maestro Mateo, said to be the greatest single surviving work of Romanesque art in the world, with 200 especially imaginative and detailed sculptures. To celebrate their arrival in the Holy City, pilgrims traditionally touch the base of the **Tree of Jesse** on the central column, accordingly known as the 'Pilgrim Pillar', and deeply worn down by millions of fingers over the centuries. On the other side of the pillar, facing the altar, is a figure of the **sculptor Mateo**, popularly known as the 'Saint of bumps on the head', as people knock heads with him in the belief that his talent is contagious. The interior is dominated by a silver Mexican altar and a dazzling 17th-century baroque altarpiece.

Four plazas surround the cathedral, each architectural gems in themselves. On the largest, the pigeon-populated **Praza do Obradoiro**, stand the impressive Hostal de los Reyes Católicos (the former hospital for pilgrims, now a parador) and the classical **Pazo de Raxoi** of 1772 (now the town hall). The Old City is tiny and everything of interest is easily accessible on foot.

ARRIVAL, INFORMATION, ACCOMMODATION

⇌ Rúa do Hórreo, 1 km south of the Old Town. Bus 6 goes into the centre, but it's quicker to walk ✈ 10 km from the centre, bus takes 25 mins. 🚌 Bus station: Estación Central de Autobuses, Praza de Camilo Díaz Baliño, bus 5 runs from Praza de Galicia. There is a good local bus system and route plans are posted at most stops. ❶ Tourist office: R. do Vilar 63 (www.santiagoturismo.com). From the station turn left up R. do Hórreo to Praza de Galicia.
⇤ During the three weeks leading up to the feast of St James on 25 July, the town is absolutely packed and you should book well in advance. Accommodation ranges from the 5-star **Hostal de los Reyes Católicos**, Praza do Obradoiro 1, ☎ 98 158 22 00 (www.parador.es), a magnificent 16th-century pilgrim hostel built by Ferdinand and Isabella, to an array of small, relatively inexpensive guest houses in both the old and new parts of the city. For budget accommodation in the Old Town, try around Rúa do Vilar and Rúa Raiña. A good mid-range option is the comfortable **Altair Hotel**, R. Loureiros 12, ☎ 98 155 47 12 (www.altairhotel.net). Good value for money and located in the Old Town, just a short walk from the Cathedral, is the stylish boutique **Hotel San Bieito**, R. San Bieito 1, ☎ 98 15 72 890 (www.ebrweb.eu/e). ✗ There are plenty of budget restaurants around the Old Town, especially on the streets leading south from the cathedral. Slightly further out of town, the Praza Roxa area, near the university, is very cheap.

CONNECTIONS FROM SANTIAGO

You can join **Route 16** and continue south through Galicia into Portugal. Although Santiago is no longer served directly by night trains, there are two excellent connections onto night trains. A local train shuttles down to Ourense, where passengers can join the *Galicia* night train to Barcelona. A separate train runs to Redondela de Galicia, giving a perfect connection onto the *Rías Gallegas* **overnight service** to Madrid. Both night trains mentioned here offer a choice of comfortable sleeping cars or second-class seats. Timings are in ERT 680.

Frequent trains from Santiago de Compostela run north to the coast at **A Coruña** (ERT 680), a lively port with particularly fine beaches. The very best excursion from Santiago will however require you forsake the train in favour of the bus. Six buses daily run west to **Fisterra**, a two to three-hour journey (see www.monbus.es). This takes in some fabulous rural Galician landscapes, ending on the Finisterre Peninsula. From Fisterra village, it is a 30 to 40-minute walk to **Cape Finisterre** – the remote headland which was for many centuries regarded as the very end of the world.

Route 16: The Atlantic coast of Iberia

CITIES: ★★★ CULTURE: ★★ HISTORY: ★★ SCENERY: ★★
COUNTRIES COVERED: SPAIN (ES), PORTUGAL (PT)
JOURNEY TIME: 6 HRS | DISTANCE: 616 KM | MAP: WWW.EBRWEB.EU/MAP16

Cast back to the mid-19th century and overland travel in Portugal was formidably difficult. The opening of the first railway in 1858 heralded a new era in Portuguese communication, giving inland communities access to the country's great ports at Porto and Lisbon.

Today, the railway is a fine way to **take the pulse of Portugal** and this route is designed to do just that. Route 16 is the sole journey in this book which crosses the **Spanish-Portuguese border**, but it is not the only way to reach Portugal by train. Bear in mind that there's also the excellent *Lusitania* hotel train, which leaves both Madrid and Lisbon every evening to give an overnight link between the two Iberian capital cities (ERT 45). Plans to link Madrid and Lisbon with a new high-speed line for daytime trains have stumbled with the Portuguese government refusing to fund the route on their side of the border.

The route described here starts in Spain at the lovely pilgrimage city of **Santiago de Compostela**, which lies at the end of **Route 15** in this book. Heading south, the train crosses into Portugal, taking in the beautiful coastal resort of Viana do Castelo the port-producing city of **Porto** and the old university town of Coimbra.

SUGGESTED ITINERARY

With the much improved cross-border train service these days, it is now possible to take a morning train from Santiago de Compostela and be in the Portuguese capital by early afternoon. With a day or two to spare though, you might profitably stop off here and there on the journey south. Porto would be our top choice for an intermediate stop. If you have time for a longer stop in northern Portugal, then you may want to venture inland from Porto to explore the scenic and deeply rural **Douro Valley**.

South through Galicia

For more on **Santiago de Compostela** see p167. Train services running south from the city were radically improved in 2015 with the modernisation of the line to Vigo. It is certainly an impressive piece of engineering, and it has trimmed the travel time between Santiago and Vigo, but it'll take a few years for the line to settle into the landscape. At the moment, the cuttings and embankments all look a little raw. Older parts of the route which meandered through the hills have been replaced by dead-straight tunnels. But there are still some good views, especially as the railway bridges major valleys on the run south and at one point (just beyond Padrón) follows the **River Ulla**. Sit on the right for the best views.

Route details

Santiago de Compostela to Vigo Guixar		ERT 680
Frequency	Journey time	Notes
6–8 per day	1 hr 30 mins	A

Vigo Guixar to Porto Campanhã		ERT 696
Frequency	Journey time	Notes
2 per day	2 hrs 20 mins	R

Porto Campanhã to Lisbon Santa Apólonia		ERT 690
Frequency	Journey time	Notes
Hourly	2 hrs 45 mins – 3 hrs 10 mins	R

Notes

A – In addition to the trains to Guixar station in Vigo, there are also direct Media Distancia (MD) trains from Santiago de Compostela to Vigo Urzáiz. These MD trains run 11 times each day and take 50–65 mins for the journey to Vigo. Advance reservation is required.
R – Reservation compulsory

RAILWAY STATIONS IN VIGO

Vigo's main railway station is called **Vigo Urzáiz**. It reopened in 2015 after **major refurbishment**, but many trains are still using the temporary station (called Vigo Guixar and located closer to the waterfront) which was constructed to allow trains to still serve Vigo during the Urzáiz closure. As of late 2019, the trains to Portugal still leave from **Vigo Guixar**. If you arrive in Vigo on a fast train from Santiago (ie. one with the prefix MD), then it will run to Urzáiz station. But if you travel from Santiago de Compostela on a slow train (any service taking more than 70 minutes), you'll arrive at Vigo Guixar. If you do need to change stations in Vigo, note that it takes 12 to 15 minutes to walk from Urzáiz to Guixar.

The principal town of note between Santiago and Vigo is **Pontevedra** which began life as a port, but its importance dwindled as the old harbour silted up. Although surrounded by a new city, the compact **Old Town** is pretty much intact, with parts of the original walls still visible around a maze of cobbled streets, arcaded squares with carved stone crosses and low houses with flower-filled balconies. **Iglesia de la Virgen Peregrina**, an unusual chapel with a floor plan in the shape of a scallop shell, is situated by the partly arcaded main square, Praza da Ferrería, on the boundary between the Old and New Towns. The railway station is a 12-minute walk south-east of the centre.

When following Route 16, it is always necessary to change trains at **Vigo**. The town is a major fishing port and lies on a beautiful sheltered bay. It's a clamorous, busy place built of grey granite, not immediately attractive except in the old, sloping quarter near the seafront. **Castro Castle**, the ruined fort on a hill just above the town, provides a fine view. The wonderfully unspoilt **Islas Cíes archipelago**, reached by ferry from Vigo from June till the end of September and during the Easter Week, is the main reason for stopping here. Designated a national park, the islands have white sands and rugged hilltops, with enough trails to provide a day's walking on the main two isles (which are joined together by a sandbank).

The Celta train to Portugal

The fortunes of the rail route from **Vigo to Porto** have ebbed and flowed over the last 50 years. Like many rural **cross-border** rail links in Europe, there has been talk of closure including serious discussions in 2012. That the route has survived has been mainly due to the dedicated support of local activists in the Minho region — the portion of north-west Portugal which abuts onto the Spanish border. The line was happily reprieved, with a renewed commitment by the regional authorities in both **Galicia and Minho** to improving services between Vigo and Porto.

In summer 2013, the service was relaunched under the *Celta* brand. It is a name which nicely appeals on both sides of the border, for residents of the Minho and Galicia regions are justifiably proud of their Atlantic heritage, communicated through maritime links along the seaways which connect the major Celtic regions of Europe. Football supporters of **FC Porto** do however have to endure the oft-repeated jibe that the new train service is named in honour of their rivals **Celta Vigo** on the Spanish side of the border.

The current timetable (ERT 696) shows that the trains maintain a decent pace — indeed, a positive dash compared with the timings of yesteryear. Cast back to 1965, and the morning train from Vigo to Porto took over six hours. Ten years ago, it still took over three hours. Today, trains on this route take little more than two hours.

The first part of the run out of Vigo follows the estuary upstream until the train turns south at **Redondela**, cutting through soft hill country to reach the Minho Valley and the Portuguese border. The last place in Spain is the tiered town of **Tui**, from where there's a road and rail bridge across the Minho to **Valença** in Portugal. Remember to set your watch back by one hour for Portuguese time.

The next stretch of the route is very pleasant as the railway runs beside the Minho down to the coast, following the Costa Verde south to the old fortress town and resort of **Viana do Castelo**, with the beach on one side of the River Lima and the charming little town – noted for its Renaissance and Manueline architecture, which appeared when trade began with the great Hanseatic cities of northern Europe – on the other.

With the exception of Santa Luzia on the top of the **Monte de Santa Luzia** (accessible by funicular from its beautifully restored station on Avda. 25 de Abril; excellent view), all of Viana do Castelo's interesting sights are walkable. The central square, **Praça da República**, has a 16th-century fountain that has been copied all over the region. If you are looking for a quiet place to stop for a day or two, we can especially recommend the *pousada* by the basilica at Santa Luzia.

South from Viana do Castelo, the railway runs inland before returning to the coast at **Porto**. The train terminates at **Campanhã** where the station facade, with its Romanesque windows and imposing station clock, exudes quiet authority. Do take a look and then, if you are heading for the city centre, take the local train (not shown in ERT) which runs four times each hour to **São Bento station** in the very middle of Porto.

Porto (suggested stopover)

Portugal's seductive second city, Porto (sometimes Oporto in English), is spectacularly sited on the steep banks of the **River Douro**. It gives its name to the fortified wine the English-speaking world knows as port (fortuitously invented by two Englishmen who used brandy in an attempt to preserve Portuguese wine).

Get your bearings by climbing the **Torre dos Clérigos**, Porto's symbol, an 18th-century granite bell tower that gives a magnificent view. Below, the characterfully **fading Old Town**, with its pastel shades and changes in level, is strongly atmospheric, notably in the Ribeira riverside area. The **Soares dos Reis Museum** (closed Mon), housed in the Carrancas Palace, is acclaimed for its collection of decorative arts, including Portuguese faience.

For an astonishing temple to money-making, take the guided tour of the centrally located **Palácio da Bolsa** (former Stock Exchange, now headquarters of the Chamber of Commerce, www.palaciodabolsa.com), rather grey and boring-looking from outside but revealing a lavish interior which includes the Arabian Hall, a 19th-century gilded evocation of the Alhambra in Granada. The nearby **Church of Santa Clara** is a fine example of the Manueline style and has a dazzling baroque interior.

The **vineyards** themselves are a long way upriver in the magnificently scenic Douro Valley, but most of the port is aged in the numerous lodges in the district of **Vila Nova de Gaia**, linked to the city centre by the double-decker coathanger-shaped Dom Luís I Bridge; walk over on the top level for dizzying views. Many lodges offer tours with **tastings** and booking is not generally necessary. Some are closed at weekends outside the main season. Some lodges levy a small charge, often as little as €3, but with the option to upgrade if you wish to taste more illustrious wines.

Having visited many of the **lodges**, the three we especially recommend to get a sense of port and its history are those at Taylor's, Ramos Pinto (which has a wonderful small museum on wine) and Graham's, where the guides are especially good and show amazing prowess in many different languages. Moored on the river, small barrel-laden sailing craft (*barcos rabelos*), last used in 1967, serve as a reminder of how the young ports used to be brought downriver from the vineyards.

In Porto, we have a nice instance of a railway station being a sight in its own right. The city's more central station at **São Bento** celebrated in 2016 the centenary of the opening of the current building. With its spectacularly painted glazed tiles (known as *azulejos*), São Bento is one of Europe's truly great railway stations. It may lack the grandeur of other notable stations (see our **Sidetracks** feature on p176), but the elaborate tiling in the main reception hall is something very special.

ARRIVAL, INFORMATION, ACCOMMODATION

⇬ **Campanhã**, Rua da Estação, near the south-east edge of town, serves trains from Lisbon and Vigo (local train or metro to the city centre). **São Bento**, near Praça da Liberdade, handles local/regional services. Frequent connections between the stations, taking 5 mins.

EXCURSIONS FROM PORTO

Do explore the mountain-backed **Douro Valley** east of Porto (ERT 694), with its many **vineyards** as well as some enchanting places accessible by train. Even if you are pushed for time, consider at least taking the train up the Douro Valley to **Pinhão** and back. It takes two-and-a-half hours each way. Sit on the right for the best views and certainly plan to spend a couple of hours or more in the riverside town which is dedicated entirely to the production, marketing and consumption of port.

North-east of Porto, **Guimarães** (ERT 695a) was once the Portuguese capital and contains a nice mediaeval core despite the unpromising industrial outskirts. Another excellent outing from Porto is to join pilgrims looking for absolution from their sins in **Braga**, little more than an hour away by train (ERT 695). The real draw in Braga is the monumental **Bom Jesus do Monte** shrine in a wonderful wooded setting on the hills east of the town. Braga rates alongside Međugorje (Bosnia & Herzegovina), Knock (Ireland) and Częstochowa (Poland) in hosting some of the best penitential theatre in Europe.

✈ Francisco Sá Carneiro, 11 km outside Porto (www.ana.pt). Metro line E links the airport with the city centre. 🛈 Tourist office: R. Clube dos Fenianos 25 (www.visitporto.travel). Tickets for Porto's public transport system are sold at STCP kiosks. The city has three tram lines and six metro lines. For information on public transport see www.stcp.pt. The **Museu do Carro Eléctrico** is a vintage tram that tours the city from near the Church of São Francisco (www.museudocarroelectrico.pt; closed Mon mornings). ⛴ 50-min boat trips depart from Praça da Ribeira, touring the River Douro.

🛏 For cheap lodgings, try the central area around Av. dos Aliados. Avoid the dockside Ribeira. Located between the Ribeira and São Bento station in the historic centre is the very welcoming **InPatio** guest house, Pátio de São Salvador 22, ☎ 222 085 477 (www.inpatio.pt). Or try the elegant **Porta Azul** B&B, R. Dom Manuel II, 204, ☎ 224 037 706 (www.porta-azul.com), close to the Jardins do Palácio de Cristal. The **Spot Hostel**, R. de Gonçalo Cristóvão 12, ☎ 224 085 205 (www.spothostel.pt), is a firm favourite on the European hostelling circuit.

Onward to Lisbon

The train journey from **Porto to Lisbon** is an interesting transect from north to south, with a strong sense of entering gentler, sunnier landscapes. Although the initial stretch is along the coast, the railway quickly turns inland. It is pleasant, undemanding terrain.

The first major city south of Porto is **Coimbra**, a centre of the Portuguese Renaissance and the seat of one of the oldest universities in the world. Set on a hillside above the **River Mondego**, the town is packed with mediaeval character; in term time it has a lively, youthful air. Coimbra has its own version of the **fado**, a melancholic, monotonous and sentimental chant originally sung by sailors in the 18th century.

From Coimbra, there is an alternative route south along the coast to Lisbon (ERT 693), but the main line takes a more easterly course to reach the **Tejo Valley** which it then follows downstream to Lisbon. All trains stop first at Lisbon Oriente station, a striking modern design by **Santiago Calatrava**, with most services then continuing to Santa Apolónia station in the city centre.

Lisbon

The Portuguese capital is a city on a human scale, and its immediately **likeable atmosphere** is the gateway to a rich cultural background. History and politics are inscribed on its soul and written into its unique geography. Get up high on the **Elevador de Santa Justa** and look out over the cobbled, hilly streets and hotchpotch of roofs and alleyways that cover Lisbon's seven hills. At one end of the city you'll see the **Castelo de São Jorge**, towering over an area that forms a powerful historical and architectural reminder of the city's reclamation from the Moors. At the other end of Lisbon, the 1960s Padrão dos Descobrimentos is a monument to its maritime glories.

Located at the mouth of the Rio Tejo (River Tagus), the city has a rich gastronomy influenced both by the sea and by its imperial history. In the streets you'll smell **roasting chestnuts** and freshly baked custard tarts, and in the restaurants they'll serve up salted cod or fresh sardines washed down with young vinho verde wine and fiery after-dinner **ginjinha**. Fado music and other sounds fill the air in the historic **Bairro Alto**. However you like to spend your days and evenings, immerse yourself in Lisbon's enticing atmosphere and you're sure to find something to entertain you.

ARRIVAL, INFORMATION, ACCOMMODATION

⇌ **Santa Apolónia** station, on the banks of the Tagus near Alfama, is the main station, handling all international trains and those to east and north Portugal. All trains to and from Santa Apolónia also call at the **Gare Intermodal do Oriente**, where there is an interchange with the metro system. From Oriente take the metro (changing at Alameda) to Rossio or Baixa-Chiado, the main areas for accommodation. **Cais do Sodré** station doubles as the quay for the Tagus ferries and as the station handling the local coastal services. ✈ Lisbon Portela Airport (www.ana.pt) is 7 km north of the city, with a metro connection to the city centre (Saldanha).

Public transport in Lisbon is cheap, efficient and varied, consisting of buses, trams, the metro and funiculars (*elevadores*) between different levels of the city. Make a point of getting a walking map of the labyrinthine Alfama district. The metro is fast, frequent... and cool! Trams are still an integral part of the city and easy to use. Tickets for single trips on buses operated by Carris cost €2 on board and trams €3 (www.carris.pt), cheaper fares can be obtained by buying and charging a 7 Colinas / Viva Viagem card. ℹ The main tourist office is in the Lisboa Story Center, at Praça do Comércio 78–81 (www.visitlisboa.com); also one at Santa Apolónia station.

🛏 Accommodation is scarcest and priciest at Easter and in summer. The vast majority of cheap places are in the centre of town, on and around Avda Liberdade or the Baixa. In the latter, head for the three squares Praça da Figueira, Praça dos Restauradores and Praça Dom Pedro IV. A comfortable B&B near Rossio Square is the **Lisbon Story Guesthouse**, Largo de São Domingos 18, ☎ 218 879 392 (www.lisbonstoryguesthouse.com). Cheap it may not be, but for the amazing public spaces alone, try the elegant **Hotel Avenida Palace**, r. 1 Dezembro, 123, ☎ 213 218 100 (www.hotelavenidapalace.pt), in a great central location. A friendly and quiet guest house in the Bairro Alto district is the **Casa do Bairro**, Beco Caldeira 1, ☎ 914 176 969 (www.shiadu.com/casa-bairro-overview).

CONNECTIONS FROM LISBON

From Lisbon you can travel by direct overnight train to Burgos (on **Route 15**), Madrid (on **Route 14**) and Irún (on **Route 10**). The times for all these are in ERT 45. The overnight train to Hendaye in France has good onward connections by TGV to Bordeaux and Paris.

But if you have followed Route 16 all the way to Lisbon, you may want to linger in Portugal. A good day trip by train from Lisbon is to **Évora** (ERT 698), the capital of the Alentejo region and one of the nicest places in the entire country. This walled city, with its distinctive whitewashed houses with tile work and balconies, is inscribed on UNESCO's List of World Heritage Sites.

Looking south from Lisbon, there are fast trains down to **Faro** (ERT 697) on the Algarve, from where there are local trains along the coast, running west to Lagos (ERT 697) and east to Vila Real de Santo António (ERT 697a), a small town right on the Spanish border. Ferries shuttle over the border to Ayamonte in Spain. There are direct buses from Faro and Vila Real to **Seville** (ERT 676), where you can join **Route 13**.

SIDETRACKS: GRAND STATIONS

Even in the earliest days of train travel, railway stations were more than merely functional. In great cities, the principal termini made **bold statements** about style, status and ambition.

On rural rail routes in country areas, the **design of stations** was often equally symbolic though usually more geared to communicating a sense of domesticity and order. Here was the railway as part of the community, sometimes adapting the best of regional **vernacular architecture** to its own purposes and in other cases deploying standard designs which reminded villagers in far-flung parts of the network that they, too, were now connected to 'the centre' – be it a pivot of art and culture or a great centre of **imperial power**. Many rural railway stations in Finland date from the tsarist period and even today look like stage sets for 19th-century Russia while some country stations in south-west Poland – in territory which until 1945 was German – still have echoes of Prussian authority.

Yet it was in Europe's cities that railway stations were at their most opulent and eclectic. The railway reshaped geography and used architectural whimsy to create a kaleidoscope of exotic design. Travellers arriving in **Liverpool** on the world's first passenger railway were greeted by a Moorish Arch. In London the station at **Euston**, with its glorious Doric *propylaeum*, may have seduced some passengers into thinking that they had been magically transported to Rome.

Sadly, both the Liverpool and Euston structures are long gone. But the last 20 years have seen a happy renaissance of interest in early railway architecture. The restoration in London of **St Pancras** has been so beautifully executed that this station attracts many visitors who have no intention of catching a train. It is an exuberant starting point for **Route 6** in this book. Across the continent, many other grand termini have been restored. **Antwerp Centraal** (on **Route 17**) once again looks as splendid as it did on the day it first opened. Its extraordinary main reception hall and bold facade, Mannerist in style, may have a few too many gilded trophies for some tastes, but it is a space that can only be approached with reverence. To these outstanding examples of recent **landmark renovations**, we might add in a handful of other grand termini where a missed connection gives good cause to just sit and look at the extravagant space around you: Leipzig Hauptbahnhof, Milan Centrale, Limoges-Bénédictins, Paris Est and Moscow Kazanskaya all deserve a place on any list of Europe's great stations.

Sometimes it is just one aspect of a station which commands attention: the delicate lattice facade at Porta Nuova station in Turin, the **decorative ceilings** and stained glass at Groningen, the superb tile work at Estació del Nord in València or at **São Bento station** in Porto, the covered plaza and indoor garden in the old part of Atocha station in Madrid and the art nouveau interiors at Vitebsky station in St Petersburg.

Of course, not all of Europe's grand stations are old. Our home city of Berlin has in its Hauptbahnhof (opened in 2006) a very fine modern cathedral devoted to trains. Other modern stations which invite **comparison with cathedrals** are Liège-Guillemins and Lisbon Oriente, both soaring structures designed by Santiago Calatrava. If you find yourself travelling through any of the stations mentioned here, why not stop off for an hour and take a look around?

THE LOW COUNTRIES AND THE RHINE
An introduction

In the heyday of the **Grand Tour**, affluent young Englishmen (and they were almost always men!) set out to complete their education by exploring the continent. The goal was usually Italy, but the first staging post was invariably the Rhineland – and that meant passing through the Low Countries along the way. It's no surprise that when **Thomas Cook** wrote his first travel guide in 1873, this was the region on which he focused as he bundled the River Rhine in with the Low Countries. We do just the same here.

This is generally good territory for holders of **rail passes** (such as Eurail and Interrail), as very few trains require advance reservation or supplements. Provided you avoid Thalys trains, you can roam at will throughout the Netherlands, Belgium, Luxembourg and adjacent areas of Germany. If you venture into nearby areas of France (as **Route 19** does in this section) then you'll never need to bother about advance reservations or supplements as long as you stick to regional trains (ie. TER services) and avoid TGVs.

There is one **absolute classic journey** in this section of *Europe by Rail*. That's **Route 20** which follows the Rhine upstream from Cologne and then continues through Heidelberg and the **Black Forest to Switzerland**. With the development of the railways in the 19th century it was this itinerary which pulled the crowds. More than a century and a half later, it's still a very fine journey, though nowadays often missed by travellers who make haste to get to the Alps.

Rural diversions

Equally, there's a tendency these days to just dash through the Netherlands and Belgium and to skip Luxembourg altogether. All three countries deserve more. Make time for small towns in the Netherlands. Harlingen, Delft and Middelburg are among our favourites; all three are easily reached by train. There are some **delightfully rural rail routes** in south-east Belgium and Luxembourg. **Route 19** follows one of these on the leg from Liège to Luxembourg.

Once in Germany, remember that the tributaries of the Rhine are often as engaging as the main river. We make mention of the **Moselle** (see p206) and **Route 20** takes in part of the Neckar Valley around Heidelberg. But there are others. In summer 2017, we explored the rail routes around the **Main Valley** upstream from Frankfurt. The rural route from Aschaffenburg to Wertheim (ERT 926) is a gem. The Black Forest's dense network of rural railways offers much scope. Over on the west bank of the Rhine, there's an exceptionally pretty railway running up the Bruche Valley from **Strasbourg into the Vosges**, though trains are infrequent (ERT 388). ∎

Route 17: Through Flanders to Holland

CITIES: ★★★ CULTURE: ★★ HISTORY: ★★ SCENERY: ★
COUNTRIES COVERED: FRANCE (FR), BELGIUM (BE), NETHERLANDS (NL)
JOURNEY TIME: 6 HRS | DISTANCE: 368 KM | MAP: WWW.EBRWEB.EU/MAP17

We like this route. Of course, we like all the routes in this book, but we *especially* like this one. It's short and sweet, taking in a **feast of fine cities** as well as, especially in the early stages, some **engaging rustic landscapes**. It's not a route where you need ever bother about advance booking and, if you are travelling with a Eurail or Interrail pass, there are no supplements to pay on any trains you'll use in taking this journey.

The Huguenot leader **Henri de Rohan** remarked that "he who expects any good to come from living in a land which lies lower than the sea, that in winter is a vast layer of ice and in summer a swamp, must go to Holland." So in this journey, we'll follow Henri's advice and take the train **to Holland**. Our journey starts in Flanders, in the great city of Lille – once home to many Huguenots who variously moved to Switzerland, Prussia and eastern England to escape religious persecution. Read more on Lille on p185.

RECOMMENDED ITINERARY

This journey is split into a number of shortish legs; any of the cities along the way are worthy of a stopover. If you like the buzz of big cities, then Antwerp and Rotterdam are good options for **overnight stops**. But our top choices would be two smaller communities, namely Bruges (in Belgium) and The Hague/Den Haag (in the Netherlands).

Hourly trains run along the entire length of Route 17, even at weekends. You can follow the route with just three **easy changes of train**, viz. at Kortrijk, Bruges and Antwerp. You can of course cut corners and use high-speed trains to skip parts of our recommended journey. And if all you want to do is to dash from Lille to Amsterdam, twice-daily Thalys trains will get you there in less than three hours. But of course you'll miss all manner of good things along the way.

You can tell that Route 17 has promise when you arrive at **Lille Flandres** station to start the journey. It's an elegant old-style terminus. The Flandres suffix was added to the name in 1993 when the nearby Lille Europe station was opened. While the latter is brash, bold and cosmopolitan, Lille Flandres has a homely, regional feel.

The cross-border rail route to **Kortrijk** (Courtrai in French) is run by the Belgian national rail operator SNCB. The train heads north through industrial edgelands, **crossing into Belgium** just beyond Tourcoing. At Kortrijk, it is always necessary to change onto another regional train for Bruges. At one level, there is something very ordinary about these **Flemish landscapes** – but that prosaic quality is exactly what inspired the artists who lived and worked in the region. Whether it be a line of poplars with a ruined cottage or a lone Bruegelesque tree by a waterway, the everyday scenes of this region were a source of wonder for some of Europe's most celebrated artists.

Notes

A – Most journeys require a change of train at Rotterdam Centraal.
B – Most trains from Den Haag to Amsterdam stop at Leiden Centraal 12 mins after leaving Den Haag HS or Den Haag Centraal.
C – There are in addition two trains each hour from Den Haag Centraal to Amsterdam Centraal.
X – On all journeys from Lille Flandres to Bruges, a change of train at Kortrijk is necessary.

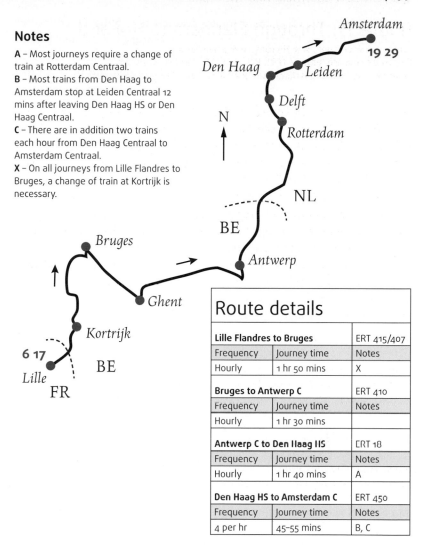

Route details

Lille Flandres to Bruges		ERT 415/407
Frequency	Journey time	Notes
Hourly	1 hr 50 mins	X

Bruges to Antwerp C		ERT 410
Frequency	Journey time	Notes
Hourly	1 hr 30 mins	

Antwerp C to Den Haag HS		ERT 18
Frequency	Journey time	Notes
Hourly	1 hr 40 mins	A

Den Haag HS to Amsterdam C		ERT 450
Frequency	Journey time	Notes
4 per hr	45–55 mins	B, C

Bruges (Brugge) – (suggested stopover)

A powerful trading city 500 years ago, Bruges became an economic back-water and the industrial age largely passed it by. Located **in the heart of Flanders**, Bruges is one of northern Europe's most impressive surviving mediaeval cities. A **boat trip** on the extensive and pretty canal system is a good introduction to the town, with frequent departures from quays along Dijver which, along with Groenerei and Rozenhoedkaai, provide some of the vintage views of Bruges.

 Markt, Bruges' large, lively and impressive main square, is surrounded by guild buildings, many of which have been converted into restaurants and bars. The Burg, the other main square, features the **Heilig Bloedbasiliek** (Basilica of the Holy Blood), with an early 12th-century stone chapel below a 16th-century chapel. Bruges' historic centre was inscribed on the UNESCO World Heritage List in 2000. Dijver is the central canal and the road that parallels it (scene of a weekend antiques and flea market) is home to several museums. **Groeningemuseum** (closed Mon) houses a fine collection of Flemish art from the 15th century to the present.

Don't forget to take a walk around the walled religious village of the **Begijnhof**. The houses where Beguine nuns lived, as well as other single women or widows who opted for living within the community, are neatly arranged near the **Minnewater**, a tranquil, swan-populated lake.

ARRIVAL, INFORMATION, ACCOMMODATION

⇌ A 20-min walk south-west of the centre; buses stop in front (tickets and a free route map from the De Lijn kiosk). Tickets can also be purchased from the driver or at a ticket machine. To the right as you leave the station is a branch of the tourist office. ⓘ Tourist office: Markt 1 (www.visitbruges.be).

⇥ A duo of reasonably priced B&Bs are the stylish and friendly **Charming Brugge**, Komvest 13 (www.charmingbrugge.be), and the **Huis't Schaep**, Korte Vuldersstraat 14, ☎ 050 34 06 30 (www.huishetschaep.be), which is conveniently located for both the station and the city centre. Or try the **Hotel Fevery**, Collaert Mansionstraat 3, ☎ 050 33 12 69 (www.hotelfevery.be), a short walk north of the market square.

CONNECTIONS FROM BRUGES

Note that in the ERT or in online journey planners, the city's name is usually rendered in its Dutch form, Brugge, rather than the French toponym Bruges, which we use in this book as that French version has wider currency among English speakers. Bruges has excellent connections with **the coast**. Ostend (ERT 400, 407 & 410) and Knokke (ERT 405) are both just about 20 minutes away. You can connect in either with the **Belgian coastal tramway**, a rather surreal route which extends the entire length of the Belgian coast. Read more in our **Sidetracks** feature on p184.

There are three trains per hour from Bruges to Brussels (ERT 400 & 405), where you can connect onto **Route 18** to Germany. From Bruges there is also an hourly train to Liège (ERT 400), to connect into **Route 19** to Luxembourg, Alsace and Switzerland. Bruges is closer to England than you may think. A bus leaves the station at 17.30 for nearby **Zeebrugge** to connect into the P&O overnight sailing to Hull (ERT 2250).

From Bruges, it's a pleasant ride east **across Belgian Flanders** to Antwerp, along the way passing through **Ghent** (Gent in Dutch), a pleasant Flemish university city, rich in culture and very lively during term time. The 12th–17th-century guild houses along the Graslei quay and the old houses by the Kraanlei quay provide two of the city's classic views. The main station, Gent-St-Pieters, is south of the city centre.

Belgium's second city, **Antwerp** (Antwerpen/Anvers) has an extensive old Flemish quarter, a rich Jewish heritage and is at the cutting edge of diamonds and fashion. Nowhere else in Belgium is so thoroughly dedicated to being cool. Even the moment of arrival is something special. The trains

THE BACK-DOOR ROUTE TO HOLLAND

Travellers heading north from Bruges into Holland have an alternative to that described in Route 17. Instead of looping east through Antwerp, take the hourly bus to **Breskens**, a port on a sliver of Dutch territory on the south side of the Westerschelde Estuary (ERT 499). Bus 42 leaves from Stand 7 outside Bruges railway station. The bus connects perfectly with a **ferry to Vlissingen** (also ERT 499), from where trains run every half hour to Rotterdam and Den Haag (ERT 450). This route affords fine views of watery Zeeland landscapes. **Middelburg** (seven minutes from Vlissingen on the train) is wonderful, one of the nicest Dutch towns we know.

from Bruges always arrive on the uppermost level of Antwerpen Centraal station, usually on Platform 1. This is **one of Europe's great railway stations**. The platforms are on three levels and your onward train to Rotterdam and Den Haag will leave from the lowest level. But take time to look around the station and this famously tolerant city on the River Schelde. Antwerp hit the headlines in 2011 with the opening of the **Museum aan de Stroom**, Hanzestedenplaats 1 (www.mas.be; closed Mon) in the Eilandje district of the city's old port. It is dedicated to the city's connections with the world. Just take trams 3/5/9/15 to 'Linkeroever' from Antwerpen Centraal station, alighting at 'Meir'. The Royal Museum of Fine Arts (KMSKA) is currently closed for major renovations. It is expected to open again in 2021.

North into Holland

The hourly Intercity train service from Brussels and Antwerp to Amsterdam is often called the *Beneluxtrein* or in Belgium sometimes the *Amsterdammer*. It is a hop-on and ride service, unlike the competing and faster Thalys trains which speed across the border. But its very flexibility is what makes the *Beneluxtrein* so popular. We can follow it the whole way to Amsterdam via Rotterdam and Den Haag. It is a largely urban route, but you'll still see those **staples of the Dutch landscape**: windmills, canals and glasshouses. Parts of the route really are below sea level, crossing reclaimed land which relies on dykes for protection.

Rotterdam was virtually flattened in the Second World War, but much of its modern architecture is strikingly innovative (**Lijnbaan** was the European pioneer of shopping precincts, for example). Situated at the delta of the rivers Rhine, Maas and Waal, **Europoort** is the world's largest container port. Rotterdam Centraal is located on the northern edge of the centre (on the city's blue metro line).

Long famed for **Delftware porcelain** and birthplace of the artist Vermeer, **Delft** is an elegant town with old merchants' houses lining the canal. It has a number of porcelain factories where you can watch production; the oldest is De Koninklijke Porceleyne Fles (Rotterdamseweg 196), but more central is Aardewerkfabriek de Candelaer (Kerkstr. 13). **Nieuwe Kerk** (New Church) houses the huge black-and-white marble mausoleum of Prince William, and its 109-m spire provides great views.

Den Haag – (suggested stopover)

Den Haag (The Hague) is the **administrative capital** of the Netherlands and a pleasant town, spread over a wide area of parks and canals and centred around the **Binnenhof**, home of the Dutch parliament, just a short walk from the station (or take trams 2/3/4/6 to 'Spui' and walk from there). Most of the city's palaces can be viewed only from the outside. An exception is the huge **Vredespaleis** (Peace Palace), Carnegieplein 2 (tram 1, 🚌 24), which houses the International Court of Justice and the Permanent Court of Arbitration. It's a strange architectural mishmash, with a display of items donated by world leaders. It is open Tues–Sun 10.00–17.00 (Nov–Mar 11.00–16.00); guided tours need to be pre-booked at www.vredespaleis.nl.

Make time to visit the seaside town of **Scheveningen**, which is effectively part of Den Haag. The pretty fishing port which inspired 17th-century Dutch artists is still there, but nowadays surrounded by all the commerce and attractions which sustain Scheveningen's reputation as a great place for sun, sea and sand.

ARRIVAL, INFORMATION, ACCOMMODATION

≈ Centraal (CS) is a 7-min walk from the centre and serves most Dutch cities. Fast services for Amsterdam and Rotterdam use HS (Hollands Spoor) station (1 km south). Centraal and HS are linked by frequent trains and by tram 9 or 17. 🚺 Tourist office: Spui 68 (www. denhaag.com). There is an excellent bus and tram network. A rechargeable OV-chipkaart is required to travel on public transport (available at the station). 🛏 Very comfortable is the privately run **Paleis Hotel**, Molenstraat 26, ☎ 070 362 46 21 (www.paleishotel.nl). Just a short walk from the city centre towards the beach in Scheveningen is the **Hotel Pistache**, Scheveningseweg 1, ☎ 06 152 169 41 (www.hotelpistache.com), which offers apartments for 2-6 people. Or try the friendly boutique hotel **La Paulowna**, Anna Paulownaplein 3, ☎ 070 450 0091 (www.lapaulowna.com) which also has a good restaurant.

Birthplace of Rembrandt, **Leiden** has a mediaeval quarter, centred on the vast Pieterskerk, plenty of studenty haunts and some excellent museums, covering archaeology, local history and art. In the Boerhaave, Lange St Agnietenstr. 10, is an **anatomical theatre**, complete with skeletons and displays of early medical paraphernalia. The university, founded in 1575, includes the world's oldest botanical gardens.

Amsterdam

Amsterdam has always been a city that has attracted outsiders, whether tourists, philosophers, immigrants or hippies. **Romantic and laid-back,** what makes Amsterdam so special is its combination of a beautiful setting with a **vibrant and youthful street life** that reflects Dutch society's culture of tolerance. Yes, the red-light district and the 'coffee shops' will not be to everyone's taste, but thankfully Amsterdam is much more than just sex and smoking, and if you give yourself the time to explore you will discover a city that is home to marvellously varied **museums and galleries**, as well as leafy parks and a network of canals lined with elegant gabled brick houses that rivals Venice in its beauty. The **Rembrandt House Museum** (www. rembrandthuis.nl) marked the 350th anniversary of Rembrandt's death in 2019 with special exhibitions devoted to the life and work of the artist.

The city centre is wonderful for walking, and there is a series of **sign-posted walking routes** to help you find your way. It is useful to grab one of the maps from the tourist office, as Amsterdam's layout can be confusing; bear in mind that *gracht* means 'canal' and that the centre follows the horseshoe shape dictated by the **ring canals**. The entire central area of the city was inscribed on the UNESCO World Heritage List in 2010.

ARRIVAL, INFORMATION, ACCOMMODATION

Centraal is the terminal for most trains and a 5-min walk north of Dam (the central area). Amsterdam Airport Schiphol (www.schiphol.com) is about 14 km south-west of town. Transfers by train to/from Centraal are the cheapest: at least every 10 mins 06.00–24.00 (hourly 24.00–06.00); journey time 15 mins.

Tourist office: Stationsplein 10, opposite Centraal station (www.iamsterdam.com). You can cross Amsterdam's central canal hub on foot in about an hour and walking is a pleasant way of getting around. Regarding regular public transport, the **tram** is the easiest and the most popular option. The network (www.gvb.nl) covers the city centre, with 14 lines running until 00.30. Buy a rechargeable OV chipkaart at GVB ticket machines or service desks. There's a **metro** within the city centre, designed mainly to access the suburbs. Three lines (51, 53 and 54) run between Centraal Station, Nieuwmarkt and Waterlooplein, the city centre stops most likely to interest visitors. A new north-south metro line opened in 2018.

Otherwise just do as the locals do and get on your **bike**. MacBike (five locations, including Centraal Station), www.macbike.nl, is open daily and prices for bike rental start at €9.75 per day, although the longer period you book, the cheaper the daily rate becomes.

Amsterdam is a small, old city but a popular one and there isn't really enough accommodation to deal with the huge numbers of visitors on peak days. Book well ahead, especially at weekends and in summer, and don't expect to find anything really cheap. A converted 1672 canal house is home to the welcoming **Keizershof**, Keizersgracht 618, ☎ 020 622 28 55 (www.hotelkeizershof.nl). A good B&B with strikingly quirky interiors is the **Barangay**, Herenstraat 26, ☎ 062 504 54 32 (www.barangay.nl), conveniently located close to the station. Or try the cozy and friendly **The Neighbour's Magnolia**, Willemsparkweg 205, ☎ 020 676 93 21 (www.magnoliahotelamsterdam.com), close to the Vondelpark and the Van Gogh Museum.

AMSTERDAM CONNECTIONS

You can connect here into two other routes in this book. **Route 19** runs south through the Ardennes region of eastern Belgium to Luxembourg and beyond. **Route 29** runs through Germany and Denmark to Norway. There's a wide choice of direct trains from Amsterdam Centraal station, including regular departures to Berlin (ERT 22) and Cologne (ERT 28).

Sidetracks: Coastal Tramway

Belgium's Coastal Tramway (*Kusttram*) is the **world's longest tram route**. And it confers on Belgium the distinction of being the only country on the planet where the entire coastline can be surveyed in a single tram ride. From the French border near **Plopsaland** to the dune landscapes of **Knokke** on the Dutch border it is about 70 kilometres, and the Coastal Tramway takes in the entire coast, with about 70 tram stops along the way.

The first section of Belgium's Coastal Tramway was opened in 1885, with most of the existing route being completed by the First World War. The extension south from the coast at De Panne to serve the theme park of Plopsaland and the railway station at **Adinkerke** was opened only in 1998.

The tram links into the Belgian national railway network at each end of its route (viz. at De Panne station in Adinkerke at the western end and at Knokke-Heist station at the eastern end). It also stops outside the rail stations at **Ostend** and **Blankenberge**.

Some countries are best understood by their coastlines. **Paul Theroux** in *The Kingdom by the Sea* came to terms with Britain by exploring its coastline. Some authors even invented coastlines for landlocked countries. Didn't **Shakespeare** in *The Winter's Tale* make reference to travelling by ship to Bohemia? But no one needed to invent the Belgian coast. It is magnificent, all 145 minutes of it.

The tram ride is one of Europe's most engaging pieces of cinema. Rattling down the main street of De Panne, cutting through the forest at Koksijde, speeding along the coastal promenade east of **Middelkerke**, lurching through the streets of Oostende and slipping past back gardens on the final run into Knokke.

All Belgian life is captured in this run along the coast, from gnomes at Plopsaland to a hundred tearooms where people linger for hours over a coffee or a Leffe beer. Kings, mainly called Leopold and occasionally Albert, make cameo appearances in **showpiece monuments** along the way. The backdrop changes dramatically by the minute: one moment a feast of classical colonnades and now piles of containers arranged like **avant-garde art** as the tram skirts the edge of the docks. You get glimpses of art nouveau villas, Gothic town halls, geometric art deco, and heaps of monstrous modern concrete. As a perfectly framed piece of cinema, the journey is utterly engaging. The best 145-minute distraction anywhere around the North Sea.

De Haan is easily the most attractive of the communities along the coast. Until the coastal tram arrived in 1886, De Haan was a poor seaside village, populated by shrimp fishermen and their families. It was just a scattered collection of huts, regarded with disfavour by folk in neighbouring villages who judged De Haan to be the haunt of scoundrels and thieves. After the arrival of the tram, De Haan developed into a select coastal resort – one that was later to number **Albert Einstein** among its visitors.

The coastal tram is very **modestly priced**. A day pass which allows you to travel the entire length of the route, hopping on and off at will, is just €7. Trams operate from before 06.00 until about midnight – every 10 minutes in the summer season and every 20 minutes in winter.

Route 18: From Flanders to the Rhine

CITIES: ★★★ CULTURE: ★★ HISTORY: ★★ SCENERY: ★
COUNTRIES COVERED: FRANCE (FR), BELGIUM (BE), GERMANY (DE)
JOURNEY TIME: 3 HRS | DISTANCE: 357 KM | MAP: WWW.EBRWEB.EU/MAP18

Lille and Cologne are two cities with very **strong regional identities** within their respective countries, but they could scarcely be more different. With a historical legacy dating back to the Romans, Cologne makes great play of its long-standing importance as an ecclesiastical and cultural centre. Lille is altogether more downbeat. Coal mining eclipsed textiles as Lille's economic mainstay in the 19th century, bringing with it a new politics of dissent. Lille is radical while Cologne is conformist.

This is one of the shorter journeys in this book. We include it because of its importance for travellers heading from London or Paris to eastern Belgium and the Rhineland. **Route 6** from London to Nîmes via Paris passes through Lille. When the **high-speed line** from Lille into Belgium opened in 1997, it transformed the geography of the Flanders region.

This route, and other new lines from Brussels running east towards Germany, have brought Lille and Cologne much closer together.

ITINERARY AND TICKETS

The journey is so short that it can easily be accomplished in a morning. There are however two cities which cry out for a stopover. They are **Brussels and Aachen**. So you could use this journey as the basis for a more thorough exploration, but we give only a brief introduction to intermediate cities on this route. If you are no great fan of the fast trains used on this journey, it is possible to make the entire trip from Lille to Cologne on slow trains using legacy railway lines which quite closely parallel the route described here. The journey by slow trains requires four changes of train (at Tournai, Brussels, Welkenraedt and Aachen), and takes over five hours – that's two hours more than the fast option we commend below, which requires just an easy change between high-speed trains in Brussels.

This journey illustrates the perversity of **railway ticketing in Europe**. Two high-speed rail operators compete on the Lille to Brussels leg (Eurostar and SNCF). Two quite different companies compete with fast services between Brussels and Cologne (Deutsche Bahn and Thalys). Tickets on these routes are normally limited to a specific operator. None of these operators offer through tickets from Lille to Cologne. This is one of those cases where an independent ticket retailer like Loco2, now part of Rail Europe (www.raileurope.co.uk), might be the best bet if you are keen to book from Lille right through to Cologne in a single transaction. If you have an Interrail or Eurail Pass, and want to avoid supplements altogether, you'll need to use the slower services mentioned in the preceding paragraph.

Flanders

The largest city in French Flanders is too often underrated. Lille is good for more than merely changing trains. **Flemish touches** are everywhere, whether in the exuberant architecture on the Grand Place or in the Flemish flavours on the menus, which include leek tart (*flamiche*), waffles and *potjevleesch*.

Route details

Lille Europe to Brussels Midi	ERT 16	Brussels Midi to Cologne Hbf	ERT 20
Frequency	Journey time	Frequency	Journey time
Hourly	35 mins	9–12 per day	1 hr 50 mins

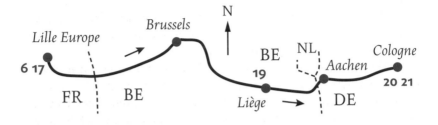

Central Lille is very easy to explore on foot, and lies just a ten-minute walk west of **Lille Europe** station (which is where all Eurostars, Thalys and most TGVs stop). There is a second, much older station called **Lille Flandres**, which is even more convenient for the city centre. That station is used by a small number of TGVs and most local trains. If you want to avoid the high-speed line and take a slow train to Belgium, then you'll depart from Lille Flandres. Our recommended journey for Route 18 starts at Lille Europe.

You'll find a higher level of security at Lille Europe than at most other French stations. If you are travelling to Brussels on a Eurostar train, you'll need to arrive at least 30 minutes prior to the advertised departure time. If your journey to Brussels is on a SNCF TGV train, then 10 minutes suffice.

The journey between Lille and Brussels illustrates how **high-speed rail travel** has transformed this part of Europe. In 1990, there were just five trains each day from Lille to Brussels. Today there are over 20 trains on weekdays. The fastest services take just 34 minutes and at peak times pull crowds of cross-border commuters. The journey starts by running south from Lille to the **Frétin Triangle**, where Brussels-bound trains turn decisively east and cross into Belgian territory. For one stretch just beyond Enghien, the railway parallels a motorway, the train easily outpacing even the fastest-moving cars. All too soon, the pace slows as the train leaves the fast line and follows the Senne Valley into the centre of Brussels.

The Belgian capital

As the administrative hub of the European Union, and with residents who can trace their origins around the world, **Brussels** is an exceptionally cosmopolitan city. It may not be regarded as the most glamorous or romantic of Europe's capitals – after all, its two most famous monuments are a statue of a urinating boy and an outsized 1950s atomic model – but take time to explore and you will find some **great art galleries**, abundant greenery, a majestic central square, and many excellent restaurants. The city is officially bilingual and so street and station names appear in two versions (e.g. French Rue Neuve is Dutch Nieuwstraat).

The main rail route through Brussels runs just east of the city centre, partly underground, but here and there above the surface for long enough to afford some tantalising views of the city.

The fast trains from Lille Europe all arrive at **Brussels Midi** (Zuid in Dutch) and serve no other station in the city. But from Midi it is just four minutes on frequent local trains to Centraal station, from where it's a short walk down to the **Grand Place** – the magnificent square which is the hub of Brussels life. Read more on Brussels stations in our 'connections' section below.

Hotel prices are high in Brussels but they are often greatly discounted on Fr, Sat and Sun nights. If you decide to stay overnight in the Belgian capital, the Novotel Brussels off Grand Place, 120 r du Marché aux herbes, ☎ 026 20 04 29 (www.accorhotels.com) is in a good location between Centraal station and the Grand Place.

CONNECTIONS FROM BRUSSELS

Eurostar trains to France, England and the Netherlands, as well as all TGVs and Thalys services bound for destinations in France serve only **Brussels Midi**. The same applies to Thalys trains for all destinations in Germany and the Netherlands. Deutsche Bahn trains (eg. to Cologne and Frankfurt) serve both Midi and **Brussels Nord**.

All other international trains make three stops in Brussels, viz at Midi, Centraal and Nord. So if you are taking the hourly Intercity *Beneluxtrein* to Rotterdam or Amsterdam (ERT 18), you can board at any of the three stations. The same applies to the Intercity trains to Luxembourg (ERT 445) and to the frequent trains to most destinations within Belgium. These include direct services to Bruges and Ostend (both ERT 400), Antwerp (ERT 420), Liège and Verviers (both ERT 400), Mons (ERT 422), Namur (ERT 440) and Charleroi (ERT 420). Trains to **Brussels Airport** also serve all three stations in the Belgian capital.

The Thalys and Deutsche Bahn trains from Brussels to Cologne all follow the same route. They dash across the flatlands of Brabant to reach **Liège** (Luik in Dutch and Lüttich in German), an industrial city that sprawls along the west bank of the River Meuse.

In Liège, all trains stop at **Guillemins railway station**, a stunning piece of design by Santiago Calatrava. The building is best appreciated from the road outside rather than from the platforms, but on a sunny day the play of light and shade on the platforms is quite seductive. The station is a reminder that Liège is a city which has always had strong railway connections. Read more in our **Sidetracks** feature on p176.

CONNECTIONS FROM LIÈGE
You can connect at Liège Guillemins with **Route 19** in this book, which follows a lovely line south through the Ardennes to Luxembourg and beyond (see ERT 446 for Liège to Luxembourg). There is a useful hourly train to Maastricht, just 32 minutes from Liège on the other side of the Dutch border (ERT 436).

A new **high-speed line** from Liège to Aachen opened in 2009, thus marking the end of a slow dawdle through the hill country of eastern Belgium to reach the Germany border. Nowadays, the fast trains dive through tunnels and miss the best of the scenery. Of course, you can if you wish still follow the old line via Verviers to Aachen. There are hourly trains on this route, all requiring a change of train at Welkenraedt (ERT 400 & 438).

Into Germany

A frontier town close to the point where the borders of Belgium, the Netherlands and Germany converge, **Aachen** (formerly known as Aix-la-Chapelle) was already a great city 1,000 years ago when Emperor Charlemagne enjoyed the thermal springs here and made it the capital of his empire.

The **Aachener Dom** is the oldest cathedral in northern Europe and inspiring more for its historical associations than for any great beauty. You can see Charlemagne's gilded tomb and the imperial throne. Nowadays, in a post-Schengen Europe largely free of border controls, Aachen thrives as the main city in the three-country Euregio district. The quirky **Dreiländerpunkt** (three-country point) on the edge of town is worth a visit in fine weather. Take 🚌 350 from the railway station in Aachen to Vaals Bussttaion from where it is a 10-minute uphill walk. From Aachen, it is just 40 minutes on the fastest trains to Cologne.

Cologne (Köln)

During World War II, nine-tenths of what was Germany's largest **Altstadt** (Old Town) was flattened by bombing, and the quality of reconstruction has been patchy. But there's much to enjoy, in the cathedral, churches and museums, and Kölners themselves have an irresistible verve, exemplified in the city's pre-Lent carnival, reaching its peak on Shrove Tuesday. The **twin spires of the Dom** (cathedral), one of the world's greatest Gothic buildings, soar over the Rhineland capital, and greet the visitor arriving at Cologne's main station. Climb the tower for a splendid view of the city, the River Rhine and a largely industrial hinterland. Lively Cologne has a large Turkish minority. The city boasts **excellent beer** (look for the local *Kölsch*).

Roman traces include remnants of the original 5th-century city wall. The excellent **Römisch-Germanisches Museum**, Roncallipl. 4, holds many of the finds of the ancient town, including an arched fortress gate and the famous Dionysus Mosaic. By the 13th century, Cologne was a thriving metropolis of 40,000 people, protected by Europe's longest city walls – a 6-km rampart pierced by 12 massive gates. Within the original city wall stand a dozen Romanesque churches, Germany's finest such architectural concentration. The most striking are Gross St Martin, overlooking the Rhine in the Altstadt, and St Aposteln.

From 321 until 1424, the city was home to one of the most important **Jewish communities** in Germany. The remains of a mikvah (a Jewish ritual bath) dating from 1170 are preserved under a glass pyramid in the middle of the square of the City Hall. Nearby, the **Museum Ludwig** (closed Mon) houses 20th-century works including those of Kirchner, Beckmann and Dix and an excellent collection of pop art (Warhol, Lichtenstein and more). The outstanding **Wallraf-Richartz-Museum**, with superb 14th- to 16th-century paintings by the Cologne school and an excellent café, is at Martinstr. 39, about a 10-min walk from the Dom. For information about all these museums, and more, check out www.museenkoeln.de. The Kwartier Latäng – around Rathenauplatz and Zülpicher Strasse – and the Südstadt are good places to chill out.

ARRIVAL, INFORMATION, ACCOMMODATION

≈ Köln Hbf, centrally placed, right by the cathedral with a huge shopping centre, left luggage, information desk, currency exchange and service point. ✈ Flughafen Köln–Bonn, south-east of the city (www.koeln-bonn-airport.de). S Bahn trains take 15 mins and run every 20 mins, direct to Köln Hbf (see ERT 802). 🛈 Tourist office: Kardinal-Höffner Pl. 1 (www.cologne-tourism.com), by the Dom. The comprehensive public transport system includes U-Bahn (underground), S-Bahn (surface suburban trains), trams and buses (see www.kvb.koeln).

🛏 A good-value option also close to the station is the small, family-run **Hotel Domstern**, Domstr. 26, ☎ 0221 16 800 80 (www.hotel-domstern.de). Or stay at the **Eden Hotel Früh am Dom**, Sporergasse 1, ☎ 0221 27 29 20 (www.hotel-eden.de) within sight of the cathedral. The **Hotel Drei Kronen**, Auf dem Brand 6, ☎ 0221 258 06 92 (www.hotel-drei-kronen.de) is a good option not far from both the railway station and the Old Town with views of the River Rhine. ✗ A typical Cologne dish is *Sauerbraten*, a 'sour roast', with beef soaked in vinegar and stewed, served with *Kartoffelklösse* (potato dumplings) and apple sauce. *Blootwoosch* (black pudding) makes a snack served with mustard on a bread roll, known as 'Cologne caviar'. A dish that sounds like half a chicken (*Halve Hahn*) is actually just a cheese roll. Many pubs (*Brauhäuser*) offer local beer and good-value food.

CONNECTIONS FROM COLOGNE

You can connect in Cologne onto two other journeys in this book: **Route 20** runs up the Rhine Valley to the Black Forest and Switzerland, while **Route 21** crosses the flatlands of northern Germany to Berlin.

A **high-speed line** running south-east from Cologne (opened 2002) has transformed the railway geography of the Rhine-Main region. The fastest ICE trains now dash to Frankfurt in just an hour (ERT 910), with some trains continuing to Stuttgart and Munich (also ERT 910). Looking north, there are fast trains from Cologne to Hamburg (ERT 800), from where **Route 28** and **29** will take you on into Scandinavia.

Sidetracks: Creature comforts

We never pass through Liège without thinking of **Georges Nagelmackers** – a name which for devotees of comfortable rail travel immediately evokes a dose of nostalgia. Georges Nagelmackers was **born in Liège in 1845** into an affluent banking family with interests in the then flourishing Ardennes iron industry. The young Nagelmackers, deciding banking was not for him, trained as an engineer. As a young man he travelled to America, returning to Liège in 1868 to run the family ironworks. But he was distracted by trains, possibly a result of growing up just outside Liège where the main railway line from Brussels to Cologne and Berlin cuts across the corner of the family estate at Angleur.

While in America, Nagelmackers had travelled in George Pullman's saloons, which offered greater comfort than that provided in the regular carriages of the railway companies. Nagelmackers built upon the **Pullman principle**, but took it a stage further. In his purpose-built carriages Nagelmackers offered not just a Pullman-style open saloon, but separate compartments with proper beds. And thus it was that on 1 October 1872, at an office in Liège, the **Compagnie Internationale des Wagons-Lits** was founded. Among the very first services to use Nagelmackers' new *Wagons-Lits* carriages was that from Ostend through Brussels and Liège to Cologne and Berlin. Within ten years the *Wagons-Lits* Company had a fleet of over a hundred carriages, providing **sleeping cars** for many of the continent's premier railway companies.

Despite competition from George Pullman, who attempted to emulate in Europe his successes across the Atlantic, Nagelmackers' concern flourished through successive **waves of innovation**. It may seem extraordinary nowadays, but in the late 1870s, fully a half century after train travel had been invented, no one had thought of providing hot food to passengers on the trains.

Nagelmackers sensed a market opportunity, and before long *Wagons-Lits* passengers were being served both luncheon and **dinner on board** his trains. With plush upholstery, even an occasional Gobelin tapestry, polished mahogany and crystal glasses, Nagelmackers ensured that his clients had **all the very best en route**. His most stylish carriages were reserved for the premium routes: Paris to the French Riviera, the *Nord Express* to Berlin and Riga and the *Rome Express*. In 1883, *Wagons-Lits* pioneered what became the most famous named train of them all: the *Orient Express*.

Nagelmackers' concern for comfort was not restricted just to the rails. The company also **opened fine hotels** at spots served by its trains; the first two were the Avenida Palace in Lisbon and the Riviera Palace in Nice. By the time Nagelmackers died in 1905 the midnight blue and gold carriages of his company reached as far afield as Siberia, Iberia and the Bosphorus.

Today, one will scan the **departure boards at Liège** in vain for trains to distant lands. Long gone are the through sleeping cars to Copenhagen, Vienna and Moscow. Indeed, nowadays, there are simply no overnight trains with sleeping cars from Liège to anywhere. Belgium has scrapped all night trains. The **last survivor** was a seasonal ski train from Brussels to Austria. It was discontinued in 2016. It didn't even have proper sleeping cars, merely humble couchettes. Georges Nagelmackers is probably turning in his grave.

Route 19: South to Switzerland

CITIES: ★★ CULTURE: ★ HISTORY: ★ SCENERY: ★★
COUNTRIES COVERED: NETHERLANDS (NL), BELGIUM (BE), LUXEMBOURG (LU), FRANCE (FR),
SWITZERLAND (CH)
JOURNEY TIME: 12 HRS 30 MINS | DISTANCE: 1,020 KM | MAP: WWW.EBRWEB.EU/MAP19

This route describes a journey which draws upon a wealth of railway history. In spring 2016, the last direct Eurocity trains from the **Low Countries to Switzerland** slipped quietly from the pages of the *European Rail Timetable*. *Iris* and *Vauban* – those were the names of the twice daily Eurocity services which pottered south through Luxembourg and Strasbourg to Basel – were unloved and neglected in recent years. But they were a good reminder that, in the last century, the route south via the **Ardennes and Alsace** was a popular choice for Swiss-bound travellers from the Low Countries and, for that matter, from England too.

Picture the scene. Fifty years ago on a summer morning at Amsterdam Centraal station. Families bound for holidays in the Alps and the Mediterranean are climbing aboard train D315: the 10.24 to Basel and beyond.

The journey to Basel stayed entirely west of the Rhine, traversing Belgium, Luxembourg and France along the way. The through trains have gone, but the railways are still there. **Regular regional trains** – all offering a high level of comfort – still ply the entire route. So let's hop aboard and make tracks south, following a route which will lead us all the way from Amsterdam to the shores of **Lake Geneva**.

RECOMMENDED ITINERARY

Route 19 is an antidote to the modern fad for high-speed trains. You can travel end-to-end on services which don't need to be booked in advance; it's a chance to rediscover **the joy of travelling spontaneously**. If you are using a Eurail or Interrail pass, you'll not need to pay any supplements or bother making seat reservations. This is a route which could easily be spun out over a full week, so why not think of stopping off at three cities along the way: **Maastricht, Nancy and Strasbourg** would be our top choices. Luxembourg and Berne would be good additional overnight stays.

The railway heads south-east from **Amsterdam** (more on p182) to Utrecht, paralleling the Rijnkanaal, a waterway opened in 1952 to provide a direct link between the River Rhine and the port of Amsterdam. Tree-lined canals encircle the historic heart of Utrecht; it's not a major tourist destination but we rather like it – and it's a good choice if you are keen to stay in this part of Holland but want to avoid pricey Amsterdam hotels.

Running south from Utrecht, crossing the River Lek and the River Waal, the countryside changes slowly in **Noord-Brabant**. No longer is it quite so pancake flat and the geometric rigour of fields in the Amsterdam area gives way to a less orderly landscape. Crossing the **River Maas**, the train

Route details

Amsterdam Centraal to Maastricht		ERT 470
Frequency	Journey time	Notes
2 per hr	2 hrs 25 mins	

Maastricht to Liège-Guillemins		ERT 436
Frequency	Journey time	Notes
Hourly	35 mins	

Liège-Guillemins to Luxembourg		ERT 446
Frequency	Journey time	Notes
Every 2 hrs	2 hrs 35 mins	

Luxembourg to Nancy		ERT 384
Frequency	Journey time	Notes
Hourly	1 hr 35 mins	A

Nancy to Strasbourg		ERT 383
Frequency	Journey time	Notes
Every 1–2 hrs	85 mins	

Strasbourg to Basel SNCF*		ERT 385
Frequency	Journey time	Notes
1–2 per hr	80 mins	B

Basel SBB* to Berne		ERT 560
Frequency	Journey time	Notes
2 per hr	55–60 mins	

Berne to Lausanne		ERT 505
Frequency	Journey time	Notes
2 per hr	65–70 mins	

Notes

A – Some journeys may require a change of train in Metz.
B – Some journeys may require a change of train in Mulhouse.
* – The SNCF (French sector) and the SBB (Swiss sector) stations at Basel/Bâle are adjacent.

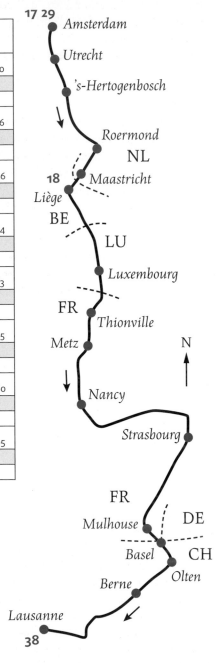

reaches **'s-Hertogenbosch** (often called Den Bosch); always worth a stop if only to take a peek at the town's magnificent market square. There is no reason to pause at the industrial town of Eindhoven, but if you take a couple of hours out at **Roermond**, you'll discover that this southernmost province of the Netherlands – called Limburg – is a world apart from Amsterdam and the North Sea coast. Roermond has a strong Catholic heritage, and that still inflects many aspects of Roermond life.

Maastricht (suggested stopover)

Step off the train in Maastricht and you may wonder if you really are still in the Netherlands at all. The city has a distinctly 'southern' feel. Tucked into a mildly hilly corner of the Netherlands, the provincial **capital of Limburg** is a busy university town. With its **lively squares**, distinctive stone houses and arty boutiques, it really is most appealing. You can get a great view from the tower of **Sint Janskerk**, next to huge Sint Servaasbasiliek (see the 11th- and 12th-century crypts).

As Roermond, this is a largely **Catholic town**. At Museumkelder Derlon, there are *in situ* remnants of Roman Maastricht, while centuries-old fortifications abound in and around the city, notably at Fort Sint Pieter. **St Pietersberg Caves** are the result of centuries of excavation of marl stone, which have left a labyrinth of more than 20,000 passages; you can visit two sections (check details with the local tourist office).

ARRIVAL, INFORMATION, ACCOMMODATION

A 10-min walk east of the centre. Tourist office: Kleine Staat 1 (www.visitmaastricht. com). The small, cozy **Hotel Les Charmes**, Lenculenstraat 18 (www.hotellescharmes.nl), is located in a historic 17th-century building in a quiet area in the heart of the Old Town. Or try the friendly **Maison Haas**, Vrijthof 20A, ☎ 043 852 43 53 (www.haashustinx.nl), which is equally central and close to Sint Janskerk. The **Townhouse**, St Maartenslaan 5, ☎ 043 323 30 90 (www.townhousehotels.nl), is very convenient for the station and offers individually styled rooms.

Through the Ardennes

From Maastricht, our route follows the River Maas (Meuse in French) up-steam over the Belgian border to **Liège** (see p187), where you can connect onto **Route 18**, running east to Cologne or west via Brussels to Lille. You'll need to change trains in Liège; that's a good chance to see the station which is quite magnificent – a building without evident facades and a monumental roof which dips and curves and then soars skyward. Down on the platforms, the trains come and go: a red Thalys bound for Paris, a sleek silver ICE heading for Frankfurt-am-Main and the occasional Intercity to Luxembourg. That's the train we want, so climb on board and enjoy the ride on one of **Europe's finest rural rail routes**.

Today's eight daily trains from **Liège to Luxembourg** are usually formed of a rake of four Belgian carriages, three second class and one first, all comfy Intercity stock from the 1980s. The electric locomotive at the head of the train works through to Luxembourg. Long gone are the days when there was a change of engine at the border.

Leaving **Liège-Guillemins station**, the line immediately crosses the River Meuse – eyes left for a superb view downstream – and then tracks south up the Ourthe Valley. Twenty minutes out of Liège, the train pauses at Rivage before turning east into the hills. The scenery becomes ever more dramatic as the train climbs slowly into the **Belgian Ardennes**. About 75 minutes into the journey, the train stops at **Gouvy**, the last station before the border with the Grand Duchy of Luxembourg. At 466 metres above sea level, Gouvy is the highest station on the 160-km route from Liège to Luxembourg. The journey south from the border through tilted hill country to the city of Luxembourg is a sheer delight with a medley of **castles, gorges and waterfalls**. If you are minded to break your journey, **Clervaux** is a good place to stop. It's a hike from the station into the town centre, but you'll be rewarded by a world-class photographic exhibition (called *The Family of Man*) at Clervaux Castle.

One of Europe's smallest capitals, **Luxembourg** is a pleasant place to pass a day or two. The city was founded in Roman times and is dramatically sited on a gorge cut by the **rivers Alzette and Pétrusse**. It falls naturally into three sections: the old centre (north of the Pétrusse Valley and home to most of the sights), the modern city and station (south of the gorge), and Grund (the valley settlement), reachable by deep escalators or lifts from the central part of town. Descending to Grund ('the ground') is like entering a different, darker city, and it is this area that houses most of Luxembourg's racier nightlife.

CONNECTIONS FROM LUXEMBOURG

Hourly trains from Luxembourg slip over the German border to Trier (ERT 915), and then continue down the **Moselle Valley** to Koblenz (also ERT 915), where you can connect into the next route in this book; follow **Route 20** south up the Rhine Valley to the **Black Forest** and Switzerland. Read more on the Moselle Valley in our **Sidetracks** feature on p206.

Luxembourg has long had direct TGVs to Paris (ERT 390), but the high-speed train offering was enhanced in spring 2016 with the introduction of direct TGVs to Strasbourg, the **Rhône Valley and Provence** (ERT 379). Cross-border links to Lorraine are also much improved with better services on the busy Luxembourg – Metz – Nancy axis (ERT 384).

The train ride into the city of Luxembourg from the north may have seduced you into thinking that the **Grand Duchy** consists entirely of lush green valleys and striking castles. Travelling south to the French border, you see a more industrial side of Luxembourg. The **steel industry**, once so important in southern Luxembourg and adjacent areas of Lorraine (in France), has declined, leaving the region with significant economic challenges. Over the border, the first French town of any size is **Thionville**. This is not the prettiest introduction to France, but it's nonetheless an interesting ride up the Moselle Valley through **Metz** to Nancy.

Nancy (suggested stopover)

The French city of Nancy is a little off the beaten track. But it deserves to be better known. Those who visit are universally impressed by its **striking architecture** which sweeps from elegant 18th-century classicism to art nouveau. Nancy's pre-eminent position in architecture and the decorative arts has earned it a place on UNESCO's World Heritage List. The star of the show is the **neoclassical place Stanislas** in the middle of the city. It is locally referred to just as Stan. Its entire south side is taken up by the palatial Hôtel de Ville. Behind is the pl. d'Alliance, and to the north, through the **Arc de Triomphe**, the 15th-century pl. de la Carrière. A good overnight option in the historic Old Town is the Hôtel de Guise, 18 r. de Guise, ☎ 03 83 32 24 68 (www.hoteldeguise.com), about a 15-min walk from pl. Stanislas.

Territorial reforms in France in 2016 nudged Lorraine and Alsace into a single mega-region (which also assimilated the Champagne-Ardenne region to the west of Lorraine). Nancy, the proud capital of Lorraine, lost out to Strasbourg in the bid to be top dog in the new order.

Nancy may be miffed, but there's still an excellent train service running **east to Strasbourg**. It's a pleasant old-style main line, once used by the *Orient Express* and still used today by the weekly Paris to Moscow train (ERT 24), though nowadays all other long-distance trains use a new high-speed line to Strasbourg which opened in summer 2016. But the regional TER services from Nancy still use the old route to Strasbourg which meanders delightfully through the **Vosges hills**, paralleling the canal which links the River Marne with the River Rhine.

Strasbourg (suggested stopover)

The old capital of Alsace, once a mere fishing village, has grown into a **most attractive city**, successfully combining old with new. The town is best known today as the seat of the European Parliament, housed in an imposing new building on the city outskirts. The prettiest area of town is **Petite-France**, where 16th- and 17th-century houses crowd around narrow alleys and streams. The river is spanned by the picturesque **Ponts Couverts**, a trio of mediaeval covered bridges with square towers. The **Cathédrale Notre-Dame** is a Gothic triumph with a carved west front. Highlights include the 13th-century Pilier des Anges (Angels' Pillar) and the 19th-century Horloge astronomique (astronomical clock), which strikes at 12.30 each day. The tower, a 332-step climb, provides a marvellous city view.

Exploring the Vosges

To see something of the beautiful wooded hills behind Strasbourg (called the Vosges), take the local train which runs up the **Bruche Valley** to Saint-Dié-des-Vosges (ERT 388), from where you can continue to Épinal (ERT 388a) in the upper reaches of the **Moselle Valley** before cutting south to Belfort (ERT 386a). This is one of those lovely branch-line escapades which take time but are unfailingly rewarding.

Arrival, information, accommodation

≋ Pl. de la Gare, 10-min walk to the centre. 🚹 Tourist office: 17 pl. de la Cathédrale (www. otstrasbourg.fr).

🛏 Conveniently located close to the station is the **Monopole Métropole**, 16 r. Kuhn, ☎ 03 88 14 39 14 (www.bw-monopole.com). Or try the elegant and good-value **Gutenberg**, 31 r. des Serruriers, ☎ 03 88 32 17 15 (www.hotel-gutenberg.com), or the stylish and more upmarket **Rohan**, 17–19 r. du Maroquin, ☎ 03 88 32 85 11 (www.hotel-rohan.com), both close to the cathedral. ✗ There are plenty of cafés and *winstubs* (traditional Alsatian restaurants) near the cathedral, on r. des Tonneliers and in the Petite-France quarter.

Connections from Strasbourg

From Strasbourg it is just a short hop over the River Rhine to Offenburg (ERT 912), where you can connect with **Route 20** (running north to Cologne and south through the Black Forest to Zurich). German ICE trains appeared in Strasbourg for the first time on regular scheduled services in summer 2016; they are used on the Paris to Stuttgart and Frankfurt routes (ERT 32). SNCF's smart TGVs also run across the German border with direct trains to Frankfurt and Munich (also ERT 32).

Strasbourg has TGVs to **Paris** (ERT 390) and a good range of **provincial cities across France**, including Nantes and Bordeaux (both ERT 391), and Lyon and Marseille (ERT 379). International destinations, beyond those already mentioned in Germany, include Brussels (ERT 391), Basel (ERT 385) and a **direct night train** to Berlin, Warsaw and Moscow (ERT 24).

The journey south from Strasbourg keeps well west of the River Rhine and you'll not see the river at all. To the right of the train, the Vosges mountains nudge ever closer and south of **Sélestat** there are especially fine views of the hills with some of **Alsace's finest vineyards** on their lower slopes. From the train, it's easy to pick out some of the most distinguished wine-making villages in the region, such as Riquewihr and Hunawihr.

Unlike their colleagues to the east of the river in Germany, who work with similar soils, Alsatian winemakers prefer strong, dry wines which are the perfect match for the bold flavours of the local cuisine. **Colmar** is a good place to stop and try those classic Alsace wines. It is the nicest small town on this route. Beyond Colmar there is no particular reason to stop until Basel.

Into Switzerland

Wedged into the corners of Switzerland, France and Germany, **Basel** (Bâle in French) is a big, working city (the second largest in the country after Zurich). It has long been a crossroads for European culture. The main station, Bahnhof SBB, is a 10-min walk south of the city centre (5 mins by tram from the front of the station), and handles Swiss and main-line German services.

A separate adjacent station, Bâle SNCF, hosts French regional trains. Both stations evoke the heady old days of train travel. For a spell there were even direct overnight trains from here to London (shipped on a ferry across the Channel). The town's **mediaeval centre** is on the south bank, in Grossbasel. Kleinbasel is the small modern area on the north bank.

Connections from Basel (Bâle)

A glance at the ERT reveals that Basel offers a greater choice of **international rail services** than many European capital cities. All trains mentioned here leave from the main SBB station. TGVs dash to Paris in just three hours (ERT 40). There are fast trains to Berlin and Hamburg (both ERT 912), to Milan via either the Simplon or Gotthard routes (both in ERT 82) and a direct Eurocity service to Munich (ERT 75), which takes a very pretty route around the east side of **Lake Constance**, touching Austrian territory on the way.

The main rail route from Basel to Berne makes a dog-leg to the east, picking up a high-speed line from **Olten to Berne**. It's not particularly special, and if you want a prettier alternative you might consider taking the route via Delémont (ERT 505a) which cuts through splendid Jura landscapes. Basel to Berne via this routes requires just a single change of train (at Biel / Bienne). It takes one hour more than the faster Basel to Berne route through Olten.

One of Europe's more relaxed capitals, **Berne** is rightly fêted as a wonderfully appealing city. Its **handsome Old Town**, tucked into a big meander of the River Aare, features on the UNESCO World Heritage List. The Alps are often visible in the distance, though the immediate rural hinterland of the city is unremarkable.

It is little more than an hour from **Berne to Lausanne**. Don't expect dramatic views of the distant Alps until the very end. The appeal of most of this route is in the pastoral beauty of the landscape closer to hand. The line climbs to the Vauderens Tunnel and drops down gently through the **Lavaux vineyards** (see p338) towards Lake Geneva. Near **Grandvaux**, a wonderful vista over the lake opens up, on clear days affording views of Mont Blanc. This is one of **Europe's great arrivals** by train. For travellers of yesteryear arriving in Lausanne on the prestigious *Rheingold Trans-Europe Express* (first class only with every creature comfort), this descent into Lausanne was the highlight of the entire run from Amsterdam. However humble the train you choose for the final leg of this route, the arrival in Lausanne will still surely be a moment to remember.

At **Lausanne** (see p338) you can connect into **Route 38** to Geneva (with the option of joining there **Route 12** to the south of France and Spain). Or follow **Route 38** in reverse from Lausanne back to Zurich, a journey that takes in one of the finest mountain rail routes in the Alps.

Route 20: Touring the Rhine Valley

Cities: ★★ Culture: ★ History: ★★ Scenery: ★★
Countries covered: Germany (DE), Switzerland (CH)
Journey time: 7 hrs 30 mins | Distance: 611 km | Map: www.ebrweb.eu/map20

This is one of Europe's classic rail journeys, as the route south from Cologne hugs the River Rhine and then, once past Koblenz, follows the **dramatic Rhine Gorge** upstream. Moving over the imperceptible divide from northern into southern Germany (read more on the *Weißwurstgrenze* on p220), we leave the Rhine Valley and continue through the **Black Forest** into Switzerland. Once in Switzerland, at Schaffhausen, our route takes in one of Europe's most celebrated waterfalls en route to our final destination in Zurich.

No other journey in this book quite so perfectly recalls the wholesale changes in travel patterns which took place in the early and mid-19th century. The end of the **Napoleonic Wars** heralded a wholly new era in travel – one where many people travelled purely for the sake of it. The restless English were in the vanguard of this movement and many looked to the Rhine as a easy-to-reach continental destination. The liberalisation of steamer traffic on the river, coupled with the completion of new railways stretching from the Belgian coast to Cologne, encouraged the more monied classes from London and the Home Counties to take short breaks to see the **mediaeval castles** and **Rhine landscapes** which poets and artists had helped inscribe on the Romantic imagination.

Clutching their Murray guides, the English sallied forth in the first clear example of international mass tourism in Europe. The extension of rail networks throughout Germany, and the advent of all-inclusive tour arrangements of the kind pioneered by **Thomas Cook**, served only to augment the flow of travellers. By the mid-1870s increasing numbers of visitors were pushing well beyond the Rhine Gorge into central Germany, the Black Forest and the Alps. Thomas Cook pioneered his *Tourist Handbooks* series, which described routes rather than merely places, in much the same way as we do in this book. The very first Cook *Handbooks* covered railways in the territory traversed by Route 20.

There are railways on both sides of the River Rhine from **Cologne upstream to Mannheim**. Our journey here follows the left bank of the river, that is, the west bank, which generally offers a better choice of trains than the east bank.

Suggested itinerary

Our starting point is **Cologne**, which is nowadays just a short hop on regular high-speed trains from Amsterdam (ERT 28), Brussels and Paris (both ERT 20). Travellers from Britain can leave London on a morning departure on Eurostar and, with just one change of train in Brussels, be in Cologne to start Route 20 by early afternoon.

Route details

Cologne Hbf to Koblenz Hbf		ERT 800/802
Frequency	Journey time	Notes
3–4 per hr	55–90 mins	

Koblenz Hbf to Mainz Hbf		ERT 911/914
Frequency	Journey time	Notes
3–4 per hr	50–85 mins	

Mainz Hbf to Mannheim Hbf		ERT 911/911a
Frequency	Journey time	Notes
2–3 per hr	40–80 mins	

Mannheim Hbf to Heidelberg Hbf		ERT ***
Frequency	Journey time	Notes
4–6 per hr	15–20 mins	

Heidelberg Hbf to Karlsruhe Hbf		ERT 912/913
Frequency	Journey time	Notes
1–2 per hr	35–45 mins	

Karlsruhe Hbf to Singen		ERT 916
Frequency	Journey time	Notes
Hourly	2 hrs 45 mins	

Singen to Schaffhausen		ERT 939/940
Frequency	Journey time	Notes
3–4 per hr	15–20 mins	

Schaffhausen to Zurich HB		ERT 940
Frequency	Journey time	Notes
3 per hr	35–55 mins	

Note

*** – ERT 912/913/918/919/923/924

Cologne
18 21
N
Bonn
Koblenz
Boppard
Mainz
Mannheim
Heidelberg
Karlsruhe
Baden-Baden
Offenburg
Triberg   DE
Singen
CH
Zurich   **35 36 38**

There are no **compulsory seat reservations** on any of the trains on this route. Holders of Interrail and Eurail passes can thus follow the entire route without paying a cent in supplements. This is, therefore, a journey well suited to spontaneous travel. Cheap tickets, valid only on regional trains, are available for all but the final leg from Schaffhausen to Zurich. Read more on these slow travel deals in the box on p222.

Heidelberg is the obvious place for an **overnight stop**. If you decide to travel from Cologne to Heidelberg in a day, we especially recommend using one of the two morning

Eurocity trains which run up the Rhine Valley from Cologne. These two trains (EC7 and EC9 respectively) are both formed of very comfortable Swiss carriages; both trains have excellent restaurant cars.

A **Swiss panorama carriage** (first class only) has been included in the EC9 throughout 2019 (we do not yet know if this will continue in 2020). It is a two-and-a-half hour journey from Cologne to Mannheim, where you'll need to change for a connecting train to Heidelberg, just a dozen minutes away.

If the weather is good and time no object, think of doing part of the **journey by boat** up the Rhine; the best place to do this is definitely between Boppard and Bingen (ERT 914a). Holders of Eurail and Interrail passes receive a 20% discount on the regular fares on all shipping services shown in ERT 914a.

In his *Tourist Handbook* of 1873, Thomas Cook remarked on the extraordinary amount of traffic to be observed on the River Rhine as the traveller heads south from **Cologne** (see p188) to Bonn. He noted in particular the timber rafts on which entire families had built simple shelters. Modern German officialdom brooks no such improvisation, but the river still bustles with traffic today. The stretch immediately upstream of Cologne towards Bonn wins no prizes for beauty.

With its small-town atmosphere, it is hard to believe that **Bonn** was still a capital city just 25 years ago. Packed with students and top-notch cultural attractions, Bonn is a lively stopover for a day or two. All the central areas are walkable, and the pubs near the river do a roaring trade at night.

Deprived of its capital city status, Bonn now makes the most of its musical connections, of which Beethoven is the biggest. The **Beethoven-Haus-Museum**, where the composer spent the first 22 years of his life, is at Bonngasse 20 and contains his instruments and a rather sad collection of ear trumpets testifying to his irreversible decline into total deafness.

Upstream from Bonn, the landscape perks up as we pass **Königswinter** with its seven hills of which the most striking (though actually the lowest of the seven) is the Drachenfels, the "castled crag" promoted to stardom by Byron in *Childe Harold's Pilgrimage*. Byron sailed up the Rhine in spring 1816.

Koblenz is a name intimately associated with travel: it was here that Karl Baedeker started publishing his famous guidebooks to Europe in 1823, taking advantage of the first of the great wave of visitors then discovering the Rhine.

The Moselle and Rhine rivers meet in Koblenz at the **Deutsches Eck** (the German Corner), marked by a massive, heavy-handed monument to Kaiser Wilhelm I. The pleasant gardens that line the banks of both rivers combine to provide an attractive 8-km stroll. **Ehrenbreitstein** (across the Rhine, ferries in summer) is dominated by an enormous fortress, begun in the 12th century, but grown to its present size during the 16th century. An incline elevator, opened in 2011, grants barrier-free access to the fortress. From the left side of the Rhine, a cable car leads from Koblenz up to the plateau. As well as providing a superb panorama, the fortress contains two regional museums and a youth hostel. A big firework display (the most important of the 'Rhein in Flammen' series) is staged here on the second Saturday in August.

The Moselle Valley is of course a tempting diversion, and it is followed in part by trains running up the valley to Trier and beyond (ERT 915). Read more on the Moselle in our **Sidetracks** feature on p206.

The Rhine Gorge

English travellers in the 19th century always travelled with their sketch pads, recording Rhenish landscapes with varying degrees of artistic competence. Not all were as good as **JMW Turner** who visited in 1817. No castles or crags were more frequently sketched than those which line the 60-kilometre stretch of the river between Koblenz and Bingen.

In the space of just 25 years, from 1825 to 1850, the number of travellers taking boats along this stretch of the river increased 30-fold, most of these tourists anxious to discern a rich mediaeval past in the time-worn villages which line the banks of the Rhine. The lure of myth has not quite faded, and today even regular users of the railway still crane their necks to catch a glimpse of the slaty summit of the **Loreley** above Sankt Goarshausen on the east bank. The drama of the Rhine castles may have faded, but this is still a tremendous ride.

Our favourite villages along this stretch of the river are **Boppard** and **Oberwesel** on the west bank and Lorch on the east bank. These, and most other villages on both banks, have railway stations served by local trains shown in ERT 914 (a single table covering the railways on both banks). At almost every village, there are ferries over to the opposite bank of the river.

The mood of the landscape changes dramatically beyond **Bingen** as the railway runs through flat terrain to **Mainz**, a city which stands centre stage in German history as the place where Gutenberg invented printing. Our route continues south, still with occasional glimpses of the Rhine through Worms to Mannheim (where a change of trains is often necessary). Beyond Mannheim, we follow the River Neckar to Heidelberg.

Heidelberg (suggested stopover)

Heidelberg's romantic setting, beneath wooded hills along the banks of the **River Neckar** and overlooked by castle ruins, makes it a magnet for tourists and moviemakers. Expect packed streets in the summer high season. The town has a long history and is home to Germany's oldest university, founded in 1386, but there's little that's ancient in the centre, as most of it was rebuilt in the 18th century following wholesale destruction by Louis XIV's troops in 1693. The city's most famous sight is the part-ruined **pink sandstone castle,** high above the town. From its terraces, you get a beautiful view over the red rooftops and the gently flowing river.

Many fine old mansions are scattered around the **Altstadt** (Old Town). The buildings around Marktplatz include the Renaissance Haus zum Ritter and the 14th-century Heiliggeistkirche (Church of the Holy Spirit). Universitätsplatz, which has the **Löwenbrunnen** (Lion Fountain) in the centre, is the location of both the 'old' and 'new' universities. Until 1914, students whose high spirits had got out of hand were confined to the special students' prison round the corner in Augustinerstr. 2. Incarceration was regarded as an honour and self-portraits are common in the graffiti on the walls. Highlight of the summer is the castle festival, when opera, theatre and dance performances are staged outdoors in the cobbled courtyard.

Across the river, over the **Alte Brücke**, the steep Schlangenweg steps zigzag up through orchards to the Philosophenweg (Philosophers' Path). This is a scenic lane traipsing across the hillside, so-called because the views allegedly inspired philosophical reflection.

ARRIVAL, INFORMATION, ACCOMMODATION

≋ Heidelberg Hbf, 10-min walk to the edge of the pedestrian district; or 25 mins to the heart of the Old Town (or 🚌 32). 🄸 Tourist office: Willy-Brandt-Pl. 1, directly in front of the station (www.heidelberg-marketing.de). Accommodation booking service. Guided walking tours of the Altstadt (Old Town) in English (Thur, Fri & Sat at 10.30, Apr–Oct) from the town hall on Marktplatz (€9). A network of buses and trams serve the pedestrianised Altstadt, where a funicular ride saves the 300-step climb up to the castle. It's also possible to tour by bike; rentals available from Eldorado, Felix-Wankel-Str. 1 (www.eldorado-hd.de), particularly pleasant for exploring the banks of the Neckar.

🛏 Heidelberg is a prime tourist destination, so the later you book during the summer, the further from the centre you will find yourself. Located right at the Alte Brücke in the Old Town is the comfortable **Holländer Hof**, Neckarstaden 66, ☎ 06221 60 50 0 (www.hollaender-hof.de). Also in the Old Town, in a quiet side street, is the **Backmulde**, Schiffgasse 11, ☎ 06221 53 66 0 (www.gasthaus-backmulde.de), which has a good restaurant and 26 individually furnished rooms. More upmarket is the chic and stylish **Arthotel**, Grabengasse 7, ☎ 06221 65 00 60 (www.arthotel.de), which has spacious rooms.

✗ The Altstadt is very touristy and its restaurants lively with a student atmosphere. Many spill out onto the traffic-free streets. This is also the nightlife hub. You are spoilt for choice along Heiliggeiststr. and Untere Str.

The Black Forest

From Heidelberg, it is a short run south to **Karlsruhe** where the most interesting sight is the palace built in 1715 by Margrave Karl Wilhelm; it is an enormous neoclassical pile with extensive formal gardens. From the tower, you see clearly how he designed the entire city to radiate out from it like a fan and Karlsruhe's grace derives from that ambitious urban plan.

Directly across from the north entrance of the Hauptbahnhof (mind the trams) and right next to the tourist office is the **Zoologischer Stadtgarten**.

Much more than a regular zoo, it offers expansive parks and is a wonderful place for walks. There is a boating lake and, in season, outdoor cafés and a blaze of flowers.

Connections from Karlsruhe

Fast trains run non-stop to Strasbourg (ERT 912) where you can connect onto **Route 19**. There's a very useful direct TGV to Lyon and Marseille, affording a connection in both cities to the French routes featured in this book. TGV and ICE trains dash to Paris (ERT 32). There are frequent services up the **Rhine Valley** to Freiburg and Basel (ERT 912). Karlsruhe has direct trains to Berlin and Hamburg (both ERT 912), Stuttgart (ERT 931), Munich (ERT 930) and Nuremberg (ERT 925). The most exotic destination to feature on the Karlsruhe departure boards is the weekly train to Warsaw, Minsk and Moscow (ERT 24).

Some of the **trams** which depart from the station forecourt are shape-shifters, morphing magically into trains once they escape the city. Pick of the bunch is the S41 which makes a two-hour journey up the Murg Valley to the Black Forest town of **Freudenstadt** (ERT 943), from where you can take a connecting train (ERT 942) to rejoin Route 20 at Hausach (just north of Triberg).

Just south of Karlsruhe, **Baden-Baden** is the European spa town par excellence. Ever sniffy about modernity, the locals kept the railway at a distance and the station is inconveniently far away from the town. Almost oppressively elegant and full of visitors dripping with money, Baden-Baden is a throwback to an earlier age.

But it has a compelling appeal, and nowhere else in Germany offers the same opportunities for people watching (or even snaring a rich, aged spouse). The city has snob appeal and everything is overdone, but it's all the more fabulous for that. You half expect to bump into the Russian tsar or a Hungarian countess as you stroll into the casino.

Beyond Baden-Baden, our route turns into the hills following the **Schwarzwaldbahn** (Black Forest Railway) through glorious wooded hills towards the Swiss border. **Thomas Cook** travelled the route just after it opened in 1873 and remarked on the unusual density of red waistcoats, velvet breeches and cuckoo clocks.

The waistcoats and breeches have slipped from fashion, but the cuckoo clocks are still everywhere, most particularly in **Triberg**, where you'll find

Danubian diversion

Running south from the Black Forest, many travellers are surprised to discover that the **source of the River Danube** lies so far west (and so close to the Rhine). Lovers of rural railways (and Danube hunters) can easily follow much of the course of the river through southern Germany and beyond. You need to leave Route 20 at **Immendingen**, from where a delightful railway follows the Danube down to Ulm (ERT 938). From there, continue via Donauwörth (where you cross **Route 23**) to Regensburg (ERT 945), where you can connect into the Vienna-bound ICE trains (ERT 920) which broadly follow the Danube downstream via Passau and Linz.

fabulous displays of Black Forest kitsch. Known for the purity of its air, this touristy spa town is actually very pleasant; it's been a centre for **cuckoo clock production** since 1824, when Josef Weisser started his business in the *Haus der 1000 Uhren* (House of a Thousand Clocks). The **Schwarzwaldmuseum** (www.schwarzwaldmuseum.de; closed Mon from Oct–Mar) is full of woodcarvings, some splendid local costumes and, inevitably, clocks.

The summit of the *Schwarzwaldbahn*, at over 800 metres above sea level, is about a dozen kilometres beyond Triberg, after which the railway drops down into the **Danube Valley**. The railway parallels the youthful river, here no more than a stream. At **Singen**, it is always necessary to change trains. Running west from Singen, the train slips through Gottmadingen where the station starred in political history. It was here that in 1917 Lenin – en route from Switzerland back to Russia – changed trains, boarding the famous sealed carriage in which he was forced to remain for the long journey across German territory to the Baltic island of Rügen.

All trains stop at **Schaffhausen**, a Swiss town which unusually, though not uniquely, is located on the right bank of the River Rhine, hemmed in by German territory. The one big reason for stopping here is the famous waterfall, that great obstacle to shipping on the Rhine which has been turned into a lucrative economic opportunity. Schaffhausen thrives on tourists intent on getting soaked by the spray from the Rhine. Thomas Cook underplayed the appeal of the spot: "At the outset, let me warn the tourist not to build his hopes too high," wrote Cook in 1873. "They are not equal to Niagara," he continued. Maybe not, but the **Rhine Falls at Schaffhausen** are extraordinarily beautiful, and the town itself, likeable rather than picturesque, has a useful range of onward connections. The two stations nearest the falls are called Schloß Laufen and Neuhausen am Rheinfall, the latter being possibly a shade better placed. The stations are on opposite banks of the river. Both are served by half-hourly local trains from Schaffhausen.

From Schaffhausen it is less than an hour on to Zurich – criss-crossing the **Swiss-German border** a number of times along the way – with a tremendous view of the Rhine Falls to the left just after leaving Schaffhausen. Note that some slower trains from Schaffhausen to Zurich, viz. those routed via Winterthur, do not give the same splendid view of the falls.

SCHAFFHAUSEN CONNECTIONS

Hourly trains run west to **Basel** (ERT 939), sticking to the right bank (ie. the German side) of the River Rhine. Sit on the left for best views of the river. There's a lovely minor route that runs east along the left bank (ie. the Swiss side) of the Rhine to Kreuzlingen and beyond (ERT 538). It's possible to continue right through to Bregenz in Austria, returning to Schaffhausen by train via **Lindau**. This three-country tour is a grand circuit of Lake Constance. There is an integrated road-rail ticketing scheme covering the entire **Lake Constance** area. For longer journeys, the Bodensee Ticket undercuts regular fares (see www.bodensee-ticket.com). With a bit more time, you might consider setting out from

Schaffhausen to explore Lake Constance by boat. Schaffhausen to **Konstanz** takes 4hrs 40mins, from where it's about another four hours on to Bregenz in Austria.

Zurich (Zürich)

There's more to Switzerland's largest town than gold bars and chocolate bars. It's a classical city with a **contemporary edge**, preserving its architectural and cultural heritage, yet surprising the world with the latest innovations in art and architecture, fashion, shopping and design. Most of Zurich's sights fall within a compact, walkable area on either side of the Limmat River, which bisects the city centre. Next to the Hauptbahnhof on Museumsstrasse is the **Swiss National Museum** (www.nationalmuseum.ch; closed Mon). Once you have a grasp of the nation's colourful history, walks around town are all the more rewarding.

The ancient hilly **Niederdorf district** to the east is a veritable labyrinth of old, cobbled lanes brimming with trendy bars, cafés and quirky shops. Here you will find the Romanesque **Grossmünster**, the city's cathedral and the birthplace of the Swiss Reformation. Climb the tower for the best views over the city. To the west, the **Altstadt** (Old Town) contains many of the city's finest historic buildings, and broad, leafy **Bahnhofstrasse** counts among the world's most sophisticated shopping boulevards. The trendy former industrial quarter of Zurich West reflects the city's radical change in recent years, while the lake, with its beautiful grassy parks and waterfront promenades, is framed by majestic, snow-capped mountains.

ARRIVAL, INFORMATION, ACCOMMODATION

≋ Zurich Hauptbahnhof (HB) is on the west side of the River Limmat, leading out onto Bahnhofstrasse, the city's main shopping street. ✈ Zurich Airport is 10 km north-east of the city centre (www.zurich-airport.com). There are 10 to 13 trains an hour from the rail station, taking approx. 12 mins (ERT 529). The centre of Zurich is small enough to explore on foot. All buses and trams, run by VBZ Züri-Linie (www.ebrweb.eu/zuri), leave the terminal outside the HB frequently. Buy your ticket from machines at stops before boarding or online. 🛈 Tourist office: on the station concourse at the Hauptbahnhof (www.zuerich.com).

🛏 Staying in Zurich is not cheap. However, if you are design conscious and enjoy a relaxed and friendly atmosphere you might like the **25hours Hotel Langstrasse**, Langstrasse 150, ☎ 044 576 52 55 (www.25hours-hotels.com), located not far from the main station. The stylish **St Josef**, Hirschengraben 64/68, ☎ 044 250 57 87 (www.st-josef.ch), is between the station and the university. Just a few steps from the Bahnhofstrasse, the friendly **Townhouse** boutique hotel, Schützengasse 7, ☎ 044 200 95 95 (www.townhouse.ch), has rather memorable wallpaper.

ZURICH CONNECTIONS

The Hauptbahnhof in Zurich is the place to connect onto **Route 35, 36** and **38** in this book. All three offer great opportunities for **exploring the Alps** by train. There are hourly trains to Geneva (ERT 505), where you can connect onto **Route 12**. ÖBB Railjet trains speed east to Vienna, Budapest and Bratislava (ERT 86). There are night trains to Berlin and Hamburg (both ERT 54), as well as to Ljubljana, Zagreb, Vienna, Graz and Budapest (all ERT 86). Eurocity trains run south from Zurich via the new Gotthard Base Tunnel to Milan (ERT 82).

SIDETRACKS: RHINE VERSUS MOSELLE

Travellers who progress up the Rhine Valley from Cologne face a big decision at **Koblenz**. Most continue up the Rhine and indeed that is just what **Route 20** does. But you might forsake the Rhine in favour of the Moselle, following the lesser river upstream towards Trier and Luxembourg (where you can join **Route 19** in this book). **Mary Shelley** commended a Moselle excursion as a device to enhance still more "the prouder and more romantic glories of the Rhine." The Moselle landscape, Shelley suggested, possesses "an inferior beauty".

We disagree. The Moselle's lazy sinuous course, occasionally rocky and wild, sometimes densely hung with forests and often gently clad with vines, makes for one of the most seductively beautiful waterways in Europe. The **Moselle** might well lay claim to being the **most European of rivers**. It crosses boundaries; its management is a model of international cooperation, and it even has, on its west bank (in Luxembourg territory), a village whose name is now known through the continent: **Schengen**. The eponymous treaty was signed in 1985 on the *MS Princess Marie-Astrid* which bobbed mid-stream in the Moselle just at the point where the German, French and Luxembourg borders converge. The village of Schengen is nearby.

The **Moselle villages** boast a high density of timber-framed buildings. There are mighty fortresses too. Some, like the ruins of **Grevenburg** above Traben-Trarbach, hint of former glories. The grandest are secluded, like Burg Eltz, hidden away in a tiny side valley above Moselkern. And then there are the enigmatic silhouettes, like **Burg Thurant** above Alken with its double keep. Did one side of the family fall out with the other, one wonders! There are fabulous town gates, like the Roman **Porta Nigra** in Trier, the decorative Brückentor in Trarbach and the elegant Graacher Tor (Graach Gate) in **Bernkastel**. But this is no mediaeval landscape preserved in aspic for the traveller's camera. The Moselle was and is an **industrial river**. The ironworks at Alf were opened in 1824, and with the opening of the river to steamers in 1839, the Moselle quickly developed into a great industrial thoroughfare. True, the boatbuilders who once populated the banks of the river have long since turned to other trades. The Romans brought walnuts and vines to the valley, and two millennia of careful cultivation have given the Moselle region a premier position in **European viticulture**.

It takes less than two hours to reach either Trier or Traben-Trarbach from Koblenz. The latter involves an easy change of train at Bullay (ERT 915). Opt for **Traben-Trarbach** if you want to catch the flavour of a classic Moselle wine town. Trier is less evidently connected to the Moselle than Traben-Trarbach, but offers a big dose of history and culture. The Porta Nigra is one of the most impressive Roman structures north of the Alps. Sedate **Trier** was the birthplace of Karl Marx, and the house where he was born at Brückenstr. 10 has a superb exhibition on his life and work (closed Monday mornings Nov–Mar).

There are excellent **boat services** along the Moselle. ERT 914a shows just one example, viz. the five-hour trip from Koblenz up to **Cochem**. But there are many more. Our favourite is the Sunday sailing (summer only) on the *MS Princess Marie-Astrid* from Trier to Schengen. Read more details on www. entente-moselle.lu.

PRUSSIA, BAVARIA AND BEYOND
An introduction

There are a few **echoes of history** in this section of *Europe by Rail*. It's a chance to reconnect with the political entities of yesteryear. The Kingdom of Prussia and the Kingdom of Bavaria both slipped into history in 1918, as their respective royal families – the Hohenzollerns in Prussia and the Wittelsbachs in Bavaria – were unceremoniously despatched. But there's more recent history too, for all three routes in this section of the book breach a fracture line which divided Europe in the second half of the 20th century, namely the **Iron Curtain**. **Route 21, 22** and **23** all cross the former border between the Federal Republic of Germany (or West Germany) and the German Democratic Republic (or East Germany).

The lines on the maps may have disappeared but, a generation on from the **unification of the two German States** (in 1990), the lingering effects of the post-war division of Germany are still evident. Attitudes to life, family and work are often different in the former East, and many older citizens hanker after the good times when jobs were secure and the pace of social change less troubling. Those worries find expression in continuing strong political support for left-wing parties (ie. *Die Linke*) and latterly for the extreme right (the AfD secured a majority in some electoral districts in eastern Germany in the September 2019 elections).

In spring 1991, in the wake of German unification, there were just three trains each day from **Berlin to Munich**; the fastest of these services took ten hours for the journey. Today, there are hourly departures on the route; December 2017 saw the first sub-four-hour timing between the two cities (though in fairness most trains on the route still take closer to five hours).

Our routes in this section criss-cross territory where the Deutsche Bahn's showpiece **ICE trains** are commonplace on main-line routes. But, to catch a sense of the landscape, it's better to stick to slower trains. In **Route 22**, there's a chance of an ultra-slow travel experience, as we explore the Harz Mountains, taking advantage of the network of **narrow-gauge railways** which serve that region. It's a reminder that Prussia, Bavaria and many other territories in Germany once had very extensive networks of *Kleinbahnen* (literally 'small railways', often constructed to a narrower gauge than the main routes). Almost all these minor routes have disappeared, but the Harz network is a chance to recapture an earlier spirit of rail travel.

There are other routes in this region, ones we know well, for which we might well try and make space in a future edition of *Europe of Rail*. The German state of **Thuringia** has some wonderful lesser routes. The 3-hour-35-minute journey from Eisenach to Neuhaus am Rennweg is a gem. There's also a fine network of rural routes in south-west Bavaria (ERT 935). ∎

Route 21: Across northern Germany

Cities: ★★ Culture: ★ History: ★★ Scenery: ★
Countries covered: Germany (DE)
Journey time: 6 hrs | Distance: 612 km | Map: www.ebrweb.eu/map21

This is one **big leap across Germany**, west to east, but let's not beat about the bush. The main rail route linking Cologne with Berlin will hardly inspire you with fine scenery. A sleek ICE train leaves Cologne Hauptbahnhof (Hbf) hourly for the German capital and the journey takes about five hours. Since mid-2019, the route is also served by Flixtrain. There's a delicate beauty to the landscape here and there, particularly around the Weser Hills and in the watery **flatlands of western Brandenburg**. But ultimately this is a journey where few will be spellbound by the scenery beyond the carriage window.

Recommended itinerary

The particular itinerary we describe here is a variant of that followed by the direct ICE trains from Cologne to Berlin. We leave the fast main line at Hannover, favouring instead the old line via Helmstedt. That's the route taken during the **Cold War years** by the **transit trains** which linked West Germany with West Berlin. The only through train from Cologne to Berlin which, in late 2019, still follows this precise route is the overnight ICE train between the two cities (which is a no-frills affair with just seats and no sleeping cars). You'll always need to make a couple of changes of train along the way to follow this itinerary by day. You can transform this rather prosaic journey into a real adventure by combining it with **Route 22**, which describes a modest detour through the Harz Mountains.

Our journey starts at **Cologne** Hauptbahnhof (see p188 for more on the city), and almost immediately there is one of the route's best moments as the train crosses the Hohenzollern Bridge over the River Rhine. Look behind you for great views of the Cologne riverfront with its cathedral and splendid Romanesque churches. The run north to Düsseldorf takes in a number of industrial communities, not always pretty, but interesting in their own way.

Too often derided as being too commercial and industrial, **Düsseldorf** has moved quite upmarket, its transition exemplified by the Königsallee (generally termed the 'Kö'), one of the most elegant shopping streets in Germany. The city has a substantial Japanese population, who appear to have learnt the art of drinking beer in the same quantities as the German natives – especially the local 'Alt'. Most of the areas of interest are along the Rhine, itself spanned by the graceful **Rheinkniebrücke** (bridge) with the Rhine Tower prominent on the skyline. Marked by the Schlossturm, all that remains of the original 14th-century castle, the **Altstadt** (Old Town) is small and walkable. One of the most attractive corners is the Marktplatz (Market Square), brimming over with outdoor cafés and restaurants.

The city is also the birthplace of **German punk**. Along with Hamburg and Berlin, Düsseldorf nurtured the nascent punk culture, most notably at the Ratinger Hof, which is still an important music venue in the Old Town.

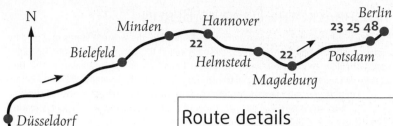

Route details

Cologne Hbf to Düsseldorf Hbf		ERT 800/802
Frequency	Journey time	Notes
3–6 per hr	25–30 mins	

Düsseldorf Hbf to Hannover Hbf		ERT 800
Frequency	Journey time	Notes
Hourly	2 hrs 35 mins – 3 hrs 5 mins	

Hannover Hbf to Magdeburg Hbf		ERT 866
Frequency	Journey time	Notes
Hourly	1 hr 20 mins	H

Magdeburg Hbf to Potsdam Hbf		ERT 839
Frequency	Journey time	Notes
Hourly	70–75 mins	

Postdam Hbf to Berlin Hbf		ERT 839
Frequency	Journey time	Notes
5–9 per hr	25–40 mins	

Notes

If you are heading for Berlin and are pressed for time, bear in mind that there are fast ICE trains direct to Berlin from Cologne and Düsseldorf (ERT 810, hourly from both cities, travel time about 4 hrs 40 mins). These Berlin-bound express trains use the new high-speed line which runs east from Hannover to Berlin via Wolfsburg (where there is a fine view of the Volkswagen factory which you can admire as you ponder the ethics of a company which said its cars were less polluting than they in fact were).

H – Only alternate trains between Hannover and Magdeburg stop at Helmstedt.

To the Weser and beyond

The main rail routes running north-east from Düsseldorf skirt once **heavily industrialised valleys** (the Ruhr, Wupper and Emscher). Much of this area has been creatively rescued from its industrial past with impressive new green landscapes. The route then opens out onto the **Westphalian Plain**. You can detour via the old cities of Münster and Osnabrück (ERT 800 then 811), both with a rich religious history: Münster Protestant and Osnabrück Catholic. The fastest ICE trains speed east on a more southerly route through Bielefeld (ERT 810), a town which is so uncharismatic that Germans often question whether it really exists at all.

The scenery perks up beyond **Herford**, as the train follows the Werre Valley down towards the Weser. Suddenly, and all too briefly, there is a glorious view of the Weser meadowlands and Wiehen Hills. This is the **Porta Westfalica**, the ancient gateway to Westphalia – the historically Prussian province which the railway is now leaving. In the Romantic imagination, the gentle ripples of hills here were magnified into mighty mountains, but

FLASHBACK: THE D243 TO BERLIN

Cast back over 30 years and Germany was still divided, the western states occupied by American, British and French forces; the east, called the German Democratic Republic, stood shoulder to shoulder with the Soviet Union in comradely solidarity. The **Iron Curtain** divided the country. Special transit trains linked West Germany with West Berlin.

Imagine yourself standing on the platform at Cologne Hauptbahnhof in the chill of a March morning in 1981. The first hints of spring are in the air and just a stone's throw away, the great Gothic cathedral looks splendid. But now all eyes are on the train pulling into your platform. This is the D243, an overnight service from Paris which stops briefly in Cologne just after six in the morning and then continues to Berlin. It is one of many **lifeline rail services to West Berlin** in the Cold War years. The passengers at Cologne climb onto the train, taking their seats in the East German (Reichsbahn) carriages for the eight-hour journey to Berlin. Some make for the Mitropa restaurant car where breakfast is already being served.

Travel across the inner-German border between the two German states wasn't easy. There were complicated **border formalities**, with the *Trapos* (the East German transport police) and their dogs carefully checking the train as it entered the territory of the German Democratic Republic. The French couchette carriages and sleeping cars from Paris were removed from the D243 when it stopped at Hannover around ten in the morning. Only the first and second-class seated carriages from Paris continued right through to West Berlin – along the way passing without halt through a medley of East German towns.

In this journey for *Europe by Rail*, we follow exactly the same route as that taken by the D243 from Cologne to Berlin. The **Mitropa restaurant car** is gone too, as is that slightly antiseptic smell which was a feature of East German railway carriages. The fierce fences which once divided Germany have disappeared. Nowadays Europe finds other uses for fences which so cruelly hinder mobility.

even without the hyperbole it's all very fetching. Away to the north (ie. on the left side of the train), you cannot miss the huge monument to Kaiser Wilhelm I on the Wiehen Hills. From mid-May to mid-September, there are river cruises on the Weser which depart from **Minden** (details on www. mifa.com). Just half an hour after crossing the River Weser, your train is approaching Hannover, the capital city of the German state of Lower Saxony.

With over half a million residents, **Hannover** is a major centre for education, commerce and culture. It has many fine historical buildings and some world-class landscape gardens. The city certainly deserves a brief stop and the key sights can be seen within a couple of hours. From the station, Bahnhofstraße leads to the **Kröpcke piazza**, in the heart of the largely reconstructed Altstadt; the Kröpcke clock is the most prominent rendezvous point in town. The high-gabled, carefully restored Altes Rathaus is a splendid edifice with elaborate brickwork. Alongside is the Marktkirche, with 14th- to 15th-century stained glass and a bulky tower that is the city's emblem. An absolute must-see are the **Royal Herrenhäuser Gardens**, 10 mins by urban rail line 4 or 5 from Kröpcke (station: Herrenhäuser Gärten) – four once-royal gardens, two of which are the English-style landscaped

Georgengarten and the formal Grosser Garten with spectacular fountain displays in summer. The Herrenhäuser Gardens are often acclaimed as the finest early baroque gardens in Germany.

CONNECTIONS FROM HANNOVER

You can join **Route 22** here. It's a good option for Berlin-bound travellers who have time to detour into the **Harz Mountains** and see some real forest wilderness. As the largest rail hub in Lower Saxony, Hannover offers plentiful onward connections. There are two or three trains each hour north to Hamburg (ERT 900 or 903), the fastest taking just 75 minutes to reach the great port city on the Elbe. Southbound you can choose from hourly departures to Frankfurt-am-Main, Nuremberg and Munich (all ERT 900). Trains to Stuttgart and Basel both leave every two hours (ERT 900).

Closer to hand, there are hourly trains to **Goslar** and Bad Harzburg, both in the Harz Mountains (ERT 860). Another **regional route** (ERT 809) runs south-west to Hameln – that's the Hamelin of pied piper fame. The real gem though, when it comes to the local lines radiating from Hannover, is the minor route which runs north via Soltau to Buchholz (from where it is but a short hop on to Hamburg). This line is not shown in the ERT. Trains for **Buchholz** depart hourly (every two hours at weekends) from Hannover Hauptbahnhof; it's a fine two-hour journey which takes in the Böhme Valley and skirts the great Lüneburg Heath. Flat lands, you'll discover, can indeed be winsomely beautiful.

A tale of two Germanys

German unification in 1990 spawned a number of major rail infrastructure projects to improve communications across the former border between the two German states. The most important of these came to fruition in 1998 with the opening of a new fast line from Hannover to Berlin. Trains now dash between the two cities in just 95 minutes (ERT 810). That's the way to go if you are pressed for time. Along the way, you'll get a great view (left side of the train) of the **Volkswagen factory** at Wolfsburg. It's just one of many striking buildings in a city which has some first-rate architecture.

But we'll stick to the old main line, the one once followed by the transit trains to West Berlin, which runs south-east from Hannover through Braunschweig and cuts through pleasant beech forests to reach **Helmstedt**, the last town on the former territory of West Germany. It's a pleasant place with some fine examples of late 16th-century Weser Renaissance-style architecture – well east of the area where that architectural fashion flourished. During the Cold War, Helmstedt benefited from its position close to the **East German border**. Trade was good with border hoppers often stopping in Helmstedt to stock up on goods which were less readily available in the German Democratic Republic. Helmstedt was a busy crossing point for road traffic too. The border post where eastbound travellers left West Germany was known as Checkpoint Alpha. Border antics and the sorrows of living in a divided country are recalled in the **Zonengrenz-Museum** (literally Zonal Boundary Museum) in Helmstedt. It is in a villa just a five-minute walk north of the station at Südertor 6 (closed Mon).

Nowadays, many fast trains speed through Helmstedt without even stopping. It is just six minutes on a local train from Helmstedt to Marien-born, which was the entry point into East Germany. The Berlin-bound transit trains and all other eastbound expresses used to stop at **Marienborn** for checks by the East German authorities. Nowadays this is no more than an inconsequential country railway station, served only by the hourly local trains from Braunschweig to Magdeburg.

The border between the two German states may have gone but, if you take time to explore smaller communities in the eastern part of the country, you'll still find very different attitudes compared to the west. And, as the train rattles east towards **Magdeburg**, you'll notice a string of quiet villages where it looks as though the clocks may have stopped 30 years ago. Magdeburg is always worth a stop, if only to take a look at the city's remarkable cathedral. The city's position on the navigable **Elbe** gave Magdeburg's traders a mighty boost in the Middle Ages; the city was an important player in the Hanseatic League. Today the Elbe is a mixed blessing. The city has on a number of occasions suffered catastrophic flooding and the last of them were in 2013.

CONNECTIONS FROM MAGDEBURG

At Magdeburg, you can connect onto **Route 22** and follow it (in reverse direction) through the **Harz Mountains** back to Hannover. Regional Express trains run north to Wittenberge every hour or two (ERT 841), from where it is just a short hop to Hamburg (ERT 840). Fast double-deck Intercity trains run direct to Leipzig and Dresden (ERT 866), where you can connect with **Route 25** to Prague and Budapest (Table 60).

Brandenburg and Potsdam

From Magdeburg, Deutsche Bahn's red double-decker Regional Express (RE) trains run hourly to Berlin. Grab a seat on the upper deck as the train cruises east through the Brandenburg flatlands towards the German capital. Brandenburg is the name of the German state which entirely surrounds Berlin; the capital has the status of a state in its own right. All Berlin-bound RE trains from Magdeburg stop at the town of **Brandenburg**, which gave its name to the eponymous state. With a watery setting on the Havel, Brandenburg is an appealing mid-sized town. The nicest areas are around the cathedral, well north of the station.

The next town of any size is **Potsdam** which nudges up so close to Berlin that you might be inclined to see it as no more than a suburb of the German capital. But that's to mistake the historical importance of Potsdam – it was the home of the Hohenzollern family and the hub of imperial power – and the city's status today as the capital of Brandenburg, the largest state in eastern Germany. Potsdam is an absolute 'must see'. The town centre has been superbly restored with two areas especially worthy of a visit. In the very centre is the **Dutch quarter**, a neat area of high-gabled houses with a fabulous mix of small shops and cafés. After wandering through the Dutch quarter, walk north to **Alexandrowka**, once home to the city's Russian community. With its wooden houses, orchards and serenity, Alexandrowka gives a real sense of being a Russian village. There is a delightful Russian café at Alexandrowka Haus 1 (closed Mon).

But Potsdam has of course a real trump card in its **array of palaces and gardens**. The great writer on parks and gardens, Charles Quest-Ritson, lavishes praise on Potsdam in *Gardens of Europe*: "Sanssouci Park is by far the most beautiful, exciting and rewarding garden in Germany and, in my view, the world... It is a series of stupendous palaces and gardens joined together by Peter Joseph Lenné's brilliant, fluid, landscaping." Go judge for yourself. Fast trains link Potsdam and Berlin in less than half an hour. We find Potsdam so beautiful, so exceptional, that we think it worth stopping off there for a night or two. Indeed, some travellers prefer to stay in Potsdam and use it as a base for day trips to Berlin. A good area of town to stay is on or around the **Luisenplatz** close to Potsdam's Brandenburg Gate and the Sanssouci Gardens. Try the Hotel Am Luisenplatz, Luisenplatz 5, ☎ 0331 97 19 00 (www.hotel-luisenplatz.de), or the Steigenberger Hotel Sanssouci, Allee nach Sanssouci 1, ☎ 0331 90 910 (www.steigenberger.com).

Berlin

Rich history, fabulous art, **alternative culture** – all in the broadest sense – combine to make the city of Berlin a destination that is a little out of the ordinary. The city's turbulent past and cosmopolitan citizens are its main draw; at every corner a piece of modern history plays out in front of you – whether it's the intrigue of the Cold War or the violent trauma of Nazism, it's all represented here.

But Berlin is more than just wars and destruction. Berlin is a city that is always evolving, never stagnant. If you have time to visit just one museum, make it the **Jewish Museum** on Lindenstrasse 9–4 (U-Bahn: Hallesches Tor). Berlin's hottest complex of boutiques, galleries, bars and cafés is the area around **Hackescher Markt**. For a more edgy urban feel head for Schönhauser Allee. The city's latest attraction, the **Humboldt Forum,** will open in phases from autumn 2020 on the site of the former Hohenzollern city palace as both an exhibition and a discussion space.

Rail travellers will most likely enter the city through the **Hauptbahnhof**, a stunning glass-and-steel construction. Indeed, it can be said that Berlin as a city only truly came of age in the era of the railways, and its rich history in this regard is reflected in some wonderful railway architecture, including the Hamburger Bahnhof, now converted into a museum of modern art, the red-brick **Oberbaumbrücke** lifting the elevated U-Bahn tracks across the River Spree, and the ruined facade of the Anhalter Bahnhof.

Also worth searching out is the small memorial by Friedrichstraße station. It shows the two sides of the railway's role during the Nazi era in Germany, from the evacuation of 10,000 Jewish children to England in 1938 on the one side, to the many others who were **deported by train** to the concentration and extermination camps of the Third Reich on the other.

For a cheap sightseeing trip, avoid the tourist buses and take 🚌 100 from Alexanderplatz to Zoo Station. Travelling along Unter den Linden and through the Tiergarten, the bus takes in most of central Berlin's sights at a fraction of the cost.

ARRIVAL, INFORMATION, ACCOMMODATION

🚄 Berlin's impressive **Hauptbahnhof** (Hbf) is the city's main railway hub. Note that the railway platforms are not all on the same level, so changing trains, particularly if you are unfamiliar with the station, might take a while. Avoid tight connections. The other stations served by various long-distance services and night trains are **Ostbahnhof** (Ost), **Südkreuz**, **Gesundbrunnen** and **Spandau**. Some regional trains may also serve **Zoologischer Garten** (Zoo), **Lichtenberg** or the newly opened regional rail platforms at Berlin Ostkreuz.

✈ The much publicised grand opening of Berlin's new airport (BER) in June 2012 was deferred at the last minute. Now there's talk of the first planes landing in late 2020 – but don't bet on it. The major budget airlines all serve **Schönefeld Airport** (SXF), about 20 km south-east of the city centre (trains 04.45–22.45 to Zoo, Hbf and Ost stations; ERT 847). Berlin's second airport is at **Tegel** (TXL), about 12 km north-west of the city centre. 🚌 TXL connects Tegel Airport with Hauptbahnhof (20 mins), S-Bahn Brandenburger Tor (28 mins) and Alexanderplatz (35 mins). Airport information at www.berlin-airport.de.

ℹ Berlin infostores offer city information and accommodation services (www. visitberlin.de). They are located at the Hauptbahnof, in the Europa Center on Kurfürsten-damm, the Brandenburg Gate and the Park Inn at Alexanderplatz. The city's efficient public transport system combines buses, trams, underground (U-Bahn) and surface trains (S-Bahn). Tickets are valid on all means of transport mentioned, and you can get them on station platforms, from machines on the trams, or from bus drivers.

🛏 Berlin has some wonderful hotels and, although prices are creeping up, the German capital remains surprisingly reasonable. Hotels in Mitte are best placed for the majority of Berlin's sights, and a recommended option in the area is the stylish and friendly **Circus Hotel**, Rosenthaler Strasse 1, ☎ 030 200 039 39 (www.circus-berlin.de). A no-frills but functional and cheap alternative is the **EasyHotel**, Rosenthaler Strasse 69, ☎ 030 400 065 50 (www.easyhotel-berlin.de), which is in an good location. If you want to treat yourself, the **Casa Camper**, Weinmeisterstrasse 1, ☎ 030 200 034 10 (www.casacamper. com), has brought their extremely popular boutique hotel concept to Berlin from Barcelona.

CONNECTIONS FROM BERLIN

The German capital is of course a **major rail hub** with direct trains to Dresden (ERT 840) Prague (ERT 60), Warsaw (ERT 1001), Leipzig (ERT 850) and Munich (ERT 850). The very fastest trains to Munich now take just four hours to reach the Bavarian capital. Berlin has a superb choice of regional services with direct trains to the **Baltic towns** of Rostock and Stralsund (ERT 835 & 845), Kostrzyn in Poland (ERT 832) and Cottbus in Lusatia (ERT 837).

Berlin also has a number of **night trains**. The list includes a seasonal service to Malmö in Sweden (ERT 50, couchettes only) and a very comfortable year-round link with Minsk and Moscow (ERT 24 or 56). There are also direct night sleepers to Basel and Zurich (ERT 54) as well as new direct night trains to Vienna, Budapest, Kraków and Przemyśl (all in ERT 77, a welcome new ERT table added when these sleeper services launched in 2019).

Route 22: The Harz Mountains

CITIES: ★★ CULTURE: ★ HISTORY: ★★ SCENERY: ★★★
COUNTRIES COVERED: GERMANY (DE)
JOURNEY TIME: 9 HRS | DISTANCE: 302 KM | MAP: WWW.EBRWEB.EU/MAP22

The figures quoted for end-to-end journey time and distance for this route exclude the side trip on the steam railway from Drei Annen Hohne to the summit of the Brocken and back.

Every day, thousands of travellers speed across northern Germany on the main rail routes from Cologne or the Ruhr region towards Berlin. The previous route in this volume describes one such journey. It covers a lot of ground at speed, but it's hardly a great rail adventure.

Yet so often in Europe, even just a modest diversion from the main line can transform a prosaic run into something very special, and nowhere is that better illustrated than in journeys **across northern Germany**. You can cut off to the south of the main railways which link Hannover with Berlin to discover the glorious landscapes of the Harz Mountains, a region which boasts Europe's finest network of **narrow-gauge steam railways**. Even if you are not a train buff, the scenery alone justifies an **excursion into the Harz region**. Moreover, the Harz steam trains always go down a treat with children and families.

The entire journey relies on **private rail operators**, rather than the Deutsche Bahn. Interrail, Eurail and other passes are accepted from Hannover as far as Wernigerode and again from Quedlinburg to Magdeburg. For the journey on the Harz narrow-gauge rail routes from Wernigerode to Quedlinburg, rail passes are not recognised and separate tickets must be purchased. There are useful passes allowing unlimited travel on the Harz narrow-gauge network (for fares and rover tickets see www.ebrweb.eu/3).

RECOMMENDED ITINERARY

You could follow this entire journey, from Hannover to Magdeburg via the Harz Mountains in one long day. But it deserves much more time. We suggest making at least two overnight stops along the way. **Drei Annen Hohne** and **Quedlinburg** are good choices.

The best of the scenery is on that part of the journey served by the Harz narrow-gauge trains. Note that there are only very limited services on this network in late autumn, with some routes usually closed completely for a spell between early November and mid-December. Trains to the **summit of the Brocken** are always steam operated, but bear in mind that services may be disrupted by heavy snow or high winds.

We think that this is a route best tackled in the months from May to October inclusive – and, in our view, the Harz Mountains region is at its loveliest in spring or early autumn, so if you can travel in May or October you are in for a treat. Arrange your journey so that the section from Drei Annen Hohne to Quedlinburg is on a Thursday, Friday or Saturday when there is a much better choice of steam-operated services. On other days, diesel railcars operate far more trains on the **Selke Valley railway** to Quedlinburg. Quite apart from the allure of steam, the railcars used on the Harz network just aren't very comfortable. The timetables for the Harz narrow-gauge network are online at www.ebrweb.eu/hrs. They clearly indicate whether **diesel railcars** or **steam trains** are used on particular services.

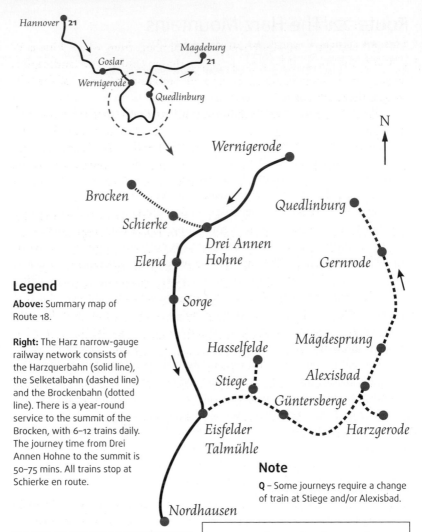

Legend

Above: Summary map of Route 18.

Right: The Harz narrow-gauge railway network consists of the Harzquerbahn (solid line), the Selketalbahn (dashed line) and the Brockenbahn (dotted line). There is a year-round service to the summit of the Brocken, with 6–12 trains daily. The journey time from Drei Annen Hohne to the summit is 50–75 mins. All trains stop at Schierke en route.

Note

Q – Some journeys require a change of train at Stiege and/or Alexisbad.

Route details

Hannover to Goslar		ERT 860
Frequency	**Journey time**	**Notes**
Hourly	70 mins	

Goslar to Wernigerode		ERT 860
Frequency	**Journey time**	**Notes**
Hourly	35 mins	

Wernigerode to Drei Annen Hohne		ERT 867
Frequency	**Journey time**	**Notes**
6–9 per day	40 mins	

Route details (cont.)

Drei Annen Hohne to Eisfelder Talmühle		ERT 867
Frequency	**Journey time**	**Notes**
4 per day	70 mins	

Eisfelder Talmühle to Quedlinburg		ERT 867
Frequency	**Journey time**	**Notes**
4 per day	2 hrs 15 mins – 3 hrs 15 mins	Q

Quedlinburg to Magdeburg Hbf		ERT 862
Frequency	**Journey time**	**Notes**
Hourly	70–80 mins	

Towards the hills

The journey starts at **Hannover** Hauptbahnhof, from where blue-and-yellow trains operated by erixx leave hourly for Goslar. The landscape is initially unremarkable, but soon there are tantalising glimpses of the hills away to the south-east.

All trains pause at **Hildesheim**, a mid-sized town that's worth a stop. It's a busy town, at first glance quite uninviting, but wander into the centre (a 10-min walk south from the main station) and you'll discover a very handsome central area, with two spectacular churches – both inscribed on UNESCO's World Heritage List. Hildesheim is one of northern Germany's best-kept secrets.

From Hildesheim, it is just a short hop on the erixx train to **Goslar** which boasts a well preserved mediaeval centre full of half-timbered houses. It owed its prosperity to silver and lead mining in the Middle Ages. At its heart is the **Marktplatz**, presided over by the Rathaus and Marktkirche. It is all very fine, but in our view a shade too touristy. Quedlinburg (further east on this route) offers the same architectural feast but without the crowds. But Goslar is a good jumping-off point for hikes into the hills to the south.

From Goslar, our route continues with a train run by Abellio Rail across the former border between West Germany and East Germany to **Wernigerode**, another historic half-timbered town, notable for what might well be the finest town hall (Rathaus) in all Germany. That, and the extravagant castle, justify a stop. It is here in Wernigerode that the fun begins, as the journey south into the mountains is on the **narrow-gauge Harzquerbahn** (Trans-Harz Railway).

Exploring the Harz Mountains

Trips on the **Harz region steam trains** will appeal to those inclined to savour the ride as much as the destination. You'll have time aplenty to enjoy the journey on trains which chug through woodlands and valleys, for the average speed is only about 25 kilometres per hour.

The network formerly extended into the western Harz, but the routes that ran through West Germany were axed between 1958 and 1963 after harsh cost-benefit analyses which failed to appreciate the potential of the railways as shared community assets. The German Democratic Republic saw the value of **rural railways** in a region that lagged far behind the West in terms of levels of car ownership.

This network (see sketch map on p216) includes a celebrated mountain railway, with steam trains climbing to the highest point in the Harz Mountains which is called the **Brocken**. At 1,141 metres the Brocken is the greatest elevation in northern Germany.

Drei Annen Hohne (suggested stopover)

Drei Annen Hohne is a good base for exploring the region. This railway junction is also the starting point for the branch line (called the **Brocken-bahn**) to the summit of the Brocken, an excursion we've made several times. We've found journeys around dusk by far the most memorable. Travelling at that time you'll have the advantage of a completely empty train on the uphill journey, but it does mean that you'll not have much time at the summit before catching the last train back down to Drei Annen Hohne.

Arrival, information, accommodation

Drei Annen Hohne is just a small community with a handful of houses, large car parks and a lovely station building that houses a ticket office and information centre for the Harzquerbahn and a café. ⋈ The hotel **Der Kräuterhof**, ☎ 0394 558 40 (www.hotel-kraeuterhof.de), is a good place to stay and ideally located just behind the station. Ask for a room with a view of the station to watch the trains go by. The hotel has a restaurant.

The Selke Valley

Whether or not you include the Brocken excursion, our main route follows the **Harzquerbahn** south from Drei Annen Hohne. The start is stunning, as the railway weaves through varied Harz landscapes.

We rate the 29-km stretch from Drei Annen Hohne to Eisfelder Tal-mühle as one of Europe's finest short train journeys. At **Eisfelder Talmühle**, the main station building houses a decent bar and restaurant if you are minded to break the journey. It is at this station that you switch from the Harzquerbahn to the **Selketalbahn** (Selke Valley railway) for the onward journey to Quedlinburg.

The Selketalbahn traverses landscapes of delicate beauty with many fine opportunities for lineside photography if you are tempted to stop off. The nicest of the many small communities along this line is **Alexisbad**, a small spa town where life is as leisurely as the pace of the trains which stop at the local station. Beyond Alexisbad, the railway drops steeply down from the hills to **Gernrode** on the North German Plain, from where it's just a few minutes across flat country to Quedlinburg.

Quedlinburg (suggested stopover)

The railway station in Quedlinburg is in a wretched state of decay and gives no hint of the beauty of all that waits in the centre of town, just a 12-minute walk north-west of the station. This is one of northern Germany's most engaging small towns. With its remarkable ensemble of **mediaeval buildings**, Quedlinburg knocks spots off the Bavarian competition, yet it still seems undiscovered by non-Germans despite its UNESCO World Heritage status.

ARRIVAL, INFORMATION, ACCOMMODATION

⇌ The station is a 12-min walk south-east of the main square. ⓘ Tourist office: Markt 4 (www.quedlinburg.de). ⤳ The hotel **Zum Bär**, Markt 8–9, ☎ 03946 7770 (www.hotelzumbaer.de), is located right on the main square and offers good rooms in a historic building. Other good options are the friendly **Hotel Domschatz**, Mühlenstr. 20, ☎ 03946 70 52 70 (www.hotel-domschatz.de), close to the castle in a quiet location just a 7-min walk from the main square and the **Hotel am Hoken**, Hoken 3, ☎ 03946 525 40 (www.hotel-am-hoken.de), next to the town hall on the main square.

CONNECTIONS FROM QUEDLINBURG

If you want to return to Wernigerode without having to retrace the route by train through the Harz Mountains, there is a useful direct bus from Quedlinburg to **Wernigerode**. Bus service 230 leaves hourly (every 2 hrs on Sat & Sun) from the bus stop by the railway station, and takes about 55 minutes to reach Wernigerode.

On Friday, Saturday and Sunday afternoons, rail operator Abellio runs a great-value express train from **Quedlinburg to Berlin**. See timings in ERT 862. The one-way fare (just pay on the train) is €16. This train is marketed as the *Harz-Berlin Express*. Note that rail passes (Interrail, Eurail etc.) are not recognised, nor are Deutsche Bahn train tickets.

To the Elbe Valley

From Quedlinburg, our journey tracks north-east across the plain to **Magdeburg**, where it rejoins **Route 21** in this book. There is nothing to detain you on the short run from Quedlinburg to Magdeburg, but the latter is definitely worth a look. Approaching Magdeburg from the south, on the train from Quedlinburg, you get little sense of the city's riverside location. But Magdeburg's historical influence and commercial affluence derives entirely from its position on the **River Elbe**. From the main station, it is a 10-minute walk east along Ernst Reuter Allee to the west bank of the river. Take time to wander through the centre and see the city's showpiece Gothic cathedral.

CONNECTIONS FROM MAGDEBURG

Magdeburg is a **major railway junction**. You can follow **Route 21** in this book east to Berlin or west to Hannover and beyond. There are departures at least hourly in both directions (ERT 839 to Berlin & ERT 866 to Hannover). Regional trains leave every hour for Erfurt in Thuringia (ERT 861). Fans of **Bauhaus architecture** and design may be tempted by the hourly trains to Dessau (ERT 848), which is less than an hour away. Read more on Dessau on p223. There are also regular direct trains from Magdeburg to Halle and Leipzig (ERT 866), with some services continuing beyond Leipzig to Dresden.

EAST GERMAN STEAM

Apart from the Harz region, there are a number of other narrow-gauge steam railways in eastern Germany. You might want to explore the **Rügensche Bäderbahn** which runs through lovely beech woods on the island of Rügen (ERT 844a). In Saxony, steam still runs year-round on a line which climbs into the hills behind **Zittau** and on another at **Radebeul** in the Elbe Valley near Dresden. Times for both are in ERT 853.

Route 23: From Prussia to the Alps

Cities: ★★★ Culture: ★ History: ★★ Scenery: ★★
Countries covered: Germany (DE), Austria (AT)
Journey time: 10 hrs | Distance: 943 km | Map: www.ebrweb.eu/map23

This long journey from **Berlin to Bavaria** and on across the Austrian border to **Salzburg** takes in some very fine German cities (including Leipzig, Weimar and Munich) and some decent countryside – of which the two highlights are the hill country of Thuringia in the middle of the route and the Chiemgau area of Upper Bavaria. The latter gives a grand finale to the journey on the approach to Salzburg.

Route 23 is one of two in this book which lead travellers from northern Germany to the Alps. The other is **Route 20** from Cologne to Zurich via the Rhine Valley and the Black Forest. Both these routes are ideal components in longer itineraries extending from **northern Europe to the Mediterranean** (or vice versa). As you travel the length of Route 23 there is a real sense of swapping cool and practical Prussian restraint for the more easy-going southern pieties.

This route takes in both halves of Germany, viz. the former German Democratic Republic (DDR) and the western part of the country. That erstwhile political division slips slowly into history. Not so the **north-south culinary divide**. Our journey starts in undisputed *Currywurst* territory – although the traditional Berlin curried sausage is not a snack of great antiquity. In the late 1940s American soldiers added ketchup and British forces threw in curry powder and Worcester Sauce to give a much-needed kick to Berlin's anaemic pork sausages. Few Berliners would give shelf space to a Bavarian white sausage (*Weißwurst* in German), any more than lads from Munich would resort to a *Currywurst*.

Route 23 breaches the **Weißwurstgrenze**, that never quite defined but universally acknowledged frontier which will forever separate Prussia from Bavaria, north from south, Protestants from Catholics. Our journey traverses various sausage territories. In Weimar and Erfurt, look out for the famous grilled *Thüringer*; as you move south don't miss the spicy *Würzburger* and the finger-sized *Nürnberger*. Having sucked on mushy *Weißwurst* in Munich, you'll be all set to tackle the celebrated Salzburg *Bosna*, served in a roll much like a hot dog.

ITINERARY NOTES

The beauty of rail travel in Germany is that seat reservations are never compulsory on daytime trains, and there are no supplements for those travelling with Eurail and Interrail passes. So this is a good route for just **hopping on and off at will**. You have a choice of fast services (ie. Intercity or ICE) and slower trains for most legs of the route. It's a journey which could so easily be spun out to a week or more. If you can afford just **three overnight stops**, we would opt for Weimar, Würzburg and Munich.

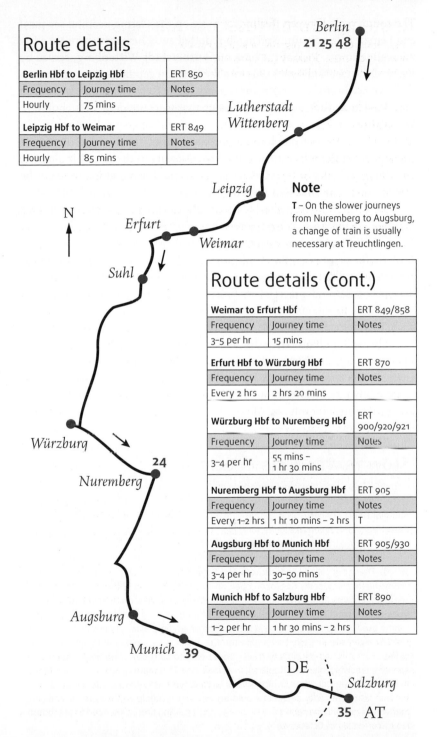

Route details

Berlin Hbf to Leipzig Hbf		ERT 850
Frequency	Journey time	Notes
Hourly	75 mins	

Leipzig Hbf to Weimar		ERT 849
Frequency	Journey time	Notes
Hourly	85 mins	

Berlin
21 25 48

Lutherstadt
Wittenberg

Leipzig

N

Erfurt

Weimar

Suhl

Note

T – On the slower journeys from Nuremberg to Augsburg, a change of train is usually necessary at Treuchtlingen.

Route details (cont.)

Weimar to Erfurt Hbf		ERT 849/858
Frequency	Journey time	Notes
3–5 per hr	15 mins	

Erfurt Hbf to Würzburg Hbf		ERT 870
Frequency	Journey time	Notes
Every 2 hrs	2 hrs 20 mins	

Würzburg Hbf to Nuremberg Hbf		ERT 900/920/921
Frequency	Journey time	Notes
3–4 per hr	55 mins – 1 hr 30 mins	

Nuremberg Hbf to Augsburg Hbf		ERT 905
Frequency	Journey time	Notes
Every 1–2 hrs	1 hr 10 mins – 2 hrs	T

Augsburg Hbf to Munich Hbf		ERT 905/930
Frequency	Journey time	Notes
3–4 per hr	30–50 mins	

Munich Hbf to Salzburg Hbf		ERT 890
Frequency	Journey time	Notes
1–2 per hr	1 hr 30 mins – 2 hrs	

Würzburg

24

Nuremberg

Augsburg

Munich **39**

DE

Salzburg

35 AT

The countryside between **Berlin** (for more on the German capital see p213) and Leipzig is largely uninspiring, but dotted away here and there are a few interesting towns. Pick of the bunch is **Lutherstadt Wittenberg**, served by many of the fast trains en route from the German capital to Leipzig. In 2017, the town celebrated the 500th anniversary of the Reformation. It was in 1517 that **Martin Luther** pinned his famous theses to the door of a church in Wittenberg.

This handsome small town is worth a visit not merely on account of its Luther connections and the inevitable memorials to the reforming pastor, but also as a chance to see a former East German town that is a little off the beaten track. The **Haus der Geschichte** (House of History) at Schlossstr. 6 gives rich insights into everyday life in the German Democratic Republic from 1949 to 1989.

Leipzig has been a cultural centre for many centuries, famous particularly for its music: numerous great 19th-century works were premiered at the **Gewandhaus**, Augustuspl. 8. The original building is long gone, but the current Gewandhaus is a very fine piece of DDR architecture from 1981. Second only to Vienna for its **musical tradition**, the city was the home of Bach, Mendelssohn and Schumann.

The Gewandhaus Orchestra, Opera House and the Thomanerchor (St Thomas's Church Choir), which was conducted by Bach for 27 years, have a world-class reputation. Take a stroll around the **pedestrianised centre**, where many long-neglected buildings and arcades are fast acquiring rows of smart shops, restaurants and offices. Yet Leipzig retains some of the grace of an old European city.

SLOW TRAVEL DEALS IN GERMANY

Germany has some amazingly good deals for rail travellers prepared to avoid the fastest trains (generally those with an ICE, IC or EC prefix) and stick only to **local or regional train services**. This is a train category called *Nahverkehr* in German. Many of these regional trains make quite long journeys, with many routes extending to well over 300 kilometres.

There are regional tickets covering each German state (or two or more adjacent states). These are called **Ländertickets**. The **Bayern Ticket**, which gives unlimited travel in Bavaria for a day, costs €25 for one person or €49 for a group of five (for more details see www.ebrweb.eu/5). There is a useful one-day pass valid for nationwide travel. The **Quer-durchs-Land Ticket** (QdL) is priced from €44 for one to €76 for five travellers; it can be used on Mondays to Fridays after 09.00 or anytime at weekends.

You can see just what a bargain the QdL ticket is by looking at its potential use in Route 23. It is just possible to travel from Berlin to Salzburg using only *Nahverkehr* services, precisely following Route 23, in a single day. That journey takes 16 hours. Make that trip with the QdL ticket, which is valid beyond the Austrian border to Salzburg, and the one-way fare for one person would be €44, for a couple €52 and for a family of four with two children under 15 years of age just €52. And there's **no need to pre-book**. Prices correct as of October 2019.

BAUHAUS ARCHITECTURE

Lutherstadt Wittenberg is a good jumping-off point to visit **Dessau**, the UNESCO World Heritage city that is so popular with fans of 20th-century architecture, but curiously unknown among a wider public. Dessau is the **Bauhaus town** par excellence. Trains from both stations at Wittenberg run at least hourly to Dessau, about 40 mins distant (ERT 848). The main Bauhaus building is just a 4-min walk from the back entrance of Dessau Hauptbahnhof. Catch it on a good day, and the glass curtain facade looks superb against a blue sky.

Other Bauhaus highlights include the **Meisterhäuser** (Masters' Houses), a 20-min walk from the station. These classic Bauhaus buildings were once the homes of the architects, artists and designers who brought such revolutionary impetus to the Bauhaus movement. The roll call of illustrious residents includes Paul Klee, Wassily Kandinsky and Walter Gropius. And don't miss the **Kornhaus Restaurant**, a classic piece of Bauhaus style, on the bank of the Elbe. Take 🚌 10 or 11 from Hauptbahnhof directly to Kornhaus. The new Bauhaus Museum (www.bauhaus-dessau.de) which opened in September 2019 in time for the centenary celebrations of the Bauhaus school, is also on those bus routes. There is no need to return to Lutherstadt Wittenberg to continue your journey, for Dessau is served by direct local trains to Leipzig (ERT 848).

In 1989, the mass demonstrations and candlelit vigils in Nikolaikirche, Nikolaikirchhof 3, were the focus for the city's peaceful revolt against the East German state authorities. The Stasi 'Power and Banality' Museum, Dittrichring 24, in the former **Ministry of State Security**, reviews the apparatus of State surveillance and control.

On the edge of the **Innenstadt** (city centre), a 10-min walk to the middle, Leipzig's station is an attraction in its own right, and is one of Europe's biggest and most impressive. Built in 1915, it was recently refurbished. If you are minded to stay in Leipzig, the Hotel Living Bach14, Thomaskirchhof 13/14, ☎ 0341 496 140 (www.bach14.arcona.de) is in a great location just opposite the Thomaskirche in a listed building. Very convenient for the station is the modern and comfortable Seaside Park Hotel Leipzig, Richard-Wagner-Str. 7, ☎ 0341 985 20 (www.parkhotelleipzig.de).

A **new high-speed line** from Leipzig to Erfurt opened in late 2015, so the fastest trains now bypass Weimar, but we think it's worth taking the old line which follows the River Saale and then the Ilm upstream to Weimar – along the way passing the first large vineyards on this route.

Weimar (suggested stopover)

Smart shops, pavement cafés and a lively Onion Fair, which takes over the town for the second weekend in October, are outward signs of Weimar's vitality. But, famously, Weimar is steeped in German culture, having been the home of two of the country's greatest writers, **Goethe and Schiller**, as well as the composers **Bach, Liszt and Richard Strauss**, the painter **Lucas Cranach** and the philosopher **Nietzsche**.

Weimar was also where the pre-Nazi Weimar Republic was founded. The entire town centre, with its wide tree-lined avenues, elegant squares and fine buildings, is designated a historic monument. Architecture fans should not miss Weimar's Bauhaus connections. Look out for the **Haus am Horn** (Am Horn 61), a modernist prototype of Bauhaus demeanour that relieves the tedium of Weimar's baroque mansions.

The baroque mansion where Goethe lived, **Goethehaus**, Frauenplan 1 (closed Mon), displays furniture, personal belongings and a library of 5,400 books. A stroll across the little River Ilm in the peaceful **Park an der Ilm** leads to the simple Gartenhaus, his first home in town and later his retreat. Goethe himself became a tourist attraction: people travelled from afar to glimpse the great man. In the **Marktplatz** a plaque marks the house in the south corner where Bach lived when he was leader of the court orchestra. The Liszthaus (closed Tues), on the town side of the park at Marienstr. 17, is the beautifully maintained residence of the Austro-Hungarian composer Franz Liszt. He moved to Weimar in 1848 to direct the local orchestra and spent the last 17 summers of his life here.

Ten kilometres north of Weimar is the memorial museum and site of **Buchenwald concentration camp**, a grim reminder of the horrors of the Nazi regime during the Second World War (closed Mon, easily reached by 🚌 6 from Goetheplatz and the railway station; see www.buchenwald.de).

Arrival, information, accommodation

🚃 A 20-min walk north of the centre (🚌 6/7). 🅸 Tourist office: Markt 10 (www.weimar.de). They can arrange hotel and private accommodation. City tours 10.00 and 14.00 (Apr–Dec) or 11.00 (Jan–Mar) for a fee of €8.

🛏 A good choice in the centre of town is the **Hotel Kaiserin Augusta**, Carl-August-Allee 17, ☎ 03643 2340 (www.hotel-kaiserin-augusta.de) or try the **Anna Amalia**, Geleitstr. 8–12, ☎ 03643 495 60 (www.hotel-anna-amalia.de). Spacious and comfortable rooms are available at the **Hotel Villa Hentzel**, Bauhausstr. 12, ☎ 03643 865 80 (www.hotel-villa-hentzel.de), located between the Park an der Ilm and the city centre.

Just 25 kilometres beyond Weimar, **Erfurt** has shot to prominence as a tourist attraction, with its substantial variety of attractive old buildings from mills to monasteries, much spruced up since German unification. A flight of 70 steps leads up to Dom St Marien, the hilltop Gothic cathedral beside the Domplatz, a large marketplace and useful tram stop.

An array of decorative buildings surround **Fischmarkt**. To the west is Krämerbrücke, a 14th-century river bridge lined with old houses and shops, best seen from the river itself. In the 15th century, Erfurt was noted for its altarpieces and a superb example can be seen in Reglerkirche, Bahnhofstr.

Connections from Erfurt

New **high-speed railway lines** have given Erfurt added prominence as a rail hub. The new fast line to Halle and Leipzig has brought Erfurt within two hours of Berlin (ERT 850). In late

2015, a new non-stop service to Frankfurt-am-Main was launched (ERT 850). In late 2017, a new 190-km long fast line from Erfurt to Bamberg in Bavaria opened (also ERT 850).

Erfurt is a stop on the Moscow to Paris service (ERT 24). The westbound train gives a convenient weekly overnight link from Erfurt to **Paris**. Closer to hand, there's a useful local service running north to Nordhausen (ERT 868), giving a link onto the **Harz narrow-gauge network** described in **Route 22**. By far the prettiest of the local lines spanning out from Erfurt is that via Suhl to Würzburg (ERT 870), which is followed by Route 23.

The next leg of our journey, from **Erfurt on to Würzburg** reveals just how unhelpful online journey planners can be. Most websites will suggest taking a fast ICE and changing at either Fulda or Bamberg to reach Würzburg. You could do very much better by sticking to regional train services which take a more direct route through the hills.

True, it'll take 20 to 30 minutes longer but you'll be rewarded by some fabulous scenery. **Gently rounded hills**, dense forests and folded valleys are the landscape themes in a region which is home to lynx and wolves. As you travel through this part of Thuringia, you'll see small villages which evoke images of mediaeval Europe.

Leaving Erfurt, the regional train to Würzburg crosses gently undulating terrain to reach Arnstadt, a beautiful small town which makes much of its Bach connection: the composer spent four productive years there. Pausing at Plaue, the railway then cuts through the **Thüringer Wald** (Thuringian Forest) nature reserve – relying part on deep cuttings and tunnels, but there are stretches with good views.

Beyond the hills, the train stops at **Suhl**, an improbably large place given its relative remoteness. It greatly expanded in the 1960s as an important administrative centre in East Germany. It is, to be frank, quite an eyesore. The railway then tracks south-west through pleasant countryside, partly forested, to cross the former border between East Germany and West Germany and reach the first stop in Bavaria at Mellrichstadt. From there, it's a easy run south to Schweinfurt and Würzburg.

Würzburg (suggested stopover)

Würzburg is a university town where in autumn the **Winzerfest**, a traditional annual harvest festival, celebrates the (justly famous) Franconian wines – one of the most celebrated of the local vineyards rises up by the station.

The rebuilt domes, spires and red roofs are seen at their best from the terrace battlements of **Festung Marienberg**, an impressive white fortress on a wooded hill above the River Main. Converted to baroque style in the 17th century, little remains inside, though the **Mainfränkisches Museum** (www.museum-franken.de, closed Mon) displays a large collection of works by Franconian artists, including superb 16th-century woodcarvings by one of the city's most famous sons, Tilman Riemenschneider. The Festung is best reached by 🚌 9 (from Apr–Oct) in just a 10-min ride. Otherwise it is a 40-min walk.

The marketplace is notable for the **Marienkapelle**, a 14th-century church with more Riemenschneider carvings, and the richly decorated 18th-century Falkenhaus, which houses the tourist office. The town's main sight is the massive sandstone **Residenz** on the eastern edge of town. Built as the new palace of the prince-bishops in the 18th century by Balthasar Neumann, it has been given World Heritage Site status. Statues line the roof facade, symbolising the Church's wealth and power. The rooms are sumptuously decorated with frescos and sculptures by leading artists of their day, including the Venetian master Tiepolo (guided tours in English, daily at 11.00 and 15.00; also 13.30 and 16.30 from Apr–Oct). **Evening bevvies** aplenty in and around Sanderstrasse, popular with students.

ARRIVAL, INFORMATION, ACCOMMODATION

🚆 Würzburg Hbf, at the foot of vineyards on the northern edge of the town centre, a 15-min walk. 🛈 Tourist office: in the Falkenhaus, Marktplatz 9 (www.wuerzburg.de).

🛏 There is no shortage of hotels. If you don't mind the atmosphere of a large, modern business hotel, then go for the **Ghotel**, Schweinfurter Str. 3, ☎ 0931 359 620 (www.ghotel.de). Or stay at the very centrally located **Hotel Alter Kranen**, Kärrnergasse 11, ☎ 0931 35 18-0 (www.hotel-alter-kranen.de) right on the bank of the River Main. If you are looking to splurge, try the **Rebstock**, Neubaustr. 7, ☎ 0931 309 30 (www.rebstock.com), with its rococo facade.

It is a hop of just a hundred kilometres from Würzburg to Nuremberg, cutting through the gentle **Steigerwald Hills** which lie to the south of the Main Valley. The poet Henry Wadsworth Longfellow had mixed feelings about **Nuremberg** (Nürnberg), calling it "a quaint old town of toil and traffic." Nowadays the city of **Lebkuchen** (a speciality Advent gingerbread) is trying to cast off its associations with Nazi rallies and war trials. Heading north from the station, you immediately enter the **Old Town** with its impressive Stadtbefestigung (city wall). Beyond the Schöner Brunnen (Beautiful Fountain), the spacious **Hauptmarkt** (market square) makes a perfect setting for one of Germany's liveliest Christmas markets.

Hitler's mass rallies were held in the vast **Reichsparteitagsgelände** (in the Luitpoldhain, in the south-eastern suburbs), a huge area with a parade ground, stadium and the shell of a massive congress hall that was never completed. One of the remaining parts, the **Zeppelin grandstand** (S-Bahn line 2 to Frankenstadion) hosts an exhibition called *Faszination und Gewalt* (Fascination and Violence).

If you've used this book to plan your travels to Nuremberg, chances are you will be interested in the **Nuremberg Transport Museum** (Verkehrsmuseum Nürnberg), just five minutes from the station at Lessingstr. 6 (www.dbmuseum.de; closed Mon). The major exhibits are managed by Deutsche Bahn and give a good account of German railway history. A second exhibition focuses on other aspects of communication and includes an excellent display of old post coaches. For a note on Nuremberg's identity as a central European city, see p230.

CONNECTIONS FROM NUREMBERG

You can connect in Nuremberg onto **Route 24** to Prague. Nuremberg is a major hub on Gemany's ICE network, with fast trains to most principal German cities, among them Hamburg (ERT 900), Cologne (ERT 910) and Munich (ERT 904). The latter is just an hour away on the fastest trains. There are also direct trains to Vienna (ERT 66).

If you can resist the temptation of taking the fast train to Munich (see 'connections' above), then there's much to be seen on the 'old' Nuremberg to Munich line which runs via **Augsburg**. It runs south through pleasant Franconian countryside, crossing the River Danube at Donauwörth and then following the Lech Valley upstream to Augsburg.

Just a stone's throw from Munich, Augsburg nowadays is overshadowed by its larger Bavarian neighbour. But there was a time when Augsburg was respected as one of the largest and most influential centres in all Europe. Be it as a hub for finance and trade, in its social programmes to alleviate poverty or as a centre of Jewish life and culture, Augsburg towered above its rivals. The key to this were two families, the **Welsers** and the **Fuggers** who, in the early 16th century, dominated Augsburg life.

There is a predictably imposing cathedral on the hilly north side of the city centre, and, just a stone's throw from the Hauptbahnhof (on Halderstr. 8), one of Germany's most remarkable **synagogues**.

KING LUDWIG'S CASTLES

Many visitors to Bavaria feel compelled to make an excursion to the royal castles at Füssen, the most famous of which was built at preposterous expense by King Ludwig II. The easiest way of getting to **Neuschwanstein** and **Hohenschwangau** is to take a train to Füssen, an attractive old town beneath the mountains, served by direct trains from both Augsburg and Munich (both ERT 935). The journey from Augsburg is rather shorter.

Hohenschwangau and Neuschwanstein are within walking distance of each other (involving a modest climb). Tudor-style Hohenschwangau, built in the early 19th century by **Maximilian II**, was an attempt to recreate the romantic past and was adorned with Wagnerian references by his son, **King Ludwig II**. Ludwig then surpassed his father by building the fairy-tale neo-Gothic Neuschwanstein on a rocky outcrop high above. It might be read as a clever postmodern fantasy, but the great majority of visitors perceive Neuschwanstein as a **Disneyesque** dive into mediaeval Germany. Hohenschwangau, a real castle which was a family home, has been upstaged by an utter fabrication which was never completed – hence the throne room without a throne, and doorways leading to suicidal drops.

Neuschwanstein is really best seen from a distance. If you've a head for heights, the best vantage point is the Marienbrücke, a bridge spanning a huge gorge. The really sad thing is that Germany has real mediaeval castles aplenty, yet it is a fake castle that pulls the crowds.

Munich (suggested stopover)

The less you know about Munich (München), the easier it is to define. Right – it's the **Oktoberfest** city, full of ruddy-cheeked people in lederhosen singing 'ein prosit, ein prosit' with foaming steins raised. But after a few trips – or even a few days – you'll soon discover that Munich is more than just beer. Munich is **affluent and stylish**, with a world-class cultural scene, superb museums, and some of Germany's best restaurants. Join students, artists, musicians and Munich's young crowd on the city's left bank. Schwabing is north of the centre, and a good way to get there is to take the U-Bahn to Münchner Freiheit.

Try Bavarian specialities or pick up the makings of a picnic from around the world at the **Viktualienmarkt** – one of Europe's finest produce markets, right in the heart of the city. Exit Marienplatz to the east and then walk around the corner. Munich's **Lenbachhaus** by the Königsplatz houses the world's largest collection of works by the avant-garde **Blue Rider group** and further 20th-century art (www.lenbachhaus.de; closed Mon).

Munich's location is also a huge asset, with easy access to lakes and mountains, and superb transport connections to Italy, Switzerland, Austria and destinations further south as well as the rest of Germany.

ARRIVAL, INFORMATION, ACCOMMODATION

≉ München Hauptbahnhof (Hbf), about 1 km due west of Marienplatz in the city centre is the city's main railway station; ✈ Franz Josef Strauss Airport, 30 km north-east of Munich city centre (www.munich-airport.de). S-Bahn lines S1 and S8 run every 10 mins from the rail station via the Ostbahnhof and city centre to the airport (see ERT 892), taking 40 mins.

🛈 The main tourist office is at Bahnhofplatz 2, outside the main railway station (www.muenchen.travel). For a walking tour with a knowledgeable English-speaking guide, try **Munich Walk Tours**, ☎ 089 24 23 17 67 (www.munichwalktours.de), which also cover Dachau, a brewery tour, a cycle tour and a Third Reich Tour.

🛏 Finding accommodation is rarely a problem except during the city's biggest tourist attractions, the annual Oktoberfest beer festival (mid Sept–early Oct) and Fasching, the bacchanalian carnival that precedes Ash Wednesday. The biggest choice of hotels is around the rail station in streets like Schillerstr. and Senefelderstr.; it's a rather drab area but handy for the centre. A mid-range one is the **Leonardo Hotel München City Center**, Senefelderstr. 4, ☎ 089 551 540 (www.leonardo-hotels.com). A comfortable option not far from the city centre is the **Admiral**, Kohlstr. 9, ☎ 089 21 63 50 (www.hotel-admiral.de). Or try the **Cocoon Hauptbahnhof**, Mittererstraße 9, ☎ 089 54 80 18 9905 (www.cocoon-hotels.de) with its Alpine-themed design, just a short walk from the station.

It is just 150 kilometres from Munich to Salzburg, but what a journey! Sit on the right side of the train for fine views of the Alps as you approach **Salzburg** (more on the city on p317). Closer to the railway, and on both sides of the train, are the delicate landscapes of the **Chiemgau**. It is a stunning end to a journey which started on the banks of the River Spree in Berlin and ends by the Salzach near the Austrian-German border.

CENTRAL EUROPE
An introduction

It is amazing how geographical horizons change through time. In the heyday of the **Austro-Hungarian Empire**, every educated European would have shared some tacit understanding about where central Europe was. True, they may have squabbled over where its boundaries lay. In the salons of Vienna those inclined to geographical debate questioned frontiers and languages: "Should we include Lusatia and Lodomeria? And what about Podlachia and the Posavina? Are they part of central Europe?"

The Habsburg flame was snuffed one hundred years ago, and with it died a peculiarly central European *zeitgeist*. A generation later, in the wake of the Second World War, Europe was split asunder, rent in two by the **Iron Curtain**. A more binary view of Europe gained ascendancy: there was western Europe and eastern Europe. That was the geopolitical reality of the **Cold War years**.

The quiet revolutions of 1989 and the years immediately thereafter allowed for the re-emergence of central Europe, redeeming a number of countries from the eastern Europe label. They included Czechoslovakia (as it was until 1993), Hungary, Slovenia and other parts of fragmenting Yugoslavia, and a swathe of other towns and cities with former Habsburg connections. In Chernivtsi and Trieste, as in a thousand other places in between, there was a sudden recognition of **shared history and heritage**.

We explore these ideas more in the first route in this section. We have five routes in this part of *Europe by Rail*, but you can also look elsewhere in the book for more routes that touch places with a strong *Mitteleuropa* feel. For example, **Kraków**, once part of the Austro-Hungarian Empire, has more than a dash of Habsburg flair woven into its Polish style. Kraków is on **Route 48** and **49** in this book.

Many who know their trains far better than we wax lyrical about rail travel in central Europe. **Old-style Eurocity services** ply main lines with engines pulling colourful carriages which, though they have seen better days, are often incredibly comfy. Cut off the main lines and you'll discover ancient diesel railcars trundling through the countryside. See our 'Slow train through Bohemia' box on p232; experiences akin to that Bohemian adventure are there for the taking across central Europe.

Had we had more space, we would surely have included a long west to east leap across Slovakia: the single-track non-electrified railway running east from Banská Bystrica is superb (ERT 1188). For a nicely retro rail experience, try the morning train from **Sopron to Pécs** which follows a medley of minor routes through south-west Hungary, paralleling the Croatian border for a spell (ERT 1235 & 1237). ■

Route 24: Bohemian byways

CITIES: ★★ CULTURE: ★★ HISTORY: ★★★ SCENERY: ★★
COUNTRIES COVERED: GERMANY (DE), CZECH REPUBLIC (CZ)
JOURNEY TIME: 9 HRS 30 MINS | DISTANCE: 560 KM | MAP: WWW.EBRWEB.EU/MAP24

This route represents our first serious encounter with Central Europe, a geographical notion which has enjoyed a renaissance in recent years. When Europe was divided by the Iron Curtain, during those decades when the continent was so markedly fractured into East and West, there was no space in our imagination for Central Europe. But 'twas not always so: from the mediaeval period until shortly after the demise of the Habsburg Empire in the last century, there was always a region with distinctive geography, culture and traditions which was unmistakably *Mitteleuropa*.

In this journey from **Nuremberg to Prague** we take in spa towns and synagogues, make time for coffee and cake, and explore some deeply rural areas of **Bohemia** – the latter another of those cartographic entities which have always played both real and imaginary roles in the lives of Europeans. Nuremberg is a good spot to embark on our journey, as it is a city which for centuries strongly played the *Mitteleuropa* card (although American occupation after 1945 very firmly 'pulled' Nuremberg westwards). The city has always taken geography seriously; it was here in Nuremberg in the 15th century that **Martin Behaim** created the first globe (his Erdapfel, literally 'earth apple'). Early modern cartographers from the city always placed Nuremburg in the very middle of Central Europe, much to the annoyance of their rivals in Prague and Budapest. This route is your chance to take the pulse of one of Europe's most elusive regions.

ITINERARY NOTES

Even if the social rhythm of spa life has no appeal, you should definitely think of stopping off for a night in either Mariánské Lázně or Karlovy Vary – perhaps even in both as the two towns are very different from each other. The **finest stretches** of the train journey are the section over the German-Czech border (ERT 885) and the short hop from Mariánské Lázně to Karlovy Vary (ERT 1123).

Don't be waylaid by the **express coach** (run jointly by Deutsche Bahn and its Czech counterpart) which runs non-stop from Nuremberg to Prague (ERT 76). Taking only 3 hrs 40 mins to speed along the boring motorway between the two cities, crossing into the Czech Republic at Waidhaus, the bus greatly undercuts the fastest train travel time to Prague. Take the bus if time is all that matters. But if you have the slightest interest in landscape and culture, then the train is the way to go.

From Bavaria to Bohemia

The rail journey through the hills east from **Nuremberg** (see p226 for more on the city) into the Czech Republic is superb. The train follows the Pegnitz Valley before cutting through the **Bayerischer Wald** (Bavarian Forest) to

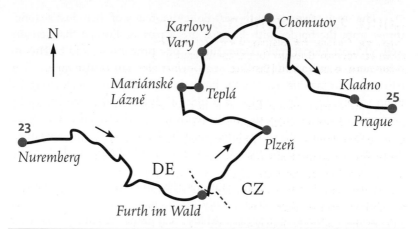

Route details

Nuremberg Hbf to Furth im Wald		ERT 886/885
Frequency	Journey time	Notes
Hourly	2 hrs 10 mins – 2 hrs 30 mins	A

Furth im Wald to Plzeň hlavní		ERT 885
Frequency	Journey time	Notes
8 per day	1 hr 10 mins – 1 hr 45 mins	B

Plzeň hlavní to Mariánské Lázně		ERT 1121
Frequency	Journey time	Notes
Every 1–2 hrs	50–70 mins	

Mariánské Lázně to Karlovy Vary		ERT 1123
Frequency	Journey time	Notes
8 per day	75 mins	

Karlovy Vary to Chomutov		ERT 1110
Frequency	Journey time	Notes
Every 1–2 hrs	50–90 mins	

Route details (cont.)

Chomutov to Prague Masarykovo		ERT 1105
Frequency	Journey time	Notes
3–4 per day	2 hrs 40 mins	C

Notes

A – On most journeys, a change of train is necessary at Schwandorf.
B – A change of train in Domažlice is sometimes required.
C – On our recommended route from Chomutov to Prague, a change of train is required at Lužná u Rakovníka. There is an alternative route from Chomutov to Prague via Ústi. Trains on this route run every two hours, taking 2 hrs 25 mins. These trains run direct from Chomutov to Prague hlavni.

reach the Czech border at Furth im Wald. Very few trains run right through. Travellers from Nuremberg normally need to change trains in Schwandorf.

Once **over the border**, the train passes through the enigmatically named community of Babylon and then descends steeply towards **Domažlice**, the first place of any size in the Czech Republic. This is Chod country. The Chods were an early version of border guards. They made a decent living by keeping an eye on the borderlands where Bohemia runs up against Bavaria. Imagine a militia armed with bagpipes which kept Bavarian aspiration in check and so secured the independence of Domažlice.

The small towns of south-west Bohemia, many of them just a stone's throw from the border with Bavaria, are a part of Europe that remains well off most tourist trails. Domažlice, a one-time stronghold of **Hussite reformers**, is well worth visiting in its own right, but is also an excellent base for exploring this area (see the box below). The town's nicely elongated main square, lined by arcades, is a place to linger and watch life go by. **Domažlice's museum**, located in the renovated castle, tells the story of the region, explaining the history of the local Chod minority, and making much of a fine collection of bagpipes that ranges from the Magyar duda to the Swedish säckpipa.

Domažlice has two railway stations. The direct trains from Munich, Nuremberg and Prague all stop only at the main station, simply called Domažlice, 1 km east of the centre. Many local trains, including those from Furth im Wald, also serve Domažlice město, a small halt located 500 metres south of the main square.

From Domažlice, it's downhill all the way to **Plzeň**, where you might expect the most striking building to be a brewery. The name of the fourth largest Czech city (often rendered Pilsen in German and English) is synonymous with good beer. The distinctive **golden lager** known as pilsner (or often just pils) has been brewed in the city for about 140 years.

But there's more to Plzeň than beer. From the **main railway station** (hlavní nádraží), walk west over the river into the city centre. This road is called Americká, having previous been called Moskevská. You'll quickly reach the main north-south thoroughfare, which is called Klatovská. Gaze up beyond the tacky shop fronts and there are some remarkable embellishments to the peeling facades of the buildings that line **Klatovská**. For those who pause to look, there's everything from baroque to art nouveau.

SLOW TRAIN THROUGH BOHEMIA

For devotees of slow trains, Bohemia is well served by a dense network of **rural railway lines** (many not shown in the ERT). Some services are still operated by antiquated red railcars which trundle through the forests stopping off here and there at tiny wayside halts. **Domažlice** is a good base for exploring such rail routes. Just a short hop from Domažlice is **Horšovský Týn**, the most attractive small town in the region abutting the border with Bavaria (with a fine sloping main square). Domažlice to Horšovský Týn takes less than an hour, with a change of train at Poběžovice.

If you fancy a **longer rural excursion** and do not mind missing Plzeň, you can cut the corner on Route 24 and travel north on characterful minor railways through Bor to Mariánské Lázně. These lesser rail routes in Bohemia recall an era of rail travel which has long disappeared in western Europe. It is a region to which we return time and time again, and so dense is the rail network, we rarely cover the same ground twice. If, like us, you find yourself becoming addicted to **Bohemian branch lines**, then it's worth investing in a printed copy of the Czech national rail timetable (jízdní řád in Czech). It costs just 99 CZK (about €4) and makes splendid fireside reading for winter evenings.

But one building outshines any other in Plzeň. It is one of the most impressive pieces of sacred architecture anywhere in Europe: the **Great Synagogue**. It is majestic! In terms of size, it is surpassed in Europe only by the Dohány Synagogue in Budapest. There are too few surviving synagogues in the cities of Central Europe. And even fewer which can match Plzeň's Great Synagogue for its artistry. Pause in the choir loft and gaze over to the **Aron Kodesh** – the Holy Ark in which the Torah scrolls are traditionally kept. It looks peculiarly Indian in style. Touch the cantor's platform which is carved from the finest mahogany. Raise your eyes aloft to the Heavens and ponder the golden stars set in a dome of **celestial blue**.

More's the pity that it's all too rare these days that the Great Synagogue in Plzeň echoes to the chanting of the psalms. One hundred years ago, this was one of the largest *kehillot* in central Europe. During the 19th century, Plzeň's growing Jewish population had consistently outgrown smaller synagogues. The Great Synagogue was triumphantly opened in 1892, its Moorish Revival style eliciting much praise from local citizens of all religious persuasions.

That the building survived the onslaughts of **Nazi Germany** is remarkable. But it emerged from the war in bad shape, and has benefited in recent years from extensive renovation. Now it once again stands proud on the city's principal thoroughfare as a witness to the civic influence and the economic power once wielded by the city's Jewish community.

Spa diversions

Our journey from Nuremberg has thus far been entirely on secondary rail routes, none of them electrified. That changes in Plzeň as we join a main line which runs to the north-west corner of Bohemia, home to some outstanding examples of **European spa culture**. All have their origins in the Austro-Hungarian spa tradition, and all were once favoured holiday destinations for Europe's royalty. These are not places for Bohemian excess. But colonic irrigation is not mandatory, and these three towns are just wonderful places to hole up and relax for a day or two.

Travelling north-west on the main railway from Plzeň, the line follows the beautiful winding **Mže Valley** to Planá – where the station is signed as Planá u Mariánských Lázní. How misleading! This is not Mariánské Lázně – that's another ten minutes up the line.

Mariánské Lázně has a feast of *belle époque* decadence, a lovely Russian Orthodox church and the town is surrounded by some beautiful parks and woodland. There is still all the *fin de siècle* charm of old Marienbad, the hideaway in the hills which once attracted monarchs from across Europe. If you are minded to stay overnight, try the central and comfortable Villa Patriot, Dusíkova 62, ☎ 354 673 143 (www.villa-patriot.cz) which also has a good restaurant.

A TRIO OF SPA TOWNS

The three most famous spa towns of Bohemia, from the smallest to the largest, are (with their old German-language names in brackets): Františkovy Lázně (Franzensbad), Mariánské Lázně (Marienbad) and Karlovy Vary (Karlsbad). Each has its own charm.

Visiting **Františkovy Lázně** means deviating from the route we describe here. It's an easy day trip from either Mariánské Lázně or Karlovy Vary – about 90 minutes by train from either of those towns, in each case normally with a change of train at **Cheb** – where the retro atmosphere of the railway station will evoke a wave of nostalgic memories for travellers who experienced travel in Czechoslovakia in the 1970s and 1980s. Františkovy Lázně is a tiny picture-perfect community with the air of an outdoor sanatorium and a nice line in erotic sculptures. **Fertility treatments** are one of the town's specialisations and this gives Františkovy Lázně a more youthful air than the other spa towns mentioned here.

From Mariánské Lázně, it is an entertaining ride on a branch line to Karlovy Vary. These trains start at the main railway station (simply called Mariánské Lázně), but they also stop at Mariánské Lázně město station, which is much closer to the town centre. It's a **request stop**, so just stand on the platform and stick out your hand, as one might for a bus. The line climbs steeply up through forests to over 700 metres above sea level. It's a fine piece of Habsburg engineering. The stations ooze **faded Habsburg style**, their former German names eclipsed by Czech renderings. The highest station on the line, once Habakladrau, is now called Ovesné Kladruby. Prosau has morphed into Mrázov.

Once over the summit, away to the right of the railway are the imposing twin towers of the abbey church at **Teplá**. The line then runs down the Teplá Valley to Karlovy Vary – through richly varied forests of pine, sycamore, spruce, elm and birch.

The hills rise up steeply on either side of **Karlovy Vary** with the River Teplá running through the heart of the town. The therapeutic qualities of these waters have created a sanctuary which pulls visitors from far and wide. Nowadays the town is particularly popular with Russian visitors. They follow a tradition extending back to **Peter the Great**, who first took the waters here in 1711.

In Karlovy Vary, very much larger than the other Bohemian spa towns, the real world intrudes on the pursuit of health and recuperation, and there's a bustle about the place, especially during the **annual film festival** which takes place in July each year. The Hotel Embassy, Nová Louka 21, ☎ 353 221 161 (www.embassy.cz), is extremely friendly and located right in the heart of the spa zone. The excursion up the funicular railway (called the 'Diana') to the viewing tower is a must in Karlovy Vary.

All three spa towns offer good-value hotels, often more geared to long-stay clients nursing their ailments than passing trade, but if space is available casual guests are accepted. Plan for **leisurely days** taking the waters, going for healthy walks, and enjoy afternoon tea and waltzes aplenty! If you really want to catch the spa atmosphere, head for Františkovy Lázně or Mariánské Lázně. If you're uncertain whether you can cope with such unalloyed commitment to healthy living, Karlovy Vary makes for a good compromise. At least there you can sup on something stronger than the spa waters. Try the **Jan Becher Museum** on TG Masaryka 57, which provides an interesting history of the locally produced **Becherovka** spirit, as well as ample opportunity to sample the product itself.

Karlovy Vary connections

With all those **Russian guests** in Karlovy Vary, it's no surprise that the city has good connections with Russia. Indeed, the local airport only has flights to and from Russia. The railway station offers more variety. Though the direct trains to Minsk and Moscow were cut in 2016, Karlovy Vary still has a range of connnections to cities across the Czech Republic.

Close at hand, there is a lovely route north from Karlovy Vary; it runs through the mountains via Johanngeorgenstadt to Zwickau in Saxony (ERT 884), from where it is a short hop east to **Dresden** to connect with **Route 49** to Poland and **Route 25** to either Budapest or Hamburg. Plenty of trains run from Karlovy Vary to Cheb (ERT 1110), from where there are three local rail routes across the border into Germany (ERT 1122).

From Karlovy Vary, you have a number of options for the onward journey to Prague. There are direct trains which run east to Ústí nad Labem and then follow the Elbe Valley upstream towards the Czech capital. A more interesting route is to cut off to the south at **Chomutov** and taking the old main line through Žatec and Kladno to Prague. The fast trains on this route were axed in 2008, but there are still local services. It's a fascinating journey, passing through a major area of **hop cultivation** (essential for the Czech beer industry). By contrast, you'll see some of the worst industrial dereliction anywhere in central Europe. Towns which were surely never beautiful in the Communist period have decayed even more under capitalism. It's a good reminder that market economics cut two ways. **Prague** (see p240), a city so full of creative energy, is just one face of the modern Czech Republic. The view from Kladno looks rather different.

Connections from Prague

In Prague you can connect with **Route 25** which runs north to Hamburg via Berlin (ERT 60) or south to Budapest (ERT 1175). Railjet trains run south to Vienna (ERT 1150), most of these continuing beyond the Austrian capital to Graz in Styria (ERT 60). There is an especially nice route south from **Prague to Linz** in Austria (ERT 1132), It runs via **České Budějovice**, where brewing has been a habit since the 13th century. The town created and still brews the original Budweiser (Budvar) beer. From České Budějovice, it is just a short hop to Český Krumlov (ERT 1131), a sererely beautiful (but in mid-summer often busy) south Bohemian town which boasts one of the most-photographed castles in the Czech Republic.

Russian Railways offer direct services from Prague to Minsk, Moscow and St Petersburg (ERT 95). There is a good choice of **night trains** with direct services leaving most evenings for Warsaw and Kraków (both ERT 99) and Zurich (ERT 52). There are direct overnight trains to Poprad (for the Tatra Mountains) and to Košice.

Route 25: Four capitals in a day

CITIES: ★★★ CULTURE: ★★ HISTORY: ★★★ SCENERY: ★
COUNTRIES COVERED: GERMANY (DE), CZECH REPUBLIC (CZ), SLOVAKIA (SK), HUNGARY (HU)
JOURNEY TIME: 13 HRS 45 MINS | DISTANCE: 1,291 KM | MAP: WWW.EBRWEB.EU/MAP25

The rail journey from **Hamburg to Budapest** can be completed in a long day. The sole direct service between the two cities takes just under 14 hours for a journey of about 1,300 km. It really does take in four capital cities in a day. Travel all the way through if you will, but the great majority of travellers will stop off en route, usually at one or more of the following cities: Berlin, Dresden, Prague or Bratislava. On this journey from the banks of the **Elbe to the Danube**, there is a strong sense of swapping the cultural realm of northern Europe for that of *Mitteleuropa* (Central Europe).

Trains over this entire route run at least every two hours throughout the day. So, if you do break your journey along the way, you'll find a wide choice of onward services.

FAST TRACK ALTERNATIVES

If you are in a hurry to get from Hamburg to Budapest, there is an **alternative route** which tracks south through western Germany to Bavaria, and then continues through Austria to Vienna and beyond. It gives a slightly faster journey time, but always requires a change of trains along the way (normally at Vienna).

Bear in mind, too, that there are overnight possibilities covering parts of this route. There is a **nightly sleeper service** from Hamburg to Vienna (from where it's just a short hop on to Budapest in the morning). A happy innovation for 2019 has been the reinstatement of the direct night train from Berlin to Bratislava and Budapest.

The Hungaria

The direct train from Hamburg to Budapest is a Eurocity service called the *Hungaria*. It has run from Berlin to Budapest for over half a century; only in late 2015 was it extended to start from Hamburg. Cast back to the **Cold War days**, and the *Hungaria* carried East German families off for summer holidays in Hungary — where Lake Balaton was a favourite destination. It was also the train that transported government officials and party stalwarts carrying fraternal greetings between the Warsaw Pact capitals. The *Hungaria* was much favoured by spies too. In the 1980s, it still carried through carriages from Sweden to Yugoslavia, both non-aligned countries, and the train was a good spot for discreet exchanges of intelligence as it trundled through the central European countryside.

The Europe traversed by the *Hungaria* has been utterly transformed over the last 30 years. The **Iron Curtain** has gone and borders have melted. That's not to say that you'll necessarily be able to travel from Berlin to Budapest without once being asked to show your passport. In the northbound direction this rail route is one that has been much used in

Notes

Table 60 in ERT gives a useful summary of principal trains along the entire length of the journey from Hamburg to Budapest.

Please note that 'Hbf' in the route details (bottom left) stands for Hauptbahnhof (main station).

X – There is an alternative, more rural, route between Prague and Brno which cuts the corner south of Kolín, serving Kutná Hora along the way. The travel time from Prague to Brno via this route is 3 hrs 5 mins. Trains run every 2 hrs (ERT 1151).

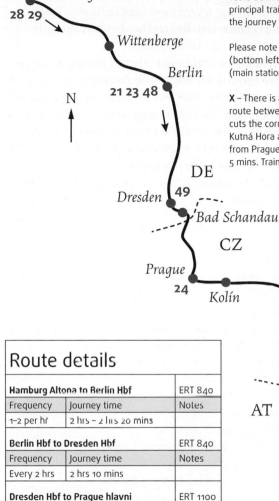

Route details

Hamburg Altona to Berlin Hbf		ERT 840
Frequency	Journey time	Notes
1–2 per hr	2 hrs – 2 hrs 20 mins	

Berlin Hbf to Dresden Hbf		ERT 840
Frequency	Journey time	Notes
Every 2 hrs	2 hrs 10 mins	

Dresden Hbf to Prague hlavni		ERT 1100
Frequency	Journey time	Notes
Every 2 hrs	2 hrs 25 mins	

Prague hlavni to Brno hlavni		ERT 1150
Frequency	Journey time	Notes
Hourly	2 hrs 30 mins	X

Brno hlavni to Bratislava hlavna		ERT 1150
Frequency	Journey time	Notes
Every 2 hrs	1 hr 30 mins	

Bratislava hlavna to Budapest Nyugati		ERT 1175
Frequency	Journey time	Notes
Every 2 hrs	2 hrs 20 mins	

The **numbers in red** adjacent to some cities on our route maps refer to other routes in this book which also include that particular city.

The ERT numbers in our route details refer to the table numbers in the *European Rail Timetable* (ERT) where you will find train schedules for that particular section of the route.

2015 by refugees from Syria heading for the German capital (the overnight *Metropol* service from Budapest to Berlin was also a popular choice).

The *Hungaria* train which once served three capitals (Berlin, Prague and Budapest) now stops at four. The **velvet divorce** that divided Czechoslovakia gave Bratislava capital city status on 1 January 1993.

The route from Hamburg to Budapest is shaped by two of Europe's great rivers, with the *Hungaria's* **blue-and-white carriages** following the Elbe Valley (Labe in Czech) on its route south from Germany into the Czech Republic. The latter part of the journey plays cat and mouse with the Danube, never actually crossing the river, but on several occasions running close by the river banks. Indeed at one point, just north of Bratislava, you can look across the river to Austria in the distance.

Across eastern Germany

The *Hungaria*, like almost all trains from **Hamburg** (see p270) to Berlin, departs from Hamburg Altona station. It is in an erstwhile working-class area of the city which has recently seen fractious debates over gentrification. It's worth joining the train here if you have time as the ten-minute journey to Hauptbahnhof (where all trains to Berlin also stop) affords excellent views of the wider Hamburg cityscape.

The train crosses the one-time border between the two German states about half an hour after leaving Hamburg Hauptbahnhof. The open **meadowlands and forests** of this part of eastern Germany possess a rare beauty which is hard to appreciate through the train window. Make a note to come back and explore some time. There is a good network of minor rail routes through the region. Some Hamburg to Berlin fast trains (including the *Hungaria*) stop at **Wittenberge**, from where there is an alternative route via Wittstock to Berlin which traverses beautiful swathes of forest. This rural line is not shown in ERT, but trains leave Wittenberge hourly (every 2 hrs on Sat & Sun) and take 2 hrs 30 mins to reach Berlin.

If you stay on the main line, less than an hour after Wittenberge you are approaching **Berlin** (see p213) where most trains from Hamburg arrive at the lower-level platforms of Hauptbahnhof station.

EASTERN CONNECTIONS FROM BERLIN

Change at Berlin to connect into **eastbound services** to Poznań, Warsaw, Minsk and Moscow (ERT 56 & 1001). There are many other direct trains from Berlin to Poland, including hourly services from Berlin Lichtenberg to Kostrzyn (ERT 832) which follow the **Ostbahn**, the railway which once ran all the way from Berlin to Königsberg in East Prussia (now Kaliningrad in Russia). There are also occasional direct trains from Berlin to the Polish cities of Bydgoszcz, Gdańsk and Gdynia (all ERT 51) and to the port city of Szczecin (ERT 949).

All Dresden-bound trains from Berlin pick up passengers at both Hauptbahnhof and Südkreuz stations. There's a remarkable mixture of trains on this route. Strangely, German trains are a rarity but Polish, Czech and Hungarian trains all make daily appearances on this line – all with restaurant cars and menus reflecting their respective national culinary traditions. It's an easy run south from Berlin through largely **rural terrain**, with the train crossing the River Elbe on the approach into Dresden.

The capital of Saxony for four centuries, **Dresden** will long be remembered for one of the great tragedies of the Second World War. In February 1945, the city was carpet-bombed by the Allies, and some 35,000 people died. But despite the devastation, the city has risen from the ashes, and is once again a major cultural destination — although still with its difficulties. The **Elbe Valley** is very prone to flooding, and many areas have from time to time been catastrophically inundated. And the city was rightly criticised when it pressed ahead with plans to ruin the Elbe Valley by building a new road bridge through the heart of a UNESCO World Heritage Site. UNESCO responded to such civic vandalism by stripping the city of its World Heritage status — making Dresden the only place in Europe to have been so publicly humiliated. Dresden continues to attract negative publicity for the right-wing rallies organised by the anti-immigrant *Pegida* group.

The baroque magnificence of the city's centre is best appreciated from the raised terraces on the south bank of the Elbe, with views of the **Residenzschloss** (the tower of which gives another good view), and the spire of the early 18th-century Catholic **Hofkirche** (royal cathedral). By the cathedral are the **Semper Opera House** and the **Zwinger**, a gracious complex of baroque pavilions, fountains and statuary.

Out of the centre, Dresden is just as interesting. Follow the River Elbe upstream for gorgeous views of villas perched on the hillside on the opposite bank, and within minutes of the centre you are virtually into countryside as you head east. Forests and vineyards aplenty. Further on, **Schloss Pillnitz** was the only baroque building in Dresden to have escaped bombing; entry is free.

Connections from Dresden

There are thrice-daily trains from Dresden to Węgliniec in Poland, with a good onward connection to Wrocław (ERT 1085). This journey forms the initial part of **Route 49** in this book.

There is an hourly service from Dresden to Hof in Bavaria (ERT 880) with onward connections to Nuremberg (ERT 880), Regensburg and Munich (both ERT 879). Leipzig is little more than an hour from Dresden (ERT 842). There is a very attractive route which runs from Dresden to Zittau (ERT 855), briefly cutting through a finger of Czech territory on the approach to Zittau. Some trains continue beyond Zittau to Liberec (ERT 1117).

The Elbe Gorge

The stretch of the Elbe Valley upstream from Dresden has the **finest scenery** on this entire journey. Heading south, sit on the left side of the train. You may wish to consider taking slow trains for the cross-border leg from Dresden to

Děčín. While the fast services take just 45 mins, the slow trains take twice the time and usually require an en-route change of train at **Bad Schandau**, a small town in southern Saxony that has become a Mecca for hikers wanting to explore the sandstone hills which tower over the Elbe Valley. A **ferry** across the river links the station with Bad Schandau's small town centre. The train slips across the border into the Czech Republic at **Schöna**. The landscape south towards Prague becomes slowly more industrial, but still full of interest, as the train cruises past Bohemian riverside villages full of timber-framed houses and tottering barns. These landcapes of northern **Bohemia** inspired Smetana's music *Má vlast* (which means 'My Country').

Prague (suggested stopover)

Even in the '70s and early '80s, a steady stream of travellers of all ages were making for Prague (Praha) from the West. Before the Iron Curtain wavered in 1989, Prague was for many Westerners the only glimpse they'd had of life in 'the other Europe'. Three decades on and the stream of travellers has become a flood. During the spring and summer months, Prague is packed. Yet, for all the crowds, the Czech capital has a **very special appeal**.

You'll find architectural styles galore, everything from Gothic to cubist, on both sides of the **Vltava River**, which languidly loops through town. Plenty of parks, a pulsing nightlife and a galaxy of classical music offerings all add to Prague's heady mix. **Václavské náměstí** (Wenceslas Square) is the Czech Champs-Élysées and the biggest and busiest shopping plaza in Prague, as well as being the focal point for political rallies, protests and parades, such as the unrest in 1968/1969 and the Velvet Revolution of 1989. Take the metro to Muzeum and then walk down the length of the square towards the **Old Town**.

Possibly the largest ancient castle complex in the world, **Pražský hrad** (Prague Castle) boasts a magnificently elevated cliff-top position and is crammed with artistic and architectural treasures. Cross the bustling **Karlův most** (Charles Bridge) from the Old Town and walk up through the narrow, picturesque streets. At a hight of 318 m, **Petřín Hill** is covered in eight parks and topped with a 62-m copy of the Eiffel Tower. It offers fabulous views of Prague and the surrounding area. Trams 9/12/20/22 will get you to the start of the funicular – re-launched after reconstruction work in spring 2016 – up Petřín Hill at Újezd.

ARRIVAL, INFORMATION, ACCOMMODATION

≈ **Praha hlavní nádraží** (Prague Main Station) is on Wilsonova, not far from the top end of Wenceslas Square. Prague's efficient, fast and clean public transport system is a good choice if you need to speed across town. There are three metro lines and more than twenty tram routes (some running all night). You will need to buy an extra ticket for a large backpack or luggage. Remember to validate your ticket by stamping it once at the outset of your journey in the yellow machines at metro entrances and on trams. 🚻 The main tourist office is located in the Old Town Hall (Staroměstská radnice), Staroměstské náměstí 1 (www.prague.eu). There is also a branch at Václav Havel Airport and on Wenceslas Square.

🛏 Prague is no longer as cheap as it once was, but there are good-value options throughout the city. Some recommended hotels that might be worth trying include the small, quiet and perfectly located **Hotel Antik**, Dlouhá 22, ☎ 222 322 288 (www.hotelantik.cz). Another reasonably priced option is the **Hotel Jungmann**, centrally located on a quiet square at Jungmannovo náměstí 2, ☎ 224 219 501 (www.hotel-jungmann.cz). The classic art nouveau **Hotel Paříž**, ul. Obecního domu 1, ☎ 222 195 195 (www.hotel-paris.cz), is close to all the main sights and worth the financial splurge.

CONNECTIONS FROM PRAGUE

Prague's role as a **rail hub** has, along with cheap beer, propelled the city into the premier league of destinations favoured by young travellers (many of them using Interrail passes). There are **night trains** from far and wide, with direct overnight services to Budapest, Košice, Kraków, Moscow, Warsaw and Zurich.

Vienna is just four hours away from Prague, with a choice of two operators on that route (ERT 1150). As an alternative to the main line south to Vienna, travellers bound for Austria might consider the more rural line through České Budějovice to Linz (ERT 1132). Apart from the obvious main routes out of the city, there are a number of lesser lines which deserve to be better known. **Private operator** ALEX (part of the Arriva group, rail passes are valid) offers a beautiful route to Munich (ERT 76) which is a much better bet than the express buses (also shown in ERT 76) that run from Prague into Bavaria.

From the Czech capital, the train heads past **Kolín** (from where there is a connection to Kutná Hora, with its mediaeval Old Town huddled around a superb Gothic church), through the **Bohemian-Moravian uplands** to Brno in South Moravia. This is a land of rolling hills, dotted with elegant châteaux and mediaeval castles where many Czech and foreign films are set; if you've time to stop off, you'll discover peaceful nature reserves and areas with karst limestone scenery and underground caves. It's also the main **Czech wine-growing region** (with attractively painted wine cellars dotting the hills).

High-rise blocks and an unmistakably industrial look might tempt you to skip **Brno**, which expanded in the 19th century as a textile-making centre. But the town does have a scattering of good sights (most are closed Mon, and are either cheap or free) within 1 km of the station in the largely traffic-free centre. The neo-Gothic **Katedrála sv. Petra a Pavla** (Cathedral of Sts Peter and Paul) crowns Petrov Hill, while the 13th-century **Špilberk Castle** was the most notorious prison in the Austro-Hungarian Empire – you can visit the horrifying prison cells (closed Mon Oct–Mar). A little way south-west is the Augustinian Monastery, where in 1865 the monk Mendel studied genetics, breeding pea plants in the garden. Garden and plants remain, and there's also a small museum, the **Mendelianum**, Muzejné 1 (www.mendelianum.cz; closed Mon).

The city's **Old Town Hall** at Radnická 8, is a combination of Gothic, Renaissance and baroque style and displays a 'dragon'; a stuffed crocodile from 1608. Brno's most bizarre sight is the crypt of the **Kapucínský**

klášter (Capuchin Monastery) close to the station on Kapucínské náměstí, containing 150 mummified bodies, air-dried since 1650.

Through Slovakia

Beyond Brno, the landscape becomes more subdued as the railway follows the flatlands around the **River Morava**, dropping down slowly to the Danube. For a 200-km stretch, the train cuts through Slovakian territory, along the way passing through the capital Bratislava.

Overshadowed by Prague, it has sometimes been hard for **Bratislava** to make its mark. But the city enjoys a superb location, where the last ripples of the Carpathians reach the Danube. It is midway between Prague and Budapest, and less than an hour by train east of Vienna. Bratislava fans argue that the city has all the merits of Prague without the crowds.

The scenery through the **Danube Lowlands** east from Bratislava is largely unexceptional, so what follows comes as a surprise. Shortly after leaving the last station in Slovakia at **Štúrovo**, there is a magnificent view south across the Danube to Esztergom in Hungary. The vista is dominated by **Esztergom Basilica**, the tallest building in Hungary and an impressive symbol of ecclesiastical power in the Danube town that for 250 years served as capital of Hungary. Seen in the right light, we would really rate that view of Esztergom from Slovakia as one of the finest anywhere on Europe's rail network. Within a few minutes, the train crosses into Hungary (but still does not cross the Danube) and there is a superb stretch with the train running through small **Hungarian villages** surrounded by vineyards. Not many long train journeys across Europe have quite such a rousing finale.

Budapest

Budapest is a **grand city**, and was always the most westernised of the Warsaw Pact capitals. In the two decades since the fall of the Iron Curtain it has demolished many of its communist monuments, while moving others, such as the Liberation Monument, to be reassembled in a statue park. Within a medley of Habsburg and Ottoman influences, Budapest is now a city to indulge yourself, in spas, Hungarian cuisine and the city's thriving cultural scene.

The grey-green Danube splits the city into **Buda**, on the west bank, and **Pest** on the east. Buda is the photogenic, hilly Old Town, with its pastel-coloured baroque residences, gas-lit cobblestone streets and hilltop palace, while Pest is the thriving, mostly 19th-century commercial centre, with the imposing riverside **State Parliament building**, its wide boulevards and **Vörösmarty tér**, the busy main square. Between Buda and Pest, Margaret Bridge gives access to Margaret Island (Margit-sziget), a green oasis and venue for alfresco opera and drama in summer. The city's **Museum of Fine Art** opened again at the end of 2018 after major reconstruction work. It houses the Romanesque Hall which served as a storage space but has now been restored to its original splendour. Szent István Bazilika (St Stephen's Basilica), Mátyás Templom (Matthias Church) and Nagy Zsinagóga (Great Synagogue) are just three lavishly decorative places of worship that reflect the diverse paths of religion in Budapest. Take the **Budavári Sikló** (Buda Castle Funicular) up to the **Halászbástya** (Fishermen's Bastion).

Budapest has excellent rail connections to the rest of central Europe, the Balkans and destinations further east, and if your enthusiasm for railways is unbounded, don't miss the Magyar Vasúttörténeti Park (Hungarian Railway History Park) on Tatai út 95 (www.vasuttortenetipark.hu; closed Mon).

Arrival, information, accommodation

≋ There are three major stations: **Nyugati pályaudvar** (Western Station), designed in 1877 by the Eiffel firm from Paris; **Keleti pályaudvar** (Eastern Station); and **Déli pályaudvar** (Southern Station). All three are fairly central, close to hotels and on the metro: Keleti on lines 2 and 4, Déli on line 2, Nyugati on line 3. ✈ **Budapest Airport** (www.bud.hu), 16 km east from the centre at Ferihegy. There's a rail service 2–6 times an hour from Ferihegy station, near Terminal 2, to Budapest Nyugati station, taking 25 mins. To get to Ferihegy station from the airport, take the frequent 🚌 200E. A new bus service connecting Deák Ferenc tér with the airport started in July 2017. 🚌 100E connects Deák Ferenc tér with the airport (every 10 mins during the day), stopping at Kálvin tér along the way (buy tickets before bording). The **metro** is fast and cheap and runs 04.30–23.30 (buy tickets from kiosks or machines inside stations; individual tickets or blocks of ten). Tickets must be stamped in the machines at the station entrance. The southern section of metro line 3 is currently being refurbished (bus replacement service is in operation). Information on public transport at www.bkk.hu. Outside winter, **boat services** operate from the southern end to the northern end of Budapest, from Haller utca to Újpest, Árpád út and Római türdő, daily 08.00–18.35. The **funicular** (*sikló*) from the Buda side of the Chain Bridge to Buda Castle runs daily 07.30–22.00.

🛈 Budapest tourist offices: Sütő ut. 2 (Deák Ferenc tér) and Olof palme sétány 5 (www.budapestinfo.hu). ⌑ Budapest has a wide range of hostels and hotels in all categories, as well as pensions and private rooms. The **Casati Budapest Hotel**, Paulay Ede ut. 31, ☎ 1 343 11 98 (www.casatibudapesthotel.com), is on a quiet street, yet centrally located in Pest. Close to the Danube and overlooking the Parliament building, is the chic and modern **art'otel budapest**, Bem rakpart 16–19, ☎ 1 487 94 87 (www.artotels.com). **Bo18**, Vajdahunyad ut. 18, ☎ 1 783 20 07 (www.bo18hotelbudapest.com), offers comfortable, modern rooms. ✗ Enjoy traditional Jewish-Hungarian fare at the **Rosenstein** restaurant, Mosonyi ut. 3, ☎ 1 333 34 92 (www.rosenstein.hu), close to Keleti station.

Connections from Budapest

You are spoilt for choice when it comes to moving on beyond Budapest. There are direct services to Belgrade (ERT 1360), Lviv and Kiev (both ERT 96), Bucharest (ERT 1280), Zurich (ERT 86), Ljubljana (ERT 1313) and Zagreb (Table 89). During the summer season, there are through carriages to various destinations on the **Adriatic coast**. In 2019, these included Bar (Montenegro), Koper (Slovenia), Rijeka and Split (both in Croatia). When planning onward journeys, check the Budapest departure station carefully. You can continue from Budapest on **Route 26, 45** and **46**.

SIDETRACKS: NAMED TRAINS

Train names can be very **powerful brands**, and some names – such as *Orient Express* and *Flying Scotsman* – were mainstays of the European railway scene for decades. Named trains have inspired art. Thus the luxurious *Train Bleu* which ran overnight from Calais and Paris to Nice in the **heyday of the Riviera** inspired Sergei Diaghilev's 1924 ballet of the same name.

It's been a two-way process. While a train sparked Diaghilev's creative instincts, so art and music have inspired the naming of trains. Until 1987, the daytime train from Hoek van Holland to Basel took its name from *Das Rheingold*, the first of the four operas in Richard Wagner's Ring Cycle. No doubt images of Wagner's Rhine maidens helped **market the train**, which for much of its route ran along the banks of the River Rhine. All good romantic stuff, and perhaps it cheered up passengers from England who found themselves riding the Rheingold through Holland's bleak estuarial landscapes at dawn after a short night on board the packet boat from Harwich to the Hook.

If the train names of yesteryear were impossibly romantic, some of those we have come across more recently are prosaic in the extreme. We made an early morning journey in the Austrian Vorarlberg region a few years ago on a train named after a **brand of Tyrolean ham**. We could never see Diaghilev cooperating with Pablo Picasso, Jean Cocteau and Coco Chanel (as he did in *Le Train Bleu*) to stage a ballet named after a piece of bacon. We note that *Handl Tyrol Speck* quickly disappeared from the Austrian timetables, presumably because the eponymous company terminated the sponsorship agreement. Other **bizarrely named Austrian trains** in recent years have included *A1 Blackberry*, the *Hotel Ibis* and the deeply theological *Licht für die Welt* (Light for the World).

Composers, artists and writers have always been **safe choices** for named trains. You can never go wrong with Chopin, Rembrandt or Goethe. One of the morning trains from Berlin to Prague is called *Carl Maria von Weber*. A later train on the same route is the *Johannes Brahms*.

Mountains and lakes are also sound bets. Shift to more abstract concepts and you get into tricky territory. In the 1980s, the afternoon train from **Prague to Berlin** was called the *Progress*, a name that sounded, well, nicely progressive in Czechoslovakia and East Germany. After the political reforms of 1989, progress became all-too-retro and the train name was quietly dropped.

Other names that initially had a **political edge** to them have however survived. When the *Krasnaya Strela* (Red Arrow) started operating in 1931, it was hailed by Soviet commentators as a great socialist achievement. Curiously, the train's carriages were blue in the early days. Only in 1949 were they changed to red – the shade carefully matched to the same red that dominated the Soviet flag. Both the train name and its distinctive colour have outlived the Soviet Union. Train number 1, the *Krasnaya Strela*, still pulls out of **St Petersburg** at five minutes to midnight every evening, just as it did in the days of the Soviet Union. And the musical accompaniment has not changed either. The station still resounds to Reinhold Glière's *Hymn to the Great City*, the orchestral piece which has signalled the departure of the *Krasnaya Strela* for over half a century. It remains one of Europe's great overnight journeys.

Route 26: Through the Carpathians

CITIES: ★★ CULTURE: ★★★ HISTORY: ★★★ SCENERY: ★★
COUNTRIES COVERED: HUNGARY (HU), UKRAINE (UA)
JOURNEY TIME: 14 HRS | DISTANCE: 607 KM | MAP: WWW.EBRWEB.EU/MAP26

The journey from **Budapest** to the Ukrainian city of **Lviv** (Львів) takes in Habsburg lands not often visited by travellers from western Europe. It crosses just one international frontier, but that glosses over the appeal of the journey: this is a route which traverses religious, linguistic and cultural borderlands. For these considerations alone, it really is a journey well worth making.

Do keep an eye on the **political situation in Ukraine** before venturing over the border. But, as of autumn 2019, the westernmost part of the country remains entirely untouched by the conflict and unrest which has brought such hardship and uncertainty to the Donbass region of eastern Ukraine. Citizens of EU nations enjoy visa-free access to Ukraine, as do US and Canadian nationals. Most other passport holders require a visa, though citizens of ex-Soviet states can still enter Ukraine visa-free. There were reports that the Kiev government might impose a visa requirement on Russian citizens in 2019, but so far this has come to nothing.

Fallout from the conflict in eastern Ukraine has shaped patterns of rail services across all Ukraine's borders. Until 2014, all trains from Budapest to Lviv continued right through to Moscow. Now they run only as far as Kiev.

PRACTICAL DETAILS

Twice-daily direct trains run from Budapest to western Ukraine (see ERT 96 for an overview). The direct daytime train is called *Latorca*; that is the Hungarian name for the river which drains down from the **Carpathian Mountains** through the town of **Mukachevo** (Мукачево). That's where the daytime train from Budapest terminates, with a good onward connection to Lviv. This daytime service from Budapest leaves from Nyugati station in the Hungarian capital. The overnight direct train is of course less conducive to sightseeing, but it's a pleasant enough journey and might be a good choice for a full moon night in mid-summer. The **night train** leaves Budapest Keleti around 19.40 (and, if you want to join it in Vienna where it starts, then about three hours earlier from the Austrian capital). The downside of the timetable is being awoken for customs formalities as the train only crosses the Ukrainian border well after midnight.

Our recommendation is to opt for a morning departure from Budapest and then travel just as far as Mukachevo on the first day. The best of the scenery is on the stretch just beyond Mukachevo, as the railway cuts through the Carpathians. So it may make good sense to break your journey in Mukachevo and then continue next morning from there to Lviv.

Leaving Budapest

If you are making the journey by day go to **Nyugati station** in Budapest, not Keleti (for more on Budapest see p242). Nyugati means 'western' — that's

Route details

Budapest Nyugati to Nyíregyháza		ERT 1270
Frequency	Journey time	Notes
1–2 per hr	3 hrs – 3 hrs 50 mins	R

Nyíregyháza to Záhony		ERT 1270
Frequency	Journey time	Notes
Every 1–2 hrs	50–70 mins	R

Záhony to Chop		ERT 1270
Frequency	Journey time	Notes
7 per day	20 mins	

Chop to Mukachevo		ERT 1700
Frequency	Journey time	Notes
8 per day	60–90 mins	R, E

Mukachevo to Lviv		ERT 1700
Frequency	Journey time	Notes
6 per day	2 hrs 30 mins – 5 hrs 30 mins	R, E

Notes

E – The slower services on this leg are not shown in ERT. These are *elektrichka* (електричка) services (ie. local trains) which do not need to be booked in advance.

R – Advance reservation is required for the faster trains on this route.

entirely misleading as the station lies on the east bank of the Danube (in Pest) and it's the jumping-off point for many journeys to the east. There are hourly fast trains to Nyíregyháza via Debrecen, and at least every two hours there's a train running right through to Záhony on the Ukrainian border.

Make time to take a good look at this **grand terminus** before hopping on the train. It is a remarkable glass and iron structure flanked by two monumental pavilions. Opened in 1877, it was one of the first major contracts secured by Gustave Eiffel's Paris-based company. Although now uncomfortably attached to a large shopping mall, parts of the station still drip with nostalgia for a past era of rail travel. Even the McDonald's has a certain charm not usually associated with fast food. That's not to suggest you should eat there.

Faith on the Great Plain

The railway runs south-east from Budapest, stopping at Ferihegy station (for the airport). Slowly urban Hungary is eclipsed by the far horizons of the **Great Plain**, which stretches east from the Danube to the River Tisza and beyond. About two-and-a-half hours after leaving Budapest, the train stops at **Debrecen** (see p440), Hungary's second city and a place with a strong Jewish and Protestant heritage. It is a good reminder that Hungary is by no means entirely Roman Catholic. The Jewish community is tiny nowadays, but Calvinist traditions still run deep in Debrecen. For an alternative, and much longer, journey from here to Lviv see **Route 52** in this book.

The religious mix of this part of Hungary is exemplified in the next town along the railway which is **Nyíregyháza**. The town has Roman Catholics, Calvinists, Lutherans and even a sizeable Uniate population. Uniates (sometimes misleadingly described as Greek Catholics) use Orthodox rites but recognise the Roman pontiff. In many ways, they bridge the religious traditions of western and eastern Europe. From Nyíregyháza it is about an hour across the plain to **Záhony**, the last station in Hungary.

Bridging two worlds: into Ukraine

Crossing the **River Tisza** on a girder bridge, the train enters Ukrainian territory. The riparian landscapes are very beautiful just here, despite the proximity of huge railway shunting yards on each side of the river. The modern border along the River Tisza marked, until 25 years ago, the frontier with the Soviet Union. A few minutes after slipping over the river, the train arrives at **Chop** (Чоп in both Ukrainian and Russian), where signage in Cyrillic is a reminder that you really have entered another world.

At Chop, the bogies of through trains from Hungary and Slovakia running beyond Mukachevo are adjusted to allow those trains to run on the wider-gauge railway tracks which are the norm in much of eastern Europe. Passengers remain on the train while this takes place. Trains which only go as far as Mukachevo don't need to **switch bogies** as a long abandoned standard-gauge stretch of track from Chop to Mukachevo was reactivated in 2019 — all part of the political project of binding western Ukraine more into the European Union's sphere of influence.

CONNECTIONS FROM CHOP

If you want only the merest taste of Ukraine (viz. no more than the railway station at Chop), there is a quick escape route to Slovakia. There is a thrice-daily service from Chop which runs west via Čierna nad Tisou to **Košice** (ERT 1195), with good onward connections from Košice to Prague and Bratislava (both on **Route 25**).

For some itineraries, cutting through this south-west corner of Ukraine makes perfect sense. If you do change trains at Chop, take time to walk out to the front of the station, which has a very imposing Soviet-era neoclassical facade with a monumental portico.

The main line from **Chop to Lviv** certainly affords good views of the Carpathians as it cuts through the hills north of Mukachevo. But if you are a fan of rural railways, there is a very appealing alternative route from Chop to Lviv which runs much closer to the borders with both Slovakia and Poland. This 291-km route (not shown in ERT) from Chop to Lviv via **Uzhhorod** (Ужгород) and **Sambir** (Самбір) climbs to 850 metres above sea level as it crosses Užok Pass. The mainly single-track rail route passes through a very remote region, at one point skimming (but not crossing) the frontier with Poland. If you opt for the **Užok Pass route**, daytime journeys require changes of train at Uzhhorod and at Sianky (Сянки) which is just north of Užok. There are night trains on the Užok Pass route which run right through from Chop to Lviv.

East to Mukachevo

There is often a festival of shunting at Chop as carriages are marshalled onto the trains to Lviv and Kiev. Once that's done, you'll be on your way again, running east from Chop through the flatlands around the Latorycja River to **Mukachevo** (Мукачево).

Within sixty kilometres of Mukachevo, there are borders with four other countries: Romania, Hungary, Slovakia and Poland. It is easy to lose count of how many flags have fluttered from the ramparts of **Palanok Castle** that stands on a knoll overseeing this lively city on the River Latorycja.

In the 17th century the Kingdom of Hungary and the Principality of Transylvania tussled over Mukachevo, and later it was part of the Austro-Hungarian Empire. At the end of World War I, Mukachevo found itself free of Romanian occupation and part of the newly constituted state of Czechoslovakia. Less than thirty years later, Europe's national boundaries were again redrawn after World War II, and Mukachevites woke up one morning to find the flag of the USSR flying from their castle. And, 25 years ago, there was more change as Mukachevo celebrated the new-found independence of the Ukrainian Republic.

There may be few reminders nowadays of the once thriving **Jewish community** in Mukachevo, so it's easy to forget that this was the place that was known as an Iyr Imahot B'Yisroel ('a mother city of Israel'). To the Jewish community, their home town was called Munkacs and, a hundred years ago, it was a regional focal point for Jewish literary and cultural activity, and renowned worldwide for its Jewish commercial creativity.

Serenity was not the watchword, though, for Munkacs was home to **very different Jewish traditions**, which often stridently opposed each other. The heady mix of assimilationists and Zionists, Orthodox Jews and neologues made for some tough tussles. In the late thirties, well over a third of the town's population was Jewish, but most perished in the concentration camp at Auschwitz. Nowadays, you won't hear much Yiddish in Mukachevo, but Ukrainian, Russian, Hungarian and Slovak voices intermingle. And even, now and again, the local Rusyn language, which is still spoken in the Carpathian borderlands. If you are tempted to stop in Mukachevo, you will

Joseph Roth

"For seventeen hours, Lieutenant Trotta sat in the train. In the eighteenth, he reached the most easterly railway station in the Austrian empire. And there Trotta alighted." The name of the town matters not, but it could so easily have been Brody. The quote above is taken from *Radetzky March*, a novel by Joseph Roth who was born in Brody in 1894.

Brody is 90 km north-east of Lviv, nowadays little more than an hour on a fast train. Services are much faster than in Lieutenant Trotta's day. *Radetzky March* is a tale which plays out at the nerve ends of the Habsburg Empire, in communities very like Joseph Roth's birthplace in **eastern Galicia**. It is a great book to take along when travelling through western Ukraine. On our route from Budapest to Lviv, you enter the erstwhile territory of Austrian Galicia when the train passes through the Beskid Tunnel as its cuts through the **Carpathians** north of Mukachevo. If you travel more widely through this region, you'll discover former Jewish *shtetls* which recall the edgy townships described by Joseph Roth in *Radetzky March*. Brody was just such a place. In Roth's day, it was a classic border town, and for Jews fleeing pogroms in Russia, Brody was often the first stop.

Rail travel features regularly in the writing of Joseph Roth. A remarkable 1924 essay called *Gleisdreieck* captures the intriguing appeal of a triangular junction on an elevated railway in Berlin.

discover a pleasant town which has a very *Mitteleuropa* feel. Accommodation is scarce but the excellent value Tonal, Vokzalna ul. 3, ☎ 031 31 312 11 is a good option right by the station.

Through the Carpathians

On leaving Mukachevo, the train enters **hilly terrain** as the railway climbs up into the Carpathians. The next two hours of the journey are great, as the train cuts through remote hill country with **traditional wooden villages**. The renaissance of religion in this part of western Ukraine means that there are many new churches under construction. Seen from the railway, most have domes which hint of Orthodox affiliation, but many are in fact Uniate. Faith and identity are closely intertwined in this area of Ukraine.

The daytime through train from Budapest makes seven intermediate stops on its journey between Mukachevo and Lviv; the last stop before the summit of the line is at **Volovets** (Воловець), once favoured by Austrian monarch Franz Joseph I as a place to escape from the pressures of courtly life. A dozen kilometres beyond Volovets, the railway dives into the Beskid Tunnel, emerging a few minutes later in the upper part of the Opir Valley which drains north towards Lviv. That tunnel is a real bottleneck on this main rail route. It is currently being widened to accommodate two tracks rather than just one. The first stop on the descent is at **Slavske** (Славське), a small ski resort with some very kitsch mock-Bavarian architecture. Thereafter the landscape slowly becomes more open as the railway winds north through the hills towards Lviv.

Lviv (Львів)

If Lviv were just 100 km further west, it would be in the premier league of European tourist destinations. The problem is, that while Poland oozes youthful chic from every cobblestone, Ukraine struggles with its international image. Lviv's attempts to style itself as 'the new Kraków' have yet to bear fruit. While Kraków pulls the crowds, **Lviv slumbers**.

The two cities share a common history, both having been part of the Austro-Hungarian province of **Galicia**. And both have that same Italianate flair in their central square and some of the surrounding courtyards. The centre of Kraków was the very first place in Poland to be inscribed on the UNESCO List of World Heritage Sites. That was back in 1978. Lviv had to wait another 20 years to receive the same accolade.

Lviv boasts a galaxy of fine churches and civic buildings. 'Must sees' include the **Armenian Cathedral** and the over-the-top baroque St George's Cathedral. The latter was the traditional hub of the Ukrainian Uniate Church which dominates religious affairs in western Ukraine. Following the Orange Revolution, the Archeparchy was transferred to Kiev.

Above all, Lviv is a fine place just to wander. In good weather the Italian Yard is a spot to linger over coffee; it is a superb Renaissance courtyard. Or watch the sunset from **Vysoky Zamok** (Castle Hill) when the view of the city takes on a dreamy quality. For a more macabre take on life (or death), don't miss **Lychakivsky Cemetery**, a magnificent wooded parkland east of the city full of crumbling memorials to poets, philosophers and soldiers.

ARRIVAL, INFORMATION, ACCOMMODATION

≥ West of the city centre. Trams 1 and 9 get you to the town centre at Rynok Square.
🛈 Tourist office: in the city hall, opposite the Neptune Fountain (www.lviv.travel).

⊨ Lviv is happily very cheap. Even such a venerable institution as the **George Hotel**, Mickiewicz sq. 1, ☎ 032 232 62 36 (www.georgehotel.com.ua), is very affordable. We very much enjoyed staying at the **Swiss Hotel**, 20 Knyazya Romana ul., ☎ 032 240 3777 (www.swiss-hotel.lviv.ua), which is close to the centre and has a wonderful restaurant. Or opt for the **Vintage Boutique Hotel**, 11 Serbska ul., ☎ 032 235 68 34 (www.vintagehotel.com.ua), just a short walk from Rynok Square in the heart of the city.

CONNECTIONS FROM LVIV

Lviv is the **principal rail hub** in western Ukraine and so offers a wide range of long-distance trains. There are overnight trains to Wrocław, Kraków and Košice. Since 2018, there are much better daytime services to Przemyśl in Poland, giving good connections onto the new night train to Berlin and possibly (from early 2020) a new direct daytime train to Vienna. There are direct rail links from Lviv to **Kiev** (details on next page) and to many provincial cities not affected by the current conflict. So you can board trains in Lviv which will take you directly to the Black Sea port of **Odessa** (ERT 1700) or to the country's second largest city, Kharkiv (also ERT 1750).

There is still a once-daily direct service from Lviv to **Moscow** (ERT 1740). And there is an overnight service to **Minsk**, leaving Lviv on alternate mornings. Note that most travellers continuing beyond Ukraine to either Belarus or the Russian Federation will need visas.

SIDETRACKS: THROUGH UKRAINE

If you arrived in Lviv following our recommended journey from Budapest on **Route 26**, you'll already have seen some very rural areas of south-west Ukraine. That route from Budapest featured in *Europe by Rail* for the first time in 2016, and we retained it as that particular journey, ending with a stay in Lviv, gives a good introduction to the country. Ukraine of course deserves more. The country is vast, twice the size of Poland and nearly five times larger than England.

If you enjoy Lviv, you may be tempted to explore further. Most of the country is very safe for travellers, provided you avoid the easternmost districts of Luhansk and Donetsk. Wherever you are, be cautious about engaging in fiery political debate. It's wise to take along a Ukrainian (or Russian) dictionary and phrase book, and it's essential to be able to read the Cyrillic alphabet.

Long train journeys are a quintessential part of the Ukrainian experience. Remember that all long-distance journeys in Ukraine must be pre-booked. After Lviv, **Kiev** (Київ) is the obvious next stop. There are fast daytime Intercity services from Lviv to Kiev, the fastest of which make just two intermediate stops, taking five hours for the 572-km journey to the Ukrainian capital. The trains offer a choice of first and second-class seated accommodation and you'll find timings for selected services in ERT 1700.

There are several **overnight trains** from Lviv to Kiev, a selection of which are shown in ERT 1700. On these overnight services there are no carriages with seats, and every traveller is allocated a sleeping berth. This may be in a 2 or 4-berth compartment or in an open-plan carriage with about four dozen bunks. This last is effectively third class; it is called *platskartny*. We've used it, and it certainly feels safe, but you'd be wise not to leave valuables lying around in what is effectively a dormitory on wheels.

The Ukrainian capital is set on wooded hills around the **River Dniepr** and has an altogether grander and more eastern demeanour than Lviv. It boasts impressive squares, graceful boulevards and magnificent churches and museums. Star of the show is the **Kyievo-Pecherska lavra**, in English dubbed the Monastery of the Caves, one of the highest-ranking ecclesiastical foundations in the Orthodox world. It includes a number of churches, a newly rebuilt cathedral, a curious, tiered bell tower, and a vast complex of underground corridors that travel writers of yesteryear often suggested led to Moscow. Be not fooled. If you are bound for Moscow, it is best to take the train.

Visitors to Kiev should not miss **Maidan Nezalezhnosti** (Independence Square), which was the focal point in Kiev for the Orange Revolution in 2004 and the Euromaidan demonstrations in the winter of 2013–2014. Spend any time in Kiev and you'll appreciate how much Ukraine is split. You'll realise in retrospect that Lviv was very western in orientation. Kiev is different. There's a more palpable eastern influence and more Russian spoken. Move further east and the Russian thread becomes yet more dominant.

To learn more about life in eastern Ukraine in these times of civil strife and discord, turn to *In Wartime: Stories from Ukraine* by Tim Judah. This compelling account of how the conflict has affected ordinary people was published by Allen Lane in December 2015.

Route 27: Historic Habsburg cities

CITIES: ★★ CULTURE: ★★ HISTORY: ★★ SCENERY: ★★
COUNTRIES COVERED: ITALY (IT), SLOVENIA (SI), CROATIA (HR)
JOURNEY TIME: 11 HRS | DISTANCE: 430 KM | MAP: WWW.EBRWEB.EU/MAP27

Fifty years ago, there were four direct trains each day from **Venice to Zagreb**. The pick of the daytime services was the *Simplon Express*. It pulled into Santa Lucia station on the bank of the Grand Canal in Venice at 08.42, after an overnight journey from Paris. At 09.28 the *Simplon Express* left again, now running east around the head of the Golfo di Venezia to Trieste and then crossing the border into Yugoslavia at lunchtime. It reached Zagreb at 18.25. All very civilised. Even in a Europe divided by the **Iron Curtain**, reasonably good train services connected the two halves of the continent.

A dozen years ago, we travelled on a daytime train direct from Venice to Zagreb. The train was named after the 18th-century Venetian playwright **Carlo Goldoni**, who is best remembered for his comedy *Il servitore di due padroni* (Servant of Two Masters). That train no longer exists. In recent years, many of Europe's rail operators have struggled to reconcile public service interests with the need to make a decent profit. The service ethos has slipped down the agenda and international rail services have often suffered. Today, we have a Europe shaped by a commitment to coordination and integration. Except when it comes to railways. There are some woeful gaps in our rail infrastructure. Not a single main-line train service now crosses the border between Italy and Slovenia. A twice-daily regional train from **Trieste to Ljubljana**, reintroduced in late 2018, goes some way to bridge the gap but it's not enough.

In this journey for *Europe by Rail*, we follow the exact route taken by the old *Simplon Express* and later by the EC *Goldoni*. It's an amazing ride, in which we'll discover Habsburg ingenuity while cursing EU transport policy.

This route starts with a train journey along the coast to **Trieste**, from where we zigzag up into the hills to reach the dry *karst*. After that we travel east to the Slovenian capital Ljubljana, then follow a scenic rail route down the **Sava Valley** towards the Croatian capital, **Zagreb**. We are, in effect, following in reverse the journey described by Ian Fleming in *From Russia with Love*, where James Bond took the train out of Yugoslavia (though not, as it happens out of danger).

SUGGESTED ITINERARY

It is perfectly possible to complete this journey in a longish day. It takes about 11 hours and requires three trains. But with two great cities on this route, we suggest you take your time, **stopping overnight** in both Trieste and Ljubljana. Both cities drip with Habsburg charm and each has a clear *Mitteleuropa* feel. Whether you travel direct or stop off along the way, this is not a route where there is huge advantage to booking in advance. If you buy tickets as you go along, the entire journey will still cost less than €40.

Route details

Venice Santa Lucia to Trieste Centrale		ERT 601
Frequency	Journey time	Notes
Hourly	2 hrs 5 mins	M

Trieste Centrale to Villa Opicina		ERT 87
Frequency	Journey time	Notes
2 per day	30 mins	T

Villa Opicina to Sežana		ERT 1305
Frequency	Journey time	Notes
6–8 per day	10 mins	

Sežana to Ljubljana		ERT 1305
Frequency	Journey time	Notes
5-13 per day	1 hr 45 mins – 2 hrs	X

Ljubljana to Zagreb Glavni		ERT 1300
Frequency	Journey time	Notes
5 per day	2 hrs 20 mins	

Notes

There is a useful express coach from Trieste to Ljubljana. This twice-daily service is operated by Slovenian Railways. The one-way fare is €9. The coaches depart from Trieste bus station.

M – There are additional trains from Venice Mestre to Trieste Centrale, the fastest of which take only 1 hr 25 mins.
T – In addition to the train, 🚌 2 runs every 20 minutes from Via Galatti (by Piazza Oberdan) in Trieste up to Villa Opicina, with some journeys detouring via Villa Opicina station. As a possible alternative to the bus, do check if the Villa Opicina tram link is running again. It is likely to be reinstated during 2020.
X – A small number of journeys on this leg require a change of train at Divača.

II = Italy
SI = Slovenia

Trieste (suggested stopover)

Arriving by train in Trieste from Venice is something special. Sit on the right and you'll see Miramare Castle (more on which below). Italy's atmospheric easternmost city looks more Austrian than Italian, a reminder of its former role as the entrepôt of the Austro-Hungarian Empire (up to 1918). Rebuilt in the 19th century in a **grand gridiron plan**, it relishes its role as a cross-roads between East and West. Trieste is stately rather than intimate, with six-storey palazzi, **art nouveau** and classical facades. It's set on a beautifully curving bay, with the rugged limestone heights of the **arid Carso** an impressive backdrop to the city.

Trieste is a place which makes you think about issues of identity and heritage. **Habsburg history** is just one part of the Trieste mix. Today, the Slavic and Latin worlds mingle in Trieste. The city has a substantial Slovene minority. Throw in a dash of Italian flair and you begin to see why Trieste is so appealing. The 'must read' book for any visit to the city is Jan Morris' *Trieste and the Meaning of Nowhere* (published in 2001 by Faber & Faber).

The port of Trieste has long been important in the **coffee trade**, so it's no surprise that the Triestini cherish their city's café culture. Perhaps the most evocative café, one much favoured by the literary set, is the Caffè San Marco, Via Cesare Battisti 18, with its high-ceilinged art nouveau interior. One of Trieste's oldest cafés, the **Caffè degli Specchi** (1839), is on the majestic central square, Pza dell'Unità d'Italia, presided over by the vast **Palazzo del Comune del Governo**, aglow with its mosaic ornamentation.

A pleasant area for strolling is the Capitoline Hill, the heart of Roman and mediaeval Trieste. On top, beside the remains of the Roman forum, stands the 11th-century Cathedral of San Giusto, founded in the 5th century on the site of a Roman temple and containing early mediaeval mosaics and frescos.

A short bus ride west from Trieste (🚌 6 towards Grignano) leads to **Miramare Castle**, a white marble pile in a stunning coastal location. Built 1856–60 for Maximilian of Habsburg as a love nest for him and Charlotte of Belgium, it reveals astonishingly ornate marquetry interiors. There's free entry to the surrounding park, which slopes down from the main road (get off the bus after going through two tunnels; retrace through one tunnel to reach the park gates). It is laced with trails and has many rare Mediterranean broadleaf trees, as well as a pond and a grotto.

ARRIVAL, INFORMATION, ACCOMMODATION

🚃 Stazione Centrale, Pza della Libertà 8. Adjacent to the bus station. 🅸 Tourist office: V. dell'Orologio 1, Pza Unità d'Italia (www.turismofvg.it).

🛏 A very comfortable and friendly B&B not far frm the station is **Atelier Lidia Polla**, Via del Coroneo 1, ☎ 0334 715 0231 (www.atelierlidiapolla.com). More upmarket, but also very close to Pza dell' Unità Italia is the design-centric **Urban**, Androna Chiusa 4, ☎ 040 302 065 (www.urbanhotel.it). Or try the similarly central and stylish hotel **Vis à Vis**, Pza dello Squero Vecchio 1, ☎ 040 760 0011 (www.hotelvisavis.net).

BOAT CONNECTIONS FROM TRIESTE

Trieste is the jumping-off point for some wonderful local boats trips. For a short excursion take the ferry over to **Muggia** (30 mins), a characterful community on the far side of the bay, close to the Slovene border.

Liberty Lines (www.libertylines.it) offer summer-season scheduled boats from Trieste (Pier 4) to Istria. The nearest destination is the beautiful Slovenian port of **Piran**. There are also direct sailings to Poreč and Rovinj – both towns in **Croatian Istria** – and even a twice weekly sailing to Mali Losinj, from where there's an onward boat connection to Zadar. As befits a great port, there are also some long-distance shipping links from Trieste. Adria Ferries (www.adriaferries.com) has a weekly sailing, usually on Tuesdays, to **Durrës** in Albania.

Border business

There are twice-daily direct trains from Trieste Centrale to Ljubljana. The train labours in great curves up into the hills above the port city to reach **Villa Opicina**, a northern suburb of Trieste, which already has a fair density of Slovene speakers. There are additional local trains from Villa Opicina across the border, so for extra choice you may want to consider taking the local bus from the centre of Trieste up to Villa Opicina.

As of autumn 2019, the **marvellous old tramway** from Trieste to Villa Opicina is closed, but it is tentatively slated for reopening in mid-2020. It's an ingenious creation of Habsburg engineers, originally constructed as a cog railway. and later it was converted into a hybrid tram and funicular railway. If it's running again, it's worth the ride. It is a one-kilometre walk from the upper terminal of the Opicina Tramway to the railway station. Walk north from the tram stop to the roundabout, where you turn slightly left into Via di Prosecco. Later turn right on Via della Ferrovia to reach the station.

The station is a shadow of its former self, but has still not quite lost the sense of intrigue and mystery which surrounded it in the Cold War years. If you delve into spy novels, Villa Opicina plays a bit-part role in many plots – often featuring under its former name **Poggioreale Campagna**. The station name was changed to Villa Opicina in the late 1960s. When Ian Fleming wrote about James Bond's arrival from across the border in From Russia with Love, the station revealed "the first smell of the soft life with the happy jabbering Italian officials and the carefree upturned faces of the station crowd." How times have changed. When we last were at Villa Opicina, the platform was deserted and we were the only people to board the evening train across the border to Sežana in Slovenia.

You can also take a direct bus from **Trieste to Sežana** instead and join the train to Ljubljana there. Buses depart about eight times every weekday from the bus station near Trieste Centrale (Sunday services are sparse).

Serene Slovenia

Whether you take the train or the bus over the border from Italy, your first encounter with Slovenia is at **Sežana**. A short walk around town is a nice reminder that you have crossed one of Europe's great cultural frontiers and are now definitely in the Slavic world. Burek replaces pizza as a favoured snack, and there are memorials to the Yugoslav Partisans (who liberated Sežana). The **botanical park** at the top end of town is a nice spot to while away an hour while waiting for the onward train. Sežana lies at the southern end of a great rural rail route to Bled and Jesenice (ERT 1302).

The journey from Sežana to Ljubljana leads across **dry limestone terrain** – which is locally known as *karst*. Building a railway across this area was a considerable feat (see the box below). If you wish to stop en route from Sežana to Ljubljana, the obvious choice is Postojna, famous for its remarkable cave complex.

Ljubljana (suggested stopover)

The capital of Slovenia is a lively university town dominated by a hilltop fortress. The **River Ljubljanica** divides the city into two parts, joined in the city centre by an attractive and unique triple bridge, the **Tromostovje**. This links the city's old heart, Stari Trg, on the right bank, built below the hilltop castle, to Novi Trg on the left bank. The **Old Town**, on the right bank, is an inviting maze of cobbled streets with historic buildings. Recent years have witnessed a renaissance with the opening of numerous shops, restaurants and bars, many with river views and generally reasonably priced. It is a gentle stroll up to the castle, which gives a good view of the city below. Beyond, on Vodnikov Trg, lies the **central food market** (open every day); good for picnic shopping.

On the river's left bank, the 17th-century Franciscan church dominates Prešernov Trg. The left bank of the city serves a generous portion of museums, including the **Museum of Contemporary Art Metelkova** and the **Museum of Modern Art** (both at www.mg-lj.si; closed Mon).

CROSSING THE KARST

Few of the passengers on the train even noticed **Gornje Ležeče**. The train had twisted and turned through valleys where the hillsides tilted sharper and sharper, screeches of wheels on ancient rails, and the wind blowing madly through open carriage windows. And then, after a long climb, just on the edge of the karst, the slow train stopped. The wind dropped, and for a moment, there was just the rasping sound of a lone cicada in the distance. A goat crossed the railway and paused beside the tracks to glance at the train before running off to safety behind a mountain ash laden with red berries. For a while, we were alone in the Slovenian karst, Vremščica's gentle slopes to the north and, in the opposite direction, the land tumbling away to the Reka Valley far below. A hundred years ago, Gornje Ležeče was at the hub of a great system of aqueducts that provided water to this arid land of potholed limestone. Here, the steam engines of the **Austrian Southern Railway**, labouring through the mountains and valleys from Trieste to Vienna, would stop for water. Near the railway tracks, a handsome building with blue doors housed the old water reservoir. Today it is half covered in ivy – a silent tribute to a wonderful piece of Habsburg hydrological engineering that made it possible for steam trains to traverse the arid karst.

Our slow train waits at Gornje Ležeče in the late summer sunshine. A minute stretches into five, and then, as the cicada ticks away the seconds and the dregs of morning coffee are drained, the door of the white station building opens and a clean-shaven man in a smart green uniform and red cap emerges. He walks with slow precision across to our train and gives a wave. Suddenly we are rattling along once more, towards Postojna and Ljubljana.

Arrival, information, accommodation

≥ Trg Osvobodilne Fronte 6, a short walk south to the Old Town. ✈ Ljubljana Jože Pučnik Airport, 24 km north-west of Ljubljana, 45 mins by bus (hourly Mon–Fri 05.20–20.10; every 2 hrs Sat & Sun 09.00–19.00; www.fraport-slovenija.si). 🛈 Tourist office: Adamič-Lundrovo nabrežje 2 (www.visitljubljana.com).

🛏 A good-value choice in the centre of town is the B&B **Petra Varl**, Vodnikov trg 5a, ☎ 01 430 3788 (www.petravarl.com). The **Hostel Celica**, Metelkova ul. 8, ☎ 01 230 9700 (www.hostelcelica.com), is housed in a former prison and is an excellent choice located in the heart of the popular artist-run Metelkova quarter. More upmarket and perfectly located close to the Old Town is the friendly and stylish boutique hotel **Cubo**, Slovenska cesta 15, ☎ 01 425 60 00 (www.hotelcubo.com). ✗ The riverside zone between Stari Trg and Novi Trg is the centre for friendly bars and reasonably priced eating places.

Connections from Ljubljana

There are direct daytime Eurocity services from **Ljubljana to Budapest** (ERT 89), Vienna (ERT 91) and Munich (ERT 62). You also find a number of useful overnight trains, with a departure each evening for Innsbruck and Zurich (both ERT 86). If you **yearn for the sea**, take the direct train from Ljubljana down to Rijeka (ERT 1305), whence there is a year-round fast catamaran link to the Croatian islands of Rab and Pag.

Into Croatia

The entire journey from Ljubljana to Zagreb follows the **Sava Valley**. This river, a tributary of the Danube, is often seen as marking the border between Central Europe and the Balkans. Running east from Ljubljana, the railway hugs the south bank of the river, but just short of Litija it crosses over onto the north bank and remains there for the entire run downstream into Croatia. So sit on the right side of the train for the best views of the Sava.

All trains stop at **Dobova** for border formalities, which are very light touch. Croatia, although a member of the European Union, is not yet a member of Schengen, although it is gearing up to join in the coming years. Until that happens, passports are routinely checked at the country's frontiers.

From Dobova, it is just another 30 minutes to **Zagreb** (p393). You'll find a few thoughts on the area immediately around the main station (called Zagreb glavni kolodvor) on p397.

Connections from Zagreb

At Zagreb you can connect onto two other routes in this book. For a real Balkan adventure, take **Route 47** south to Bulgaria and Greece. Or follow **Route 46** down to the Adriatic coast at Split (ERT 1330) or north to Budapest (ERT 89).

There is a daytime train (augmented on some dates by a seasonal overnight train) running east across the Pannonian Plain to Belgrade (ERT 1320), where you can connect onto **Route 45** which runs south to the port of Bar on the coast of Montenegro.

If Zagreb marks the easternmost extent of your explorations, you'll find very useful direct daytime Eurocity services from Zagreb to Vienna (ERT 91) and Munich (ERT 62). You can also join the *Alpine Pearls* **overnight train** which leaves Zagreb in the early evening for the 15-hour journey to Zurich.

SCANDINAVIAN FORAYS
An introduction

In this section of *Europe by Rail*, we include six journeys to and through **Denmark, Norway, Sweden and Finland**. One of the six journeys (**Route 33**) crosses Finland's eastern border to end in the Russian city of St Petersburg. Rail travel is extremely efficient in the Scandinavian countries and, though seat reservations may be advisable at busy periods, there are few trains where it is required that you book in advance. The latter are mainly **premium fast services** such as the Pendolino trains in Finland and the X2000 routes in Sweden (including the fast trains from Stockholm to Copenhagen). Note that journeys on the **high-speed Allegro services** from Finland to Russia all require advance reservation, and rail passes are not accepted on the route to St Petersburg. But tickets, if booked in advance, are modestly priced with one-way journeys from Helsinki to St Petersburg starting at just €39.

There's an oddity in **names of train classes** in some routes in this region. Here's an example. Finland avoids use of the terms second and first class, instead calling its standard class of travel *Eco*, while the more expensive premium class is called *Extra*. Pass holders with a first-class pass are thus entitled to use the *Extra* seating on Finnish trains.

Shift to Norway, though, where the premium class is called *NSB Komfort* and the rules for pass holders are very different. Holders of first-class passes can ride in *NSB Komfort*, of course, but so can those with second-class passes (and, for that matter, most kinds of second-class ticket) subject to payment of a small supplement.

Other options to consider

There are many routes in Scandinavia which deserve exploring for which we just couldn't find space in this book. We are great fans of some of the **rural railways in central Sweden**, particularly those around Lake Vänern. You'll get a glimpse of that lovely region if you follow the main line between Stockholm and Oslo which forms the final part of **Route 51**.

There's a **classic slow journey** much favoured by many devotees of Sweden for which we didn't have enough space in this book. It is the *Inlandsbanan* which runs up to Gällivare. It is open to passenger traffic for just nine weeks each year (details in ERT 766) and, for those who love trees, it's hard to beat. Yet perhaps the most celebrated Scandinavian slow journey of all is not a train but a shipping service. If you tire of trains, make time for the **Hurtigruten ships** which ply the Norwegian coast from Bergen all the way to Kirkenes near the Russian border (ERT 2240). Two journeys in this volume (**Route 31** and **32**) take in the **Lofoten Islands**, an archipelago often acclaimed as the most scenic stretch of the entire Hurtigruten itinerary. ∎

Route 28: Through Denmark to Sweden

CITIES: ★★ CULTURE: ★ HISTORY: ★★ SCENERY: ★
COUNTRIES COVERED: GERMANY (DE), DENMARK (DK), SWEDEN (SE)
JOURNEY TIME: 12 HRS | DISTANCE: 997 KM | MAP: WWW.EBRWEB.EU/MAP28

This journey takes us right across northern Europe – from the banks of the **River Elbe** in northern Germany to the Swedish capital. You'll not be craning your neck to see passing mountains, as the journey is across largely flat terrain, but it is nonetheless a **very interesting route**. There are excellent coastal and lake views and some fine cities. There's a pleasant short hop on a ferry thrown in too – though from mid-December 2019 you'll no longer get the decidedly oddball experience of seeing an entire train transported on a ship. The through trains from Hamburg to Copenhagen are now routed via Flensburg and Odense. But the journey described here, using the ferry from Germany to Denmark, is much more scenic.

RECOMMENDED ITINERARY

Lübeck and **Copenhagen** both deserve an overnight stop. We like to linger on all journeys and would probably take a week to travel from Hamburg to Stockholm. If time is tight, you could travel right through to Stockholm, using daytime trains from Hamburg via Copenhagen to Malmö, connecting there with the overnight train to **Stockholm**. That night train leaves Malmö daily except Saturdays; there is a choice of sleepers, couchettes and seated accommodation. Or you could travel entirely by day, leaving Hamburg at breakfast time and reaching Stockholm by mid-evening.

The short hop on the **Scandlines ferry** does not require advance booking. Seat reservations are compulsory year round on the fast Snabbtåg trains from Copenhagen or Malmö to Stockholm. If you have an aversion to ever making advance reservations, then bear in mind that one can make the entire journey from Hamburg to Stockholm using local trains and the ferry.

From the North Sea to the Baltic

Our journey starts in **Hamburg** (read more about the city on p270), where all trains for Lübeck and Copenhagen depart from the Hauptbahnhof. Suffice to say here that it is a city shaped by its history as an important North Sea port. The destiny of Lübeck, just 65 kilometres away to the northeast, has also been forged by the sea, but here the maritime connections are Baltic. If you only have time to visit one of the old **Hanseatic towns**, make it Lübeck, a city that has cut a dash in commerce, trade and the arts for seven centuries.

Lübeck (suggested stopover)

The 12th-century **Altstadt** (Old Town), on a moated island in a river, has been beautifully restored. Between this and the main station is Lübeck's emblem, the twin-towered **Holstentor**, a 15th-century structure and now

Route details

Hamburg Hbf to Lübeck Hbf		ERT 825
Frequency	Journey time	Notes
2 per hr	40–60 mins	

Lübeck Hbf to Puttgarden		ERT 825
Frequency	Journey time	Notes
Every 1–2 hrs	60–100 mins	

Puttgarden to Rødby Færge		ERT 2375
Frequency	Journey time	Notes
2 per hr	45 mins	B

Rødby Færge to Copenhagen H		ERT 720
Frequency	Journey time	Notes
Every 2 hrs	2 hrs 10 mins	

Copenhagen H to Stockholm C		ERT 730
Frequency	Journey time	Notes
4–6 per day	5 hrs 20 mins	

Notes

The through trains from Hamburg to Copenhagen via the Puttgarden to Rødby ferry run for the last time in December 2019. Our grid reflects the revised timings applicable from December 2019. To compensate for the loss of these direct trains, there will be a limited direct train service from Hamburg to Copenhagen via Flensburg, Fredericia and Odense.

B – By Scandlines ship.

museum, that was one of the four city gates. It's a fine example of the **Brick Gothic style** which secured for Lübeck a place on UNESCO's World Heritage List. Get your bearings by taking the lift up the 50-metre spire of the Gothic Petrikirche; from the observation platform you'll see the Baltic Sea on a clear day. Take a look inside the church below too; nowadays it's a non-denominational centre for culture and ethics, which often hosts innovative art displays.

The **Marktplatz** is dominated by the striking L-shaped mediaeval Rathaus, typical of Lübeck's affection for alternating red unglazed and black glazed bricks, a trick later copied by the Dutch. Opposite the east wing is **Niederegger Haus**, Breitestrasse, renowned for displays of marzipan (the town's speciality and produced since the Middle Ages). Opposite the north wing is the brick-built 13th-century Marienkirche that was the model for many churches in the area. For a glimpse of Lübeck's watery hinterland, consider a boat trip to the nearby port of **Travemünde**. It's a 90-minute one-way journey. If you do not have time to make the round trip, there are plenty of trains from Travemünde back to Lübeck (ERT 825).

ARRIVAL, INFORMATION, ACCOMMODATION

≥ Lübeck Hbf, a 10-min walk west of the Old Town. 🛈 Tourist office: Holstentorpl. 1 (www. luebeck-tourismus.de). ⨝ There are several reasonably priced hotels around the station (Hbf). Just a few minutes from the railway station is **Hotel Excelsior**, Hansestr. 3, ☎ 0451 880 90 (www.hotel-excelsior-luebeck.de). A central budget option is the **Hotel zur alten Stadtmauer**, An der Mauer 57, ☎ 0451 737 02 (www.hotelstadtmauer.de). The **Atlantic Hotel Lübeck**, Schmiedestraße 9-15, ☎ 0451 38479-0 (www.atlantic-hotels.de) is an up-market option with a modern feel in the Old Town.

From Lübeck it is an hour on a Copenhagen-bound train to **Puttgarden**, and it's a lovely ride through the placid landscapes of eastern Holstein. Away to the west you see a gentle ripple of hills known as the **Holsteinische Schweiz** (Holstein Switzerland). That's a fine piece of northern hyperbole, as the hills are no more than pimples on the landscape. But it's all very pretty with water meadows, glimpses of the sea and abundant bird life. The railway crosses a very graceful bridge onto the pancake-flat island of **Fehmarn** (see box on next page).

To speed up services between Hamburg and Copenhagen, there are plans to build a tunnel under the arm of the Baltic which separates the island of Fehmarn from Denmark. Until the tunnel opens, you either swim or take the ferry. The latter is the more advisable option. It's a chance to catch the Baltic breeze on the open deck or enjoy a snack in the ship's cafeteria.

Through Denmark

Landfall in Denmark is at the port of **Rødby**, where you join a Danish train which tracks north through undemanding rural landscapes towards

GERMAN ISLANDS

Germany has an ambiguous relationship with its islands. Rather than enjoying the inherent isolation of island communities, Germans prefer to tame their islands by robbing them of their island status. **Fehmarn** (traversed by the rail-ferry route from Hamburg to Copenhagen) is one of several offshore islands connected by fixed links to the German mainland. You also travel in the comfort of an Intercity train all the way to Westerland on the North Sea island of **Sylt** (ERT 821) or to Binz on the Baltic island of **Rügen** (ERT 844) – the latter has two dozen stations and trains aplenty. The star turn on Rügen is the line from Putbus to Göhren (ERT 844a), where all trains are hauled by steam locomotives. Services run year round through fabulous beech woods and meadows in the eastern part of the island. If you can be weaned off trains and want to visit a German island which still has a strong sense of isolation, head for **Helgoland** (ERT 2242, see also 'Connections from Bremen' on p269).

Two other German islands, closer to the mainland than Helgoland, which are easily reached by ferries from a mainland port and with good rail connections include the North Sea outposts of **Föhr** and **Amrum**. Boats depart from Dagebüll (ERT 822), where the trains pull up right on the quayside. Another island community well deserving of a visit is car-free **Hiddensee** in the Baltic, which in summer has a direct ferry from Stralsund, itself a old Hanseatic town with some stunning brick Gothic architecture.

Copenhagen. Of the small towns along the way, Næstved is notable for its brick architecture. It was a member of the Hanseatic League just like Lübeck and its far-flung web of trading links gave the town an importance way beyond its size. **Næstved** has never really featured on mainstream tourist trails, so it's a pleasant place to stop for an hour or two.

Slightly further on, and much more impressive, is **Roskilde** which was Denmark's first capital. The town is rich in history, with a magnificent brick cathedral that is the traditional burial place of Danish royalty. The impressive **Viking Ship Museum**, one kilometre north of the centre on the shore of Roskilde Fjord, exhibits the intact remains of five original ships and shows a film about their excavation in the 1960s (www.vikingeskibsmuseet.dk). The famous open-air **Roskilde music festival**, which has done so much to put Roskilde on the map, is held in late June and early July (www.roskilde-festival.dk); it features some of the biggest international rock groups as well as lesser-known Scandinavian bands.

Copenhagen (København) – (suggested stopover)

Copenhagen is a refined and **vibrant city** of great Renaissance architecture, cobbled pedestrian walks and meandering canals and lakes, with a distinct, easy-going and friendly atmosphere that is a joy to take in, especially in the summertime. Cruise boats tour the canals that thread through the historic core, revealing an appealing diversity of open spaces, spires, towers and statuary. Cycling is encouraged here and the outdoor, almost Mediterranean, feel is compounded by an effervescent street life and excellent nightspots.

In spring 2018 a new urban space opened on the city's harbour waterfront. **BLOX** is home to the Danish Architecture Centre and its exhibitions, but also aims to be a meeting and living space for Copenhagen's citizens.

For an evening of mindless pleasure, do not miss the **Tivoli Gardens** and its stomach-churning rides, giant puppets, kitsch merry-go-rounds and all the fun you would expect of the fair in what is one of Europe's oldest, and best-loved amusement parks. Or have a stroll through **Christiania**, a unique social experiment, and enjoy a picnic on the lakeside, sip on a beer with the curious array of locals and visitors, or just browse through the market stalls.

ARRIVAL, INFORMATION, ACCOMMODATION

≋ The main rail station is **København Hovedbanegård** (København H; www.dsb.dk), with an S-train (urban train) station of the same name. Buses to districts in and around Copenhagen stop right outside and the city centre is a 5-min walk away. ✈ Copenhagen Airport Kastrup (www.cph.dk) is 8 km south-east of town. Trains to København H every 10 mins, taking 14 mins, and the metro every 2–6 mins (every 15 to 20 mins at night; details on www.m.dk), taking 15 mins to Nørreport; you must buy your ticket before boarding the train or metro. ⓘ Tourist office: Vesterbrogade 4B, opposite the station, by Tivoli's main entrance (www.visitcopenhagen.dk).

Buses, trains and the driverless metro all form part of an integrated system in the Copenhagen area and tickets are valid on all. Most attractions are central, so for a single journey you will probably only need the cheapest ticket, 24 DKK, which covers travel in two zones for 1 hr 15 mins. Or buy a 24-hr City Pass for 80 DKK. Validate your ticket in the machines on board buses and on S-train platforms. Bus tickets can be purchased on board, but train tickets must be purchased at one of the automated machines at the station. An electronic ticketing system called Rejsekort covers all modes of public transport. Two new metro lines are scheduled to be opened in September 2019 (M3) and in 2020 (M4).

⌕ Copenhagen has a wide range of accommodation options, although turning up without a reservation – especially during the summer months – can be risky. **Hotel Absalon**, close to the Centralstation, is a reasonably priced option in Helgolandsgade 15, ☎ 33 31 43 44 (www.absalon-hotel.dk). Basic, but quite affordable are the three huge **WakeUp Copenhagen** hotels at Carsten Niebuhrs Gade 11, ☎ 44 80 00 10, at Bernstorffsgade 35, Tel. 44 80 01 10 and at Borgergade 9, ☎ 44 80 00 90 (www.wakeupcopenhagen.dk). If you are in the mood for something extra special, opt for the **Hotel Nimb**, Bernstorffsgade 5, # 88 70 00 00 (www.nimb.dk), a fabulous piece of stylish escapism just opposite the train station's eastern exit, close to the Tivoli Gardens. If like us you can't afford the room prices, just have a peek around.

CONNECTIONS FROM COPENHAGEN

Take the local train to **Helsingør** (ERT 703), a relaxed small town on the shores of the Øresund with a spectacular castle (called Kronborg Slot), which features centrally in Shakespeare's *Hamlet*. From Helsingør, Scandlines ferries shuttle frequently over the Øresund to Helsingborg on the Swedish side (ERT 2345), where there is a connection into **Route 30** north to Göteborg and Oslo.

Over the Øresund into Sweden

If you travel east from Copenhagen on one of the Stockholm-bound trains shown in ERT 730, you need to be at the station 15 minutes before departure;

there is usually an ID check before you board the train. If you take any other eastbound service from Copenhagen or Kastrup (that's the airport station now increasingly referred to in timetables as CPH Lufthavn) expect a cursory ID check on the train. This may change in 2020, so our advice is to allow an extra hour for all journeys between Copenhagen and **Malmö** on local trains on the Øresund route (shown in ERT 703, 735, 737, 745 and 746). This doesn't apply if you are pre-booked on one of the fast Stockholm-bound services. As of late 2019 there are no ID checks on the reverse route, ie. from Sweden to Denmark, but that too could change in 2020.

Route 28 shares a common stretch with **Route 30** between Copenhagen and Lund (for more on Malmö and Lund – including connections from Malmö – see pp277–79). Beyond **Lund**, the two routes diverge, Route 30 heading north-west through rolling agricultural land towards Göteborg and our train running north-east through pleasant countryside towards Stockholm.

There are a number of unremarkable small towns, but none that really cries out for a stop until **Linköping**, where the prime attraction is Gamla Linköping, an ambitious living museum that seeks to recreate the 19th-century town, much of which was painstakingly relocated piece by piece and rebuilt here. Linköping's Domkyrka is one of Sweden's oldest cathedrals, with a 107-m green spire visible from far outside the town, and containing fine stone carvings along the south doorway.

The next place of any size is **Norrköping**, a prosperous textile centre, with a museum celebrating the town's industrial legacy. The cluster of old mills around the Motala river is truly impressive. Beyond Norrköping, the surrounding countryside becomes more densely populated as the train gets closer to Stockholm. The Swedish capital is reached in about 80 minutes on the fastest trains from Norrköping.

Stockholm

Spread over **14 islands** with countless inlets, Stockholm has a stunning waterfront that rivals those of San Francisco and Sydney, and most visitors would probably rate it the most rewarding of the Scandinavian capitals. At its heart is the impressively intact original part of the city, **Gamla Stan**, with an enticing blend of dignified old buildings, cafés, and craft and designer shops; in contrast, the **Djurgården** is a huge natural park where the city comes to swim, canoe, fly kites, visit the zoo and the superb outdoor museum **Skansen** (www.skansen.se), or just admire the views. Stockholm is airy and very much a harbour capital. It's a lovely place to be outdoors in summer (winter is perfectly romantic, if a bit austere), whether listening to an outdoor concert or taking a cruise, but there are also plenty of superb indoor attractions, such as the Nationalmuseum and the historic Vasa warship – dredged from the mud and restored to reveal its full 17th-century glory. The **Vasa museum** (www.vasamuseet.se) that houses the ship is located on the island of Djurgården, which can be reached by boat from Nybroplan, Slussen or Steppsholmen or by tram no. 7 from Norrmalmstorg.

ARRIVAL, INFORMATION, ACCOMMODATION

⇌ Centralstation has a bus information/ticket office and good food stalls (train information at www.sj.se). Stockholm City station is located below the T-Central station (for metro services) that is part of Stockholm's central railway station. Stockholm City serves all commuter train services. ✈ Stockholm Arlanda (www.swedavia.se/arlanda) is 45 km north of Stockholm. The Arlanda Express rail link (www.arlandaexpress.com), takes 20 mins to Centralstation (every 10–15 mins, daily, 04.50–23.05, then every 30 mins until 01.05). 🛈 Visitor centre: Kulturhuset, Sergels Torg 3–5 (www.visitstockholm.com).

Storstockholms Lokaltrafik (SL; www.sl.se/en/) runs the excellent bus and metro (T-bana) network. Buy tickets for buses and the T-bana at SL Centers, newsagents, at machines on T-bana platforms or commuter train stations, by SMS or the SL App. The zonal fare system was abandoned in January 2017. An smart card system is now in place (SL Access card), but you can also buy a single journey ticket (SEK 45) which is valid for unlimited travel on all SL services for 75 minutes. Note that tickets cannot be purchased on the bus. Validate your ticket before you enter the T-bana or bus, or bypass the machines by buying a pass for free transit within 24 hours or 72 hours. The **T-bana** has three main lines (red, green and blue). Trains are fast and frequent, 05.00–01.00. Metro stations display a blue 'T' on a white circle. The decor on some lines is among the most imaginative in Europe: walls are moulded to look like caves, are painted in strident colours or hold original murals.

🛏 Staying in Stockholm is certainly not cheap, especially in the city centre. A good-value option right on Gamla Stan and thus not far from Centralstation is the atmospheric **Sven Vintappare**, Sven Vintappares gränd 3, ☎ 08 22 41 40 (www.hotelsvenvintappare. se), housed in a renovated, early 17th-century building. About a 15 min walk north of Centralstation, the **Hotel Tegnérlunden**, Tegnérlunden 8, ☎ 08 545 455 50 (www.birgerjarl. se/hotel-tegnerlunden), is a comfortable and functional option. The well located **Story Hotel Riddargatan**, Riddargatan 6, ☎ 08 545 039 40 (www.storyhotels.com), north-east of Gamla Stan offers smart design and arty details – perfect for guests who like their hotel room to be modern and trendy.

CONNECTIONS FROM STOCKHOLM

From Stockholm, you can fast-track north on an overnight train to **Swedish Lapland**, which continues over the frontier to Narvik in northern Norway (ERT 767). This journey is described in **Route 32** in this book. Another useful direct link to Norway, tamer in character but still very pretty, is the line to Oslo (ERT 750), which part of **Route 51**. Train services up Sweden's Bothnian coast are much improved. It's now much quicker to head north to Sundsvall and Umeå (ERT 760). Ten years ago, the journey from Stockholm to **Umeå** took over ten hours. Today it takes less than five hours.

Stockholm offers a good range of **shipping connections**. There are overnight services leaving late afternoon every day for both Helsinki (ERT 2465) and Tallinn (ERT 2475) run by Tallink Silja, all making a brief call in the Åland Islands along the way. St Peter Line sails at least weekly to **St Petersburg**, serving **Helsinki** along the way (ERT 2482). This is an excellent way to make a visa-free visit to Russia.

Another useful overnight route from Stockholm is the link to Riga in Latvia (ERT 2464). Sailings for Riga leave on alternate days. Finally, you have a choice of both daytime and overnight crossings from Stockholm to the Finnish port of Turku (ERT 2480), all stopping in the **Åland Islands** en route.

Route 29: Maritime cities

CITIES: ★★ CULTURE: ★ HISTORY: ★ SCENERY: ★★
COUNTRIES COVERED: NETHERLANDS (NE), GERMANY (DE), DENMARK (DK) NORWAY (NO)
JOURNEY TIME: 24 HRS | DISTANCE: 1,611 KM | MAP: www.ebrweb.eu/MAP29

One of the longer journeys in this volume, this is a route full of **rich maritime character**. Most of the cities along the way have developed through sea trade or through their links with the sea – in the case of Aalborg, for example, the city's prosperity depended for a period on the herring industry. You'll still find the humble herring aplenty on this journey; it is a staple on the breakfast table in this part of Europe.

We'll visit ports shaped by the **Hanseatic League** and feel the sea breeze on this journey through four countries. It's a route which wouldn't be complete without a short sea journey, so we include a hop by boat across the Skagerrak; that's the name of the strait separating northern Denmark from Norway. A highpoint of the journey (literally) is the **Rendsburger Hochbrücke** (Rendsburg High Bridge) on the railway between Hamburg and the Danish border. This extraordinary piece of railway architecture, which bridges the **Kiel Canal**, embodies a compromise between shipping interests and those of the railway magnates.

There was a time when Dutch clippers regularly sailed directly from Amsterdam to Oslo Fjord. No longer. True diehards wanting to travel by sea from the Low Countries to Norway can opt for a weekly cargo vessel which leaves Ghent (in Belgium) every Friday evening and reaches Brevik on Eidangerfjord on Sunday morning. The vessel is operated by DFDS Tor Line, and still makes space for a few passengers.

RECOMMENDED ITINERARY

If you are in a rush, you could complete the journey described here in just two days, leaving Amsterdam at breakfast time and reaching Oslo in time for dinner the following day. You'll need to make an overnight stop along the way, and that break of journey might best be made in the appealing Danish city of Aarhus. But – and you know what comes next – this route deserves more time. It could easily be spread out over a week or more, with stops of a day or two in Bremen, Hamburg, Aarhus, Aalborg and Kristiansand.

From Amsterdam to Bremen

Who said that the Netherlands are pancake flat? Watch closely as the Intercity train rattles east from Amsterdam towards the German border and you'll see that beyond Amersfoort the landscape rises and falls in gentle ripples. The train crosses the **River IJssel** just before Deventer and an hour later reaches the border at Bad Bentheim. The prefix 'Bad' in the town's name reveals its status as a spa town. If brine and sulphur are your thing, **Bad Bentheim** might be worth a stop.

Route details

Amsterdam Centraal to Osnabrück Hbf		ERT 22
Frequency	Journey time	Notes
Every 2 hrs	3 hrs 5 mins	

Osnabrück Hbf to Bremen Hbf *		
Frequency	Journey time	Notes
Hourly	2 hrs 15 mins	

Bremen Hbf to Hamburg Hbf		ERT 800/801
Frequency	Journey time	Notes
2–3 per hr	55–90 mins	

Hamburg Hbf to Flensburg		ERT 823
Frequency	Journey time	Notes
Hourly	2 hrs	

Flensburg to Aarhus		ERT 710/700
Frequency	Journey time	Notes
Every 2 hrs	3 hrs 35 mins	F

Aarhus to Aalborg		ERT 701
Frequency	Journey time	Notes
2 per hr	80–90 mins	

Aalborg to Hirtshals		ERT 701/728
Frequency	Journey time	Notes
Hourly	75 mins	X

Hirtshals to Kristiansand		ERT 2350
Frequency	Journey time	Notes
2 per day	3 hrs 15 mins	S

Kristiansand to Oslo S		ERT 775
Frequency	Journey time	Notes
4–8 per day	4 hrs 30 mins – 5 hrs	

Notes

* – Our recommended route is not shown in the ERT. Times for the main line are in ERT 800 & 815.
F – Many journeys require a change of train at Fredericia.
S – The journey time and frequency refers to the year-round Color Line shipping service. The summer-season Fjord Line catamaran operates 2–3 times per day and takes 2 hrs 15 mins.
X – A change of train at Hjørring is always required.

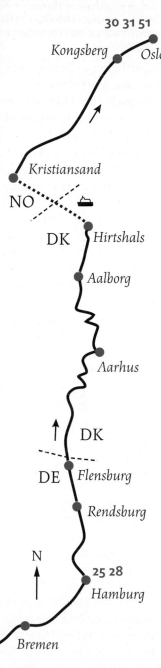

TICKET TIPS: AMSTERDAM TO OSLO

This is a journey which can be done **remarkably cheaply**. Tickets from Amsterdam to Bremen, using the route described below, can be purchased at www.bahn.de for as little as €19.90 one way. The onward fare from Bremen to Hirtshals is just €39.90 if booked well in advance. That latter ticket allows a break of journey of one or two nights in Hamburg, so long as that is specified when booking the ticket. Once into Denmark, you can stop off as often as you wish, without needing to specify anything in advance, provided only that you complete your journey from Bremen to Hirtshals within 4 days. Ferry tickets from Hirtshals to Kristiansand start at €21. A *Minipris* fare on the train from Kristiansand to Oslo is just 249 Norwegian kroner (about €24.90). Tot up those four fares, and you'll see that you can travel from Amsterdam to Oslo for just about €106. Not bad for a journey which might easily be spread over a fortnight or more.

Running east from the border, the landscape becomes more three-dimensional. The forested hills to the right are the Teutoburger Wald. Next stop is the genial university city of **Osnabrück**, where the scale of the late 19th-century station building is a reminder that this is one of the major railway junctions in western Germany. You'll arrive on the lower level of this two-tier station, and you'll need to change trains here for an onward service to Bremen.

CONNECTIONS FROM OSNABRÜCK

Osnabrück used to be a **paradise for insomniac train spotters**. They would gather at all hours of the night to watch the long-distance expresses leaving for Copenhagen, Paris, Warsaw and Moscow. The departure boards have been tamed, but there's still a good range of connections from Osnabrück. There is a fast train every two hours to Hannover and Berlin (ERT 810). There are hourly fast trains to Cologne (ERT 800), most of which continue up the Rhine Valley to Koblenz, Mainz and beyond. **Private rail operator** NordWestBahn has an hourly slow train on a scenic line which runs all the way to Wilhelmshaven on the North Sea coast (ERT 814).

The easy choice from Osnabrück to Bremen is the hourly Intercity train which usually leaves from Platform 3 (on the upper-level platforms). But there is a much more interesting alternative, namely the **slow trains** operated by NordWestBahn (which depart from Platform 13 or 14, both located on the lower level; see www.nordwestbahn.de). Rail passes are accepted on this privately operated rail service. Timings are not shown in the ERT, but the timetable is simple. Trains depart Osnabrück hourly (usually at 26 minutes past each hour) and take 2 hrs 12 mins to reach Bremen Hauptbahnhof.

The NordWestBahn trains take in some of the **finest countryside** in Lower Saxony. Don't expect anything dramatic, but sit back and relax as the slow train to Bremen wends its way through landscapes of delicate beauty. The train wanders past arable land, forests and heath with lots of pretty farms. All too soon, you'll be running into Bremen where the train crosses the **River Weser** on its approach to the city's Hauptbahnhof.

Bremen is one of Germany's foremost maritime cities. It boasts a rich Hanseatic history and the city's links with the Americas brought great wealth to Bremen. Coffee and cotton were key to the transatlantic trade and many of the **merchants' houses** from the 16th century survive. Together with Bremerhaven, its outer harbour some way downstream towards the mouth of the Weser River, Bremen is one of the Länder (states) that make up Germany, continuing a proud tradition of self-government that dates back to the Middle Ages.

The **Old Town**, on the north-east bank of the river, is the main area of historical interest. The wide **Marktplatz** is dominated by the **Rathaus** (town hall), a 15th-century structure overlaid with a Renaissance facade. It's worth joining a tour to see the splendid interior. Don't miss the quirky statue of the **Four Musicians of Bremen** on Marktplatz, which recalls a Grimm Brothers' tale.

The 11th-century twin-spired **St Petri Dom**, Sandstr. 10–12, is sombrely beautiful. In the Bleikeller (basement, open Apr–Oct) are some ghoulish corpses, preserved from decay by the lack of air. To the south side of Marktplatz is Böttcherstrasse with its eclectic mix of Jugendstil (Germany's version of art nouveau) and art deco. Today it houses cafés and artisans' workshops, making it a fine part of town to wander and feel the relaxed pulse of Bremen life. Bremen has accommodation options to fit all wallets.

CONNECTIONS FROM BREMEN

Trains leave Bremen twice-hourly for **Hannover** (ERT 813). If you've tired of northern flatlands and crave some hills, you can escape from Bremen with a direct ICE to Munich (ERT 900). This route runs every two hours and the journey to the Bavarian capital takes under six hours.

There are hourly regional trains to Cuxhaven (ERT 815), serving Bremerhaven along the way. Cuxhaven itself is uninspiring, but it's the departure point for boats to **Helgoland** (ERT 2242), an extraordinary hulk of red rock in the North Sea which was variously Danish and British, before becoming German territory in 1890 – as part of a deal whereby the German Kaiser relinquished claims on Zanzibar.

Two great trade cities

It'll be no surprise to learn that Bremen and Hamburg are great rivals. Both were key members of the **Hanseatic League**, and both have privileged status as city states in modern Germany. Berlin is the only other city in the country which is also a Bundesland in its own right.

The train journey from Bremen to Hamburg takes less than a hour, speeding you from the **Weser to the Elbe** – the latter is the river which defines so much of Hamburg life. Along the way, the train to Hamburg passes through Scheeßel, a small town which springs to life in June each year when it hosts the *Hurricane* music festival. Some say it's Germany's version of Glastonbury.

Hamburg (suggested stopover)

Hamburg's long maritime history and its status as Germany's media capital means that it has grown to become one of the country's richest, most **cosmopolitan and sophisticated** cities. It has everything you would expect of a port city – with a multicultural population, red-light district centred on the infamous Reeperbahn and a waterfront of hulking warehouses and storerooms – but the city is much more than that. For a start, Hamburg is surprisingly green, with leafy streets and pleasant parks, and its location on the water provides plenty of opportunities to take boat trips on the Alster Lakes. Take a tour of the city's huge **harbour** with boats leaving from St Pauli Landungsbrücken. It's worth bearing in mind that Hamburg has several ferry routes which are fully integrated into the city's **public transport network** (and are thus very cheap). A good choice is the hour-long ride on ferry route 62 from the Landungsbrücken (Pier 3) to Finkenwerder and back.

As Germany's second largest city after Berlin, Hamburg also offers up a wealth of cultural attractions, including a vibrant and hedonistic nightlife, a fine collection of museums and plenty of events and festivals taking place throughout the year. The city on the **River Elbe** has a fascinating combination of historic and modern architecture, including many former warehouses now renovated to house some of the city's top cultural and tourist attractions. Among them is the **largest model railway** in the world (www. miniatur-wunderland.com; Kehrwieder 2–4 in Hamburg's Speicherstadt).

ARRIVAL, INFORMATION, ACCOMMODATION

≋ The **Hauptbahnhof** (Hbf) handles most long-distance trains. It's huge, central and on the U-Bahn and S-Bahn. ⓘ The Hauptbahnhof houses the main tourist office (www. hamburg-tourism.de) and a wonderfully cosmopolitan selection of eateries. **Altona** station, in the west of the city, is the terminal for most trains serving Schleswig-Holstein.

✈ Hamburg International Airport (www.hamburg-airport.de), is 8 km from the town centre. Rapid-transit S-Bahn line S1 runs every 10 mins for most of the day and takes 25 mins to and from Hamburg Hbf. 🚌 HVV (Hamburg Transit Authority) run efficient buses, U-Bahn (underground) and S-Bahn, as well as a night bus service to most city districts (www.hvv.de).

🛏 Hamburg has a wealth of mid-range accommodation options, including the boutique hotel **Henri**, Bugenhagenstr. 21, ☎ 040 554 357 0 (www.henri-hotel.com), a 10-min walk from the Hauptbahnhof. The friendly hotel **St Annen**, Annenstr. 5, ☎ 040 317 71 30 (www.hotelstannen.de), is centrally located between the St Pauli district and the Schanzenviertel (yet far enough from the Reeperbahn). For a bit of luxury take a look at **Hotel Side**, Drehbahn 49, ☎ 040 309 990 (www.side-hamburg.de).

CONNECTIONS FROM HAMBURG

You can connect in Hamburg onto **Route 25** to Berlin, Prague and Budapest and onto **Route 28** to Copenhagen and Stockholm. There are departures at least hourly from Hamburg Hauptbahnhof for Berlin (ERT 840), Frankfurt-am-Main (ERT 900) and Munich (ERT 900). There are several trains each day to Copenhagen (ERT 50 & 720) although from late 2019, the train is no longer shipped on a ferry across the 18-km wide strait separating Germany and Denmark. Other international departures from Hamburg include direct trains to the

Swiss cities of Basel, Chur, Interlaken and Zurich (all ERT 73) and a choice of daytime or overnight services to Vienna (ERT 53 and 64). Closer to hand, there are good links to Germany's **Baltic and North Sea coasts** with direct trains to the resorts of Westerland (ERT 821) on the North Sea island of Sylt and to Binz (ERT 830) on the Baltic island of Rügen. The notion of trains running to offshore islands may test your credulity, but Sylt and Rügen are both linked respectively by bridges to the German mainland.

German-Danish borderlands

The entire 600-km long peninsula which juts north from Hamburg is the historic territory of **Jutland**. In mediaeval times Scandinavian influence extended much further south than today.

Yet as the train heads north from Hamburg towards the Danish border, there is a strong sense of entering a different cultural realm. Germany's northernmost state of **Schleswig-Holstein** really has a sense of being a place apart – all the more so if you take time to explore away from the main rail routes. Saxons, Danes and Angles tussled for centuries over the southern part of Jutland. The current line of the border between Germany and Denmark is less than one hundred years old and even today there are Danish-speaking villages on the German side of the border and a vocal German-speaking minority in Danish Jutland.

Our journey north from Hamburg runs the **entire length of Jutland** to the northernmost city on the peninsula at Aalborg. It then crosses a bridge onto North Jutland, an island created in the 19th century when the northernmost part of the peninsula was severed from the rest in a great storm. This is a part of Europe where the sea has long had the upper hand.

The Rendsburg Bridge

The bridge over the **Kiel Canal** at **Rendsburg** is one of Europe's most striking civil engineering achievements. Like all great railway bridges, it is best seen from the ground rather than from the train itself. But the experience of travelling by train over the bridge is nonetheless extraordinary. The canal links the North Sea with the Baltic and is thus a major artery for trade. It dates back to the late 19th century; in the early days low-level swing bridges carried the railway over the canal, but that meant that ships had to be stopped to allow the passage of trains. In 1913 a much higher bridge was opened that is still in use today. But so flat is the terrain in these parts that an elaborate girder structure is necessary for the railway to gain sufficient height to reach the deck of the bridge. The **descent on the north side** is especially impressive as the train circles in a grand spiral over the rooftops of Rendsburg.

Take time to look at the bridge from the canal bank too. It is a 15-minute walk from Rendsburg station down to the canal. A **gondola** hangs from the railway bridge; it shuttles to and fro, ferrying cars and pedestrians across the canal without any charge. Sadly, it is out of service following an accident in early 2016, when a mariner rammed the gondola. The historic gondola is currently rebuilt – it is planned to go into service again in 2020. Until then, a boat service shuttles pedestrians and bikes over the canal. There's a pleasant restaurant and café right under the northern end of the bridge by the canal bank (www.brueckenterrassen.de).

Rendsburg's fine suite of technological assets is not limited to the bridge and unusual ferry. There is a **long pedestrian tunnel** under the Kiel Canal, accessed by escalators which, when the tunnel was first opened in 1965, claimed records as the longest in Europe.

Into Denmark

About 40 minutes north of Rendsburg, the train reaches **Flensburg**, the last stop on German territory before the Danish border. A couple of trains each day run right through from Hamburg to Denmark (see ERT 823). If you are arriving in Flensburg on one of the regional German trains shown in ERT 823 or 824, you need to allow about 20 minutes to transfer to the onward train to Denmark (ERT 710).

Beyond Flensburg, the railway tracks north through dull country, only returning to the coast at **Kolding**, a small port in a lovely setting at the head of Kolding Fjord. If you have an hour to stop, it's a fine first encounter with Denmark, with a very appealing Old Town just five minutes west of the railway station. Just a dozen minutes beyond Kolding the train pulls into **Fredericia**, another town deserving of a short stop. Kolding and Fredericia are as different as chalk and cheese. While Kolding is a mediaeval jumble (and all the better for that), Fredericia is a well-ordered garrison town dating back to the 17th century. Make time to wander along the grassy ramparts which surround the town; it is a fine walk on a clear, still day.

CONNECTIONS FROM KOLDING AND FREDERICIA

From Kolding there are regular trains west to **Esbjerg** (ERT 705) with connections at Bramming for **Ribe** (ERT 709), which we rate as the loveliest small town anywhere in Jutland. There are direct trains to Odense and Copenhagen from both Kolding (ERT 710) and Fredericia (ERT 700). Fredericia is also the departure point for trains to Struer and Thisted (ERT 715) in west Jutland.

From Fredericia, it is just an hour on to **Aarhus**. Although there are occasional tantalising glimpses of coastal inlets and harbours, the railway is inland for most of the journey. All trains serve a medley of small towns along the way, among them the neat little harbour town of **Vejle** which once mainstreamed on bargain-basement sausages and nowadays exports improbably large quantities of chewing gum.

Aarhus (suggested stopover)

Denmark's second largest city changed the spelling of its name in 2011 from Århus to Aarhus. You'll arrive at the main station, nowadays part of a modern shopping centre. It gives an oddly consumerist first impression of the city, but there's more to the city than shops. Aarhus was **European Capital of Culture** in 2017 and you'll find culture aplenty in this fascinating port city. Most sights are within easy walking distance.

Old Aarhus holds the monopoly on nightspots as well as a few museums, including the **Kvindemuseet** (Women's Museum, www.kvindemuseet.dk; closed Mon), Domkirkepladsen 5, which examines the role of women through history. Aarhus' renown art museum, **ARoS**, is just a 10-min walk from the railway station at Aros Allé 2 (www.aros.dk; closed Mon). Its collections showcase both national and international artists.

The city's major attraction is Den Gamle By, an open-air ethnographic museum featuring close to a hundred traditional half-timbered Danish homes. Located about 10 km south of the city, the superb **Moesgård Museum** (closed Mon) is home to the 2,000-year-old preserved Grauballe man, discovered in a nearby peat bog in 1952 (www.moesgaardmuseum.dk); take 🚌 18 from Aarhus Park Allé. In the centre, you can use any of the city bikes from 56 special stands around town, free of charge. Insert a 20 DKK coin into the bike's slot and get it back when returning the bike to a stand.

ARRIVAL, INFORMATION, ACCOMMODATION

🚆 The station is just south of the centre, buried away in the Bruuns Galleri shopping complex. 🚉 Tourist office: Dokk 1, Hack Kampmanns Plads 2 (www.visitaarhus.com).

🛏 Just round the corner of the station is the functional but friendly **Hotel Ritz Aarhus City**, Banegårdspladsen 12, ☎ 86 13 44 44 (www.millinghotels.dk). A good mid range option a short walk from the station in a quiet location is **Hotel Oasia**, Kriegersvej 27, ☎ 87 32 37 15 (www.hoteloasia.dk). If you want to splash out, try the stylish design hotel **Villa Provence**, Fredens Torv 12, ☎ 86 18 2400 (www.villaprovence.dk), in the heart of the city.

All trains reverse direction in Aarhus and then **head decisively inland** for the run north to Aalborg. It's best to opt for an Intercity train for this leg of the journey, rather than the faster Lyn services. The slower services are better for appreciating the quiet beauty of the heath and forest landscapes of Jutland, of which you'll have hitherto seen very little on the long journey north from Hamburg.

There's an **especially pretty stretch** as the railway winds through woodland just beyond Hadsten. That's just a foretaste of what is to come, namely a glorious few minutes as the train cuts through **Rold Skov**, one of the last remaining areas of true wilderness in Jutland. It's all too brief, and if you want to explore this area a little more, alight at Skørping from where there's ample scope for walks and cycle rides through the region. **Skørping** is not included in ERT 701, but all Intercity trains stop there.

Aalborg (suggested stopover)

Herring brought prosperity to this north Jutland town in the 17th century, and the legacy of that boom is the **handsome Old Quarter** with finely preserved merchants' houses, such as the spectacularly ornate Jens Bangs Stenhus. **Kunsten** (Museum of Modern Art, www.kunsten.dk; closed Mon) is home to one of the nation's foremost collections of 20th-century art and has a sculpture garden too. The museum is located at Kong Christians Allé 50. After the sun goes down, **Jomfru Ane Gade** is the street to hit for restaurants, music and bars (be sure to sample the local spirit, Akvavit). The Aalborg Carnival takes place in late May every year, and throughout the summer open-air rock concerts are held in Mølle Park and in Skovdalen.

ARRIVAL, INFORMATION, ACCOMMODATION
➤ A short walk south down Boulevarden from the town centre. 🛈 Tourist office: Kjellerups Torv 5 (www.visitaalborg.com).
🛏 Just opened in 2019 and a good value option is the **Zleep Hotel Aalborg**, Jyllandsgade 6, ☎ 70 23 56 35 (www.zleep.com). Or try the **Comwell Hvide Hus Aalborg**, Vesterbro 2, ☎ 98 13 84 00 (www.comwell.com). More upmarket is the **Scandic Aalborg City**, Europa Plads 1, ☎ 70 12 51 51 (www.scandichotels.com). All three hotels are on the functional side, but are located conveniently close to both the railway station and the city centre.

North Jutland

Leaving Aalborg, the railway crosses a low girder bridge which spans **Limfjord**, here at its narrowest point, to reach the island of North Jutland. Most trains on this route running north from Aalborg – called the **Vendsyssel Railway** – are bound for Frederikshavn, whence there are useful ferry links to Göteborg (ERT 2320) and Oslo (ERT 2368), both operated by Stena Line. Our journey requires alighting before Frederikshavn at the small town of **Hjørring**, and then taking the local train down to the coast at Hirtshals. If time permits, you might enjoy a walk through Hjørring, the centre of which exemplifies the laidback charm of the communities in North Jutland.

The port of **Hirtshals** boldly styles itself as "a geographical turntable close to some of Europe's best fishing." It's certainly true that Hirtshals has been shaped far more by its maritime connections than by its hinterland. It has long been, and still is, an important port. A small museum in Hirtshals (at Sophus Thomsens gade 6) nicely documents the manner in which fishing has long been an economic mainstay.

Our journey continues with a short **sea crossing to Kristiansand** in Norway. Fjord Line (www.fjordline.com) runs fast catamarans from mid-April to early September, while Color Line (www.colorline.com) has year-round services using very comfortable ships. We find the latter, although slower, preferable to a bumpy catamaran. For other connections from Hirtshals, see the **Sidetracks** feature on p276.

Arriving in Norway

A little over three hours relaxing on the ferry from Hirtshals will leave you well prepared to enjoy **Kristiansand**, a working port and resort town at the southernmost tip of Norway. In summer, the town's pleasant beaches are busy. Much of the town was laid out in the 17th century by Christian IV, after whom it is named. His plan included the **Christiansholm Festning**, built to guard the eastern approach to the harbour; the circular fortress is the major sight with views to match. Forming the north-eastern part of the Old Quarter, **Posebyen** has many carefully preserved little wooden houses. The fish market on the quay, called Fiskebrygga, is a good place to pick up some smoked salmon or prawns for a picnic lunch. If you are minded to stay overnight, the Comfort Hotel Kristiansand, Skippergata 7–9, ☎ 38 07 94 00 (www.nordicchoicehotels.com), is a good-value option just 200 m from the station.

If you are expecting a pleasant run along the Norwegian coast from Kristiansand to Oslo, you'll be disappointed. Construction of the 266-kilometre stretch of the **Sørlandet Line** from Kristiansand to Kongsberg was only started after the First World War; the route was not completed until 1938. The Norwegian authorities were worried about the risk of invading forces taking control of a coastal railway, so the line was routed well inland. Although this did not help communication to the small towns around the coast, it does mean that the line cuts through lovely **wilderness areas**.

The nicest town on the journey to Oslo is **Kongsberg**, a township which grew following the discovery (in the early 17th century) of silver deposits of unique purity in the nearby mountains. Mining remained the town's raison d'être for three centuries: most of the mines closed early in the 19th century, but the last one survived until 1957. Just out of town are the disused **silver mines at Saggrenda** (8 km west, 🚌 Vy express line Vy1 from Kongsberg centre; tours available) take you by train into the mountain to 560 m below sea level. In the town centre a striking legacy of the silver-boom heyday is the Kongsberg Kirke, a sumptuous triumph of baroque church architecture on a grand scale. Close to Nybrufoss waterfall is the **Norsk Bergverksmuseum** (Norwegian Mining Museum), housed in an old smelting works. Den Kongelige Mynts Museum (Mint Museum) is an offshoot of the industry: coin production moved to Kongsberg in 1686 (the National Mint is still here). From Kongsberg, it is little more than an hour to **Oslo** (see p281) where the train terminates at the Sentralstasjon, usually abbreviated as Oslo S.

CONNECTIONS FROM OSLO

You can continue from Oslo on **Route 31** to the Arctic or on **Route 30** through Sweden to Copenhagen. Or follow **Route 51** (in reverse) to Riga and Tallinn.

Sidetracks: Slow boat to Iceland

As we travel north through Jutland on **Route 29**, we have a sense of going to the very end of the world. With changes of train in Aarhus, Aalborg and Hjørring, we are at last on the branch line which leads to the port of **Hirtshals**. There the *Norröna* is at the quayside, preparing to depart for Iceland. This is just one of many inviting shipping links from Hirtshals. Another is the ferry to Kristiansand (ERT 2350), a short sea crossing which forms part of **Route 29**. There is also a very useful Fjord Line sailing each evening from Hirtshal to Stavanger and Bergen (ERT 2237). It connects nicely in **Bergen** with the northbound *Hurtigruten* ship to northern Norway (ERT 2240). Adventurers can thus travel by boat all the way from Hirtshals to Kirkenes on the Barents Sea coast near the Russian border, with just one easy change of boat in Bergen. That entire journey requires seven nights afloat.

But let's take a closer look at the *Norröna*. The ship's funnel is embellished with a merlin (*smyril* in Faroese). The small bird of prey is common in the North Atlantic region served by **Smyril Line**. The company is based in the Faroes, a scatter of mountainous islands midway between Iceland and the Shetlands. The company's sole ship is called *Norröna*, a name that underlines the vessel's role as an ambassador for the north.

Within an hour or two of boarding the *Norröna*, everyone has found or created a tolerable lair. For some it is the secure luxury of a cabin. For others it is a couchette deep in the bowels of the ship or an improvised arrangement of rucksacks and deck chairs on an upper deck. **Wind and waves** are a good prelude to geysers, glaciers and icy tundra wilderness.

Denmark recedes to nothingness, and the *Norröna* is soon alone among the waves. Distant views of oil rigs, supper in the *Simmer Dim* – a chic onboard restaurant that takes its name from the short summer nights in Shetland where dusk never quite gives way to true darkness. A day out from Hirtshals and a **Shetland outpost** hoves into view on the port side. **Fair Isle** hovers in the mist, ethereal and other-worldly. Many hours later a first glimpse of the east coast of the island of Sandoy signals that the Faroese capital of **Tórshavn** is only an hour or two away. Travellers bound for Iceland can go ashore in the Faroese capital, wander the streets of Tórshavn and explore Europe's smallest cathedral.

Soon the *Norröna* is on her way again, threading a course through the beautiful Faroe Islands. The great ridge that defines **Kalsoy** is on the starboard side, its steep slopes entirely uninhabited. Another night on board, then all thoughts are on Iceland. Eventually the land of elves reveals herself, and soon the *Norröna* is sliding up one of the eastern fjords in absolute silence. On either side of the great loch there are the ruins of long deserted farmsteads while naked crags dominate the skyline. This is for the *Norröna* the very end of her journey to Iceland. She docks in **Seyðisfjörður**.

See ERT 2285 for details of Smyril Line sailings to the Faroes and Iceland. Note that in winter storms the leg between Tórshavn and Seyðisfjörður is liable to delay or cancellation.

Route 30: Sampling Scandinavia

CITIES: ★★ CULTURE: ★ HISTORY: ★ SCENERY: ★★★
COUNTRIES COVERED: DENMARK (DK) SWEDEN (SE), NORWAY (NO)
JOURNEY TIME: 14 HRS 30 MINS | DISTANCE: 1,192 KM | MAP: WWW.EBRWEB.EU/MAP30

This long route from Copenhagen to Bergen via Oslo is a journey of extremely varied character. It starts with a tame prelude but develops into a great symphony of lakes, snowfields and mountains. Along the way, you have in Oslo a very pleasant (but expensive) capital city.

SUGGESTED ITINERARY

The **two principal cities** on this journey are Göteborg and Oslo, both certainly deserving of an overnight stop. If you follow this route from end to end, you will in any case need to change trains in those two cities. We really judge this entire journey to be one well worth taking. If time is tight, you could at a pinch consider taking the **DFDS boat to Oslo**. It leaves Copenhagen every afternoon, sailing overnight up the Kattegat to reach Oslo just before ten the next morning (ERT 2360), in sufficient time to catch the midday train to Bergen. If you hate fine scenery, but love **night trains**, you can sleep your way from Oslo to Bergen on a comfortable overnight service which departs every evening except Saturdays.

The first part of the journey from **Copenhagen** is sometimes complicated by the ID checks recently introduced for travellers using the **Øresund link** from the Danish capital to the Swedish city of Malmö. This stretch of the railway is also followed by **Route 28** in this book, so take a look at pp263–64 to see what we say there about the journey.

Malmö is Sweden's fast-growing third city and a lively place, with plenty of good bars, clubs and coffee houses, and an excellent festival in August. Capital of the Skåne province, the city was part of Denmark for much of the Middle Ages and came under Swedish sovereignty in 1658: even today the Skåne accent has something of a Danish tinge. Recently, many young Danes have moved here to avoid strict Danish marriage laws.

Enclosed by a canal that loops round through a park and doubles as the castle moat, the city's well-groomed historic centre dates back to Danish times and features a pair of **fine cobbled squares**. Leaving the station southwards along Hamngatan, you soon reach the large central square, **Stortorget**, presided over by the statue of Carl Gustav, who won Skåne back from Denmark. The square is flanked on the east by the 1546 Rådhuset (town hall), just by Södergatan, the main pedestrianised street. Behind stands **St Petri Kyrka** (St Peter's Church) – Sweden's second-largest church – its whitewashed Gothic interior complementing its baroque altar and mediaeval frescos.

CONNECTIONS FROM MALMÖ

Malmö has a feast of rail connections. The most important is the trunk route which runs north-east to Stockholm (ERT 730). It is followed by **Route 28**. Malmö also has an overnight

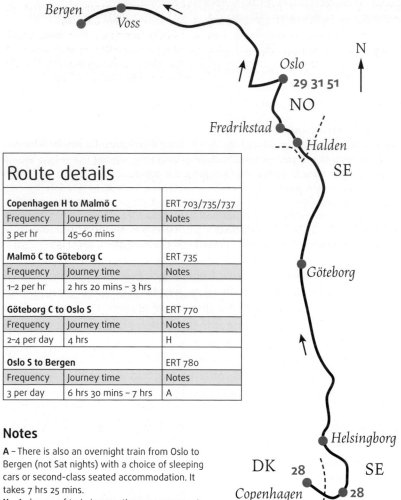

Route details

Copenhagen H to Malmö C		ERT 703/735/737
Frequency	Journey time	Notes
3 per hr	45–60 mins	

Malmö C to Göteborg C		ERT 735
Frequency	Journey time	Notes
1–2 per hr	2 hrs 20 mins – 3 hrs	

Göteborg C to Oslo S		ERT 770
Frequency	Journey time	Notes
2–4 per day	4 hrs	H

Oslo S to Bergen		ERT 780
Frequency	Journey time	Notes
3 per day	6 hrs 30 mins – 7 hrs	A

Notes

A – There is also an overnight train from Oslo to
Bergen (not Sat nights) with a choice of sleeping
cars or second-class seated accommodation. It
takes 7 hrs 25 mins.

H – A change of train is sometimes necessary at
Halden.

The **numbers in red** adjacent to some cities on
our route maps refer to other routes in this book
which also include that particular city.

The ERT numbers in our route details refer to the
table numbers in the *European Rail Timetable*
(ERT) where you will find train schedules for that
particular section of the route. Do note that ERT
table numbers may change occasionally with
successive editions of the timetable.

train (leaving every evening during the summer season and Mon–Fri & Sun otherwise) to Stockholm (ERT 730). There is a **seasonal overnight train** from Malmö to Berlin. It is called the *Berlin Night Express* and even in mid-summer runs only three times per week. It conveys only couchettes (so no sleeping cars and no seated accommodation), which are shipped on a ferry over the Baltic to the port of Sassnitz in northern Germany.

Closer to hand, there are good **regional rail links** fanning out from Malmö, with hourly direct trains to the windy east coast towns of Karlskrona (ERT 745) and Kalmar (ERT 746). Local trains run every half hour from Malmö down to the attractive port of Ystad (ERT 731), whence there are regular boats to the Danish island of **Bornholm** (ERT 2494).

Lund and Helsingborg

From Malmö, it is just ten minutes on frequent trains to the handsome ancient university town of **Lund**, which is one of the most rewarding spots to visit in southern Sweden. A religious centre in the 12th century, much of mediaeval Lund is still visible.

From Lund, the railway returns to the coast and runs north to **Helsingborg**. Don't be put off by Helsingborg's subterranean train station as the city is well worth a stop. During much of the Middle Ages, Helsingborg was Danish and functioned a+s an important garrison town; the massive fortified keep, the Kärnan, still dominates the place. The bustling port is a pleasant enough base, with an **Old Quarter** to explore. If you decide to get off the train here, you should pay a visit to the rewarding 15th-century Church of St Maria and the entertainingly eclectic **city museum** in Dunkers Kulturhus on Kungsgatan 11 (www.dunkerskulturhus.se; closed Mon outside Jul–Aug).

CONNECTIONS FROM HELSINGBORG

There is a **car ferry** which breezes across the narrowest point of the strait to Helsingør in Denmark (ERT 2345), from where there are frequent trains to Copenhagen (ERT 703). Helsingør is a great place to visit in its own right, so this boat trip makes a fine afternoon out from Helsingborg.

Running north from Helsingborg, the railway leaves the historic territory of Scania and crosses into Halland where all but the fastest trains stop at **Varberg**, which made its mark in the late 19th century as a bathing station, attracting many prominent artists.

Göteborg (suggested stopover)

The huge cranes and shipyards that greet visitors arriving at **Scandinavia's biggest port** mask the fact that this is one of Sweden's most attractive old cities, one that grew rapidly when Dutch merchants settled here in the early 17th century. Boat tours take in the best of the waterside views from the old canals, while elsewhere there are atmospheric squares and numerous leafy parks that have earned Göteborg (also called Gothenburg in English) the nickname 'Garden City'. To get your bearings, go up **Skanskaskrapan** (Skanska Skyscraper) – a striking red-and-white skyscraper, 86 m high, which has a lookout (Göteborgsutkiken; opening hours vary) and is locally referred to as 'lipstick'. It has a small café (June–Aug only) near the top, giving superb views over the harbour. It's situated in **Lilla Bommen**, itself a charming area, with shops and craft workshops. Dominating the whole scene here, however, is the spectacular waterside opera house – its postmodern design is a fine instance of form matching function.

Kungsportsavenyen, usually known simply as 'Avenyn' (The Avenue), is the hub of the city, a 50-m-wide boulevard lined with lime trees, shops and eateries, further enlivened by buskers and ad hoc street stalls. It leads up to Götaplatsen, the city's cultural centre, fronted by Carl Milles' fountain of Poseidon. Just off Avenyn is **Trädgårdsföreningen** (turn right into Nya Allén towards Slussgatan), a fragrant park full of flora and birdsong, speckled with works of art and other attractions.

The city's oldest secular building (1654) is **Kronhuset** (Crown Arsenal; closed Sun), close to Gustaf Adolfs Torg at Postgatan 6–8. Around it is Kronhusbodarna, a courtyard bounded by handicraft boutiques in 18th-century artisans' dwellings. Other good places for browsing are the Antikhallarna antique market in Västra Hamngatan, and Haga Nygata, a renovated historic area of cobbled streets, lined with craft, second-hand, antique and design shops, as well as cafés and restaurants. Opposite, across the water, the **Feskekörka** resembles a 19th-century church, but is actually a thriving fish market (open Mon–Sat). It's a fine place to sample local seafood, either in the restaurants or from the stalls.

Some city museums close on Mondays but open daily in summer. Don't miss Göteborg's **maritime museum** at Packhuskajen next to the opera house (open daily), the **Konstmuseet** (Art Museum; www. goteborgskonstmuseum.se; closed Mon), Götaplatsen, and the Universeum (the National Science Centre), Södra vägen 50.

ARRIVAL, INFORMATION, ACCOMMODATION

≥ Centralstation, a short walk north-east of the centre. Most buses stop at Nils Ericsonsplatsen, next to the station. ✈ Landvetter Airport is 20 km south-east of Göteborg (www.swedavia.se/landvetter); buses every 12–30 mins, depending on time of day, to Centralstation, taking 20 mins. ⛴ Stena Line (www.stenaline.se), to/from Germany (Kiel), sail from Elof Lindälvs Gata, on the western edge of Göteborg; Stena ships to/from Denmark (Frederikshavn) sail from Emigrantvägen, at the western end of the centre.

🛈 Tourist office: Kungsportsplatsen 2 (www.goteborg.com). The centre's attractions are quite close together, but there's also an excellent tram network (buy tickets in advance at Västtrafik sales outlets or via the ToGo App). 🛏 Not far from Göteborg's cathedral is the comfortable **Hotel Vanilla**, Kyrkogatan 38, ☎ 31 71 16 220 (www.hotellvanilla.com). Just 300 m from Centralstation, **Scandic No. 25**, Burggrevegatan 25, ☎ 31 75 15 500 (www.scandichotels.com), is a good budget option. Located in the station building, the **First G**, Nils Ericsonsplatsen 4, ☎ 31 63 72 00 (www.firsthotels.com), is a quiet mid-range place.

LAKE VÄNERN RAIL TOUR

Göteborg is also the jumping-off point for a wonderful rural rail adventure around **Lake Vänern**, Europe's largest lake outside the Russian Federation. Only two Karelian lakes, Lagoda and Onega, are larger. Travel out from Göteborg to **Karlstad** along the south side of the lake via **Mariestad** (ERT 736 then 750; see also p438 in this book), returning on the direct train from Karlstad back to Göteborg (ERT 751) which skirts the north side of Lake Vänern. We made this **circular journey** as a day trip a year or two ago; it was just at the time that winter thawed into slushy spring, but the sun shone and we recall it as a journey through landscapes of considerable beauty.

✖ The seafood is excellent, most restaurants clustering along the waterfront. For other types of cuisine, try around Avenyn or in Linnéstaden. The Nordstan complex offers a lot of eateries, including a good supermarket, Hemköp. Try the indoor Stora Saluhallen market, Kungstorget, for a tempting range of goodies.

CONNECTIONS FROM GÖTEBORG

From Göteborg, multiple rail operators compete on the busy route to Stockholm (ERT 740). Given Göteborg's port status, it's no surprise to find plenty of **boat connections**. The most interesting are the DFDS Tor Line sailings (not shown in ERT) to Ghent in Belgium and Brevik in Norway. A small number of passengers are accepted on both routes. There are daily departures each week to Ghent, but services to Brevik only leave Göteborg on Thursdays. Stena Line offer a regular overnight sailing to Kiel (ERT 2335). Several ferries a day cross from Göteborg to Frederikshavn on the coast of Danish Jutland (a useful link to connect into **Route 29** in this volume; see ERT 2320).

At Göteborg, the railway to Oslo tracks inland, passing close to the southwest corner of Lake Vänern before heading north through bleak terrain to the Norwegian border. The first community of any size beyond the border is **Halden**, an old border post on the attractive Iddefjord, overlooked by the star-shaped **Fredriksten Fortress**, a huge 17th-century castle east of the town. Other highlights include the Fredrikshalds Teater, with its fully restored baroque stage, and **Rød Herregård**, a furnished 18th-century manor house with an enviable collection of art.

Cutting down to the east shore of Oslo Fjord, the train stops at **Fredrikstad**, a town still protected by fortified walls. Fredrikstad guarded the southern approaches to Oslo and its Old Town has survived as one of the best-preserved fortress towns in Scandinavia. It's conducive to wandering, particularly around the walls and along the cobbled alleys of **Gamlebyen** (the Old Town) over on the east bank. Fort Kongsten is a pleasant 15- to 20-min stroll.

OSLO (suggested stopover)

Hemmed in by water, forests and rolling hillsides, Oslo is a pleasant and laid-back modern city. It is not a big place − nor is it as architecturally captivating as the other Scandinavian capitals – but it is definitely worth a stop before venturing out to experience Norway's great outdoors. The city has a number of outstanding art museums – with attractions such as Edvard Munch's *The Scream* – as well as great harbour views from the **Akershus Fortress** and a **lively nightlife** scene in the central districts of Grünerløkka and Grønland. The fortress is still used for state occasions and contains the Resistance Museum, which gives a startlingly forthright account of the German occupation of Norway. In **Vikingskipshuset** (Viking Ship Museum) on the Bygdøy peninsula, the well preserved Gokstad, Tune and Oseberg Viking ships, all dating from 800–900, are on display.

Oslo is connected by **ferry** to Germany and Denmark, and you can catch trains via Sweden to Denmark and on to the rest of Europe. Oslo is also the starting point for some spectacular train journeys to the Norwegian fjords, mountains and on to the Arctic, which are also featured as routes in this book.

ARRIVAL, INFORMATION, ACCOMMODATION

⇝ The main rail station is the central Oslo Sentralstasjon (known as Oslo S). All long-distance trains stop here, as well as some local services. This modern construction feels more like an airport than a train station, and it is crammed with facilities of every kind. The T-bane (metro) is to the right as you leave the station.

⛴ There are usually daily sailings to Germany (Kiel) by Color Line (www.colorline.no). DFDS Seaways sail daily to Copenhagen (www.dfdsseaways.no) and Stena Line sail to Frederikshavn (www.stenaline.no). 🚌 Long-distance buses use Bussterminal, which is easily reached from Oslo S by an enclosed walkway. ✈ Gardermoen (50 km north; https://avinor.no/flyplass/oslo). Airport express trains take 20 mins to Oslo (www.flytoget.no); buses take 45 mins but are cheaper. From the airport there are also direct trains to Lillehammer and Trondheim (ERT 785). Ryanair and Wizz Air flights land at Oslo Torp (www.torp.no), which has bus connections with Ryanair flights (booking not necessary); buses to Oslo Torp leave Oslo's main bus terminal around 3 hrs before flight departure (www.torpekspressen.no) and take 1 hr 40 mins for the journey.

Oslo's centre is relatively small and outlying attractions are easily reachable on the excellent public transport system (www.ruter.no). Single tickets are valid for 1 hr (plus 30 mins per extra zone). Oslo's metro lines converge at Stortinget and Jernbanetorget (T-bane: Oslo S). Most trams converge at Oslo S and most city buses around the corner on Schweigaardsgate (on Vaterland, by Oslo S). Pre-purchase your ticket at kiosks or Ruter service points or use the RuterBillett App. ⛴ Ferries to Bygdøy, Hovedøya, Langøyene and other islands in the Oslo Fjord leave from the Rådhusbrygge. 🛈 Visitor centre: right next to Oslo S in Østbanehallen (www.visitoslo.com).

🛏 Recently refurbished and very centrally located is the boutique hotel **Christiania Teater,** Stortingsgata 16, ☎ 21 04 38 00 (www.christianiateater.com), housed in a former theatre. For a good budget option try the **Citybox Oslo**, Prinsensgate 6, ☎ 21 42 04 80 (www.citybox.no), just a 10 min walk from Oslo S station. Head for the **Saga Hotel Oslo**, Eilert Sundts gate 39, ☎ 22 55 44 90 (www.sagahoteloslo.com) if you are looking for a smaller hotel. It's a friendly and stylish place in a quiet area not far from the Royal Palace.

CONNECTIONS FROM OSLO

You may wish to return to Copenhagen by ship (ERT 2360) and there is also a useful daily ship to Kiel in northern Germany (ERT 2372). You can connect in Oslo onto three other routes in this book. Follow **Route 31** north through Norway to beyond the Arctic Circle, take **Route 29** in reverse back to Kristiansand for boat connections to Danish Jutland or take **Route 51** in reverse to Riga & Tallinn which starts with the train from Oslo to Stockholm (ERT 750).

Fjells and fjords

The railway from Oslo to Bergen is one of Europe's most remarkable mainline journeys. It climbs to an altitude of over 1,200 metres, crossing a starkly beautiful mountain plateau called **Hardangervidda**. All trains on the route stop at Finse, which at 1,222 metres claims the record as the highest railway station in Scandinavia. Many communities along this route rely entirely on the railway for their links with the outside world – and the **Bergensbanen** (as the line from Oslo to Bergen is called) has served them well, providing reliable service in all but the very worst of winter weather. Snow fences and avalanche protection along long stretches of the railway give a hint of the hazards which are part of everyday life in this region.

For a rail route which has been so showered with superlatives, you might expect the Bergensbanen to be sheer beauty from end to end. In fact, the entire first half is unexceptional. Only beyond the ski resort of **Geilo** (three-and-a-half hours out of Oslo) does the scenery really pick up, switching from prosaic to stunning in a space of just a few kilometres. Now's the moment to forsake your phone or laptop and just focus on the landscape slipping by beyond the carriage window.

At the lonely railway junction at **Myrdal**, a branch railway (called the **Flåmsbana**) cuts north, dropping down steeply to Flåm (ERT 781). The descent offers superb views of towering cliffs, chasms and cascades. There are 16 tunnels on the route, including one where the line makes a 360° turn completely within the mountain. Most trains stop briefly at the spectacular **Kjosfossen waterfall**. This 20-kilometre railway is unashamedly touristy, but still fun. It is often marketed as 'Norway in a nutshell' and is a popular day trip for cruise ship passengers from Bergen. From **Flåm** there is a direct bus to Bergen (ERT 782).

Staying with the main Bergensbanen line at Myrdal, the only place of any size before Bergen is the lakeside resort of **Voss**, where water sports and skiing are the principal seasonal distractions. From there, it is a pleasant run down through gentler terrain to Bergen.

Bergen

Norway's appealing second city is the gateway to some of the country's most magnificent fjords. Perched on a peninsula and **surrounded by mountains**, Bergen has meandering cobbled streets lined with gabled weatherboard houses and dignified old warehouses.

The city centres on the waterfront **Torget**, a working fish (and various other things) market open Mon–Sun 08.00–23.00 May–Sept (otherwise Mon–Sat 09.00–21.00, Sun 11.00–21.00). At the centre of the Old Quarter, **Bryggen** contains a fine row of mediaeval houses designated a UNESCO World Heritage Site. When the Bryggens Museum was being constructed, the remains of the original city of 1050–1500 were found and incorporated.

Ole Bulls Plass, south-west of Bryggen, is good for bars, as is the area behind Torget. There are more student-frequented bars and cafés up towards the university. Look out for events at **USF Kulturhuset** (www.usf. no), on an old wharf to the south. You can get almost everywhere on foot in Bergen, but take the **Fløibanen** (funicular) from the centre up Mt Fløyen (320 m), for a panoramic view. At the top there's scope for pleasant picnics and walks in the woods.

Arrival, information, accommodation

≋ Strømgaten, a 10-min walk east of the centre; walk straight ahead down Marken and keep going. ⛴ Most ferries and local boats leave from Strandkaiterminalen and Skoltegrunnskaien. Hurtigruten leaves from Nøstegate.

🛈 Tourist office: Strandkaien 3 (www.visitbergen.com). ✉ Advance booking is recommended since Bergen is often chock-full of tourists and conference-goers. Located on top of a hill in the vicinity of the university is the friendly and quiet family-run **Hotel Park**, Harald Hårfagresgate 35, ☎ 55 54 44 00 (www.hotelpark.no). If you are looking for a good budget option, try the clean and friendly **Marken Gjestehus Hostel**, Kong Oscars gate 45/Tverrgaten, ☎ 55 31 44 04 (www.marken-gjestehus.com) well located between the station and Torget. Just opposite Bryggen and overlooking the harbour and bay, the **Clarion Hotel Admiral**, C. Sundts gate 9, ☎ 55 23 64 00 (www.nordicchoicehotels.com), is a good choice.

Connections from Bergen

The **quaysides at Bergen** still appeal to lovers of ferries, even though some of the more interesting sailings have slipped from the schedules. No longer does the P&O ship *St Clair* weigh anchor at two on a Sunday morning (as she did in summer 1996) for the voyage to Aberdeen via the Shetland Islands. Sadly, Bergen nowadays has no direct ferry links to Britain. The Bergen to Newcastle route was axed after 140 years in service.

But the town still has a feast of Scandinavian connections. **Fjord Line** depart every lunchtime for Stavanger and Hirtshals (ERT 2237), where you can join **Route 29** and follow it in reverse to Hamburg and Amsterdam. The cruise south from Bergen to Stavanger is a fine trip for a summer afternoon; it takes about six hours. From Stavanger you can return east to Oslo by either daytime or overnight train (ERT 775).

Fjord Line also now offer a **daily sailing** (not shown in ERT) from Bergen to Langesund; it takes 24 hours, but is another good option for travellers returning to Oslo who don't want to retrace their outward train journey. There are bus and train connections from Langesund via Porsgrunn to Oslo.

Bergen's most distingushed shipping link is of course the **Hurtigruten** service which departs every evening and runs north all the way up the Norwegian coast to far beyond the Arctic Circle. After six nights on board and over 30 stops along the way, the voyage ends at the **Barents Sea** port of Kirkenes. This is one of Europe's finest coastal journeys. ERT 2240 shows the timetable for this year-round route.

Route 31: North to the Lofoten Islands

CITIES: ★ CULTURE: ★ HISTORY: ★ SCENERY: ★★★
COUNTRIES COVERED: NORWAY (NO)
JOURNEY TIME: 20 HRS | DISTANCE: 1,450 KM | MAP: WWW.EBRWEB.EU/MAP31

If you follow just one Norwegian route in this book, make it this journey from Oslo to beyond the **Arctic Circle**. This long ride north nicely reveals the variety and scale of Norwegian landscapes. The appeal of this journey beyond the Arctic Circle is undoubtedly the scenery and the real sense of remoteness that you encounter along the way. Townies may get jittery with such **vast expanses of wilderness** and begin to yearn for concrete (of which there is plenty in some of the townships of northern Norway). In mid-summer you will experience perpetual daylight, but this is a journey for winter too, when the subdued, sometimes even ethereal, character of very short days bring a special quality to the landscape.

The scene outside the carriage window evolves from gentle and bucolic pasturelands near Oslo to breathtakingly **dramatic fells and lakes** in the northernmost reaches. This is territory inhabited by reindeer and by the **Sámi** (the more common term Lapp is considered a shade derogatory) – the Nordic region's indigenous inhabitants. The journey ends with a short trip on a boat from Bodø to Svolvær on the **Lofoten Islands**.

SUGGESTED ITINERARY

The journey from Oslo to Bodø is best spread over two full days, with an intermediate stop of one night (or more) in **Trondheim**. There are direct overnight trains from Oslo to Trondheim (departures every evening except Saturdays) and also from Trondheim to Bodø (every night). Yet the scenery on this route is too good to be missed in sleep.

But here's an idea for a **midsummer journey**. You can leave Oslo on the early afternoon train which arrives in Trondheim about three hours before the overnight train to Bodø leaves. So you'll have ample time for dinner. After a meal, join the night train north – but don't even think of sleeping for in mid-summer dusk will morph into dawn and you can savour the real beauty of the northern night. You'll arrive in Bodø in good time to have a look around and then join the afternoon boat to the Lofoten islands.

Lake Mjøsa and beyond

For a relatively small capital, Oslo's main station has a remarkably large number of railway tracks. Arrive in good time to find the right platform. You may want to consider taking regional train services for the first part of the journey north, only changing onto the main-line service to Trondheim at Hamar or Lillehammer (ERT 785).

Shortly after the airport (served by all trains), the slower services pause at **Eidsvoll**, a small town know to every Norwegian as the place where Norway's first constitution was hammered out, way back in 1814. It's a

Route details

Oslo to Trondheim		ERT 785
Frequency	Journey time	Notes
2–3 per day	6 hrs 30 mins – 6 hrs 50 mins	A, C
Trondheim to Bodø		ERT 787
Frequency	Journey time	Notes
1 per day	9 hrs 55 mins	B, D
Bodø to Svolvær		ERT 2239/2240
Frequency	Journey time	Notes
2 per day	3 hrs 30 mins – 6 hrs	

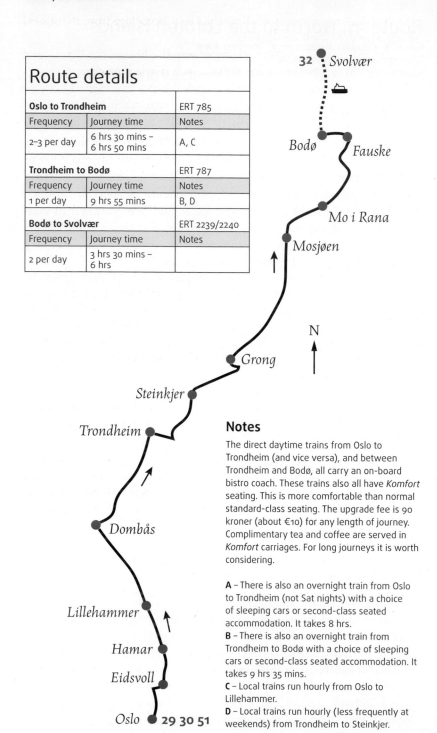

Notes

The direct daytime trains from Oslo to Trondheim (and vice versa), and between Trondheim and Bodø, all carry an on-board bistro coach. These trains also all have *Komfort* seating. This is more comfortable than normal standard-class seating. The upgrade fee is 90 kroner (about €10) for any length of journey. Complimentary tea and coffee are served in *Komfort* carriages. For long journeys it is worth considering.

A – There is also an overnight train from Oslo to Trondheim (not Sat nights) with a choice of sleeping cars or second-class seated accommodation. It takes 8 hrs.
B – There is also an overnight train from Trondheim to Bodø with a choice of sleeping cars or second-class seated accommodation. It takes 9 hrs 35 mins.
C – Local trains run hourly from Oslo to Lillehammer.
D – Local trains run hourly (less frequently at weekends) from Trondheim to Steinkjer.

pleasant small town; the centre is reached by a footbridge from the station which leads over the River Vorma.

Running north from Eidsvoll, the railway also bridges the Vorma, and then hugs the east bank of **Lake Mjøsa**, which is by a long chalk Norway's largest lake. For a closer look at this beautiful region, we suggest taking a three-hour boat trip from Eidsvoll to Hamar. A remarkable heritage paddle steamer (the *DS Skibladner* built in 1856) plies the route in mid-summer. It has an excellent, though pricey, restaurant (see www.skibladner.no).

At the northern tip of Lake Mjøsa lies **Lillehammer** which is both a major skiing centre and an appealing lakeside town, typified by winsome wooden houses that cling to the hillside. It hosted the 1994 Winter Olympics and many of the facilities can now be visited – and in some cases used.

Into the hills

Running north from Lillehammer, the railway parallels the E6, the main highway which extends from southern Sweden to Kirkenes in the far north-east corner of Norway, a distance of 3140 km. Distances can be deceptive in Scandinavia. Whether you travel by rail or road, be prepared for very long hops between settlements. About 30 minutes north of Lillehammer, you'll catch a glimpse of a typical Norwegian **stave church** on the hillside on the far side of the lake.

All trains pause at **Dombås**, junction for the 114-km long branch line to Åndalsnes, a small town at the head of a coastal fjord. The ride to Åndalsnes on the **Rauma Railway** (ERT 785) is an epic one, plunging through tunnels, across bridges, past cascading waterfalls and the highest vertical canyon in Europe. Beyond Dombås, the main line to Trondheim changes in character, swapping the soft, green landscapes of the Gudbrand Valley for much harsher terrain as the railway cuts through **Dovrefjell-Sunndalsfjella National Park**. Home to eagles, reindeer and musk ox, this wild area is a foretaste of what's to come as we head north towards the Arctic Circle.

Just after the railway crosses the boundary of the Trøndelag region, the train reaches **Kongsvoll station**, a handsome essay in wood with neat blue shutters and delicate red moldings. If your trip has been too full of city stays, this is your chance to redress the balance. There is an attractive hotel

TWO LINES TO TRONDHEIM

The town of **Hamar** on the east shore of Lake Mjøsa is the starting point for an alternative and rather slower route north to Trondheim via **Røros** (ERT 784). There's a bigger dose of stark wilderness on the Røros route but, if you are following this journey all the way to Bodø, you'll get wilderness aplenty on the run north from Trondheim. However, if your travels merely take you to Trondheim and then back to Oslo, we strongly recommend that you travel out on the main line via **Lillehammer** and then back via Røros.

just a five-minute walk from the station. Cross the River Svåne on the bridge then turn right onto the main road (our old friend the E6 again). Kongsvold Fjeldstue has a homely, welcoming feel and there's a good restaurant (open March to mid-November, ☎ 90 08 48 02, www.kongsvold.no).

Trondheim (suggested stopover)

From Kongsvoll, it's just two hours more to the city which prides itself on being Norway's first capital. Trondheim was founded in 997 by **King Olav Tryggvason**, whose statue adorns the market square, and the city still has strong royal connections. Monarchs are crowned in the cathedral and Trondheim has been the seat of the monarchy since the 12th century. This major university town, with more than 20,000 students, boasts some of the best nightlife in Norway – not quite what you expect at over 63° north. The narrow streets of the compact centre make for a pleasant strolling ground.

Nidaros Domkirke (cathedral), Bispegata, is cavernously Gothic in design, and well worth seeing for its decorative stonework and elegant stained-glass windows. Northwards from the cathedral lies **Torvet** (main square), while further on at the water's edge is Ravnkloa, home to a fish market. From here, hourly boats run, usually mid-May to mid-Sept, to the island of Munkholmen, a monastery-cum-fortress-cum-prison; it's now a popular place for swimming.

Trondhjems Kunstforening (Trondheim Art Gallery, www.tkf.no), Bispegata 9a, exhibits some of Norway's greatest art, including a few works by Munch, while the **Nordenfjeldske Kunstindustrimuseum** (National Museum of Decorative Art; www.nkim.no), Munkegata 3–7, has a collection of contemporary arts and crafts (closed Mon from late Aug–late May). Other sights include the **Gamle Bybro** (Old Town Bridge), with views of the wharf and its 18th-century warehouse buildings.

ARRIVAL, INFORMATION, ACCOMMODATION
≋ The train and bus station is just a short walk north of the city centre. 🚹 Tourist office: Nordre gate 11 (www.trondheim.no); entrance from Torvet (market square).
🛏 Centrally located next to the River Nid and not far from the station is the **Scandic Bakklandet**, Nedre Bakklandet 60, ☎ 72 90 20 00 (www.scandichotels.com). If you don't mind the slight cool of a business hotel, then the **Clarion Hotel Trondheim**, Brattørkaia 1, ☎ 73 92 55 00 (www.nordicchoicehotels.com) is a good option just north of the station. Or try the welcoming **Clarion Collection Grand Olav**, Kjøpmannsgata 48, ☎ 73 80 80 80 (www.nordicchoicehotels.no) well located close to the Olavshallen concert hall.

CONNECTIONS FROM TRONDHEIM
If the lure of the North means less to you, there is a useful escape route running east from Trondheim into Sweden. Twice daily diesel railcars climb up into the hills on the **Meråker Railway**. They cross the Swedish frontier (ERT 761) and connect in Storlien with Norrtåg electric trains (also ERT 761) to Östersund and Sundsvall. At **Sundsvall**, you can join a fast train to Stockholm (ERT 760). The entire cross-country journey from Trondheim to

BOATS FROM TRONDHEIM

If you have had enough of trains by the time you reach Trondheim, bear in mind that the city is a major port-of-call on the **Norwegian coastal shipping service** (ERT 2240). A southbound Hurtigruten boat sails at 9.45 each morning, taking 28 hours to reach Bergen. The northbound vessel leaves at noon, bound for Bodø (24 hrs), Svolvær (33 hours) and a medley of other northern ports on its way around the top of Norway to the Russian border. Closer to hand, smart cyan-and-white twin-hulled **Kystekspressen catamarans** speed twice or thrice daily down the coast from Trondheim to Kristiansund, a west-coast port city which is not to be confused with Kristiansand on the south coast. This latter route is not shown in ERT. The catamaran journey from Trondheim to Kristiansund takes three-and-a-half hours.

Stockholm via this route takes 10 hours. At Östersund, you can connect in summer onto the seasonal *Inlandsbanan* trains which run north to **Gällivare** in Swedish Lapland (ERT 766).

The Arctic Circle and beyond

One of the most remarkable rail trips we have made in Europe was a June overnight journey from Trondheim to Bodø. Yes, the sun did set, but only just, and the light had a peculiar quality all of its own. Since then, we have made this same journey by day in deep mid-winter and it was every bit as engaging as on the first occasion. This line is called **Nordlandsbanen**.

Here is an instance where the journey is the thing. There is no particular reason to break the ten-hour journey from Trondheim to Bodø. The towns along the way are unprepossessing and it comes as a surprise that they are quite industrial. The journey starts by skirting Trondheim Fjord, taking two hours to reach **Steinkjer**, a small town which lies at the very head of the longest arm of the fjord. Beyond Steinkjer, the railway takes to the hills, traversing increasingly desolate country.

The train may stop here and there at country halts, and you may notice the great variety of station buildings: a neat pastel-green building in Grong, bold fiery red at Harran and a startling shade of flamingo pink at **Mosjøen**, where the stark rurality of this part of Norway is suddenly interrupted by the sight of an aluminium smelter which relies on copious supplies of water from the adjacent fjord.

An hour beyond Mosjøen is **Mo i Rana** (usually dubbed Mo for short) which has a steel works. In terms of scenery, we rate the stretch beyond Mo as the finest of the journey. Here the railway skirts the **Saltfjellet–Svartisen National Park**, along the way going to within five kilometres of the Swedish border and shortly thereafter crossing the **Arctic Circle**. For more on this magic line of latitude which seems to exert so strong a pull on travellers' imaginations, see p295 in **Route 32** in this book.

We now run back down towards the coast. The train drops down through Saltdal to reach the shores of Skjerstad Fjord, on the north shore of which lies the small town of **Fauske**. You can take the express bus to Narvik (ERT 787) from here, to connect with the Ofoten Railway to northern Sweden (ERT 765). For passengers bound for Bodø, this is a last glimpse of the E6 highway, before the train turns west and hugs the fjord on the way to its final destination.

After such a remarkable journey, a trip so rich in landscape and scenery, the railway station at **Bodø** comes as something of a let-down. It is an uninspiring piece of 1960s architecture.

Bodø (suggested stopover)

Bodø is a busy little port and departure point for ferries to the Lofoten Islands. The Domkirke (cathedral) is notable for its unusual detached spire, while the **Norsk Luftfartsmuseum** (Norwegian Aviation Museum), Olav V gata, has a fine collection of **civil and military aircraft** from various eras (www.luftfartsmuseum.no).

ARRIVAL, INFORMATION, ACCOMMODATION

⇟ Centrally located, 300 m east of the tourist office. ⓘ Tourist office: Tollbugata 13, by the waterfront (www.visitbodo.com). ⛴ Hurtigruten cruises and ferries to the islands leave from quays on the road near the station. 🚌 Long-distance bus station is on Sjøgata close to the tourist information centre.

⇟ The friendly family-run **Bodø Hotell**, Prof Skyttensgt. 5, ☎ 75 54 77 00 (www.bodohotell.no), is a good-value central option. Or try the **Opsahl Gjestegaard** B&B, Prinsens gate 131, ☎ 75 52 07 04. The **Scandic Havet**, Tollbugata 5, ☎ 75 50 38 00 (www.scandichotels.com), has great views over the harbour.

By boat to Lofoten

From Bodø, it is 130 kilometres across the open waters of the Vestfjord to the port of **Svolvær** on the Lofoten Islands. This great open bight is part of the Norwegian Sea and in a south-westerly gale the water can be very choppy. If you are a nervous sailor or like your creature comforts, the best bet is the northbound **Hurtigruten ship**, which leaves Bodø at three every afternoon (ERT 2240). It makes one stop on the way to Svolvær; that's at Stamsund. On a summer evening there is no nicer way to arrive in Svolvær.

There is a another departure from Bodø, usually at 18.00, but later on Sundays (ERT 2239). This service is operated by a **fast ferry**, taking three to four hours for the crossing. The boat will normally make between three and seven intermediate stops (not shown in ERT), so you'll catch a glimpse of some remote coastal communities along the way.

Arrival in **Svolvær** (see also p296) marks the end of an extraordinary journey. You'll surely want to spend a day or two exploring the Lofoten Islands, but rather than retracing your outward route from Oslo, why not think of following **Route 32** in reverse all the way to Stockholm?

Route 32: Night train to Narvik

Cities: ★ Culture: ★ History: ★ Scenery: ★★★
Countries covered: Sweden (SE), Norway (NO)
Journey time: 21 hrs | Distance: 1,735 km | Map: www.ebrweb.eu/map32

No ifs, no buts! This route showcases one of Europe's great train journeys. There is a once-daily direct train from Stockholm which runs north to **Swedish Lapland**, crossing the **Arctic Circle** and continuing over the Norwegian border to Narvik. That's a journey of about 1,500 kilometres; it takes over 20 hours. The service is run by SJ, who now market the train, even within Sweden, as the very English-sounding *Arctic Circle Train* (replacing the previous name *Norrlandståget*).

While we normally encourage travellers to linger over journeys and stop off along the way, the very character of this route suggests a different strategy. The overnight journey to Swedish Lapland is worth doing in one long hop. Most places of real interest lie beyond **Kiruna** – in the final three hours of the journey.

The departure time from Stockholm varies by season and day of week; it's usually between four and six in the afternoon (ERT 767). You can board the train about four to five hours later in **Sundsvall**. Some travellers prefer taking an early afternoon fast train to Sundsvall, then enjoy a wander around this handsome city before joining the night train later in the evening.

The nature of this route demands a different approach in our description. So, just for once, we use a more narrative style to present the journey from Stockholm to Narvik.

From Stockholm to Boden

The adventure of the *Arctic Circle Train* is to a good degree all in the imagination, for in truth the first dozen hours of the journey are mainly a matter of watching the birch trees get smaller and the snow get deeper. Or eating and sleeping. But that's not to belittle the experience of travelling so far north, a journey which starts in the rather prosaic surroundings of **Stockholm Central** station. While city shoppers make haste for home, another kind of passenger makes for the *Arctic Circle Train*. There are people wearing fur hats and sheepskin coats, soldiers on their way to one of the bases in the far north and families with skis. Some travellers opt for the comfort of the sleeping cars; those of a hardier disposition may book an ordinary seat. Few of those climbing aboard the night train to Narvik don't share in the communal **sense of adventure**.

The train rattles north through Stockholm's suburbs, pausing at Arlanda Airport and the university town of **Uppsala** to pick up passengers. Then suburbs give way to country, with forests, pulp mills and a tantalising

JUST FOR FOODIES

The **bistro service** on the *Arctic Circle Train* is perfectly adequate, but don't expect haute cuisine. You'll find tempting shrimp sandwiches (pricey, and bizarrely deploying words from three different languages to describe them on the menu: *Räksmörgås à la Arctic Circle Train*). Try the tasty elk burgers with tatties and lingonberry sauce, though if you spot elk through the train window you may think differently about this menu option.

If you are tempted by our idea of joining the overnight train in **Sundsvall** (see the introduction to this route on p291), make time for dinner at *Saffran*, a wonderful restaurant just a five-minute walk from the station at Nybrogatan 25 (☎ 060 17 11 07; www.saffran.nu; closed Sun). With a fine **choice of tapas** for all tastes, a relaxing meal at *Saffran* could be a great prelude to the overnight train journey.

glimpse of the sea just beyond Skutskär. This is the route north followed by **Lenin** on the evening of Good Friday 1917 on his long journey back from exile in Switzerland to a Russia on the brink of revolution. Lenin was engrossed in the Russian newspapers he had picked up in Stockholm; most travellers making the journey today, even those who have travelled north many times before, are **spellbound by the scenery** slipping by beyond the window.

Moving north, the train enters a land which might have been slumbering for years. The train pauses. No one boards or alights, and nothing stirs in the churchyard that lies beside the tracks. Just a distant church, a pale shade of pink that catches the dipping sun, and the gravestones in this village of the dead. "Saliga äro de vilkas väg är ostrafflig," reads the inscription on one of the stones. "Happy are those whose way is perfect." That seems as good a motto as any for this long ride north. There is a jolt as the train starts to move again.

Pines and birch trees with a tumble of lichen-covered granite boulders poke up through the last remnants of winter snow. Every now and again, glimpses of lakes in the evening sunshine. Dusk settles, but seems to linger forever. Night never really comes. Just a dreamy bluish twilight. Time for some hours of sleep with an occasional twitching of the curtain to glimpse the rocks and the trees, and see the birches sink ever deeper into the snow.

Overnight, little changes. More rocks and forests. But the trees have thinned out, the birches have shrunk and the snow has become deeper. The **lakes have frozen**. Dawn comes before anyone awakes. Those who stir in the small hours stare out into the dim of the northern night and might glimpse moose, deer or a fox.

In early morning, the bistro car staff are up and about and there is a smell of fresh coffee. Those who curl under blankets begin to move. After hours of gently sliding through rocks and trees, the train slithers to a halt in **Älvsbyn**, a place where winter snow has been bulldozed into neat piles. Men in fur coats chat on the platform, their breath making a hoary mist that hangs steady in the still air. A white van speeds up to the train and

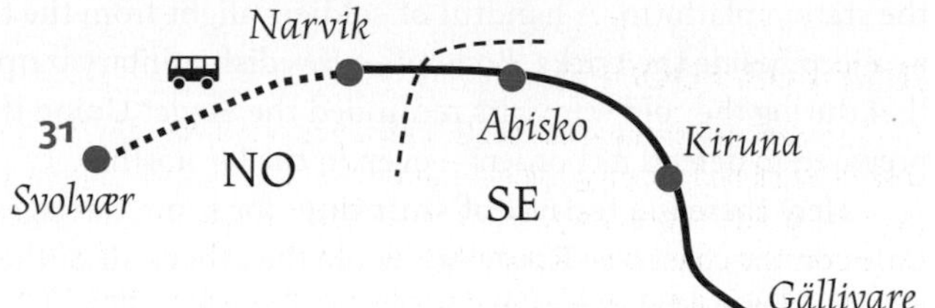

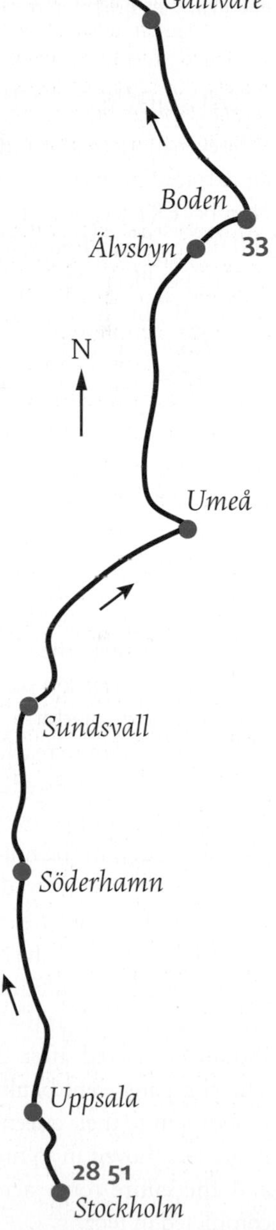

Narvik

Abisko Kiruna

31

NO

Svolvær

SE

Gällivare

Route details

Stockholm Central to Narvik		ERT 767
Frequency	Journey time	Notes
1 per day	18 hrs 50 mins	B
Narvik to Svolvær		ERT 787
Frequency	Journey time	Notes
2–4 per day	3 hrs 50 mins – 4 hrs 40 mins	direct bus

Note

B – There is a second overnight train from Stockholm to northern Sweden. It travels as far north as Boden, then runs down to the coast to terminate at Luleå (ERT 767). It connects very neatly at Boden with a day train to Narvik (ERT 765). So this gives, effectively, a second option from Stockholm to Narvik, albeit with a change of train at Boden.

Boden

Älvsbyn   33

N

Umeå

delivers the morning newspapers. Within a few minutes, folk on board are browsing the *Norrländska Socialdemokraten*, one of those old style dailies which speak to local values in this land of rocks and trees. There is news of the spring thaw, adverts for flights that hop over the Arctic Circle and obituaries for men and women who lived long lives and never left their northern homeland.

Sundsvall

The train jogs on through the forest and soon arrives in **Boden** (where there is a connection onto the next route in this book, which follows Lenin's April 1917 route on over the border into Finland). A longer stop at Boden gives passengers the chance to emerge from their sleeping compartments and taste the bitter cold of a clear northern morning. A man wearing a Stetson stands on

Söderhamn

Uppsala

28 51
Stockholm

the station platform. A handful of soldiers alight from the train. Others sit in a jeep beside the tracks. Boden is a Swedish military outpost. A bastion, that during the cold war years reminded the Soviet Union that Sweden was prepared to defend its borders – even in the far north.

Here there is a **festival of shunting**, for some carriages are bound for Luleå on the coast (see **Route 33**), while the other half of the train will head even further north, across the Arctic Circle to Narvik.

From Boden to the Norwegian coast

Whoever thought of building a railway over the mountains to Norway? It is an extraordinary route. The train takes about seven hours from **Boden to Narvik** (ERT 765) – and with every mile that passes, the scenery gets better and better. Seven hours of some of the most beguilingly beautiful landscape in Europe. Placid to begin with, to be sure, with more rocks and forest, but by now the birch trees have thinned out.

Now there is the anticipation of the **Arctic Circle**. How odd it is that we ascribe such significance to a particular line! Old hands can ignore this arbitrary rite of passage. "But it's not arbitrary at all," protests a bespectacled student in the bistro car. "The Arctic Circle is a loxodrome, the precise line of which is determined by the obliquity of the ecliptic."

Reindeer obviously understand all about loxodromes and the obliquity of the ecliptic. No sooner has the train passed a sign that marks the line of the Arctic Circle (well, the current line, because it is moving north) than there is a first encounter with a small herd of **reindeer** standing around rather aimlessly in the snow.

A little reception party waits at **Gällivare** to greet travellers who alight onto the snowy platform. From Gällivare the railway runs through formidably bleak terrain to reach **Kiruna**. The railway route from Kiruna through the mountains of Swedish Lapland and over the Norwegian border to Narvik was built just over a hundred years ago. Valuable deposits of iron ore were found in the hill country of northern Sweden in the 17th century. Pioneer miners used to drag sledges laden with the valuable ore over the mountains to the ice-free waters of the Norwegian coast.

In the late 1880s the Norwegian railway engineer **Ole Lund** marked out possible routes for a railway, and English investors provided the capital – on the condition that the marine terminus of the railway on the Ofot Fjord should be named after the then English monarch. Hence Victoriahavn. The company went bankrupt and English aspirations to create an Arctic monument to their queen were quickly eclipsed as Swedish and Norwegian financiers moved in to finish the task. **Victoriahavn** was renamed Narvik, and the entire route across the mountains to the Norwegian port was completed in 1902.

The wandering Arctic Circle

As the train crosses the Arctic Circle near the appropriately named hamlet of **Polcirkeln**, the driver usually gives a loud blast on the engine's horn. The Serbian climatologist **Milutin Milanković** calculated how variations in the tilt of the earth's axis – a sort of astronomical wobble – cause the Arctic Circle to move around. Fortunately, the good folk in Polcirkeln recognise that visitors are not satisfied with being told that the Arctic Circle is somewhere nearby, but want to see the exact line. So they have obliged by erecting signs that show where the Arctic Circle was in 2005 and 2015, and also exactly where it will be in 2025. Just now, it seems, this elusive line of latitude is heading north at a rate of about a metre a month.

The railway traverses some of Europe's wildest country. For travellers today, enclosed in the cosseted comfort of the train, it is difficult to imagine the hardships endured by the navvies who for a dozen years laboured to build the railway line. Ole Lund oversaw construction work on the Norwegian section of the line. It would be, he said, a perfect piece of engineering. Lund's daughter, Hanna, meticulously documented many of the ballads sung by the navvies as they carved out the route of the railway. A young Swedish railway worker, **Manne Briandt**, who later became an accomplished musician in his own right, studied the navvies' songs on the Swedish section of the building project. That work by Hanna and Manne became an important milestone in Scandinavian ethnomusicology, and much of the atmosphere of those early days on the **Ofoten railway** is captured in recordings of the *Rallarviser* (Ballads of the Navvies).

There is a lyrical quality to these northern landscapes, ever more so as the railway skirts the shoulders of mountains and creeps up narrow valleys where the hillsides tilt ever sharper. For over 50 kilometres the train runs along the south shore of **Torneträsk**, a magnificent glacial lake which is frozen for more than half the year. Black dots on the ice mark the spots where fishermen have carved holes in the ice and cast their rods in the hope of catching tonight's supper.

In **Abisko**, nowadays a major resort on Torneträsk, most of the passengers alight. As the railway heads up into the hills at the western end of Torneträsk lake, there is a little cemetery beside the tracks with the remains of the navvies who died in the construction of the Ofoten railway. Simple white crosses poke up through the snow. Some died in accidents; others perished from typhus.

At **Riksgränsen**, a station that balances on the very border of Norway and Sweden and the highest point of the route, several skiers alight. The train tunnels through deep snow, and then begins the long and winding descent to the Ofot Fjord. Avalanches and landslides play havoc with the line, and the route has been rebuilt many times. Away to the right there is a glimpse of the old **Norddal bridge**, which once carried the railway but now stands protected as a national monument. Views then of the great fjord in the distance, more tight curves and steep drops until, bang on time, the sleek carriages of the night train from Stockholm to Narvik come gently to a halt at their final destination.

You might take some pleasure in noting that on its **approach to Narvik** the train traverses the northernmost passenger rail route anywhere in Scandinavia, reaching a latitude of 68° 27' N. Serious record chasers must go to Russia, though, where passenger trains edge even closer to the North Pole.

Narvik

This small modern port wins no prizes for its architecture, though the setting is magnificent. Narvik was invaded in 1940 by the Germans in a bid to control shipments of iron ore; within days the British destroyed the German fleet and the Allies recaptured the town. The first section of the **Narvik Krigsmuseum** (Narvik War Museum; www.krigsmuseet.no) commemorates the town's important role in the Second World War as well as the work of the Resistance. Narvik's prosperity owes virtually everything to the Ofoten railway line, which transports iron ore from Sweden, then ships it out to sea from town; the **Ofoten Museum**, Administrasjonsveien 3, provides a thorough overview of the industry and its history.

The overnight train from Stockholm arrives in Narvik in sufficient time to connect with the afternoon bus to the Lofoten Islands. If you are tempted to stay in Narvik, we suggest the Breidablikk Gjestehus, Tore Hunds gate 41, ☎ 76 94 14 18 (www.breidablikk.no).

NARVIK CONNECTIONS

See our **Sidetracks** feature on p298 for details of connections beyond Narvik to North Cape and the Norwegian Barents Sea region, the easternmost part of Norway which shares a common border with the Russian Federation.

There are twice-daily buses from **Narvik to Fauske** and Bodø (ERT 787), which connect at Fauske into southbound trains to Trondheim (see **Route 31**). These buses leave from the bus station near the AMFI shopping centre, as do the Lofotekspressen services to Svolvær.

The bus journey from **Narvik to Svolvær** (Veolia Transport bus route number 23-760, see timings in footnote to ERT 787) is truly remarkable. With sub-sea tunnels and magnificent bridges, this new road connection has transformed access to the once-remote Lofoten region.

Svolvær

Svolvær is the islands' main town (pop. 4,500) and located on **Austvågøy**. The spectacular **Lofoten Islands** are a chain of improbably jagged glacially-sculpted mountains that shelter fishing villages, farms, sheep and thousands of birds. This is Norwegian scenery at its best – mild climate, comparatively uncrowded and a sense that you are with nature at its purest. It is excellent terrain for walking, horse riding and cycling (it is possible to hire bicycles), and there are some great boat trips – including to the beautiful cliffside bird colonies of Værøy and to **Trollfjord**. Røst and Værøy support colonies of puffins; both have accommodation.

Don't miss the picturesque fishing village with the modest name of Å, 5 km south of the island of Moskenes, with cottages, an HI hostel (Å Vandrerhjem, ☎ 76 09 12 11) and a campsite. Fishing, caving and hiking trips can all be arranged here.

ARRIVAL, INFORMATION, ACCOMMODATION

🚢 Hurtigruten boats dock in the centre at Fiskergata; the bus station where the express bus to Lofoten stops is just a short walk away. Boats to Skutvik and Skorva leave from Svolværveien on the E10.

ℹ Tourist office: Torget 18 (www.lofoten.info). Public transport information can be found on the excellent website of Nordland county at www.177nordland.no. ⛴ The small island of Lamholmen which overlooks Svolvær harbour and is connected to the town by road has two good accommodation options. We stayed at the **Scandic Svolvær**, Lamholmen, ☎ 76 06 82 00 (www.scandichotels.com). Or try the **Anker Brygge**, ☎ 76 06 64 80 (www.anker-brygge.no), which has cosy *rorbuer* (each with a kitchen) and other hotel accommodation. Despite being in the harbour, both places are quiet and close to Svolvær's centre. They also allow you to watch the comings and goings of the Hurtigruten boats.

CONNECTIONS FROM SVOLVÆR

You can connect in Svolvær with the previous journey in this book by following **Route 31** backwards to Oslo. Svolvær is of course on the main **Norwegian Coastal Voyage** route. Hurtigruten boats leave daily, sailing south to Trondheim and Bergen and north to Tromsø and Kirkenes (ERT 2240).

AN ALTERNATIVE FINALE: BY BOAT

Route 32 concludes with the long ride on the *Lofotekspressen* bus to Svolvær. But there is an alternative, one we took ourselves and really found a worthwhile detour, as it includes a superb leg on a **Hurtigruten ship**. Instead of taking the bus all the way to Svolvær, alight at Tjeldsund Kro, whence there is a connecting bus to Harstad. You can check bus times on www.177nordland.no. You'll need to overnight in Harstad; we stayed at the **Thon Hotel** by the harbour (Sjøgaten 11, ☎ 77 00 08 00; www.thonhotels.com). Next morning, take the southbound Hurtigruten boat which leaves at 08.30. The ten-hour trip to Svolvær is in our view the finest stretch of the entire Norwegian Coastal Voyage. It takes in the scenic drama of **Raftsundet** and, if you are lucky, a foray into Trollfjorden.

If you just want to get a taste of Hurtigruten, this daytime sailing from Harstad to Svolvær is the perfect opportunity. There are brief stops at three small ports along the way. All in all, you'll see a greater variety of Lofoten communities and landscapes than if you stick to the express bus from Narvik to Svolvær.

SIDETRACKS: NORWAY'S FAR NORTH

Whether you approach **Narvik** on the direct overnight train from Stockholm or on the bus that runs up the Norwegian coast from Bodø and Fauske, you are sure to have that distinct feeling of having reached somewhere very far from civilisation. Narvik is the end of the line, and the spectacular **Ofoten railway** that runs over the mountains from Sweden (part of **Route 32**) is the northernmost rail journey included among the 52 routes in this book.

End of the line does not mean end of the road, and true adventurers can continue beyond Narvik to explore Norway's two northernmost *fylker* (or counties): **Troms** (or Romsa in the Sámi language) and **Finnmark** (Finnmárku in Sámi). If you are tempted to head north from Narvik, don't underestimate the formidable distances involved.

There is a bus connection from **Narvik to Kirkenes**, the last community of any size in Norway before the border with Russia. The journey takes over 30 hours. That long haul includes a ten-hour overnight stop in Alta, a superbly located but utterly dreary town on Altafjord.

An alternative route north is by the regular coastal shipping service called **Hurtigruten**. Ships operate daily in each direction, but do not serve Narvik. You can board the Hurtigruten boats in **Bodø**, whence it is 67 hrs around the northern Norwegian coast to the Barents Sea port of Kirkenes. If you are in Narvik, your best bet is to take the direct bus to **Tromsø** (4 hrs) and join the Hurtigruten boat there. Tromsø to Kirkenes by ship takes 40 hrs. Hurtigruten schedules are shown in ERT 2240.

Travel right to the furthest reaches of eastern Finnmark and you'll realise that remoteness is utterly relative. Experience those long bus and boat journeys to **Kirkenes**, and now Narvik will retrospectively glow in your memory as a bustling hub of northern life. Kirkenes is further east than Istanbul, while Vardø is further east than the Egyptian city of Alexandria.

Like Kirkenes, **Vardø** is also served by the Hurtigruten boats. The town, located on a small offshore island linked by an undersea tunnel to the mainland, is an important fishing port. "Cod is great," reads a sign by the harbour. But Vardø has a dark secret. in the 16th century, 77 women and 14 men were **condemned as witches** and burned. A new shoreline memorial is a moving tribute to these poor souls. Nowadays there's witchcraft of another kind in the array of electronic gadgetry that sits atop a hill on the mainland. Officials say the **radar facility** is there to keep an inventory of satellites in the heavens above. Locals say the dishes point only at Russia.

For **Russia** really is just over the horizon. Kirkenes is a great jumping-off point for journeys into Russia. A 15-min drive from Kirkenes harbour and you can be eye-to-eye with a Russian border guard across a wire-mesh fence. If you have a Russian visa, you can cross the frontier at **Boris Gleb** (Борисоглебский). We used this backdoor route into Russia in 2014 and were impressed by the speed with which one could cross the border – just 10 minutes. Direct buses run daily from **Kirkenes to Murmansk** in Russia (5 hrs, ERT 789) where you can hop on a train for the 24-hour journey to St Petersburg (ERT 1905) and join **Route 50**, following it in reverse direction back to Poland and beyond.

Route 33: Around the Gulf of Bothnia

Cities: ★★ Culture: ★ History: ★★★ Scenery: ★★
Countries covered: Sweden (SE), Finland (FI), Russia (RU)
Journey time: 18 hrs 30 mins | Distance: 1,598 km | Map: www.ebrweb.eu/map33

This journey starts in northern Sweden and tracks around the northern edge of the **Gulf of Bothnia** to reach Finnish territory. On the long journey south, we take in Finland's three largest provincial cities (Tampere, Oulu and Turku). But there's more than city streets on this fine trip: you'll see lakes and forests aplenty and learn a thing or two about Finland's history. For devotees of traditional wooden architecture, we suggest two little detours off the main route: to the church town of Gammelstad and the port of Jakobstad (in a mainly Swedish speaking area of Finland).

In the last edition of *Europe by Rail*, published on the centenary of the autumn **1917 Bolshevik Revolution** in Petrograd (St Petersburg), we extended this route to run beyond Finland into the Russian Federation. Our route broadly follows that taken by **Lenin** for the final part of his journey when he returned to Russia in spring 1917, swapping exile in Switzerland for the fiery politics of Petrograd. Pack a copy of Catherine Merridale's excellent *Lenin on the Train* (published by Penguin in 2017).

Looking at the route map on the next page, Lenin effectively cut the corner from **Tampere** to Lahti, so missing both Turku and Helsinki. Lenin's loss! But he had more on his mind than sightseeing. Don't forget that most nationalities need a visa to take the train to Russia. Lenin turned up to a rapturous reception in **St Petersburg** when he arrived without official permission. The Russian authorities won't be so wild if you arrive without the proper papers. Although a new e-visa scheme for visits to St Petersburg will launch in late 2019, we don't yet know if it will cover arrival by train.

Suggested Itinerary

The **four major Finnish towns** on this route are the obvious stopovers, viz. Oulu, Tampere, Turku and Helsinki. If you are pressed for time, as Lenin was, you could cut out Turku and instead travel directly from Tampere to Helsinki. High-speed Pendolino trains dash between the two cities in 90 mins. Another possibility, which would mean sacrificing **Tampere**, is to travel by overnight train from Kemi or Oulu to Turku (ERT 794 & 795). With a journey time of over 12 hours from Kemi (over 10 from Oulu), it's a long enough leg to justify a night in a sleeping car.

To the Finnish Border

The start of this journey is unusual in that nowadays you simply cannot take a train from the Swedish town of **Boden** to the Finnish border. Forty years ago, twice-daily trains still ran east from Boden to **Haparanda**, from where there was a connecting onward train to Finland. The 200-kilometre train journey from Boden to **Kemi**, the first town of any size in Finland,

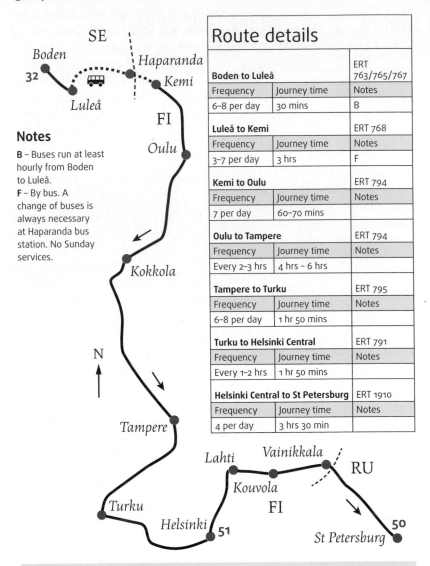

Route details

Boden to Luleå		ERT 763/765/767
Frequency	Journey time	Notes
6–8 per day	30 mins	B

Luleå to Kemi		ERT 768
Frequency	Journey time	Notes
3–7 per day	3 hrs	F

Kemi to Oulu		ERT 794
Frequency	Journey time	Notes
7 per day	60–70 mins	

Oulu to Tampere		ERT 794
Frequency	Journey time	Notes
Every 2–3 hrs	4 hrs – 6 hrs	

Tampere to Turku		ERT 795
Frequency	Journey time	Notes
6–8 per day	1 hr 50 mins	

Turku to Helsinki Central		ERT 791
Frequency	Journey time	Notes
Every 1–2 hrs	1 hr 50 mins	

Helsinki Central to St Petersburg		ERT 1910
Frequency	Journey time	Notes
4 per day	3 hrs 30 min	

Notes

B – Buses run at least hourly from Boden to Luleå.
F – By bus. A change of buses is always necessary at Haparanda bus station. No Sunday services.

GETTING TO BODEN

Boden is probably not a town where anyone lingers, although its setting – perched between two lakes – is very pleasant. The town is an **important railway junction** and has a very useful direct overnight train from Stockholm (ERT 767). That overnight journey is described in **Route 32** in this book, to which Route 33 is thus a natural extension.

With recent improvements to the *Botniabanan* (along Sweden's Gulf of Bothnia coast), it is now also possible to travel by day from **Stockholm to Boden** (a journey of 10–11 hours), with just one change of train in Umeå (ERT 760 & 763). Other direct links to Boden include an overnight train from Göteborg (ERT 767) and a twice-daily link from Narvik (ERT 765). If you need to stay overnight in Boden before joining Route 33, try the Hotell Nivå, ☎ 0921 558 60 (www.hotellniva.se), right by the station.

took five hours. Today, apart from the short hop by train from Boden down to the coast at Luleå, you'll need to travel by bus all the way to Kemi, picking up the train there for the journey south through Finland.

There are plans to reconnect the **passenger rail networks of Sweden and Finland** with a renewed service across the border between Haparanda and Tornio, but that is but a distant dream – and its realisation is not made any easier by the fact that Sweden's railways use the standard gauge common in much of western Europe while Finland's railways were built to the broader Russian gauge.

The journey starts by following the east bank of the **River Lule** from the railway junction at Boden to the port city of Luleå. It's just a half-hour journey with a choice of frequent buses or all-too-infrequent trains. If you do take the train, look out on the left for a glimpse of the church town of **Gammelstad**, a purpose-built township constructed to allow worshippers who made long journeys through difficult terrain to attend Sabbath services to stay overnight by the church. As an example of the *kyrkstad* tradition, once widespread in northern Scandinavia, Gammelstad features on UNESCO's World Heritage List. It is easily reached from Luleå by frequent local buses.

Luleå itself is a workaday port and industrial city, but it's instantly appealing as a welcome haven in a sparsely populated region. Buses from Luleå to Haparanda leave from the bus station (🚌 20 or 100). Sit on the right for good views of the brackish Gulf of Bothnia as the bus skirts a number of bays on the journey east along the E4 highway to Haparanda. Approaching the bus station in **Haparanda** you'll see on the left the enterprise which makes this town tick – the huge branch of IKEA which attracts customers from the entire Bothnia and Barents regions. It's not at all unusual to see vehicles with Murmansk license plates in the car park. Haparanda seems rather proud to host the world's northernmost IKEA.

One senses that Haparanda is no longer the exotic outpost it was when **Thomas Cook**, 150 years ago, commented that those who were really well-travelled would surely have set foot in Timbuktu, Samarkand and Haparanda.

Over the River Torne

From Haparanda, you can gaze over the River Torne to Finland. Changing buses at Haparanda bus station for the onward journey to Kemi, you'll be **over the border** within minutes. Don't forget to advance your watch by one hour. Summer or winter, Finnish time is always an hour ahead of Sweden.

Nowadays one hops with such ease across this border that it's easy to forget that this was once a difficult frontier. The River Torne marked the border of the Russian Empire, of which the **Grand Duchy of Finland** was a part until 1917. When Lenin arrived in Haparanda early on the morning of

15 April 1917 (Easter Sunday in the Orthodox calendar) on his journey from Switzerland back to St Petersburg, he had to hire horse-drawn sledges to take his party across the frozen river. It was at **Tornio** on the east bank that Lenin first touched Russian territory after his long exile.

The chances are that you'll not actually touch Finnish soil until you alight from the bus at Kemi. 🚌 70 runs regularly from the Haparanda bus station to **Kemi** (ERT 768). At Kemi, undistinguished and memorable mainly for the smell of wood pulp, the best thing is to get the first train out of town towards Oulu.

CONNECTIONS FROM KEMI

Kemi is a significant railway junction. There's a morning train running north to **Pello** and **Kolari** (ERT 794), two small towns buried away in the forests of the Torne Valley. Both lie north of the Arctic Circle. Kolari has the distinction of being Finland's northernmost railway station. If you are arriving from Sweden via Haparanda, note that you can walk over the frontier and join the Kolari-bound train at Itäinen station in Tornio. There are occasional trains from Kemi which follow the Kemi Valley upstream to **Rovaniemi** (ERT 794) from where there are onward bus connections to northern Finland and in summer also to northern Norway.

The train journey from Kemi to Oulu will be for many travellers a first chance to experience a railway which is thoroughly **Russian in design**. The line dates from the late-Tsarist period, having been completed in 1903. Although it has been completely modernised – it was electrified in 2004 – there is still a distinct Russian ambiance about the route, evident most particularly in the design of station buildings (like those at Simo and Haukipudas).

Oulu (suggested stopover)

The railway station at Oulu is a welcoming wooden structure with a nicely retro feel. The city it serves is much more modern. Oulu is one of Finland's **high-tech industry** hubs. A few of the town's older buildings, such as the city hall, recall the 19th-century tar boom – in which Oulu was a world leader. A short walk away is the **Science Centre Tietomaa**, Nahkatehtaankatu 6, an interactive science and technology museum that's entertaining even for non-kids. There's an assemblage of Sámi artefacts and other local miscellanea at the nearby **Pohjois-Pohjanmaan Museo** (Northern Ostrobothnia Museum), Ainola Park (closed Mon, free Fri).

ARRIVAL, INFORMATION, ACCOMMODATION

🚆 Rautatienkatu, east of the centre. 🅹 Tourist office: Torikatu 18 (www.visitoulu.fi). 🏨 **Best Western Hotel Apollo**, Asemakatu 31–33, ☎ 08 522 11 (www.hotelapollo.fi), is a no-frills option close to the railway station. Or try the stylish **Lapland Hotel Oulu**, Kirkkokatu 3, ☎ 08 881 11 10 (www.laplandhotels.com), not far from the station and close to the cathedral. Centrally located, the **Scandic Oulu City**, Saaristonkatu 4, ☎ 08 543 10 00 (www.scandichotels.com), is comfortable and reliable.

CONNECTIONS FROM OULU

Take your pick from comfortable daytime Pendolinos or overnight trains with sleeping cars to Helsinki (ERT 794). You'll also find a direct overnight service to **Turku** (ERT 794 & 795). At Turku this train runs right through to the quayside, connecting with the Viking Line daytime sailing to Mariehamn (in the Åland Islands) and Stockholm. If you are Helsinki-bound and are in no great rush, why not consider following the inland route from Oulu via Kajaani and Kuopio to the Finnish capital, taking in some deliciously rural countryside along the way (ERT 798). You can now travel the entire line in the comfort of a smart Pendolino train. It takes 8 hrs 30 mins.

Ostrobothnia

It's a long haul south through the lowlands of Ostrobothnia from **Oulu to Tampere** – almost 500 kilometres and a journey of about five hours. The countryside is not riveting, but it has a serene charm, seen at its monochromatic best in the depths of winter.

From Oulu, the railway heads inland, only returning to the coast much further south at **Kokkola**. Slightly further down the coast is the predominantly Swedish-speaking town of **Jakobstad** (the Finnish name is Pietarsaari), in our view easily the nicest spot on the Ostrobothnian coast. This delightful small town is full of unpretentious wooden architecture – a good place to relax for a day or two, especially in good summer weather when you can explore the beaches along the coast. To reach Jakobstad, alight from the train at Pännäinen, from where there are good bus connections for the ten-kilometre hop to Jakobstad. If you are minded to stay overnight, the Hotel Epoque, Jaakonkatu 10, ☎ 06 788 71 00 (www.hotelepoque.fi), is a good option just a short walk from the Old Town.

Tampere (suggested stopover)

Finland's second city was once the nation's industrial fulcrum, but the **atmospheric red-brick factory buildings** and warehouses have since been converted into museums, galleries and shopping centres, and Tampere (Tammerfors in Swedish) today stands as a surprisingly attractive place, flanked by lakes and graced with abundant green spaces.

From the station, Hämeenkatu leads across the **Tammerkoski**, a series of rapids that connect the city's two largest lakes and provide it with hydroelectric energy. For an entirely different take on faith on Tampere (and more generally in Finland), take a peek at the ornately **Byzantine Orthodox church**, which lies on Suvantokatu just a couple of minutes south of the railway station. It's a wonderful fantasy of domes and turrets in the Russian Romantic style. Although now owned by the Orthodox Church of Finland, it's a reminder of former Russian influence here.

Tsar Alexander I encouraged the Scottish Quaker industrialist James Finlayson to develop the mills at Tampere. You cannot miss the former

Finlayson factory, now a centre for crafts and artisan works. More on the life of the factory's workers can be found at **Amurin Työläismuseokortteli**, Satakunnankatu 49 (Amuri Museum of Workers' Housing; closed Mon). There's a **Lenin Museum** in Hämeenpuisto, near the end of Hämeenkatu (www.lenin.fi; closed Mon outside summer). This marks the spot where Lenin met Stalin at the Bolshevik Congress in 1905 — Lenin lived in Tampere after the 1905 revolution. The museum is a remarkable survey of European socialist history as seen from a Finnish perspective. It's worth remembering that after centuries of subservience to Sweden (until 1809), and then 108 years in an ambiguous and often difficult relation with Russia, the Bolsheviks were the midwives of the first truly independent Finnish state.

ARRIVAL, INFORMATION, ACCOMMODATION
A 5-min walk east of the centre. ☒ Tourist office: Kelloportinkatu 1B (www.visittampere. fi). ☒ A good and modern budget option not far from the station is the **Dream Hostel**, Äkerlundinkatu 2, ☎ 0452 360 517 (www.dreamhostel.fi) that also has private rooms and apartments. Right by the station is the comfortable **Scandic Tampere Station**, Ratapihankatu 37, ☎ 03 339 80 00 (www.scandichotels.com). Also close to the station is the stylish **Sokos Hotel Villa**, Sumeliuksenkatu 14, ☎ 020 123 46 33 (www.sokoshotels.fi), next to the landmark Torni Hotel.

CONNECTIONS FROM TAMPERE
There are regular fast trains to Helsinki (ERT 790). A very useful cross-country line runs east from Tampere to **Pieksämäki** (ERT 795). There are connections in Pieksämäki to Kuopio (ERT 798) and **Joensuu** (ERT 793), the latter a lakeshore town which is a good jumping-off point for exploring Finnish Karelia.

The train journey from Tampere to Turku traverses forests and comfortable agricultural country. This region in the south-west is Finland's farming heartland. Finland's oldest city and its capital until 1812, **Turku** (Åbo in Swedish) is home to the country's oldest university and is a vibrant commercial and cultural centre, with a pulsating nightlife.

Turku's much-rebuilt but nonetheless impressive **Tuomiokirkko** (cathedral) is easily spotted by the tower's distinctive face, the result of several fires over the centuries. The cathedral is the seat of the Lutheran Archbishop of Finland and very much the centre of Protestant life in Finland. The **Sibelius Museum**, Piispankatu 17 (www.sibeliusmuseum.fi; closed Mon), displays over 350 musical instruments, as well as memorabilia of the great composer (although he had no connection with Turku itself).

If you want to spend the night in Turku consider staying at the Park Hotel, Rauhankatu 1, ☎ 02 273 25 55 (www.parkhotelturku.fi). This early 20th-century villa has art nouveau galore and offers individually styled rooms in a good central location.

CONNECTIONS FROM TURKU
The busy port of Turku has plenty of **ferries to Stockholm**, usually with a choice of four daily sailings (ERT 2480). It's about an 11-hour crossing, and you can opt for either a daytime or

overnight sailing. There is a very useful morning boat to Mariehamn in the **Åland Islands**, a scattered archipelago which is an autonomous region of Finland with strong cultural and linguistic links to Sweden.

To the Finnish Capital

The removal of the Finnish capital from Turku to Helsinki in 1812 was at the behest of the Russians. It suited the tsar to have the administrative centre of the **Grand Duchy** closer to St Petersburg, and the move had the effect of diminishing Swedish influence in Finnish affairs. Turku has never quite forgiven Helsinki. That's a fact to ponder as Finnish and Swedish voices intermingle on the two-hour ride to Helsinki. Just short of the capital, the railway passes for a dozen kilometres through an area that until 1956 was leased by the **Soviet Union**. Trains travelling on this route in those days had dark window blinds which were pulled down as the train traversed that area. We surely would not have been able to resist the temptation to take a peek into another world. For more on **corridor trains** – that's the name for services which criss-cross borders and traverse the territory of another country on a domestic journey – see our **Sidetracks** feature on p421.

Helsinki (Helsingfors) – (suggested stopover)

Built on a series of peninsulas, Helsinki is first and foremost a city of the sea. It has a gritty, north-meets-east flavour, but in recent years this modern city has become one of the most culturally pulsating capitals in Europe. Helsinki was rebuilt to a **grand grid plan** in the 19th century when it became capital of the Grand Duchy of Finland.

With its public buildings standing proud upon great granite steps, Helsinki's architecture has a distinctly Russian air – the city itself was originally modelled on St Petersburg. The wide boulevards are lined with cobbles and tramlines and exude a liberating sense of space. Don't miss **Uspenski Cathedral**, the showpiece centre of the Finnish Orthodox Church. Located near the harbour, its golden cupolas and red-brick facade are widely visible.

The real heart of Helsinki is **Kauppatori** (Market Square) and the harbour. This is where locals, visitors, craftspeople and traders meet. Take a boat trip around the harbour and enjoy some tasty fresh fish cooked to order. Those interested in railway architecture should certainly not miss Saarinen's **Central Railway Station**, a theatrical art nouveau design dominated by the granite giants that flank the main entrance.

ARRIVAL, INFORMATION, ACCOMMODATION

Helsinki Central Station, right in the heart of the city. ✈ Helsinki-Vantaa Airport (www.finavia.fi/fi/helsinkivantaa) is 20 km north of the city. A train service between the airport and the city centre opened in July 2015. Trains run every 10 mins Mon–Sat during the day (every 15 mins in the evenings and Sun), taking about 30 mins to Helsinki Central station. 🚊 Many of the sights are in the area between the station and Kauppatori, and trams are a quick way of reaching most of the others. Buy single tickets on the tram or bus or from blue HSL ticket machines or R-kiosks (www.hsl.fi). Daytickets are also available (buy at ticket machine or the tourist information). 🛈 Tourist office: at Helsinki Central Station (www.myhelsinki.fi).

🛏 A short walk west of the train station is the good-value **Hotel Helka**, Pohjoinen Rautatiekatu 23, ☎ 09 61 35 80 (www.hotelhelka.com). Or try the sleekly-designed boutique hotel **Glo Kluuvi**, Kluuvikatu 4, ☎ 010 344 44 00 (www.glohotels.fi). Very central and not far from the harbour in a quiet location is the upmarket **Hotel Lilla Roberts**, Pieni Roobertinkatu 1–3, ☎ 09 6824 28 60 (www.lillaroberts.com).

CONNECTIONS FROM HELSINKI

You can connect here with **Route 51** to Tallinn, Riga and then on by ferry to Stockholm. Helsinki has a tantalising range of ferry connections, ranging from short hops over the Gulf of Finland to **Tallinn** in Estonia (ERT 2410), and longer-distance crossings to **Stockholm** (ERT 2465) and a daily service to the German port of **Travemünde** run by Finnlines (ERT 2485).

On to Russia

In Helsinki, you are on Russia's doorstep. St Petersburg is less than four hours away on the **Allegro high-speed service** (ERT 1910). The *Leo Tolstoy* overnight train, which departs each evening for Moscow (ERT 1910) also serves St Petersburg, but it passes through the city by dead of night, so the chances are that you'll conclude Route 33 with a ride on the Allegro, a boldly styled train sporting Russian colours on the exterior of the carriages.

The first part of the route from Helsinki via Lahti to Kouvola follows the line travelled by Lenin in April 1917. Beyond Kouvola, the Russian-bound Allegro train continues east, stopping just once before the border. That stop is at **Vainikkala**, a wee village right on the Russian frontier. A huge shunting yard is a reminder of the vast quantities of freight that are shipped via this route. The train continues along a single-track railway which cuts through the forests into Russia. The border is just past the point where a metal footbridge crosses the track. You'll see both Finnish (blue/white) and Russian (red/green) border markers by the track on the right side of the train.

It is just 80 minutes from the border to St Petersburg, with an en route stop at **Vyborg** (Выборг), a town with a striking waterside setting. There are fine views of Vyborg from the train. In **St Petersburg**, the Allegro train from Helsinki terminates at the Finland Station (Финляндский вокзал), which has a very special place in Russian history, for it was here that Lenin's arrival in 1917 heralded the imminent revolution. A fine series of sculptures at the station recall the **October Revolution**. It's unlikely that you'll receive quite the same ecstatic welcome that Lenin did, but St Petersburg remains a friendly city, a perfect place for a first taste of Russia (read more on p429).

ALPINE ADVENTURES
An introduction

Many veterans of European rail travel assert that the sheer joy of exploring Europe by train reaches its apotheosis in the Alps. We agree! Throughout the region, and most particularly in **Switzerland and Austria**, the traveller is spoilt for choice with a dense network of rail routes, the great majority of which are served by frequent, modern and utterly reliable trains.

Bar for a few services intended primarily for tourists (eg. the long-standing **Glacier Express** and **Bernina Express** services and the new **Gotthard Panorama Express**, launched in 2017), there are no trains in Switzerland where a seat reservation is required for domestic journeys. Much the same is true in Austria. The Alps of course extend across borders into the Savoie area of France, Oberbayern in Germany, the hill country of northern Italy and western Slovenia. In all these areas, you can travel on all local and regional trains without any need to reserve seats in advance.

We include a choice of six Alpine adventures in this section of *Europe by Rail*. Of these, **Route 36** and **39** are both north to south routes over the Alps; both end in northern Italy, leaving you well placed to embark on itineraries which lead deeper into Italy. **Route 34** over Austria's **Semmering railway** can of course also be used as a gateway to Italy. The other three routes (**Route 35, 37** and **38** respectively) are more in the nature of Alpine tours in their own right, rather than being designed to lead beyond the Alps. Pushed to nominate our favourite route in this section of the book, we would opt for **Route 36** - the roundabout journey from Zurich to Milan via the classic Bernina railway (ERT 545).

Beware the tunnels

We have not included some of the classic Alpine railways, such as the **Simplon and Gotthard routes**, because — let's face it — you don't see much Alpine scenery when travelling through a long tunnel. The new Gotthard Base Tunnel, opened in late 2016, is 57 km long. That's 57 kilometres of Alpine darkness which is pretty much indistinguishable from any other variety of darkness. Yet **long tunnels** are in vogue — especially in Austria, where two new tunnels are due to open in 2026: one bypassing the finest section of the Semmering route and another, south of Innsbruck, giving faster journey times over the Brenner route (**Route 39**). Let's hope that the traditional railways are retained for those who favour scenery over speed.

A number of other Alpine lines cried out for inclusion in this book, but we just couldn't find the space. You might want to make time for the fine route which runs west from Lienz into Italy (ERT 596). And don't miss the **narrow-gauge railway** from Martigny to Chamonix (ERT 572). ■

Route 34: The Semmering railway

CITIES: ★★★ CULTURE: ★★ HISTORY: ★★ SCENERY: ★★★
COUNTRIES COVERED: AUSTRIA (AT), ITALY (IT)
JOURNEY TIME: 7 HRS 40 MINS | DISTANCE: 620 KM | MAP: WWW.EBRWEB.EU/MAP34

This is a tremendous journey over one of **Europe's first mountain rail routes** and links two very fine cities: Vienna and Venice. The railway between the two was fostered by imperial ambition, with the Austrian authorities keen to see a rail link between the capital and the country's only major port at Trieste. (For more on Trieste as an important Adriatic outpost of Austrian life and culture see p253). But the notion of building a main-line railway over the rugged Alpine terrain south-west of Vienna was daunting. In 1844 **Carlo Ghega** stepped up to the challenge. Ghega was born in Venice of Albanian parents; as a young engineer he has worked on several early railway projects in Moravia.

The **Semmering Railway** opened in 1854. In 1998, it was inscribed on UNESCO's World Heritage List. The citation commends the route as "one of the greatest feats of civil engineering during the pioneering phase of railway building. Set against a spectacular mountain landscape, the railway line remains in use today thanks to the quality of its tunnels, viaducts, and other works, and has led to the construction of many recreational buildings along its tracks."

A number of other **Alpine excursions** in this book (eg. **Route 36, 37 & 38**) follow routes which are wholly or partly narrow-gauge. The Semmering is different: it was designed from the outset as a main-line route carrying heavy passenger trains and lots of goods traffic. It is the best route in this book for capturing that sense of cruising gently through the Alps on a comfortable long-distance train.

Fifty years ago, the Semmering Railway was used by the twice-weekly Moscow to Rome service. As recently as 2013, the Moscow to Nice train ran over the Semmering, although it's now routed via the Brenner route (ERT 25). Today, the Semmering Railway is well used by regular Railjet trains from Vienna to Graz and **Klagenfurt**, respectively the provincial capitals of Styria and Carinthia. It carries night trains from Vienna to over a dozen cities in Italy. And it's used by the daytime trains from Vienna to Venice.

ITINERARY HINTS

This is a journey you'll definitely want to do by day – although there is an **overnight train** which leaves Vienna every evening for **Venice**. Until recently, there was just one direct daytime train in each direction between Vienna and Venice. That sole daytime train left Vienna at 06.25 in the morning – far too early for most travellers. It still runs, but happily there is now a second daytime train with a civilised lunchtime departure time.

There are of course fast trains over the Semmering Railway every two hours throughout the day, so you have plenty of choice for the first part of the journey. We

Route details

Vienna Hbf to Klagenfurt Hbf		ERT 980
Frequency	Journey time	Notes
Every 2 hrs	3 hrs 55 mins	
Klagenfurt Hbf to Venice Santa Lucia		ERT 88
Frequency	Journey time	Notes
2 per day	3 hrs 45 mins	X

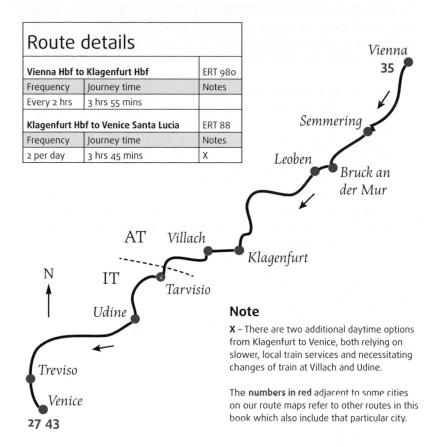

Note

X – There are two additional daytime options from Klagenfurt to Venice, both relying on slower, local train services and necessitating changes of train at Villach and Udine.

The **numbers in red** adjacent to some cities on our route maps refer to other routes in this book which also include that particular city.

suggest taking a lunchtime or early afternoon fast train from **Vienna to Klagenfurt** and staying there overnight, joining the onward Eurocity to Venice when it stops at Klagenfurt just after ten the following morning. Klagenfurt makes a good one-night stopover.

Over the Semmering

Our journey to Venice starts at Vienna's striking new main station (Wien Hauptbahnhof). For more on **Vienna** itself see our comments on the city on p320. This is, from the outset, a journey with great promise. Escaping the suburbs, there are fine views of the Wienerwald hills to the right, the lower slopes close to the railway draped with vineyards. After a stop at **Wiener Neustadt**, the railway begins to climb the first ripples of the Alps. The next hour is superb, with the line skirting the Schwarza and Auerbach Valleys to gain height. The landscape is in constant flux, here and there dense forest interspersed with fleeting views of dramatic mountains and Alpine meadows.

The **Semmering Tunnel** marks the summit of the line. The villages close to the railway display a fine mix of architectural styles, with some fabulous turn-of-the-century villas built for wealthy Viennese who were delighted that the new railway brought the Alps within striking distance of the capital. These communities assumed immense importance in the literary and cultural imagination of *fin de siècle* Vienna, as artists and writers discovered the mountains – in much the same way as in Poland the Tatra resort of Zakopane (see p310) was crucial in reshaping Polish identity. Semmering was a rural annex to the coffee houses and salons of the capital. Freud was a regular in Semmering. So too was **Arthur Schnitzler**. Semmering was not an *escape* from Vienna. It *was* Vienna in the mountains (just as Trieste was Vienna by the sea).

From Semmering, the railway drops down towards the **Mürz Valley**, following the river towards the railway junctions at Bruck an der Mur and Leoben.

BRUCK AND LEOBEN CONNECTIONS
Bruck an der Mur is the junction for Graz (ERT 980) and direct Eurocity services to Ljubljana and Zagreb (ERT 91). Connect at Leoben onto a **beautiful line** running west towards Salzburg (ERT 975). This latter route is used by a number of long-distance services with Eurocity trains running direct from Leoben to Munich, Frankfurt-am-Main and Innsbruck. There is a once-daily Eurocity and an overnight Nightjet from both Bruck and Leoben to Zurich.

From **Leoben**, the railway climbs again to reach a gentle saddle at Neumarkt – actually just as high as Semmering, albeit with less drama in the scenery. This summit marks the border with **Carinthia**, and it's downhill all the way to the provincial capital at Klagenfurt.

Klagenfurt (suggested stopover)
The city centre is just a ten-minute walk north of the station. Klagenfurt communicates a **quiet sense of prosperity**, and local life centres around the predictably named Neuer Platz and Alter Platz – the latter surrounded by a selection of handsome cafés. Klagenfurt is an excellent taste of provincial Austria, in many ways as likeable as Innsbruck or Salzburg but without the crowds. If you are minded stay overnight, the Hotel Goldener Brunnen, Karfreitstraße 14, ☎ 0463 57 380 (www.goldener-brunnen.at), is a good option with a nice courtyard. It is well placed for both the station and Klagenfurt's Old Town.

West from Klagenfurt, the railway skirts the Wörthersee to reach Villach, the second city of Carinthia and an important railway junction.

CONNECTIONS FROM VILLACH
Villach is a good jumping-off point for journeys to the **Balkans** with direct daytime trains to Ljubljana, Zagreb and Belgrade (all in ERT 62). There is a summer-only direct train to **Edirne**

in Turkey. This extraordinary long hop covers the territory of six countries. It's intended first and foremost for families wanting to take a car, but it can be booked by travellers without a vehicle. Details at www.optimatours.de.

There are tamer destinations too. Villach has a useful **overnight train** to Zurich (ERT 86) and there are direct daytime trains to Salzburg (ERT 970) and many German cities, including Munich, Stuttgart and Cologne (ERT 62). Finally there are regular regional trains running west to Lienz (ERT 971) in the **Austrian East Tyrol** region, with onward connections on through the beautiful Pustertal to the Italian South Tyrol (ERT 596).

From Villach, the railway climbs to the third and last summit of the journey, cresting the **Italian border** and reaching Tarvisio, where the railway station is an assertively modern affair inconveniently situated about a 40-minute walk from **Tarvisio** itself. It's a nice example of a frontier station that clearly made an architectural statement, designed to impress travellers who have just crossed the border. Other border stations in the same vein (albeit very different in design) include Cheb, Jesenice, Chop (on **Route 26**) and Terespol (on **Route 50**).

From Tarvisio, we follow the **Pontebbana Railway** down to the Veneto lowlands, stopping at the busy provincial town of Udine on the way to Venice (for connections to nearby Trieste, see ERT 601). The Pontebbana line has been thoroughly rebuilt in recent years, with six long tunnels which are together about 40 kilometres in length. It is a far cry from the wonderful scenic line that Carlo Ghega built over the Semmering.

But the journey ends on a high as the train traverses the Ponte della Libertà – fine views of the Venetian lagoon on either side – to reach its final destination at **Venice Santa Lucia** station. Arrivals just don't get any better than this. Just in front of the station, the Grand Canal awaits.

Venice

Venice can play cultural one-upmanship better than most cities. Even the cafés of **St Mark's Square** (Piazza San Marco) are awash with famous ghosts, and tourism is almost as ancient as the city itself. Built on 118 tiny islands, this former maritime republic once held sway over an empire stretching from northern Italy to Cyprus. Around 1,000 residents leave each year, driven out by exorbitant rents. Ironically, for a city built on water, Venice numbers around 450 souvenir shops but fewer than ten plumbers. Most day trippers fail to stray far from Piazza San Marco with its famous basilica, which is a huge mistake. Beyond the crowds at the major sights, especially around St Mark's and the **Rialto Bridge**, Venice exudes a village-like calm. Even a 15-minutes walk from the main drag can deposit you alone in a Gothic square, with just pigeons for company.

Surprisingly for a city built on water, the best way to explore is on foot. Prepare yourself for serious walking as there are 400 bridges and around 180

VENICE: WHERE THE 'REAL' PEOPLE LIVE

The Strada Nova is a broad, hectic street running along the Grand Canal, leading from the Rialto Bridge to the Ca' d'Oro museum and packed with shops and cafés as well as tourists. Equally bustling is the Lista di Spagna near the railway station, full of touristy cafés and shops. To see a bit more of the 'real' Venice you have to venture away from these streets. The district of Cannaregio, once Venice's main manufacturing area, is spacious and pleasant with broad canal sides and a fairly simple layout. Shops, bars and hotels tend to be cheaper and the area is more popular with locals than the city centre. The backstreets here in **Cannaregio**, where over a third of the city's population live, are where you will find the 'real' people in Venice.

The Fondamenta della Sensa and the parallel **Fondamenta della Misericordia** both offer peaceful walks. From the quayside of Fondamente Nove you can get fine views of the lagoon, the cemetery island of San Michele and, beyond it, Murano.

canals to discover. Expect to get lost, especially at night, which is part and parcel of the charm of this mysterious lagoon world. However, you're never far from the **Grand Canal**, which snakes through the centre, and Venice is perfectly safe. The best way to feel the spirit of the city is simply to wander its narrow streets (*calli*), popping into churches as you pass and pausing to sit at a waterside café whenever the whim takes you.

A visit to the tiny islands of **Murano** and **Burano** (from Fondamente Nove by *vaporetti* 12 to Burano and 4.1/4.2 to Murano) reveals that the traditional skills of glass- and lace-making still thrive today. Pay a visit to Venice's finest collection of modern art in the **Peggy Guggenheim Collection** on the Grand Canal at Dorsoduro no. 704 (closed Tues).

ARRIVAL, INFORMATION, ACCOMMODATION

≋ Mestre station is on the mainland; to get to Venice itself, take a train to Santa Lucia station. A local service operates between the two stations (*vaporetto* stop, at the north-west end of the Grand Canal). ✈ Marco Polo International Airport is 13 km north-east of Venice (www.veniceairport.it). The regular motorboat service of Alilaguna operates from the airport (year-round, www.alilaguna.it) via the Lido to the Pza San Marco in the heart of Venice, and costs €15 for a one-way trip.

Venice's sturdy waterbuses (*vaporetti*) are operated by ACTV (http://actv.avmspa.it) and run at 12- to 20-min intervals in daytime with a break from about 23.00–05.00. Lines 1 and 2 run the length of the Grand Canal, connecting Santa Lucia station to Pza San Marco. Piers bear the line numbers – but make sure you go in the right direction. The city's 400 gondolas, which can take up to six passengers each, provide a costly, conceivably romantic, means of getting around. Rates are fixed. You can also try the short gondola ride on the *traghetto* (gondola ferry), which crosses the Grand Canal at eight points (signposted traghetto) for €2 (residents pay less).

ℹ Tourist office: Pza San Marco 71 and at Santa Lucia station (www.venice-tourism.com). ⊨ The **Agli Alboretti**, Dorsoduro, Accademia 884, Rio Terrà Foscarini, ☎ 041 523 0058 (www.aglialboretti.com), is a popular hotel with a good restaurant and pleasant rooms. A recommended B&B within walking distance of the station is **Campiello Zen**, Santa Croce, 1285 Rio Terà, ☎ 041 710 365 (www.campiellozen.com). Splurgers should head for the **Novecento Boutique Hotel**, San Marco 2683/84, ☎ 041 241 3765 (www.novecento.biz), a small, family-run place in a central but quiet location.

Route 35: The Arlberg route

CITIES: ★★ CULTURE: ★★ HISTORY: ★ SCENERY: ★★★
COUNTRIES COVERED: SWITZERLAND (CH), LIECHTENSTEIN (LI), AUSTRIA (AT), SLOVAKIA (SK)
JOURNEY TIME: 11 HRS | DISTANCE: 911 KM | MAP: WWW.EBRWEB.EU/MAP35

The very mention of the word Arlberg evokes memories of a *belle époque* of continental rail travel. The Arlberg is the rugged mountain region which separates Austria's westernmost province, Vorarlberg, from the Tyrol. The mountains achieve no spectacular heights – there are no summits in excess of 3,000 metres. But the difficult terrain was for centuries an obstacle to travel until the **Arlberg Railway** opened in 1884. It is the principal west to east line through the Alps, a railway noted for its remarkable beauty, and it is the highlight of this route from **Zurich to Vienna** and **Bratislava**.

The Arlberg railway has long been a major artery for international traffic. One of the many versions of the legendary *Orient Express* took this route, and the modern *Venice-Simplon Orient Express* (VSOE) tourist train is normally routed via the Arlberg line on its run from Paris to Venice (the train's name is thus misleading as it does not normally take the Simplon route at all).

But no one complains over that detail for, when it comes to the **quality of the scenery**, the Arlberg route knocks spots off the Simplon (more about the Simplon line in the Sidetracks on p341). The Arlberg is, quite simply, the finest mainline rail route **through the Alps**.

There are five direct Austrian Railjet trains each day from Zurich to Vienna, with one continuing to Bratislava. There is also an overnight train from Zurich to Vienna (operated as part of ÖBB's Nightjet network).

The daytime **Railjets** from Switzerland to Innsbruck and beyond are perfectly functional, but they don't quite have the character of the old express trains which plied the route. The Railjets also take a short cut between Innsbruck and Salzburg, slipping through a corner of German territory which is much less scenic than the classic line described here.

RECOMMENDED ITINERARY

This is a superb journey to do in a **single day**. Choose your trains carefully. By far the best option is the 08.40 departure from Zurich. It's not a Railjet, but a very comfy Eurocity service with large windows which are perfect for sightseeing. All the better if you have a first-class ticket or rail pass, as there is a recently refurbished Swiss observation car on this train. This particular Eurocity train (EC163 in ERT 951, 960 & 975) runs to Graz. But with a change of train in Schwarzach-St Veit, you'll be Salzburg by late afternoon and reach Vienna by 18.30, from where it's just an hour on to Bratislava.

If you want to break your journey, there are of course three premier-league cities on this route: **Innsbruck, Salzburg** and **Vienna**. If you favour smaller towns as stop-off points, then Feldkirch is a good choice, with the option of a day exploring the Principality of Liechtenstein. We also recommend Kitsbühel which ticks all the boxes if you are looking for a dose of small-town Alpine fantasy.

Coffee in three countries

Our route leaves Zurich (see p205) heading south-east; the first 90 km out of Zurich parallel **Route 34** in this book (which runs via the Bernina Pass to northern Italy). The train skirts the Zürichsee and then the Walensee, entering an area which **Thomas Cook** describes (in his 1874 Swiss guide) as "the Lancashire of Switzerland." If you follow this route and spot any resemblance at all to Lancashire, let us know! We're inclined to write off Cook's comparison as a bit of wishful thinking. At **Sargans**, the railway turns north, following the Rhine Valley downstream. Until Buchs, the railway stays in Swiss territory, with Liechtenstein on the far bank of the Rhine. At Buchs the train reverses and then crosses the river into Liechtenstein.

If you buy a coffee in the train's restaurant car at **Buchs**, you'll have travelled on the territory of three countries by the time you've drained the cup. The train takes all of nine minutes to traverse mighty Liechtenstein. This is the sole railway which crosses the territory of the principality. Slow trains from Buchs to Feldkirch stop (weekdays only) at three minor railway stations in Liechtenstein. Shortly after crossing the **Austrian border**, the railway line performs a graceful pirouette around the Ardetzenberg to reach the station at Feldkirch.

Even in these days of light-touch borders, **Feldkirch** still has the feel of a border town – a place which is not quite Austrian. If the international community had listened to the locals, it wouldn't be Austrian at all today. In 1919, the people of the **Vorarlberg region** voted overwhelmingly to leave post-Habsburg Austria and become a canton of Switzerland. Their wishes were not granted. The train taking Emperor Charles and his wife Zita to exile in Switzerland stopped in Feldkirch in March 1919 and the unhappy monarch issued a manifesto declaring that he had been illegally deposed. No one in Feldkirch paid much notice.

Interestingly, a plaque at the railway station recalls literary rather than political events. For James Joyce, Feldkirch was the last stop on Habsburg territory as he fled with his family from Trieste to Switzerland in 1915. He was nervous that they would not be permitted to leave Austria. Returning to Feldkirch after the war, he recalled that "Over there, on those tracks, the fate of *Ulysses* was decided in 1915."

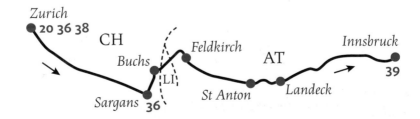

There are two very good reasons for pausing at Feldkirch. First, it happens to be a very pleasant small town. Second, Feldkirch is by far the best jumping-off point to **explore Liechtenstein** by bus. Although there are bus connections into the principality from Sargans and Buchs, we think the approach from Feldkirch is just much prettier.

Tucked in against the hills, Feldkirch is a place to linger and wander through the nicely arcaded main streets. It is worth climbing up to the Schattenburg, not so much for the contents of the museum now housed in the old fortress, but more for the views. Don't miss **St Nikolaus Cathedral** (Domkirche), with its odd double nave and flamboyant 1960s stained-glass windows. If you want to stay overnight, try the family-run Hotel Bären, Bahnhofstr. 1, ☎ 05522 355 00 (www.hotel-baeren.at), close to the station.

Route details

Zurich Hbf to Feldkirch		ERT 86
Frequency	Journey time	Notes
Every 2 hrs	1 hr 30 mins	

Feldkirch to Innsbruck Hbf		ERT 951
Frequency	Journey time	Notes
Hourly	1 hr 55 mins – 2 hrs 25 mins	

Innsbruck Hbf to Kitzbühel		ERT 960
Frequency	Journey time	Notes
Hourly	70–80 mins	W

Kitzbühel to Salzburg Hbf		ERT 960
Frequency	Journey time	Notes
Every 2 hrs	2 hrs 30 mins	X

Salzburg Hbf to Vienna Hbf		ERT 950
Frequency	Journey time	Notes
2–3 per hr	2 hrs 25 mins – 3 hrs	

Vienna Hbf to Bratislava hl. st.		ERT 996
Frequency	Journey time	Notes
Hourly	65–70 mins	Z

Notes

W – On many journeys a change of train at Wörgl Hbf is necessary.

X – There are additional options requiring a change of trains at Schwarzach-St Veit or Bischofshofen.

Z – Additional trains run between Vienna and Bratislava by a more southerly route, taking about one hour and terminating in Bratislava at Petržalka station, on the south bank of the Danube. 🚌 94 runs every few minutes from Petržalka station into the heart of the Old Town.

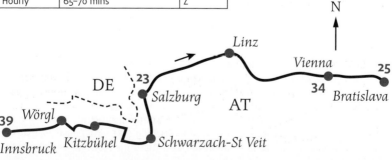

Over the Arlberg

The 160-kilometre stretch of railway from **Feldkirch to Innsbruck** is the best part of this entire route. Time and technology have tamed the mountains. In the early days of the line, specially designed locomotives were needed to cope with the gradients. Today, the trains slide with seeming ease through the mountains, with the fastest trains taking under two hours to travel from Feldkirch to Innsbruck.

The line climbs through **glorious Alpine scenery** to over 1,300 metres, passing under the watershed in a ten-kilometre long tunnel. It all seems too easy, compared with the arduous rigours of travel in the region before the coming of the railway. An early John Murray guide recalls the days when travellers perished in the Arlberg snows, their corpses left to rot by the side of the path with birds pecking at their eyes.

On the west side of the Arlberg, the waters drain to the Rhine and thus eventually to the North Sea. On the east side, the clear mountain streams flow east, joining the Inn and eventually follow the Danube down the Black Sea. Emerging from the **Arlberg Tunnel**, the train stops immediately at St Anton am Arlberg – an upmarket ski resort as full of glitz and gloss as the ultra-modern station building suggests.

Beyond St Anton, the railway follows the River Rosanna downstream through lovely Tyrolean landscapes to the town of **Landeck**, which would hardly warrant a mention, were it not for its key position on the Tyrolean transport network. It's the jumping-off point for buses which follow the Inn Valley up to Nauders (ERT 954), from where there are onward bus connections to the Engadine area of eastern Switzerland and to Malles in Italy. You can read more in our **Sidetracks** feature on p348.

The Inn Valley

Beyond Landeck, the railway follows the valley downstream through Imst, a town which once thrived on the twin industries of mining and breeding canaries, prosecuting the latter with such success that birds from Imst were once delivered on foot to potentates across the Middle East. East from **Imst**, the valley becomes more heavily industrialised on the approach to Innsbruck. You'll find a short description of **Innsbruck**, one of our recommended stopovers on this route, on p345.

CONNECTIONS FROM INNSBRUCK

Innsbruck Hauptbahnhof is the place to join **Route 37** in this book, following it north around the Karwendel Alps to Garmisch and Munich (ERT 895), or south over the **Brenner Pass** to Verona (ERT 595). Sticking with the present route towards Salzburg and Vienna, you'll find a choice of two lines to Salzburg. The fastest trains cut through German territory, giving passengers a glimpse of Bavaria on the way to Salzburg (ERT 951). Purists will stick to the classic line which remains on Austrian territory. That's the route we describe below.

There are very few direct trains from Innsbruck to Salzburg which follow the traditional line through Kitzbühel and **Zell am See** – so it's usually necessary to change trains at Wörgl and Schwarzach-St Veit. One of the few through trains from Innsbruck via Zell to **Vienna** is a weekly service run by Russian Railways (RZD), but it has recently changed from being a daytime train to a night service which is hardly conducive to watching the Alpine landscapes beyond the window.

An Austrian rail cruise

So you opted to stick with our recommended route on the classic line through Kitzbühel to Salzburg! Good for you. You're in for a treat. The initial stretch down the **Inn Valley** to drab Wörgl is nothing special. In Wörgl, we branch off east to follow the 200-kilometre long *Giselabahn* to Salzburg. The railway is named after the second daughter of Austrian Emperor Franz Josef I. The first place of any size is the pleasant old town of **Kitzbühel** which, with its mountain backdrop and tree-lined streets of steeply gabled pastel-coloured buildings, is one of Austria's prettiest and largest ski resorts (though the snow's not that reliable; main season Christmas–Easter). Don't miss the **Kitzbüheler Hornbahn cable car** to the summit of the Horn; near the top, some 120 species of flowers bloom in an **Alpine Flower Garden**, 1,880-m high and open from spring to autumn (free guided tours 11.00 in July and August). The ski elite arrive in January for the Hahnenkamm ski competition, a World Cup leg, down one of the world's trickiest ski runs. If you are tempted to break the journey, try the family-run Hotel Resch, Alfons-Petzold-Weg 2, ☎ 05356 62294 (www.hotel-resch.at), in a good central location.

There are fine views of the **Kitzbühel Alps** as the train climbs east towards the Griessen Pass and then drops down towards the Pinzgau region. Zell am See is a good spot to stop for an hour or two. Beyond Zell, the railway follows the **Salzach Valley**, eventually turning north for the run into Salzburg.

Connections from the Giselabahn

There are two important railway junctions on the **Gisela Railway** east of Zell. Connect at Schwarzach-St Veit for trains to Villach (ERT 970). This is a very useful link to the Balkans. There is a direct daytime train from Schwarzach-St Veit to Ljubljana and Zagreb (ERT 62). At **Bischofshofen**, you can connect onto the beautiful line which runs along the Enns Valley with trains running right through to Graz (ERT 975).

Salzburg (suggested stopover)

Wonderfully sited between the Alps and the lakes of the **Salzkammergut**, Salzburg lies on one of the major trading routes through the Alps. The city's wealth was rooted, as its name implies, in the salt trade. It's a place which has always buzzed with the ebb and flow of ideas and people – though not always with great tolerance. When a good percentage of the population

switched allegiance to the Protestant faith, the Catholic authorities promptly expelled them en masse. These refugees found sanctuary in Prussia.

Salzburg is renowned as **Mozart's birthplace**. Much of the city's appearance dates from the 17th century, when many of the old buildings were
pulled down and others given a baroque makeover to create Italian-style
squares with spectacular fountains. Salzburg's entire **Old Town** (Altstadt)
is designated a UNESCO World Heritage Site and much of it is sweetly
beautiful, although some find it cloying and the crowds can be oppressive.
The **compact centre** is largely pedestrianised; the main shopping street is
narrow Getreidegasse, bordered by elegant old houses, decorative wrought-
iron signs and mediaeval arcades, which now house jewellery shops or
boutiques. Mozarts Geburtshaus, No. 9, where the composer was born in
1756 and spent most of his first 17 years, is now a museum.

On **Mönchsberg** (Monk's mountain), high above the Altstadt, looms
the formidable **Festung Hohensalzburg**, Mönchsberg 34 (entry fee), once
the stronghold of the Archbishops of Salzburg. Built over six centuries,
it's almost perfectly preserved, with early Gothic state rooms, and a 200-
pipe barrel organ that booms out once the 7th-century 35-bell carillon of
the **Glockenspiel**, Mozartplatz, has pealed (at 07.00, 11.00 and 18.00). The
castle can be reached on foot from Festungsgasse behind the cathedral,
or by the **Festungsbahn**, Austria's oldest cable railway dating from 1892.
Alternatively, the Mönchsbergaufzug (Mönchsberg Lift) operates from
Gstättengasse 13 (by Museumplatz) and takes you to the uncompromisingly
minimalist contemporary art museum, the Museum der Moderne, from
whose café terrace there are great views over the city. The big event is the
Salzburg Festival, mid-July to late August. For major performances, tickets
must be booked months ahead (www.salzburgerfestspiele.at).

ARRIVAL, INFORMATION, ACCOMMODATION

⇜ **Salzburg Hbf**, Südtiroler Pl. 1, 20-min walk from the Old Town (or take 🚌 1/3/5/6/25 to
Makartplatz or Theatergasse). The station was thoroughly renovated in 2014, but it's still a
confusing place. Take care to arrive early if you are boarding a train bound for Germany, as
there are occasionally still ID checks prior to boarding the train. ✈ Salzburg Airport, 4 km
west of the city (www.salzburg-airport.com), 🚌 2 connects the station with the airport
every 10 mins (evenings and Sun every 20 mins), taking about 25 mins for the journey. 🚌
10 runs every 10 mins to the city centre, taking 15 mins.

🛈 Tourist offices: Mozartplatz 5 and at the station (www.salzburg.info). Bus and
trolley bus tickets: from vending machines or kiosks; more expensive from driver (punch
ticket on boarding). Day passes also available. 🛏 During festivals, it pays to book early
as accommodation often gets very scarce. Salzburg is not a cheap place to stay, especially
during the summer season. **Hotel Weisse Taube**, Kaigasse 9, ☎ 0662 842 404 (www.
weissetaube.at), in the centre of the Old Town, is a friendly and good-value place close
to the cathedral and Mozartplatz. Or try the comfortable **The Mozart**, Franz-Josef-Str. 27,
☎ 0662 872 274 (www.themozarthotel.com). For an upmarket option in a great location
close to Mozartplatz try the stylish **Art Hotel Blaue Gans**, Getreidegasse 41–43. ☎ 0662
842 491 (www.blauegans.at).

CONNECTIONS FROM SALZBURG

As befits a major rail hub, there is a wealth of onward connections. You can join **Route 19** in this book at Salzburg, following it in reverse all the way to Berlin. **Munich** is the nearest large city to Salzburg, and there are plenty of cross-border trains. The journey to Munich takes less than two hours (ERT 890). There are direct Eurocity services to Stuttgart, Frankfurt-am-Main and Cologne. **Budapest** is little more than five hours away on a fast Railjet train (ERT 86).

Towards Vienna

The 300-km journey from Salzburg to Vienna is for many visitors from western Europe (who often arrive in Salzburg from Munich) their first taste of rail travel in Austria. In 1873, when Vienna hosted the World Exposition, the fastest run on the route was the lunchtime express from Salzburg, which dashed to the Austrian capital in just under eight hours. Today it takes just two-and-a-half hours on the fastest trains.

The first part of the run out from Salzburg is superb, with the railway following the narrow valley of the **River Fischach** up to Wallersee. The train skirts the shores of the lake before climbing steadily towards the summit of the line at just over 600 metres above sea level – and that barely 20 minutes out of Salzburg. From here it is downhill all the way to the Austrian capital, with the rail route dropping down through the Vöckla, Ager and Traun Valleys to reach the Danube at **Linz**.

Linz, Austria's industrial third city, is gradually reinventing itself with ultra-modern museums and events, such as the **Ars Electronica Center**, Ars-Electronica-Str. 1 (www.aec.at; closed Mon), Europe's first museum dedicated to virtual reality. Facing it across the river, the sleek **Lentos Kunstmuseum**, Ernst-Koref-Promenade 1, glows with changing colours after dark. Hauptplatz blends colourful baroque and rococo facades around the baroque marble Trinity column. In 1938, **Hitler** – who grew up here – stood on the balcony of Hauptplatz 1 (now the tourist office) to inform the Austrians that the Nazis had annexed their country.

CONNECTIONS FROM LINZ

Linz is the place to connect onto direct ICE trains to many **destinations across Germany**, including Berlin, Hamburg (both ERT 64), Frankfurt am Main, Koblenz, Cologne and the Ruhr region (all ERT 66). There are direct services to **Prague** (ERT 1132), Budapest (ERT 65) and Graz (ERT 974), the latter taking a very scenic route through Selzthal. Another fine rural route is that which leads south from the Enns Valley to Steyr and beyond (ERT 976). If you want a closer look at the River Danube, Linz is a good place to forsake the train and switch to **water transport**. From late April until October there are boats running upstream to Passau and downstream to Melk and Vienna (ERT 999).

Leaving Linz, travellers anticipating an early glimpse of the Danube will be disappointed. When it was opened in 1861, this line was one of the best engineered routes in the **Habsburg Empire**, and part of the line's success was keeping a safe distance from the Danube, so averting the risk of flooding. But there are fine views of the handsome little town of **Enns** just before crossing the river of the same name to enter the province of Lower Austria.

After playing cat and mouse with the little stream called the **Ybbs**, the train eventually plucks up courage to confront the Danube, giving a fleeting view of the **monastery at Melk**. This is one of those great moments of European rail travel where patience is eventually rewarded by something far more uplifting than one might ever have dared to imagine. It is a feast for the eyes and for the soul, so much so that most travellers will hardly notice the tunnels and cuttings that dominate the last part of the run into Vienna.

Vienna (Wien) – (suggested stopover)

Not for nothing does Austria's capital regularly top lists revealing Europe's most liveable city, for Vienna is an enviably **civilised place**, safe and manageable yet rarely dull. The **Altstadt**, or historic core, is traffic-calmed if not entirely pedestrianised, with cobbled streets, old merchants' houses, spacious gardens and hundreds of atmospheric places to eat and drink, though some of the most charming – and least touristy – lie in the districts just beyond the ring.

A visit to one of the classic coffee houses for coffee and home-made cake is *de rigueur*. Most sights are on or inside the famous **Ringstrasse**, which encircles the city centre. For architectural splendours of the late 19th century, take trams 1 or 2, passing the neo-Gothic Rathaus (City Hall), Burgtheater, Parlament and Staatsoper. Or admire the lavish state apartments and some seriously glittering crown jewels at the vast **Hofburg** (Imperial Palace) complex, which was once home to the Habsburgs. The **Albertina Museum** opened as a new home for contemporary art in the centre of Vienna in 2018.

Vienna is extremely well placed to be part of a rail tour of Europe, with good connections to Germany, the Czech Republic, Slovakia, Hungary, Slovenia, Switzerland, Italy and beyond.

ARRIVAL, INFORMATION, ACCOMMODATION

≉ A new main station (**Hauptbahnhof**) opened in 2014 and all international services had transferred to the new station by the end of 2015. **Westbahnhof**, once so important for travellers arriving in Vienna from the west, is now relegated to secondary status although private operator Westbahn still uses Westbahnhof for some trains to Salzburg (ERT 950). Some long-distance trains arriving in Vienna now run beyond Hauptbahnhof to terminate at the newly expanded airport station (shown in timetables as Flughafen Wien).

The U-Bahn (underground trains), S-Bahn (suburban trains) inside the city limits, trams and buses all use the same tickets, with transfers allowed. Under-6s travel free, under-15s travel free on Sundays, public holidays and school holidays; photo ID required. You can get a 24 hour (€8), 48 hour (€14.10) or 72 hour (€17.10) rover ticket. Just before travelling, validate (time-stamp) the ticket. 🄳 Tourist office: Albertinapl., corner of Maysedergasse (www.wien.info) and at Hauptbahnhof.

Art in Vienna

Unrivalled in the art department, Vienna offers a kaleidoscopic palette of Old Masters and new talent. Start off at the **Hofburg**, which showcases glittering jewels and Biedermeier portraits, then head over to the Albertina, with its riot of Rembrandts, Picassos and Warhols, or gaze on the **Kunsthistorisches Museum's riches**, which include works by Velázquez and Caravaggio. Design reaches a peak at the MAK (Museum of Applied Arts), which houses precious Wiener Werkstätte pieces. Visit the Upper Belvedere for great Impressionist works and a fine Klimt collection; or see Hundertwasser's colours make a secessionist splash at **KunstHaus Wien**. For a modern twist to the city's art offerings visit the MuseumsQuartier. Take a trip to the cube-shaped Leopold Museum, which houses an impressive collection of Egon Schiele paintings, or the Kunsthalle Wien where contemporary art comes boldly to the fore. The monolithic **MUMOK** (Museum of Modern Art Ludwig Foundation) gives you a shove into the 20th century with works by Warhol, Magritte and Kandinsky.

✉ A comfortable and very central option is **Hotel Austria**, Fleischmarkt 20, ☎ 01 515 23 (www.hotelaustria-wien.at). Close to the new Museumsquartier, **Pension Wild**, Lange Gasse 10, ☎ 01 406 5174 (www.pension-wild.com), has great rooms and is both backpacker- and gay-friendly. In the vicinity of Westbahnhof is the eco-friendly boutique hotel **Stadthalle**, Hackengasse 20, ☎ 01 982 42 72 (www.hotelstadthalle.at).

Vienna connections

In Vienna you can connect onto **Route 32**, which takes the famous Semmering railway through the Alps and leads to Venice. Vienna is the best-connected city in central Europe when it comes to railways. From the city's impressive new Hauptbahnhof, there are direct trains to Budapest (ERT 1250), Belgrade (ERT 61) and Bucharest (ERT 61). Ljubljana and Zagreb (both in ERT 91) are each just a few hours away on comfortable Eurocity services. **Railjets** run to Prague (ERT 1150) and Zurich (ERT 86). There are **night trains** to Bucharest (ERT 61), Rome (ERT 88), Kraków (ERT 99), Berlin (ERT 77) and Moscow (ERT 95).

Closer to hand, Vienna is the hub for a fine network of regional and local services, many of which cross nearby borders into **Slovakia and Hungary**. This area has benefited enormously from the enhanced mobility afforded by the Schengen Agreement. Trains apart, from Vienna you can cruise up the Danube to Krems an der Donau (ERT 999) or speed downstream on a fast hydrofoil to Bratislava or Budapest (also ERT 999).

From Vienna there are two rail routes east to Bratislava. We strongly recommend that you use the more northerly of the two, shown in ERT 996. This route is more rural and beyond **Marchegg** affords good views of the water meadows that surround the Danube. On the final approach into Bratislava, you'll see the last whisper of the **Carpathians** to the left. Our journey ends at the main station (Hlavná stanica).

Bratislava

Overshadowed by Prague, it has sometimes been hard for the Slovak capital to make its mark. But the city is **superbly placed** midway between Prague and Budapest, and is less than an hour by train east of Vienna. Bratislava fans always argue that the city has all the merits of Prague without the crowds.

There will not be a lot to detain you in the dreary suburbs, but the **Old Town** (Staré Mesto) is a gem. The main sights cluster within the old city walls on the east side of **Staromestská**. West of that is a prominent hill topped by the rather austere **castle** (Bratislavský hrad). The Danube riverfront is dominated by the modernist **New Bridge** (Nový most) that leads over to the huge Petržalka estate.

The Old Town is full of atmospheric lanes. In and around Ventúrska, Michalská and Panská you'll find excellent **baroque palaces**. Look out for the Mozartov dom (which has only the most tenuous of links with the composer), the rococo Mirbach Palace and the **Pálffyho Palace** that houses part of the Bratislava City Gallery (closed Mon). Noteworthy Gothic structures include the Franciscan church and the striking tower of St Klara's Convent (today not a convent at all but a library).

Climb **St Michael's Tower** at Michalská 22 for a great panoramic view. At the west side of the Old Town stands the Gothic St Martin's Cathedral, nowadays rather hemmed in by Staromestská. Immediately on the west side of Staromestská, under the shadow of the castle, is Bratislava's **old Jewish Quarter**. The castle itself houses extensive museums. Information on the various exhibitions and locations of the **Slovak National Museum** on www. snm.sk. Bratislava's Old Town is full of bars, cafés and restaurants that spill out onto the streets on sunny evenings, with the highest concentration on Ventúrska.

ARRIVAL, INFORMATION, ACCOMMODATION

� Bratislava has two main train stations. The chief one, **Hlavná stanica**, is used by almost all trains and is 1.5 km north of the Old Town (tram 1 provides a reliable link). A second station at **Petržalka** (3 km south of the city centre on the south side of the Danube) has fewer facilities, but it is the terminus for an alternative service from Vienna via Kittsee (ERT 997). ⓘ Tourist office: Klobučnícka 2 (www.visitbratislava.com) and at Hlavná stanica.

⊨ Budget accommodation is hard to find in Bratislava. Just a ten-minute stroll from the Old Town is the comfortable **Loft Hotel Bratislava**, Štefánikova 4, ☎ 02 57 51 10 03 (www.lofthotel.sk). Or try the equally central **Danubia Gate Bratislava**, Dunajská 26, ☎ 02 20 66 55 00 (www.danubiagate.sk). Just around the corner of the Old Town and close to the bank of the Danube is the modern **Hotel Avance**, Medená 9, ☎ 02 59 20 84 00 (www. hotelavance.sk).

CONNECTIONS FROM BRATISLAVA

You can connect in Bratislava into **Route 25** in this book. Take your pick from the impressive range of **international trains** serving Bratislava. You can travel directly to both Dresden and Berlin (ERT 60) or to Polish cities including Kraków, Warsaw (both ERT 99) and Wrocław (ERT 77). Bratislava is also the jumping-off point for journeys to the **Tatra Mountains** and eastern Slovakia (see trains to Poprad-Tatry and Košice in ERT 1180). Prague (ERT 1150) and Budapest (ERT 1175) are both just a short ride on regular Eurocity services.

Smaller cities in Slovakia are often exceptionally pleasant, and several are easily reached by train from the capital. Two we particularly like are the picturesque university town of **Trnava** and the genteel spa at **Piešt'any**, a place where relaxation has been refined into a high art. Both can easily be combined in a day trip from Bratislava (ERT 1180).

Route 36: Over the Bernina Pass

CITIES: ★ CULTURE: ★ HISTORY: ★★ SCENERY: ★★★
COUNTRIES COVERED: SWITZERLAND (CH), ITALY (IT)
JOURNEY TIME: 8 HRS 30 MINS | DISTANCE: 415 KM | MAP: WWW.EBRWEB.EU/MAP36

The high point of this journey, indeed its entire *raison d'être*, is the Bernina Railway which links the **Engadine** area of eastern Switzerland with the Valtellina region in **Lombardy**. The Bernina is in our view far and away the finest of the three north-south rail routes connecting Switzerland with Italy. Just for the record, the other two are through the Gotthard (ERT 550) and Simplon tunnels (ERT 590), each of them routes well woven into the rich tapestry of Alpine transport history. You can read more about the Simplon route in particular in our **Sidetracks** feature on p341.

Of these three main rail links across the Alps from **Switzerland to Italy**, the Bernina is the youngest. Unlike the Simplon and Gotthard routes, it has never echoed to the rumble of distinguished international expresses. It has from the outset been a rural railway carrying only local trains. The fact that it is of a different gauge — much narrower than the standard and thus better suited to a railway line with tight curves in challenging mountain terrain — has meant that long-distance trains linking Europe's great cities have never been able to use the Bernina route.

While the Gotthard and Simplon routes tunnel *through* the mountains, the **narrow-gauge Bernina Railway** (since 2008 included on the UNESCO World Heritage List) climbs high *over* a mountain pass at **Ospizio Bernina**, reaching an elevation of 2,253 metres. If you are heading from Basel or Zurich for Milan or elsewhere in northern Italy, the Bernina route means quite a detour, but it is extra time well spent. Route 36 is special at any time of year, but the Bernina stretch is really at its very best in deep mid-winter.

ITINERARY SUGGESTIONS

This journey can be done in a single day, but we think it deserves more. Why not think of staying **overnight at St Moritz**? The advantage of spreading the journey over two days is that you'll be able to make short breaks, perhaps just an hour or two, at interesting points along the way. With trains every hour or two along much of the route, it's easy to continue your journey on the next train. **Zernez** deserves just such a stop-off. On the Bernina Railway itself, we recommend a short stop at **Alp Grüm**, where the views are stunning. Purists may want to stop instead (or as well) at the highest station at **Ospizio Bernina**. At both these stations, public facilities (in each case a cosy restaurant with rooms for those wanting to stay overnight) are only open from mid-May to early November. At other times of the year, only alight if you have appropriate boots and warm clothing for harsh winter conditions.

Our experience is that the carriages on the **regular local trains** are more fun than the slick observation cars on the trains shown in ERT 545 as *Bernina Express*. And no supplement is payable to ride the slow trains routinely used by locals travelling between remote communities along the route. So opt for the slow train, throw open the window, take a deep breath of mountain air and enjoy the ride. It is pure magic.

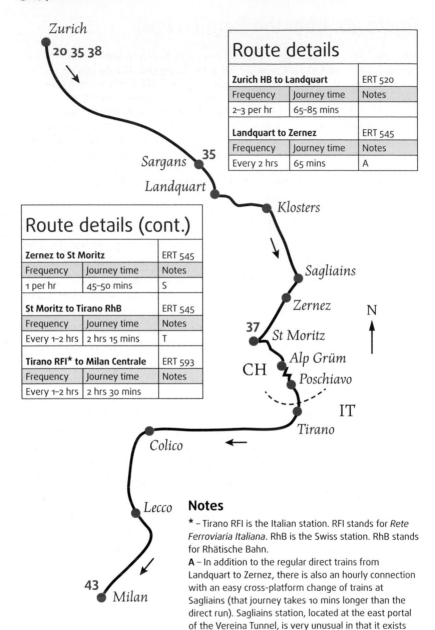

Route details

Zurich HB to Landquart		ERT 520
Frequency	Journey time	Notes
2–3 per hr	65–85 mins	
Landquart to Zernez		**ERT 545**
Frequency	Journey time	Notes
Every 2 hrs	65 mins	A

Route details (cont.)

Zernez to St Moritz		ERT 545
Frequency	Journey time	Notes
1 per hr	45–50 mins	S
St Moritz to Tirano RhB		**ERT 545**
Frequency	Journey time	Notes
Every 1–2 hrs	2 hrs 15 mins	T
Tirano RFI* to Milan Centrale		**ERT 593**
Frequency	Journey time	Notes
Every 1–2 hrs	2 hrs 30 mins	

Notes

* – Tirano RFI is the Italian station. RFI stands for *Rete Ferroviaria Italiana*. RhB is the Swiss station. RhB stands for *Rhätische Bahn*.

A – In addition to the regular direct trains from Landquart to Zernez, there is also an hourly connection with an easy cross-platform change of trains at Sagliains (that journey takes 10 mins longer than the direct run). Sagliains station, located at the east portal of the Vereina Tunnel, is very unusual in that it exists purely for the purpose of changing trains. There is no public access to or from the platform.

S – On many journeys a change of train is necessary at Samedan (which is just before St Moritz).

T – Note that there are no evening trains running through to Tirano. The last departure from St Moritz is usually before 17.00.

RAILWAYS TO THE ENGADINE

The Engadine is the name given to the Inn Valley area of eastern **Graubünden**. It takes its name from the Romansh name for the valley: Engiadina. The importance of the **Rhaetian Railway's network** in the economy and social life of this valley cannot be overemphasised. Prior to the coming of the railway, the canton of Graubünden was a Swiss paradox, a mountain fortress which was barely accessible from the rest of the country. The Inn Valley, accessible in winter only from Austrian territory, was a world unto itself. But the arrival of the **Albula Railway** (which is described, travelling north from St Moritz, in the next route in this book) in 1903, ended the isolation of the Inn Valley. The opening of the Vereina Tunnel in 1999 gave the Engadine a second year-round rail link to the Rhine Valley and thus on to the rest of Switzerland.

Through Graubünden

Our journey starts in **Zurich** (for more on the city, see p205), for the first hour running in parallel with **Route 35**. There is a short account of the stretch from Zurich to Sargans on p314. It is at **Sargans**, a stone's throw from the tiny Principality of Liechtenstein, that **Route 35** (to Vienna and Bratislava) and our current journey diverge, as we follow the River Rhine upstream towards the cathedral city of Chur. But, just short of Chur at **Landquart**, we change trains, swapping a main-line Swiss train for a **Rhaetian Railway** narrow-gauge one for the onward journey deep into the mountains of eastern Switzerland.

The red train climbs slowly up the **Prättigau Valley**, lush green pastures slowly giving way to rockier terrain. Just beyond the chic ski resort of Klosters, the line dives into the long Vereina Tunnel to reach the Inn Valley, which it then follows upstream to **Zernez**. If you are tempted to stop for an hour or two, Zernez is a very good choice. This pretty village lies at the heart of the Romansh-speaking area of Graubünden canton. It is the jumping-off point for excursions into Val Müstair, which we rate as one of the most beautiful of all Swiss valleys. The post bus for **Val Müstair** leaves from outside Zernez station. It continues on to Malles in Italy. Read more on border hopping by bus in this area in our **Sidetracks** feature on p348. From Zernez, the railway parallels the River Inn up to St Moritz.

St Moritz (suggested stopover)

Even with competition from the likes of Zermatt, Gstaad and Davos, St Moritz still pretty much leads the way as a **Swiss winter sports resort**, with a breathtaking location and an enviable sunshine record. It is the starting point for the famous *Glacier Express* rail journey (ERT 575), which features as the next route described in this book.

St Moritz divides into **Dorf** (village) on the hill, and **Bad** (spa) 2 km downhill around the lake. A long escalator leads up from the station to St Moritz Dorf. You'll find the main hotels, shops and museums in Dorf (including the Engadine Museum, offering an absorbing look at the furniture and house interiors of the area).

The centre for downhill skiing is **Corviglia** (2,486 m), but even if you're not skiing it's worth the 2-km funicular trip for the views and a glimpse of the 'beautiful people' at play. From there, take the cable car up to **Piz Nair** (3,057 m) for a panorama of the Upper Engadine. **Muzeum Susch** (www.muzeumsusch.ch; Thu, Fri, Sun 12.00–17.00; Sat 11.00–18.00) with its art exhibitions and experimental performances is only a rail trip away from St Moritz (50 mins, ERT 545). Located in the remnants of a mediaeval monastery, it opened its doors to the public in January 2019.

ARRIVAL, INFORMATION, ACCOMMODATION

≋ The station is close to the centre of town (St Moritz Dorf). 🛈 Tourist office: Via Maistra 12 (www.stmoritz.com).

🛏 Accommodation and food are generally expensive, but less so in St Moritz Bad than in St Moritz Dorf. For great views over the lake, try the **Waldhaus Am See**, Via Dimlej 6, ☎ 081 836 60 00 (www.waldhaus-am-see.ch). Located in St Moritz Bad, the **Hotel Piz**, Via dal Bagn 6, ☎ 081 832 11 11 (www.piz-stmoritz.ch) is a good, functional option. A comfortable and very central hotel in St Moritz Dorf is the **Hotel Eden**, Via Veglia 12, ☎ 081 830 81 00 (www.eden.swiss).

Over the Bernina Pass

You can board the Bernina Railway train in St Moritz, from where it's just ten minutes to **Pontresina**, a small town where creative types once came to relax long before St Moritz became famous (see box on p327).

The 55 kilometres of the Bernina railway from Pontresina to the Italian town of Tirano are almost all above ground. With gradients at over seven per cent, the railway leads passengers from Pontresina up into a high Alpine environment of icy glaciers and rocky moraines before plunging in a great series of loops down into the **Poschiavo Valley** which it then follows south to the Italian Valtellina.

Until the opening of the railway, only the most adventurous visitors to Pontresina contemplated the arduous excursion to **Alp Grüm**, which was commended by **Baedeker** for its restaurant and fine view of the Palü glacier. Now the railway transports tourists from Pontresina up to the front door of the restaurant at Alp Grüm in just forty minutes, and the view is every bit as magnificent as it was in Baedeker's day. The **Palü glacier** has receded a little, and Mr Baedeker might well be bemused by the signs in Japanese on the railway station platform, but otherwise it is much the same. A place for deep snow in winter with gentian, edelweiss and moss campion in summer.

This railway line offers a **kaleidoscope of scenery** from rocky gorges to carefully tended vineyards. The descent into Italy communicates a sense of entering the sunny south.

CHANGING TIMES IN PONTRESINA

Hans Christian Andersen stayed in Pontresina. So did Richard Wagner. Stefan Zweig was a regular, giving a wonderful account of hotel life in Pontresina in his novel *The Post Office Girl* – one of two Zweig books which influenced Wes Anderson's film *Grand Hotel Budapest*. **Mrs Gaskell** started writing *Wives and Daughters*, her gossipy tale of scandal and intrigue in an English country town, while holidaying – with all her daughters – in Pontresina. But Pontresina's star faded as the **literary crowd** shifted their affections elsewhere. A certain class of English traveller stayed loyal to Pontresina, but that class dwindled and eventually there was no one left to attend the English church there. So in 1974 it was demolished.

Pontresina has slipped out of fashion, but its fate is a nice reminder of how travel fads come and go. That said, the place still has a certain charm, and its setting in the shadow of the **Bernina Alps** is superb. If you are inclined to stay – it's a cheaper alternative to St Moritz – we can recommend the guest house right by the station, ☎ 081 838 80 00 (www.station-pontresina.ch).

In **Tirano**, the train runs through the streets. Traffic waits, not always patiently, as it moves smoothly past shops and houses, then on past the great pilgrimage church of the **Madonna di Tirano**, before coming to a halt at the Rhaetian Railway's own little station just beside the Italian station. If you feel it's time for a meal, then you can enjoy the down-to-earth simplicity of the **Ristorante Sale e Pepe** right by the station.

The Bernina trains terminate at Tirano. Walk over to the adjacent Italian railway station for onward services to Milan. The journey first follows the vineyard-clad **Adda Valley**, and then runs down the east side of **Lake Como** and Lake Lecco. Sit on the right for the best views. If your appetite for good scenery has not been entirely satiated by the Bernina Railway, then pause at **Colico**, at the north-east end of Lago di Como and continue by boat to Como (ERT 599). Even if you stick with the train, you'll still be in for a treat. This is a wonderful ride as the train follows the lakeshore. If you have time to stop, we suggest **Varenna-Esino** as the place to alight (all trains from Tirano stop at that station). From the station it is a seven-minute walk down to the village, following a path along the shoreline. You'll find that Varenna is picture-perfect, made all the more appealing by the coming and going of ferries serving other communities around the lake. It is worth taking a ride over to **Bellagio** and back; the ferry takes just 15 minutes each way.

Although a busy road and railway skirt Varenna, it is still possible to discern in the centre of the village something of the serenity so characteristic of the Lake Como region prior to the advent of major roads and railways.

You'll arrive in **Milan** at Centrale station (more on the city on p327). In Milan, you can connect onto **Route 43** in *Europe by Rail* which runs in one direction to Verona and Venice and in the other direction down to the Mediterranean at Genoa. For other direct connections by train from Milan see pp371–72.

Route 37: Following the Glacier Express

CITIES: ★ CULTURE: ★ HISTORY: ★ SCENERY: ★★★
COUNTRIES COVERED: SWITZERLAND (CH)
JOURNEY TIME: 8 HRS 15 MINS | DISTANCE: 290 KM | MAP: WWW.EBRWEB.EU/MAP37

The historical rise of mass tourism in Switzerland has changed our understanding of **mountain landscapes**. In the decades after the Napoleonic Wars, before the railways had extended their networks into remote valleys, travel through the Alps was arduous and slow. Representations of the mountains in Romantic literature and picturesque art (think Turner and Ruskin) gave travellers some inkling of what to expect. By the mid-19th century, the developing rail network widened possibilities and in 1863 **Thomas Cook** was offering a 16-day excursion through Switzerland which he billed as "fulfilling the wishes of a lifetime, in a pleasant duty never to be repeated."

A century and a half after Cook, with myriad **editions of Baedeker** in those intervening years, the *Glacier Express* is the epitome of the constructed tourist experience. Ruskin's descriptions of the Alps echo down through the generations: "Infinitely beyond all that we had ever thought or dreamed... lost Eden could not have been more beautiful to us." And the marketing men and women have moved in to give the affluent visitor to the **Swiss Alps** an experience which transcends even Cook and Ruskin. Here is a case of what the American historian Rudy Koshar described as externally directed tourism: "You go not where you want to go, but where the industry has decreed you shall go... Tourism requires that you see conventional things and that you see them in a conventional way."

Glaciers and brooding mountain valleys are Swiss staples and the conventional way of seeing them is through the panoramic windows of a train full of other tourists. Indeed, the *only* Swiss train trips sold by thousands of travel agents in North America are packages with a journey on the *Glacier Express* or the *Bernina Express* (this latter train features in the preceding route in this book).

All of which might lead you to wonder why we have Route 37 in this book at all. Until 2016, the *Glacier Express* route from **St Moritz to Zermatt** was not included in *Europe by Rail*. And that, we decided, was an oversight because it is a truly amazing rail journey. It runs through high mountain scenery from the **Engadine to the Valais**. It takes in valleys whose water drain down towards the Black Sea, and it touches the upper reaches of both the Rhine – which flows to the North Sea – and the Rhône, which runs eventually into the Mediterranean.

The important thing to remember about Route 37 is that it's not compulsory to take the tourist train which plies this route. Read more in our itinerary notes on the next page.

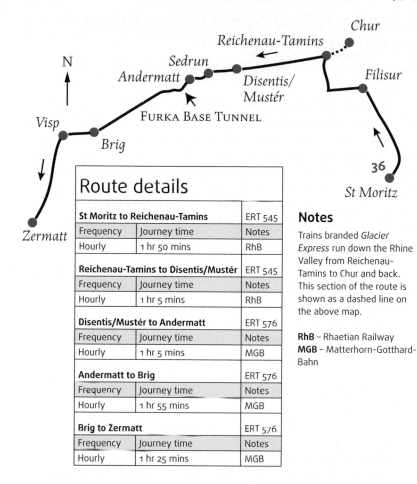

Route details

St Moritz to Reichenau-Tamins		ERT 545
Frequency	Journey time	Notes
Hourly	1 hr 50 mins	RhB

Reichenau-Tamins to Disentis/Mustér		ERT 545
Frequency	Journey time	Notes
Hourly	1 hr 5 mins	RhB

Disentis/Mustér to Andermatt		ERT 576
Frequency	Journey time	Notes
Hourly	1 hr 5 mins	MGB

Andermatt to Brig		ERT 576
Frequency	Journey time	Notes
Hourly	1 hr 55 mins	MGB

Brig to Zermatt		ERT 576
Frequency	Journey time	Notes
Hourly	1 hr 25 mins	MGB

Notes

Trains branded *Glacier Express* run down the Rhine Valley from Reichenau-Tamins to Chur and back. This section of the route is shown as a dashed line on the above map.

RhB – Rhaetian Railway
MGB – Matterhorn-Gotthard-Bahn

THOUGHTS ON ITINERARY

The train known as the *Glacier Express* runs year round bar for a seven-week break in the autumn. A supplementary fare is payable; this includes a reserved seat. The one-way fare varies from 175 Swiss francs (second class, low season) to 301 Swiss francs (first class, high season) (€160 to €276). In 2019, a new Excellence Class service was launched under the banner "the most sought-after seats in Switzerland". The 688 Swiss franc (€631) one-way fare includes champagne, a five-course lunch and pampered service.

The *Glacier Express* leaves St Moritz and Zermatt (at either end of the route) each morning and takes just over eight hours to cover the entire 290-kilometre journey. The number of *Glacier Express* trains in each direction increases to three per day in mid-summer (see ERT 575 for details). It's a packaged experience with a **rather cinematic quality**.

All that stacks up to an interesting day out, but **there is an alternative**. Why not just take the **regular local trains** which ply the entire *Glacier Express* route all year? There are hourly services along the full length of the route from St Moritz to Zermatt (see table above). You will need to change trains a number of times along the way but trains always connect perfectly – this is Switzerland after all, a country which has refined train connections into a high art. We find that the local trains have far more character than the

Glacier Express. And guess what? Unless you decide to stop off along the way, the journey from St Moritz to Zermatt relying on local trains will not take a minute longer than if you had opted for the *Glacier Express.*

If you use local trains as we suggest, your trains will be run by the **Rhaetian Railway** (RhB) from St Moritz to Disentis/Mustér. There RhB hands over the baton to the **Matterhorn-Gotthard-Bahn** (MGB) which runs the onward trains via Andermatt to Brig and Zermatt. RhB accepts both Interrail and Eurail passes. MGB has historically been rather sniffy about rail passes but happily changed its policy in 2017, so that holders of Interrail and Eurail passes can now travel for free on all MGB trains (except for the *Glacier Express* where a seat reservation fee is still payable by pass holders – as indeed by all other travellers).

Is it worth stopping off? Well, we think it really is possible to overdose on too much fine scenery, and the entire run from St Moritz to Zermatt takes in a vast number of mountains, gorges, meadows and glaciers. Why not break the journey and spend a night at **Andermatt**?

Profile of the route

This journey starts high and ends high. St Moritz, in Switzerland's Engadine region, lies at a breezy 1,775 metres above sea level. Zermatt is only slightly lower. But during the journey we'll dip down twice to about 650 metres, once into the **Rhine Valley** and then later into the Rhône Valley. Between the two, the railway climbs over the mighty **Oberalp Pass**, which marks the boundary of two Swiss cantons: Graubünden to the east (Grisons in French) and Uri to the west. The Oberalp Pass railway station at the summit is the highest point on our journey: 2,033 metres above sea level. The journey thus has a profile shaped like the letter W.

Highlights

On a route which is so full of scenic superlatives, we are not sure that a blow-by-blow account of the journey serves any great purpose. But it's surely useful to say something of the landscapes you'll encounter along the way.

Our journey starts in **St Moritz** (read more on this stylish mountain resort on p325), and initially follows the **Albula Railway** down towards the Rhine Valley. This mountain railway was added to UNESCO's World Heritage List in 2008 (along with the Bernina Railway on **Route 36**). It's a tremendous engineering and architectural achievement, and one which in its design and execution shows great sensitivity to the environment. As visitors, it's easy to forget that this, like other rail routes through the Alps, does not exist purely for the benefit of tourists. These are key links in the local transport infrastructure, all the more so in winter when roads may be blocked by snow. A museum by the station at **Bergün** tells the remarkable story of the Albula Railway (www.bahnmuseum-albula.ch; closed Mon).

If you are using local trains for the journey to Zermatt, the first place to change trains is at **Reichenau-Tamins** station, where an inconveniently

CONNECTIONS WITH THE *GLACIER EXPRESS*

The very nature of the *Glacier Express* route, running as it does from east to west across part of Switzerland, means that it intersects several north-south transport arteries along the way. The eastern end of the route in St Moritz is easily reached from either Zurich or Milan, the latter taking in the celebrated Bernina Railway along the way. The **Zurich – St Moritz – Milan** journey features as **Route 36** in this book.

From Reichenau-Tamins it is just a short ride down the Rhine Valley to nearby Chur where you can connect onto regular direct trains to Zurich and Basel (both ERT 520). From Andermatt, a mountain railway drops down steeply to Göschenen (ERT 576), just 14 minutes away, giving easy connections into trains on the **Gotthard route** (ERT 550a) running north to Lucerne and south to Locarno. This is not the new Gotthard Base Tunnel line, which opened in December 2016, but its predecessor.

In Brig, there are good connections north to Berne, Basel and Zurich (all in ERT 560) and south via the Simplon Tunnel to Milan (ERT 590). There is even a direct train from Brig via the Simplon to Venice (ERT 82). For more on the **Simplon route**, see our **Sidetracks** feature on p341.

The fast northbound trains from Brig all use the Lötschberg Base Tunnel which opened in 2007. Happily, the old **Lötschberg pass railway** was not abandoned and that makes a splendid route north via Kandersteg to Spiez, Berne and beyond (ERT 562). There are also connections in Brig or Visp onto the main-line trains down the Rhône Valley to Lausanne and Geneva (ERT 570). Zermatt is very much the end of the line. If you follow Route 37 to its very end, you'll have no choice but to return back down into the Rhône Valley, connecting in Visp or Brig through to your next destination.

positioned main road makes it difficult to reach the bank of the River Rhine which is just a few metres north of the railway station. From Reichenau-Tamins, sit on the right of the train bound for **Disentis/Mustér** for the best views of the Vorderrhein; it's not always pretty with scars of huge rockslides, many very ancient, on the north side of the valley.

Beyond Disentis, now on a MGB train, the line climbs steeply towards Oberalp Pass. Look out for the village of **Sedrun** which lies immediately above the north-south Gotthard Base Tunnel which opened to passenger traffic in June 2016. An ambitious plan to build a passenger station on the new link – 800 metres beneath Sedrun – had been shelved. The Swiss authorities even went so far as to give the station a name: Porta Alpina. Had the station been built, it would surely have transformed this remote mountain valley for ever.

The most **dramatic mountain scenery** is in the section of the journey between Sedrun and Andermatt. This sense of desolation in the winter is quite terrifying. Dropping down from the summit, the town of **Andermatt** makes a good overnight stop. It's a place which has moved dramatically upmarket in recent years – helped by substantial investments from the Middle East. The **Chedi Hotel** (which you cannot miss as you walk from the station into town) was the first manifestation of a revolution which has transformed Andermatt from a sleepy mountain village to a high-end resort. Take a look at the Chedi, Gotthardstr. 4, even if like us you couldn't possibly afford to stay there (www.thechediandermatt.com). Its 'Andermatt-meets-Arabia' design is captivating. There's a good choice of cheaper accommodation. We can recommend the River House, Gotthardstrasse 58, ☎ 041 887 00 25 (www.theriverhouse.ch).

Running west from Andermatt, the railway to Zermatt affords fleeting views of the glaciers away to the north before diving into the **Furka Base Tunnel**, at 15 kilometres by far the longest tunnel on the entire route. Emerging from the tunnel into the Rhône drainage basin it's downhill all the way to **Brig** (Brigue in French), an amiable small town dominated by the Italianate-style **Stockalper Castle**. It is worth wandering up Brig's main street, which is lined by merchants' houses, and taking a look at the arcaded courtyard of the castle. Kaspar Stockalper controlled the Simplon trade from his base in Brig. Today, the town remains an important transport hub (see the connections box on p331).

Beyond Brig, the valley scenery down to **Visp** is unexceptional, but there the line to Zermatt turns south and climbs steeply up into the mountains. It's a **dramatic finale** to a journey full of scenic wonder. Yet the final stretch is not without surreal touches, such as the vast car parks at **Täsch** where even the most determined motorists are forced to abandon their cars and take to the train.

Zermatt

No matter how chic your Mercedes, there's no way you'll be allowed to drive into Zermatt. The only way to Zermatt is by train. It's much to the credit of local planners that the town has not been completely wrecked by mass tourism – and the car-free atmosphere is one of many things which make Zermatt special. The **Pennine Alps** rise up steeply behind the town, from where on clear days there are superb views of the **Matterhorn** and the Dufourspitze. And you don't need an ice axe and crampons to really get up high. The **Gornergrat mountain railway** (ERT 578) climbs up from Zermatt to well over 3,000 metres above sea level.

ARRIVAL, INFORMATION, ACCOMMODATION

≈ The train station is just a short walk south along Bahnhofstr. into the centre of Zermatt.
🚹 Tourist office: Bahnhofplatz 5 (www.zermatt.ch).

🛏 There is no shortage of accommodation, but prices in Zermatt can be a challenge and it's best to book well ahead. Many of the hotels are closed for part of the year (usually in the quieter months in late spring and late autumn). A good and comfortable mid-range option is the **Hotel Alpenrose**, Oberdorfstr. 79, ☎ 027 966 40 40 (www.alpenrose-zermatt.ch), beyond the centre, a 20-min walk from the station. Or try the friendly, family-run **Bella Vista**, Riedweg 15, ☎ 027 966 28 10 (www.bellavista-zermatt.ch). The welcoming **Hotel Parnass**, Vispastr. 4, ☎ 027 967 11 79 (www.parnass-zermatt.ch), is another good, central option.

Route 38: Swiss lakes and mountains

CITIES: ★ CULTURE: ★★ HISTORY: ★ SCENERY: ★★★
COUNTRIES COVERED: SWITZERLAND (CH)
JOURNEY TIME: 7 HRS 30 MINS | DISTANCE: 338 KM | MAP: WWW.EBRWEB.EU/MAP38

In our opinion, this is one of the finest one-day train journeys in Switzerland, certainly on a par with the much-vaunted **Glacier Express** from St Moritz to Zermatt (the route of which is described in the preceding journey in this book). When **Thomas Cook** escorted his first tours to Switzerland, his itineraries focused on the territory traversed by this route. To English travellers in the Victorian period, Switzerland meant the Alps. This understanding of Switzerland was not peculiar to the English. The Alps are still as essential an element as ever of the Swiss psyche, even though more Swiss citizens now live in city apartment blocks than on farms in remote Alpine valleys. The myth of the *Dörfli* under the shadow of an alp is a very powerful image, and many Swiss who live in cities still assert that their hearts lie in a small village in the hills.

This route nicely explores the Switzerland of the imagination – a place full of **Alpine meadows**, cow bells and snow-capped peaks. With some of Europe's most efficient rail services running even into remote Alpine valleys, there is plenty of scope for really getting off the beaten track. We start in **Zurich**, heading south for a brief but tantalising encounter with Lake Lucerne, before striking south-west into one of the most serenely beautiful parts of the Alps. You'll see a lot of the **Bernese Oberland** on this route.

Our favourite section is the steep drop down to Montreux on the shores of Lake Geneva. West from Montreux we cruise through the **Lavaux Vineyards** to reach Lausanne, before embarking on the final leg along the lakeshore to Geneva.

THOUGHTS ON AN ITINERARY

We have twice in recent years made this journey from end to end without an overnight stop – once in each direction. It's a long ride, seven to eight hours, but it's **utterly captivating**. If you want to split the journey into two, then Interlaken is a good place to stop. With a

ALL A QUESTION OF WIDTH

There is an oddity about this journey which may appeal to rail buffs but may be judged a modest inconvenience by others. You will have to change trains along the way.

There are **two narrow-gauge sections** of line: 74 kilometres from Lucerne to Interlaken Ost and a further stretch of 62 kilometres from Zweisimmen via Gstaad to Montreux. The rail operators which ply different sections of Route 38 are evaluating new rolling stock with wheels that slip ingeniously from standard-gauge to narrow-gauge track and back again – a piece of engineering magic which can be seen in action from December 2020 when, if all goes to plan, a through service will be introduced from **Interlaken to Montreux**, obviating the need to change trains at Zweisimmen.

two-night stop in Interlaken you might use the free day to travel to the **Jungfraujoch** (see box on p336). That line is pictured on the front cover of this book. Towards the end of Route 38, you might think of spending a night in Lausanne, well worth exploring in its own right, but also a perfect jumping-off point for visiting the Lavaux Vineyard region or for **excursions by boat** on Lake Geneva (ERT 506).

Journeys on the Lucerne – Interlaken – Montreux axis, the central portion of Route 38, are now being marketed under the banal name *GoldenPass Line* (www.goldenpassline.ch). We suspect that there might be another Glacier-Express-style packaged tourist experience in the making here. So take this journey soon, before the crowds arrive.

On the first part of the run out of **Zurich** (see p205) the train speeds under the balconies of multicoloured apartment blocks, before plunging into a long tunnel. There are stops in lakeside **Thalwil** and affluent **Zug** before, less than an hour after leaving Zurich, the train arrives at Lucerne for the first of several changes of train along the route.

Lucerne straddles the River Reuss, itself crossed by quaintly roofed mediaeval footbridges, at the end of Lake Lucerne. Characteristic of Old Lucerne are its many elaborately painted houses, its cobbled squares, its fountains, its Renaissance town hall by the Kornmarkt, and the two bridges over the Reuss. The city's mascot, the **Löwendenkmal** (Lion Memorial), Löwenstr., is a massive but movingly portrayed dying lion carved in the cliff-side, commemorating the Swiss Guards massacred at the Tuileries in Paris during the French Revolution. Nearby is the **Gletschergarten** (Glacier Garden), Denkmalstr. 4, a bed of smooth rocks pitted with holes, created by glacial erosion. There's an ingenious mirror-maze here too.

Anyone with an interest in transport in all its guises and vintages should make for the **Verkehrshaus** (Swiss Transport Museum), Lidostr. 5 (www.verkehrshaus.ch), 2 km east of town, reached by a pleasant lakeside walk (or 🚌 6/8/24); it's one of Europe's leading museums on the theme, with exhibits covering locos, vintage cycles, space rockets and more, plus an IMAX movie theatre, a 360-degree cinema with a huge, almost vertigo-inducing screen.

The Zentralbahn

The **narrow-gauge railway** from Lucerne to Interlaken is called the Zentralbahn (literally Central Railway) or sometimes the **Brünig Railway**, taking

that name from the line's summit. The old surface line through Lucerne's suburbs was rerouted underground in 2012. Soon we are above ground again, with the hills slowly closing in. After skirting the **Sarnersee**, the railway climbs steeply to Brünig Pass, where the summit station is called **Brünig-Hasliberg**.

This is an extraordinary spot, not so much for the scenery as for the huge bric-a-brac shop now housed in the station buildings. Austrian cook Josef Hechenberger ('Brünig Sepp') has run the place for twenty years, and when we stopped off at Brünig in 2011, Hechenberger's stock included a ship's bell, an artificial leg, a life-size model of Jesus Christ with a penguin,

Route details

Zurich to Lucerne — ERT 555
Frequency	Journey time	Notes
2 per hr	45–50 mins	

Lucerne to Meiringen — ERT 561
Frequency	Journey time	Notes
Hourly	70 mins	

Meiringen to Interlaken Ost — ERT 561
Frequency	Journey time	Notes
2 per hr	35 mins	

Interlaken Ost to Spiez — ERT 560
Frequency	Journey time	Notes
2–3 per hr	20 mins	

Spiez to Zweisimmen — ERT 563
Frequency	Journey time	Notes
1–2 per hr	35–45 mins	

Zweisimmen to Montreux — ERT 566
Frequency	Journey time	Notes
Hourly	1 hr 50 mins	

Route details (cont.)

Montreux to Lausanne — ERT 570
Frequency	Journey time	Notes
4–5 per hr	20–30 mins	

Lausanne to Geneva — ERT 570
Frequency	Journey time	Notes
4–5 per hr	35–45 mins	

20 35 36
Zurich
Thalwil
Zug
Lucerne
N
Brünig-Hasliberg
Interlaken — Meiringen

and a fabulous collection of books ranging from Karl May to Karl Marx (plus a very handsome edition of *Sexual Splendours of the Erotic East*). This delicious emporium is open every day of the year.

From Brünig, it's downhill all the way to **Meiringen**, a town that claims to be the birthplace of meringue (the confection rather than the Caribbean musical genre). From Meiringen, opt for a seat on the left for lovely lake views on the run west, skirting the north shore of the **Brienzersee**, to Interlaken.

Interlaken (suggested stopover)

This **lively resort**, strategically placed between two lakes, boomed in the 19th century when it became popular with British visitors as a base for exploring the mountains, and fanciful hotels sprang up along the **Höheweg**, the town's principal avenue (which links the two stations). It's still virtually unrivalled in the country as a centre for scenic excursions.

You don't need transport for getting around town, but hiring a bike to explore the adjacent lakeshores can be fun. From the Höheweg a wonderful, uninterrupted view extends across the undeveloped meadow where the original 12th-century monastic site of the town once stood, to **Jungfrau** (4,158 m) and other peaks looming beyond – especially magnificent in the later afternoon Alpenglow.

One of the period pieces in town is the distinctive 19th-century **Kursaal** (Casino), which in addition to gambling stages concerts and folklore evenings (www.casinosswitzerland.com). Across the River Aare is the old part of town known as Unterseen, with the oldest buildings

---

TO EUROPE'S HIGHEST STATION

A **popular excursion from Interlaken** is the journey to **Jungfraujoch**, the highest railway station in Europe at 3,454 m. Services (ERT 564) leave from Interlaken Ost at least hourly, and two changes of train are usually necessary: first in either Lauterbrunnen or Grindelwald and then always in **Kleine Scheidegg**. The earlier you start the better, to increase the chance of clear views. Dedicate a whole day to the trip, if the weather warrants it, as stops can be made en route.

This trip is undeniably breathtaking, but also very expensive (210.80 CHF return, passes not valid), although you can save around 30% by splashing out on a *Good Morning Ticket* (valid only on 08.00 or 08.30 train from Kleine Scheidegg from May to October – and you must start your descent from the Jungfraujoch by 13.00). On a good day, you'll see the best of Switzerland on this route. The little **rack-and-pinion railway** then goes into the face of the Eiger, emerging from the long tunnel at the summit. If you are put off by the high fares, consider at least travelling as far as Kleine Scheidegg, much more modestly priced at 82.80 CHF return, but with no discounts for early risers. This little community, dominated by the North Face of the **Eiger**, is a great place for mountain walks (including many easy strolls amid dramatic scenery).

in the region. Cross the bridge and walk along the river to Obere Gasse, with its 17th-century **town hall and palace**, 14th-century church and the **Tourismuseum**. The latter charts the rise of Interlaken's tourist industry (www.tourismuseum.com; open May–Oct, Wed–Sun).

ARRIVAL, INFORMATION, ACCOMMODATION

≋ Ostbahnhof at the western end of Höheweg, a 10-min walk from the centre. Westbahnhof is central. The two stations are 15 mins apart on foot, 4 mins by rail. It is the Ostbahnhof that connects with the railway to Jungfraujoch. From Berne, Westbahnhof is the first stop and the journey, by hourly trains, averages 50 mins. 🛈 Tourist office: Marktgasse 1 (www.interlaken.ch).

▶ There's no shortage of hotels, many catering largely for tour operators, but private rooms can be better value. A reasonably priced and comfortable hotel is **Arnold's Bed & Breakfast**, Parkstr. 3, ☎ 033 823 64 21 (www.arnolds.ch). Or try the cozy **Sunny Days Bed & Breakfast**, Helvetiastr. 29, ☎ 077 456 23 38 (www.sunnydays.ch), in Unterseen. More upmarket, in a great location between the two stations on the far side of the River Aare is the **Aparthotel Goldey**, Obere Goldey 85, ☎ 079 385 77 86 (www.goldey.ch).

To Spiez and beyond

Our train runs west from Interlaken to **Spiez** with fine views over the Thunersee en route (sit on the right). Crossing the main Brig to Berne railway at Spiez, the railway then climbs the **Simmen Valley**.

At **Zweisimmen** travellers change onto a narrow-gauge train. Hills roll into more hills and the train traverses several ridges, passing the resort town of Gstaad, before a spectacular descent down to Montreux on the shores of Lake Geneva. Stylish **Gstaad** is a pleasant spot to pause for a couple of hours. For an overnight stay here, the small, family-owned Hotel Restaurant Alphorn, Gsteigstrasse 51, ☎ 033 748 45 45 (www.alphorn-gstaad.ch), is a good option.

Montreux is the best-preserved of the Lake Geneva resorts and blessed with a mild climate, with palm trees, magnolias and cypresses along its long waterfront promenade – a lovely place for strolling. Smart hotels make the most of the views, while the rest of the town rises in tiers up the hillside. The effect is slightly spoiled by a garish casino.

Our route west from Montreux skirts Switzerland's largest lake for much of the 85-km journey to Geneva. The best of the scenery is between Vevey and Lausanne where the railway skirts the **Lavaux Vineyard Terraces**, affording good views of a cultural landscape that dates back to mediaeval times (read more in our box 'Train des Vignes'). The Lavaux Vineyard is included on UNESCO's World Heritage List.

There are some lovely set-piece villages which are delightful places to stop. Our favourite on the main lakeshore railway is **Saint-Saphorin**, the first stop west of Vevey. The place is served only by hourly local trains (service S2).

Lausanne (suggested stopover)

A city of two moods, half Alpine and half Riviera, Lausanne is perched on the **hills above Lake Geneva**. Some of the best views of this university city are from the cathedral high above the Old Town. The steepness of the place is part of its appeal, and if you don't fancy the trudge up from the lakeshore suburb of Ouchy, with its grand hotels and large park, up to the Old Town, there's a **useful metro** linking the top, middle and lakeshore districts of Lausanne. The partly pedestrianised **Old Town** is small enough to be explored on foot.

The upper metro terminal (Flon) is located just south of the main area of interest and dominated by the 15th-century steeple of the Église St-François (St Francis' Church). The **Cathédrale de Notre-Dame**, a 10-min walk up into the town, was consecrated in 1275. Italian, Flemish and French craftsmen all had a hand in its construction, and it is accepted as a perfect example of Gothic architecture. The night watch is still called from the steeple every hour from 22.00 to 02.00.

Escaliers du marché, a wooden-roofed mediaeval staircase, links the cathedral square to Pl. de la Palud, an ancient square surrounded by old houses. West of the cathedral, the Palais de Rumine, Pl. de la Riponne, was built by a Russian family at the turn of the last century. It now houses a number of museums, including the cantonal museum of fine art. Take a 10-min walk north-west (or 🚌 2/3/21) to the **Collection de l'Art Brut**, av. des Bergières 11 (www.artbrut.ch), housed in the Château de Beaulieu (closed Mon except July–Aug). This compelling post-war gallery was founded by a local collector, who sought the works of anyone who was not a trained or formal painter, from amateur dabblers to the criminally insane.

The **quai de Belgique** is a shady, flower-lined, waterside promenade, looking towards the Savoy Alps. The 13th-century keep of Château d'Ouchy is now a hotel. Baron Pierre de Coubertin, founder of the modern Olympics

TRAIN DES VIGNES

The journey from **Vevey to Lausanne** along the lakeshore is all too brief. Even the stopping trains take only 20 minutes. For much better views of the Lavaux area, take the *Train des Vignes* (service S7) which runs slightly higher up the hillside and cuts through the middle of the vineyards. This line is not shown in the ERT, but the *Train des Vignes* runs hourly from Vevey to **Puidoux**, where there's an easy connection onto the S4, S5 or S9 which drop back down through Grandvaux to Lausanne.

For something really special consider an overnight stay at the **Auberge de la Gare** which is right by the railway station at **Grandvaux** (just one stop along the line from Puidoux). It's a place to try the delicate fillets of perch which are a Lake Geneva speciality and local Lavaux region wines. Check out the chasselas (white) and pinot noir (red). With a great view over the railway, it is also a sure hit with train spotters (☎ 021 799 26 86; www.aubergegrandvaux.ch).

in 1915, chose Lausanne as the headquarters of the International Olympic Committee. The **Musée Olympique**, quai d'Ouchy 1, is a large modern complex, cleverly designed to retain the natural beauty of its surrounding park (www.olympic.org). Boats can be hired near the 'cruise' pier.

ARRIVAL, INFORMATION, ACCOMMODATION

Between the centre and Ouchy, connected by metro. Left luggage facilities and bike rental. **i** Tourist office: in the main hall of the railway station (www.lausanne-tourisme. ch). Close to the railway station and within walking distance of the centre, the **Agora Swiss Night**, Av. du Rond-Point 9, ☎ 021 555 59 55 (www.byfassbind.com), is a good option. Or try the **Hotel Élite**, Av. Sainte-Luce 1, ☎ 021 320 23 61 (www.elite-lausanne.ch), just north of the station. Newly refurbished in 2015 and in a quiet location in the Old Town, just a few minutes' walk from the Flon metro station is the boutique **Hotel des Voyageurs**, r. Grand-St-Jean 19, ☎ 021 319 91 11 (www.voyageurs.ch).

CONNECTIONS FROM LAUSANNE

In Lausanne, you can connect onto **Route 19** in this book, following it back through France to the Low Countries. There are fast trains north from Lausanne to Berne and Zurich (ERT 505). Or follow the lakeshore railway west to Geneva (ERT 505). **Compagnie Générale de Navigation sur le lac Léman** (CGN), av. de Rhodanie 17, ☎ 0900 92 92 92 (www.cgn.ch), operate ferries (ERT 506) from Ouchy to Geneva, Montreux and Évian-les-Bains (in France on the south shore of the lake).

The final leg of our journey from Zurich follows the north **shore of Lake Geneva** (Lac Léman) all the way to Geneva itself. Sit on the left for the best views of the lake.

Geneva (Genève, Genf)

Geneva is a cosmopolitan, comfortably prosperous city, with promenades and parks beautifying the shores of Lake Geneva. The River Rhône splits the city into two distinct sections, with the international area on the **Rive Droite** (right bank, to the north) and the compact Old Town on the **Rive Gauche** (left bank, to the south).

On Rive Droite (🚌 5/8/15/F/Z) is Pl. des Nations, near which most of the international organisations are grouped. The **Musée International de la Croix-Rouge et du Croissant-Rouge**, av. de la Paix 17 (www.redcrossmuseum.ch; closed Mon), is a stern building with high-tech exhibits tracing the history of the Red Cross and its Islamic offshoot, the Red Crescent. Profoundly moving, it covers natural disasters and man's inhumanity to man. Close by, the **Palais des Nations**, av. de la Paix 14, is home to the European headquarters of the United Nations, which replaced the League of Nations in 1945; there are guided tours. Between here and the lake is the lovely **Jardin Botanique**, a perfect place for a quiet stroll (once you're away from the main road) and featuring a rock garden, a deer and llama park and an aviary.

On Rive Gauche, south of the centre, the **Jardin Anglais**, on the waterfront, is famous for its Horloge Fleurie (floral clock), while the city's trademark, the 140-m high fountain (**Jet d'Eau**), spouts from a nearby pier.

At the heart of the Old Town is the lively **Place du Bourg-de-Four**, Geneva's oldest square. Take rue de l'Hôtel de Ville to the 16th-century Hôtel de Ville (town hall), where the first Geneva Convention was signed in 1864. Adjacent is the former arsenal and the 12th-century **Maison Tavel**, Geneva's oldest house and now an evocative museum, with several period rooms and exhibits covering the 14th–19th centuries.

Calvin preached in the **Cathédrale de St-Pierre** and his chair has been saved for posterity. The north tower, reached by a 157-step spiral staircase, offers a great view of the Old Town. Beneath the cathedral is the *Site Archéologique*, where catwalks allow you to see the result of extensive excavations, including among others a 4th-century baptistery and a 5th-century mosaic floor.

If you come to Geneva with your family, head for **Exploracentre** (www. exploracentre.ch), a venue for children aged five and above, opened in October 2018, which promises a fun way to discover science.

ARRIVAL, INFORMATION, ACCOMMODATION

≋ Gare de Cornavin is the main station, a 10-min walk north of the centre (🚎 5/8/9). Gare Genève Eaux-Vives, south-east of the lake, is the terminal for SNCF trains from Annecy and St Gervais (30-min walk from Cornavin station or 🚎 9 & 12 via Pl. des Eaux-Vives). ✈ The airport has its own station (Genève Aéroport), with frequent trains into central Geneva taking 6 mins; services continue to all major cities in Switzerland. ❚ Tourist office: r. du Mont-Blanc 18 (www.geneve.com). When staying in a hotel, campsite or youth hostel in Geneva, you get free use of local public transport (transport info at www.unireso.com).

⊨ Most hotels are expensive, but there are plenty of hostels and private rooms. During summer, the **CAR** (Coordination Accueil Renseignement à Genève), located in a trailer in the pedestrian area opposite the station, offers accommodation booking and other advice to young people. A simple but comfortable option in the Old Town close to the r. de Rive is the **Bel Espérance**, r. de la Vallée 1, ☎ 022 818 37 37 (www.hotel-bel-esperance.ch). A bit more upmarket is the welcoming boutique hotel **La Cour des Augustins**, r. Jean-Violette 15, ☎ 022 322 21 00 (www.lacourdesaugustins.com). Well regarded and conveniently located close to the railway station is the **Kipling**, r. de la Navigation 27, ☎ 022 544 40 40 (www.hotelkiplinggeneva.com).

✗ Capitalising on the proximity to France, Geneva claims to be the culinary centre of Switzerland. The majority of places cater for the international business market. Look for reasonably priced restaurants on the r. de Lausanne (turn left out of Gare de Cornavin) and around place du Cirque (blvd Georges-Favon). A great place for tapas and mezzes is the very relaxed **Cottage Café** by the Brunswick Monument (www.cottagecafe.ch).

CONNECTIONS FROM GENEVA

Geneva is the starting point for **Route 12** in this book, which leads across France to Spain. Frequent trains cross the border to France including TGV services direct to Paris (ERT 341), Lyon (ERT 346) and Marseille (ERT 350). There are also very good connections with regional trains running south from Geneva into the French Alps, with direct trains to Aix-les-Bains and Chambéry (ERT 364).

SIDETRACKS: THROUGH THE SIMPLON

Roman Catholic bishops do not normally incline to subterranean exploits. But on a spring Sunday morning in 1905, Bishop Jules-Maurice Abbet skipped his normal duties at the **cathedral in Sion** in Switzerland's Valais canton. Instead of celebrating Holy Mass at his cathedral he travelled deep into the bowels of the Lepontine Alps to bless the **new Simplon rail tunnel**. The Bishop of Sion embraced an Italian bishop deep below Mount Leone at the point where the tunnel crosses the Swiss-Italian border.

A small band played the *Marcia Reale* and the *Cantique Suisse* – so appealing to the national sentiments of all present. Bishop Abbet dowsed the tunnel with **holy water** and said nice things about technological progress – perhaps wondering if the new rail tunnel would mean redundancy for the Augustinian canons who offered shelter and succour at the hospice on the difficult carriage road which climbs over the Simplon Pass.

The first trains did not run through the Simplon Tunnel until a year after Bishop Abbet's subterranean excursion. The train service was inaugurated to coincide with the start of the **Milan EXPO** in late April 1906. In those days, it was expected that each new World Fair (or EXPO) would celebrate a particular technological achievement: examples included the Eiffel Tower at the Paris *exposition* in 1889 and the motor car at the Brussels fair in 1897.

The 1906 EXPO focused fair and square on transport and the showpiece achievement associated with the Milan fair was the Simplon Tunnel – when it opened it was the longest railway tunnel in the world. It kept that record for 76 years. The **official medallion** of the 1906 EXPO showed the Italian portal to the tunnel near Iselle. Promotional posters urged Parisians to take the train to the Milan exhibition

The Simplon route from **Paris to Milan** was faster than the Mont Cenis route. The latter relied on the Fréjus Tunnel which had opened 35 years earlier. Travellers to the 1906 Milan EXPO could leave Paris on a *train de luxe* just after eight in the evening, and by breakfast time the following morning their train was cruising gently through the towns of the Valais: Sion, Visp and **Brig**. The latter was the last station in Switzerland prior to the Simplon Tunnel. Departure from Brig was at 08.40, giving an arrival in Milan just after midday – a total journey time from Paris of slightly over 16 hours.

The **Thello overnight service** from Paris to Venice (see ERT 44) still uses the Simplon route to Italy – though, as the train now slips through the Simplon Tunnel in the wee small hours, most of those on board are surely quite unaware that they have slept through a medley of Swiss cantons. The Simplon route remains today one of the trunk rail routes **through the Alps**. It is well used by the direct Eurocity services from Geneva to Milan and Venice (ERT 82) as well as by car trains which ferry motorists from Brig through the tunnel into Italy. For a real engagement with Alpine landscapes, it's not our top choice – the Bernina Railway described in **Route 36** gets that prize. But the Simplon is a fast route south, and gives a magical introduction to northern Italy as the train skirts the western shore of **Lago Maggiore**.

Route 39:
Across the Alps: Bavaria to northern Italy

CITIES: ★★ CULTURE: ★ HISTORY: ★ SCENERY: ★★
COUNTRIES COVERED: GERMANY (DE), AUSTRIA (AT), ITALY (IT)
JOURNEY TIME: 6 HRS 20 MINS | DISTANCE: 434 KM | MAP: WWW.EBRWEB.EU/MAP39

This route is a very useful fast hop south **over the Alps** from southern Germany to Italian sunshine. But it is also worth doing in its own right for Route 39 packs in an astonishing variety of scenery. **Munich and Verona** could hardly be more different and each city deserves a few days of exploration. Along this route, the Alps change in character almost from one valley to the next.

ROUTE OPTIONS

Innsbruck makes a marvellous overnight stop along the way (where there is a connection with **Route 35**). Should you wish to extend this journey into a longer trip, then Garmisch, Mittenwald and Bolzano all commend themselves as good places to stop off. If you have had many city stays during your explorations of Europe by rail then Mittenwald, with its homely small-town feel, is the perfect antidote to big city blues.

There are direct Eurocity trains every two hours from Munich to Verona (ERT 70), but it's worth noting that these services take a completely different route from Munich to Innsbruck than suggested here in Route 39. They loop well east of the **Karwendel Alps** and then approach Innsbruck via the *Unterinntalbahn* (Lower Inn Valley Railway). This route, which gains Austrian territory at Kufstein is not a patch on the journey described below, which is shorter in distance but takes longer than the route via Kufstein.

Beyond Innsbruck, there is no choice of route to Verona, so the Eurocity service is a fast option for the journey over the **Brenner Pass** into northern Italy – though the slow trains which ply the same route are more of an adventure.

Through Upper Bavaria

The journey from **Munich** (p228) to the Austrian border runs entirely through a part of Bavaria known as Oberbayern (Upper Bavaria). The ride south is dominated by the approaching Alps, but don't focus merely on the mountains in the distance.

There are glimpses of lakes, baroque churches, neat farmsteads and half-timbered houses – the latter invariably decorated with the wall murals which are so typical of this region. This local form of vernacular art is called **Lüftlmalerei**; it celebrates religious and moral themes, and often depicts local crafts and agricultural practices. It speaks volumes about a community and its relationship with the land. Critics note that it is also deeply conservative and to non-Catholics even possibly oppressive. Make what you will of this local take on graffiti.

Before long, the train is running up the Loisach Valley, the mountains closing in on either side as you approach **Garmisch-Partenkirchen**. Once

Route details

Munich Hbf to Garmisch-Partenkirchen		ERT 895
Frequency	Journey time	Notes
Hourly	75–85 mins	M

Garmisch-Partenkirchen to Mittenwald		ERT 895
Frequency	Journey time	Notes
Hourly	20–25 mins	

Mittenwald to Innsbruck Hbf		ERT 895
Frequency	Journey time	Notes
Every 1–2 hrs	60–70 mins	S

Innsbruck Hbf to Bolzano		ERT 595
Frequency	Journey time	Notes
Every 1–2 hrs	2 hrs – 2 hrs 10 mins	T

Bolzano to Verona Porta Nuova		ERT 595
Frequency	Journey time	Notes
Hourly	1 hr 20 mins to 1 hr 50 mins	

Notes

M – Most trains from Munich to Garmisch depart from platforms 27 to 36 at Munich Hauptbahnhof. Note that these platforms are a five-minute walk from the main station concourse.

S – On some journeys between Mittenwald and Innsbruck, a change of train may be necessary at either Scharnitz or Seefeld in Tirol.

T – Some journeys between Innsbruck and Bolzano require a change of train at Brenner/ Brennero (on the Austrian-Italian border).

two quiet Bavarian villages at the foot of the 2,962-m Zugspitze, Germany's highest mountain, Garmisch and Partenkirchen were officially united to host the 1936 **Winter Olympics**. Though now separated only by the railway line, they retain individual personalities. Partenkirchen is more modern and upmarket while Garmisch has much more of a traditional Bavarian character – the most appealingly rustic part is around Frühlingstraße.

Garmisch is Germany's most popular ski resort, with downhill and cross-country skiing on offer. The **Bayerische Zugspitzbahn** rack railway leaves from its own dedicated station just by the main railway station, with the journey to the summit of the Zugspitze taking 75 minutes. On the way, the train stops at **Eibsee**, an idyllic mountain lake, where you can transfer onto the Eibsee cable car (often crowded) to reach the summit much quicker than remaining on the train.

If summit bagging is not your thing, there are good walks around Eibsee. The seven-kilometre lake circuit is an undemanding but beautiful stroll on an easy path.

CONNECTIONS FROM GARMISCH

From Garmisch-Partenkirchen, you can cut off to the west on a **beautiful branch railway** which runs through Austrian territory en route to the **Allgäu** region of southern Germany. It is a two-and-a-half hour journey from Garmisch to Kempten, with a change of train at the Austrian town of Reutte (ERT 888). From Kempten there are fast trains back to Munich (ERT 935), or you can continue west to Lindau (ERT 935) on the shores of Lake Constance.

The Innsbruck-bound railway heads east from Garmisch, cresting a gentle col and dropping down into the Isar Valley. Close to the Austrian border, **Mittenwald** is perhaps the most attractive town in the German Alps, with an abundance of character in its gabled, whitewashed houses, hung with green shutters and sporting creaky wooden balconies.

The town has some of the most elaborate Lüftlmalerei anywhere in Oberbayern, but Mittenwald's main claim to fame is in its violins. **Matthias Klotz** (1653–1743), a pupil of the great Amati, began Mittenwald's tradition of high-quality violin making that continues to this day. If you are tempted to stop overnight you might try the Hotel Alpenrose, Obermarkt 1, ☎ 088 23 92 700 (www.hotel-alpenrose-mittenwald.de) right in the centre.

The Tyrol

The Tyrol (Tirol in German) reveals a medley of influences which mark it out as being palpably different from the rest of Austria. It was an important **Habsburg** *Kronland* (crown land) but the area has also been variously under Bavarian and Italian control.

Our journey beyond Mittenwald cuts through a beautiful part of the Austrian Tyrol, continuing over the Brenner Pass into the region known as

South Tyrol, a predominantly **German-speaking region** which was ceded to Italy under the terms of the Treaty of Saint-Germain-en-Laye in 1919. Frontiers are fragile in this part of Europe, and political authority waxes and wanes. The historical development of communities along this route (such as Mittenwald, Innsbruck, Bolzano) has been governed not by distant emperors or kings, but by trade. This has for centuries been one of the most important **trading routes** through the Alps.

Innsbruck (suggested stopover)

The 800-year-old Tyrolean capital on the River Inn is a bustling, amiable Austrian city overlooked by the **Karwendel Mountains** to the north and the Patscherkofel Mountains to the south – making the town an excellent base for walks and other activities in the Alps.

The **Hungerburgbahn** cog railway, which ascends from the Alpenzoo on the edge of the city on to the Hungerburg plateau – a superb place for walks and views – opened in 2007, following the earlier rebuilding of the **Nordkettenbahnen**, which take visitors from the Congress Centre up onto the Hafelekar by cable car (more on www.nordkette.com/en).

Innsbruck's Altstadt (Old Town) is dotted with 15th- and 16th-century buildings, many with elaborate stucco decorations and traditional convex windows to catch extra light on the narrow streets. Its most famous sight is the 15th-century **Goldenes Dachl**, Herzog-Friedrich-Str. 15 (www.goldenes-dachl.at), a roof of 2,657 gilded copper tiles covering a balcony, which Emperor Maximilian I (the subject of an exhibition inside) added in 1500 to the Neuhof, the residence of the Tyrolean princes. The **Stadtturm** (city tower) opposite the balcony offers views across the rooftops to the mountains. Nearby is the Dom zu St Jakob, a striking baroque cathedral.

Near the Hofgarten (court gardens), the revamped **Tiroler Volkskunst Museum** (www.tiroler-landesmuseum.at) concentrates on Tyrolean culture, displaying traditional costumes and wood-panelled rooms. The Tiroler Ferdinandeum, Museumstr. 15 (closed Mon), is more diverse, with beautiful stained glass, mediaeval altars and works by Cranach and Rembrandt.

ARRIVAL, INFORMATION, ACCOMMODATION

≥ Innsbruck Hauptbahnhof (Hbf) is about a 10-min walk south-east of the city centre.
➤ Innsbruck Airport (www.innsbruck-airport.com), 4 km west of the city centre (🚌 F from the station).
🛈 Tourist office: Burggraben 3, on the edge of the Altstadt (www.innsbruck.info). 24 hr ticket (also for families) for use on trams and buses (www.ivb.at).
🛏 Right in the Old Town, the characterful, family-run **Hotel Weisses Kreuz**, Herzog-Friedrich-Straße 31, ☎ 0512 594 79 (www.weisseskreuz.at), is offering something for every budget. Apparently it is where Mozart stayed when his family visited Innsbruck in 1769. The stylish **Hotel Maximilian**, on the edge of the Old Town at Marktgraben 7–9, ☎ 0512 599 670 (www.hotel-maximilian.com), is a good up-market choice. Right in the

Old Town, the **Hotel Goldener Adler**, Herzog-Friedrich-Strasse 6, ☎ 0512 57 11 110 (www. goldeneradler.com), offers comfortable rooms in a historic building. ✖ The Altstadt area is generally expensive. **Café-Konditorei Munding**, Kiebachgasse 16 (www.munding.at), is the oldest Tyrolean café and pastry-shop, and serves fabulous cakes.

INNSBRUCK CONNECTIONS

Our journey crosses **Route 35** in Innsbruck, which you can follow east through Salzburg to Vienna, or west through Liechtenstein to Switzerland. The **Railjet** services on the important Alpine east-west axis (Zurich-Innsbruck-Salzburg-Vienna) are shown in ERT 86.

As a major rail hub, Innsbruck has a tempting range of connections, the most exotic of which is a train every Sunday evening direct to Warsaw, Minsk and Moscow (ERT 25). There are direct **Nightjet** sleeper services leaving every evening for Hannover, Hamburg, Koblenz, Cologne and Düsseldorf. These trains convey sleeping cars, couchettes and seats.

If you decide to stick with Route 39 to Verona, then you will head south over the **Brenner Pass** into Italy. By Alpine standards, the Brenner is a modest affair. No great tunnels as on the Simplon and Gotthard routes and no great heights as on the Bernina. The Brenner route tops out at just 1,370 metres, but what it lacks in height is made up for by the beauty of the landscape.

If you have the time, take slow trains south from Innsbruck, changing at Brennero and usually Bolzano to reach Verona. Once over the top, you can cut off to the east at Fortezza to follow a beautiful branch line back over the border at **San Candido** (Innichen in German) to reach the Austrian town of Lienz (ERT 596), from where there are good onwards connections to Villach (ERT 971) and even a daily Railjet to Vienna (also ERT 971).

Although in Italy and with street names in Italian, **Bolzano** (Bozen in German) looks decidedly Austrian, with its pastel-coloured baroque arcades and Austrian menu items; for centuries Bolzano was part of the South Tyrol region of Austria. Set beneath Alpine slopes in a deep valley, it's handy for exploring the Dolomites. Pza Walther (named after the poet Walther von der Vogelweide) is the focus of the town's outdoor life.

CONNECTIONS FROM BOLZANO

From Bolzano, there are trains at least hourly up the **Adige Valley** to Merano (ERT 597), where you can connect onto the local service, more a tram than a train, which runs west through Val Venosta (Vinschgau in the local German dialect) to Malles (ERT 598). This is a glorious ride through vineyards and orchards, a joy at any time of year but certainly at its very best in spring. Malles (Mals in German) is the jumping-off point for the bus links to Switzerland and Austria explored in our **Sidetracks** feature on p348. There's an hourly direct bus to Zernez (to connect with **Route 36**) and a less frequent connection via Martina to Landeck (on **Route 35**).

Remaining with the main line south towards Verona, the railway parallels the E45 highway as it runs down the Adige Valley. All daytime trains pause at Trento, a handsome regional centre and a good base for exploring the Dolomites. Beyond **Trento**, the landscape becomes gentler for the final stretch down to Verona.

Verona

Placed on an S-bend of the **River Adige** and best explored on foot, this beautiful city of pastel-pink marble thrives on the story of Romeo and Juliet, but the real attractions are its elegant medieval squares, fine Gothic churches and massive a **Roman amphitheatre** – the Arena – which comes alive during the annual opera festival in July and August (ticket office ☎ 045 800 5151, www.arena.it; the cheapest seats are unreserved, so arrive early). Dominating the large **Piazza Brà**, it has 44 pink marble tiers that can accommodate 20,000 people – incredibly, the singers and orchestra are perfectly audible.

Via Mazzini, which leads off Piazza Brà, is one of Italy's smartest shopping streets. This leads to Piazza delle Erbe, which is surrounded by faded Renaissance palaces. Originally the Roman forum, the square is now a daily market. An archway leads to a serener square, **Piazza dei Signori**, the centre of mediaeval civic life, and framed by the 15th-century Loggia del Consiglio and the crenellated Palazzo del Capitano.

Across the river, over the partly **Roman Ponte Pietra**, Verona's best-known bridge, are the remains of the Roman theatre (where plays were performed, as opposed to the amphitheatre, which held coarser public entertainments); although smaller than the amphitheatre, there's rather more to see, as entrance includes admission to the **Archaeological Museum**, housed in an old convent with great views of the city.

ARRIVAL, INFORMATION, ACCOMMODATION

🚄 Stazione Porta Nuova, a 10 to 15-min walk south of the centre (🚌 11/12/13/51/52). ✈ There are two airports: the main one is Valerio Catullo, (www.aeroportoverona.it), with a shuttle bus running every 20 mins to Port Nuova station 🏢 Tourist office: Via Degli Alpini 9 (www.turismoverona.eu). For information on public transport see www.atv.verona.it.

🛏 Try the friendly and highly regarded **B&B Agli Scaligeri**, Vicolo Ponte Nuovo 2, ☎ 0347 4765089 (www.agliscaligeri.it), well located in Verona's historic centre, west of Piazza delle Erbe. Another good and comfortable option is **Hotel Torcolo**, Vicolo Listone 3, ☎ 045 800 75 12 (www.hoteltorcolo.it), just north of Piazza Brà. Overlooking the Piazza delle Erbe, the central **Hotel Aurora**, Piazzetta XIV Novembre 2, ☎ 045 59 47 17 (www.hotelaurora.biz), is also a good choice.

✗ For reasonably priced restaurants, look along Corso Porta Borsari, in the streets around Pza delle Erbe or the Veronetta district on the east bank of the Adige. The Pza delle Erbe's food market is also useful.

CONNECTIONS FROM VERONA

From Verona, you can speed south to **Rome** on either a Trenitalia Frecciargento service or on one of Italo's sleek red high-speed trains (ERT 600). The city lies on the main rail axis across the North Italian plains, with regular services running west to Milan and Turin or east to Venice and Trieste (both directions are shown in ERT 605).

Verona has direct night trains to Paris (ERT 44), Rome (ERT 595), Vienna (ERT 88) and Munich (ERT 70). Closer to hand, there is a very **good network of regional trains**; destinations include Bologna, Mantua, Padua, Vicenza and Modena.

SIDETRACKS: THE ALPS BY BUS

The area where Switzerland, Austria and Italy conjoin is one of the most beautiful areas of the Alps. Several railways penetrate this region, but they do not connect in a manner which allows **cross-border train journeys**. So travellers must perforce resort to buses – which is just what we did when exploring this mountainous area a year or two ago.

Bolzano (on **Route 39** in this book) is a good starting point for rural cross-border adventures. First take the train to Merano (ERT 597), a graceful German-speaking spa town in the Adige Valley, which is worth a stop. From Merano, take the **Vinschgaubahn** (ERT 598), a local railway which happily reopened in 2005, to Malles (Venosta). German is very much the *lingua franca* here, and the town is shown on many maps and in timetables by its German name: Mals im Vinschgau.

There are some very tempting local bus routes which start outside the station in **Malles**. Swiss post bus (route number 811) runs hourly from Malles to Zernez via beautiful **Val Müstair** and the Ofen Pass (every two hours in winter). You may want to stop off at the UNESCO-listed Benedictine monastery in Val Müstair (closed Sundays and on major Catholic feast days). Most people in the Müstair Valley speak Romansh. The principal village of **Santa Maria**, just west of the monastery, is well worth a wander. The bus from Malles to Zernez in Switzerland takes 95 minutes. In **Zernez**, you are on the Rhaetian Railway network (and on **Route 36** in this book). See ERT 545 for train times.

Another equally appealing option is bus 273 which runs north from Malles along the east side of the **Lago di Resia** and on over Reschen Pass to Nauders in Austria. From there the bus drops down steeply into the Inn Valley, and terminates at Martina in Switzerland. Buses on this route run hourly all year round (less frequently on Sundays in winter). On the run north alongside the lake, you'll see an **extraordinary spectacle**: an eerily beautiful campanile projecting from the waters of the reservoir. It is a reminder of the fate of the Italian village of Graun which was flooded in 1950, when the valley was dammed to enlarge a pre-existing natural lake – curiously to provide water for Switzerland. The scene at Graun is so striking that you may want to alight from the bus and take a look around.

The journey from Malles to **Nauders** takes 37 minutes; from Malles to Martina takes 48 minutes. This bus route is operated by Servizi Autobus Dolomiti (times in ERT 954). In **Martina**, bus 273 connects with an hourly Swiss post bus which runs 17 kilometres down the Inn Valley to the Engadine railhead at **Scuol-Tarasp**, from where the Rhaetian Railway has two trains an hour (ERT 545) for your onward journey through Switzerland.

If you want to move north into the **Austrian Tyrol**, there are Austrian post bus services from both Nauders and Martina (times for both in ERT 954) on to Landeck – on the Arlberg rail route (ERT 951) – which is featured in **Route 35** of this book.

Our experience is that bus to bus, bus to train and train to bus connections in this region generally work perfectly. Only in severe winter weather, when snow may close even major roads, is there any serious risk of disruption.

ROAMING ITALY
An introduction

It is a shade under 1,000 kilometres by train from Naples to Turin. The fastest expresses dash between the two cities in under seven hours. If money is no object, you could book an **Executive Class** ticket on one of the smart NTV Italo trains. Sink deep into one of the train's posh leather armchairs and let yourself be pampered with complimentary coffee and snacks while losing yourself in Italo's entertainment system. It'll surely be a fun ride, but Italy won't stand centre stage in your memories of the trip. We've never travelled in Italo's Executive Class, but we have meandered through Italy on the slowest of slow trains, stopping off here and there along the way.

The fast train services in Italy are very fast, and seats always need to be booked in advance. The **slow trains** are wonderfully cheap and only very rarely need reservations. Just buy a ticket, hop on and ride. Slow trains are a chance to see the real Italy. We have **five routes in this section** of *Europe by Rail*, three of which (**Route 40, 41 and 42**) are old favourites. The other two were designed from scratch for the 2016 edition of the book. All five routes have been updated anew for this 16th edition.

As ever, it has been tough to decide which journeys to include here. With a few more pages, we'd have loved to cover more of the country's Adriatic coast, culminating with a tour of Apulia on the network of branch railways run by **Ferrovie del Sud Est** (FSE). But FSE was in dire straits in 2018, with some services suspended. During 2019, the company was integrated into Trenitalia's operations and, with the return of some stability, we might well include a journey through Apulia in a future edition of the book. Meanwhile, you can see times for a selection of FSE trains in Table 636 of the monthly *European Rail Timetable*.

Many travellers in Italy **combine rail and ferry travel**. There are excellent onward Adriatic shipping connections with direct services from Ancona, Bari and Brindisi to Croatia, Albania, Montenegro and Greece. Some ferry companies offer railpass holders free deck passage on sailings between Italy and Greece. **Overnight boats** make sense even for some inner-Italian journeys, particular on routes to and from Sicily.

Rail services to Italy are generally on the up. A direct daytime train from Frankfurt-am-Main to Milan was launched in December 2017. A new twice-daily service from **Ljubljana to Trieste** started in autumn 2018, thus linking up the latterly disconnected rail networks of Slovenia and Italy. With comfortable **Nightjet** trains from Germany and Austria to many Italian cities, the long-standing Thello sleeper from Paris to Milan and Venice, plus of course the weekly direct train from Warsaw to Verona, Milan and Genoa, it's easier than ever to reach Italy by train. ∎

Route 40: Through Liguria to Tuscany

Cities: ★★ Culture: ★★ History: ★★ Scenery: ★★★
Countries covered: France (FR), Monaco (MC), Italy (IT)
Journey time: 6 hrs | Distance: 370 km | Map: www.ebrweb.eu/map40

Travel writers rarely attain celebrity status nowadays. But in the early 19th century, as continental Europe once again became accessible to English travellers in the new political equilibrium which prevailed after the Napoleonic Wars, a number of British writers became household names for their tenacity in exploring far and wide and for their diligence in recording their experiences for the public. The **Riviera coast** attracted almost all budding authors of guidebooks, and one of the first was **Mariana Starke** whose perceptive accounts of Italy made her famous. Of the journey from **Nice to Pisa** along the coast, Starke remarked that the rough terrain was in many places impassable for carriages and the route was suitable only for mules.

It was the railway which created the Riviera and by 1874 it was possible to travel by train all the way from Nice to Pisa. Mariana Starke never lived to see the day. When she died in 1838, Italy did not have a single railway. Our journey from Nice to Pisa needs no mules and there are no arduous feats of endurance. Just grab a seat on the **seaward side of the train** and sit back as we rattle east along a coast where the place names alone conjure up images of style and elegance: Monte Carlo, Sanremo, Portofino and more.

Along this entire route, the hills rise steeply into **wild country**, but the coastal littoral itself is seductively mellow. Vineyards, olive groves and palms flourish in the mild climes that attracted English visitors to Alpes-Maritimes and Liguria in the 19th century. Genoa is gritty but engrossing, and Pisa is a fine introduction to **Tuscany**.

Itinerary notes

There is some **wonderful scenery** on this short journey, though to see the best of it, you'll really need to get off the train and linger. Genoa is an obvious choice for an **overnight stop**, but you may want to be more creative and choose one or two smaller communities to stay for a day or two. Smaller towns which are among our personal favourites are Menton, Sanremo, Albenga, Santa Margherita Ligure and Vernazza, though the last of these is so formidably busy in summer that we would not even think of stopping there other than in the depths of winter.

Slowish regional trains run at least every couple of hours along every section of this route, so it's perfectly possible to **travel spontaneously** and just buy tickets along the way. If you are in a rush, you can travel from Nice to Pisa in about six hours, with just a single change of train in Genoa.

This journey from Nice is a natural extension of **Route 8** in this book which runs from Marseille east through Provence to Nice. If you were taken with the scenery on that journey, then you'll find the coast east from Nice in

Route details

Nice-Ville to Menton		ERT 361
Frequency	Journey time	Notes
2–3 per hr	30–40 mins	A

Menton to Ventimiglia		ERT 361
Frequency	Journey time	Notes
1–2 per hr	15 mins	

Route details (cont.)

Ventimiglia to Sanremo		ERT 580
Frequency	Journey time	Notes
1–2 per hr	15–20 mins	

Sanremo to Genoa Piazza Principe		ERT 580
Frequency	Journey time	Notes
Every 1–2 hrs	1 hr 45 mins – 2 hrs	

Genoa Piazza Principe to Santa Margherita Ligure		ERT 610
Frequency	Journey time	Notes
Hourly	30–45 mins	

Santa Margherita Ligure to La Spezia Centrale		ERT 610
Frequency	Journey time	Notes
Hourly	55–75 mins	B

La Spezia Centrale to Pisa Centrale		ERT 610
Frequency	Journey time	Notes
1–2 per hr	40–70 mins	

Notes

It is possible to travel right through from Nice to Genoa on Route 40 using one of the thrice-daily Eurocity services operated by Thello (ERT 90). Note that these trains do not stop at Menton.

A – All trains between Nice and Menton serve Monaco-Monte Carlo.
B – Many journeys between Santa Margherita Ligure and La Spezia require a change of train at Sestri Levante.

many ways even more impressive. Hardly has the train left **Nice** (more on which on p118) that it reaches **Villefranche-sur-Mer** with its precariously tall ochre houses and one of the deepest harbours on the coast. Once leased to the Russian Navy, it's now a favoured stop for cruise ships. Away to the right you'll see **Saint-Jean-Cap-Ferrat**, a peninsula with gorgeous beaches plus some of the world's most expensive and closely guarded properties. **Beaulieu-sur-Mer** means 'beautiful place' – the name was bestowed by Napoleon. It's a tranquil spot full of affluent retired people, and palms flourish profusely in its mild climate.

Now we reach the tiny **Principality of Monaco** which has been a sovereign state ruled since 1297 by the Grimaldis, a family of Genoese descent. Later the family grew rich on gambling and banking, and now high-rise buildings crowd round the harbour, some built on reclaimed land which extends into the sea. Whatever the geographical and aesthetic limitations of the place, its curiosity value is undeniable. Old Monaco is the touristy part, but still very much worth a wander with its narrow streets, the much-restored **Grimaldi Palace**, and the 19th-century Cathédrale de Monaco, containing the tombs of the royals, including Princess Grace. In av. St-Martin is the **Musée océanographique**, in the basement of which is one of the world's great aquariums, developed by Jacques Cousteau (www.oceano. org). Monte Carlo is the swanky part, with its palatial hotels, luxury shops and the unmissable, world-famous **Casino Café de Paris**, pl. du Casino, which is worth a look for the interior gilt alone. Oddly, you'll see none of this from the train. Land is so expensive in Monaco that the railway was long ago buried underground. The sole railway station in the principality is called Monaco-Monte Carlo.

Back on French territory (albeit only briefly), **Menton** is a retirement town full of Italianate charm, endowed with long stony beaches and full of lemon, orange and olive trees. Wander around the **hilly Old Town**, constructed by the Grimaldis in the 15th century. The former summer residence of the Grimaldi family, the **Palais Carnolès** at 3 av. de la Madone, is now an excellent museum of fine art. For a very different take on art, visit the **Jean Cocteau museum** (www.museecocteaumenton.fr; closed Tues) by the Covered Market. In summer, the short curve of beach between the port and the marina is lined with bars, some of them pulling the rich and famous, others more the preserve of those who *wish* they were rich and famous.

From Menton it is not far to the rather scruffy frontier town of **Ventimiglia**, the first station in Italy, always packed on Friday mornings when the French invade the town for its busy market. There is a crumbling steep Old Town, a thriving cut-flower and olive-oil industry, but little to detain visitors beyond the superb market, the place to stock up on bags, clothes, Parmesan cheese, oil and picnic lunches.

INLAND FROM VENTIMIGLIA

Twice-daily trains run inland from Ventimiglia along a railway through fierce mountainous terrain to Tende (in France) and Cuneo (back in Italy). This **border-hopping railway** (see ERT 581 for times) is a very fine excursion. At Cuneo there are good onward connections to Turin (ERT 582). If you do not want to go that far, consider travelling inland just as far as **Breil-sur-Roya**, from where trains run every hour or two back down to the coast at Nice (ERT 581). If you take this route, the small town of **Sospel** in the Bévéra Valley is definitely worth a stop.

Sanremo (sometimes spelt San Remo) is the grande dame of the Ligurian Riviera – it's set in the long gentle arc of a bay. As in Monaco, the railway has been banished underground here and arriving at Sanremo station is nowadays a rather surreal experience. The old seafront route of the railway is now a pedestrian and cycle route. It's a nice thought that you can walk on the very ground over which tsars and emperors once travelled en route to Riviera holidays. Sanremo has an intriguing old quarter called **La Pigna**, full of shadowy streets, steep steps and a growing number of artisans and cafés. The **Villa Nobel**, C. Cavallotti 116, was the house of the Swedish inventor Alfred Nobel, who established the international prizes named after him; it is open to the public. In mid-February each year the town is filled with singers and musicians for a massively popular and peculiarly Italian musical event: the **Festival della canzone italiana di Sanremo**.

Beyond Sanremo the railway escapes subterranean confinement and tracks east along the coast through Imperia to Alássio and Albenga. This stretch of the Ligurian coast, from the French border to Genoa is called the **Riviera di Ponente**. Beyond Genoa, it is called the Riviera di Levante. Both sides have their highs and lows, but along the Riviera di Ponente the most immediately appealing community is the old Roman town of **Albenga**. Just before you reach it on the train, there's a stunning view to the right of beautiful Gallinara Island, a one-time monastic retreat which is nowadays a nature reserve.

Genoa (Genova) – (suggested stopover)

Sandwiched between the mountains and the sea, Genoa is a concertina of a city, with slate-topped palaces and squat churches bearing down on the old port. 'La Superba' is Italy's foremost seaport and was once, like Venice, a proud maritime republic ruled by a Doge, or elected ruler. As one of the most densely packed historic centres in Europe, Genoa is unfathomable. **Renzo Piano**, the renowned architect, sees his hometown as a 'secret, inward-looking Kasbah city'. Following the tragic collapse of the Morandi bridge in 2018, the construction of a new viaduct designed by Renzo Piano is underway. The new bridge is planned to open in 2020.

After the **restoration of the waterfront**, Genoa now has a port worthy of a maritime republic. Clustered around the Porto Antico are a traditional Genoese galleon, the **Museum of the Sea** (www.galatamuseodelmare.it; closed Mon Nov–Feb) and the superb Aquarium, designed to resemble a ship setting sail. Further west is the Lanterna (1544), Italy's oldest lighthouse. **Porto Antico**, the redesigned waterfront, functions as a new city piazza, with bars tucked into mediaeval arcades along the landward side. Much of the centre is pedestrianised, set among a maze of mediaeval alleys. The most patrician street is **Via Garibaldi**, lined with Renaissance palaces, including Palazzo Bianco (No. 11) and Palazzo Rosso (No. 18), both galleries bursting with Flemish and Italian masterpieces. The **Cattedrale di San Lorenzo**, which survived bombing by the British, is one of the most engaging churches. Pza Banchi is a lively pocket of old Genoa, with cheap cafés nearby and places to try typical pasta and pesto dishes. A funicular from Pza del Portello whisks you to Sant'Anna, high on the hill. If you fancy a swim, there are a few *bagni*, private beaches with facilities such as showers, on Corso Italia (Albaro area), like Bagni Nuovo Lido at No. 13.

ARRIVAL, INFORMATION, ACCOMMODATION

≽ There are two main stations: Principe and Stazione Brignole further east. Trains to the north use both stations; use the metro to transfer between them and to get into the city centre. ⓘ Tourist office: V. Garibaldi 12r (www.visitgenoa.it).

◤ Cheap accommodation is easy to find, but can be tacky. Try the outskirts of the Old Town, near Brignole. Close to the Pza Banchi in the Old Town is **Le Nuvole Residenza d'Epoca**, Pza delle Vigne 6, ☎ 010 251 00 18 (www.hotellenuvole.it). Conveniently located close to Stazione Principe and with that Riviera look is **Hotel Continental**, V. Arsenale di Terra 1, ☎ 010 26 16 41 (www.hotelcontinentalgenova.it). A friendly B&B right in the Old Town is the **Genova Porto Antico**, V. San Luca 1/15A, ☎ 010 301 39 05 (www.bbgenovaportoantico.it). ✘ The cheapest places for lunch are in the dock area, but most close in the evening. For Saturday night fever, head for the student-filled Via di San Bernardo and Stradone di Sant'Agostino, or stroll down the pedestrianised Via di San Lorenzo.

CONNECTIONS FROM GENOA

From Genoa, follow **Route 43** in this book via Milan to Verona and Venice. Although remote from the Italian high-speed rail network, Genoa has an excellent range of domestic rail services. Frecciabianca and Intercity services run south to Rome (ERT 610), Intercity trains run to Turin and Milan (both ERT 610). There are direct **night trains** to Naples and Sicily. Apart from the regular Eurocity trains to France, the only other **international service** from Genoa is a weekly train to Warsaw and Moscow (ERT 25). Departure times have varied, but in late 2019 the train leaves at Sunday lunchtime; it offers a fine opportunity to travel in Russian style across northern Italy. The journey from Genoa to Verona, for example, takes just over four hours.

The Riviera di Levante

The stretch of coast from Genoa down to La Spezia is dedicated to mass tourism, but that's not to say that it's not very attractive. Stop off, if you have time, at **Santa Margherita Ligure**, a laid-back resort which pulls the yacht crowd. From there it's but a short hop on a boat to impossibly beautiful **Portofino**. Back on the railway, a string of *belle époque* hotels overlook the palm-shaded promenade that defines Rapallo's long seafront. Anchoring the far end of this classic Riviera scene is a picture-perfect stone castle almost surrounded by water.

In time, we come to the **Cinque Terre** coast where, prior to the coming of the railway, a string of villages clinging to the cliffs relied entirely on boats for their connection with the outside world. Early travellers remarked on "the primitive simplicity of the inhabitants" – the words are from John Murray's 1866 guide. One hundred and fifty years later, that primitive simplicity is long gone. So too are the traditional occupations of wine making and fishing. The Cinque Terre villages are dedicated entirely to **tourism** and a visit to the

CINQUE TERRE: THE FIVE LANDS

Five villages just up the coast from La Spezia are often lauded as the most delectable on the entire coast of **Liguria**. The Cinque Terre coast is indisputably beautiful. Just imagine a summer evening in a rocky cove on this coast, preparing sauteed anchovies with wild fennel and garlic over a simple open fire of pine cones and twigs. Beautiful, yes? The problem is that thousands of others might well have the same idea.

Each of the five villages has **its own railway station**. Running from north to south they are Monterosso, Vernazza, Corniglia, Manarola and Riomaggiore. In high-season local trains stop two or three times each hour at all five stations.

region is a rite of passage for well-heeled Americans. In recent years, cruise tourism has added greatly to the pressures on Cinque Terre. Large **cruise ships** anchor at La Spezia, from where smaller boats ferry passengers up the coast to Cinque Terre. A long sequence of tunnels means that you'll see little of the area from the train, but take time to stop and explore. Vernazza is a good base; it's the prettiest of the villages and from there you can take a boat along the coast. Choose carefully and you'll find it's not all impossibly expensive. Albergo Barbara in Vernazza, Pza Marconi 30, ☎ 0187 81 23 98 (www.albergobarbara.it) has several grades of room, all at reasonable prices, with the more expensive rooms having fine views over the harbour.

Beyond Cinque Terre, the railway passes through **La Spezia**, but there's no special reason to stop until Pisa, which marks the end of Route 40, but you can connect in Pisa onto the next route in this book which leads on through Tuscany and Umbria to Rome.

Pisa

The Leaning Tower of Pisa rates among the world's most familiar landmarks, part of a magnificent triumvirate of buildings around the **Campo dei Miracoli** (Field of Miracles), by the Cathedral and Baptistry. The 11th-century, four-tiered **Duomo**, one of Italy's finest cathedrals, was the first Tuscan building to use marble in horizontal stripes, a design device popularised by the Moors. The **Leaning Tower** (Torre Pendente) began life in 1173, as a campanile for the Duomo. When it was 10 m high it began to tilt and the architect fled. Construction continued, however, with successive architects trying unsuccessfully to restore the balance.

ARRIVAL, INFORMATION, ACCOMMODATION

≋ Centrale, south of the River Arno and a 20-min walk from the Leaning Tower, or take 🚌 LAM Rossa. 🎫 Tourist office: Piazza Vittorio Emanuele II 16 (www.aboutpisa.info). 🛏 Just a short walk from the station and well placed for the city centre is the welcoming **Alessandro della Spina**, V. Alessandro della Spina 5/7/9, ☎ 050 50 27 77 (www.hoteldellaspina.it). The B&B **Villa Teresa**, V. della Foglia 13, ☎ 050 49 159 (www.villatheresa.it), is quiet but central with a beautiful garden. Or try the comfortable and friendly B&B **Cuore di Pisa**, Pza San Frediano 6, ☎ 050 57 75 21 (www.bedbreakfastcuoredipisa.com).

SIDETRACKS: WORLD HERITAGE

Securing a coveted place on UNESCO's World Heritage List is just one of many ways in which countries stage their identity. The decision about what sites to propose for inclusion is **deeply political**, but also speaks volumes about how a country perceives itself and its achievements on a global stage.

Railways have long been a component of successful **World Heritage applications**. In 1986, Britain made its first successful applications and Ironbridge Gorge in Shropshire was inscribed on UNESCO's List. The site is a fine example of creative ingenuity in the **Industrial Revolution**, and railways are part of that story. But the intention of that listing was to do far more than showcase a primitive railway network – and much the same would be true of the listing of the industrial landscapes of Blaenavon in Wales, which were added to the World Heritage List in 2000. Here too, railways are important, but not centrally so. What is perhaps surprising is that Britain has never proposed the various sites around the **Liverpool and Manchester Railway**. Opened in 1830, this was the world's first railway linking two cities. Is this not the Chartres of railway history, something which would be as deserving of recognition as Europe's great Gothic cathedrals or mediaeval townscapes?

Switzerland and India made the first successful nominations in which **railways stood centre stage**. In 1998, the *Semmering Railway* (see **Route 34**) was the first railway to secure UNESCO recognition, followed by the narrow-gauge *Darjeeling Himalayan Railway*, which was inscribed on the list the following year. That latter citation has since been extended to include two other mountain railways in India.

The third railway citation focuses on the **Rhaetian Railway** network and its surrounding landscapes in eastern Switzerland. The specific lines are on two routes from St Moritz, namely the *Albula Railway* north to Thusis (the opening section of **Route 37** in this book) and the *Bernina Railway* south to Tirano (which forms part of **Route 36**). So, of the first six railways to get a mention on UNESCO's list, all but the Semmering are narrow-gauge routes.

There have been some interesting **rail-related inscriptions**, among them the exuberant Gothic revival style Chhatrapati Shivaji Terminus in Mumbai and the **Forth Rail Bridge** in Scotland. The latter is not the only case of a World Heritage Site which is particularly well seen from a train. The final stretch of **Route 49**, as it climbs south from Kraków towards the Tatra Mountains, cuts through the middle of a remarkable cultural landscape of huge spiritual significance. This is the park at **Kalwaria Zebrzydowska**, where the landscape has been shaped into a symbolic representation of the events and scenes of Christ's passion.

In Budapest, the long-standing UNESCO listing covering the banks of the Danube and the Buda Castle complex was extended to include the first line of Budapest's underground railway. But wouldn't it be good to see **Moscow's fabulous metro stations** being added to the World Heritage List? The *art deco* columns at Mayakovskaya and the ornamentation at Kiyevskaya are just two examples from the heyday of Soviet design that might easily be grouped into a single nomination. But Russia's priorities today lie elsewhere and the Moscow metro could probably not compete with an ancient convent or monastery.

Route 41: Exploring central Italy

CITIES: ★★★ CULTURE: ★★★ HISTORY: ★★ SCENERY: ★★
COUNTRIES COVERED: ITALY (IT)
JOURNEY TIME: 8 HRS | DISTANCE: 474 KM | MAP: WWW.EBRWEB.EU/MAP41

The idea of Rome as the **Eternal City** or *caput mundi*, the capital of the world, has seduced travellers since classical times. From Virgil and Horace to Goethe and Gibbon, a phalanx of great writers have lauded the city. All roads eventually lead there, and all train journeys too perhaps – though travelling by train to Rome is not as simple as once it was. Fifty years ago, direct trains arrived from as far afield as Stockholm and Moscow. Nowadays, the Eternal City is directly connected with just one other European capital, Vienna, by the *Allegro Tosca* night train. It's run by ÖBB Nightjet.

The demise of the **long-distance links** to Rome is the direct result of the massively improved travel times due to Italy's expanding high-speed rail network. It's now possible to dash from Milan to Rome in less than three hours. In this route we offer a **slow saunter** through central Italy, a quiet and gentle journey which approaches Rome with the reverence she deserves. We start in Pisa, meander east through **Tuscany and Umbria**, then follow the Tiber Valley down to Rome.

ITINERARY NOTES

Any of the communities along this route which are mentioned in the text would well repay an **overnight stay**. We particularly commend Florence and Perugia. The journey described here can be completed without any need to use high-speed trains, or indeed any service requiring advance seat reservations. Using just local and regional services, and following this entire route, the journey from Pisa to Rome takes just under eight hours – with three changes of train along the way. There is no need to book in advance. The fare for the entire journey described here is about €40. You can, if you wish, pre-purchase tickets for each leg of your journey on Trenitalia (www.trenitalia.com).

Even if you don't have time to stop off, you certainly see a lot more of **central Italy** taking this route than if you took the fast Frecciabianca train which runs down the coast from Pisa to Rome in under three hours.

Moving inland

A railway runs east from **Pisa** (see p355), following the valley of the River Arno upstream to Florence. It's boring. You would do better by taking the alternative route via **Lucca**, which adds a little time to your journey, but gives a nicer introduction to Tuscany. The railway skirts Monte Pisano to reach Lucca, which is one of the finest small towns in the region. Even if you just stop for an hour or two, you'll be entranced by Lucca. It's just a five-minute walk from the railway station through the city's impressive bastions to the cathedral and **Piazza San Michele**. Despite its considerable beauty, Lucca never feels overrun, and the town has a leisurely, provincial feel.

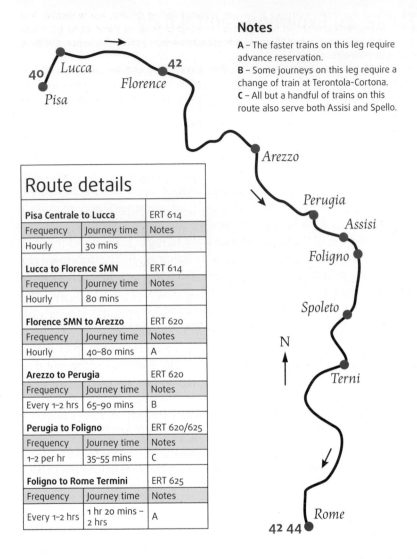

Notes

A – The faster trains on this leg require advance reservation.
B – Some journeys on this leg require a change of train at Terontola-Cortona.
C – All but a handful of trains on this route also serve both Assisi and Spello.

Route details

Pisa Centrale to Lucca		ERT 614
Frequency	Journey time	Notes
Hourly	30 mins	

Lucca to Florence SMN		ERT 614
Frequency	Journey time	Notes
Hourly	80 mins	

Florence SMN to Arezzo		ERT 620
Frequency	Journey time	Notes
Hourly	40–80 mins	A

Arezzo to Perugia		ERT 620
Frequency	Journey time	Notes
Every 1–2 hrs	65–90 mins	B

Perugia to Foligno		ERT 620/625
Frequency	Journey time	Notes
1–2 per hr	35–55 mins	C

Foligno to Rome Termini		ERT 625
Frequency	Journey time	Notes
Every 1–2 hrs	1 hr 20 mins – 2 hrs	A

From Lucca, the railway runs east, **Tuscan villas** and gardens slowly giving way to industrial estates as the train approaches **Florence**, where you'll arrive at Santa Maria Novella station (shown as 'Firenze SMN' in the ERT), which is one of those buildings you'll either love or hate. It is acclaimed by some as a fine example of Italian Modernism; others take a less positive view. For more on Florence, see p366.

ITALIAN HIGH-SPEED: FLORENCE CONNECTIONS

If you have followed our **Route 40** to Pisa, and then this current journey from Pisa to Florence, it's likely the Santa Maria Novella (SMN) station in Florence is your first encounter with **Italian high-speed trains**. This is a place to watch the ultra-modern Italo and

Frecciarossa trains come and go. If you are tempted to hop on one, just remember that Italian high-speed services all require advance booking. Some of these trains have **four classes**, the most luxurious of which is for those who evidently cannot leave home without having every possible creature comfort.

The times for all **high-speed services** serving Florence SMN are shown in ERT 600. You can speed north to Bologna, Verona, Venice, Milan and Turin. Or make tracks south for Rome and Naples. The fastest trains take less than 100 minutes to reach either Milan or Rome.

From Tuscany to Umbria

Sit on the left of the train for the journey up the Arno Valley from **Florence to Arezzo**. You'll be rewarded with fine views across the river against a backdrop of Tuscan countryside. Lots of chestnut orchards, olive groves and distant villages in serene composition. You may want to stop off at **Arezzo**, which was a major settlement in Etruscan, Roman and mediaeval times. Always a wealthy city, today its economy rests on jewellers, goldsmiths and antiques. Much of the centre is modern, but there are still attractive winding streets in the hilltop **Old Town**, with its Renaissance houses and the handsome Piazza Grande. One of the masterpieces of Italian Renaissance painting and the city's major attraction is Piero della Francesca's brilliant fresco cycle of *The Legend of the True Cross* (1452–1466), on display in the 14th-century **Basilica di San Francesco**, Pza San Francesco, in the centre of the Old Town. You'll need to make a reservation to visit the church (www.pierodellafrancesca-ticketoffice.it).

Soon after Arezzo, the railway **crosses into Umbria**, skirting the shores of Lake Trasimeno to reach Perugia. Some slower trains stop at three stations around the north and east sides of **Lake Trasimeno**. If you are tempted to stop, Tuoro sul Trasimeno is the best spot. There's access to the lake with an extraordinary set of modern sculptures overlooking the shoreline.

Perugia (suggested stopover)

Warlike and belligerent, the splendid **capital of Umbria** was smitten by strife almost until the 19th century and has a host of monuments of very martial demeanour.

Ignore the unattractive modern suburbs and head straight for the almost intact mediaeval centre. From **Piazza Italia** the pedestrianised Corso Vannucci, lined with fortified palaces, cafés and shops – the centre of activities for a cosmopolitan crowd almost around the clock – runs north to the city's heart in **Piazza IV Novembre**, where the Duomo (cathedral) is located. All the other major sights are within easy walking distance of here.

The **Duomo** is a large, plain, mediaeval building, supposedly home to the Virgin Mary's wedding ring. In the centre of the square is the 13th-century **Fontana Maggiore**, a fountain sculpted by Nicola and Giovanni Pisano. The **Museo Archeologico Nazionale dell'Umbria** on Pza G Bruno 10 includes Etruscan and Roman artefacts. And don't miss the 10th-century **Basilica of San Pietro**, south-east of the centre (Borgo XX Giugno).

ARRIVAL, INFORMATION, ACCOMMODATION

≋ 3 km south-west of the centre (an uphill walk). Use the rapid transit. 🛈 Tourist office: Pza Matteotti 18 (http://turismo.comune.perugia.it).

⊨ There is plenty of cheap, central accommodation, but book ahead if you're coming during the **Umbria International Jazz Festival** (ten days every July: www.umbriajazz.com). A friendly and central option is the B&B **Le Naiadi**, Via Bonazzi 17, ☎ 0333 74 17 408 (www.beblenaiadi.com). Or try the **Hotel Morlacchi**, V. Leopoldo Tiberi 2, ☎ 075 572 03 19 (www.hotelmorlacchi.it), a comfortable family-run hotel in the Old Town. The **Sangallo Palace Hotel**, V. L Masi 9, ☎ 075 573 02 02 (www.sangallo.it), is a smart option in the Old Town. It's in a quiet area and some rooms offer the added benefit of a balcony with great views over the town and the countryside beyond.

The valley over which Perugia presides is that of the **River Tibe**r (called the Tevere in Italian). But we'll forsake the valley and make a loop east through eastern Umbria where a number of classic hill towns all demand our attention.

The first of these, which you'll see to the left very shortly after leaving Perugia, is **Assisi**. The station is four kilometres out of town, but shuttle buses run every 20 to 30 minutes between the station and the centre.

One name is irrevocably linked with Assisi – **St Francis**. Born here in 1182, he practised what he preached: poverty, chastity and obedience, leading to a love of God and an appreciation of all living things. He founded the Friars Minor and the other Franciscan Orders. His home town became (and remains) a major pilgrimage centre, concentrated on the **Basilica di San Francesco**, erected in his memory and adorned with some of the most magnificent frescos in Italy. St Francis' life initiated a wealth of art and architecture in Assisi. Still largely mediaeval, and clinging to a side of **Monte Subasio** high above the green Umbrian countryside, the town is instantly familiar from the landscapes depicted in the frescos of the Umbrian painters.

If you worry about the crowds in Assisi, a great alternative is just ten minutes further down the line at **Spello**, a town which has an added plus: its centre is within walking distance of the station. Spello is the epitome of an Umbrian hill town, with tiers of pink houses, cobbled alleys, churches and Roman gateways. The 13th-century church of **Santa Maria Maggiore** contains a chapel full of brilliantly restored frescos by Pinturicchio and a 15th-century ceramic floor.

Just a few kilometres beyond Spello at **Foligno**, the railway line from Florence joins the main line from Ancona (on Italy's Adriatic coast) to the Italian capital.

CONNECTIONS FROM FOLIGNO

Foligno is a place to change trains – and not much more. The town was badly damaged by bombing in the Second World War. But the station, an unlovely post-war building, is fit for purpose, and from here there are regular trains to Rome and Ancona (ERT 625). The star turn of the day on the Foligno departure boards is the evening Frecciabianca train to **Ravenna**, a three-hour ride away.

The train service to **Ancona** is useful for travellers wanting to connect into the Adriatic shipping lines. There are direct ferries from Ancona to Igoumenitsa and Patras in Greece (ERT 2715), as well as a summer service to the Greek island of Corfu (ERT 2715). There are also **direct ferries** from Ancona to Split (ERT 2725) and Zadar (ERT 2732) in Croatia.

Running south from Foligno towards Rome, the first place of any size is **Trevi** which is high above the railway to the left. If you don't fancy climbing up to the heights of Trevi, you're better off to take a break at Spoleto, where the old city centre is much more accessible from the station.

Founded by Umbrians in the 6th century BC, **Spoleto** has an interesting mix of Roman and mediaeval sights, the most spectacular being the cathedral. In 1958, Spoleto secured the prize of hosting Italy's leading performing arts festival, and it has done so with considerable style in early summer each year ever since. It's an interesting case of a city reshaping its identity through a commitment to art. Spoleto's **Festival dei Due Mondi** (www.festivaldispoleto.com) transforms the tranquil town into an unrecognisably invigorated place; prices, inevitably, soar.

Part of the small **Teatro Romano**, Pza della Libertà, at the southern end of the old centre, has been carefully restored and is now used for festival performances. The **Rocca**, a huge 14th-century castle to the south-east of town, guards one of the finest engineering achievements of mediaeval times, the **Ponte delle Torri**: a 240-m long bridge, supported by ten arches, 80 metres high. From it there are magnificent views of the gorge below.

After Spoleto, the railway dives briefly through the hills to reach the **Nera Valley** where the main town of note is Terni. **Terni** has a lot to answer for, being the one-time home of St Valentine. Terni rather bravely styles itself as a city for lovers, gently overlooking the reality that it's pretty industrial with a background in steel making. If you do stop, the famously quirky attraction that brings visitors to Terni (apart from the St Valentine connection) is the entirely artificial **Marmore Waterfalls**, created more than 2,000 years ago. The falls are seven kilometres east of the town. 🚌 7 from Terni will take you there in 20 minutes.

From Terni the railway follows the **River Nera** down to the Tiber, crossing from Umbria **into Lazio**. The railway criss-crosses the Tiber on its way south to Rome, sharing the valley with the high-speed line from Florence. That line was the very first in a new generation of European high-speed railways developed in the 1970s and thereafter. This stretch down the Tiber Valley opened in 1977.

The approach into Rome is through a predictable medley of motorways and industrial estates. Most trains stop first at Tiburtina station and then continue on to Roma Termini.

Rome (Roma)

The Romans have an inbuilt resistance to schedules and short lunch breaks. Life is too Latin for a Protestant work ethic. Indeed, they have no qualms about playing the tourist in their own city, from eating ice creams on **Piazza Navona** to tossing a coin in the Trevi Fountain, visiting the Vatican museums on a Vespa, lolling around the Villa Borghese Gardens, or peeking into the Pantheon while on a café crawl. In Italy's most bewildering but beguiling city, it has somehow never made more sense to 'do as the Romans do'.

The Eternal City, dominated by its seven hills, is cut by the fast-flowing River Tiber. Don't expect Rome's legendary 'seven hills' to stand out as landmarks: they are too gentle, and merge into one another. Instead, treat the **Colosseum** and the **Forum** as the city centre, set on the east bank of the Tiber, with the Pantheon just north, and the chic Spanish Steps beyond. On the west bank of the Tiber lies bohemian Trastevere, a great restaurant and nightlife centre, with the mausoleum-fortress of **Castel Sant'Angelo** further north, and the Vatican City to the west. If this sounds exhausting (and it is), **Villa Borghese** is Rome's green heart, but with baroque fountains and galleries attached – you'll find there's no escape from several millennia of art and architecture in a city that spawned a civilisation. For a note on connections from Rome see p368.

ARRIVAL, INFORMATION, ACCOMMODATION

⇌ **Termini**, Pza dei Cinquecento, is Rome's largest station, handling all the main national and international lines; well served by buses and at the hub of the metro system. **Tiburtina**, Pza della Stazione Tiburtina, serves some long-distance north–south trains. ✈ **Leonardo da Vinci** (Fiumicino) is 36 km south-west of Rome (www.adr.it). There's a fast train service, every 15 mins (every 30 mins late evenings, Sun and holidays), to Tiburtina. Trenitalia also runs the *Leonardo Express* every 15 mins, taking 20 mins to Termini; **Ciampino** is just 16 km south-east of Rome with frequent shuttle buses to Termini station. Individual combined bus/metro tickets, called BIT (*biglietto integrato a tempo*, €1.50), are valid for 100 mins. 1–3 day tickets are also avilable. Tickets can be bought at newsstands and tobacconists or at railway and underground stations and bus termini. Validate the ticket on the bus, tram or trolleybus or at metro entrances. 🄸 Tourist information points (www.turismoroma.it) throughout the city, e.g. at Termini station and at V. Nazionale (Palazzo delle Esposizioni).

🛏 Hotels range from the opulent – mainly located close to the Spanish Steps and the Via Veneto – to the basic, largely clustered around the Via Nazionale and Termini station. Central, reasonably-priced hotels get booked quickly so reserve ahead. The very welcoming **Due Torri**, Vicolo del Leonetto 23, ☎ 06 688 069 56 (www.hotelduetorriroma.com), is in a great, quiet location north of Piazza Navona. Comfortable and tucked away in a quiet side street is the well located **Modigliani**, V. della Purificazione 42, ☎ 06 428 152 26 (www.hotelmodigliani.com). For those looking to splash out, the **Isa**, V. Cicerone 39, ☎ 06 321 26 10 (www.hotelisa.net), is a boutique hotel close to the Spanish Steps.

Route 42: Tuscany and Umbria

CITIES: ★★★ CULTURE: ★★★ HISTORY: ★★ SCENERY: ★★
COUNTRIES COVERED: ITALY (IT)
JOURNEY TIME: 6 HRS 45 MINS | DISTANCE: 562 KM | MAP: WWW.EBRWEB.EU/MAP42

Some journeys in this volume come with advice about the wisdom of procuring visas or a supply of toilet paper (or, in the case of **Route 52**, both) before setting out. This current journey from Bologna through Tuscany to Rome comes with its own special health warning. When the French author **Stendhal** visited Florence in 1817 he endured a bout of illness after looking at too much art. The malady, nowadays known as Stendhal syndrome, finds expression in dizzy spells and fainting.

Be warned! One can overdose on culture. It's not compulsory to see every painting in the Uffizi Gallery in **Florence**, nor is it necessary to explore every back alley in **Siena**. A little goes a long way in Tuscany. Bear in mind that the fact there is no conspicuous queue *outside* a church or art gallery does *not* mean that there is nothing worth seeing *inside*. Nowhere is the flocking instinct of tourists more dramatically displayed than in **Tuscany**. We have never understood why thousands of visitors huddle in San Gimignano, when a score of other hilltop towns in Tuscany are every bit as beautiful as San Gimignano, but less assailed by crowds.

So let's set off on a journey **through green hills**, striped with olive groves and vineyards, stopping off at historic towns and cities overflowing with **Renaissance art** and architecture.

ITINERARY SUGGESTIONS

Florence and Siena are the obvious **overnight stops**, but you may also want to make space for Orvieto, a city which is a little off the beaten track.

You could, if you wish, do this entire route relying only on local and regional train services – where there's no need to pre-book, fares are cheap and holders of rail passes are not burdened with supplements. If you need to cover ground quickly, then why not use a fast service for the first part of the journey? Choose between Trenitalia Frecciargento or NTV Italo trains. Either will speed you from **Verona to Florence** in about 95 minutes (see ERT 600).

Over the last dozen years, the railway between **Verona** (more on which on p347) and Bologna has been much improved, with long sections of single track being doubled and a new bridge constructed over the **River Po**. These Po Valley landscapes have been tamed by extensive land reclamation, and there is none of the sense of wilderness which early settlers would have encountered. The **drainage of the swamplands** took place from the 1880s and was the prelude to railway construction in this region.

But the latter proceeded in a lazy way; indeed the final link in the line from Verona to Bologna, namely the first bridge of the River Po between **Ostiglia** and Revere, was not completed until 1911. With dry land and access to railways, the region developed into a major agricultural area with thousands of acres devoted to wheat and sugar beet. Today, this has become a favoured region for urbanites seeking to escape city life, and increasing numbers of single-family villas (normally accompanied by a token olive grove) creep across the plains.

There is no particular reason to stop until **Bologna** which is the capital of Emilia-Romagna. The city's long-standing role as a major transport hub has been enhanced by its location on Italy's *alta velocità* spinal rail route linking the cities of the north with Rome and Naples. The city mastered the art of living in mediaeval times, when a pink-bricked settlement clustered around **Europe's oldest university**, founded in 1088.

In terms of tourism, the only reason that Bologna has languished is because Florence is a looming presence over the hills. The streetscape has real dignity in its **arcades**, red- and ochre-coloured buildings, stucco facades, greatly varied porticos, church spires, palaces and **mediaeval towers**, the latter built as status symbols by the city's wealthy nobles.

Bologna Stazione Centrale is a distinctive neoclassical building. It's not by chance that the main station clock no longer works and forever reads 10.25. That was the moment on the morning of 2 August 1980 when a bomb exploded killing 85 people. A memorial to the victims stands by the renovated station entrance.

Into Tuscany

Three different rail routes between Bologna and Florence attest to the challenge of building a railway through the rugged **Apennines**.

The **Porrettana Railway** with its complex spiral tunnels was opened in 1864, cutting the travel time between the cities to five hours. Seventy years later, the *Direttissima* was built and the travel time tumbled to under two hours. In 2009, yet a third line was opened and the fastest trains now run non-stop from Bologna to Florence in just 35 minutes. All three lines are

FROM BOLOGNA TO THE COAST AND SAN MARINO

From Bologna, it is just a short hop to **Ravenna** (ERT 621) where a stunning array of Byzantine mosaics have secured for Ravenna a place on UNESCO's World Heritage List. Or take the main line along the Adriatic coast to **Ancona** (ERT 630) and **Brindisi** (ERT 631). On the way you might pause at Rimini, a somewhat charmless resort but with an excellent beach, fine Roman bridge and lively nightlife; it's a 50-minute bus trip from Rimini to the tiny independent **Republic of San Marino**, memorably perched on the slopes of Monte Titano. We very much like San Marino, but it's definitely not at its best during the day. Most visitors spend just a few hours in the hilltop republic, and it can get very crowded. But stay overnight and you'll have a chance to see for yourself why San Marino styles itself *serenissima repubblica* – the most serene republic.

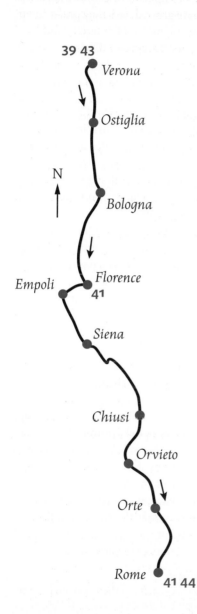

Route details

Verona Porta Nuova to Bologna Centrale		ERT 595
Frequency	Journey time	Notes
Every 1–2 hrs	50–80 mins	

Bologna Centrale to Florence SMN		ERT 600/620
Frequency	Journey time	Notes
3 per hr	35–100 mins	F

Florence SMN to Siena		ERT 613
Frequency	Journey time	Notes
Hourly	1 hr 30 mins	E

Siena to Chiusi–Chianciano Terme		ERT 619
Frequency	Journey time	Notes
Every 1–2 hrs	75–85 mins	

Ciusi–Chianciano Terme to Orvieto		ERT 620
Frequency	Journey time	Notes
Every 1–2 hrs	25–30 mins	

Orvieto to Rome Termini		ERT 620
Frequency	Journey time	Notes
Every 1–2 hrs	65–90 mins	

Notes

E – On some journeys between Florence and Siena it is necessary to change trains at Empoli.

F – A travel time of less than 45 mins between Bologna and Florence indicates that the train is routed via the new high-speed line, which is largely in tunnels (see ERT 600 for these fast trains). A longer travel time suggests that the train uses the *Direttissima* route (shown in ERT 620). We think the latter is the better choice if you want to see something of the Tuscan scenery on the approach to Florence.

The **numbers in red** adjacent to some cities on our route maps refer to other routes in this book which also include that particular city.

The ERT numbers in our route details refer to the table numbers in the *European Rail Timetable* (ERT) where you will find train schedules for that particular section of the route.

still in use. If you opt for the new high-speed route, your train will depart from the underground platforms at Bologna Centrale. That sets the tone for what's to come. It's a 92-kilometre journey, of which more than 70 kilometres are in tunnels. If you believe in staying above ground, you may prefer to opt for the *Direttissima*, which is still served by a handful of Intercity and local trains. The timings for a selection of trains are shown in ERT 620.

Florence (suggested stopover)

Most trains from the north arrive at **Santa Maria Novella station** in Florence. See what you make of the station's bold rationalist lines. Feted by some as a marvel, but derided by others, it's a building which always evokes a strong reaction.

Too many travellers arriving in Florence for the first time just dash though the station, keen to see their first Michelangelo or Giotto. The station is itself one of the city's most striking sights.

One of the greatest of Italy's old city-states, Florence has one of the richest legacies of art and architecture in Europe. Stendhal found in Florence a city of reason, intellect and order — the **epitome of Renaissance virtue**. Generations of travellers have flocked to Florence. It is so popular that, from Easter till autumn, its narrow streets are tightly crammed and major sights get extremely crowded during this period. Be prepared to wait in line to enter the **Galleria Uffizi** (www.uffizi.it) — Italy's premier art gallery — or to see Michelangelo's *David* in the **Galleria dell'Accademia** (www.accademia. org). Nevertheless, few would omit Florence from a tour of Tuscany, and it's really rewarding providing you don't overdo the sightseeing and take an afternoon siesta.

There are plenty of other galleries of world status if you cannot cope with the Uffizi crowds. Try the **Museo dell'Opera del Duomo**, the Palazzo Pitti museums or the Bargello. Enjoy the city by walking around: take in the **Ponte Vecchio**, the Duomo, the banks of the Arno or the huge **Piazza Santo Spirito**. The latter is on the south side of the river in an area known at Oltrarno. This is our favourite area of Florence; it's a little tamer than the north bank, where the main sights cluster. Wander the streets of **Oltrarno** in the evening and there is a reassuring sense of normality. It is an antidote to the over-hyped Florence-on-show style of the north bank.

ARRIVAL, INFORMATION, ACCOMMODATION

⇒ Santa Maria Novella (SMN) is Florence's main rail hub. It is a short walk from the city centre. Florence's buses are run by *Azienda Trasporti dell'Area Fiorentine* (ATAF) and *Linea*. There is an ATAF information office inside SMN railway station. Tickets need to be pre-purchased (at tobacconists, newsagents, ATAF sales points and machines at tram stops) and are valid for 90 mins. Validate them in the machine immediately upon boarding.

🄸 Tourist office: Via Camillo Cavour 1r and at the station (www.firenzeturismo. it). ⋈ Florence is one of Europe's most popular tourist destinations, and although this means that there is plenty of accommodation on offer, things can get pretty full during the summer months. Near the station is the family-run **Hotel Nuova Italia**, Via Faenza 26, ☎ 055 287 508 (www.hotel-nuovaitalia.com). Equally handy for SMN station and good value for money is the **Hotel Fiorita**, Via Fiume 20, ☎ 055 2654376 (www.hotelfiorita. com). Very upmarket, the **Gallery Hotel Art**, Vicolo dell'Oro 5, ☎ 055 272 63 (www. lungarnohotels.com), is a boutique design hotel just off the north end of the Ponte Vecchio.

FLORENTINE CONNECTIONS
There is an alternative itinerary from Florence to Rome described in **Route 41**, taking in Perugia and Assisi. From Florence you can also follow Route 41 in reverse, connecting in Pisa for the coastal route to Nice (**Route 40**). If all you want to do is head south in a hurry, a **high-speed train** will get you to Rome in 90 minutes and Naples is under three hours (ERT 600). Florence has direct night trains to Munich, Vienna and southern Italy.

The train to Siena initially runs west down the Arno Valley to **Empoli**, then turns south and climbs slowly into the hills. As you head towards Siena, the hillsides close in and you have a sense of travelling back in time. There are glimpses of **hilltop villages** and before long you arrive in Siena.

Siena (suggested stopover)

Spread over low hills and filled with robust terracotta-coloured buildings, Siena has changed little since mediaeval times. Indeed, this most beautiful of Tuscan cities is still contained within its **ancient walls** – look out from just behind the Campo, the main square, and there's a vista down a green, rural valley.

The city was Florence's tireless enemy for much of the Middle Ages, competing with it for supremacy politically, economically and artistically. Now it's a **delightful place to visit**, for its artistic treasures as well as just for the pleasures of discovering its myriad sloping alleys.

The fan-shaped **Piazza del Campo** dates from 1347 and is regarded as the focus of the city's life. The arcaded and turreted **Palazzo Pubblico**, on the south side, still performs its traditional role as the town hall, and its bell tower, the 102-m **Torre del Mangia**, soars above the town, with dizzying views. Part of the Palazzo Pubblico houses the Museo Civico, the Sala della Pace and Sala del Mappamondo which contain treasures of Lorenzetti and Martini among others. To the west stands the **Duomo**, the cathedral, with its striped marble facade studded with Renaissance sculptures.

Terzo di Città (south-west of the Campo) has some of the city's finest private palaces, such as the Palazzo Chigi-Saracini, Via di Città 89.

ARRIVAL, INFORMATION, ACCOMMODATION
⇼ 2 km north-east (in a valley below the town). There are regular city buses into the centre (tickets from the machine by the entrance). You could also take a sequence of elevators that lead from the shopping centre opposite Siena station up to Porta Camolia, just opposite the city walls.

ℹ Tourist office: Santa Maria della Scala, Palazzo Squarcialupi, Pza Duomo 1 (www. terresiena.it). ✉ Private rooms are best value, but you often have to stay at least a week and they can be full of students in term time. A good, central B&B is the **Antica Residenza Cicogna**, V. delle Terme 76, ☎ 0577 285 613 (www.anticaresidenzacicogna.it). Another nice & comfortable B&B with large rooms, located not far from the Campo is the **Palazzo Bulgarini**, V. Pantaneto 93, ☎ 0391 396 85 71 (www.bbpalazzobulgarini.com). Even closer to the Campo is the stylish B&B **Il Corso**, V. Banchi di Sopra 6, ☎ 0577 284 248 (www. ilcorsosiena.it), in a lively neighbourhood.

In a route that has a lot of only middling scenery, the stretch running southeast from Siena is quite exceptional. This area, known as *crete senesi*, is classic peaceful **Tuscan countryside**.

The 70-kilometre stretch from Siena via Asciano to **Montepulciano** is simply magnificent – in our view perhaps the finest one-hour train journey in the entire region. Many of the stations are far distant from the towns they serve; passengers alighting at Montepulciano, for example, might be surprised to find that the station is ten kilometres away from the town it serves. Buses run up to the exquisite hilltop town.

Through Umbria to Rome

Rejoining a main railway at **Chiusi**, close to the border with Umbria, it's not far to **Orvieto**. Set in a valley of vineyards, this striking cliffside town is perched above a raised tufa-stone plateau. Dominating the town is the vividly striped **Duomo**, Pza Duomo, built in honour of a 13th-century miracle. With its triple-gabled exterior of gilded mosaics, bronze doors and bas-relief by Lorenzo Maitani, as well as its outstanding interior frescos by Luca Signorelli depicting the Last Judgement, it is one of the great churches of Umbria.

Not far beyond Orvieto, the main railway towards **Rome** reaches the valley of the **River Tiber** (Tevere in Italian), which it then follows downstream all the way to the capital, in many places running parallel to the new high-speed line. The final approach to the city is shared by **Route 41**. You can read more about the Italian capital on p362 of this book.

ROME CONNECTIONS
You can return north to Florence by following **Route 41** in reverse, which takes in some very different landscapes from those seen on this journey. To continue further south, **Route 44** will escort you all the way to Sicily.

Rome has a useful range of **night trains**, with southbound departures every evening for Palermo and Siracusa (both in Sicily). Heading north, there are direct night trains to Turin, Milan, Venice, Trieste, Bolzano, Vienna and Munich.

Bear in mind that a long hop on a **ferry** can be used to create itineraries which combine very different regions of Europe. The port of **Civitavecchia**, just 45 minutes from Rome by fast train, has departures almost every evening for Barcelona (ERT 2520). There are also direct ferries from Civitavecchia to Spain, Sicily, Sardinia and Tunisia.

Route 43: North Italian cities

CITIES: ★★★ CULTURE: ★★★ HISTORY: ★★ SCENERY: ★
COUNTRIES COVERED: ITALY (IT)
JOURNEY TIME: 5 HRS 30 MINS | DISTANCE: 461 KM | MAP: WWW.EBRWEB.EU/MAP43

This route takes in several **glorious north Italian cities** from Genoa in the west to Venice in the east – a veritable feast of art and architecture, along the way swapping the Mediterranean for the Adriatic. With such illustrious art and culture hot spots as Milan, Verona, Vicenza and Padua along the way, this route is, at one level, quintessential Italy. If you really are a **city lover**, then Route 43 is for you.

But there's much here too for those who discern beauty in the **gentle alluvial landscapes** of northern Italy: the rice fields between the Ticino and Po rivers, the lakes and meadows of the Mincio Valley at Mantua, the Lessini Hills dancing on the horizon as you approach Verona from the south-west and – towards the end of our journey – the **quiet drama of the Veneto**.

ITINERARY SUGGESTIONS

Although this route has more constituent legs than many journeys in this book, each leg is quite short. With so many fine cities, it would easily be possible to spin this route out to a week or more. The train journeys are undemanding, each onward hop to the next city taking no more than an hour or two. As a bare minimum, think of **stopping off** in Milan, Mantua and Verona.

The beauty of this route is that it can be followed using only regional trains. Even if you want to **travel totally spontaneously** and not book *any* train tickets in advance, you'll still not pay the earth for the entire journey from Genoa to Venice. If you want to pre-book tickets, **Trenitalia** (www.trenitalia.com) sells tickets for all component legs of the journey for a total of about €40.

The hills which rise up immediately behind the Ligurian coast were a formidable barrier to railway magnates wanting to link **Genoa** (see p353) with the great inland cities of northern Italy. In 1853, the line running north from Genoa was eventually opened, cutting through the most rugged portion of the mountains in the **Giovi Tunnel** which, although less than four kilometres in length, was then the longest tunnel in the world.

There was widespread apprehension as to whether drivers and passengers might die of suffocation. Two catastrophic incidents in the early days of this railway demonstrated that such fears were well founded. A driver was overcome by smoke and fell from his cab; his train sped out of the steeply sloping tunnel and ploughed into a waiting passenger train at Busalla. Some years later, ten passengers died of fumes in the tunnel.

With such a painful history, the journey inland from Genoa nowadays seems all too easy. Even longer stretches are in tunnels, but soon you emerge into **Piedmont** sunshine and track north towards Milan. The train crosses the **River Po**, skirting one of the most important areas of rice production

Route details

Genoa Piazza Principe to Milan C		ERT 610
Frequency	Journey time	Notes
Every 1–2 hrs	1 hr 30 mins – 1 hr 50 mins	X

Milan C to Cremona		ERT 607
Frequency	Journey time	Notes
Every 2 hrs	70 mins	

Cremona to Mantua		ERT 607
Frequency	Journey time	Notes
1–2 per hr	40–90 mins	

Mantua to Verona Porta Nuova (PN)		ERT 609
Frequency	Journey time	Notes
Every 1–2 hrs	45–50 mins	

Verona PN to Venice Santa Lucia		ERT 605
Frequency	Journey time	Notes
2–3 per hr	70–90 mins	V, X

Riding the Frecciarossa

In recent years, Trenitalia have introduced their top-of-the-range Frecciarossa trains on the main west-east route across the North Italian Plain from Milan via Verona to Venice. In 2018 a new Genoa-Milan-Venice Frecciarossa service was added. It is an interesting move, showcasing premium rolling stock designed for high-speed travel running on traditional, low-speed railway lines. It's a prime business route, so no doubt there will be takers for the high-end executive and business-class seating. Trenitalia's move may have been prompted by the decision of competitor NTV Italo to offer the Milan to Venice route from 2018.

The Frecciarossa and Italo trains are shown in ERT 605. They take the main line running east from Milan to Verona, so they do not serve Cremona and Mantua. East of Verona, they follow the line described in **Route 41**, stopping at Vicenza and Padua on the way to Venice.

Notes

V – Most direct trains from Verona Porta Nuova to Venice Santa Lucia stop at both Vicenza and Padua along the way.
X – Some trains on this leg are premium services (eg. Frecciarossa or Frecciabianca trains) where a seat reservation is compulsory. There are however also local or regional trains, usually a little slower, where no prior reservation is needed (or even possible).

outside Asia. **Pavia**, a lovely city of quiet piazzas, might reasonably claim to be the risotto capital of the world. Just north of Pavia, to the left of the railway, you'll see one of the most notable buildings of Renaissance Italy: the **Carthusian charterhouse**, served by a railway station (local trains only) called Certosa di Pavia. It is open to visitors (May–Sept 09.00-11.30 & 14.30-17.30, free entry; closed Mon). Tours led by resident monks afford a glimpse into the rich spirituality of the Carthusians.

Approaching **Milan**, the railway cuts through areas where industrial premises have nudged aside ancient orchards and olive groves. There are pylons, piles of pallets and container parks. This is the detritus of modernity which even sophisticated landscaping can never totally conceal. The train speeds past unsung **Lombardy communities** which have long succumbed to the enveloping reach of the city.

Milan (Milano) – (suggested stopover)

Italy's second largest city is the country's **economic powerhouse** as well as its commercial, banking, fashion and design centre. Milan is less aesthetically appealing than Florence or Rome. But Italy's most **cosmopolitan city** boasts Romanesque churches, grand galleries, a superb museum of Northern Italian art (the Brera) and one of the boldest cathedrals in Christendom.

Milan's signature building is the **Duomo**. This extravagant Gothic cathedral, overflowing with belfries, statues and pinnacles, has stairs leading to rooftop views. Leading off the square is the **Galleria Vittorio Emanuele II**, an iconic 19th-century iron and glass shopping arcade lined with chic cafés and boutiques. Beyond lies Pza Scala, home of **La Scala**, the world's most celebrated opera house (www.teatroallascala.org).

Milan's finest art gallery is the **Pinacoteca di Brera**, Via Brera 28 (www.pinacotecabrera.org; closed Mon), featuring Italian artists of the 14th–19th centuries, including pieces by Mantegna, Raphael and Caravaggio. The Brera district is worth a wander for its relaxed and slightly alternative feel.

Milan's most celebrated work of art is **Leonardo da Vinci's** *Last Supper* (1495–1498), occupying a wall of a Dominican monastery refectory next to Santa Maria delle Grazie. Tickets must be booked ahead (www.vivaticket.it). Before leaving Milan, escape the urban chaos by visiting Milan's most beloved church – not the cathedral but the largely Romanesque **Sant'Ambrogio**, a basilica begun in the late 4th century by St Ambrose, Milan's patron saint and former bishop. So smooth in speech was St Ambrose that a honey liqueur was named after him.

ARRIVAL, INFORMATION, ACCOMMODATION

≋ Most long-distance trains arrive at **Stazione Centrale**, Piazza Duca d'Aosta, although a limited number of services use **Porta Garibaldi**. Both stations are north of the city centre.
🛈 The tourist offices are at V. dei Mercati 8 and Pza Duomo 14 (www.turismo.milano.it).
🛏 A comfortable and well regarded hotel close to Porta Garibaldi station is the **Berna**, V. Napo Torriani 18, ☎ 02 947 534 82 (www.hotelberna.com). A good central option is the **Hotel Cavour**, V. Fatebenefratelli 21, ☎ 02 620 001 (www.hotelcavour.it), just a short walk from the cathedral. Or try the highly regarded **Milan Suite Hotel**, V. Varesina 124, ☎ 02 33431618 (www.milansuitehotel.com), located about 4 km north-west of the city centre close to Villapizzone Railway Station. A bus outside the hotel runs into town.

MILAN CONNECTIONS

All services mentioned here depart from Milan Centrale station unless otherwise mentioned. Eurocity services tunnel north **through the Alps** (via both the Simplon and new Gotthard Base Tunnel routes) to major Swiss cities (ERT 40); other Eurocity trains run direct to Nice and Marseille (ERT 90). There are night trains to Naples and Sicily (ERT 640), Paris (ERT 44) and Vienna (ERT 88). Fast TGV services to France all depart from Milan Porta Garibaldi, running direct to Chambéry and Paris (ERT 44).

High-speed trains from two Italian operators, Trenitalia and Italo, dash south from Milan Centrale to Florence and Rome (ERT 600). There are also direct trains to many cities around the Italian Adriatic, including Trieste and Venice (both in ERT 605), Ancona (ERT 630) and both Bari and Brindisi (ERT 631).

Milan is a **hub for regional train services** to cities across Lombardy and neighbouring Piedmont. You can follow **Route 36** (in reverse) up the Adda Valley to join the Bernina Railway in Tirano (ERT 593). There are trains at least hourly from Milan to Turin (ERT 585) and Bergamo (ERT 607).

From Milan, the railway runs south-east across flat terrain to **Lodi**, then broadly follows the River Adda downstream to **Cremona**, where the railway station is as handsome as the small city it serves. To musicians, Cremona means one thing: violins. **Antonio Stradivari** lived his entire life in Cremona. Still today, Cremonese violin making is held in worldwide esteem. It's a delightful small town, well worth a few hours even if you have no interest in violins. Local life centres on the Piazza del Comune, less than ten minutes on foot south of the railway station. From Cremona it is just a short hop east to Mantua.

Mantua (Mantova) – (suggested stopover)

Mantua is one of the finest small inland cities on the **North Italian Plain**. It is a world removed from the self-conscious style of Milan and thankfully less crowded than Verona. Arriving in town on the train from Cremona, you get a hint of what makes Mantua so special: its lakeshore setting. The railway station by **Lago Superiore** is a short walk west of the city centre. The city is on a wedge of land surrounded on three sides by water.

A quartet of **pleasant squares** are the spaces where Mantovani of all ages convivially gather. Visitors usually head first for the **Palazzo Ducale**, which occupies a big chunk of land in the north-east corner of the Old Town. This one-time home of the Gonzaga family (closed Mon) is packed with Italian Renaissance art – though, let's face it, one can have too many Renaissance crucifixions, so you'll find respite in some especially beautiful Flemish tapestries.

The other 'must-see' attraction is the **Palazzo del Te** (www.palazzote.it), also a Gonzaga palace, but dedicated entirely to relaxation and the good life. Don't miss the magnificent Mannerist frescoes.

The real appeal of Mantua lies beyond the formal sights. It is a delightful place to just spend a couple of days doing nothing more demanding than **enjoying good food**, walks and boat trips. Shakespeare made a fine job of inscribing Mantua on the English imagination. There is a famous Mantua scene in *Romeo and Juliet*, though we learn little about Mantua itself. And there is a nice scene in *The Taming of the Shrew* where Tranio suggests to a Mantua pedant that leaving the town brings only death. It is a point to ponder as you stand on the station platform waiting for the train from Mantua to Verona.

ARRIVAL, INFORMATION, ACCOMMODATION

≈ The train station is just a short walk west of the centre. **ℹ** Tourist office: Pza Mantegna 6 (www.turismo.mantova.it). ⊨ A friendly, central and family-run B&B in a historic building is the **Palazzo Arrivabene**, V. Fratelli Bandiera 20, ☎ 0376 328 685 (www.palazzoarrivabene. net). The **Agorà**, V. Leon d'Oro 13, ☎ 0349 886 0410 (www.agoraresidenza.it), is another comfortable option in the Old Town. The **Residenza Bibiena**, Pza Arche 5, ☎ 0376 355 699 (www.residenzabibiena.it), is a good B&B in a quiet area.

From Mantua the train stays to the east of the **River Mincio** as it runs north through vineyards to **Verona** (see p347), where you can connect onto two other journeys in this book: **Route 39**, which runs north through the Tyrol to Bavaria, and **Route 42** which tracks south through Tuscany to Rome.

From Verona our route runs due east through **Vicenza** and Padua to Venice. Both these intermediate cities are well worth a stop. Prosperous Vicenza was largely rebuilt in the 16th century to designs by Andrea di Pietro della Gondola, better known as **Palladio**, who moved here from Padua at the age of 16 to become an apprentice stonemason. He gave his name to the Palladian style of architecture, which applied elegant Romanesque concepts to classical forms. **Corso Palladio**, the long, straight, main street, is lined with palaces.

The **Teatro Olimpico** at the eastern end was Palladio's finest work. Based on the design of ancient Roman theatres and opened in 1585, it is the oldest indoor theatre in Europe and still in use from May to early July, and from Sept to early Oct. Palladio's most famous villa, **La Rotonda**, is on a hillside about 1.5 km south-east of the centre. It has a round interior under a dome set in a cube of classical porticoes, a design often copied.

The dignified Old Town in **Padua** (Padova in Italian) has attractive arcaded streets and traffic-free squares. **Prato della Valle**, Italy's largest square, hosts a Saturday market. In the University, founded in 1222, you can see the wooden desk used by **Galileo**, who taught physics there, and visit the old anatomical theatre.

From Padua the railway runs straight as an arrow across the plain to **Mestre**, the dismal industrial town which sits on the mainland just across the lagoon from **Venice** (see p311). But don't despair. The train continues, to terminate in Venice itself at Santa Lucia station by the **Canal Grande**. You can connect in Venice onto two other journeys in this book, both full of Habsburg flavours. Choose between **Route 34** to Vienna or **Route 27**, which continues east around the head of the Adriatic to Trieste and then on to Zagreb in Croatia.

Route 44: South to Sicily

CITIES: ★★ CULTURE: ★★ HISTORY: ★★ SCENERY: ★★★
COUNTRIES COVERED: ITALY (IT)
JOURNEY TIME: 11 HRS | DISTANCE: 858 KM | MAP: WWW.EBRWEB.EU/MAP44

Is it not extraordinary how some travel trends persist over centuries? In the heyday of the Grand Tour, privileged travellers from northern Europe travelled south in their thousands to **Naples**, but very few ever went far beyond. That's still largely true today.

In the 18th and 19th centuries the city of Naples, although raucous and scruffy, tugged irresistibly on the north European imagination – and it still does today. The French poet and librettist **Auguste Creuzé de Lesser** had words for the city. "Europe ends at Naples – and it ends there quite badly," he wrote 200 years ago. Naples has tidied itself up, but not completely. The noise and bustle of the city is complemented by the dramatic landscapes of the **Sorrento peninsula** and the islands of Ischia and Capri, with the entire ensemble presided over by temperamental Vesuvius which still spits at intervals.

Our journey takes in these Neapolitan staples to be sure, but the real appeal of Route 44 lies *beyond* Naples. This is a journey which ventures past the point where most rail travellers visiting Italy turn round and head back home. It gives a taste of the fiery harsh lands of **Basilicata** and it takes in a great sweep of the **Calabrian coast**. In a word, this is the finest coastal rail journey in this book – though that's not to diminish the appeal of **Route 8** and **40**, which between them lead from Provence through Liguria to Tuscany, sticking to the Mediterranean coast for much of the way.

Route 44 includes a short **hop on a ferry** from Villa San Giovanni, at the toe of the Italian mainland, to the Sicilian port of Messina. Five trains each day are shunted onto ferries for the crossing over the Strait of Messina. The **endgame is Sicily**, the largest island in the Mediterranean (just beating Sardinia to that record). Successive invasions by Greeks, Romans, Arabs, Normans, French and Spanish have shaped the Sicilian character; the land is a strange mixture of fertile plains, volcanic lava fields and rocky desert, while Mount Etna, the great volcano, is omnipresent, smoking in the background.

ITINERARY SUGGESTIONS

You can board an Intercity train in Rome in the morning and alight in Siracusa just 11 hours later. It would most certainly be a very enjoyable journey and it needn't be expensive. **Trenitalia** (www.trenitalia.com) often have tickets for the direct daytime trains from Rome to Siracusa for about €30. But to really catch the flavours of southern Italy, it's best to take this trip slowly with one or more stops en route. **Local trains** run the entire length of the journey, although only a selection of those slower services are shown in the ERT.

If you are really **pushed for time** and want to focus on the coastal scenery well south of Naples, you can fast-track the first third of this route by taking a high-speed train which

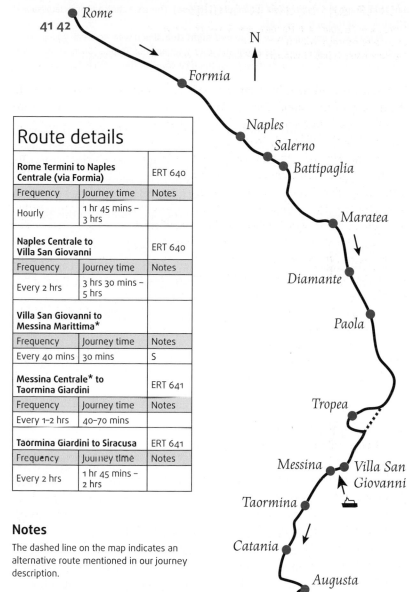

Route details

Rome Termini to Naples Centrale (via Formia)		ERT 640
Frequency	Journey time	Notes
Hourly	1 hr 45 mins – 3 hrs	

Naples Centrale to Villa San Giovanni		ERT 640
Frequency	Journey time	Notes
Every 2 hrs	3 hrs 30 mins – 5 hrs	

Villa San Giovanni to Messina Marittima*		
Frequency	Journey time	Notes
Every 40 mins	30 mins	S

Messina Centrale* to Taormina Giardini		ERT 641
Frequency	Journey time	Notes
Every 1–2 hrs	40–70 mins	

Taormina Giardini to Siracusa		ERT 641
Frequency	Journey time	Notes
Every 2 hrs	1 hr 45 mins – 2 hrs	

Notes

The dashed line on the map indicates an alternative route mentioned in our journey description.

S – Only very occasional trains are transported across the Strait of Messina to Sicily. But passenger and car ferries are frequent. The one-way fare as a foot passenger on the ferry from Villa San Giovanni to Messina Marittima is €2.50.
* – If you arrive in Sicily as a foot passenger on the boat from the mainland, you'll need to walk (5 mins) from Messina Marittima to Centrale station for the onward train journey.

runs from Rome to Salerno in just two hours (ERT 600). There's a choice of Frecciarossa and Italo trains for that initial fast hop.

Naples is an obvious choice for an **overnight stop**. If you want to break your journey on the Calabrian coast, then we suggest either Diamante or Tropea. Once in Sicily, the 'must-see' community on our journey down the east coast of the island is Taormina.

South to Naples

Our route follows the main line from Rome via Formia to Naples (ERT 640). This railway was conceived as a pioneering experiment in high-speed travel. So tortuous and slow was the old inland route through Cassino (still used and shown in ERT 626) that a new line closer to the coast was completed in 1927. Nowadays, the high-speed trains use an even newer line which opened in 2005, but we think the Formia route is the best prelude to this Sicilian adventure.

Escaping from **Rome** (see p362), you have a good view of the volcanic **Alban Hills** away to the left, then the railway skirts the wooded Lepini Hills (also to the left), before tunnelling under the great limestone massif of the Aurunci Mountains to reach the sea at **Formia**. There's no particular reason to stop, unless you want to visit Ponza, a very beautiful island served by hydrofoils from Formia. The railway briefly skirts the coast then heads in a straight line to Naples. The manner in which this railway from the 1920s defies the lie of the land is a very early example of an approach to railway engineering which returned to fashion in the new-build high-speed railways of the 1980s and thereafter.

Naples (Napoli) – (suggested stopover)

There's nowhere quite like Naples – the city is a **glorious assault on your senses**. It may have a notorious reputation as a city of crime, but its ebullience, history, cuisine and range of treasures make it a compelling stop on a southern Italian journey. The old central axis, known as **Spaccanapoli**, is a superb immersion into the Neapolitan maelstrom, so break yourself in with a pizza and a peaceful gallery visit first.

Then venture out and explore dark, crumbling, **mediaeval alleys**, with washing lines strung above and cooking smells everywhere. Watch housewives haul up bucketfuls of shopping by ropes hanging from high tenement windows. Out on the streets, you can wander for hours in the city's various districts, such as the **Sanità**, and be entertained by the performative style of daily life. All this comes with an important caveat. Petty crime is rife, notably pickpocketing and bag-snatching, so take care, especially after dark. Avoid hanging around near the Stazione Centrale. But it's by no means all edgy. Wander down to sedate **Santa Lucia**, the waterfront district to the south of the city centre, where there is a good choice of seafood restaurants.

DAY TRIPS FROM NAPLES

Naples is somewhat upstaged by its surroundings, notably the **Neapolitan Riviera** – including the beautiful but often crowded resorts of Sorrento, Positano and Amalfi, and the island of Capri, just a short boat ride away – as well as the astonishing Roman remains of **Herculaneum** and **Pompeii**.

Exploring the area is easily done by train, bus and ferry. The **Circumvesuviana** is a private venture operating local trains (half-hourly service on most routes, ERT 639) linking Naples, Sorrento, Pompeii and Ercolano (for Herculaneum). The **Sorrento Peninsula** is unbeatable if you like beaches, ancient sites, boat trips and stunning coastal scenery. Take the boat or train from Naples to Sorrento. Scenically, **Amalfi** on the south side of the peninsula has the edge over Sorrento. There are some great walks in and around Amalfi. Take the frequent bus from Amalfi up to Ravello and return by one of several very attractive paths. This delicious hilltop village has stupendous views. Lying just off the Sorrento Peninsula, the island of **Capri** has a wonderful setting, with bougainvillea, cacti and jasmine growing everywhere around the Greek-looking dome-roofed white houses.

ARRIVAL, INFORMATION, ACCOMMODATION

≽ All trains from Rome (whichever of the three lines you use) arrive at **Stazione Centrale**, which is the hub for most long-distance trains. Most Circumvesuviana services, including those to Pompeii and Sorrento, start at **Napoli Porta Nolana** station (often locally referred to as Circumvesuviana) and then stop 2 mins later at Piazza **Garibaldi**, which is very close to the main-line station at Centrale. The two stations are linked by a moving walkway. ℹ Tourist office: Via San Carlo 9 (www.visit-napoli.com).

The city centre is best explored on foot, but if you tire there is an excellent metro network. Four **funicular railways** (Funicolare di Montesanto, Centrale, Mergellina and Chiaia) link the Old City with the cooler Vomero Hill – take the funicular from Montesanto metro station to admire the views. Buy train tickets at kiosks and validate them in the machines near each platform. Buy bus tickets from news kiosks, tobacconists and bars.

⊨ If you like to experience the flavour of a lively neighbourhood full of local colour, try the friendly Hotel **Il Convento**, V. Speranzella,137/a, ☎ 081 403 977 (www.hotelilconvento.it), located in Naples' Spanish Quarter. The **Hotel Piazza Bellini**, Via SM di Constantinopoli 101, ☎ 081 451 732 (www.hotelpiazzabellini.com), is in a good, central location. Some of the higher rooms have balconies. For a dash of antique flair, try the family-run and very comfortable **Atmosfere del Centro Storico**, Corso Umberto I, 23, ☎ 0339 300 00 56 (http://bbatmosfere.blogspot.com), near the university.

The Tyrrhenian coast

Most trains running south-east from Naples duck round the back of **Vesuvius**, passing to the north of the volcano. A small number of trains (mainly local services to Salerno) take the old coastal railway, which is slower but much recommended. Opened in 1839, this was the very first railway in Italy. The slopes of Vesuvius rise up to the left and there are fine views to the right across the **Gulf of Naples** to Sorrento and Capri. The way to discern if a train takes the coastal line is to see if it stops at Torre Annunziata. If a train doesn't stop there, then it almost certainly follows the less interesting inland route.

Whichever way you skirt Vesuvius, the two routes from Naples converge in **Salerno**, a port city which is altogether more ordered than Naples. Salerno marks the start of the best section of this route. The Intercity trains take about four hours for the run south down the coast to **Villa San Giovanni**. Choose a seat on the right side of the train for great sea views. If you really want to make the most of the journey, consider using one of the slower trains on this route. The semi-fast RV services (shown in ERT 640 but not identified as such) add an hour to the journey time and require a change of trains at Paola.

True **slow travel aficionados** might opt for the local trains which run the whole way down the coast (not shown in ERT). With four dozen intermediate stations between Salerno and Villa San Giovanni, it'll take a day or two and you'll need to change trains several times along the way.

The railway heads inland, turning south at Battipaglia, where in the distance – on the lower slopes of the **Monti Picentini** – you'll glimpse **Eboli**, the village which inspired Carlo Levi's *Christ Stopped at Eboli*. When Levi arrived in handcuffs in remote Basilicata in 1935, the locals were quick to remind him that theirs was a region beyond the edge of civilisation, abandoned by God and the authorities. For the writer-in-exile, this was another world, one "hedged in by custom and sorrow, cut off from history and the State, eternally patient." Italy's southern provinces of **Basilicata** and **Calabria** have benefited in recent years from massive investment, not least in transport infrastructure and that sense of isolation from civilisation, captured so well by Carlo Levi, is no longer very evident. But it is still a place apart, a region where the values and norms of the north seem very foreign.

To the right of the railway is the small walled town of **Paestum**, once one of the most important cities of **Magna Graecia**, the territory of the ancient Greeks which included Sicily and the southernmost shores of mainland Italy. Beyond Paestum, the railway cuts through **Cilento National Park**, a wilderness area of rare beauty which figures centrally in Greek mythology. The appeal of this stretch of the railway is the manner in which it plays cat and mouse with the coast, swapping views of azure seas for glimpses of wild defiles and mountain streams. The province of Basilicata touches the **Tyrrhenian coast** only briefly (though it has beaches aplenty away to the east on its Ionian coast), but it presents in **Maratea** a good spot to break the journey. A huge statue of Cristo Redentore (Christ the Redeemer) dominates the town; it is easily visible from the train. One glance at the marina – which has its own small railway station just south of Maratea itself – will convince you that this short stretch of Basilicata coast has been discovered by the chic set.

South of Maratea, the railway sticks firmly to the coast until Gizzeria, a stretch of about 130 kilometres. Only occasional tunnels interrupt the sea views. Of the various small communities along the coast, **Diamante** is the best choice for an overnight stop. Citrons and peperoncini are culinary staples in Diamante and you'll find **seafood aplenty** in this engaging small town. A safe hotel choice is the Stella Maris, V. Cavour 12, ☎ 0985 87 70 52 (www.stellamarisdiamante.it), on the seafront, where it is definitely worth paying the small supplement to secure a room with sea view.

Much further down the coast, another fine spot to stop off for a day or two is **Tropea**. With a fine setting on a rugged stretch of coast, this is a resort justifiably popular with Italians. It is worth checking accommodation availability before arriving. We've never stayed in Tropea ourselves, but hear good reports of the Residenza Il Barone, Largo Barone, ☎ 0963 60 71 81 (www.residenzailbarone.it). Note that only slower trains serve Tropea; the faster services cut south from Pizzo, avoiding the coastal loop around Capo Vaticano which serves Tropea and a number of other beach communities. The two lines converge again at Rosarno.

Beyond **Rosarno**, there are many more tunnels but still sufficient open stretches, as the train skirts the Costa Viola, to afford fine views across to Sicily. At **Villa San Giovanni**, there is the rare pleasure of watching your train being shunted onto a ferry for the short voyage to Sicily.

Sicily

Messina, Sicily's nearest port to the mainland, was the victim of an earthquake in 1908 that shook for two months and claimed 84,000 lives, and of a massive attack by US bombers in 1943. But even those events could not take away its glorious setting beneath the mountains. Much has been rebuilt in a stable, squat style. Trains from the mainland arrive on the ferry at Stazione Marittima, and continue to Stazione Centrale.

CONNECTIONS FROM MESSINA AND MILAZZO

From Messina Centrale, a railway runs along the north coast of Sicily to the island's capital at **Palermo** (ERT 641), along the way stopping at Milazzo, the departure point for the ferries and hydrofoils to Lipari and its neighbouring islands (ERT 2570).

If you have travelled all the way to Sicily by train and fancy returning to **Naples by boat**, we especially recommend the twice-weekly ship (operated by *Siremar*) from Milazzo to Naples (www.carontetourist.it). The 18-hour journey starts with an afternoon cruise through the Aeolian Islands, stopping off at four or five small ports along the way. The last island stop is at Stromboli, from where the vessel continues overnight to Naples. Sicily is also well placed for onward travel to **Sardinia** (see our **Sidetracks** feature on p381).

Sit on the left side of the train for the onward journey to Siracusa. Once we escape Messina's dismal suburbs, there are fine views over the **Ionian Sea**. The first place of note is **Taormina**, a pretty town on a hillside overlooking Sicily's east coast with some striking Greek and Roman ruins. Mount Etna makes a beautiful backdrop to the south. Taormina is a picture-postcard spot. It is the ideal place to slip into the slow Sicilian way of life.

Taormina's only drawback is that the railway station (called Taormina Giardini) is on the coast way below the town itself. But you'll be rewarded for your effort in climbing up to the town by **breathtaking views**. And, if you don't fancy the climb, there's a useful shuttle bus that connects the station with the centre of Taormina. If you are minded to stay overnight, we can recommend the Villa Fiorita, V. L Pirandello 39, ☎ 0942 24 984 (www.villafioritahotel.com), which is very comfortable and has ample, well-furnished public spaces.

Beyond Taormina, you may want to shift to the right side of the train for views of **Mount Etna**. The last two hours of the journey, from Taormina down to Siracusa are dominated by the volcano. The principal city is **Catania** where you can connect onto a local railway which circles around the back of Mount Etna (ERT 644). It's a brilliant circuit, affording views of Etna from all angles.

South of Catania, the railway slips by the **Gulf of Augusta**, its coast much despoiled by some hideous chemical plants. It makes arrival in Siracusa seem all the better.

Siracusa

The city marking the end of our long journey from Rome is superb, one which in its history captures the entire Mediterranean experience. For **Cicero**, Siracusa was "the greatest Greek city and the most beautiful of them all." The sights are all gathered on **Ortygia Island**, just a short walk south-east of the main railway station and linked by two bridges to the mainland. There is a lively **daily fish market** on V Emanuele de Benedictis as you cross from the mainland onto Ortygia. Vegetables, fruit and dairy products are traded too, but fish stands centre stage.

Don't miss the impressive **cathedral**; it is essentially a baroque design, but it incorporates ancient columns which were once part of a Greek temple on the same site. That building encapsulates what is so very special about Siracusa. It is a city which has reinvented itself a dozen times over the centuries. Had the devotees of the **Grand Tour** ever ventured beyond Naples and come this far south, they would have discovered something well worth writing home about.

ARRIVAL, INFORMATION, ACCOMMODATION

≽ On the mainland, north-west of the Old Town. 🚹 Tourist office: V. Roma 31 (www. siracusaturismo.net). ⊨ A friendly B&B on the Island of Ortygia, overlooking the channel between the island and the mainland is **L'Approdo delle Sirene**, Riva Giuseppe Garibaldi 15, ☎ 0931 248 57 (www.apprododellesirene.com). Also a good option right in the heart of the Old Town is the **Archimede Vacanze** B&B, Pza Archimede 2, ☎ 0339 140 98 09 (www. archimedevacanze.it). Or try the stylish **Palazzo del Sale B&B**, V. Santa Teresa 25, ☎ 0931 659 58 (www.palazzodelsale.com), on the western side of Ortygia, well placed for the evening *passeggiata* along the Foro Vittorio Emanuele II.

SIDETRACKS: BY SEA TO SARDINIA

When Sicilian winter weather became too overbearing for the English writer **DH Lawrence** and his wife Freda, the couple took a break in Sardinia (Sardegna), taking care to make bacon sandwiches and prepare a thermos of tea before setting out from their home in Taormina in the east of **Sicily**. First they took the train to Messina ("dreary, dreary hole" wrote Lawrence), and then journeyed by train along the north coast to Palermo.

DH Lawrence wrote a wonderful account of the couple's journey by **train through Sicily**, the crossing by ship from Palermo to Cagliari and their nine days exploring Sardinia, much of the latter by train. *Sea and Sardinia* was published in 1921 and remains a classic piece of travel writing. It is witty, insightful and tells us as much about Lawrence as it does about Sardinia. Definitely a volume to pack if you branch off from **Route 44** and head by train from Messina to Palermo (ERT 641), thinking that you might board the ferry for Sardinia.

In Lawrence's day, the boat ran just fortnightly. Nowadays there is a service from Palermo leaving on Saturdays. The route is operated by Tirrenia (see ERT 2675). The **ferry route** takes you to Cagliari, by far the largest and most modern-looking city on the island.

Cagliari was much rebuilt following wartime bomb damage, but there's a compact Old Town inside the imposing 13th-century walls, with a warren of brick-paved lanes and two Pisan towers, Nuraghic artefacts in the **National Archaeological Museum** (closed Mon) and a Roman amphitheatre. As the capital of Sardinia, Cagliari offers the greatest opportunity to sample the fine cuisine and wines that are so characteristic of the island.

From **Cagliari**, one rail route heads west and another heads north. The latter is much the finer of the two options. DH Lawrence perfectly caught the flavour of rail travel in Sardinia when he wrote: "It is a queer railway. I would like to know who made it. It pelts up hill and down dale and round sudden bends in the most unconcerned fashion." The rail network is more limited today than it was when Lawrence visited, but it's still fun. Outline schedules are shown in ERT 629.

Sardinia's second city, **Sassari**, is an obvious place to head for. It is a busy commercial, administrative and university town. You can experience real Sardinian life here in the knot of medieval streets before taking the train on to either Porto Torres or Olbia, both of which offer a wealth of onward shipping connections.

You might, by way of example, consider taking the regular daytime ferry from **Porto Torres to Barcelona**, a longish route across the Mediterranean that thrives because of the long-standing cultural and trade links between Catalonia and north-west Sardinia. At Barcelona you can connect onto **Route 13** and **14**. Both Porto Torres and Olbia have ferries to Genoa (for **Route 40** and **43**). Details of all ferry routes mentioned above are in ERT 2675.

If travelling through Sicily and Sardinia has not exhausted your appetite for islands, then **Corsica** beckons. The French island is less than an hour from Sardinia by boat (ERT 2566).

BALKAN JOURNEYS
An introduction

The Balkan region is for many rail travellers a **taste of a more exotic Europe**. But rail travel in this region has been sorely hit by troubled public finances, lack of investment and sometimes even downright bad management. So many **journeys require careful planning** and, with timetables liable to change at short notice, it's essential to double check your itinerary just before travelling. There have been times when we might have found ourselves stranded on Balkan journeys were it not for the fact that the region is generally well served by buses.

Rail fares are so cheap throughout much of south-east Europe that rail passes are really redundant. Those valuable passes are best reserved for journeys in parts of Europe where train fares are more expensive. In many areas, there may be no first-class seating on trains and, even where there is a designated first-class carriage, it may be no more comfortable and just as crowded as second class. But there are always the exceptions which prove the rule. There are comfortable **Spanish-built Talgo trains** which trundle through Bosnia with improbably luxurious seating in first class. There are some nicely retro first-class Romanian carriages where you can sink into plush red seats and enjoy watching the hills slip by beyond the window.

Lack of connectivity

Easily the most frustrating element of rail travel in the region is the propensity of operators to just cancel entire routes without any consultation or advance notice. In 2017, the cross-border trains from Vršac to Timişoara were axed, so severing the last direct passenger train service between **Serbia and Romania**. A pretty poor show, all the more so when one considers that there were once eight separate railways crossing the border between the two countries.

Successive editions of this book have been bedevilled by the sheer perversity of national rail administrations in the Balkans whose vision rarely extends beyond national borders. **Croatia** scrapped a swathe of services, so putting an end to *inter alia* the Belgrade-Sarajevo and Budapest-Sarajevo trains which both briefly traversed Croatian territory. The **Bosnian authorities** have axed the last international train service from Sarajevo, namely the daily train to Zagreb. Things are no better in **Albania**, which has no rail link crossing its borders. International services to and from **Greece** are patchy, while as of late 2019 there is just one train each day from **Kosovo**; it runs from Prishtinë/Pristina to North Macedonia. But it's not all doom and gloom. In **Hungary** and Romania, you'll find extensive rail networks with some of the finest rural rail experiences in Europe. ■

Route 45: The long haul south

CITIES: ★ CULTURE: ★ HISTORY: ★★ SCENERY: ★★
COUNTRIES COVERED: HUNGARY (HU), SERBIA (RS), BOSNIA & HERZEGOVINA (BA),
MONTENEGRO (ME)
JOURNEY TIME: 21 HRS | DISTANCE: 874 KM | MAP: WWW.EBRWEB.EU/MAP45

Leon Trotsky travelled south from Budapest in 1912 in order to report on the Balkan Wars for the newspaper *Kievskaya Mysl*. Trotsky nicely captured the essence of the journey with the observation in his diary that "although the railway line from **Budapest to Belgrade** proceeds mainly in a southerly direction, from the cultural standpoint one moves eastward." Trotsky went on to remark on the kaleidoscope of cultures and languages that he saw as his train paused at wayside stations along the route. More than a century later, the ride south from Budapest to Belgrade and beyond is still remarkable for the same reasons.

The first part of the journey wins no prizes for dramatic scenery. It traverses landscapes that are often pancake flat. The **Pannonian Plain** is the dried-up bed of a vast inland sea that once lay between the Carpathian Mountains and the uplands of southern Serbia. Although the route as far as Belgrade has Danubian landscapes aplenty, you will not see a lot of the river itself, but there is a dramatic **crossing of the Danube** at Novi Sad. Beyond Belgrade, which is most definitely worth a stop, the scenery picks up as we travel through the hill country of western Serbia, slipping by stealth (and only briefly) into Bosnia & Herzegovina, then continuing through rugged terrain to reach the coast of Montenegro at the port of Bar. There are good bus connections up and down the Adriatic coast from Bar, as well as a regular ferry link over to Bari in Italy.

A CAUTIONARY NOTE

Note that a major programme of **track renewal** has been taking place in Serbia throughout 2019, particularly north of Belgrade. So there have been no through trains from Budapest to Belgrade during much of 2019. Normal services should be reinstated by early 2020. Other major Serbian rail infrastructure projects, funded in part by China or Russia, are planned for 2020 and beyond. These may affect services running south from Belgrade to Bulgaria, North Macedonia and the route to Montenegro described here. Check the *European Rail Timetable* or www.srbvoz.rs for details (click on the flag for English-language pages).

Leaving Budapest

Our journey starts at **Keleti station** in Budapest, which has a touch of old-style grandeur about it. Statues of James Watt and George Stephenson adorn the neoclassical facade, inviting travellers into this great cathedral of transport. Well... most passengers. The world saw another rendering of Hungarian hospitality in summer 2015, when thousands of Syrian refugees were denied access to Keleti station.

Route details

Budapest Keleti to Subotica		ERT 1295
Frequency	Journey time	Notes
3 per day	3 hrs 50 mins	
Subotica to Belgrade Centar		ERT 1360
Frequency	Journey time	Notes
6 per day	3 hrs 45 mins – 4 hrs 40 mins	
Belgrade Topčider to Bar		ERT 1370
Frequency	Journey time	Notes
2 per day	11 hrs	A

Note

A – Additional trains run on both the Serbian and Montenegrin sections of the route, but it is only the twice-daily direct trains from Belgrade to Bar which cross the Serbian-Montenegrin border. There are, for example, four local trains per day from Belgrade Centar to Užice, and three per day from Užice to Prijepolje. There are five local trains per day along the Montenegrin section of the line (in addition to the Belgrade to Bar expresses).

HU = Hungary
RS = Serbia
BA = Bosnia & Herzegovina
ME = Montenegro

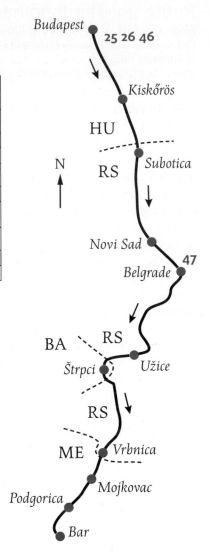

THE ROUTE TO SAFETY

This initial part of this route, from Hungary to Serbia, is precisely that which in 2015 was followed in the reverse direction by **thousands of refugees** looking to find safety and security in Germany. It's interesting to reflect that the rights which we enjoy to roam across Europe at will are not shared by all travellers. The curtailment of some train services in the Balkans was a measure used by the rail operators in 2015 to stem the flow of refugees travelling north from Greece towards Hungary and beyond. The flow of refugees has abated, but some train services were never restored.

Heading **south from Budapest** (read more on the Hungarian capital on p242), you might well wonder why Hungarians refer to this great plain as *puszta*, a term that has only derisory connotations. This is no arid wasteland at all, but a varied landscape with areas of productive farmland, prairie-like grasslands, forests and great saline depressions, often filled with brackish waters. There is something of the Hungarian soul in these sweeping landscapes. They have inspired Csontváry's art and Sándor Petőfi's poetry.

The poet and revolutionary Petőfi was born in **Kiskőrös**, and there is hardly a Hungarian alive who has not made a pilgrimage to his birthplace. Unless you are a real Petőfi fan, we would say it is hardly worth the stop, but you'll get serious kudos from Hungarian fellow passengers if you can recite a line or two of Petőfi's *Nemzeti dal*, which holds revered status as Hungary's national poem. An hour or two south of Kiskőrös, the train approaches the border with Serbia. **Kelebia** is the last stop in Hungary, and the train waits here for 30 minutes. Kelebia is a straggly village dominated by railway sidings. It makes a living from its position by the international border. This is an old-style frontier where passports really are properly checked.

Subotica (Суботица) is a strange introduction to Serbia, but it is a very fine place to start **exploring the Vojvodina**, that region of northern Serbia which celebrates its peculiarly multicultural character. Subotica is full of surprises, and top of the list is the extraordinary mix of languages you will hear in the streets, typical of Serbia's semi-detached northern province which has several official languages (see box on next page). The town has a Habsburg feel to it, more central European than Balkan in character. Indeed, enjoying coffee and cake in the many outdoor cafés, you might easily imagine you were in a provincial city in Austria. Subotica offers a feast of art nouveau architecture, among them the lovely town hall (with a gorgeous blue fountain outside) and the more restrained synagogue. Near the station is another striking art nouveau building, the **Raichle Palace**, which houses a gallery of modern art (closed Sat afternoon & Sun).

South through the Vojvodina

The train journey south from Subotica traverses pretty Vojvodina agricultural landscapes with villages clustered around monumental churches. There are Slovaks, Croats, Rusyns and many other ethnic groups. The first station stop south of Subotica is named **Bačka Topola** (Бачка Топола) on Serbian maps, but the Hungarians who form the majority of the population in the town call it Topolya. Next stop is **Vrbas** (Врбас), a town full of Rusyns, Montenegrins and Serbs. This is one of Europe's most strikingly multi-ethnic areas.

The Vojvodina capital of **Novi Sad** (Нови Сад) is a bustling city, though it takes a vivid imagination to understand why the locals call it the Serbian

LANGUAGES OF VOJVODINA

The **cultural mosaic** of Vojvodina is sometimes difficult for outsiders to fathom. Six official languages with daily or weekly newspapers in all of them, and a long tradition of multilingual education suggest that Vojvodina is something quite extraordinary. Beyond the six official languages (Serbian, Hungarian, Rusyn, Slovak, Romanian and Croatian), a handful of other tongues crop up in isolated villages. But **multicultural Vojvodina** is not always a place full of happy interactions between its constituent communities. If you take time to explore the region, you'll discover that specific villages are often home to just one language group – many of whose members might well be hard pushed to have any sensible conversation with speakers of another language living in the next village down the road.

Athens. The city suffered terribly in the NATO bombing of Yugoslavia in 1999, rather surprisingly in view of the fact that the authorities in Novi Sad and much of the local population had little time for the Milošević government in Belgrade. Mention Novi Sad to young people across Europe and you'll quickly discover that the Danube city is intimately associated with one annual event: the **Exit music festival** (www.exitfest.org) that is staged every July in the Petrovaradin Fortress, located on the south bank of the Danube opposite Novi Sad. You'll get a glimpse of the fortress when you leave Novi Sad on the Belgrade-bound train as it crosses Drumsko-železnički most, an improvised structure that carries rail and road traffic over the Danube. To the right of the train, as it rumbles over the blue girder bridge, you'll see **Petrovaradin Fortress** in the distance. The train then skirts the eastern edge of the Fruška Gora hills, with fleeting glimpses of the Danube to the left. It takes just 90 minutes to travel from Novi Sad to Belgrade.

On the final approach into the Serbian capital you cross the **River Sava**. The old main station close to the city centre has been sacrificed to property developers. All trains from the north run to the new Belgrade Centar station (often referred to as Prokop) which is now Belgrade's major rail hub.

Belgrade (Београд) – (suggested stopover)

Wandering around Belgrade's relaxed **Old Town**, with its chic restaurants, galleries and boutiques, it's almost impossible to imagine that it's less than 20 years since the city endured heavy bombardment by NATO planes. Today the Serbian capital is generally a serene metropolis, particularly as two of its main districts are pedestrianised – the Roman-era streets around Knez Mihailova, home to many of the city's best shops, eateries and museums, and the bohemian restaurant district **Skadarlija**. Despite – or perhaps because of – what they have suffered over the years, the citizens of Belgrade now seem focused on life's simple pleasures, socialising at the many tiny bars and clubs dotted around, shopping or just sitting and watching the world go by in a café or in **Trg Republike**.

As a destination, Belgrade ticks all the boxes. It's positively brimming with culture – not only is the city a living historical site in itself, but it boasts museums on everything from African art and the football club Red Star Belgrade to the weird and wonderful gifts given to President Tito during his decades in power. There are plenty of pleasant outside spaces for strollers to enjoy, from the car-free centre to various city parks and gardens, topped off by the showpiece **Belgrade Fortress** in **Kalemegdan Park**, a large green area popular with families, couples and walkers. South of Kalemegdan, Princess Ljubica's Konak is a superb example of 19th-century Serbian architecture.

Arrival, information, accommodation

 Most main-line trains now arrive at **Beograd Centar**, some way south of the centre. But there are some important exceptions. Locals trains to Vršac depart from **Dunav** station. International direct trains bound for final destinations in Montenegro, North Macedonia and Bulgaria normally depart from **Topčider** station, which is even further out from the centre than Centar. The station name may evoke images of an apple beverage, but it's actually a small but historic station once used as the base of Tito's presidential *Blue Train*. The station reopened to regular passenger traffic in 2018.

 Belgrade's Nikola Tesla Airport is 18 km west of the city centre (www.beg.aero). 72 runs to the airport from Zeleni venac market every 35 mins with a stop in Novi Beograd, taking 30–40 mins for the run. The city has an integrated and comprehensive public transport system of buses, trolleybuses (except in Novi Beograd) and trams. Buy tickets in advance from a kiosk or on board (valid for 90 mins). Tourist office: Knez Mihailova 56 (www.tob.rs).

 Well located close to Knez Mihailova is **Kopernikus Hotel Prague**, Kraljice Natalije 27, 011 321 4444 (www.hotelprag.rs), a good mid-range option. Conveniently located not far from Beograd Centar station and the city centre is the friendly **Hotel Argo**, Kralja Milana 25, 011 364 0425 (www.argohotelbelgrade.com). One of the city's most famous landmarks, the **Moskva**, Terazije 20, 011 364 2069 (www.hotelmoskva.rs), is more expensive, but the art nouveau building offers rooms of character and class.

Belgrade Connections

You can connect in Belgrade onto **Route 47** in this book, following it north-west to Zagreb in Croatia (ERT 1320) or south via Sofia to Thessaloniki. Belgrade Centar station has useful direct services to Slovenia and Austria. Note that the direct rail route from Belgrade via Vršac to Timișoara in Romania, featured in recent editions of *Europe by Rail*, has sadly been closed. It was the last remaining passenger service linking two countries which once enjoyed a rich network of cross-border connections. Serbian Railways continue to offer a service as far as **Vršac** (ERT 1365) which departs from Belgrade's incredibly run-down Dunav station. Vršac (Вршац) is well worth a visit; it's a laid-back place with faded Hapsburg style, a Romanian minority and some decent local wines.

In a Balkan region with generally poor rail services – though renewed investment now promises improvements in the years ahead – it's no surprise that Belgrade is a **major hub for express coach services**. So there are useful direct services from Belgrade Bus Station (at Železnička 4, www.bas.rs) to Split on Croatia's Adriatic coast and on **Route 46** (12 hrs); major cities in Bosnia & Herzegovina, including Banja Luka (6 to 9 hrs) and Sarajevo (7 hrs); Skopje in North Macedonia (6 to 9 hrs); and various destinations in **Kosovo** including Pristina/Prishtinë (6 to 8 hrs) and Prizren (8 hrs). Those with a real appetite for long-distance bus travel may want to hop on the weekly overnight direct service to Athens, 1,200 km and 16 hours away.

Belgrade to Bar

Belgrade is the jumping-off point for one of Europe's finest rail journeys. It's the route from Belgrade to Bar in **Montenegro**, and this is the first time we've featured this journey in *Europe by Rail*. It's a magnificent ride through scenery that gets ever better as you progress south. Along the way we'll cross three international frontiers and over 400 bridges.

The construction of this extraordinary railway in the 1970s was first and foremost a political project, one conceived as part of **Josip Broz Tito's great nation-building agenda** in socialist Yugoslavia. Communications served to unite Tito's far-flung federal republic, and the route from Belgrade to Titograd (as Podgorica, nowadays the capital of independent Montenegro, was called in Tito's day) and Bar was pure political ambition. It even had an international dimension, as Yugoslavia agreed to fund a branch railway running south from Titograd into Albania – in those days a brave political move given Yugoslav worries about Albanian irredentism in Kosovo and the serious ideological disputes between the authorities in Tirana and Belgrade. For more on rail travel in socialist Yugoslavia see the box on p396.

PRACTICALITIES

It's about 520 km from Belgrade to Bar by train. The route is served by two direct trains daily. There is an overnight service called the *Lovćen*, named after a mountain in Montenegro. The daytime train is called the *Tara*. These two trains are the only services of the day to cross the border from **Serbia to Montenegro**. Both these trains leave from Topčider station on Belgrade's southern fringes. All local trains, terminating at Serbian stations along the first half of the route (such as Užice), leave from Belgrade Centar.

Our view is that it'd be a pity to miss on the glorious scenery on this route, so **take the day train** if you can. It leaves Topčider at 09.00 (but check times before travelling). The one-way fare to **Podgorica** is €19.20, to Bar €21.

It's not worth buying a first-class ticket. If there are first-class carriages on the train (it does happen!), our experience is that there's a sign on them indicating they may be used by holders of 2nd-class tickets. Given that it's an 11-hour run to Bar, you may want to consider breaking the journey overnight. This is best done once in Montenegro, as from Bijelo Polje there are five daily trains down to the coast. **Mojkovac** is a good choice. The Hotel Dulović, Trg Ljubomira Bakoča, ☎ 067 631 654 (www.hoteldulovic.me) is a 15 minute walk from the station. From Mojkovac, there's a conveniently timed morning train which takes three hours to reach Bar.

From the flatlands around Belgrade, the train to Bar takes slowly to the hills. There is no great drama for the first 200 km or more of the route, but it's a pleasant enough ride, especially as the railway cuts through the hills south of **Valjevo** (Ваљево). It's beyond Užice (Ужице) that the railway starts to tussle with the landscape.

Beyond Jablanica, the railway makes a 13-km detour into eastern Bosnia & Herzegovina. While the *Tara* slips through Bosnia without stopping, the thrice-daily local trains from Užice to Prijepolje do pause at **Štrpci** station. It's an interesting backdoor route into Bosnia, although one tainted by a terrible massacre at Štrpci in February 1993, when non-Serb passengers travelling on a train from Belgrade to Bar were abducted and murdered by a Serbian paramilitary brigade. For more on trains which make short cross-border diversions into another country, see our Sidetracks feature on p421.

Returning to Serbia, the train to Bar follows the **Lim Valley** upstream to the border with Montenegro. Just by the railway station at Vrbnica, the last stop in Serbia, is the Kumanitsa Orthodox monastery. After Bijelo Polje, the railway forsakes the River Lim, taking to the hills as it skirts the **Biogradska Gora National Park**. Mojkovac, though hardly inspiring, is good for an overnight stop (see note above), then come the finest three hours of the journey. Snatches of virgin forest, then great canyons and stark limestone ridges as the railway climbs to over 1,000 metres high above the Tara Gorge just beyond Kolašin. Then the train sweeps down through long tunnels and dramatic loops, crossing the **Mala Rijeka Viaduct** (Europe's highest railway viaduct), to reach tamer terrain around **Podgorica** (Подгорица).

PODGORICA CONNECTIONS

Podgorica is the hub of Montenegro's sparse rail network. The railway station in Podgorica is quite unwelcoming. But it is the starting point for a pretty branch line which runs north-west up the Zeta Valley to **Nikšić** (ERT 1370). The railway from Podgorica into Albania didn't open until long after Tito's death, and it has never carried passenger traffic. But the capital of Montenegro is still the best jumping-off point for excursions south into Albania. There are direct buses to **Shkodër** (2 hrs) and **Tiranë** (4 hrs). The morning bus from Podgorica reaches Shkodër in time to connect onto the lunchtime train to **Durrës**.

From Podgorica, the railway parallels the River Morača to reach beautiful **Lake Skadar**, one extremity of which the train crosses on a causeway, along the way passing (on the right) the island fortress at Lesendro. Then the train plunges under the Dinaric Alps in the 6-km Sozina Tunnel, emerging on the shores of the Adriatic at the unpretentious small resort of Sutomore. This final hour from Podgorica to Bar really is pure theatre. **Bar** itself is sadly something of an anticlimax. If you are tempted to stop, **Sutomore** may be the better bet.

BAR AND SUTOMORE DETAILS

⮈ The station in Bar is 1.5 km south-east of the modern city centre (which is close to the port) and about 3.5 km west of the Old Town, Stari Bar. **Jadrolinija** (www.jadrolinija.hr) sails from Bar to Bari in Italy (ERT 2738).

There are hourly direct buses from Bar down the coast to Ulcinj (40 mins away), for onwards bus connections into Albania. There are direct buses from both Bar and Sutomore to Kotor (2 hrs), with two buses per day continuing to Dubrovnik (4hrs) where you can connect onto **Route 46**. The bus station in Bar is close to the railway station. If you want to stay in Bar, try the **Hotel Princess**, Jovana Tomasevica 21, ☎ 030 300 100 (www.hotelprincess.me), located close to the beach and the city centre.

⮈ The station in Sutomore is at the southern end of the city centre, with the bus station nearby. Right on the beach front, the **Sea Fort**, ul. Obala Iva Novakovica bb, ☎ 069 314 888 (www.seafort.me) offers large and comfortable rooms in Sutomore.

Sidetracks: Through Albania

Comb the various online travel forums that focus on Adriatic travel and there is one question that recurs with unfailing regularity: "How do I get from Dubrovnik to Greece without going through Albania?" And of course the travel pundits who haunt those virtual communities give all the right advice. There are **direct boats from Dubrovnik to Bari** (ERT 2795), from where there is an onward ship to Greece (ERT 2755) serving Corfu, Igoumenitsa (in the Thesprotia area of north-west Greece) and Pátras (in the northern Peloponnese, about 200 km west of Athens). But few on those online forums query why one would ever want to avoid Albania. True, a couple of days making an Adriatic dog-leg to reach Greece by ship from Dubrovnik would surely be very relaxing. But to skip Albania (and for that matter Montenegro too) is to miss two of Europe's most intriguing countries.

In this edition of *Europe by Rail*, we've included a rail journey from Belgrade to the Montenegro coast for the first time. But what if you follow the next route in this book and end up in Dubrovnik? How do you head down the coast? And can you really cut through Albania to reach Greece? The answer to that last question is yes. And here's how to do it.

You can make the entire journey **south from Dubrovnik through Montenegro into Albania** on local buses. But we suggest relying instead on longer-distance bus services; it means you spend less time sitting on buses, but it does require a couple of overnight stops with plenty of time for sightseeing. Those overnight stops are probably best made in Kotor and Tiranë.

Times given here are correct in October 2019. There are direct buses from **Dubrovnik to Kotor** at 11.00 and 15.00. The journey takes two hours. Tickets can be booked on www.buscroatia.com. The lovely Bay of Kotor is a real highlight of Montenegro, and the UNESCO-listed town of Kotor on the shores of a great fjord surrounded by high mountains is stunning. If you have time, spend two nights in Kotor and use the intervening day to make a side trip to the mountain town of **Cetinje** (Цетиње), which flourished in the late 19th century as the capital and principal centre of Montenegrin culture. It is not for nothing that many Montenegrins still refer to Cetinje as the honorary capital of their country.

From Kotor, there is a direct bus at 08.00 every morning to **Tiranë**. The journey takes six hours, and the bus routes via Podgorica to enter Albania by the north-east corner of **Lake Shkodër**. Details on www.kotortotirana.com. From Tiranë there are direct coaches to Athens, but that's the boring option. Far better to take the Riviera Bus service which now runs daily from **Tiranë to Sarandë**. It leaves the Albanian capital at 10.00 (details and bookings on www.rivierabus.com), routing via Vlorë and the spectacular coast road to reach Sarandë from where there is now a year-round direct **hydrofoil to Corfu**. The crossing takes just 35 minutes; you'll find details on www.ionianseaways.com.

Once in Corfu, you can plot your onward journey to the Greek mainland, whether with just a short ferry hop over to Igoumenitsa or a longer sea passage down to **Pátras**. Whatever you decide, you'll have the satisfaction of having made a journey through a part of Europe which is well off the beaten track.

Route 46: From the Danube to Dalmatia

Cities: ★★ Culture: ★★ History: ★★ Scenery: ★★
Countries covered: Hungary (HU), Croatia (HR)
Journey time: 17 hrs 30 mins | Distance: 1,037 km | Map: www.ebrweb.eu/map46

Hungarians have always looked towards the Adriatic. Until the First World War, Hungary effectively controlled the seaport of Fiume (nowadays Rijeka in Croatia), with Budapest financiers promoting **Fiume** as a rival to the great Austrian port of Trieste (see p253). The tradition of leaving the Budapest heat and decanting to the coast for the summer was as established a seasonal rhythm as the Parisian flight to the Riviera. Those who could afford it followed the Hungarian nobility to the resort they called Abbázia (still as lovely a place as ever, and now known more widely as Opatija). Other Hungarians would make for resorts down the **Dalmatian coast**: Crikvenica, Zadar, Šibenik or Split.

This journey for *Europe by Rail* retraces a pilgrimage of yesteryear – but one which remains enduringly popular with residents of Budapest today. It is a mark of Hungarians' continuing affection for the Adriatic that there are many special summer-only direct trains from Budapest to cities on the coast of Slovenia, Croatia and Montenegro. Of course, not everyone can afford to travel so far, but closer to home is **Lake Balaton**, often affectionately referred to as the Hungarian Sea. Landlocked countries have to use their watery assets as best they can.

So, on our journey from Budapest to **Split**, we shall cruise the south shore of Lake Balaton and stop off in the largest city on the way: Zagreb. We'll then take the slow train down to the coast at Split and conclude the journey by travelling by bus or fast ferry to **Dubrovnik**.

By day or by night: thoughts on itinerary

For an authentic **meet-the-locals experience**, you could book a seat on the Friday night holiday special from Budapest to Split. This train is called the *Adria*, and it runs daily for an 11-week summer season. But the Friday departure is your chance to catch the *Adria* at its surreal best. It is packed to the gills with families looking forward to a week of sun, sea and sand.

As the train tracks out through Budapest suburbs, hearty picnics are being shared and before long parents are telling their kids bedtime stories. But no one sleeps and neither will you. After a 14-hour journey, you'll arrive in Split dog-tired in the morning.

So, yes, you could take the *Adria*. But you probably won't, because there are sensible daytime alternatives. In summer, there is a good crack-of-dawn train from **Budapest to Zagreb** which takes the lakeshore route past Balaton (ERT 1220). The year-round afternoon train from Budapest to Zagreb takes a less interesting route which misses the lake. Stop off in Zagreb, continuing at will by day train to Split and then on to Dubrovnik. If you take the boat rather than a bus for that last leg to Dubrovnik, you're in for a real treat.

The early train from Budapest to Zagreb is called the *Agram*, recalling the name which German-speaking elites in Vienna often used for Zagreb. It's

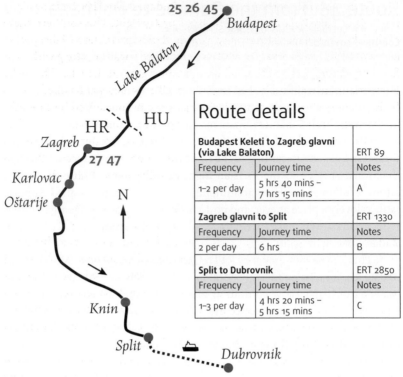

Route details

Budapest Keleti to Zagreb glavni (via Lake Balaton)		ERT 89
Frequency	Journey time	Notes
1–2 per day	5 hrs 40 mins – 7 hrs 15 mins	A

Zagreb glavni to Split		ERT 1330
Frequency	Journey time	Notes
2 per day	6 hrs	B

Split to Dubrovnik		ERT 2850
Frequency	Journey time	Notes
1–3 per day	4 hrs 20 mins – 5 hrs 15 mins	C

Notes

In summer 2019, Split had direct holiday trains from Budapest. This service will most likely be again on offer in summer 2020.

A – There is an additional year-round direct daytime train from Budapest to Zagreb. It also departs from Budapest Keleti station, taking a more southerly route to the Croatian border which does not pass Lake Balaton.
B – There are also overnight trains from Zagreb to Split.
C – Seasonal service by catamaran with a choice of two operators. In 2019, the catamaran link from Split to Dubrovnik ran from mid-April until late October. A year-round bus service is available as an alternative to the boat.

not a name which ever found favour with the locals, so there's a touch of imperial posturing in using it today as a train name. Expect a mix of older Hungarian and Croatian carriages, some with separate compartments, others open-plan. If you are inclined to travel first class, bear in mind that the seating there is entirely in compartments – if you don't like compartments, it's definitely not worth paying the extra. For **good views** of Lake Balaton, sit on the right side of the train. The *Agram* leaves from the **Déli station** in Budapest: it has none of the antique grace of the city's two other main termini. For more on Budapest see p242.

Little more than an hour after leaving Budapest, you'll be cruising along the bank of **Lake Balaton**. It's not always a pretty sight. This southern shore of the lake was the focus for intense organised tourism in the socialist period of the last century. Workers needing a well-earned vacation, along with their families, would flock to cheap accommodation around the lake. The lucky ones had vouchers which guaranteed an all-expenses-paid holiday – no frills, of course. Comradely solidarity has since been eclipsed by capitalist avarice and the area has paid a heavy price for overdevelopment.

Once past Balaton, it's not far to the **Croatian border**, where there's usually a quick check of passports. Over the border, the train cuts through the hills separating the Drava from the Sava Valley to reach Zagreb.

Zagreb (suggested stopover)

Zagreb has a distinctly **Austro-Hungarian flavour**, both in architecture and, on first impression, the restrained manners of its citizens. Its oldest and most beautiful quarter is **Gornji grad** (Upper Town), with the cathedral-dominated Kaptol area. To reach it, begin from Trg Bana Jelačića, the main square, and follow Ilica, to reach Tomićeva, where you can take the funicular up to Strossmayer promenade for one of the best views over the city. A cannon is fired daily at 12.00 from **Lotrščak Tower**.

Next take Ćirilometodska to St Mark's Church, noted for its extraordinary 'coat of arms' red, white and blue tiled roof, and follow Kamenita to pass through an archway, housing a shrine complete with altar, flowers and flickering candles. Turn left up Radićeva, and take one of the series of steep wooden stairways to your right, which link the upper town to **Kaptol**. In the cathedral look for the inscription of the Ten Commandments on the northern wall, written in 12th-century Glagolitic characters unique to the old Slavic language. Zagreb's fine art collection is in the **Mimara Museum**, Rooseveltov Trg 4 (www.mimara.hr; closed Mon).

Despite its straight-laced image, Zagreb is culturally quite mixed. For more on social divides in Zagreb, see our further comments on the city at the very start of **Route 47**.

ARRIVAL, INFORMATION, ACCOMMODATION

⇌ In the centre of town. 🅸 Tourist offices: Trg Bana J Jelačića 6 (www.infozagreb.hr) and at the railway station. ⊨ Try the **Jägerhorn**, Ilica 14, ☎ 01 483 3877 (www.hotel-jagerhorn.hr), Zagreb's oldest hotel, in the heart of the Old Town. Close to the main square and within walking distance of museums, eateries and cafés is **Hotel Dubrovnik**, Ljudevita Gaja 1, ☎ 01 486 35 12 (www.hotel-dubrovnik.hr). A simple, friendly B&B is the central **Lobagola**, Bosanska 3, ☎ 01 580 19 90 (www.lobagola.com).

✗ The central and certainly most obvious destination for coffee by day and beer by night is popular Tkalčićeva street, leading from Trg Bana J Jelačića up to Gornji grad. For a good introduction to Croatian cuisine and wines, head for the well regarded, family-run **Trilogija**, Kamenita ul. 5, ☎ 1 4851 394 (www.trilogija.com) in Zagreb's Old Town.

ZAGREB CONNECTIONS

You can connect in Zagreb onto two other journeys described in this book: **Route 27**, which you can follow (in reverse) back to Venice, and **Route 47**, which runs right through the Balkans to Greece. Zagreb has an excellent range of train services. There are direct daytime trains from Zagreb to Belgrade (ERT 1320), Ljubljana (ERT 1300), Munich (ERT 62) and Vienna (ERT 91). For travellers heading to the Alps and western Europe, there is a very useful overnight train from **Zagreb to Zurich** (ERT 86).

Over the hills to Split

We have mixed feelings about the long leg from Zagreb to Split. In the **depths of winter**, it can be a stunning ride. In mid-summer, the train is often very crowded. The train journey to Split has become a rite of passage for large numbers of young and often affluent travellers from western Europe. Anyway, this is a route where you should definitely **reserve a seat** in advance, even if only on the eve of your departure from Zagreb.

The railway parallels the motorway as far as **Karlovac** and then takes to the hills. The journey up the Mrežnica Valley is very pretty, but the best is yet to come. South of **Oštarije**, the train runs the entire length of the **Lika Railway** (Lička pruga in Croatian) through formidably desolate terrain which can be very snowy in winter. The summit of the line at Rudopolje is at 870 metres above sea level.

As the railway drops down towards the **Krka Valley**, the train crosses territory which in the 1990s was part of the Republic of Serbian Krajina (RSK). It was formally assimilated back into Croatia in 1998. It is still a region where the scars of the terrible war years are all too evident. All trains stop at **Knin**, the former RSK capital. It is an unloved town, but it does have a useful bus connection to Zadar (ERT 1330). From Knin, it is less than two hours down to the coast. From the right side of the train you'll get good views of Split on the approach.

Split (suggested stopover)

Split's old core is built around the remains of **Diocletian's Palace** which was constructed 2,000 years ago for the Roman emperor's retirement. The waterfront **Riva** buzzes all day with a string of pavement cafés. The traffic-free Old Town consists of narrow paved alleys, opening out onto ancient piazzas. From here the tourist office's self-guided walk leads through town; a series of information boards highlight Split's Roman roots, the Cathedral of St Duje, and the various buildings dating back to the times of Venetian and Austro-Hungarian rule. Climb the **cathedral bell tower** for fine views.

Continue through the area of Varoš, where steep winding steps take you to the wooded Marjan peninsula. One of Split's best museums is the **Meštrović Gallery** (www.mestrovic.hr) in Šetalište Ivana Meštrovića 46.

EXCURSION FROM SPLIT: TROGIR

The **UNESCO** World Heritage-listed city of Trogir lies just 30 km west of Split. Buses leave from Split's main bus station every 30 mins, taking half an hour for the ride. Wander around Trogir's narrow cobbled streets, stopping off at the cathedral and the **Kamerlengo Fortress**. The waterfront fills at night with pavement cafés and seafood restaurants in summer and there are regular boat excursions to the nearby islands. The tourist office in Trogir is at Trg Ivana Pavla II 1 (www.visittrogir.hr).

Ivan Meštrović was a Split-born sculptor whose work can be seen all over the country and overseas, with one of the most striking examples being the hulking statue of **Grgur of Nin** on the northern edge of Diocletian's Palace.

ARRIVAL, INFORMATION, ACCOMMODATION

≥ Trains, buses and ferries all arrive in the same area, overlooking Gradska Luka, the town's harbour. The historic centre is just 100 m away to the north-west. ✈ Split Airport (www.split-airport.hr), 20 km from Split. Buses to and from Split every 30 mins. 🚹 Tourist office: Peristil bb (www.visitsplit.com), situated close to the seafront (or Riva).

⊨ A friendly B&B, close to the harbour on the edge of the Old Town, is **Kastel 1700**, Mihovilova Sirina 5, ☎ 021 343 912 (www.kastelsplit.com). It varies from quite affordable to pricey depending on season. Split has a number of apartments for rent which can be good value. Try the **Split Apartments Peric**, ul. Lučićeva 13, ☎ 098 331 475 (www. splitapartments-peric.com), just a few minutes' walk north of the Old Town. Well located just a few minutes east of the Old Town is the friendly and very affordable **B&B House Sandra**, Nincevica 11, ☎ 099 685 21 99 (www.housesandra.com).

✕ Simple eating places offer a fixed menu at budget prices. For typical Dalmatian food join the locals at **Kod Jose**, Sredmanuška 4, behind the market. For a cheap stand-up lunch with locals try *ribice*, tiny fishes deep fried and served with a glass of red wine, in a canteen-style establishment opposite the fish market (**Ribarnica**), Kraj Sv. Marije 8. Get ultra-fresh fruit and veg and local smoked cheeses at **Stari Pazar**, the colourful open-air green market held each morning just next to the east wall of Diocletian's Palace.

Coast and islands

The onward journey from Split to Dubrovnik is a stunning ride on a very smart catamaran which weaves its way between some of Croatia's most beautiful islands – including Hvar and Korčula. It is an utterly memorable ride but it's not cheap. The one-way fare from **Split to Dubrovnik** is 210 Croatian kuna (about €28.50). It's a seasonal service which in 2019 ran from April to October (see www.krilo.hr and www.jadrolinija.hr for timetables). The boat trip from Split to Dubrovnik takes four or five hours (ERT 2850).

If you are travelling off-season, when there is no boat service, you'll need to take the bus from Split to Dubrovnik. The bus runs down the **Adriatic Highway** (Jadranska magistrala in Croatian), cutting through a little sliver of Bosnian territory at Neum. Most buses take just over four hours. Sit on the right side for views of the coast. It's a fun ride, but not a patch on the boat.

Dubrovnik

Dubrovnik is one of the most impressive mediaeval fortified cities on the Mediterranean. The best way to get a feel of the place is to walk the full 2 km circuit of the **walls** (open summer 08.00–18.30, winter 09.00–15.00), but do avoid the hottest hours, especially if you've sampled Dubrovnik's atmosphere to the full the night before. For centuries Dubrovnik was a refined and prosperous trading port, which managed to keep its independence by paying off various would-be conquerors. Buildings such as the **Rector's Palace**, the **Sponza Palace** and **Jesuit Church** still bear witness to this glorious past. There's a major festival, mid-July to mid-Aug, with outdoor theatre, jazz and classical music (www.dubrovnik-festival.hr).

ARRIVAL, INFORMATION, ACCOMMODATION

🚌 Autobusni kolodvor is on the harbour front of Gruž port, 3.5 km from the Old Town. 24-hr left luggage. Take local bus 🚌 1a/1b/1c/3/8 to the Old Town. Bus timetables for city and regional services at www.libertasdubrovnik.com. ✈ Dubrovnik Airport is 20 km south of Dubrovnik and 5 km from Cavtat, 30 mins by bus. ⛴ Gruž port, Gruška obala; Jadrolinija runs a service to Bari in Italy (limited services in winter; see www.jadrolinija.hr); the Krilo catamaran to Split and the local boat service from Dubrovnik to Šipan also leave from here (www.krilo.hr). 🛈 Tourist office: Brsalje 5 (www.tzdubrovnik.hr) and at the port building.

🛏 A good option in Babin Kuk (near Gruž port) is **Hotel Perla**, Šetalište kralja Zvonimira 20, ☎ 020 438 244 (www.hotelperladubrovnik.com), or try **Hotel Lapad**, Lapadska obala 37, ☎ 020 455 555 (www.hotel-lapad.hr), on the harbourside overlooking Gruž port. The family-run B&B **Pension Stankovich**, ul. Matije Gupca 15, ☎ 098 182 73 38 (www.pension-stankovich.weebly.com), is a friendly and comfortable place in a central location with great views of the Old Town of Dubrovnik. ✗ Try along Prijeko, parallel to the central street, Placa, the main area for eating out within the city walls.

CONNECTIONS FROM DUBROVNIK

The trains that once served Dubrovnik are long gone. But you can leave by boat. Jadrolinija run a seasonal ferry service over to Bari in Italy (ERT 2795). For advice on travelling down the coast to Albania, see our **Sidetracks** feature on p390.

THE TRAIN TO DUBROVNIK

The last train left Dubrovnik 43 years ago. The railway to Dubrovnik was part of an extensive **narrow-gauge network** which once extended from Sarajevo to Podgorica. In 1965, the fastest train from Dubrovnik to Sarajevo took over ten hours. In 1966 the narrow-gauge line from Sarajevo to Mostar and Ploče was converted to standard gauge, leaving only peripheral fragments of the old narrow-gauge network (like the Dubrovnik branch). The narrow-gauge railways of the region were a legacy of **Austro-Hungarian influence**. The demise of the network was born of good intentions. In Tito's Yugoslavia, there was a strong commitment to renewing aged rail infrastructure and building new lines – of which the most celebrated was the line from **Belgrade to Bar** (ERT 1370), newly included in this edition of *Europe by Rail* as part of **Route 45**. The new line to Bar opened in May 1976 in the same week as the last train ran to Dubrovnik. Had the Bosnian narrow-gauge network survived, it would surely today be a cherished asset in promoting tourism – much like the Rhaetian Railway network in eastern Switzerland.

Route 47: Through Balkan byways to Greece

CITIES: ★★ CULTURE: ★★ HISTORY: ★ SCENERY: ★★
COUNTRIES COVERED: CROATIA (HR), SERBIA (RS), BULGARIA (BG), GREECE (GR)
JOURNEY TIME: 25 HRS | DISTANCE: 1,166 KM | MAP: WWW.EBRWEB.EU/MAP47

Cast back half a century and, in the late 1960s, you could board the *Direct Orient Express* when it stopped in Zagreb in the wee small hours of the morning and be in Sofia by early evening. Today's travellers don't have it quite so easy, but this route repays time and effort on a journey that takes in **three capitals** (Zagreb, Belgrade and Sofia) and concludes with a ride through the **fine hill country** of south-west Bulgaria to reach northern Greece.

RECOMMENDED ITINERARY
This journey is best tackled over three days, with overnight stops in **Belgrade** and **Sofia**. If you share our affection for more rural landscapes, then you might consider stopping off in the beautiful **Struma Valley** for a night or two. The Bulgarian spa town of Sandanski (Сандански) would be a good choice for this, all the more so if you can take time for an excursion by bus to the vineyards around **Melnik** (Мелник).

The main railway station in **Zagreb** was made for grand departures. This neoclassical Habsburg building is one of the finest stations designed by Hungarian architect Ferenc Pfaff. Half a century ago, the departure boards at Zagreb Glavni recorded the passage of trains to Athens, Hamburg, Istanbul and Paris.

Around Zagreb station

Take a look around the vicinity of the station before leaving Zagreb (read more on the city itself on p393). The north is the posh side of the railway tracks. The distinguished Croatian writer **Miroslav Krleža** wrote a damning essay on social (and spatial) divides in Zagreb in 1937. To the north of the station, he found "hot water, roulette, lifts, *on parle français*, Europe, good!" Over on the south side of the railway there were "open cesspits, malaria... Balkan, a sorry province." To Krleža, those quarters of Zagreb beyond the railway were "the back of beyond, Asia." That from a left-leaning writer who was keen to shock the Zagreb bourgeoisie – all by definition residing north of the railway – out of their complacency.

Nowadays, the cesspits south of the tracks are long gone and the district between the railway and the river, while not pretty, is an edgy part of town where activists protest against real estate speculators. Even Zagreb has its rebel zone. If you incline towards more sedate cityscapes, stick to the north side of the station where the **Esplanade Hotel** still has uniformed bellboys and the Paviljon restaurant attracts an affluent elite who like elaborate cakes and seem not to have noticed that the Habsburg Empire disappeared a while

Route details

Zagreb to Slavonski Brod — ERT 1320

Frequency	Journey time	Notes
Every 2 hrs	2 hrs 50 mins – 4 hrs	

Slavonski Brod to Belgrade — ERT 1320

Frequency	Journey time	Notes
1–2 per day	3 hrs 40 mins	

Belgrade to Niš — ERT 1380

Frequency	Journey time	Notes
7 per day	4 hrs 20 mins – 5 hrs 20 mins	C

Niš to Dimitrovgrad — ERT 1380

Frequency	Journey time	Notes
4–5 per day	2 hrs 45 mins – 3 hrs 30 mins	

Dimitrovgrad to Sofia — ERT 1380

Frequency	Journey time	Notes
1 per day	2 hrs	X

Sofia to Blagòevgrad — ERT 1560

Frequency	Journey time	Notes
7 per day	2 hrs 10 mins – 3 hrs 20 mins	

Blagòevgrad to Kulata — ERT 1560

Frequency	Journey time	Notes
6 per day	1 hr 20 mins – 2 hrs	Y

Kulata to Thessaloniki — ERT 1560

Frequency	Journey time	Notes
1 per day	3 hrs 15 mins	Z

Notes

C – Most services now leave from Beograd Centar which, despite its name, is not at all central. It lies well south of the city centre. The summer-only direct train from Belgrade to Sofia departs not from Centar but from Topčider station.

X – Remember that clocks advance by one hour as trains cross the Bulgarian border just after leaving Dimitrovgrad.

Y – All trains on this route stop at Sandanski. Some journeys from Blagòevgrad to Kulata require a change of train at General Todorov.

Z – Passengers may be conveyed by bus from Kulata (Bulgaria) across the border to Strimon in Greece. The bus leg is about 15 km long.

back. Both the Esplanade and the Paviljon are visible from the front of the station. It's also impossible to miss the statue of **good old King Tomislav** and his horse which arrived here in 1947 and commemorates the tenth-century monarch who is credited with having created the first coherent Croatian state. Whatever you make of Tomislav, the statue was a good way of recycling old cannons which were melted down to secure the bronze needed.

Through Slavonia

The chances are that you'll take the main daytime train from **Zagreb to Belgrade** (Београд). It carries sleeping cars from Zurich which have traversed five countries on their overnight journey from Switzerland to the Croatian capital. It is only the Serbian carriages on this train which continue to Belgrade, so take care to join the correct part of the train. Our experience is that these carriages usually only have second-class seating, so it's definitely not worth paying extra for a first-class ticket on this leg.

The six-and-a-half-hour journey from Zagreb to Belgrade runs through mainly flat terrain – part of the **great Pannonian Plain** – but that's not to say it's boring. The railway line traverses the easternmost of Croatia's four historic provinces: the region called **Slavonia**.

The first scheduled stop for the fast train is at **Dugo Selo** where the pavilion-style station building is a taste of what's to come. The train runs south-east, to the right the motorway and to the left land rising gently to the **Moslavina vineyards**. All the while, the railway nudges ever closer to the border with Bosnia & Herzegovina. If you are tempted to do a little pedestrian border hopping, your chance comes at **Slavonski Brod**. This is an interesting community, a town divided by the Sava River, which itself forms the border between Croatia and Bosnia. The area on the far bank is called Brod to distinguish it from its Croatian counterpart on the north bank. It's an easy 20-minute walk from the station down past the ruined fortress to the bridge over the River Sava. If you take the early morning slow train from Zagreb (it leaves at 07.41 in October 2019, but that may change in 2020), you'd have two-and-a-half hours in Brod before joining the fast train for the onward journey to Belgrade. Would that it were possible to actually travel by train across the border from Croatia into Bosnia! The last passenger rail service between the two countries, a once-daily train from Zagreb to Sarajevo, was withdrawn in December 2016.

From Slavonski Brod, the railway runs north-east through a region scarred with the legacy of the war in the early 1990s, when Croatia strenuously asserted its independence from federal Yugoslavia. Multicultural Slavonia was ravaged by strife between Serbs and Croats. Just over half an hour from Brod, the train stops at **Vinkovci**, the largest city in Slavonia. The railway station seems unduly large for the few trains which now serve the town, but that's a mark of Vinkovci's historic role as a transport hub. If you are tempted to stop, you'll find a surprisingly elegant traffic-free central area.

The train to Belgrade rolls on across the dark plain to reach **Tovarnik**, a village which would barely warrant a stop bar for the important fact that it's the last community in Croatia. Just over the fields lies the **border with Serbia**. It's not so many years since minefields in this border region continued to pose a major danger. Today, all is calm and the border formalities, conducted at Tovarnik and at Šid (Шид) on the Serbian side are invariably civil and often even good-humoured.

Sedately through Serbia

The fast train from Zagreb takes under two hours to travel from **Šid to Belgrade**, with five scheduled stops along the way. It doesn't rush. This is pleasant, undemanding country: the **Sava flatlands** drifting away to the southern horizon on the right side of the train, while to the left there are the distant ripples of the forested hills known as Fruška Gora. The first stop is at **Sremska Mitrovica** (Сремска Митровица), the biggest community in Serbia's Srem region and a relaxed riverside town which traces its history back to the Roman settlement of Sirmium.

Beyond Sremska Mitrovica, agriculture slowly gives way to more urban development. This final stretch of the journey from Zagreb ends with a nicely dramatic moment as the train crosses the **River Sava** on its approach into Belgrade. It is this river which has set the geographical tone for the entire journey from Zagreb, but it is only now as we near Belgrade (more on which on p386) that we cross the Sava for the first time. Note that Belgrade lies on another journey featured in this book: **Route 45**.

From Belgrade to Sofia

Throughout summer 2019 there was a **once-daily direct train** from Belgrade to Sofia. It ceased operating in mid-September, but with some reassurances from the Serbian and Bulgarian railway authorities that it would be reinstated for the 2020 summer season. If it does indeed return, that will be a blessing, but there are alternatives. Throughout the year, you can travel by train from Belgrade to Sofia with two changes of train along the way, viz. at Niš (Ниш) and Dimitrovgrad (Димитровград). The direct train, if and when it runs, follows the same route.

Within twenty minutes of leaving Belgrade on the southbound train, you are passing **Rakovica** (Раковица), famous for the Orthodox monastery and infamous for its abandoned factories. Skirting low wooded hills, the rail route drops down into the Morava Valley which it then follows upstream for some hours towards the border with North Macedonia. The communities along the valley are unremarkable places, yet this valley is seen by many Serbs as constituting the historic heartland of Serbian life and culture. Parts of central Kosovo are accorded similar iconic status.

There is no special reason to break your journey until **Niš** (Ниш), a major regional centre and the largest city in southern Serbia. Yet Niš has a couple of very unusual sights. Devotees of dark tourism should not miss the **Skull Tower** (Ćele Kula), a grisly memorial on the edge of town at Bulevar Dr Zorana Đinđića erected by Ottoman forces who suppressed a Serbian uprising here in 1809. The skulls of dead Serbian forces were mounted on a tower as a cautionary reminder of the folly of contesting Ottoman supremacy in the region. A chapel protects the remains of the tower. 🚌 1 from the city centre runs to the Skull Tower.

Only slightly less dark than the Skull Tower is the **Nazi concentration camp**, located north of town on Bulevar 12 Februar in the Crveni Krst (Red Cross) district of Niš, which offers frightening insights into the horrors of war. Between 1941 and 1944, many Roma, Jews and Yugoslav communists were interned and murdered here. The site hosts a museum (closed Mon).

Leaving the main line at Niš, there is immediately a sense of entering another world. We've swapped a double-track electrified railway for a humble single-track rural line where trains are hauled by an ancient blue diesel engine which was once reserved for use on the luxury *plavi voz* (Blue Train) which ferried Yugoslav leader President Tito around the country. But there is no hint of luxury on the slow train to Dimitrovgrad. The railway follows the Nišava Valley up into increasingly rugged hills, along the way passing through **Bela Palanka** (Бела Паланка) and **Pirot** (Пирот), the latter newly raised to city status and still noted for its fine traditional woven carpets. From Pirot it is just a short hop onto Dimitrovgrad, the last station before the Bulgarian border, and a community where ethnic Bulgarians outnumber Serbs by two to one. The language spoken in this border region is Torlak, a South Slavic transitional dialect which has elements of both Serbian and Bulgarian.

At **Dimitrovgrad**, the Serbian diesel engine is swapped for an electric Bulgarian one and before long the train is running south-east, paralleling the main road across the border. In just another hour, we are running through the suburbs of the Bulgarian capital. The train terminates at Sofia's newly renovated main railway station.

Sofia (София) – (suggested stopover)

Nudging up against the slopes of **Mount Vitosha**, the Bulgarian capital enjoys a fine setting. But the city itself, it must be said, is unremarkable. It's a perfectly good spot to spend a day or two, but it certainly doesn't have the multicultural appeal of Budapest, the entrepreneurial spirit of Tirana or the historical riches of Thessaloniki. The newly renovated central railway station is nowadays much smarter than it was a few years back. Most newcomers to Sofia make first for **Alexander Nevsky Cathedral**, where if you can spare the time it is worth staying for a service. Orthodox liturgies include some fine ecclesiastical theatre. Don't miss the impressive collection of icons in the crypt. Of the museums, the one that really stands out is **Muzeiko** (www. muzeiko.bg; closed Mon), an interactive science centre for kids which opened in late 2015 and has quickly become a hit with visitors of all ages.

While many east European capitals have wantonly destroyed statues from the Communist period, Sofia has sensibly gathered them together in a statue park adjoining the **Museum of Socialist Art**, 7 Lachezar Stanchev (closed Mon). This really is one of the most ambitious museums in the city, one which has pulled much critial praise since opening in 2011. The real appeal of Sofia is the residents' laid-back approach to life, and it's a fine place to drift from café to café. If you need respite from the city heat, make for the slopes of Mount Vitosha.

ARRIVAL, INFORMATION, ACCOMMODATION

≋ bul. Mariya Luiza, a 20 min walk north of the centre. **ℹ** Tourist office: bul. Tsar Osvoboditel 22 (www.visitsofia.bg).

⊨ A good budget option, a short walk to the centre yet in a quiet area, is **Hotel Light** (Лайт), ul. Veslets 37, ☎ 02 983 12 43 (www.hotellight.com). Well located for the railway station is the comfortable and highly regarded **Hotel Favorit** (Фаворит), ul. Knyaz Boris I 193, ☎ 02 931 93 91 (www.hotelfavorit.bg). Or try the more upmarket and recently renovated boutique hotel **Les Fleurs**, bul. Vitosha 21, ☎ 02 810 08 00 (www.lesfleurshotel. com), located right on Sofia's main shopping street.

CONNECTIONS FROM SOFIA

Sofia's location in western Bulgaria means that the capital is not really a natural hub for rail traffic in the country. That said, there are some onward connections. The country's second city, **Plovdiv** (Пловдив), which in many respects has more to offer to visitors than the capital, is just a short hop away by fast train (ERT 1500). It makes a good day trip from Sofia. If you are heading for Bulgaria's **Black Sea coast**, don't underestimate journey times. Journeys from Sofia to both **Burgas** and **Varna** take about eight hours (ERT 1500).

There are also some useful international links, among them the overnight train to Halkalı, on the outskirts of Istanbul (ERT 1550), and a seasonal daytime train to **Bucharest** (ERT 61).

South to Greece

The onward journey to Thessaloniki starts by skirting the north-west side of Mount Vitosha and passing through the industrial town of **Pernik** (Перник). The route then follows the valley of the River Struma downstream the entire way to the Greek border and beyond. **Dupnitsa** (Дупница) is the first place of note, surrounded by fields of tobacco with the Rila Mountains rising up impressively to the east. Tucked away in those hills is the most celebrated of the Orthodox monasteries of Bulgaria. For seven centuries or more, the

Monastery of St Ivan of Rila has been a beacon of Orthodox faith in the southern Balkans. For Bulgarians, it is much more. It has been the custodian of Bulgarian history, literary tradition and language. No surprise perhaps that on high days and holy days, great crowds of visitors from Sofia and other Bulgarian cities flock to Rila. It's definitely worth a visit, ideally off-season (it's open all year). The **nearest railway station** (served by all trains on the Struma Valley rail route) is Kočerinovo (Кочериново), from where it's 30 km to Rila Monastery. A taxi might be your best bet, though for the journey down from the monastery an inducement of a few leva will easily secure a lift from the monastery car park back down to the Struma Valley.

The largest town in the Struma Valley is **Blagòevgrad** (Благòевград). First impressions may not tempt you to stop, but give Blagòevgrad a chance. It's a lively, amiable spot, and the upper part of town blends nicely into the surrounding hills. An hour south of Blagòevgrad is **Sandanski** (Сандански). It's a short hop by bus from the railway station to the town centre (4 km away). This leafy spa town is a nice place to relax for a day. The real reason most people stop off, however, is to make a day trip by bus to **Melnik** (Мелник), 17 km east of Sandanski. Melnik has a spectacular setting amid **deeply eroded sandstone hills**, with a landscape dominated by bare ridges and *coulisses*. You don't need to be a geomorphologist to be impressed. Throw in some fine vernacular architecture and a **local viticultural tradition**, which dates back to antiquity and produces splendid red wines, and you begin to see why Melnik is such a magnet. The local grapes are unusually small, but they produce hefty tannic wines which find favour on dinner tables far beyond the Balkan region.

From Sandanski, it's just 20 minutes down to the Greek border at **Kulata** (Кулата) and from there not far to Thessaloniki. As of October 2019, passengers on this route are required to change from the train to a **rail replacement bus** at Kulata. The bus runs down the main E79 highway, which is a fast dual carriageway weaving between forested hills with the River Struma to the right. After about 20 minutes, the bus reaches the railway station at Strimon where a local Greek train awaits for the onward ride to Thessaloniki.

Thessaloniki (Θεσσαλονίκη)

The second largest city in Greece was founded in 315 BC. Many of the interesting sights are within a 10- to 15-min walk of the **Plateia Aristotelous**, an elegant pedestrian-only square opening onto the sea and rimmed by popular open-air cafés. The Old Town was destroyed by fire in 1917 and suffered a severe earthquake in 1978. Thessaloniki today is a modern, busy city, laid out along a crescent bay – yet it's a worthwhile place to stop over, with some elegant corners and a lively night scene (thanks primarily to the large number of young people who study here). A good area to eat and go out at night is **Ladadika**, a short taxi ride west of the centre, where former warehouses have been refurbished to house countless bars, tavernas and small clubs. Alternatively, try the bustling tavernas that line the narrow alleys of Athinos, just off Plateia Aristotelous in the centre.

The city became strategically vital to the Romans, straddling the **Via Egnatia**, their highway between Constantinople and the Adriatic, and later to the Byzantines and their Turkish conquerors. It was one of the greatest cities of the Ottoman Empire, rejoining Greece only in 1913. On the seafront promenade, the **White Tower**, the most prominent surviving bastion of the Byzantine-Turkish city walls, stages an exhibition tracing the city's history.

A five-min walk north-east from here, the vast **Archaeological Museum** (www.amth.gr) houses finds from different parts of Macedonia. The city's **Roman heritage** includes remains of the Forum, Odos Filipou, the Palace of Galerius, Plateia Navarinou, the Baths, the 4th-century Rotonda, and the Arch of Galerius, beside Odos Egnatia, near Plateia Sintrivaniou.

The city also has a fine collection of Byzantine churches (giving Thessaloniki's status as a **UNESCO World Heritage Site**), the most notable of which are the restored 4th-century Agios Dimitrios, and the 8th-century Agia Sofia, decorated with stunning golden mosaics. Those who enjoy food shopping should also check out the colourful **Modiano** covered market between Vasileos Irakleiou Str and Ermou Str.

ARRIVAL, INFORMATION, ACCOMMODATION

✈ 1 km west of the centre on Monastiriou Str. (take 🚌 3 to the centre via Plateia Aristotelous). ℹ Tourist office: Plateia Aristotelous (www.thessaloniki.travel).
🛏 A good-value option between the station and the city centre is **Hotel Colors Central**, Oplopoiou 1 & Katouni, ☎ 231 600 7676 (www.colorscentral.gr). Or try the stylish **Hotel Olympia**, Olympou Str. 65, ☎ 231 036 6466 (www.hotelolympia.gr), well located north of Plateia Dikastirion. Also central and close to both the Roman Forum and Agios Demetrios, **Hotel Orestias Kastorias**, Agnostou Stratiotou 14 str. & Olympou str., ☎ 231 027 6517 (www.okhotel.gr) offers good, comfortable rooms.

CONNECTIONS FROM THESSALONIKI

Thessaloniki is the **gateway to Greece**. Athens is just over four hours away on a direct Intercity (IC) train (ERT 1400). In addition to the five daytime IC trains each day, there is an overnight service from Thessaloniki to Athens (though, in these days of austerity in Greece, there are no sleeping cars or couchettes on this night train).

Another possibility from Thessaloniki is to head west: there are five direct trains each day to beautiful **Edessa** (ERT 1410). Visit Edessa (Έδεσσα) to discover just how water can transform a cityscape. With its rapids and old mills, Edessa is strangely redolent of Tampere in Finland (see p303). The railway continues beyond Edessa to drab **Florina** (also ERT 1410), about which the best we can say is that it's just a short hop over the border to Bitola in the **Republic of North Macedonia**, where you can pick up a train to Skopje (ERT 1385). There are connections from Thessaloniki to Kalambaka, changing at Paleofársalos (ERT 1400 and 1408), for the gravity-defying monasteries of the **Meteora**. Services from Thessaloniki to Turkey have not run for many years.

SIDETRACKS: SOUTH FROM SERBIA

During 2019, a new country name appeared on the political map of Europe, as the Former Yugoslav Republic of Macedonia morphed into the **Republic of North Macedonia**. It signalled a rapprochement in the long-standing squabble between Greece and its northern neighbour over the use of the name Macedonia.

It's very easy to visit North Macedonia as an adjunct to **Route 47**. During the summer months, there's a direct overnight train from Belgrade's Topčider station to Skopje, the capital of North Macedonia (ERT 1380). This train follows Route 47 to Niš, where it arrives just after eleven in the evening. This seasonal overnight service is the only scheduled passenger train from Serbia into North Macedonia. It is no surprise, therefore, that most locals use buses rather than trains for cross-border travel. On the train, there's a choice of second-class seating or couchettes. **Frontier formalities** take place at an hour when you would rather be asleep at Preševo (Serbia) and Tabanovce (North Macedonia). At the latter, the locomotive is usually changed, and a little railway ritual of yesteryear is played out as men in overalls walk the length of the train carefully tapping each wheel – presumably to check it is still intact. The train reaches Skopje about 04.30, and continues south to the **Greek border**, from where there is a connecting bus to Thessaloniki in Greece (which is at the end of Route 47).

That pre-dawn arrival in **Skopje** may not be for those who value uninterrupted sleep, but on a summer morning there's a real pleasure in watching the capital of North Macedonia slowly awake. The city centre lies south of the **Vardar River** in a part of the city which is modern, chaotic and generally Christian. Walk over the old stone bridge, itself the most well-known North Macedonian landmark, to the north bank of the Vardar and you'll discover quite another Skopje, a city that is ancient, in the main Muslim and as chaotic as the south bank. For all the bustle, Skopje is a great place just to wander. North-bank highlights are the **Kale Fortress** and the **Mustafa Pasha Mosque**, opposite the main entrance to the fortress, which has an especially lovely rose garden. From the mosque there are good views over the Old Bazaar. Dive into this area to discover back lanes, several very fine mosques, old Ottoman inns (often with wonderfully secluded courtyards overlooked by wooden balconies) and a covered market.

If you've had your fill of Skopje, the next obvious destination is another newish state, namely **Kosovo**. There's a train each afternoon from Skopje to **Prishtinë/Priština** (ERT 1375), capital of the fledgling state where the fault lines of faith and culture still have to be carefully negotiated. An hour after leaving Skopje, the train is approaching the border with Kosovo, where the frontier formalities at **Hani i Elezit** are very smooth. It is necessary to change trains there. Hani i Elezit is an unlovely sprawl, dominated by a cement factory. But within a few minutes, the railway runs up a beautiful wooded valley towards Kaçanik.

Beyond **Kaçanik** the landscape opens out as the train crosses flatter terrain. There are houses that were half-destroyed in the Kosovo War. And there are half-built houses, mere shells of bricks and mortar whose owners wait for remittances from abroad to fund the windows, doors and utilities. As so often in the Balkans, there's a lot of unfinished business.

EXPLORING EAST
An introduction

For many residents of western Europe, the eastern boundaries of their home continent are vague and imprecise. Few have any inkling that the centre of Europe lies well east of Warsaw. Villages in Lithuania and Ukraine both stake credible claims to being right in the middle of the continent. The combined area of Ukraine, Moldova, Belarus and that part of the Russian Federation which lies geographically within Europe is larger than the entire European Union (EU) – although, with just 165 million people, notably less densely populated than the EU which has, at least until Britain leaves the fold, just over 500 million residents.

The truth is that Europe east of the old **Curzon Line** – that line on the map of Europe which in 1919 rather arbitrarily defined the western borders of the Soviet Union – is, bar for the Baltic States and a handful of major Russian cities, rather *terra incognita* for most who live and work in the westernmost regions of the continent. That's a pity, as those who venture east invariably comment on the **warm reception** they receive, especially in rural regions, and the ease with which one can explore much of eastern Europe by train.

In this section of *Europe by Rail*, we nudge our readers to expand their eastern horizons but we make no great forays into the Russian Federation. If and when Russia relaxes its visa regime, we may be tempted to include more Russian routes. For now, we include just one itinerary running beyond Warsaw, namely **Route 50** to **St Petersburg**, from where one can follow **Route 33** (in reverse) west to Helsinki. We also include in this section a journey through the **Baltic States**, now extended to include a ferry journey to Stockholm. And we have two routes to western Ukraine.

As ever, there were many routes we would gladly have included had more space been available. With time, **travellers might consider** other routes east through Poland beyond those mentioned here. One can track east from Hamburg via Stralsund and Szczecin to Gdańsk and beyond (although bear in mind that there is currently no passenger rail route from Poland into Russia's Kaliningrad region). The **reinstatement in 2016** of direct trains from Białystok (in north-east Poland) to both Belarus and Lithuania opens up a raft of new journey possibilities. The improvement in 2019 of cross-border train services from Przemyśl (in south-east Poland) into western Ukraine makes the final leg of **Route 48** so much easier than when we first introduced that route into *Europe by Rail* in 2016. So there are some good news stories that give every incentive to venture east. Chances are that, once you made your first trip into the **former territory of the Soviet Union**, you'll be tempted to return time and time again. ∎

Route 48: Through Poland to Ukraine

CITIES: ★★ CULTURE: ★ HISTORY: ★★★ SCENERY: ★
COUNTRIES COVERED: GERMANY (DE), POLAND (PL), UKRAINE (UA)
JOURNEY TIME: 15 HRS | DISTANCE: 1,207 KM | MAP: <u>WWW.EBRWEB.EU/MAP48</u>

Route 48 is a journey full of historical overtones. In 1701, the Elector of Brandenburg decided to style himself King of Prussia, thus creating a new monarchy – one with no precedent, but one which developed into a great dominion with its pivots in the twin centres of Berlin and Königsberg (now Kaliningrad in Russia). Our journey starts in Berlin, the city which was Prussia's real political powerhouse.

This route ends in a city whose inhabitants know a thing or two about empire. The first railways to **Lviv** were all planned in Vienna for, after the partition of Poland in 1772, Lviv was part of the **Austrian Empire**, where it remained until the collapse of Habsburg authority at the end of the First World War. Lviv was the capital of Galicia, an Austrian crown land – not to be confused with the region in north-west Spain still known today as Galicia. Between the two world wars, Lviv was part of Poland, then in 1946 it found itself in the Soviet Union. Borders have shifted, empires have come and gone yet, in the cities on Route 48, the echoes of history, sometimes even the burden of history, still inflect everyday life.

Between Berlin and Lviv, Route 48 takes in two particularly **fine Polish cities**, Poznań and Kraków – both with magnificent central squares. Not to mention the capital Warsaw too. Like every route in the book, this journey is not just about getting from A to B. It's better to linger and take a few days exploring places along the way. **Kraków** deserves at least a couple of nights. If you want to make an interesting rural diversion, it is an easy journey south from Kraków to visit the Tatra Mountains (that rail excursion is described towards the end of **Route 49**).

Across the border

Our journey starts in **Berlin** (see p213) – at the glitzy Hauptbahnhof. The Russian trains on this route are very fine, but only run east from Berlin three times each week. So the chances are you'll find yourself in ageing Polish carriages for the journey to Poznań. They are comfy, but often crowded. The 19th-century writer **Erasmus Wilson** commented that only Russian princes and English tradesmen travel first class. Our view is that, if you are travelling at a peak time, it might be worth paying the modest extra charge to rub shoulders with princes (or tradesmen) on the ride to Poznań. The train passes through tame countryside, with lots of forest. Highpoint is the crossing of the **River Oder** into Poland (where that river is called Odra).

Polish steam

Western Poland is the last remaining area in Europe to retain steam locomotives for hauling scheduled standard-gauge passenger trains. In autumn 2019, steam was used on two return workings from Wolsztyn to Leszno on Mondays to Fridays, and on the Wolsztyn to Poznań line on Saturdays. Whether steam will continue beyond May 2020 is uncertain. **Wolsztyn** lies just south of Zbąszynek on the Berlin to Warsaw main railway line. See ERT 1099 for train times from Zbąszynek and Poznań to Wolsztyn.

That the Wolsztyn area survives as an outpost of standard-gauge steam trains, long after they have disappeared elsewhere in Europe, is the result of cooperation between the Polish railway authorities and **British train enthusiasts** (find out more about that venture at www.thewolsztynexperience.org). The latter have provided financial support to ensure that the locomotive depot at Wolsztyn is kept operational. Local Polish staff retain the necessary skills to keep old locomotives in good order.

The steam trains seen around Wolsztyn are immensely evocative of a bygone age of European rail travel. The area is often blanketed in winter by deep snow and in such conditions the engines are seen at their best.

Poznań (suggested stopover)

The **capital of Wielkopolska** is one of Poland's most engaging and oldest cities. It was the seat of Poland's first bishop in the 10th century. Its status as a great mercantile centre (it's still an important centre for trade fairs) has contributed to the architectural heritage of its Old Town.

The city's focal point is **Stary Rynek**, a spacious square with gabled burghers' houses and a spectacular multicoloured 16th-century Renaissance **Town Hall**, where at midday two mechanical goats emerge from above the clock to lock horns. Inside is the Chamber of the Renaissance with its beautifully painted, coffered ceiling (1555).

Several churches form an outer ring around the market square. Of those, the baroque **Poznań Parish Church** (Kolegiata Poznańska) at the southern end is dedicated to St Mary Magdalene. The Jesuit College next door, once Napoleon's residence, now hosts Chopin concerts. A short walk north-east of the centre is **Ostrów Tumski**, the oldest part of the city on an island in the River Warta; here stands the cathedral, fronted by a huge but gentle statue of Pope John Paul II.

Arrival, information, accommodation

⇌ Poznań Główny is a 10-min walk to the centre or take tram 3. Buy tickets from one of the kiosks at the western exit. All international and domestic trains call here. ℹ Tourist office: Stary Rynek 59/60 (www.poznan.travel) and at the station.

✉ We very much recommend staying at the **Brovaria**, Stary Rynek 73–74, ☎ 61 858 68 68 (www.brovaria.pl), and if you can secure one of the few rooms that overlook the Stary Rynek, then it is worth every złoty. The friendly **City Solei Boutique Hotel**, ul. Wenecjańska 10, ☎ 512 36 88 18 (www.citysolei.pl), has individually styled rooms and is well located just a short walk east of the Stary Rynek. A modern and stylish option in the old Jewish quarter close to the Old Town Square is the **Puro Hotel Poznan**, Stawna 12, ☎ 61 333 10 00 (www.purohotel.pl).

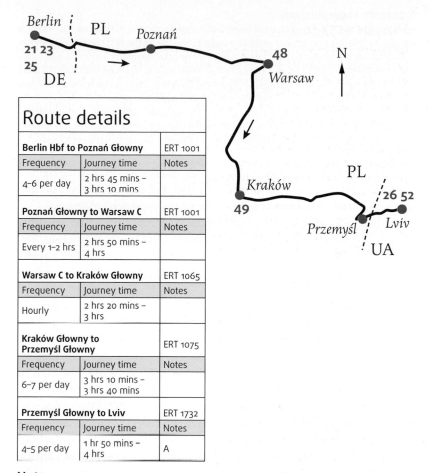

Route details

Berlin Hbf to Poznań Głowny		ERT 1001
Frequency	Journey time	Notes
4–6 per day	2 hrs 45 mins – 3 hrs 10 mins	

Poznań Głowny to Warsaw C		ERT 1001
Frequency	Journey time	Notes
Every 1–2 hrs	2 hrs 50 mins – 4 hrs	

Warsaw C to Kraków Głowny		ERT 1065
Frequency	Journey time	Notes
Hourly	2 hrs 20 mins – 3 hrs	

Kraków Głowny to Przemyśl Głowny		ERT 1075
Frequency	Journey time	Notes
6–7 per day	3 hrs 10 mins – 3 hrs 40 mins	

Przemyśl Głowny to Lviv		ERT 1732
Frequency	Journey time	Notes
4–5 per day	1 hr 50 mins – 4 hrs	A

Notes

If you like the idea of travelling from Berlin to southern Poland and Ukraine, but don't have time to follow the whole route described here, you can use the new night train which leaves Berlin every evening for Kraków and Przemyśl (ERT 77). This train conveys both seated and sleeping car accommodation. The train leaves Berlin Charlottenburg station at 18.22 and reaches Przemyśl at 09.05 the next morning (times correct as of October 2019).

A – Train services between Przemyśl and Lviv have much improved in 2019 with the introduction of new daytime trains with sensible timings. You might also consider taking a bus from Przemyśl to Lviv. There are five direct buses each day leaving from the bus station in Przemyśl. The journey takes about three hours. The one-way fare is 30 złoty (about €7).

The ERT numbers in our route details refer to the table numbers in the *European Rail Timetable* (ERT) where you will find train schedules for that particular section of the route. Do note that ERT table numbers may change occasionally with successive editions of the timetable.

Sidetrips from Poznań

From Poznań, there is a very nice rail route which runs north-east to **Gniezno** (ERT 1020), a handsome little town which can justifiably claim to have been the first capital of Poland. In a route largely dominated by big cities, albeit very fine ones, a night in Gniezno would make a worthwhile diversion and give a taste of small-town Poland. Trains on this route continue beyond Gniezno to **Toruń**, a wonderful city on the River Wisła with a rich Hanseatic history or to Gdańsk on the Baltic – another city with a proud Hanseatic past.

Another option from Poznań is to go south to **Wrocław** (ERT 1070), a university city on the Odra River which is on **Route 49**. If, having visited Poznań, you are keen to head straight for Kraków (ie. skipping Warsaw), you find direct trains to Kraków in ERT 1080.

As the train leaves Poznań, there is a tantalising glimpse (back to the right of the train) of that city's remarkable Town Hall. Before long you are running through pleasant **Mazovian countryside** on the approach to Warsaw.

There are glimpses of rural estates and manor houses, wistfully beautiful meadows and concrete apartment blocks – a very Polish mix. The melancholic, plaintive melodies of the region found expression in **Chopin's music**; the composer was born in Żelazowa Wola, about 45 kilometres west of Warsaw.

Warsaw (Warszawa) – (suggested stopover)

Warsaw, capital of a resurgent Polish nation, is once again punching its weight as a major European city. Straddling the **River Wisła** (Vistula), its location between the old powers of Germany and Russia has ensured that the city has been a victim of history on more than one occasion. After the horrors of the Second World War, the communist period saw the meticulous reconstruction of the city's historic buildings and a rash of new Socialist Realist buildings. Among the latter is the widely visible **Palace of Culture and Science**, Stalin's gift to Poland.

The city's reconstructed **Old Town** is a bewitching network of cobbled streets, church spires and hidden courtyards. Take some time to explore the churches and cathedrals, of which Poland has no shortage, making sure not to miss St John's Cathedral in the Old Town. One of the city's highlights is the **Muzeum Sztuki Nowoczesnej** (Museum of Modern Art) with cutting-

Warsaw jazz

Although it comes as a surprise to most Western Europeans, jazz has a **long tradition** in Poland. Pre-war dance club bands in Warsaw and other cities got Poles moving to swing-based jazz in the 1930s. In the early 1960s the first Warsaw Jazz Jamboree Festival was staged. In 1992, the idea of the annual **Warsaw Summer Jazz Days** was born (www.adamiakjazz.pl). The festival quickly became an important event on the jazz circuit. Innovation is the watchword and the main location is the awe-inspiring Congress Hall within the Palace of Culture and Science. Even outside the festival season, Warsaw has a vibrant year-round jazz scene.

edge contemporary Polish art located not far from the Palace of Culture and Science on ul. Pańska 3 (www.artmuseum.pl; closed Mon). There is a further exhibition space called the Museum on the Vistula. **Muzeum Powstania Warszawskiego** (Warsaw Uprising Museum) recalls Warsaw's most heroic moment relived inside one of Poland's finest museums, located on ul. Grzybowska 79 (www.1944.pl; closed Tues). Don't miss **POLIN**, the Museum of the History of Polish Jews, ul. Mordechaja Anielewicza 6 (www. polin.pl; closed Tues).

Warsaw is the hub of modern Polish culture and Poland's centre of academia. The large student and young professional contingent has ensured one of Europe's most happening nightlife scenes. For real Warsaw buzz, explore the area well south of the tourist-focused Old Town. Poznańska and the streets around are where the locals gather. Enjoy **Koszyki Market Hall**, just beyond the southern end of Poznańska, with its eateries, food stalls, trendy bars and a bookshop.

ARRIVAL, INFORMATION, ACCOMMODATION

≥ **Warszawa Centralna** is the principal rail station at Al. Jerozolimskie 54 in the city centre. Other large stations in the city are: **Warszawa Wschodnia** on the east bank of the River Wisła, and the western suburban station, **Warszawa Zachodnia**, 3 km west of Centralna, opposite the PKS bus station. → Warsaw Frédéric Chopin Airport lies 10 km south of the city (www.lotnisko-chopina.pl). Line S3 of Szybka Kolej Miejska (SKM – Rapid Urban Railway) links the airport with Warszawa Centralna, S2 with Warszawa Zachodnia and Wschodnia. Or take the KML airport train run by Masovian Railways.

Trams and buses operate on a frequent network (www.ztm.waw.pl). Prepaid tickets (from kiosks etc.) are cheaper than paying on the bus. There are frequent services on Warsaw's two metro lines which run from north to south and east to west through the centre of the city (stations are marked with a red 'M' on yellow background). Covering all public transport, 24 hr tickets are excellent value (available for one or two zones). 🛈 Tourist office: pl. Defilad 1 in the Palace of Culture and Science (www.warsawtour.pl).

🛏 For rail travellers, an excellent choice just a short walk from Centralna station is the very stylish **H15 Boutique Hotel**, ul. Poznańska 15, ☎ 22 553 87 00 (www. h15boutiqueapartments.com). Don't miss the H15's excellent *Signature* restaurant. An upmarket hotel close to the Old Town in a quiet area is the very welcoming **Le Regina**, Kościelna 12, ☎ 22 531 60 00 (www.mamaisonleregina.com). Not far south of the Old Town, the **Residence Diana**, ul. Chmielna 13A, ☎ 22 50 59 100 (www.mamaisondiana.com), is a comfortable and welcoming mid-range option.

EXPLORING BEYOND WARSAW

In Warsaw you can connect onto **Route 50** to Minsk and St Petersburg. There are useful eastbound sleepers from Warsaw with afternoon departures to Moscow and Kiev (both in ERT 56). From Warsaw, there are good rail links to the north-east corner of the country, an area of Poland not much visited by tourists. **Białystok** (see ERT 1040 for trains from Warsaw) is the main regional centre, but it's worth cutting off the main routes to explore the Masurian lakeland (where Mikołajki is the best base) and the **Tatar villages** close to the Belarusian border. Kruszyniany and Bohoniki both have traditional wooden mosques and Muslim cemeteries. It's an interesting reminder that Poland has a centuries-long Islamic tradition. Train services beyond Białystok are few and far between, but a once-daily direct service from Warsaw via Białystok to Hrodna (Гродна) in Belarus (ERT 1042) was reinstated in 2016. Another link which happily was recently restored is the service from Białystok into Lithuania (also ERT 1042), with local trains now shuttling between Białystok and Kaunas at weekends.

The Central Trunk Line to Kraków

There surely could not be a less romantic name for a railway than the Central Trunk Line – in Polish *Centralna Magistrala Kolejowa*, often just abbreviated to CMK. This could so easily have been Europe's first modern-era high-speed railway. It was designed to a very high engineering specification with a view to trains running at over 200 kilometres per hour. But in the 1970s, when Poland had no trains capable of achieving such speeds, the Central Trunk Line was used mainly for freight. Not until late 2014 was a respectably fast passenger train service introduced, with **Pendolinos** speeding non-stop between Warsaw and Kraków. The fastest trains are branded **Express Intercity Premium** (EIP); seat reservation is compulsory. The CMK route wins no prizes for scenery, but before long you'll be in Kraków, where you can connect onto **Route 49**.

Kraków (suggested stopover)

Kraków is by far the most **popular tourist destination** in Poland. The city's main square rivals St Mark's in Venice as one of the finest piazzas in Europe. Kraków was once Poland's capital, and, though it lost that status in 1596, much of Polish history has been forged here. After Poland was partitioned, it was briefly an independent city-state, and then became part of the Austro-Hungarian province of Galicia. During the 20th century, Kraków was Poland's pre-eminent city of ideas. Be it in the arts, politics, commerce or in church affairs, the town has always punched above its weight.

Kraków is also an important centre of industry and home to the huge steelworks at **Nowa Huta**, north-east of the city. As a tourist attraction, the Nowa Huta district offers a very different experience from its romantic counterpart, but this fascinating, carefully designed socialist suburb is more than concrete blocks and just a tram-ride away from the beaten path.

The city's main sights are concentrated on the north bank of the River Wisła (Vistula). Focal points are the Old Town Square and **Wawel Hill** with the castle and cathedral within walking distance of each other. The **Old Town Square** (Rynek Główny) is a gem, but to experience it at its best you will have to see it at dead of night or at dawn on a sunny spring morning. No other space in Poland is so utterly dedicated to tourists, and the impact of the square's magnificent architecture is often lessened by the sheer number of visitors. The centrepiece is the **mediaeval cloth hall** (Sukiennice), a fine covered market in 16th-century Renaissance style.

An easy 20-min walk due south from the Old Town Square will bring you to **Kazimierz**, once a separate community outside the walls of Kraków, and later the city's **Jewish quarter**. There are several synagogues and a number of restaurants that proclaim their Jewish credentials (some not as kosher as they may seem).

ARRIVAL, INFORMATION, ACCOMMODATION

≋ Kraków Główny (main station) is a short walk north-east of the centre. Head left from the station, turn right down Basztowa, enter the large underpass and head for the Planty/Basztowa exit to the right. Główny has services to Oświęcim (for the Auschwitz memorial), Zakopane and Wieliczka, as well as long-distance trains. ℹ Tourist office: on Rynek Główny in the cloth hall (www.krakow.pl).

🛏 If you've travelled around Poland and become used to good-value accommodation, prepare for a shock if you arrive in Kraków in high season. Market rules apply, and prices rocket. A centrally located option is the **Hotel Saski**, ul. Sławkowska 3, ☎ 12 421 48 65 (www.hotelsaski.com; note the antique lift) or try **Ascot Hotel**, ul. Radziwiłłowska 3, ☎ 12 384 06 06 (www.hotelascot.pl), a mid-range hotel just outside the Old Town walls. A friendly and cozy option is the **Tango House B&B**, Szpitalna 4, ☎ 12 429 31 14 (www.tangohouse.pl), right in the Old Town. ✗ Rynek Główny and the surrounding streets are packed with restaurants. For premium locations on the Old Town Square, expect to pay premium prices. Make for the small streets around the university to find the best deals. Enjoy excellent Polish-Mediterranean cuisine at the **Farina**, ul. św. Marka 16, ☎ 12 422 16 80 (www.farina.com.pl), close to the Old Town Square.

If you stop at just one place between Kraków and Lviv, make it **Przemyśl**, a small town on the River San just short of the Ukrainian border. Frontier-hopping shoppers have boosted the economy of this **border town** that has a delightful centre just a 5-min walk south-west of the railway station. The **main square** (Rynek) doesn't match up to those in Wrocław and Kraków, but the real draw in Przemyśl are the churches, where you will find western-style Roman Catholicism merging gently into Eastern Orthodoxy. The Uniate (or Greek Catholic) Church bridges the divide and commands a great following in this area of eastern Poland.

Przemyśl is a chance to experience another side of Poland before taking a deep breath and leaping over the border into **Ukraine**. Make sure that you have your passport to hand and check that the visa requirements have not changed. As of late 2019, no visas were required of tourists holding passports from EU countries, Switzerland, Canada, the US or the Commonwealth of Independent States.

The train journey from **Przemyśl to Lviv** (Львів) is slow. But in this 98-km ride, you slip between two worlds. Just a few minutes out of Przemyśl, the train enters Ukraine and – however unholy the hour – you'll need to be awake for passport checks. Soon you'll be on the move again, trundling east through busy villages to **Lviv** (see p250), where you can connect onto **Route 26** and **52** in this book. For onward journey options from Lviv see p250 and our **Sidetracks** feature on p251.

SIDETRACKS: CARRIAGE DESIGN

Rail travel is generally very safe. But that was not the perception of Parisians in 1861 after poor **Monsieur Poinsot** was found dead in a railway carriage compartment at the Gare de l'Est. By the time Poinsot's mutilated body was discovered, the murderer had long fled, presumably having alighted at one of the stations where the train from Mulhouse had stopped on its journey to Paris.

The fate of Monsieur Poinsot made French travellers think twice about buying a train ticket. Before long, Gallic panic over the **dangers of train travel** spread to England, when a particularly gruesome compartment murder took place in London. English trains were designed on the same lines as those in France, with first-class accommodation being in separate compartments, each accessed by a door directly from the railway platform. There was in those days no connection at all between adjacent compartments.

This design was the norm across Europe for first class, in contrast to North America where the open-plan saloon car was more common. **Wolfgang Schivelbusch**, in his marvellous book *The Railway Journey*, suggests that on European trains well-to-do travellers enjoyed the privacy and style associated with travel in a horse-drawn coach on a highway. The first-class **railway compartment in Europe** imitated the coach, but Schivelbusch notes that the design of the American railroad car was inspired by the open saloons on the riverboats which plied the young nation's waterways.

"That only two cases of murder," writes Schivelbusch, "were able to trigger a collective psychosis tells us as much about the compartment's significance for the nineteenth century European psyche as does the fact that it took so long to become conscious of the compartment's dysfunctionality."

That **dysfunctionality** lay not merely in the compartment's appeal for assassins. There were surely many instances of lavatorial distress; no surprise perhaps that, when a train arrived at an intermediate station after a particularly long non-stop leg, there was often a communal rush for the station toilets.

The victim in the London murder was an unfortunate Mr Briggs; his assailant was a German villain named Franz Müller. The railways responded by introducing a small glazed peephole between compartments. These peepholes were called **Müller Lights**. Many a courting couple surely bemoaned the resulting loss of privacy. Before long, railway companies installed communication cords which passengers in distress could pull to alert the train crew to an emergency. But a German railway engineer, Edmund Heusinger von Waldegg, devised a more radical approach to mitigating the dangers of travel in compartments. He suggested an **internal corridor** down one side of each carriage, allowing passengers and train staff to move from compartment to compartment. It did not entirely erode the intimacy of the small compartment but now afforded a new sense of safety and security. It also paved the way for the introduction of on-board facilities such as toilets and restaurant cars.

European carriage design has moved on, with the open-plan saloon now much preferred by most travellers. Trains with individual compartments linked by a connecting corridor are now increasingly rare. Read more on carriage design in **Sidetracks X** (on communal carriages in Russia) on p431.

Route 49: From Saxony to the Tatra Mountains
CITIES: ★★★ CULTURE: ★★ HISTORY: ★★★ SCENERY: ★★
COUNTRIES COVERED: GERMANY (DE), POLAND (PL)
JOURNEY TIME: 11 HRS 30 MINS | DISTANCE: 685 KM | MAP: WWW.EBRWEB.EU/MAP49

Thirty years ago this autumn, some weeks before the 1989 **fall of the Berlin Wall**, Dresden's main railway station was in the news as word spread through the city that special trains carrying migrants to West Germany would stop at Dresden Hauptbahnhof. Those trains were in fact **carrying East Germans** who had spent some weeks camping in the grounds of the West German embassy in Prague. Their wish to move to the West was granted, but the East German authorities insisted that the trains transit Saxony en route to West Germany. Many thousands of **Dresden citizens** gathered at the station, some keen to join a westbound train, others just curious to see comrades deserting their country in favour of a new life in a capitalist state.

Dresden has always been a place for comings and goings. In Europe today, the principal flow of refugees is from south to north. In the last century, different patterns prevailed. In this journey we travel east through the **shatterzones of history**, through territories where tyranny and violence shaped lives and landscapes.

These are places where the past is a foreign country. That's true of Dresden and Görlitz, which a generation ago were still paid-up members of the **German Democratic Republic**. It's true of Wrocław which was for 200 years Prussian and German. Our journey east will take us through the borderlands of three empires: Germany, Russia and Austria-Hungary. Along the way we'll transit the **vanished kingdoms** of Saxony, Lusatia, Silesia and Galicia.

ITINERARY NOTES

This journey from Dresden east through Wrocław to Kraków follows a former main-line railway which has been demoted to secondary status. Train services are never fast. On the final leg from Kraków to Zakopane, trains are even slower, but the **beauty of the landscape** as the train creeps up into the hills means that the slow progress is never a burden.

Distances are not huge in Route 49, but you would still be hard pushed to cover the entire route in a day. **Wrocław** and **Kraków** both deserve an overnight stop. If you want to stop off while still in Germany, then the top choice is most certainly Görlitz.

Running **east from Dresden** (see p239), the railway cuts through the Oberlausitz (Upper Lusatia), which is home to the **Sorbian people**. The Sorbs are a linguistic minority which has survived rather against the odds, in some ways helped between 1948 and 1989 by the East German state for whom it was rather convenient to have some home-grown Slavic culture. Sorbian villages, most of them deeply Catholic, are dotted across the region, but the strongest urban presence is in the town known at **Budyšín** (Sorbian)

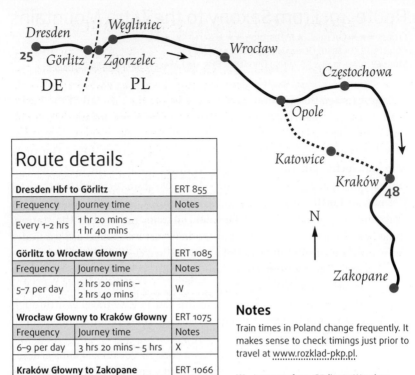

Route details

Dresden Hbf to Görlitz — ERT 855

Frequency	Journey time	Notes
Every 1–2 hrs	1 hr 20 mins – 1 hr 40 mins	

Görlitz to Wrocław Głowny — ERT 1085

Frequency	Journey time	Notes
5–7 per day	2 hrs 20 mins – 2 hrs 40 mins	W

Wrocław Głowny to Kraków Głowny — ERT 1075

Frequency	Journey time	Notes
6–9 per day	3 hrs 20 mins – 5 hrs	X

Kraków Głowny to Zakopane — ERT 1066

Frequency	Journey time	Notes
2–5 per day	3 hrs – 3 hrs 50 mins	

Notes

Train times in Poland change frequently. It makes sense to check timings just prior to travel at www.rozklad-pkp.pl.

W – Journeys from Görlitz to Wrocław require a change of train in Węgliniec.
X – Most direct trains travel via Częstochowa (shown on our map as a continuous line), others via Katowice (shown as a dashed line). Although the Katowice route is shorter in distance, the journey via Częstochowa is much faster.

or **Bautzen** (German). Bilingual station signs here, and at other stations along the line, are more than merely a token deference to the linguistic diversity of this region of Saxony.

East through Silesia

Görlitz, right on the Polish border, has one of the finest city centres in central Europe with a dazzling array of Renaissance, Gothic and baroque architecture. The best of the show is on and around the Untermarkt where you'll find courtyards with an almost Mediterranean demeanour. Although nowadays in the German state of Saxony, Görlitz was historically part of Silesia. When Germany ceded **Silesia** to Poland after the Second World

THE STORY OF THE NEISSE VIADUCT

Route 49 was only made possible by the decision of regional authorities in Germany and Poland to **reinstate train services** between Dresden and Poland. The trains started running again in December 2015, using the railway viaduct which crosses the River Neisse between Görlitz and Zgorzelec.

There were surely local voices protesting against the construction of the **viaduct across the green valley** of the River Neisse in 1847. But just as viaducts elsewhere have settled into the landscape, so too has the long railway viaduct across the Neisse. History has not always been kind to this structure or to those who travelled over it. During the **Second World War**, many trains running east over the viaduct were bound for the concentration camp at Auschwitz.

In the very final hours of the war, after the unconditional capitulation of Germany had already been agreed, Wehrmacht troops detonated the central spans of the viaduct. Only 12 years later was the railway reopened and by then the five-minute journey from **Zgorzelec to Görlitz** had become an international adventure. For the post-war Potsdam Agreement defined Germany's new eastern frontier along the Oder and Neisse rivers. Under the new order, Görlitz was now the easternmost town in the **German Democratic Republic** and the territory east of the Neisse belonged to Poland.

But slowly the traffic built up, and by 1965 there was even a train carrying through carriages from Paris which trundled over the border at Görlitz on its journey to Kraków. The journey required two nights on board in ordinary seating. There were no couchettes or sleepers running through from Paris to Kraków, so this was surely a trip only for very hardy comrades.

The political and social eruptions of late 1989 ushered in a new era of importance for the old viaduct. Suddenly **all Europe was on the move**. Those who watched the movement of trains across the Neisse Valley could occasionally spot Russian carriages slipping over the border from Poland to Germany. Even the Moscow to Geneva service came this way. This looked like a railway whose hour had eventually come.

The two German states were united in 1990. Poland joined the European Union and was later admitted to Schengen. With no frontier formalities, Görlitz and Zgorzelec moved closer. In 2012 there was a major programme of renovation, funded in part by the European Union, to create a viaduct fit for a new Europe.

That **new Europe** was still on the move, but the new Europeans had discovered discount airlines and coach services with bargain basement fares. The trains were not quite so full; profits dwindled, and the line was closed to passenger traffic. "The market is not large enough," explained officials. We suspect that half a century ago, no one ever hired consultants to evaluate the potential market for rail travel between Paris and Kraków.

It took local protests to get the line reopened. The decision 170 years ago to build a great viaduct across the Neisse Valley was **a visionary leap**. Now that elegant structure, one of central Europe's finest pieces of railway engineering, needs a dose of 21st-century vision. The trains are on the move again, but we desperately need more **creative transport policies** to boost rail travel on Europe's cross-border rail routes.

War, only those fragments of the province which lay west of the River Neisse remained German territory. Görlitz is thus the only community of any size in modern Germany which can legitimately claim Silesian heritage. But it is a whiff of 1930s central Europe, rather than the specific Silesian link, which has pulled many **filmmakers to Görlitz**, among them Wes Anderson who filmed much of *Grand Hotel Budapest* in and around the city.

If you want to stay, we can thoroughly recommend the Hotel Börse at Untermarkt 16, ☎ 03581 764 20 (www.boerse-goerlitz.de). Rooms in the main building offer a real touch of luxury, but there are also cheaper rooms in an annexe around one of the nearby courtyards.

Crossing the **Neisse Viaduct**, we enter Polish Silesia (Śląsk in Polish). The railway runs east through mixed forest and arable land, pausing here and there at railway stations in such a state of dereliction that it seems barely possible that any train might even stop.

Wrocław (suggested stopover)

Poland's fourth largest city is the **capital of Lower Silesia** and is culturally one of the most interesting oddballs in this part of Europe. Prior to the Second World War, it was a predominantly German city, then known as Breslau, which was ceded under the 1945 **Potsdam Treaty** to Poland. The Germans left, quickly to be replaced by thousands of Polish migrants from the Lwów region. Today Lwów is the Ukrainian city of Lviv, the end point of **Route 26, 48** and **52**.

With Wrocław Airport latterly much favoured by budget carriers, the city is no longer so off the beaten track as it was ten years ago. In 2016, it was one of Europe's two capitals of culture. We rate Wrocław as being almost as good as Kraków, but happily without Kraków's high prices. The central area is compact and easily covered on foot. The city is defined by its river, the Odra, which skirts the northern edge of the city centre. Apart from the **stunning main square** dominated by the magnificent town hall, our favourite part of Wrocław is the ecclesiastical and university district northeast of the centre. Head over Piaskowy bridge onto Wyspa Piasek and then right over the colourful **Tumski bridge** to reach the **cathedral**. Back on the south side of the river, you can easily spend many happy hours exploring the various streets around the central **Rynek** (main square).

One highlight not to be missed is the **Racławice Panorama** in a striking modern building in Słowackiego Park about 1 km east of the Rynek (closed Mon in winter). The panorama was produced for an exhibition in Lwów in 1893 and thus predates the heyday of cinema. Its portrayal of one of the rare glorious moments in Polish military history, the **Battle of Racławice**, where Polish peasants armed with scythes and pitchforks outwitted better-equipped Russian forces, evokes a great sense of reality that must have been truely dramatic when first viewed by late 19th-century Poles who had no experience of media we now take for granted. Today, it still is very impressive. The panorama accompanied the post-war mass movement of **Polish exiles from Lwów** to Wrocław, and is the most tangible expression of the historic connections between the two cities.

ARRIVAL, INFORMATION, ACCOMMODATION

⇌ Wrocław's main station is a Disneyesque confection about 1 km south of the heart of the Old Town. ⃞ The main tourist office is on the central square in the Old Town at Rynek 14 (www.visitwroclaw.eu).

⊨ A good central hotel just a few minutes from the main square is the **Dikul Centrum**, Antoniego Cieszyńskiego 17–19, ☎ 71 796 77 66 (www.dikul.pl). Equally central is the boutique hotel **The Granary**, Mennicza 24, ☎ 71 395 26 00 (www.thegranaryhotel. com), located in a historic building. On our most recent visit to Wrocław, we stayed at the welcoming **Jana Pawła II**, Św. Idziego 2, ☎ 71 327 14 00 (www.hotel-jp2.pl). The hotel is a real haven of calm in a busy city, right on Ostrów Tumski.

CONNECTIONS FROM WROCŁAW

There are fast trains to Poznań (ERT 1070), to link into **Route 48**, and to Warsaw (ERT 1061) where you can connect into **Route 50** to Russia. Of the many regional rail routes which fan out from Wrocław, the most interesting is that to **Szklarska Poręba Górna** (ERT 1084), a small town in the Karkonosze Mountains which straddle the Polish-Czech border. In 2010 this route was extended over the border to Harrachov in the Czech Republic (ERT 1141). There are new direct overnight trains to Vienna and Budapest (ERT 77).

All Wrocław to Kraków trains initially follow the Odra Valley upstream to Opole. Some then continue via Katowice, while others take a more northerly route through Częstochowa. You'll almost certainly want to stop overnight in **Kraków**, and you'll find a short account of the city on p412.

Into the hills

Eighty years ago, Poland's prestige *Luxtorpeda* train linked Kraków with Zakopane in less than three hours. In 1936, a *Luxtorpeda* made the run in a record time of 2 hrs 36 mins. Nowadays, things are more leisurely. The railway is a marvellous **piece of Habsburg engineering**, though no longer in great shape. Not far south of Kraków, the railway passes **Kalwaria Zebrzydowska** – best described as an early 17th-century religious theme park. Its Mannerist landscapes have earned it a place on UNESCO's World Heritage List, and it's still a major focal point for Roman Catholic pilgrimages.

The railway climbs through the hills, first following the Skawa and then the Raba Valley. Eventually it reaches the **River Dunajec**, which it follows upstream to Zakopane, along the way passing Biały Dunajec where **Lenin** once lived. "This is almost Russia," wrote Lenin of this area in 1913, referring to the fact that the border of the tsarist empire was not far away on the north side of Kraków.

Zakopane

Every Pole knows Zakopane, a resort town in the **Tatra Mountains**. It is the place to which the Kraków intelligentsia came (and still come) to rest and play. With **beautiful late 19th-century villas**, wooden churches, leafy avenues and easy access to Poland's highest mountains, Zakopane is a year-round resort: excellent winter sports, rock climbing and summer hiking.

The imprint of one man is everywhere in Zakopane: **Stanisław Witkiewicz**. At a time when Poland was partitioned between three empires, Witkiewicz promoted a new architectural grammar which spoke to a uniquely Polish identity, drawing upon the vernacular building traditions of the Carpathian region. So here, in what was at the time a remote corner of the Habsburg world, **Polish artists and writers** began to envision an independent Poland, a sovereign state which might determine its own future. A particular fussy style of wooden architecture, with plenty of art nouveau accents, became the hallmark of that emerging national spirit. It is seen at its very best in Zakopane.

As for day hikes from Zakopane, one of the best is to the summit of **Giewont** (there and back takes seven hours); there's also a cable car up to Kasprowy Wierch (1,985 m) from Kuźnice, from where there's a ridge path along the Slovakian border. The less energetic may like to take the modern **funicular railway** from the centre of town to Gubałówka (1,120 m) for excellent views south to the main Tatra range; there are cafés at the top.

ARRIVAL, INFORMATION, ACCOMMODATION

≋ It's a 15-min walk south-west to the town centre. 🚌 Buses from Kraków arrive very close by. 🛈 Tourist office: ul. Kościuszki 17 (www.zakopane.pl); arranges accommodation and has useful maps. 🛏 Book ahead, especially during the peak winter season. We can especially recommend the **Hotel Art & Spa**, Kościuszki 18, ☎ 18 200 06 70 (www.artandspa.pl), which also has an excellent restaurant. Right on Zakopane's main street (pedestrianised) and just a few minutes' walk to the funicular railway is the **Villa Vita**, ul. Krupówki 2, ☎ 18 200 06 00 (www.villavita.pl). Or try the **Sabala**, ul. Krupówki 11, ☎ 18 201 50 92 (www.sabala.zakopane.pl).

ACROSS THE TATRAS

There is a useful bus link from Zakopane, which cuts through rugged Tatra countryside to **Poprad** in Slovakia (ERT 1183). The bus stops along the way at **Starý Smokovec**, where you can connect onto the **narrow-gauge Tatra electric trains** which serve several resorts on the south side of the Tatras (ERT 1182).

In Poprad, the main railway station is a faded but still very good example of the distinctive bold style of architecture known as **Slovak East Modernism**. In Czechoslovakia, Slovak architects always had the edge over their Czech counterparts. The station is on a main rail route with direct trains to Prague, Bratislava and Košice (all ERT 1180). For those heading east, there is a very useful connection in Košice with the direct train to Lviv and Kiev (both in Ukraine).

SIDETRACKS: CROSSING FRONTIERS

The relationship between **railways and international frontiers** is always fascinating, though often not easy. Railways were the ambassadors of empire, but also served to protect imperial interests. But borders evolve and move, and railways sometimes find themselves transgressing new frontiers.

In the 1870s, **Baron Victor von Erlanger** promoted a railway which ran west from Győr via Sopron to Ebenfurth in Austria. His aim was to export Hungarian grain to Austrian markets. In the days of the Habsburg dual monarchy, Erlanger's railway flourished, but following the **First World War**, his railway was divided by a new frontier separating Austria from Hungary. That wasn't good for business, but worse was yet to come. After the Second World War the *Győr, Sopron and Ebenfurth Railway* (usually abbreviated GYSEV) was bisected by the **Iron Curtain**. Better times arrived for GYSEV when Hungary joined the European Union (of which Austria was already a member) in 2004 and three years later acceded to the **Schengen group of nations**. The fading of borders brought a big boost to business for GYSEV, and the company is now an important independent rail operator in western Hungary. It still plies Baron von Erlanger's original route to Austria (see ERT 1251 and 978).

In many parts of Europe, countries have to negotiate with their neighbours when railways criss-cross frontiers. In some cases, **privileged transit** is arranged on a railway which crosses another country – in much the same way that **Lenin** and his colleagues were given special permission to leave Switzerland in 1917 and travel across Germany in a sealed railway carriage on their way back to Russia. That was a moment of political drama, but dozens of trains across Europe enjoy a less Lenin-like form of privileged transit every day.

Nowadays, fast trains **between Innsbruck and Salzburg** (both in Austria) cut through Bavaria for 115 kilometres between Kufstein and Freilassing. Austrian Railjets running from Innsbruck to Vienna (ERT 86 & 951) use this transit corridor without stopping on German territory. Authorities which grant such privileged transit may set certain conditions. In the early 1950s, when the Soviet Union still leased the Porkkala district of southern Finland, trains running from **Turku to Helsinki** (a line which forms part of **Route 33** in this book) had window blinds which remained lowered while the train transited the Soviet zone.

Such border-hopping services are called 'corridor trains'. Borders in most of Europe are pretty relaxed these days, but in the past things were not so easy. Special **corridor trains** linking villages in Austria were given permission to transit Yugoslav or Italian territory. The train journey between Bebra and Heringen (both places in West Germany) crossed East Germany (GDR). Trains running north from **Ventimiglia to Cuneo** (ERT 581) still transit French territory. In Germany, the railway from Görlitz to Zittau (ERT 854) twice dips in and out of Poland. Perhaps the strangest corridor train of all was the Polish local train which in the 1970s and 1980s gave a **visa-free glimpse of Soviet life**. Trains from Przemyśl to Zagórz cut through the Soviet Union for 37 kilometres. For a spell, it was a favourite route with *Solidarność* activists who would throw leaflets from the train in the hope of sowing the seeds of local dissent. Moscow reacted by imposing a 'no open windows' rule.

Route 50: By train to Russia

Cities: ★★ Culture: ★ History: ★★ Scenery: ★
Countries covered: Poland (PL), Belarus (BY), Russia (RU)
Journey time: 27 hrs | Distance: 1,425 km | Map: www.ebrweb.eu/MAP50

When **Tsar Nicholas I** decided it might be fun to have a railway, he decreed that the very first line to be built in his empire should lead from St Petersburg to his summer palace at **Tsarskoye Selo** (Царское Село), about 25 kilometres south of the city. That railway opened in 1837. The tsar soon discovered that trains were more than just playthings for the aristocracy.

Before long, Tsar Nicholas was contemplating more ambitious **railway adventures**. A line from St Petersburg to Warsaw might not merely be a convenience – the tsar was after all also King of Poland – but could become a military necessity. "In the case of sudden outbreak of war," wrote Tsar Nicholas, "Warsaw, and with it our entire west, might be overrun by enemy forces before our own troops could even get from Petersburg to Luga." Luga is just 150 kilometres south of St Petersburg.

Politics and war (not in Poland, but in the Crimea) intervened, and the railway from **St Petersburg to Warsaw** didn't actually open until 1862. Tsar Nicholas never saw his railway, for he died in 1855. But his autocratic son, Tsar Alexander II, almost immediately used the railway to political and military advantage, when in 1863 he despatched troops to crush the January Uprising in Poland.

Our journey from Warsaw to St Petersburg thus recalls one of the most important rail links of **Imperial Russia**. It tracks east and north through the shatterzones of empire. But, curiously, no part of the route presented here follows the original Warsaw to St Petersburg railway of 1862. That railway has itself been the **victim of recent politics**; it ran via Białystok, Hrodna (Гродна), Vilnius and Pskov (Псков). But with the fractured disintegration of the Soviet Union, quickly followed by the aggressive eastward expansion of the European Union, new frontiers emerged in eastern Europe. And the old rail route from Warsaw to St Petersburg fell foul of those frontiers. It dipped in and out of the European Union, and at one point the border between Latvia and the Russian Federation actually ran down the middle of the railway line, so that a passenger reclining in her sleeping berth might have had her head in Russia and her feet in Latvia. The last through trains from Warsaw to St Petersburg via this **traditional route** ran more than a decade ago, and many sections of the grand railway developed at the behest of Tsar Nicholas I now lie abandoned.

The **new route** from Warsaw to St Petersburg, the one we follow in this description, takes a more southerly course, running east rather than north-east from Warsaw and **crossing the River Bug** to reach Belarusian territory at Brest. Then it's on east through Minsk to Orsha, still in Belarus

Route details

Warsaw Centralna to Brest Centralny		ERT 1050
Frequency	**Journey time**	**Notes**
3–5 per day	3 hrs 50 mins – 5 hrs 10 mins	A

Brest Centralny to Minsk Pasażyrski		ERT 1950
Frequency	**Journey time**	**Notes**
11–15 per day	3 hrs 10 mins – 5 hrs	

Minsk Pasażyrski to Orsha		ERT 1950
Frequency	**Journey time**	**Notes**
Every 1–2 hrs	2 hrs 20 mins – 4 hrs	

Orsha to Vitebsk Pasażyrski		ERT 1920
Frequency	**Journey time**	**Notes**
Every 1–3 hrs	1 hr 15 mins – 2 hrs	

Vitebsk Pasażyrski to St Petersburg Vitebski		ERT 1920
Frequency	**Journey time**	**Notes**
3–6 per day	8 hrs 40 mins – 10 hrs	

Notes

Bear in mind that the Republic of Belarus and the Russian Federation both stopped observing summer time way back in 2010. This means that cities on this route from Brest to St Petersburg are all one hour ahead of Warsaw in the summer and two hours ahead of Warsaw in winter. Adjust your watch accordingly as you travel between Terespol and Brest.

A – Some itineraries from Warsaw to Brest require a change of train in Łuków and / or Terespol.

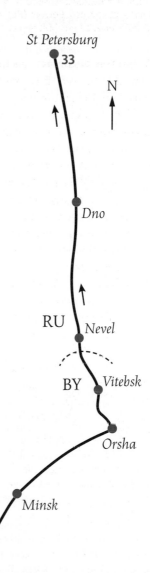

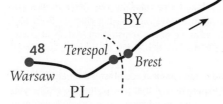

Coming from further west?

If you are travelling from Berlin, or places further west, you can easily pick up this route at the Belarusian border. On certain days, there's a direct overnight train from Berlin to Brest, leaving the German capital in the evening to reach the Belarusian border about seven in the morning (ERT 56).

but just short of the Russian border, where we turn north to Vitebsk and St Petersburg.

SUGGESTED ITINERARY

The great express trains which once linked Warsaw with St Petersburg are long gone. The last direct train connecting the two cities ran in late 2017. With fierce competition from **Baltic long-distance coach operators**, not to mention discount airlines, this is a part of Europe with where services have suffered.

Coaches run by Ecolines or Lux Express both offer Warsaw to St Petersburg in 24 to 30 hours. It won't be comfortable, so why not go by train? It just requires a bit of planning. There are good daytime options from Warsaw to Brest in Belarus (usually involving a change of train in Terespol) or you can take the *Polonez* **night train** as far as Brest, which leaves Warsaw mid-afternoon.

If you want to strike out from the main line, there's an alternative more northerly route from **Warsaw to Minsk** via **Hrodna** (Гродна). The direct train to Hrodna leaves Warsaw around 8 each morning (ERT 1042), connecting nicely in Hrodna into the mid-afternoon train to Minsk (ERT 1952). If you are tempted by this detour, do consider stopping off in Hrodna. It's a very attractive regional town, and makes a perfect first stop in Belarus.

We advise using day trains for the journey through Belarus to **Vitebsk**, staying at least one night there before boarding a night train to St Petersburg. There are no easy daytime options for the leg over the border from Vitebsk into Russia.

The two 'must see' intermediate cities on our journey from Warsaw to St Petersburg are Minsk and Vitebsk. At the end of the journey, you'll surely want to linger in **St Petersburg**, the city which was the cradle of the 1917 revolutions that deposed the Russian monarchy and brought the Bolsheviks to power.

Don't forget that most travellers will need visas for this journey. Read more in the boxed text below.

ESSENTIALS: VISAS AND MORE

Most travellers will need to do **some pre-planning** before embarking on Route 50. Both Russia and Belarus require that most visitors secure visas in advance. Visa regimes can change from year to year, so do check the current situation carefully before leaving home. The **visa requirement for Russia** is waived only for holders of passports from selected Latin American nations, some western Balkan countries and some (not all) members of the Commonwealth of Independent States. The new e-visa scheme for St Petersburg, likely to be introduced in late 2019 or early 2020, won't help you if you are following Route 50.

For **Belarus**, the visa regime is even tighter than for Russia and some travellers who might not need a visa for Russia do require one for Belarus. If you are spending no more than two days in Belarus, you may be eligible for a transit visa which is much cheaper than a normal visa. There are **relaxed visa rules** for two areas in western Belarus. Rail travellers entering by train from Poland can visit the cities of Brest and Hrodna (and their rural hinterlands) with advance online registration (details at www. belarus.by). It's a great concession, but it doesn't allow you to continue east from Hrodna or Brest to Minsk and beyond.

Take along a **Russian dictionary and phrase book**. If you master the transliteration of the Cyrillic alphabet, you'll find your experience of that part of the route after you cross the River Bug into Belarus immensely more enriching. Be aware that you may encounter very few English speakers in Belarus and rural Russia.

To the Bug and beyond

For some comments on **Warsaw** see p410. There is not a lot to detain you on the run east from the Polish capital to the Belarusian border. If you pause at any of the small communities beyond Łuków, you will surely be struck by how eastern they feel. **Biała Podlaska** is the most interesting of these small towns, a place on the main railway line from Paris to Moscow that has been trampled over by too many invading armies. Unsung, even unlovely you may say, and yet somehow immensely interesting. The town is surrounded by crumbling agricultural estates, but the real highlight is the decaying castle, once the home of the Radziwiłł family, in the heart of Biała Podlaska.

You will hear Belarusian voices too, a reminder that in this part of Europe **political boundaries**, often imposed from outside, do not always coincide with linguistic and cultural frontiers. What you will no longer hear in these small towns of eastern Poland are Yiddish voices. Prior to the Second World War, Jews numbered more than fifty per cent of the population of this part of the country. The last stop in Poland is **Terespol**. The very size of the station building, a dated piece of 1960s modernism that still bustles with peak-capped officials and sniffer dogs, is a reminder that this is one of Europe's great remaining borders. The very existence of the military border zone that extends along the valley of the **River Bug** has provided a measure of protection for the delicate environment of the area.

So the 20-minute journey from Terespol to **Brest** (Брест), when the train rumbles slowly over girder bridges spanning the river and adjacent reed beds and wetlands, affords superb views of a **watery wilderness** below. Once over on the east bank of the river, there is (on the right-hand side) a magnificent view of the striking red fortress that dominates the city of Brest. And, clearly visible from the train, there is a huge sign welcoming visitors to Belarus – in Cyrillic of course. It's a good reminder that this border is a fault line in writing conventions as well as in politics.

In Brest, most trains arriving from Poland are shunted into a shed, jacked up, and the **wheel bogies are swapped** for the wider gauge versions suited to the broader railway tracks that were the norm in Imperial Russia and remain standard throughout the former Soviet Union. The modern Russian Talgo trains (used on some Berlin-Moscow services) have inbuilt gauge-changing ability and don't need to be jacked up. Magic!

Brest is the main western **gateway to Belarus**, and the city's 19th-century fortress underlines Brest's role as the guardian of a main east-west trade route. Venture out from the railway for your first real glimpse of Belarus and you'll almost certainly be struck by the **youthful energy and gentle dynamism** of Brest. The star-shaped fortress, once dominated by four great gateways (of which just two remain), with a citadel in the centre, is the principal sight and a place to lose yourself for hours. If you want to stay in Brest – no bad idea as it's a great first taste of Belarus – try the smart Hermitage Hotel which is an eight-minute walk from the front of the station at ul. Chkalova 7, ☎ 33 327 40 00 (www.hermitagehotel.by). An equally good base for exploring Brest is the welcoming **Molodezhnaya Hotel** (Молодежная), Komsomolskaya 6, ☎ 33 351 63 76 (www.molodezhnaya.by), which is even closer to the railway station.

From Brest, the main railway runs in a generally straight line to Minsk. Look out of the carriage window and you know at once that you have entered another world. The landscapes are little different from those in eastern Poland, with a mix of forests and arable land, but the villages look smarter. **Railway stations** along the line have neat pavilion-style buildings which are often brightly painted. Monuments by the side of the line record the victories and achievements of Belarusian (or Russian) workers or, in some cases, the horrendous atrocities perpetrated by invaders.

Minsk (Мінск) – (suggested stopover)

When the writer **Colin Thubron** made his first visit to the Soviet Union, he discovered in the centre of Minsk "a ferro-concrete tundra which is crushingly shoddy and uniform." Yet **Nigel Roberts**, author of the excellent *Bradt Guide to Belarus* (the 4th edition was published in 2018) lauds Minsk as "the best example of post-war Soviet urban planning on a grand scale," noting that the Belarusian capital is a city of expansive boulevards, shady parks, neoclassical architecture, fountains and monuments.

Beauty is in the eye of the beholder, and never more so than when it comes to the **socialist architecture** of central and eastern Europe. Minsk is a great place just to wander, and you'll find splendid Stalinist architectural ensembles around **Independence Square** and along the main thoroughfares that run north-east from Independence Square towards **Victory Square**, on the far side of the River Svislach.

Whatever you make of the grand design, the really striking thing about Minsk is its unhurried feel. It is, for many visitors, one of the most appealing aspects of Belarus. Minsk has the predictable array of monuments and museums that come with a country very determined to assert its own distinctive identity and its separateness from its dominant eastern neighbour, Russia. Highlights include the **Belarusian State Museum of the Great Patriotic War** on Pobediteley Ave. 8 (closed Mon) and the **Museum of the History and Culture of Belarus** on Karla Marksa 12 (www.histmuseum.by). Don't expect sparkling displays or any glitz. Both museums rely on old-style curatorial techniques.

Several monuments commemorate the thousands of Jews in the **Minsk ghetto** who lost their lives between 1941 and 1943. Especially moving is the Holocaust memorial **Yama** (Яма) 'The Pit' on ul. Zaslavskaya.

Arrival, information, accommodation

≽ The main station on Privokzalnaya Square is right in the heart of the city, a stone's throw south from Independence Square. The city is very walkable, but do take a ride on the impressively efficient metro. A token (*jeton*) for a one-way journey, purchased at the ticket window on entering any station, costs 0.65 BYN (less than €0.30). Insert the *jeton* into the slot by the barrier, wait for the green light and go. For multiple trips you can also use a contactless smart card. ⚹ Tourist office: ul. Revolutsionnaya 13 (www.minsktourism.by/en/ and also www.belarus.by/en).

⊷ The **Hotel Belarus**, ul. Storozhovskaya 15, ☎ 17 209 71 06 (www.hotel-belarus.com), is a good mid-range choice but be aware that prices vary considerably with many grades of room. The hotel is in a great location in parkland just north of the city centre. More upmarket are the **Hotel Minsk**, Nezavisimosti Ave. 11, ☎ 17 209 90 80 (www.hotelminsk.by) and the **President Hotel Minsk**, ul. Kirova 18, ☎ 17 229 70 00 (www.president-hotel.by). A good, central place to stay is **Monastyrski Hotel**, ul. Kirilla i Mefodya 6, ☎ 17 329 03 00 (www.monastyrski.by), a converted monastery in the Old Town.

Connections from Minsk

The main railway station in Minsk is a place to watch the trains come and go. The departure boards showcase **direct services** to Milan and Murmansk, to Saratov and Strasbourg. One thing to note here, as indeed anywhere in the former Soviet Union, is that very few trains to far-flung destinations run daily. Many run only on even or odd dates (not both), others may operate only weekly. For more on long-distance hops into Russia, see our **Sidetracks** feature on p431.

In the context of this book, with its focus mainly on those parts of Europe west of Minsk, it's useful to highlight a number of good links from the Belarusian capital. There is a direct **overnight train** (normally alternate days) from Minsk to **Riga** (ERT 1850) where you can connect with **Route 51** (to Stockholm or Tallinn). Another very useful overnight link is the direct train (also normally alternate days) to **Lviv** in western Ukraine (ERT 1735), which is on **Route 26, 48** and **52**. The only downside of the overnight journey to Lviv is that you'll be woken up for border formalities (as the train enters Ukraine) at a time when you would surely prefer to be fast asleep. Lithuania has only very limited rail links with its EU neighbours, but there is an excellent train service from Minsk to Vilnius, which is less than three hours away on a newly electrified route (ERT 1950).

Gentle ripples in the landscape to the **east of Minsk**, particularly to the north of the railway, prove that Belarus is not completely flat. Some itineraries require a change of train at **Orsha** (Орша). If you have time to spare take a look at Orsha's remarkable station building, still maintained in impeccable condition and with an excellent restaurant.

Vitebsk (Витебск) – (suggested stopover)

The last major city in Belarus before the Russian border is Vitebsk. Put at its simplest, Vitebsk is superb. The **birthplace of Marc Chagall** was an important centre of Jewish life in the 19th century, a place that was still just within the permitted area of Jewish settlement (called the Pale), yet within striking distance of both Moscow and St Petersburg. Most of the main sights are on the east bank of the **Western Dvina**. The conspicuous exception is the **old Jewish quarter** which is on the west bank just an 8-min walk north-east of the railway station. The house on Pokrovskaya where Chagall lived as a child is nowadays a **museum** devoted to his work (www.chagal-vitebsk.com; closed Mon and additionally Tues Oct–Apr).

Across the river, on the east side of **Kirova Bridge**, there is a quartet of first-rate churches of which two of the most impressive are the newly renovated **Orthodox Market Church** (sometimes called the Resurrection Church) and the homely little wooden church on the river bank devoted to Alexander Nevsky. The latter looks as though it has been there for centuries, but actually was only built in 1993. The other two are the Annunciation Church, right beside and dwarfing the wooden church, and the **Church of the Dormition of Mary** which stands boldly on a bluff overlooking the river. It is worth walking up for the fine view.

Strike north from this last church past the old governor's palace to the **Marc Chagall Art Centre** on ul. Putna (opening times and website are the same as that of the Chagall house on Pokrovskaya; see above), which has a decent collection of memorabilia connected to Chagall, including some etchings and lithographs. Sadly, none of Chagall's more famous paintings are on display in his home city.

ARRIVAL, INFORMATION, ACCOMMODATION

⇄ The railway station building is one of the last gasps of Stalinist design, and most travellers nowadays walk round it rather than through it. The station is 1 km west of the centre on the west bank of the Western Dvina River. From there, just walk up ul. Kirova towards Kirova Bridge. 🛈 Tourist office: Stroityely Ave. 10 (www.vitebskcity.by).

⊨ The **Hotel Eridan**, ul. Sovetskaya 21/17, ☎ 212 60 44 99 (www.eridan-vitebsk.com), is in a prime spot by the Marc Chagall Art Centre while the **Luchesa**, Stroityely Ave. 1, ☎ 212 29 85 00 (www.luchesa.by), 2 km south of the centre, pitches more to the business market but is still good value. Or try the small **Hotel Gubernsky**, ul. Osvobozhdenije 9, ☎ 17 226 88 80 (www.ebrweb.eu/b) in the Old Town.

North to Russia

Travelling **north from Vitebsk** through gently undulating country and endless forests, you cross the border **into Russia**. The chances are you'll be doing this final leg of the journey overnight, and you'll probably not awake until the train is on its approach into St Petersburg.

By night you'll have rumbled around the shores of lakes, and past a thousand factories. The train will have slipped through towns large and small – unsung places like **Dno** (Дно), where the elegant station building has a magnificent spire; sad places like **Nevel** (Невель) where the cemetery recalls the fate of the town's Jewish population when German troops arrived in September 1941; and nameless places like the forest where the train stops in the middle of the night and you raise the blind in your sleeping compartment to see a wolf skulking by the track. But now the city is close.

It's time to stretch and smile, for the arrival in St Petersburg is one of the great delights in this book.

The train pulls into **Vitebsky station** which is a palace fit for a tsar. Take time to look around, and don't miss the magnificent art nouveau interiors. There's a bust of Tsar Nicholas I and you can see a replica of the very first train which left from here in 1837, bound for the imperial residence in Tsarskoye Selo. Whether this be your first visit to Russia or you are an old hand at Russian travel, you'll surely have that distinctive feeling of now being in a Europe very different from the one you left behind in Warsaw.

ST PETERSBURG (Санкт-Петербург)

Russia's second-largest city is first in the hearts of its population due to its collection of showpiece museums, elegant pastel-hued palaces, tree-lined parks and boulevards, not to mention its proud history of decadence and defiance. Home to the Russian tsars for over three hundred years, St Petersburg has seen more than its share of political power struggles since it was founded on the banks of the **Neva River** by Peter the Great in 1703. Sheer determination built this city up to become the fourth largest in Europe within a century of its founding – and it's also what got its citizens through such moments as the storming of the **Winter Palace** by Communist revolutionaries and the two-and-a-half year blockade by the Nazis during the Second World War.

A visit to St Petersburg will intoxicate and captivate you. Whether it's a summer night flooded with late sunlight – the so-called **White Nights** – along the banks of the river, or a winter's evening sharing a bottle of Georgian wine in a basement bar next to a cosy fireplace, you're sure to find your perfect corner.

So take a stroll down **Nevskiy Prospekt** and enjoy a caviar-covered bliny. Or sample art in the **Hermitage**, the former royal family's Winter Palace, which was transformed into the world's largest art gallery (www. hermitagemuseum.org; closed Mon). The Impressionist collection alone is worth the cost of admission (metro: Nevskiy Prospekt). From the jetty at the

RECOGNISE YOUR STATION IN ST PETERSBURG

Train station (вокзал): Moscow (Московский), Vitebsk (Витебский), Finland (Финляндский), Ladozhski (Ладожский); metro: Chernyshevskaya (Чернышевская), Elektrosila (Электросила), Gorkovskaya (Горковская), Gostinyy Dvor (Гостиный двор), Leninskiy Prospekt (Ленинский проспект), Mayakovskaya (Маяковская), Moskovskaya (Московская), Nevskiy Prospekt (Невский проспект), Park Pobedy (Парк Победы), Ploshchad Lenina (Площадъ Ленина), Ploshchad Vosstaniya (Площадъ Восстания), Proletarskaya (Пролетарская)

Hermitage, you can take a picturesque voyage by hydrofoil to **Peterhof**, the Russian palace built by Peter the Great to rival Versailles (which it certainly does!).

ARRIVAL, INFORMATION, ACCOMMODATION

≈ The train from Vitebsk arrives at **Vitebsk Station** (Vitebskiy vokzal; metro: Pushkinskaya), the terminus for all trains to and from Belarus and Poland. Use **Moscow Station** (Moskovskiy vokzal; metro: Mayakovskaya or Ploshchad Vosstaniya) for trains to Moscow and onwards to the south and **Finland Station** (Finlyandskiy vokzal; metro: Ploshchad Lenina) for trains to Helsinki. Buy your ticket at the **Central Railway Booking Office** (Tsentralnye Zheleznodorozhnye Kassy), Naberezhnaya Kanala Griboedova 24, at windows 100–104, 2nd floor (metro: Nevskiy Prospekt). ⛴ **Sea Terminal** (Morskoy Vokzal) at the western tip of Vasilievsky Island; this is where St Peter Line ferries from Helsinki dock; numerous buses, trolleybuses and *marshrutkas* from Boshoy Prospekt to Vasileostrovskaya metro station. Boats from Moscow arrive at the **River Passenger Terminal** (Rechnoy Vokzal), a 10-min walk to the Proletarskaya metro station.

✈ Pulkovo, St Petersburg's international airport is located 17 km south of the city centre. *Marshrutkas* (shared taxis on pre-defined routes) link both terminals (domestic: Pulkovo 1; international: Pulkovo 2) to Moskovskaya metro station 07.00–22.00, taking 10–15 mins. Public transport is comprehensive and very cheap. It runs 05.30–01.00, but is infrequent after 23.00. All five metro lines are colour coded, but you'll need basic knowledge of the Cyrillic alphabet. Two intersecting stations on different lines will have different names. Stations are indicated by a sign bearing a large blue letter 'M'.

Tickets for buses, trams, trolleybuses and *marshrutkas* are sold on board by conductors or the driver. For the metro, a token (*jeton*) must be dropped into the turnstiles, but most people buy magnetic cards, valid for a set number of journeys. 🛈 City Information Office: ul. Sadovaya 14/52 (www.visit-petersburg.ru); take the metro to Nevskiy Prospekt.

🛏 Unlike in Moscow, there is a broadening range of medium-price and budget hotels. For **bed and breakfast**, go for the long-established **HOFA** (Host Families' Guest Association; www.hofa.ru). They can do visas and find a room with ordinary families in St Petersburg and other cities of the former Soviet Union. The friendly, mid-range **Hotel Vera**, Suvorovsky Prospekt 25/16, ☎ 812 702 61 90 (www.hotelvera.ru), is a good central option in an art nouveau building. Or try the **M-Hotel**, ul. Sadovaya 22/2, ☎ 812 448 83 83 (http://en.mhotelspb.ru), near Nevskiy Prospekt. The **NasHotel**, 11-ya Liniya 50, ☎ 812 323 22 31 (http://nas.hotels-of-saint-petersburg.com), is a modern and comfortable option on Vasilievsky Island.

CONNECTIONS FROM ST PETERSBURG

If you have arrived in St Petersburg by train, having followed Route 50 all the way from Warsaw, you may not want to retrace your steps along that same route. For onward train travel back to the European Union, your best bet is the **Allegro high-speed service** to Helsinki (ERT 1910), under four hours away on **Route 33**. In Helsinki you can connect into **Route 51** in this book. There are also daily departures from St Petersburg to both Riga (ERT 1840) and Tallinn (ERT 1870); both cities are also on **Route 51**.

For travel within Russia, Moscow is the obvious next stop. High-speed **Sapsan trains** dash to the capital in under four hours (ERT 1900). St Petersburg has an excellent range of other connections, among them direct trains to Russia's Black Sea coast, the Russian Arctic and even Siberia. Read more in our **Sidetracks** feature on the next page.

If you've had enough of trains, consider **taking a boat** out of St Petersburg. There are regular departures to both Helsinki and Stockholm (ERT 2482). Note that the former direct ferries from St Petersburg to Germany's Baltic ports no longer operate.

SIDETRACKS: THE COMMUNAL CARRIAGE

If you have travelled by train all the way to St Petersburg on **Route 50**, you're probably game for more Russian rail adventures. One option you might consider is a direct train from St Petersburg to **Sochi** (Сочи) and **Adler** (Адлер) on the **Russian Riviera**: that's one long leap from the Baltic to the Black Sea, a trip of 49 hours on Train 115A. Train travel in the Russian Federation can be very cheap. The one-way fare from St Petersburg to Adler (including a sleeping berth in an open-plan carriage) is about €31. The same journey in the considerable luxury of a private first-class compartment will cost €140.

Perhaps you are less seduced by the idea of the warm south and would prefer to head north. Then make for Ladozhsky railway station in **St Petersburg** (Ладожский вокзал), the newest major station in the city, from where every evening Train 224 departs for **Murmansk** (Мурманск) on Russia's Kola coast. It is a 24-hour journey with some tickets costing under €20 – not bad for a trip which will take you way up north into the Russian Arctic.

The cheapest fares quoted here are for the **communal open carriages** where everyone gets a berth but not much privacy. This is third-class travel, cheap and cheerful at its best, though a long journey in a crowded communal carriage may leave you with frayed nerves. Each carriage in this class offers 54 bunks, most of them arranged in bays of four berths apiece. There has been talk of scrapping this **quintessentially Russian style of travel**, but such proposals have not been warmly received by budget-conscious Russian travellers who seem to rather enjoy the convivial mood on board these third-class carriages.

At stations along the route, passengers tumble out onto the platform in search of the roving *babushki* who sell everything from berries to beer. The third class carriage was made for sharing. It is a place where food, drink and **life stories are shared with complete strangers**.

The traditional Russian long-distance train has an interior focus. That's true of all classes of travel, but it is especially the case with the communal carriages. Sightlines to the wider world beyond the train are limited. Russia is a country with too much landscape, and the train is thus a retreat from the scenery outside into **an inner sanctuary**. The question is whether the noise and bustle of third class is anathema to inner peace.

We opted for berths in one of the communal carriages on a journey some years ago from Ukraine to Poland. But third-class carriages are rarely seen these days **within the European Union**. The overnight services from Riga to Moscow, St Petersburg (both ERT 1840) and Minsk (ERT 1850) still have them. So too do the trains from Moscow to Kaliningrad which run through Lithuania and stop in Vilnius (ERT 1950).

True devotees of the rails see the new generation of smart Russian trains as almost too comfortable. The **social magic of the Russian train** has traditionally been rooted, like so much of Russian life, in patience, endurance and discomfort. A shared commitment to those values bred solidarity and conversation. These are virtues revealed at their best in the lower travel classes, and nicely exemplified in **Dostoyevsky's 'idiot' protagonist** as he made his way back to Russia from a Swiss asylum in a third-class carriage.

Route 51: A Baltic journey

Cities: ★★ Culture: ★ History: ★★ Scenery: ★★
Countries covered: Finland (FI), Estonia (EE), Latvia (LV), Sweden (SE), Norway (NO)
Journey time: 25 hrs | Distance: 1,592 km | Map: www.ebrweb.eu/map51

For many travellers from western Europe, the **Baltic States** are a first encounter with the post-Soviet world. Estonia and Latvia, both on Route
51, are now members of the **Schengen area** and the **Eurozone**. So too is
Lithuania, the country to the south of Latvia (though sadly with only a
limited passenger rail service between the two countries). From summer
1989, the Baltic States agitated for independence from the Soviet Union.
In August that year, a human chain running from Tallinn through Riga to
Vilnius dramatically symbolised a gentle revolution. The status of Estonia,
Latvia and Lithuania as autonomous independent republics secured widespread international recognition after the August 1991 coup attempt in
Moscow. All three countries joined both the **European Union** and NATO in
2004. Since 2017, the United States have deployed new military assets in all
three Baltic countries as part of its *Atlantic Resolve* programme. It seems that,
as one empire fades, another inevitably moves in to take its place.

So Route 51 kicks off with an adventurous journey through **recent European history**, one that along the way takes in some serenely beautiful landscapes. It is a journey that will at times test the patience of travellers bent on
speed, for trains in the Baltic States are slow. We travel south from Helsinki
by boat to Estonia, then on by train into Latvia, before **continuing by sea
from Riga to Stockholm** and then on by train to **Oslo**. In designing this
revised route, we have been much influenced by two notions: viz. the idea
of a common Baltic space, and the commonality of interests shared between
the Scandinavian countries and the three Baltic States. This journey takes
in five capital cities, **lots of forests and two great boat trips**. Not to mention
the trains!

Suggested itinerary

The journey **splits neatly into six legs**: one by boat and then three by train, another boat,
then a final train from Stockholm west to Oslo. You can of course cut off the main route at
Riga and head south through Lithuania to reach Poland and join **Route 48** or **50** in Warsaw
(but you'll probably need to bus across the border from Latvia into Lithuania). Our note on
Riga connections (see p437) gives a few suggestions. From Riga you could also take the
overnight train to Minsk in Belarus (ERT 1850) to join **Route 50**. If you follow Route 51 from
end to end, we would suggest taking five to seven days over it, with stops in Tartu, Riga
and Stockholm.

By boat to Tallinn

We start with a **boat journey from Helsinki** (see p305) across the Gulf
of Finland to Tallinn. There are four different operators with a range of

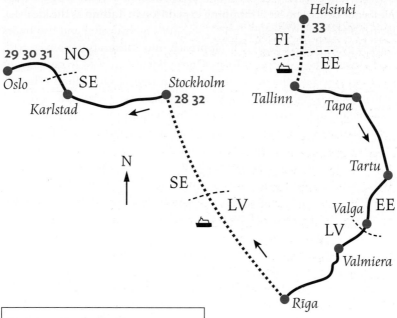

Route details

Helsinki Port to Tallinn Port		ERT 2410
Frequency	Journey time	Notes
8–15 per day	2 hrs 15 mins – 3 hrs 30 mins	

Tallinn to Tartu		ERT 1880
Frequency	Journey time	Notes
10 per day	2 hrs – 2 hrs 20 mins	

Tartu to Valga		ERT 1880
Frequency	Journey time	Notes
4 per day	1 hr 15 mins	

Valga to Rīga		ERT 1830
Frequency	Journey time	Notes
2 per day	2 hrs 40 mins – 3 hrs 10 mins	

Rīga to Stockholm		ERT 2464
Frequency	Journey time	Notes
1 per day	18 hrs	S

Stockholm to Oslo		ERT 750
Frequency	Journey time	Notes
3–5 per day	6hrs – 7 hrs	N

Notes

N – Some journeys require a change of train in Karlstad.
S – Overnight shipping service operated by Tallink Silja.

The **numbers in red** adjacent to some cities on our route maps refer to other routes in this book which also include that particular city.

hydrofoil and fast ferry services. This competition is sustained by the huge number of Finns who see a **shopping expedition to Tallinn** as the ideal day out from Helsinki. Crossing time is 100 mins by hydrofoil and two hours or more by ship (ERT 2410). The **approach into Tallinn** is impressive with good views of the walled Old Town. One option if you want to save a night in a hotel is to take the overnight ship from Helsinki to Tallinn. The MS *Viking* (www.vikingline.com) leaves Helsinski at 20.30 every evening (but at 19.00 on Sun and 21.00 on Fri) and pulls into Tallinn at 06.00 next morning.

The days of the busy shipping link from Helsinki to Tallinn may be numbered. In 2019, the Estonian and Finnish governments agreed in principle to build a 60-kilometre **rail tunnel under the Gulf of Finland** linking their two capitals, and thus extending the *Rail Baltica* project (see p439 and p524) to Helsinki. Don't hold your breath, though. The tunnel, if it ever comes to pass, will take 15 years to build.

Tallinn (suggested stopover)

Following Estonian independence, Tallinn became something of a **tourist Mecca** both for Finns on booze cruises and western Europeans exploring further afield. Lauded by some to be the Prague of the Baltic States, the old parts of the town are compact, manageable and a delight to explore on foot both during the day and at night. **Nightlife in Tallinn** goes on into the small hours particularly on the long summer nights (the summer season is very short, so locals and visitors need to take advantage of it while it is there). Live music is common and there is a vibrant atmosphere around town.

In the old part of Tallinn you will find attractive **cobbled streets**, picturesque painted houses, churches and fortifications. Against a stretch of the mediaeval wall surrounding the **Old Town**, which can be entered through a number of gates, there is a craft market, specialising in traditionally patterned fishermen's knitwear. **Katariina käik** is an atmospheric alley tenanted by craftswomen and lined with ancient gravestones.

Tallinn City Museum, Vene 17, has a section on modern history, with videos bringing to life the drama of 1989–1991 (closed Mon). From here it's a short walk through the Vana turg (Old Market) to the **Raekoja plats** (Town Hall Square), with its outdoor cafés on the cobbles, and watched over by the Gothic town hall of 1404. The tower of the Town Hall sports Vana Toomas (Old Thomas), the city guardian. Climb the tower for good views.

St Nicholas Church at Niguliste 3 houses mediaeval art, including a striking 15th-century *Dance of Death*, while the Estonian Orthodox Cathedral of Alexander Nevsky is a superb example of Russian Revival style. It has been meticulously restored over the last decades. Across Lossi plats is **Toompea Castle**, the seat of government. Walk around the building's 18th-century facade (hiding the mediaeval structure) and see Tall Hermann, the tower from which the Estonian flag, banned in the Soviet era, now proudly flies. From here Toom-kooli leads to the **cathedral** (called the Toomkirik), Tallinn's oldest church, founded by the Danes and much rebuilt. Nearby **Toompea Hill** has two good viewpoints, one over the Old Town and the other looking towards the harbour.

ARRIVAL, INFORMATION, ACCOMMODATION

≋ Near Tallinn's Old Town and harbour at Toompuiestee. Inside it has an upmarket restaurant and day spa. It's a 10-min walk to the Old Town or take tram 1 or 2. 🚌 Bus station: Lastekodu 46 (www.bussijaam.ee), some distance from the centre (take tram 2/4). To be sure of a seat, buy tickets before travel (www.tpilet.ee).

🛈 Tourist office: Niguliste 2 (www.visittallinn.ee). Trams connect harbour, rail and bus stations with Viru väljak (Viru Square); there are also buses and trolleybuses. Tickets can be bought from the driver for €2 and are valid for one journey on that vehicle. Or get a smartcard at any R-Kiosk to use the cheaper electronic ticket system.

🛏 A good budget option near the station is the **Hotel Economy**, Kopli 2c, ☎ 667 83 00 (www.economyhotel.ee). Located in a quiet area of the Old Town, the **Imperial**, Nunne 14, ☎ 627 48 00 (www.imperial.ee) is a very welcoming place. Another good option close to the Old Town square is the **Old Town Maestro's**, Suur-Karja 10, ☎ 626 20 00 (http://old-town-maestros.hotelltallinn.com).

If you are tired of Tallinn set-piece attractions and tourist-oriented craft markets, you can see another side of Estonian (or Russian) life at the market behind the main railway station. Called **Balt jaama turg**, this busy street market is popular with the city's Russian speakers.

Once you've taken a wander through the market, hop on the train for the journey south through beautiful Estonian forests to **Tartu**, Estonia's foremost university town, built into a wooded hill, with picturesque views. The university was founded by King Gustav Adolf of Sweden in 1632 (whose statue is behind it) but the classical university building dates from 1809. The **Town Hall Square** is probably the most photographed spot in Tartu. At one end is the bridge and at the other the fine neoclassical Town Hall, built in 1778–1784.

The direct trains from Tartu to Riga have long disappeared from the timetables; it is nowadays necessary to change train at **Valga**, just on the Estonian side of the border with Latvia. This small town on the River Pedeli is a border curiosity that had an untroubled life in the days of the Soviet Union. After Estonian and Latvian independence, the town found itself **split by a new border**, dividing streets in two. With both countries now members of Schengen, the border is less of an issue. Valga's railway station was recently renovated, but the train service is as dismal as ever.

Riga (Rīga)

Of the Baltic Republics, Latvia has the strongest remaining links with Russia, and roughly 30% of the country's inhabitants are **Russian speakers**.

You'll hear Russian all the time on the streets of Riga. Nevertheless, the country and its capital have asserted their independence from Russia, and Riga has witnessed a growth in tourism.

Riga has four elements – a 17th-century Hanseatic town preserved as its historic core, a large monumental Parisian-style quarter of boulevards, parks and art nouveau architecture and the odd Stalinist building beyond the fortifications, a Soviet industrial and urban wasteland and finally a new financial centre of glass skyscrapers. There is no need to stray from the northern shore unless you want to cross the bridge to look at the Old Town's church spires from a distance.

Riga's **Old Town** is a mass of winding streets, attractive old buildings and a great number of worthwhile churches. Adjacent to the rail and bus stations is the eye-opening **Central Market** on Nēģu iela. Housed in five huge former Zeppelin hangars, it's a mixture of meat, varieties of bread, dairy products, vegetables and anything else edible. The approaches often consist of lines of women selling things like outdated lingerie to make a bit of money.

Riga Castle dates from 1330 and contains the official residence of the President of Latvia and museums of Latvian history, foreign art and Latvian culture. The cathedral is the largest place of worship in the Baltics, and is renowned for its organ.

In Mazā Pils iela, the **Three Brothers** are the most famous of Riga's old houses, dating from the 15th century. For an excellent view of the city, ascend the tower of St Peter's Church on Skārņu iela. The highlight of the Town Hall Square is the restored **House of the Blackheads**, a lay order of bachelor merchants. It was blown up by the Soviets in 1948 to clear the square of any German links but was rebuilt in the 1990s. The **Occupation Museum** (free) at Strēlnieku laukums 1 displays the sufferings of the Latvian people under the Nazi and Soviet regimes.

ARRIVAL, INFORMATION, ACCOMMODATION

≈ On the south-eastern edge of the city centre. International trains are booked at windows 1–6, immediate departure tickets for local services from windows 7–12. Bear in mind that the station is now Riga's biggest shopping centre, in which trains are largely an irrelevance. Most people come here to buy designer clothes, try exotic foods or to arrange mortgages.

🚌 Bus station: Near the rail station, adjacent to the Central Market (www.autoosta. lv). ℹ Tourist office: Rātslaukums 6 (www.liveriga.com). You can buy a ticket from the driver of trams, trolleybuses and buses (€2), or purchase cheaper e-tickets. Information on public transport in Riga, including routes, timetables and ticket types is available online at www.rigassatiksme.lv. If you must take a cab, call Lady Taxi, ☎ 2780 0900, a reliable service that only employs women drivers (www.ladytaxi.lv).

✉ A good, modern option close to the railway station on the edge of the Old Town is **Hotel Avalon**, 13 janvara iela 19, ☎ 67 16 99 99 (www.hotelavalon.eu). Or try the welcoming **St. Peter's Boutique Hotel**, Peldu iela 23, ☎ 67 22 30 27 (www.stpetershotel.lv), equally well located for the Old Town. More upmarket is the modern and stylish **Neiburgs Hotel**, Jauniela 25/27, ☎ 67 11 55 22 (www.neiburgs.com).

Riga connections

There are trains beyond Riga, so you'll not necessarily need to retrace your outward route back to Estonia and Finland. There is a direct overnight train on alternate days to **Minsk** (ERT 1850), where you can connect onto **Route 50**. There are departures every day to both St Petersburg and Moscow (ERT 1840). Remember that most travellers will need to secure visas prior to travel to Belarus or the Russian Federation.

With only a very occasional train from Riga to Vilnius (a Kiev-bound Ukrainian train which runs every four days), a bus may be the best bet. Lux Express (www.luxexpress.eu) run several times daily to **Vilnius** (ERT 1800), capital of Lithuania, in four to five hours. For truly dedicated bus travellers, Ecolines offer a direct overnight bus from **Riga to Warsaw** (www.ecolines.net). The journey time is 13 hours. A more comfortable Riga to Warsaw option may be that offered by Lux Express as it is a daytime service. It requires a change of coach in Vilnius, but the journey time is the same as on the direct overnight bus.

If you want to really see an out-of-the-way Baltic spot, you might consider making for **Russia's Kaliningrad Oblast**, which is an exclave of the Russian Federation on the coast between Lithuania and Poland. The Latvian bus company Transinestra (part of the Ecolines group so bookable at www.ecolines.net) has a departure late each evening direct to Kaliningrad. The one-way fare is €20 for the eight-hour journey. Border formalities for entering Russia take place around four in the morning, so don't expect much sleep. But missing out on some sleep is a small price to pay for the chance to see this extraordinary Russian outpost. We have thoroughly enjoyed time spent exploring Kaliningrad (formerly **Königsberg**), its rural hinterland and the coastal resorts in Kaliningrad Oblast. A new e-visa scheme was launched in 2019 for visitors to Kaliningrad. It covers the entire Kaliningrad Oblast. Holders of all European passports are eligible, except for UK citizens. There is no charge for an e-visa, and there are none of the usual requirements for invites and confirmed hotel bookings.

If you are keen to head back west quickly from Riga, there's a good option from the Latvian port of **Liepāja** (200 km south-west of Riga, 3-4 hrs by regular buses), where the Stena Line freight ferry Urd accepts passengers on her twice-weekly sailings to the German port of **Travemünde** (ERT 2486).

Across the Baltic

From Riga, Route 51 embarks on the longest sea journey to form an integral part of any of our 52 routes. The **Riga to Stockholm overnight ferry** service is operated by Tallink Silja (www.tallinksilja.com), and we rate it as one of the most enjoyable of all **Baltic shipping routes**, particularly around midsummer when a long dusk never really fades to night. The MS Isabelle is the older of the two vessels on the route; she was built in 1989, and has sundecks, a pool and saunas. She was joined on this popular route in late 2016 by MS Romantika which features a beauty salon, sun bar and Turkish steam room (in addition to a regular sauna). Both ships include cabins of various categories, and if you decide to splash out on one of the Deluxe Class cabins of suites on either vessel, then you are in for a treat. One-way fares start at €69 on the MS Isabelle, €79 on the MS Romantika.

The passenger terminal in Riga is on the east bank of the **River Daugava** just north of the city centre. Trams 5, 6, 7, 9 and 11 run north along Eksporta to the terminal. The Stockholm ship normally leaves at 17.30, and you should be at the terminal about an hour in advance. The beauty of the journey to Stockholm is the real sense of being on a cruise. The ships are large and comfortable, and there is a surprising amount to see en route. In clear weather, look out for the Estonian island of **Ruhnu** off the starboard side as you sail through the **Gulf of Riga**. The vessel then cuts around the southernmost tip of **Saaremaa Island** before setting a north-westerly course for Stockholm. The last couple of hours into Stockholm are sheer joy as the vessel cruises through the archipelago to reach the dock at the chic new Värtahamnen Terminal which opened in 2017. It is a short ride by bus into the city centre (60 Swedish crowns, pay on the bus).

The ship from Riga arrives in sufficent time (usually about 10.30) to catch a same-day train to Oslo, reaching the Norwegian capital by the evening. But Stockholm is definitely worth a stop of at least one or two nights. For more information on **Stockholm** see p264. You can connect in Stockholm onto **Route 28**, following it in reverse to Copenhagen and Hamburg, or onto **Route 32** which strikes boldly north to Lapland and beyond.

West to Oslo

The train journey from **Stockholm to Oslo** (ERT 750) is a reminder that we are a long way north and in fairly inhospitable terrain. Stockholm and Oslo both lie a shade south of the sixtieth parallel, but just after crossing the border into Norway the railway goes beyond 60°N – that's just as far north as the Shetland Islands in Scotland or Cook Inlet in Alaska. **Bare rock and forests** abound. The journey starts by following the *Västra stambanan* (Western Main Line) to just beyond Hallsberg, where Oslo-bound trains branch north on the *Värmlandsbanan* (Värmland Railway) and skirt the northern edge of **Lake Vänern** to reach the Norwegian border. If you are tempted to break your journey, your best bet is **Karlstad** (served by all trains on the route), which has a fine location on the north side of Lake Vänern. It is also well placed for connecting onto the minor railway which runs down the west side of the lake (ERT 751 and p281).

From Karlstad it is just over an hour to the border with Norway, crossed at the oddly-named community of **Morokulien** (seen to the left of the train) which rates as one of Europe's more peculiar border communities. The frontier bisects the tourist office. A peace monument unveiled in 1914 is a testament to harmonious relations between Sweden and Norway. From Morokulien, the train tracks through forest and past a series of lakes to reach the **Glomma Valley** which it then follows west towards **Oslo**. Trains from Stockholm all terminate at the *Sentralstasjon*, often just referred to as Oslo S. Read more about the Norwegian capital on p281. In Oslo, you can connect onto **Route 29, 30** and **31**.

SIDETRACKS: BALTIC TRAINS

As you travel through Lithuania, Latvia and Estonia, you will frequently hear locals explaining away their abysmal rail services, with particularly poor cross-border links, as a **legacy of Soviet times**. "All lines led to Moscow, and only to Moscow," is a common phrase. That explanation, however, is all too easy.

A key factor in the Baltic countries has been **public attitudes towards the railway**. Train travel was so central a part of the Soviet experience, and remains so important in Russia today, that the post-independence political and cultural elites in the Baltic States turned their backs on the railway in much the same way that anything Russian fell into disfavour. In the new political piety, all eyes look west.

A new breed of home-grown entrepreneurs catered for the car-less by developing **long-distance bus services**. You'll find some of the most luxurious coaches in Europe in use on routes between major cities in the Baltic region.

Cast back to 1989, and the *Chaika Express* ran from Tallinn via Riga to Vilnius. From Vilnius there were also **direct trains to Warsaw and Berlin**. In the post-independence era of the 1990s, when car ownership in the Baltic States rocketed, the region's railways were left to rot. Many routes closed, and elsewhere the **lack of investment** in infrastructure meant that line speeds were so reduced that buses easily outpaced trains – so giving weight to the view that trains were an outdated relic of the Soviet period.

Various **European Union initiatives** are tempting Lithuanians, Latvians and Estonians back onto the train. The key project here is **Rail Baltica**, an ambitious plan to build a new passenger railway from Warsaw to Tallinn, serving cities in Lithuania and Latvia along the way. This new railway is being built to the standard European gauge (1,435 mm, as opposed to the wider Russian gauge), a decision driven more by politics than by engineering considerations. Having the same width tracks as most other EU countries is of great symbolic importance in the Baltic region.

Rail Baltica's first achievement was the **extension of standard-gauge tracks from Poland** over the border into Lithuania. This line reached Kaunus in 2015, and a special train carried EU officials and the media from Poland to Kaunus. In 2016, a token public service of five local trains each week was introduced between **Kaunas and Białystok**. These still run northbound on Fri, Sat and Sun; southbound on Sat, Sun and Mon. Such a minimal service hardly justifies the recent huge investment in infrastructure.

The local trains might well soon be supplemented by a once-daily through-service from **Kraków and Warsaw to Kaunas** in Lithuania; this additional link remains a possibility for late 2020. It will be a first step in realising the *Rail Baltica* dream. Keep an eye on ERT Table 1042. Advocates of *Rail Baltica* suggest that, when a standard-gauge railway line runs right through to Tallinn, fast daytime trains might dash the 970 kilometres from Warsaw to the Estonian capital in under six hours. Now that would give the operators of luxury coaches a real run for their money.

Route 52: The ultimate challenge

Cities: Culture: History: Scenery:
Countries covered: Hungary (HU), Romania (RO), Ukraine (UA)
Journey time: 22 hrs | Distance: 938 km | Map: www.ebrweb.eu/map52

Route 52 is for pros. If you are one of those people who habitually start reading a book from the back rather than the front, might we offer a word of advice? If you have never set foot on a train in Europe before, this route would not be the wisest choice for a first excursion. At 938 km, this journey is not particularly long. But it's challenging. Route 52 really takes you **off the beaten track** and it is a chance to see regions of Europe less frequented by tourists.

Route 26 is the easy way from **Debrecen to Lviv** (Львів). But Route 52 is much slower, crossing areas the very names of which evoke a sense of history: Transylvania and Bukovina. Along the way we traverse the **Carpathian Mountains** and the final section of the route, in south-west Ukraine, is through hilly country, culminating in the beautiful city of Lviv.

Do just check before setting out that **Ukrainian visa rules** are unchanged. In late 2019, no visas were required of tourists holding passports from all European Union countries or all states which were once part of the Soviet Union. However, citizens of many other countries (including many Commonwealth nations) do require a visa.

Take along both Romanian and Ukrainian (or Russian) **phrasebooks or translation apps**. You will be travelling through areas where you cannot always rely on finding English speakers (though you can get a long way with French in Romania). And once in Ukraine, it really is a huge asset if you can at least transliterate Cyrillic signs – if only to up the chances of not boarding the wrong train. And don't even think of embarking on Route 52 without a supply of toilet paper tucked away in your luggage.

Suggested itinerary

This is a route that deserves time. Yes, you could do the journey in a couple of days with overnight train journeys. But this final route in *Europe by Rail* deserves more. Take a week and give Route 52 its due. Oradea, Cluj-Napoca, **Suceava** and **Chernivtsi** are all good choices for an overnight stay. Careful planning is important because of the scarcity of trains across the two international borders crossed by Route 52.

Debrecen

You'll almost certainly **stay overnight** in Debrecen before embarking on this route. The city thrived on a heady mix of Jewish, Calvinist, Uniate and Catholic influences. These days it's a stronghold of Viktor Orbán's right-leaning nationalist Fidesz alliance. Debrecen is the most easterly of Hungary's great cities and you won't need to spend much time in Debrecen

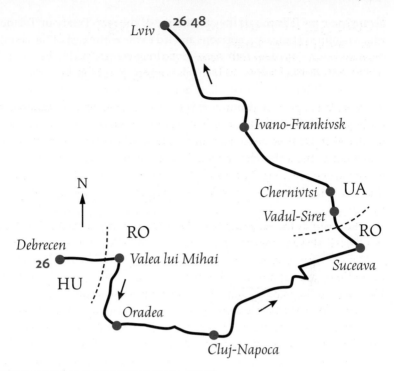

Route details

Debrecen to Oradea — ERT 1277

Frequency	Journey time	Notes
3 per day	3 hrs – 4 hrs 30 mins	Λ

Oradea to Cluj-Napoca — ERT 1600/1625

Frequency	Journey time	Notes
8–10 per day	2 hrs 40 mins – 4 hrs	

Cluj-Napoca to Suceava — ERT 1660

Frequency	Journey time	Notes
4 per day	7 hrs 10 mins	

Suceava to Vadul-Siret — ERT 1650

Frequency	Journey time	Notes
2 per day	2 hrs 30 mins	

Vadul-Siret to Chernivtsi

Frequency	Journey time	Notes
2 per day	1 hr 30 mins	

Chernivtsi to Lviv — ERT 1710

Frequency	Journey time	Notes
2–4 per day	3 hrs 50 mins – 6 hrs 30 mins	

Notes

Λ – Two of the three daily trains shown here require a change at Valea lui Mihai. There are four additional daily options from Debrecen to Oradea, taking a more southerly route and changing trains at Püspökladány (ERT 1270, then 1275). The travel time is normally about three hours.

HU = Hungary
RO = Romania
UA = Ukraine

before someone tells you of the catastrophe of the 1920 **Treaty of Trianon**, which trimmed Hungary's horizons and led to the entire east of the country being ceded to Romania. Debrecen, for so long accustomed to being in the centre of Hungarian affairs, suddenly lost a good part of its hinterland.

Kossuth tér is the great plaza dominated by the rather austere neo-classical protestant Great Church. If you were in any doubt about Debrecen's religious leanings, the next tram stop north of Kossuth tér is Kálvin tér. It's not for nothing that Debrecen often styles itself as the Calvinist Rome. Geneva may have a thing or two to say about that.

ARRIVAL, INFORMATION, ACCOMMODATION

⇌ Tram routes 1 and 2 run due north from the railway station towards the town centre. It's just four stops to Kossuth tér. Apart from the two tram routes, the city also has five trolleybus routes (ticket and route information on www.dkv.hu). Single tickets – valid for one, uninterrupted journey – can be pre-purchased at a ticket machine or post office. Tickets purchased from the driver are more expensive. Don't forget to validate your ticket when boarding the bus / tram / trolleybus. 🄸 Tourist office: Kossuth tér, in the Karakter 1517 Café (www.debrecen.hu/en/tourist).

🛏 The **Malom Hotel**, Böszörményi út 1, ☎ 52 688 850 (www.malomhoteldebrecen.hu), styled in the manner of an old mill, is a good choice. It's just west of the city centre. Or try the **Centrum Hotel**, Kálvin tér 4, ☎ 52 418 522 (www.centrumhotel.hu), which is right in the centre and has comfortable rooms.

The comings and goings by train from the town's **railway station** have not always been happy. In 1944, many thousands of Jewish residents of Debrecen were deported by train to Auschwitz. In 2015, while the media focused on refugees in Budapest, there were tense scenes at Debrecen station as local thugs taunted refugees trying to make their way to Austria.

It's just 30 km from Debrecen to the border with **Romania**. Although Hungary and Romania are both in the European Union, Romania has not yet been admitted to the Schengen area, so there are still light-touch frontier formalities, with Hungarian checks at **Nyírábrány** and the Romanian bureaucracy having its chance a few minutes later at Valea lui Mihai.

Our route then parallels the Hungarian border on the run south to **Oradea**, a Romanian city which is full of Hungarian flavours, evocatively fading baroque and secessionist buildings. A trio of synagogues attests to the city's Jewish connections, but the real star is the enormous Roman Catholic cathedral, just a 5-min walk from the train station. Look out in particular for the fine range of art nouveau architecture.

CONNECTIONS FROM ORADEA

Oradea's historic connections with Hungary are reflected in the rail schedules. Oradea has direct trains to the Hungarian capital (ERT 1275), as well as a useful once-daily Eurocity service to **Vienna**. From Oradea, there are direct trains south via Arad to **Timișoara** (ERT 1625), a striking city which serves as the capital of the Romanian Banat region. Note the onward cross-border route from Timișoara to Belgrade, featured in earlier editions of this book, no longer has any passenger trains.

East from Oradea, you quickly have a sense of heading into the hills, although the main range of the Eastern Carpathians is not till well beyond Cluj-Napoca. The railway from **Oradea to Cluj** skirts the northern edge of the Apuseni Mountains, an area of dramatic wild country. The finest part of the route is the 68-km stretch between Aleşd and Huedin.

Cluj-Napoca (Cluj) – (suggested stopover)

Cluj-Napoca is the unofficial capital of **Transylvania**. Less hyped than the famous trio of Transylvanian cities (Sibiu, Sighişoara and Braşov), and with less evidence of Saxon settlement than those more southern cities, Cluj-Napoca has the scent of Hungary in every alley and every square. In the late 19th century, Cluj oozed belle époque style and there is still more than a hint of that in the town today. The key sights are all on the south side of the river in the **Old Town**.

ARRIVAL, INFORMATION, ACCOMMODATION

≋ The main station is 20-mins north of the Old Town (walk down south along Strada Horea). **ℹ** Tourist office: Blvd. Eroilor 6–8 (www.visitclujnapoca.ro).

🛏 Try the very central and friendly **Lol et Lola Hotel**, Strada Neagră nr. 9, ☎ 0751 450 498 (www.loletlolahotel.ro), located in a quiet side street and wowing their guests with colourful interior designs. Welcoming and not far from the station in a quiet location is the **Escala**, Crisan Str. 33, ☎ 0264 444 002 (www.escala-club-vila.ro). Or try the modern and central **Capitolina**, V Babeş Str. 35, ☎ 0264 450 490 (www.hotel-capitolina.ro).

East to Bukovina

The journey east from Cluj-Napoca to Suceava crosses the main range of the **Carpathians** and takes a little planning. On most days, there is really only one option, with a departure from Cluj just after midday. The best of the landscape is the hour immediately beyond **Lunca Ilvei**, where all trains stop before tackling the steep mountain route ahead. It has been suggested that it was in these hills that **Bram Stoker** placed Count Dracula's fictional castle.

Once over the mountains, the railway descends into the Romanian region known as Moldavia – not to be confused with the Republic of Moldova, an independent country that lies further east beyond the River Prut. This area of northern Moldavia is often called **Bukovina**, recalling the former Habsburg territory which included part of south-west Ukraine and the northernmost part of present-day Moldavia. Suceava is the principal town of the Romanian Bukovina.

Suceava (suggested stopover)

There is only one real reason to visit industrial Suceava. It is the jumping-off point for tours of the UNESCO-listed **painted monasteries** of southern

Bukovina. Suceava itself is a shade run-down, but of note are the **Monastery of St John** (south-east of the city centre), the Armenian church (in the centre) and the Armenian monastery at Zamca (north-west of the centre). Suceava comes to life every Thursday morning when it hosts a **market** that attracts many traders from Ukraine and Moldova.

Arrival, information, accommodation

⇌ The old main station, locally referred to as Iţcani, is a crumbling Habsburg pile well out of the centre. It is shown as Suceava Nord in timetables. Much more convenient for the centre is Suceava station, locally called Burdujeni, north-east of the town. Its distinctive red building is one of the most handsome in town. Take the regular marshrutka (often called maxi-taxi) to the centre. 🛈 Tourist office: Str. Mitropoliei 4 (www.visitingbucovina.ro).

✉ A good option is the central but quiet B&B **Villa Alice**, Str. Simion Florea Marian 1st bis, ☎ 0230 522 254 (www.villaalice.ro). Further out, on the edge of town (500 m from the central bus station) is the comfortable **Sonnenhof**, Blvd. Sofia Vicoveanca 68, ☎ 0230 220 033 (www.hotelsonnenhof.ro), with a good restaurant.

Into Ukraine

Two daily trains leave both Iţcani and Burdujeni stations in Suceava for **Vadul-Siret** (Вадул-Сірет) in Ukraine. The lunchtime service connects into a local train to Chernivtsi. The Romanian train to Vadul-Siret requires advance reservation (but there's never a shortage of seats). The onward Ukrainian train cannot be pre-booked. These local services are not shown in the *European Rail Timetable* (ERT). On Sundays (yes, only on Sundays), through sleeping cars from Bucharest to Kiev (ERT 1670) are shunted between the two trains at Vadul-Siret – where the bogies are altered to fit the wider Ukrainian-gauge tracks at the border.

You'll need to allow about five hours for the 90-km journey from **Suceava to Chernivtsi**. If you cannot bear the slow speed, there are regular marshrutkas from Suceava to Chernivtsi, generally taking three to four hours for the journey, which includes time for border formalities. A **daily bus** leaves Suceava for Chernivtsi at 13.00 (fare €8).

Chernivtsi (Чернівці) – (suggested stopover)

Chernivtsi's distinctive **green-domed railway station** gives a hint of the city, which is one of the most attractive in Ukraine. The gracious style of Chernivtsi reflects its former status as the cosmopolitan capital of the **Bukovina** region. This is a city that has, over the last 100 years, been variously part of Austria-Hungary (until 1918), the Kingdom of Romania (from 1918 until 1940) and the Soviet Union (from 1944 to 1991). Since 1991 it has been part of an independent Ukraine.

As the crucible of so much European history, Chernivtsi distils the complex **mix of cultures** that we have experienced while travelling the 52 routes in this book. And it is appropriate that Chernivtsi be the last city of any size described in the routes section of this volume. For the city that claims to be the very **heart of Europe** is close to the geographical centre of the continent.

Chernivtsi has many pastel-coloured buildings that still have heaps of belle époque charm. Don't miss the green opera house and blue town hall. Among the many other remarkable buildings in Chernivtsi are the old **Armenian cathedral** (now a concert hall), the Orthodox cathedral with its curiously twisted towers and the university, a huge red-brick affair with Moorish elements that seems like something out of a fairy tale. There are guided tours every afternoon of the principal halls and galleries inside the building. Above all, the university gives the city much of its buzz.

Some 5 km north-west of town is **Kalynivsky market**, a huge open-air bazaar that every day attracts thousands of visitors. Marshrutkas run out to the market every few minutes from the city centre. Even if you profess to have no interest in shopping, go out to Kalynivsky. It is pure theatre, even if sometimes a trifle muddy.

ARRIVAL, INFORMATION, ACCOMMODATION

≈ 1.5 km north of the city centre on vul. Gagarina; trolleybus 3 runs between the railway station and the bus station south of the city centre. ▐ There is a tourist information office in the Hotel Bukovyna (see below).

➤ If you want to stay overnight, the **Hotel Bukovyna** in the heart of the city on Holovna St. 141, ☎ 0372 58 56 25 (www.bukovyna-hotel.com), is a safe bet. The **Allure Inn**, Tsentralnaya sq. 6, ☎ 0372 551 782 (www.allureinn.com), is a comfortable option conveniently located right in the centre. Also central is the **Georg Palace**, vul. Bohuna 24, ☎ 0372 576 116 (www.georg-hotels.com).

Beyond Chernivtsi

Chernivtsi may be the last place described in our routes, but it is not the end of the line. From Chernivtsi there are direct trains to **Lviv** (ERT 1700) where you can join **Route 26** to Budapest or **Route 48** to Kraków, Warsaw and Berlin. En route to Lviv (see p445) you may decide to stop off for a night or two in Ivano-Frankivsk (Івано-Франківськ), a good base for heading south into the Ukrainian part of the Carpathian wilderness and a town well worth exploring in its own right. There's a certain ritzy style about **Ivano-Frankivsk** which seems oddly out of place for a town in so remote a region.

But if you have followed Route 52 all the way from Debrecen to Chernivtsi, then you are clearly an independent spirit and no longer need our guiding hand. Cast an eye over the departure boards at Chernivtsi station and take your pick. Lviv is the tame option. Why not Kiev? Or even Odessa? The next 52 routes are yours to decide and plan alone, for now **the world is your oyster**. Thank you for joining us as we have roamed across Europe by train.

Gazetteer

Countries from A to Z

AlbaniaAndorraAustriaBelarusBelgium
Bosnia and HerzegovinaBulgariaCroatia
CyprusCzech RepublicDenmarkEstonia
Faroe IslandsFinlandFranceGermany
Great BritainGreeceHungaryIceland
IrelandItalyKosovoLatviaLiechtenstein
LithuaniaLuxembourgMaltaMoldova
MonacoMontenegroNetherlands
North MacedoniaNorwayPoland
PortugalRomaniaRussiaSan Marino
SerbiaSlovakiaSloveniaSpainSweden
SwitzerlandTurkeyUkraineVatican City

There is some information that is best presented on a **country-by-country basis**. In our gazetteer we give a cameo account of most European territories with key data such as language, time zone and currency. We also indicate which electrical plug types are used in the respective country. The letters A-N each represent a plug type (see www.iec.ch/worldplugs for details). For countries that feature in our **52 rail routes**, we give additional travel information. Remember that, as with everything in this book, the *European Rail Timetable* (ERT) and the accompanying *Rail Map Europe* make **good companions** to this gazetteer.

We are very aware that many readers of this book travel on tight budgets so, where appropriate in this gazetteer, we make brief mention of the availability of independent hostels – which are increasingly a canny choice for travellers looking for something different from a traditional hotel. Other types of budget accommodation are also mentioned.

Within the gazetteer, you'll find photos that **capture the flavour** of a country or region. All images, in each case duly credited to the original photographer, were sourced through www.dreamstime.com.

ALBANIA

The small republic in the **eastern Adriatic** features on few tourist itineraries, but there is no reason why it should not, for Albania offers remarkable old Ottoman towns, stunning beaches and some of Europe's finest mountain scenery. And it boasts some deliciously antiquated trains. Timetables change unpredictably (see ERT 1390). No passenger trains cross the country's borders, so the Albanian rail network is effectively isolated from the rest of Europe. Read more in our **Sidetracks** on p390.

Essentials: Local name: Shqipëria – Population: 2.9m – Capital: Tiranë – Currency: Lek (ALL) – Languages: Albanian (Italian and English often understood in main towns) – Accommodation costs: generally low – Plug types: C, F – Time zone: winter GMT+1, summer GMT+2 – International dialling code: +355 – Public holidays: 1, 2 Jan; 14, 22 Mar; Easter Mon (Catholic and Orthodox); 1 May; Eid-al-Fitr; Eid-al-Adha; 19 Oct; 28, 29 Nov; 8, 25 Dec.

ANDORRA

The mountain principality in the **Pyrenees** is one of just a handful of rail-free countries in mainland Europe. Tacky shops and concrete aplenty in the capital but fine hiking and skiing in the hills around. The nearest you'll get to Andorra by train is Andorre-L'Hospitalet, just three kilometres from the border. But the bus link from that station to Andorra was axed in 2019. Express buses run from Lleida train station (six times daily, taking 2 hrs 30 mins) and from Toulouse (thrice daily, taking 4 hrs). There are also direct buses from Andorra to Barcelona's city centre and airport (ERT 664).

Essentials: Local name: Andorra – Population: 85k – Capital: Andorra la Vella – Currency: Euro (EUR) – Languages: Catalan (Spanish, Portuguese and French also widely spoken) – Accommodation costs: generally high – Plug types: C, F – Time zone: winter GMT+1, summer

GMT+2 – International dialling code: +376 – Public holidays: 1, 6 Jan; 8 Feb; 14 Mar; Good Friday; Easter Mon; 1 May; Ascension Day; Whit Mon; 15 Aug; 8 Sep; 1 Nov; 8, 25, 26 Dec.

Austria

Austria feels very much at the **centre of Europe**. Staples in the promotional literature designed to woo visitors are lush green Alpine meadows, steep-roofed chalets with heavy wooden balconies full of geraniums, and onion-domed churches. But Austria has much more, with extremely beautiful lake regions and fine historic cities such as Salzburg and Vienna.

Essentials: Local name: Österreich – Population: 8.7m – Capital: Vienna/Wien – Currency: Euro (EUR) – Languages: German (English is widely spoken in tourist areas, Slovene minority in Carinthia) – Accommodation costs: generally high – Plug types: C, F – Time zone: winter GMT+1, summer GMT+2 – International dialling code: +43 – Public holidays: 1, 6 Jan; Easter Mon; 1 May; Ascension Day; Whit Mon; Corpus Christi; 15 Aug; 26 Oct; 1 Nov; 8, 25, 26 Dec.

Travel in Austria

Austria is most conspicuously included in this book in **Route 34** and **35**. In addition, **Route 39** crosses the country from north to south. Rail travel in Austria is very efficient. Trains are generally clean and modern, and the great majority of internal services run precisely to time.

A big plus point for touring Austria by rail is that there are no compulsory reservations or supplements on day trains, including **Railjet** high-speed trains. International services (particularly night trains) arriving in Austria from Croatia, Slovenia and Hungary are prone to delays, and you should be cautious about relying on too tight connecting times when arriving on these trains.

There is an impressive programme of **infrastructure renewal**. In Vienna, for example, the entire rail network has been remodelled with the completion of the new Hauptbahnhof in 2015. The country's principal operator is **Österreichische Bundesbahnen** (ÖBB). ÖBB's impressive range of **night trains**, branded *Nightjet*, links to Italy, Germany, Switzerland and a number of countries across central Europe. The *Nightjet* network incorporates many routes which until 2016 were run by Deutsche Bahn, so these days if you take a night sleeper train from Berlin to Zurich or from Munich to Rome, you'll be travelling on an ÖBB *Nightjet*.

Private operator **Westbahn** (WB) runs trains between Vienna and Salzburg (www.westbahn.at). **RegioJet** (www.regiojet.com) offers fast trains from Vienna to Prague, its bright yellow trains competing with Austrian and Czech *Railjet* services. RegioJet hopes to launch a Vienna-Budapest service in mid-2020. The national rail website at www.oebb.at has a good journey planner and downloadable timetables. Train categories: apart from high-speed Railjets (RJ, RJX), there are Eurocity (EC) and Intercity (IC) trains on main domestic and international routes, fast trains (D) and slower regional services (REX, R). Intercity Express (ICE) trains offer connections to and from Germany.

RAIL PASSES

Both Eurail and Interrail passes are valid (not just on ÖBB trains, but also on Westbahn and RegioJet services). Many areas within Austria have regional passes, some of which include private railways and local buses. For travel throughout the whole country, the **Einfach-Raus-Ticket** gives a day's second-class travel on regional trains for groups of 2–5 people from €34 (not before 09.00 Mon–Fri).

OTHER PUBLIC TRANSPORT OPTIONS

Austria's long-distance bus network is run by Österreichische Bundesbahnen (ÖBB) under the **Postbus** brand. Bus stations are usually based by rail stations/post offices. International services are offered by Eurolines, RegioJet, Leo Express, Flixbus and others. City transport: tickets are cheaper from Tabak/Trafik booths. Taxis are metered.

FURTHER INFORMATION

Main website for tourist information: www.austria.info. In cities, look for green 'i' sign which indicates a tourist office (called a *Fremdenverkehrsbüro*).

ACCOMMODATION

Standards of cleanliness and comfort are usually high even in simpler places. *Gasthaus/Gasthof* indicates an inn and *Frühstückspension* a bed and breakfast place. **Independent hostels** are a good bet for both private rooms and beds in dorms, although they are mainly limited to the major cities and principal tourist destinations. More widespread, but more institutional, are *Jugendherbergen* (youth hostels), of which there are more than 100 around the country (www.oejhv.at). **Camping** is popular and there are lots of sites, mostly well run, but pricey. Many sites are open summer only.

FOOD AND DRINK

Food tends towards the **hearty**, with wholesome soups and meat-dominated main courses (famously *Wiener Schnitzel* – a thin slice of fried veal or pork), while *Gulasch* (of Hungarian origin) and dumplings are also prevalent. Cakes may be sinfully cream-laden, high in calories, but are rarely sickly; *Apfelstrudel* is the best option for those watching their waistlines. A filling snack, sold by most butchers, is *Wurstsemmel* – slices of sausage with a bread roll. **Beer and wine** are equally popular. The Austrians also take their coffee seriously.

BELARUS

Rivalling Moldova for the prize of Europe's least known country, the Republic of Belarus is almost certainly **Europe's most misunderstood country**. For some the country is a reminder of what the Soviet Union was like in its heyday, but more realistically modern Belarus treads a delicate path between Russia (on its eastern border) and the European Union (to the west).

For those who take the trouble to visit, a tantalising landscape of **beautiful forests and wetlands** awaits – all nicely offset by a huge dose of history, not all of it easy to get to grips with. The country relaxed its visa regime in 2019, making it all the easier to visit. Check the current situation on www.belarus.by.

Essentials: Local name: Belarus/Беларусь – Population: 9.6m – Capital: Minsk/Мінск – Currency: Belarusian new rouble (BYN; introduced in summer 2016) – Languages: Russian and Belarusian (young people in urban areas might speak some English) – Accommodation costs: medium – Plug types: C, F – Time zone: GMT+3 (summer and winter) – International dialling code: +375 – Public holidays: 1, 7 Jan; 8 Mar; 1, 9 May; Radonista (Ancestors' Remembrance Day, 9th day after Easter); 3 July; 7 Nov; 25 Dec.

TRAVEL IN BELARUS

You will find Belarus on **Route 50** in this book. Many long-distance trains are international services to neighbouring Russia, Ukraine, Poland and Lithuania, with the capital Minsk lying on the busy Warsaw to Moscow corridor. There are high-quality daytime services on principal axes, and slow overnight trains linking provincial centres at opposing corners of the country. Reservation is compulsory on almost all **long-distance trains**.

The website of Belarusian Railways (www.rw.by) is both in Russian and English and timetable information is available. Train categories: Firménny (Fir) are fast long-distance trains; below those are trains classified as Skóry (Sko); the slowest type of long-distance train are called Passazhirsky (Pas); there are three classes of accommodation and almost all carriages are sleepers which can be converted into seated accommodation during the day. The fast international premium trains carry a dining car. Local commuter trains and shorter distance rural services are called *elektrichka*; they ooze local colour but are incredibly slow.

RAIL PASSES
Neither Eurail nor Interrail are valid. There are no local rail passes for Belarus, but fares are very cheap. The fare on the main business express from Minsk to Vitebsk is less than €4.

OTHER PUBLIC TRANSPORT OPTIONS
Buses and minibuses (*marshrutkas*) are a cheap means of travelling within Belarus. Note that *marshrutkas* can be very crowded. City transport: trolleybuses, *marshruktas* and buses.

FURTHER INFORMATION
The Republic of Belarus has a useful and informative government website at www.belarus.by/en. If you want to travel more extensively within Belarus, it is good to bring a map of the country (city maps are however easily available). Tourist offices are still rare and you might only encounter them in larger places. Nigel Roberts' *Bradt Guide to Belarus* is an excellent companion when travelling through the country.

ACCOMMODATION

Forget the normal distinction you might make, perfectly correctly in western Europe, between cheap hotels and posher top-end places to rest your head. In the bigger Belarusian cities, many hotels offer **several grades of accommodation** from simple singles with shared bathroom to luxury suites. Note that foreign visitors usually pay more than locals for the same class of accommodation. There is a buoyant market for **private apartments**, which can be let for just a night or two, and the real growth area is staying out-of-town as Belarus develops its own take on agritourism.

FOOD AND DRINK

Few options for fine dining. Smart restaurants are few and far between in Belarus, and many Belarusians never eat out. But there is no shortage of good value places where you can linger over a beer and pizza. Standard Belarusian fare mainstreams on **potatoes and root vegetables**, and you can savour a hundred varieties of *pelmeni* (пельмени) or *vareniki* (варзнікі).

When it comes to meat dishes, pork reigns supreme, often served in **hearty stews**. High-quality coffee, beer and vodka are ubiquitous. Although there is no real wine culture in Belarus, you will find in supermarkets, and sometime also in restaurants, wonderful **Georgian wines** that never seem to make it onto the west European market.

BELGIUM

If folk have told you Belgium is dull, ignore them! Belgium is homely, intimate and **immensely interesting**. It is a place to really explore, from the surreal urban landscapes of the coast, through historic cities like Bruges and Brussels, to the **hill country of the Ardennes** in the east and south-east of the country. You will find edgy modern culture cheek by jowl with magnificent mediaeval squares. Throw in some of Europe's finest art nouveau architecture and design, a population that is enviably multilingual, and you have a beguiling mix.

Essentials: Local name: Belgique/België – Population: 11m – Capital: Brussels/Bruxelles/ Brussel – Currency: Euro (EUR) – Languages: Dutch (north), French (south), German (east); many speak both French and Dutch plus often English and/or German – Accommodation costs: generally high – Plug types: C, E – Time zone: winter GMT+1, summer GMT+2 – International dialling code: +32 – Public holidays: 1 Jan; Easter Mon; 1 May; Ascension Day; Whit Mon; 21 July; 15 Aug; 1, 11 Nov; 25 Dec.

TRAVEL IN BELGIUM

Belgium is on **Route 17, 18** and **19** in his book. The country has a busy and efficient rail network, extending to the remotest corners of Belgium. All routes are served by frequent trains. In Brussels the main hub is the

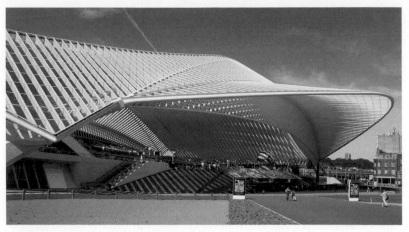

Liège Guillemins station (photo © Erzsi Molnár)

Midi/Zuid station. No reservations are required for domestic services, but seat reservations are compulsory on all **Thalys** services. The national rail operator is **SNCB** (in French) or **NMBS** (in Dutch) and has its website at www.belgianrail.be. There are two sets of timetables, one for Mondays to Fridays and another for weekends. Beware that only **Dutch or French spellings** may be shown on departure boards; for example, the French city of Lille may be rendered at Dutch-speaking stations as Rijsel.

Train categories: fast international trains connecting Belgium with its neighbours are Eurostars, Intercity Express trains (ICE), TGVs and Thalys trains. Otherwise you'll encounter regional Intercity (IC) trains and local stopping services.

Rail passes
Both Interrail and Eurail are valid. There are a number of discounted passes for people under the age of 26. **Weekend tickets** give 50% discount, and there is an off-peak fare cap for senior citizens (€6.80 single or same-day return).

Other public transport options
National bus companies are **De Lijn** (Flanders), **TEC** (Wallonia, i.e. the French-speaking area), and **STIB** (Brussels); there are only a few long-distance buses. Buses, trams and metros: board at any door with ticket or buy ticket from driver. Fares depend on length of journey, but are cheaper if bought before boarding. Tram and bus stops: red and white signs (all stops are request only – raise your hand).

Further information
Websites: www.walloniebelgiquetourisme.be (Wallonia and Brussels), www.visitflanders.com (Flanders). *Office du Tourisme* (French), *Toerisme* (Dutch) and *Verkehrsamt* (German).

Accommodation
Hotels tend to be pricey, and during the summer months it is advisable to book ahead when visiting the main cities and tourist destinations. In **business**

hubs like Brussels and Antwerp, hotels might offer greatly discounted prices on weekends. If you arrive without a reservation, the tourist office can help find a bed. As with many things in Belgium there are two official youth hostel organisations, the **Vlaamse Jeugdherbergen** (www.jeugdherbergen. be) and the **Les Auberges de Jeunesse** (www.lesaubergesdejeunesse.be). Independent hostels are often more relaxed and friendly.

FOOD AND DRINK

Most restaurants have good-value fixed-price menus (*plat du jour, tourist menu, dagschotel*). Establishments in the main squares can charge two or three times as much as similar places in nearby streets. Try waffles (*wafels/ gaufres*) and sweet or savoury pancakes (*crêpes*), mussels (*moules*) and freshly baked pastries. The **most common snacks** are *frieten/frites* (French fries with mayonnaise or other sauce). Belgium produces literally hundreds of types of **beer** (both dark and light); wheat beer (*blanche*) comes with a slice of lemon in it in the summer.

BOSNIA AND HERZEGOVINA

'The heart-shaped land' claim the tourist brochures produced by the Sarajevo government, trying to give a suitably warm and cuddly feel to a country that has had a very difficult time since the demise of socialist Yugoslavia. The country has two 'entities' which operate in many respects as independent states. One is referred to as the **Federation** and the other as **Republika Srpska**. The tiny **Brčko district** remains apart from either entity. But cut through the troubled politics and you'll discover a country with a rich Ottoman history, superb landscape and, in Sarajevo, one of Europe's most interesting capital cities.

Essentials: Local name: Bosna i Hercegovina/Босна и Херцеговина – Population: 3.9m – Capital: Sarajevo – Currency: Convertible mark (BAM) – Languages: Bosnian, Croatian, Serbian (young people will speak some English; try German in northern Bosnia & western Herzegovina) – Accommodation costs: generally low – Plug types: C, F – Time zone: winter GMT+1, summer GMT+2 – International dialling code: +387 – Public holidays: there are some national holidays, but many others are regional. National holidays: 1, 2 Jan; 1, 2 May. Entity-specific holidays include Eid ul-Fitr and Eid ul-Adha (called Bajram) or Orthodox and Catholic feast and Saint's days. Victory Day (9 May) is celebrated only in the Republika Srpska, Independence Day (1 Mar) only by the Federation.

TRAVEL IN BOSNIA AND HERZEGOVINA

Sarajevo has no international train services. Local trains run from the capital to Doboj and Mostar. The only station with international departures in the country is Štrpci on the **Belgrade to Bar railway** (ERT 1370), which is for the first time included in this edition of *Europe by Rail* (see **Route 45**). Nine new high-end Talgo trains were delivered some years ago, but they rusted in sidings in Sarajevo until eventually two trains entered regular service in 2016. They now run between Banja Luka and Sarajevo. It's a five-hour journey.

It's a mark of how desolate the state of affairs of the railways of Bosnia and Herzegovina is that the country cannot even agree on a single national operator: in the entity known as the **Federation** the railways are run by **ZFBiH** (www.zfbh.ba), whilst in the **Republika Srpska** the operator is **ZRS** (www.zrs-rs.com). Train categories: There are slow, local (*lokalni*) services and faster (*brzi*) trains. Seat reservations are not necessary except on the Talgo trains from Sarajevo to Banja Luka and Bihać.

RAIL PASSES
Eurail and Interrail global passes are valid, but there are no Interrail or Eurail one-country passes for Bosnia and Herzegovina. Domestic rail fares are very cheap. The Balkan Flexipass is valid.

OTHER PUBLIC TRANSPORT OPTIONS
Both public and private bus companies (and *marshrutkas*) connect every city and most villages within the country. Travel is cheap but standards may vary. One long-standing company with a good bus network hubbed on Sarajevo is **Centrotrans-Eurolines** (www.centrotrans.com). Bus links between the two entities may be sparse.

FURTHER INFORMATION
Website of the tourist association: www.bhtourism.ba/eng.

ACCOMMODATION

Hotels are great value, compensating for the **sparse hostel network** (though the first hostels have appeared in Sarajevo). Our experience is that there is something of a gap between scruffy one-star hotels and modern posh hotels aimed at the business market. There is a **growing B&B market**, often aimed at budget German travellers.

FOOD AND DRINK

Even the most budget-conscious traveller can eat extremely well in Bosnia and Herzegovina. **Good fresh food** costs next to nothing in local markets, and restaurant fare is very reasonably priced. Look for superb grilled lamb and other meats, good salads and the inevitable *burek* – always tasty with a variety of fillings. Good **local beer**, decent **local wines**, and wonderful Turkish coffee all add to the mix and help make Bosnia and Herzegovina a really great destination for food lovers.

BULGARIA

Bulgaria joined the EU in 2007, but is still waiting for full membership of the Schengen area. The **Black Sea nation** which has come a long way since political plurality was introduced in November 1989. The Bulgarian coast has long been popular with summer visitors, but now travellers are discovering the beauty of the Bulgarian mountains. There are remarkable **monasteries and old cities**, the latter often revealing a rich vein of Ottoman influence. Bulgaria features on **Route 47** in this book.

Essentials: Local name: Balgarija/България – Population: 7.4m – Capital: Sofia/София – Currency: Lev (BGN); credit cards increasingly accepted – Languages: Bulgarian (English, German, Russian and French in tourist areas); nodding the head indicates 'no', shaking it means 'yes' – Accommodation costs: generally low – Plug types: C, F – Time zone: winter GMT+2, summer GMT+3 – International dialling code: +359 – Public holidays: 1 Jan; 3 Mar; Orthodox Easter Sunday and Monday; 1, 6, 24 May; 6, 22 Sept; 25, 26 Dec.

TRAVEL IN BULGARIA

Bulgaria might not have the fastest, most modern or most frequent services in Europe, but the network covers the major cities and there are good services linking Sofia with the Black Sea resorts. A new rail link with Romania has recently opened, using the **New Europe Bridge** over the Danube (ERT 1520). Direct overnight trains to Turkey (ERT 1550) have been restored. A handful of the fastest trains (category Exp) have compulsory reservation and higher fares, but you may also want to reserve on other express trains as they can be busy. On-board catering is not commonplace but is improving, so best to bring your own food. The **Bulgarian State Railways** (BDŽ) website includes an English version (www.bdz.bg). Reservations can be made at Rila travel agencies as well as at stations.

RAIL PASSES
Interrail is valid, as is Eurail and the Balkan Flexipass. Domestic rail fares are cheap.

OTHER PUBLIC TRANSPORT OPTIONS
There is a **good bus network**, with buses often slightly more expensive than trains. Yet both modes of transport are very cheap compared with western Europe. Sofia: buses and trams use the same ticket but note that there are different tickets for the subway. Punch your ticket at machines after boarding and get a new ticket if you change.

FURTHER INFORMATION
The website of the Bulgarian tourist association is at www.bulgariatravel.org.

ACCOMMODATION

Beyond the main hotels, **smaller private hotels** and B&B accommdation are increasingly becoming available. As for hostels, Bulgaria is really only just getting started, although things are changing, especially in Sofia, Varna and Veliko Târnovo. Outside these cities, and particularly in rural areas, **private rooms** might be the best bet for the budget traveller.

FOOD AND DRINK

Bulgaria produces a wide variety of **excellent fruits and vegetables**. Soups are popular all year round, with yoghurt-based cold ones on offer in summer. Meat is generally pork or lamb, either cooked slowly with vegetables or grilled. Desserts include seasonal fruits, ice cream, gateaux and sweet pastries.

Vegetarians can go for the varied and generally excellent salads, as well as **stuffed peppers** or aubergine dishes like *kyopolou*. Local beers are lager-style and good value. *Grozdova*, *slivova* and *mastika* are strong spirits, served in large measures, traditionally with cold starters. **Bulgarian wine** is often of high quality, and very good value.

CROATIA

First of the countries to break from the Yugoslav fold by controversially declaring **independence in 1991**, Croatia joined the EU in July 2013. This deeply Catholic country is blessed with a vast stretch of Adriatic coast. Over a thousand islands are dotted along Croatia's sinewy littoral. The area north and west of the capital, Zagreb, is mountainous, while to the east are the vast Slavonian plains, the area worst hit by the 1990s war.

Essentials: Local name: Hrvatska – Population: 4.3m – Capital: Zagreb – Currency: Kuna (HRK) – Languages: Croatian (English, German and Italian spoken in tourist areas) – Accommodation costs: medium – Plug types: C, F – Time zone: winter GMT+1, summer GMT+2 – International dialling code: +385 – Public holidays: 1, 6 Jan; Good Friday; Easter Mon; 1 May; Corpus Christi; 22, 25 June; 5, 15 Aug; 8 Oct; 1 Nov; 25–26 Dec. Many local saints' holidays.

TRAVEL IN CROATIA

Croatia is on **Route 27, 46** and **47** in this edition of *Europe by Rail*. Hubbed on Zagreb, the Croatian rail network covers the main towns but services can be infrequent, particularly on the superbly scenic Zagreb to Split route (see **Route 46**). The modern air-conditioned diesel trains on this route (tilting trains, classified ICN) require compulsory reservation, as do a handful of Intercity (IC) trains elsewhere. For **Dubrovnik** you will need to take a bus or ferry connection. The national railway company is **Hrvatske Željeznice** (HŽ) with its website at www.hzpp.hr. In recent years, the Croatian rail network has been substantially trimmed due to public spending cuts. this has particularly affected international services. Train categories: apart from ICN and IC trains, there is a limited number of Eurocity (EC) services linking Croatia with Austria. There are slow, regional trains and slightly faster services denoted as *brzi*.

RAIL PASSES
Interrail and Eurail passes are valid; domestic rail fares are cheap.

OTHER PUBLIC TRANSPORT OPTIONS
Jadrolinija (www.jadrolinija.hr) runs many **domestic ferry lines** with hubs in Rijeka, Split and Dubrovnik. You can use the complex network of ferry services along the Dalmatian

coast to create some great sightseeing mini-cruises. We use the Split to Dubrovnik service as the final link in **Route 46**. Another of our favourites is the Zadar to Rijeka route, which gives 11 hours afloat and requires an overnight stop at the island port of Mali Lošinj (a community which was Italian until 1947). Long-distance buses are often faster than trains.

FURTHER INFORMATION

The website of the Croatian National Tourist Board is at www.croatia.hr.

ACCOMMODATION

Hotel prices, especially along the coast in high season, can be expensive, although if you travel at other times of the year some incredible bargains can be had. For those on a real budget, there are an increasing number of **hostels in Croatia**, both official (www.hicroatia.com) and independent – although the latter are concentrated in Zagreb, Dubrovnik and Split, with a handful on the islands. Private rooms (*sobe*) are also a good option, both for price and the chance to get to know your hosts.

FOOD AND DRINK

Along the **Dalmatian coast**, fish and other seafood predominate. Inland, meat in all its guises and dairy produce rule. Look out for roadside restaurants serving *janjetina* (lamb) roasted whole on a spit. Another traditional method of preparing meat is in a *peka*, a large iron pot with a dome-shaped lid, buried to cook under glowing embers. Excellent fresh produce in **local markets**.

Top-of-the-range **wines** are pricey but can be excellent. Mix with still water and enjoy *bevanda* – a less headache-inducing method of savouring rich red wine under the Adriatic sun. White wine can have similar treatment with sparkling water to make refreshing *gemišt*. Coffee (*kava*) is often served as *espresso* or *cappuccino* in bars, though some families prepare it Turkish-style at home.

CYPRUS

It's 78 years since the last passenger trains ran in Cyprus. A 122-km **narrow-gauge line** ran across the centre of the island from west to east. Interestingly, it broadly paralleled the Green Line (and the UN administered buffer zone) which now divides the Turkish Republic of North Cyprus (TRNC) from the Greek-dominated southern half of the island. Had the trains not been axed for economic reasons in 1951, the railway would almost certainly have become the victim of politics in the 1970s. The heyday of the Cyprus Government Railway (CGR) is recalled in the **Cyprus Railways Museum**, housed in the beautifully restored former railway station near Evrychou in the Troodos mountains. Nowadays, the best way to get around Cyprus is **by bus**. The website www.cyprusbybus.com is very good for planning bus journeys in the Greek-controlled part of the country. In TRNC, very cheap bus services serve all main routes.

Essentials (Cyprus): Local name: Κυπριακή Δημοκρατία – Population: 1.1m – Capital: Nicosia – Currency: Euro (EUR) – Languages: Greek (English widely spoken) – Accommodation costs: medium – Plug type: G – Time zone: winter GMT+2, summer GMT+3 – International dialling code: +357 – Public holidays: 1,6 Jan; Orthodox Ash Monday; 25 Mar; 1 Apr; Orthodox Good Friday and Easter Monday; 1 May; Orthodox Whit Monday; 15 Aug; 1, 28 Oct; 25-26 Dec.

Essentials (TRNC): Local name: Kuzey Kıbrıs Türk Cumhuriyeti – Population: 0.3m – Capital: North Nicosia – Currency: Turkish lira (TRY) – Languages: Turkish – Accommodation costs: generally low – Plug type: G – Time zone: winter GMT+2, summer GMT+3 – International dialling code: +90392 – Public holidays: 1 Jan; 23 Apr; 1, 19 May; 20 July; 1, 30 Aug; 29 Oct; 15 Nov; Mawlid; Eid al-Fitr, Eid al-Adha.

CZECH REPUBLIC

One half of former Czechoslovakia which, having defiantly despatched a lacklustre communist government with the **Velvet Revolution** in autumn 1989, then proceeded to a Velvet Divorce less than four years later. With that split from Slovakia, the Czech Republic was born. The move to a market economy hasn't always been easy. An urban elite in Prague has undoubtedly made good, but in more rural areas the supposed benefits of capitalism are not so evident. You'll run across **stunning areas of mountains and forests**, towns with delightful squares, sleepy villages and imposing castles.

Essentials: Local name: Česká republika – Population: 10.5m – Capital: Prague/Praha – Currency: Czech koruna (CZK) – Languages: Czech (English is widely spoken among young people, especially in the cities. German and Russian are also encountered, particularly among older folk) – Accommodation costs: medium – Plug types: C, E – Time zone: winter GMT+1, summer GMT+2 – International dialling code: +420 – Public holidays: 1 Jan; Good Friday; Easter Mon; 1, 8 May; 5, 6 July; 28 Sept; 28 Oct; 17 Nov; 24–26 Dec.

A rural rail route in the Czech Republic (photo © Maledictus)

TRAVEL IN THE CZECH REPUBLIC

Route 24 and **25** both traverse the Czech Republic, connecting with each other in Prague. The well-run and generally punctual rail network covers every corner of the country, with express trains hourly or every two hours on most routes. **High-speed trains** classified SuperCity (SC) are the only trains to require compulsory reservation. Smart **Railjet** (RJ) trains are used on the Prague – Brno – Vienna axis (ERT 1150). If you have time on your hands, however, there is no better way to explore than on the many slow and rural routes, often operated by **vintage railcars**, which criss-cross the countryside.

The national rail company is **České Dráhy** (ČD) with its website at www. cd.cz. The winds of competition are bringing change. ČD now competes with private operators **RegioJet** (www.regiojet.cz) and **Leo Express** (www. le.cz) on the route from Prague to Ostrava. Those two private operators also have their eyes on routes from Prague to Budapest and Berlin in 2020. Following a major revamp of the tracks around Prague, all principal trains now serve the main station, Praha hlavní, which has also been thoroughly modernised. Train categories: apart from high-speed SC and RJ trains, the Czech Republic operates fast trains ('R' for *rychlík*), semi-fast trains ('Sp' for *spešný*) and slow, local trains ('Os' for *osobný*).

RAIL PASSES
Interrail and Eurail passes are both valid. A wide range of great-value regional day passes is available, including several which include border areas of Germany or Poland. A celodenní jízdenka **one-day countrywide ticket** costs just 579 Czech crowns (about €22).

OTHER PUBLIC TRANSPORT OPTIONS
The Czech Republic has a good long-distance bus network, run by RegioJet (www.regiojet. cz) and other private companies. You can buy tickets from the driver; priority is given to those with reservations.

FURTHER INFORMATION
The website of the Czech tourism association is at www.czechtourism.com.

ACCOMMODATION

There is a **wide choice of accommodation types** in the Czech Republic, from standard hotels to private rooms and pensions, and an ever-increasing number of hostels (www.czechhostels.com). Quality in the more budget hotels can often leave a lot to be desired, so for the cost-conscious a private room might be a better choice. The well-developed network of **independent hostels** concentrates on favourite backpacker destinations such as Prague, Olomouc, Brno and Český Krumlov.

FOOD AND DRINK

Czech cuisine is **hearty**, and features lashings of meat with cream-based sauces, but vegetarian options include fried cheese (*smažený sýr*), risotto and salads. **Pork with cabbage and dumplings** (*vepřová pečeně s knedlíkem a sezelím*) is on virtually every menu, as is *guláš*, a bland beef stew. The cost of eating and drinking is reasonable. *Kavárny* and *cukrány* serve coffee and very sweet pastries. Pubs (*pivnice*) and wine bars (*vinárny*) are good places to eat. Czech beers are excellent, as is Moravian wine.

DENMARK

Situated between the Baltic and the North Sea, watery Denmark incorporates **some 400 islands**, 75 of which are inhabited, as well as the peninsula of Jutland. It is low-lying and undramatic terrain, where you sense you're never far from the sea. The **long maritime tradition** inflects the townscapes too, a reminder that even towns that now seem well inland (like Roskilde) once lived from the sea. While an impressive programme of bridge-building has linked many of Denmark's islands, you will still need to take to ferries to reach remote islands – the most distinctive of which is Bornholm.

Essentials: Local name: Danmark – Population: 5.7m – Capital: Copenhagen/ København – Currency: Danish kroner (DKK) – Languages: Danish (English is almost universally spoken) – Accommodation costs: generally high – Plug Types: C, E, F, K – Time zone: winter GMT+1, summer GMT+2 – International dialling code: +45 – Public holidays: 1 Jan; Maundy Thursday–Easter Monday; Common Prayer Day (4th Fri after Easter); Ascension Day; Whit Mon; 5 June; 24–26 Dec.

TRAVEL IN DENMARK

Denmark features on **Route 28** and **29** in this book. **Route 30** starts in Denmark but then immediately crosses the Baltic to go to Sweden and Norway. Denmark's efficient rail network relies on modern and frequent Intercity (IC) services that fan out from Copenhagen's main station, usually abbreviated to København H, which also has frequent trains **across the Øresund** to Malmö in Sweden. There is a rail-sea link to the Danish island of **Bornholm** via Ystad. There is currently quite some investment in national transport infrastructure. A new high-speed line from Copenhagen to Ringsted opened in mid-2019, and work is now underway on a new tunnel from Rødby to the German island of Fehmarn. You don't need to reserve on Intercity trains but it is recommended at busy times. Most IC trains have refreshment trolleys.

    Danske Statsbaner (DSB), www.dsb.dk, is the principal operator, although ever more regional services are run by private operators such as **Arriva** (www.arriva.dk). There is a national multi-modal **journey planner** at www.rejseplanen.dk which includes an English and a German version. Train categories: Denmark's IC services are complemented by fast Intercity Lyn (ICL) trains – which stop less frequently than ICs – and frequent, but slower RE services.

Rail passes

Interrail and Eurail are valid. Fares are based on a national zonal system. Tickets in the Greater Copenhagen area include local transport as well as trains and are available for various zones for 24 hours or, in the case of the **FlexCard**, 7 days.

Other public transport options

Long-distance travel is easiest by train but there are also excellent regional and city bus services, many dovetailing with trains. **Ferries** or bridges link all the big islands.

Further information

The website of the Danish National Tourist Board is at www.visitdenmark.com. Nearly every decent-sized town in Denmark has a tourist office (*turistbureau*), normally found in the town hall or central square; they distribute maps, information and advice.

Accommodation

Hotels in Denmark are of a high standard, and can be expensive. In rural areas the **old inns**, known as *kros*, are charming places to stay and often have good restaurants serving traditional food. There are around 100 official (HI) hostels (*vandrerhjem*), and the general standard is excellent, which might explain why the growth of independent hostels in the country has not been as dramatic as elsewhere. Check out www.danhostel.dk for more details.

If you enjoy **camping**, you will find a wide choice of campsites, many of which also offer self-catering cabins which can work out great value for those travelling in a small group.

Food and drink

Danish cuisine is simple, based on **excellent local produce**; standards are uniformly high, but with prices to match. Look for *dagens ret* (today's special), which is noticeably cheaper than eating à la carte. **Fish** features a lot – most commonly herring served in a sauce. *Smørrebrød* are elaborately topped open sandwiches of meat, fish or cheese with accompaniments, served on *rugbrød* (rye bread) or *franskbrød* (wheat bread). You can also try filling up on the ubiquitous *frikadeller* (pork meatballs). There are many **local lagers** in addition to the internationally known Carlsberg and Tuborg. The local firewater is akvavit. All alcohol is expensive.

Estonia

Smallest of the three **Baltic States**, Estonia joined the European Union in 2004. The country looks more to Finland than its Baltic neighbours to the south. Estonia offers a fetching mixture of forests with old manorial estates. You will also find some strikingly beautiful coast, desolate islands and appealing lake country. Relations with **adjacent Russia** are not always easy, but that should not deter you from combining the two countries in a single visit (provided you have a Russian visa of course).

Essentials: Local name: Eesti – Population: 1.3m – Capital: Tallinn – Currency: Euro (EUR) – Languages: Estonian, Russian (English is widely spoken, though less so in rural areas) – Accommodation costs: medium – Plug types: C, F – Time zone: winter GMT+2, summer GMT+3 – International dialling code: +372 – Public holidays: 1 Jan; 24 Feb; Good Fri; 1 May; 23 June (Victory Day), 24 June; 20 Aug; 24–26 Dec.

TRAVEL IN ESTONIA

Estonia is included on **Route 51** in this book. Whilst Tallinn has good electric suburban trains, regional train services, operated by **ELRON** (www. elron.ee), are somewhat thin on the ground, though it is possible to travel to Viljandi, Narva and Tartu by train, albeit infrequently. There is a very comfortable **sleeper train** leaving Tallinn each evening for Moscow via St Petersburg. One train a day from Tallinn to Valga connects with an onward service into Latvia. For St Petersburg, your best bet from Tallinn is really the **Lux Express bus** (www.luxexpress.eu; see ERT 1870).

RAIL PASSES
Eurail and Interrail are not valid and there are no local rail passes, but fares are cheap.

OTHER PUBLIC TRANSPORT OPTIONS
Bus services are often fast, clean and more efficient than rail services (see www.peatus. ee for routes and timetables). Book international services in advance from bus stations or online at www.luxexpress.eu. Pay the driver at rural stops or small towns.

FURTHER INFORMATION
The official tourism website is at www.visitestonia.com.

ACCOMMODATION

There should be no problem with accommodation in Estonia, which has a variety of **hostels and inexpensive hotels**. Prices in Tallinn are often twice as high as elsewhere. Home stays offer accommodation in farmhouses, summer cottages, homes and small boarding houses. For hostels, the **Estonian Youth Hostel Association** can make reservations at 40 hostels throughout the country (www.balticbookings.com/eyha), whilst Tallinn in particular has seen a massive growth in independent, backpacker-orientated establishments.

FOOD AND DRINK

Particularly outside Tallinn, many **restaurants close early** in the evenings, so you may think of lunch as a main meal opportunity. For value, look to the dish of the day (*päevapraad*). Cheap cuts of meat, particularly **pork**, with potatoes and bread are staples. Not a place for the sweet-toothed or for vegetarians. Estonian beers (both dark and light) have a growing reputation. In winter, try mulled wine or the excellent Estonian liqueur, **Vana Tallinn** (great in tea or in cocktails).

Tallinn in winter (photo © Aleksejs Stemmers)

FAROE ISLANDS

This curious little island polity in the **North Atlantic** has loose links to Denmark, but enjoys a high measure of independence with its own parliament. There are stunning wild mountain and coastal landscapes across 17 inhabited islands which are linked by efficient ferries, bridges and undersea road tunnels. Railways do not really feature, the sole exception being a winch-operated incline railway at the harbour in Gjógr on the island of Eysturoy. The Faroes are easily reached by ship from Hirtshals in Denmark (see **Route 29**). Also see our Sidetracks feature on p276.

Essentials: Local name: Føroyar – Population: 50k – Capital: Tórshavn – Currency: Faroese króna – Language: Faroese, Danish (English widely understood) – Accommodation costs: generally high – Plug Types: C, E, F, K – Time zone: winter GMT, summer GMT+1 – International dialling code: +298 – Public holidays: 1 Jan; Maundy Thur; Good Friday; Easter Mon; 22, 25 April; Prayer Day (4th Fri after Easter); 5 May; Whit Mon; 29 July; 24–26, 31 Dec.

FINLAND

Often classified as part of Scandinavia, Finland is a world apart from the two Scandinavian neighbours with which it shares common borders, Norway and Sweden. The cultural landscape reflects Finland's **historic links with Russia**, even to the extent that the Orthodox Church is an official state church. The **Grand Duchy of Finland** was part of the Russian Empire until 1917. The west of the country has a good dose of Swedish influence. Pure air, glistening lakes, an abundance of wildlife and deep winter snow all help sustain Finland's appeal to travellers.

Essentials: Local name: Suomi – Population: 5.4m – Capital: Helsinki – Currency: Euro (EUR) – Languages: Finnish (Sámi in the north, Swedish on the west coast); Swedish, the country's second official language, often appears on signs after the Finnish (English widely spoken, esp. in Helsinki) – Accommodation costs: generally high – Plug Types: C, F – Time zone: winter GMT+2, summer GMT+3 – International dialling code: +358 – Public holidays: 1, 6 Jan; Good Friday; Easter Mon; 1 May; Ascension Day; Whit Sun; Midsummer's Day (Sat falling 20–26 June); 1 Nov; 6, 25–26 Dec.

TRAVEL IN FINLAND

Finland features on **Route 33** in this book. Additionally, **Route 51** through Estonia to Latvia and beyond starts with a journey by sea across the Gulf of Finland from Helsinki to Tallinn. The modern and efficient Finnish rail system includes **Allegro high-speed trains** that have served the Helsinki to St Petersburg route since December 2010 (and included in *Europe by Rail* as the finale to **Route 33**). Some of the double-deck Intercity trains in Finland have a restaurant car on the upper level. For a small premium over the regular fare, you can reserve a seat in the restaurant area.

The premium daytime services from Helsinki to Turku, Tampere and the north use high-speed **tilting Pendolino trains**, dubbed S220 thanks to their top speed of 220 km/h (reservation is compulsory). Other than for purely local journeys, tickets are sold for specific trains, the fare level varying according to the train type: Pendolino, Intercity, Express (P), or Regional (seat reservations are included except for regional trains). Most long-distance trains have a restaurant car, buffet car or trolley service, whilst **overnight trains** to the north have sleepers, seats and a restaurant car. The national rail company is **VR** (www.vr.fi).

RAIL PASSES
Both Interrail and Eurail are valid.

OTHER PUBLIC TRANSPORT OPTIONS
There's a good long-distance bus network run in the main by **Matkahuolto** (www.matkahuolto.fi) and **Expressbus** (www.expressbus.fi). Timetables for trains, buses and boats dovetail conveniently. Matkahuolto has timetables online. Buses: stops are usually identified by the symbol of a black bus on a yellow background (for local services) and a white bus on a blue background for longer distances. It is cheaper to buy tickets from stations or agents than on board. Bus stations usually have good facilities.

FURTHER INFORMATION
Main website of Finnish tourism association is at www.visitfinland.com.

ACCOMMODATION

Hotels tend to be stylish, immaculate and pricey. Budget travellers might want to check out *matkustajakoti* (the relatively cheap guesthouses) or the nearly 50 **hostels** (*retkeilymajat*) that are well spread across the country (www.hostellit.fi). Note that not all hostels are open year-round. **Campsites** are widespread too (about 350; around 200 belong to the Finnish Campingsite Association www.camping.fi). Rough camping is generally allowed providing you keep 150 m from residents and remove any trace of your stay.

FOOD AND DRINK

Fixed-price menus in a *ravintola* (upmarket restaurant) are the best value, or you may want to try a *grilli* (fast-food stand), *kahvila* (self-service cafeteria) or a *baari* (snack bar). For **self-caterers**, try Alepa, Siwa, K-market or Valintatalo supermarkets. Some specials are *muikunmäti* (a freshwater fish roe served with onions and cream and accompanied by toast or pancakes) and for dessert *kiisseli* (literally 'berry fool'). Finns are very **dedicated coffee drinkers**. Lower-alcohol beers are sold in supermarkets, but for stronger beers and all wines and spirits, turn to **Alko**, the aptly named state-owned distributor of stronger drinks.

FRANCE

France boasts such **varied culture and heritage**, so rich a mix of scenery and architecture, that you could comfortably return every year of a long life and still discover something new. Impressive mediaeval cities in the north, although humdrum landscapes. Move to the centre for wilderness, east for the **Alps**, and south for sun, sea and sand. Throw in fine food and wine to create the perfect ensemble. But be warned! Try it once and you may become an addict who can never be weaned off the country that is by far the most popular destination for tourists on the planet.

Essentials: Local name: France – Population: 66.6m – Capital: Paris – Currency: Euro (EUR) – Language: French (many people speak some English, particularly in Paris) – Accommodation costs: generally high – Plug Types: C, E – Time zone: winter GMT+1, summer GMT+2 – International dialling code: +33 – Public holidays: 1 Jan; Easter Mon; 1, 8 May; Ascension Day; Whit Mon; 14 July; 15 Aug; 1, 11 Nov; 25 Dec. If on Thur, many places also close Mon or Fri.

TRAVEL IN FRANCE

France is on **Route 6 to 12** in this book. In addition, **Route 17, 18** and **40** all start in France but then quickly cross into neighbouring countries. France's well-developed **high-speed network** means we now take for granted that journeys such as Paris to Marseille (750 km) take little more than three hours. Many parts of France have similarly impressive journey times from Paris by high-speed TGV, although in contrast cross-country routes can often be slow and infrequent. France is not a country for hopping on and off trains at will, since reservation is compulsory on almost all **TGV** and most Intercité services; some TGV trains have only a limited allocation of seats for pass holders. Fares are higher during peak travel periods. Tickets (not passes)

The Gare de l'Est in Paris is the departure point for trains to such far-flung destinations as Munich, Minsk and Moscow (photo © Dennis Dolkens)

must be validated in the orange *composteurs* at the entrance to platforms. Domestic **night trains** have couchettes (and often reclining seats), sleeping cars being confined to international services.

The national operator is **Société Nationale des Chemins de fer Français** or **SNCF** for short with its website at www.sncf.com. Train categories: apart from high-speed TGV services, France has Intercité trains which are long-distance services running at slower speeds (they do not use the high-speed lines which are the backbone of the TGV network). In 2019, SNCF greatly extended its offering of TGVs running under the low-cost *Ouigo* brand. These can be very cheap, but Interrail and Eurail passes are not accepted at all. The country also has a good network of slower **regional services** (TER) and creative travellers (or pass holders who have an ideological objection to paying for seat reservations on high-speed services) can devise itineraries which cross the entire country on TER trains. In our view, those services – though never fast – often offer the very best rail travel in France.

RAIL PASSES

Interrail and Eurail passes are valid, but beware the supplements on French TGV services. Rail Europe market a **France Railpass** for non-European residents, valid for 1–8 days within one month. European residents should use the Interrail one-country pass. Some of the regions offer day tickets, for example the **Alsa+** 24h-ticket that allows travel throughout Alsace on local (TER) trains for €37.40. Elsewhere, such passes are generally only valid at weekends, and some are summer only; see www.sncf.com/fr/trains/ter for further details.

OTHER PUBLIC TRANSPORT OPTIONS

The **metro systems** in Paris and several other major cities are clean, efficient and relatively cheap. For urban and peri-urban transport, carnets (multiple-ticket packs) are cheaper than individual tickets. Bus and train timetables are available from bus and train stations and tourist offices; usually free. Always ask if your rail pass is valid on local transport. Bus services may be infrequent after 20.30 and on Sun. Rural areas are often poorly served.

FURTHER INFORMATION

The official website for French tourism is at www.france.fr.

ACCOMMODATION

For hotels, **half-board** (i.e. breakfast and evening meal included) can be excellent value in smaller towns and villages. As elsewhere in Europe, **budget hotels** are often clustered near stations. In summer, it is advisable to book ahead in larger towns and resort areas. **Gîtes de France** produces directories of B&Bs, *gîtes d'étape*, farm accommodation and holiday house rentals for each département (www.gites-de-france.com).

There are hundreds of hostels in France, including those which are members of **Hostelling International** (HI; www.fuaj.org) and those more independently minded. The useful website www.hostelz.com offers listings of both types. **Camping** is a national obsession, and there are hundreds of campsites all across France. Camping municipal is usually basic but cheap.

FOOD AND DRINK

France's **gastronomic reputation** often lives up to its promise, providing you're prepared to look beyond mere tourist fodder such as *steak frites* (steak and fries). In restaurants, eating à la carte can be expensive, but the *menu* (set menu, of which there may be several) or the *plat du jour* (dish of the day) is often superb value, especially at lunchtime.

Coffees and beers can be surprisingly expensive: **wine** is generally cheaper – order a *pichet* of house red (*rouge*), white (*blanc*) or *rosé*. If you ask for *café*, you'll get a small black coffee; coffee with milk is *café crème*. Tea is usually served black. **Beer** is mostly yellow, cold, French and fizzy, though gourmet and foreign beers are popular. *Une pression* or *un demi* is draught beer, better value than bottled. Baguettes with a variety of fillings from cafés and stalls are cheap – as are *crêpes* and *galettes* (sweet and savoury pancakes). **Morning markets** are excellent for stocking up on picnic items. Buy provisions before noon as shops can be closed for hours at lunchtime.

GERMANY

Germany, bang in the **middle of Europe**, is hard to miss. Nor should anyone wish to: from the heathlands of the north to the Alpine peaks of the south there is scenery galore. There are idyllic offshore islands and sandy beaches on both the North Sea and the Baltic coasts, great tracts of lakes and forests, especially in the north-east, and **three of Europe's great rivers**: the Rhine, the Danube and the Elbe. Plus a galaxy of historic cities including Cologne, Munich and Berlin.

Essentials: Local name: Deutschland – Population: 81.5m – Capital: Berlin – Currency: Euro (EUR) – Language: German (English and French widely spoken in the west, less so in the east) – Accommodation costs: medium – Plug types: C, F – Time zone: winter GMT+1, summer GMT+2 – International dialling code: +49 – Public holidays: 1, 6* Jan; Good Friday; Easter Mon; 1 May, Ascension Day; Whit Mon; Corpus Christi*, 15 Aug*; 3, 31 Oct*; 1 Nov*; 25, 26 Dec; (*religious feasts celebrated as public holiday only in certain German states.)

Travel in Germany

Germany features principally on **Route 20 to 23** in this volume. In addition, **Route 18, 24, 25, 28, 29, 39, 48** and **49** all touch German territory as part of longer international journeys. The country's comprehensive and generally efficient rail network is served by many different types of train, from sleek **high-speed Intercity Express** (ICE) trains and the less modern Intercity (IC) and Eurocity (EC) services to **sleepy rural branch lines** winding along picturesque river valleys. There are no compulsory reservations on daytime trains and no supplements for pass holders. ICE services generally have on-board refreshments (either a restaurant car or a board bistro), IC and EC trains often have a board bistro. There are good facilities at main-line stations, such as showers and lockers.

Principal operator is **Deutsche Bahn** (DB), www.bahn.de, but there are also a number of private operators. Among them are **ODEG** (www.odeg.de) with a network in eastern Germany, **Metronom** (www.der-metronom.de) operating in Germany's northern states around Bremen, Hamburg and Uelzen and **Meridian** (www.meridian-bob-brb.de) which runs services around Munich and Rosenheim, with connections from Munich to Salzburg. **NordWestBahn** has hubs in the Rhine-Ruhr area, operating from Essen, Duisburg and Düsseldorf (www.nordwestbahn.de).

National operator DB runs some overnight ICE and IC trains, but has pulled out of the market for proper **night trains** (ie. with sleepers and couchettes). The latter are run mainly by ÖBB under their *Nightjet* brand with routes from Düsseldorf, Cologne and Hamburg to Innsbruck and Vienna. There are also services from Berlin and Hamburg to south-west Germany and Switzerland, from Berlin to Vienna, Kraków and Budapest, as well as from Munich to Italy, Croatia and Hungary.

Rail passes

The full range of Interrail and Eurail passes are valid. A **German Rail Pass** is available for those living outside Europe; residents of Europe can buy the Interrail One-Country Pass. The **Quer-durchs-Land ticket** (from €44) gives one day's travel on local and regional trains for 1–5 people (buy on the day, cheapest from machines).

A range of regional **Ländertickets** is available (from €23 for one person, from €29 for groups of up to 5 people), giving the freedom to roam any day of the week on all but the fastest trains through one or more of the federal states of Germany or often even over Germany's borders. For example, the area in which the Schleswig-Holstein ticket is valid extends from Tønder in Denmark to Świnoujście in Poland. For a good summary on the Ländertickets, see www.ebrweb.eu/5. For more on cheap tickets in Germany see the box on p222.

Other public transport options

Most large cities have **U-Bahn** (U) underground railway and **S-Bahn** (S) urban rail services. City travel passes cover both and other public transport, including ferries in some cities. International passes usually cover S-Bahn. A day card (*Tagesnetzkarte*) or multi-ride ticket (*Mehrfahrtenkarte*) usually pays its way if you take more than three rides.

FURTHER INFORMATION
The website of the German National Tourist Office is at www.germany.travel. Tourist offices (marked by white 'i' on a blue background) are usually near stations and have English-speaking staff. Most offer room-finding services.

ACCOMMODATION

You'll find a range of accommodation options at **all price levels** in Germany, but prices for rooms of comparable standards vary enormously across the country. Areas that were, until 1990, part of the GDR still offer the best value, and Berlin is noticeably cheaper than, say, Munich. *Pensionen* (pensions) and *Privatzimmer* (private rooms) are particularly good value. In many cities, a new generation of **design-orientated budget hotels** are providing rooms of high quality at reasonable prices. Hostel accommodation is widely available in Germany, and the country has a **network of independent hostels** (www.german-hostels.de). There are also around 600 official (HI) Jugendherbergen (youth hostels) which often cater to school groups and can have an institutional feel. The *Deutscher Camping-Club* (DCC) (www.camping-club.de), compiles each year a list of 1,600 camping sites.

FOOD AND DRINK

Germans tend to have biological clocks that run in advance of the rest of Europe. Families at home eat early, with supper often done and dusted by soon after six. In restaurants, hotels and hostels expect breakfast from 06.30 to 10.00. Lunch is around 12.00–14.00 (from 11.30 in rural areas) and dinner 18.00–20.30 (but much later in cities). Breakfast is often substantial (and usually included in the price of a room), consisting of a variety of bread, cheese and cold meats and possibly boiled eggs. For lunch, the best value is the **daily menu** (*Tageskarte*); in rural parts of southern Germany, there's often a **snack menu** (*Vesperkarte*) from mid-afternoon onwards.

Traditional German cuisine is widespread, both in towns and rural areas, and traditional recipes, which vary greatly by region, are produced with pride. **Expect hearty fare**, with large portions, and often good value. Look for home-made soups, high-quality meat, piquant marinated pot roasts (known as *Sauerbraten*) and creamy sauces. For really cheap but generally appetising eats, there are *Imbisse* (stalls) serving *Kartoffelsalat* (potato salad) and *Wurst* (sausage) in its numerous variations, plus fish in the north. Rural Germany can be **quite challenging for vegetarians**.

GREAT BRITAIN

Great Britain consists of three countries: **England, Wales and Scotland**. And all three are handsomely featured (for the first time) in this edition of *Europe by Rail*. **Route 1** to **6** all have an English dimension. **Route 2** and **3** showcase some of Scotland's finest railways, while **Route 4** and **5** traverse rural Wales. A stunning variety of landscapes and a lavish dose of history all help make any visit to Britain very rewarding.

But it can also provoke reflection. Britain stands curiously apart from the mainstream of European life. English nationalism, even isolationism, challenges the liberal consensus which has fostered European integration over the last half-century. As this new edition of *Europe by Rail* goes to press, the **Brexit endgame** is being played out with much uncertainly about the future. Yet travel is a great way of fostering understanding – and it's for that very reason that we have now added a fine collection of British routes to this book.

Keep an eye on how the Brexit situation develops. As of October 2019, residents of most European countries outside the European Union (and EEA) already require **visas** to enter any part of the United Kingdom, and those visas are among the most expensive in the world. It is possible that a post-Brexit Britain may further tighten its visa regime. Border controls are very strict, and there's a national preoccupation with security – to the extent that security announcements on trains on some routes become a veritable litany of terror. For many Europeans, a visit to Britain is like entering another world, but it's definitely interesting. Make time to explore beyond cities, and if you can visit **rural communities** in Yorkshire, south-west England, Wales or Scotland then you're in for a treat.

Essentials: Local name: United Kingdom – Population: 65.6m – Capital: London – Currency: Pound sterling (GBP) – Languages: English, Welsh, Gaelic – Accommodation costs: generally high – Plug type: G – Time zone: winter GMT, summer GMT+1 – International dialling code: +44 – Public holidays: 1 Jan; Good Friday; first and last Mon in May; 25–26 Dec. Further regional holidays.

Britain has some very striking railway architecture, including many superb station extensions and renovations. This shot shows King's Cross station in London (photo © Rob van Esch)

TRAVEL IN BRITAIN

Britain has an **extensive rail network**, and services are by no means as bad as most British residents would have you believe. Railways extend even to the distant extremities of the British mainland and those willing to book in advance can secure some of the cheapest tickets in Europe for long-distance journeys. The downside is crowded trains. That said, the first-class service on some main-line trains really rates as among the best in Europe. Check www.raileurope.co.uk for prices and to buy tickets. Although train services are run by more than two dozen **different operators**, there's a fully integrated national ticketing scheme. Unless you board a train at a station with no facilities for ticket purchase, you are required to have a ticket before boarding the train. The penalties for infringement are unusually severe.

RAIL PASSES

Britain has been a long-standing member of the Interrail programme, and since 2019 Eurail passes are now also accepted. While you may wish to reserve a seat on busy routes, there's no obligation to do so, and the good news is that, bar for overnight sleeper services, there are absolutely **no rail pass supplements** in Britain. For travellers visiting only Great Britain, the **Britrail Pass** can be an excellent choice.

OTHER PUBLIC TRANSPORT OPTIONS

For **long-distance coach travel** in England, check www.nationalexpress.com. For main Scottish bus routes see www.citylink.co.uk. Principal Welsh bus services are covered by www.trawscymru.info (with free travel available at weekends on many Welsh routes). Britain has one of Europe's best networks of local bus services. Find times at www.traveline.info. As befits a maritime nation, there's a **good network of ferry services** in and around Britain's coastal waters. In Cornwall, for example, there are more than a dozen ferry routes which form part of the regular public transport network. Services in the Clyde and Hebrides area are provided by CalMac (www.calmac.co.uk) while ferry services to Orkney and Shetland are provided by NorthLink (www.northlinkferries.co.uk)

FURTHER INFORMATION

The official tourism website of Great Britain is available at www.visitbritain.com.

ACCOMMODATION

The British seem to particularly favour the major chains of budget hotels which are cheap but soulless. We find that small owner-managed hotels are a much better choice, but they are often not cheap. There is an excellent range of accommodation in **pubs and inns**. Major online reservations channels like www.booking.com cover the full range of options. There's a buoyant independent hostels movement (see www.independenthostels.co.uk). **B&Bs** are an especially good option in smaller communities.

FOOD AND DRINK

Standards and choice have greatly improved in recent years. The best of British cuisine now draws on a medley of Mediterranean and more exotic influences, and it's now one of the easiest regions to find top-quality **vegan and vegetarian choices**. The absence of good street markets means that many visitors are thrown back to shopping in supermarkets where too many products are chilled and pre-packed in plastic. But good, fresh produce is available and the best restaurants and inns have led the way in giving a much-needed creative edge to British dining. Expect a **brilliant range of beers**, a good choice of wines (often imported from outside Europe), endless good cups of tea and some of Europe's most insipid coffee.

GREECE

Happily recovering from financial woes, and still inexpensive, friendly and beautiful, and with a wonderful array of archaeological sites, Greece offers a seductive mix of **culture and relaxation**, with plenty of opportunity to linger in tavernas or laze on a beach as well as visiting ancient ruins. There is an edgy buzz about the capital, but it is easy to **escape to the islands**, some of which are full of cosmospolitan glitz, while others are refreshingly unspoilt and provincial.

Essentials: Local name: Elláda/Ελλάδα – Population: 11m – Capital: Athens/Αθήνα – Currency: Euro (EUR) – Language: Greek (English widely spoken in Athens and tourist areas; some German, French or Italian too, but less so in remote mainland areas) – Accommodation costs: medium – Plug types: C, F – Time zone: winter GMT+2, summer GMT+3 – International dialling code: +30 – Public holidays: 1, 6 Jan; Shrove Mon; 25 Mar; Orthodox Good Friday; Orthodox Easter Mon; 1 May; Whit Mon; 15 Aug; 28 Oct; 25, 26 Dec.

TRAVEL IN GREECE

While **domestic rail services** within Greece are reasonably reliable, the same cannot be said of international services. All **cross-border services** were axed in 2015 during the refugee crisis and have been a bit hit-and-miss ever since. As of October 2019, there are no trains across any Greek borders, but national operator **TrainOSE** (www.trainose.gr) does run a bus bridging the 15-km gap between the Greek rail network at Strimón and the Bulgarian network at Kulata. **Route 47** relies on this link. The domestic rail network is limited, but many routes around Athens and the main line to Thessaloniki have been much improved (fast Intercity trains run on main routes). Modernisation of the narrow-gauge lines in the **Peloponnese region** came to an abrupt halt during the financial crisis and these routes have not reopened.

RAIL PASSES
Interrail, Eurail and the Balkan Flexipass are all valid. The high supplements for pass holders were happily scrapped in 2019.

OTHER PUBLIC TRANSPORT OPTIONS
KTEL buses (www.ktelbus.com) provide fast, punctual, fairly comfortable long-distance services; well-organised stations in most towns (tickets available from bus terminals). The

Greek islands are connected by **ferries and hydrofoils**. City transport: bus or (in Athens) trolleybus, metro and electric rail; services are crowded. Outside Athens, taxis are plentiful and good value.

FURTHER INFORMATION
Website of the Greek National Tourism Organisation: www.visitgreece.gr.

ACCOMMODATION

Greece is over-supplied with accommodation. You should have **no problem finding a bed** in Athens, Pátra or Thessaloniki even in high summer (though the very cheapest Athens dorms and pensions are often very crowded in July and Aug). Rooms are hardest to find over the Greek Easter period (note this date is different from Easter in western Europe, as it's based on the Orthodox calendar), so try to book ahead. The **youth hostel network** is sparse, but you will find hostels in Athens, Corfu and some of the more popular islands. **Campsites** at major sights (including Delphi, Mistra and Olympia) can be good value with excellent facilities.

FOOD AND DRINK

Greeks rarely eat breakfast. Traditional Greek meals are unstructured, with lots of dishes brought at once or in no particular order. Lunch is any time between 12.00 and 15.00, after which most restaurants close until around 19.30. Greeks dine late, and you will find plenty of restaurants open until well after midnight. The best Greek **food is fresh**, seasonal and simply prepared. Fresh fish dishes are usually the most expensive. Pork, chicken and squid are relatively cheap, and traditional salad – olives, tomatoes, cucumber, onions, peppers and feta cheese drowned in oil, served with bread – is a meal in itself (though Greeks eat it as a side dish). Aniseed-flavoured ouzo is a favourite aperitif. *Retsina* (resinated wine) is an acquired taste. Greek brandy, Metaxa, is on the sweet side. **Draught lager** is not widely available and is neither as good nor as cheap as bottled beer: Amstel, Heineken and Mythos, brewed in Greece and sold in half-litre bottles.

HUNGARY

Melding central European panache with a dash of **Balkan style**, Hungary is assertively different from any of its neighbouring countries. The **Great Plain**, *Alföld*, extends across more than half this landlocked country, with the most appreciable hills rising in the far north. Hungary's most scenic moments occur along **Lake Balaton** and the Danube Bend just north of Budapest, with a trio of fine towns – Szentendre, Visegrád and Esztergom (the latter dominated by a huge basilica – see p242).

Essentials: Local name: Magyarország – Population: 9.8m – Capital: Budapest – Currency: Forint (HUF) – Language: Hungarian (English and German widely understood) –

Accommodation costs: medium – Plug types: C, F – Time zone: winter GMT+1, summer GMT+2 – International dialling code: +36 – Public holidays: 1 Jan; 15 Mar; Easter Mon; 1 May; Whit Mon; 20 Aug; 23 Oct; 1 Nov; 25, 26 Dec.

Travel in Hungary

Hungary is on **Route 25, 26, 45** and **46** in this book. In recent years the country has developed its Intercity (IC) network to link all the main towns and cities and *Railjet* (RJ) services from ÖBB are also used on international journeys from Budapest to Vienna, Munich and Zurich. Yet there are plenty of slower trains from which to savour Hungary's largely rural nature, in particular along the north and south shores of Lake Balaton.

IC trains require reservation and a supplement, whilst most of the international EC trains have a supplement but no compulsory reservation. Domestic journeys on international EC/IC/RJ/EN trains require a supplement and sometimes a seat reservation. **International sleepers** should be booked well in advance, particularly in summer. EU pensioners over 65 can enjoy **free second-class travel** on all trains (but not on cross-border services), including those run by GySEV (any supplements applicable to premium services do however still need to be paid). **Hungarian State Railways** (MÁV) owns the network and MÁV-Start runs the trains (www. mavcsoport.hu). Some cross-border services between western Hungary and eastern Austria are run by **GySEV** (www2.gysev.hu). Further train types: fast trains are called *györsvonat* (G; supplements required), semifast ones *sebesvonat* (S; subject to supplements) and very slow local trains *személyvonat* (SZ). There are also InterRegio (IR) services.

Rail passes
Interrail and Eurail passes are valid, as is the Balkan Flexipass. **Balaton Mix** gives rail and shipping services around Lake Balaton, available March to mid-October, allowing either 1 or 2 days travel, plus discounted travel to and from the area within 3 or 7 days respectively (family version also available).

Other public transport options
Long-distance buses operated by **Volánbusz** (www.volanbusz.hu). There are plenty of local boat services along the Danube, but do note that the **hydrofoil** service connecting Budapest with Bratislava and Vienna has been withdrawn. But there are still seasonal services from Budapest to Esztergom.

Further information
The website of the National Tourist Board is available online at www.hellohungary.com. *Tourinform* branches exist throughout Hungary.

Accommodation

There is a wide range of accommodation. For the medium to lower price bracket, **private rooms** are very good value, as are **small pensions**. Steer clear of the old Soviet-style tourist hotels and youth hostels as they are very

basic with limited facilities. However, in Budapest especially, a new generation of **independent hostels** are offering dorm rooms at a much higher
standard. Campsites are, on the whole, very good and can be found near the
main resorts. Many have cabins to rent.

FOOD AND DRINK

Cuisine has been much influenced by Austria, Germany and Turkey. Most
restaurants offer a cheap fixed-price menu. Lunch is the main meal of the
day, and a bowl of *gulyás* (goulash) laced with potatoes and **spiced with
paprika** is a 'must'. Try smoked sausages, soups (sour cherry soup is superb)
and paprika noodles or pike-perch. Hungary has some decent wines, such
as *Tokaji* and *Egri Bikavér* (Bull's Blood), while *pálinka* is a fiery schnapps.

ICELAND

This remote **North Atlantic island** did a great favour to railway operators
over much of Europe in spring 2010 by exporting so much volcanic ash that
flights across Europe were paralysed. Of course, you'll not get to Iceland by
train but there is an excellent **ferry link** from Hirtshals in Denmark (on
Route 29). A land of wild fjords and volcanoes awaits. And it is not quite
devoid of trains. On the dockside in Reykjavík you'll see a preserved steam
locomotive that once ran on the local harbour railway. Read more about
travelling to Iceland in our **Sidetracks** feature on p276.

Essentials: Local name: Ísland – Population: 33k – Capital: Reykjavík – Currency: Icelandic
króna (ISK) – Language: Icelandic (Danish and English are widely spoken) – Accommodation
costs: generally high – Plug types: C, F – Time zone: winter and summer GMT – International
dialling code: +354 – Public holidays: 1 Jan; Maundy Thursday; Easter Monday; 21 Apr; 1
May; Ascension Day; Whit Monday; 17 June; 25–26 Dec.

IRELAND

Much more than merely Britain's sidekick, the Republic of Ireland is assertively independent and punches far above its weight on the European stage.
Six counties in the north of Ireland continue to be administered by direct
rule from Westminster (ie. by the UK government), yet many aspects of economic, cultural and sporting life in Northern Ireland and the Republic are
seamlessly integrated. That will surely change with Brexit. There are fabulous landscapes across Ireland, with highlights being the Antrim glens in
the north and the rugged Atlantic coast, notably in Connemara and Kerry.

Essentials: Local name: Poblacht na hÉireann (or Éire for short) – Population: 4.9m – Capital:
Dublin – Currency: Euro (EUR) – Languages: Gaeilge (Irish), English – Accommodation costs:
medium – Plug type: G – Time zone: winter GMT, summer GMT+1 – International dialling
code: +353 – Public holidays: 1 Jan; 17 Mar; Easter Mon; 1st Mon in May; 1st Mon in June; 1st
Mon in Aug; last Mon in Oct; 25–26 Dec.

TRAVEL IN IRELAND

Route 4 and **5** in *Europe by Rail* explore Ireland, with one of them having originated in Rotterdam and the other in London. Ireland has a modern rail network hubbed on Dublin with one route extending across the border to Belfast (for an onward connection by rail to Derry).

RAIL PASSES

Eurail and Interrail are both valid, not just throughout the Republic but in **neighbouring Northern Ireland** too. Before investing in a first-class pass, note that first-class seating is only routine on fast trains from Dublin to Belfast or Cork. For the purposes of One-Country Passes, Northern Ireland is combined with the Republic in a single unit. That means that the One-Country Pass Great Britain (and all Britrail Passes) are not valid in any part of Ireland. Trekker and Explorer are available for unlimited rail travel in the Republic.

OTHER PUBLIC TRANSPORT OPTIONS

Cross-country rail travel in Ireland is limited, with most rail routes leading to or from Dublin or Belfast. The very comfortable **Bus Éireann long-distance coaches** nicely fill the gaps in the rail network (www.buseireann.ie). Good ferry links with Roscoff and Cherbourg (the latter on **Route 9**) allow a visit to Ireland conveniently to be combined with France. There's a wide choice of short-hop ferry links with Scotland and Wales. For those who don't mind a longer time afloat, there are direct ferries from both Dublin and Belfast to Merseyside.

FURTHER INFORMATION

The website of the national tourist board is online at www.discoverireland.ie.

ACCOMMODATION

Hotels are generally of a very high standard with a price tag to match. There are many **independent hotels**, the best of them full of character, which knock spots off the faceless chain hotels. There's at good selection at www.originalirishhotels.com. **An Óige** (www.anoige.ie) manages a network of about two dozen youth hostels and there's also a lively independent hostels scene (see www.hostels-ireland.com).

FOOD AND DRINK

The **Irish breakfast** is legendary and packed with enough calories to set you up for the day. Irish beef and lamb are renowned staples, complemented by excellent fish and seafood in coastal areas and all major cities. There are plenty of good quality cheeses, many from independent producers. As to drinks, don't miss the creamy stout (of which **Guinness** is just one example) and Irish whiskey. Despite the first class ingredients to hand, Ireland still serves up some culinary disasters. Anyone for lasagne with garlic fries?

ITALY

Italy has been on the tourist trail since the days of the 18th-century 'Grand Tour', offering a mix of **art, history and landscape** arguably unrivalled in

The Bigo in Genoa's old port is a landmark in the Mediterranean city (photo © Aniramka33)

any other European country. It is not for nothing that the pundits say 'see Rome and die'. But Italian passion and flair comes with a nice dose of chaos too, and for unhurried travellers prepared to slip gently into the Italian way of life, the country is deeply seductive.

Essentials: Local name: Italia – Population: 60.8m – Capital: Rome/Roma – Currency: Euro (EUR) – Language: Italian, German in Alto Adige (many speak English in cities and tourist areas) – Accommodation costs: medium – Plug types: C, F, L – Time zone: winter GMT+1, summer GMT+2 – International dialling code: +39 – Public holidays: 1, 6 Jan; Easter Monday; 25 Apr; 1 May, 2 June, 15 Aug; 1 Nov; 8, 25, 26 Dec. Regional saints' days: 25 Apr in Venice; 24 June in Florence, Genoa and Turin; 29 June in Rome; 11 July in Palermo; 19 Sept in Naples; 4 Oct in Bologna; 6 Dec in Bari; 7 Dec in Milan.

TRAVEL IN ITALY

Italy features principally on **Route 40 to 44** in this book. In addition, **Route 27, 34, 36** and **39**, while more focused on territory beyond Italy's borders, start or end in Italy. Although headlined by its showpiece 1,000-km-long Torino to Salerno **high-speed line** via Milan, Rome and Naples, with sleek Frecciarossa and Frecciargento trains linking the principal cities in double-quick time, there is also no shortage of railways of the slow and scenic variety in Italy. The fastest trains (at premium fares) are classified *Alta Velocità* (AV) services, and all Frecciarossa and Frecciargento trains require advance reservation, as do the Eurocity trains to Austria via Bolzano and the Brenner Pass. Frecciabianca trains are fast premium services which run on traditional rail lines. There are refreshments on most **long-distance trains**. Italy has a good **night train network** with first and second class in both sleeping and couchette compartments. Train travel in Italy is generally good value. For the best fares, book long-distance journeys well in advance.

The national rail company is **Trenitalia** (www.trenitalia.com), a division of *Ferrovie dello Stato* (FS). Private operator **NTV Italo** (www.italotreno.it) competes with Trenitalia on the high-speed routes from Turin, Milan and Venice to Rome and Naples. **Trenord** operates local services mainly in the Lombardia region (www.trenord.it). French TGVs connect Paris with Turin and Milan and direct EC services to northern Italy arrive from Geneva, Zurich, Basel, Frankfurt, Munich and Vienna. **Thello** operates an EC service from Marseille and Nice to Milan (www.thello.com).

RAIL PASSES
Interrail and Eurail are both valid. There are no locally sold national passes in Italy, but some city passes include trains and cover a wide area extending well beyond the municipal border.

OTHER PUBLIC TRANSPORT OPTIONS
Various regional bus companies operate. Buses are often crowded, but regular and serve many areas inaccessible by rail. Services are however drastically reduced at weekends.

FURTHER INFORMATION
The website of the Italian Tourist Baord is at www.italia.it. All regions and most towns have Tourist Boards and tourist offices, usually called APT or IAT but, confusingly, the name depends on the area.

ACCOMMODATION

Hotel prices are often per room rather than per person, with Venice, Florence and Amalfi Coast particularly pricey. Most establishments style themselves *hotel* or *albergo*, but some more basic hotels are still called *locande*. **B&Bs** are booming, with lists available from tourist offices. **HI youth hostels** are plentiful, with around 80 members; prices include sheets and breakfast (www.hihostels.com). **Independent hostels**, of varying standards, can be found in all the main tourist destinations. Some 'hostels' are glorified guesthouses, and are small, family-run affairs, often with restricted check-in times and lacking common rooms or other social areas.

Camping is popular, but sites are often tricky to reach without a car. Most tend to be upmarket camping villages with bars, restaurants and pools, often also with accommodation in cabins. Farm stays and B&B in cottages and estates is well-established. **Agriturismo** (www.agriturismo.it) is a good first port of call.

FOOD AND DRINK

In Italy, meals are an **important social occasion**, but food is far more varied than the pasta and pizza stereotypes. A full meal may consist of *antipasti* (cold cuts, grilled vegetables, bruschetta), followed by *pasta*, a main course, then fruit, cheese or a *semi-freddo* (cold desserts, like tiramisu) or superb ice cream (*gelato*). Much of the pleasure of eating in Italy is derived from the sheer **freshness and quality** of the ingredients. *Trattorie* are simple establishments and are cheaper than *ristoranti* while *osterie* vary from simple and unpretentious to pricey gentrified-rustic restaurants. For drinking, try an *enoteca*, a wine bar, which may do light meals. *Alimentari* stores often prepare good picnic rolls while a *rosticceria* sells meaty takeaways, and *tavole calde* have cheap self-service. Coffee (*caffè*) comes in tiny shots of espresso. There are many **fine Italian wines**, though Italian beer tends to be bottled. Bars are good places to get a snack, such as a roll or toasted sandwich. In restaurants, be aware of cover charges (*coperto*) and service (*servizio*), both of which will be added to your bill.

Kosovo

Europe's **newest nation state**, Kosovo controversially seceded from Serbia in 2008, leaving the international community divided on whether the upstart country deserved recognition.

As of autumn 2019, just over half of UN members recognise Kosovo as a legitimate sovereign state. Even the EU is divided on the issue, but 23 of the Union's 28 members have recognised Kosovo. The country is best visited by train from Skopje, so entering from North Macedonia and leaving again the same way. Read more in our **Sidetracks** on p405. Limited train services within Kosovo are operated by **Trainkos** (www.trainkos.com). An excellent website (www.kosrail.de; only in German) on the affairs of the Kosovan railways is run by Raphael J Krammer. **Serbian Railways** (ZS) operate a limited train service into Kosovo from Serbia (ERT 1375) but there is no point served by both ZS and Trainkos passenger trains. In 2019, the European Bank for Reconstruction and Development has been financing rail improvement work in Kosovo. Until the programme is complete, Kosovo offers a very retro railway experience. Enjoy it while it lasts.

Essentials: Local name: Kosovë/Kosovo (Косово) – Population: 1.8m – Capital: Prishtinë/ Priština – Currency: Euro (EUR) – Languages: Albanian, Serbian, Romani, Gorani – Accommodation costs: generally low – Plug types: C, F – Time zone: winter GMT+1, summer GMT+2 – International dialling code: +383 – Public holidays: 1 Jan; Orthodox Christmas; 17 Feb; Catholic Easter Mon; 9 Apr; 1, 9 May; Orthodox Easter Mon; Eid al-Fitr; Eid al-Adha; 25 Dec.

Latvia

Latvia secured independence from the Soviet Union in 1991 and joined the EU in 2004. Silvery beaches, the **finest forests** you've ever seen and some **showpiece cities** combine to make affordable Latvia one of Europe's most promising destinations. You'll find an interesting ethnic mix, with about one third of the population speaking Russian and preserving many aspects of Russian culture and customs.

Essentials: Local name: Latvija – Population: 2m – Capital: Riga/Rīga – Currency: Euro (EUR) – Languages: Latvian (spoken by two thirds of the population), Russian (English spoken by younger people) – Accommodation costs: medium – Plug types: C, F – Time zone: winter GMT+2, summer GMT+3 – International dialling code: +371 – Public holidays: 1 Jan; Good Fri; Easter Monday; 1, 4 May; 23–24 June; 18 Nov; 25, 26, 31 Dec.

TRAVEL IN LATVIA

Latvia is on **Route 51** in this book. Domestic train services are sparse and international services even more so. The country uses the Russian broader gauge rather than the western European standard gauge. There are very limited cross-border train services into Lithuania. Most travellers take a bus. However, comfortable **overnight trains** operate from Riga to St Petersburg, Moscow and Minsk (remember that most travellers need a visa for journeys to Belarus or Russia). Latvia's national rail operator is **Pasažieru vilciens** (PV) and has a website at www.pv.lv.

RAIL PASSES
Neither Interrail nor Eurail are valid. There are no local passes, but rail fares are unbelievably cheap.

OTHER PUBLIC TRANSPORT OPTIONS
Buses provide a more extensive service than train for journeys within Latvia and for that matter also across the country's borders. Bus tickets can be purchased at bus stations or directly from the driver. **Lux Express** (www.luxexpress.eu) buses connect Riga with St Petersburg, Kaliningrad, Vilnius, Tallinn, Moscow, Vienna, Pärnu and Budapest.

FURTHER INFORMATION
Website: www.latvia.travel.

ACCOMMODATION

The best selection of hotels in Latvia is available in Riga, the nearby seaside resort of Jūrmala and the bohemian city of Liepāja on the west coast of Latvia. Most **camping facilities** are located near the nation's 495 km of coastline, but cheap country lodging and homestays can be arranged online via **Lauku ceļotājs** (www.celotajs.lv). The Latvian capital offers dozens of good hostels.

FOOD AND DRINK

Many Latvian dishes are accompanied by a richly seasoned gravy, and are usually eaten with superb rye bread. Pork and peas are staples. **Latvian beer** (*alus*) is good and strong – try Bauskas, Tērvete or Užavas. The bitter **Riga Black Balsam** is famous throughout the former Soviet Union and is considered very good for your health. Add it to coffee, cheap sparkling wine and cocktails, or just drink it on its own, whether you're ailing or not.

LIECHTENSTEIN

The bite-sized alpine Principality of Liechtenstein is set between the River Rhine and the mountains to the east. Enigmatic Liechtenstein shares borders with Austria and Switzerland and is traversed by **Route 35** which takes in the only railway line to cross Liechtenstein territory. All rail passes valid in Austria are deemed to also include Liechtenstein.

Essentials: Local name: Fürstentum Liechtenstein – Population: 37k – Capital: Vaduz – Currency: Swiss franc (CHF) – Language: German (English is widely spoken) – Accommodation costs: generally high – Plug types: C, J – Time zone: winter GMT+1, summer GMT+2 – International dialling code: +423 – Public holidays: 1, 6 Jan; Easter Monday; 1 May; Ascension Day; Whit Monday; Corpus Christi; 15 Aug; 8 Sept; 1 Nov; 8, 25–26 Dec.

LITHUANIA

Largest of the three **Baltic States** (though only fractionally larger than Latvia), Lithuania is able to refer back to a more glorious history than its Baltic neighbours, having been part of the influential Polish-Lithuanian Commonwealth from 1569 to 1795. Nowadays a place for sculptural stork nests, Europe's finest sand spit and a glorious capital city in Vilnius, Lithuania is cheap, friendly and desperate to welcome visitors. The fact that there are almost no train services into Lithuania from its EU neighbours doesn't encourage visitors. Limited cross-border services to Poland run at weekends; they use the new *Rail Baltica* route to Białystok.

Essentials: Local name: Lietuva – Population: 2.9m – Capital: Vilnius – Currency: Euro (EUR) – Languages: Lithuanian, Russian (English is widely spoken, as is German on the coast) – Accommodation costs: medium – Plug types: C, F – Time zone: winter GMT+2, summer GMT+3 – International dialling code: +370 – Public holidays: 1 Jan; 16 Feb; 11 Mar; Easter Monday; 1 May; 24 June; 6 July; 15 Aug; 1 Nov; 25, 26 Dec.

TRAVEL IN LITHUANIA

Lithuania does not feature on any of our 52 routes. The country has a **thin domestic rail network** with services from Vilnius to Kaunas, Klaipėda and Turmantas and a new link to Vilnius airport. There is a through train to St Petersburg, as well as good services to Minsk, Moscow and Russia's Baltic exclave at Kaliningrad. The national operator is **Lietuvos Geležinkeliai** (GZ) with a website at www.litrail.lt. Most railway lines are of the Russian broad gauge. The line to Poland has been rebuilt, as part of the *Rail Baltica* project (see p439), to the standard gauge more common in western Europe.

RAIL PASSES
Both Eurail and Interrail are valid. There are no local passes, but rail fares are very cheap.

OTHER PUBLIC TRANSPORT OPTIONS
Cheap for Westerners. Long-distance buses operated by **Lux Express** (www. luxexpress. eu) provide links from Vilnius to Riga, Prague, Warsaw, Tallinn, Budapest, Berlin and Vienna.

FURTHER INFORMATION
The Lithuanian State Department of Tourism has a website at www.lithuania.travel.

ACCOMMODATION

Lithuania has an extensive system of tourist information offices that cover all the main towns and can help you find accommodation, also private **B&Bs**. The latter are mostly available in Vilnius, Kaunas, Klaipėda, Palanga and places on the Curonian Spit. Hostels of the Lithuanian Youth Hostel Association are thin on the ground.

FOOD AND DRINK

Local specialities include: *cepelinai* (the national dish – dumplings stuffed with meat), *blynai* (mini pancakes) and *kotletai* (not the cutlets you might expect, but minced meat balls). Or try *šaltibarščiai*, cold beetroot soup with cream and cold eggs usually served with potatoes. Fish and dairy products are common in all dishes. Lithuanians eat their evening meal early and in smaller restaurants you should aim to order by 19.00. Vodka is the main spirit, Lithuanian beer (try Utenos or Svyturys) is easily available.

LUXEMBOURG

The Grand Duchy of Luxembourg covers some pretty terrain for hiking, with river valleys, forests and hills, giving way to a more industrial landscape along the southern border (with neighbouring France). The **forested sandstone hills** of the north-east, abutting onto Germany, are an oasis of calm

Vianden Castle, Luxembourg. The Grand Duchy is on **Route 19** in this book (photo © Robert Paul van Beets)

rurality in an otherwise rather crowded part of Europe. The country's eponymous capital has a dramatic and picturesque setting, straddling two gorges.

Essentials: Local name: Luxembourg/Lëtzebuerg – Population: 5k – Capital: Luxembourg/ Luxemburg – Currency: Euro (EUR) – Languages: Lëtzebuergesch, French and German (most people speak some English) – Accommodation costs: generally high – Plug types: C, F – Time zone: winter GMT+1, summer GMT+2 – International dialling code: +352 – Public holidays: 1 Jan; Easter Monday; 1 May; Ascension Day; Whit Monday; 23 June; 15 Aug; 1 Nov; 25, 26 Dec.

TRAVEL IN LUXEMBOURG

The small, modern and efficient rail network links Luxembourg city with most areas, the longest line being the picturesque route northwards to the Belgian border at Gouvy and on to Liège (part of **Route 19** in this book). Most stations are small with few facilities. The national rail company is **Société Nationale des Chemins de fer Luxembourgeois** (CFL), www.cfl. lu. From 1 March 2020, all domestic rail travel will be free.

RAIL PASSES
Both Eurail and Interrail are valid. The **Dagesbilljee/Billet longue durée** gives a day's unlimited travel on all public transport throughout the country for just €4 in second class or €6 in first class. The **Saar-Lor-Lux Ticket** is available for 1–5 people in second class for weekend travel on local trains covering Germany's Saarland, Luxembourg and the French region of Lorraine.

OTHER PUBLIC TRANSPORT OPTIONS
Good bus network linking Luxembourg city with towns and villages across the Grand Duchy and into neighbouring countries. Timetables are online at www.mobiliteit.lu.

FURTHER INFORMATION
Luxembourg City Tourist Office, 30 place Guillaume II (www.luxembourg-city.com). The National Tourist Office has a website at www.visitluxembourg.com.

ACCOMMODATION

The National Tourist Office has free brochures featuring hotels (of all grades, plus restaurants), holiday apartments, farm holidays and camping in the Grand Duchy, plus a bed and breakfast booklet that covers all three Benelux countries. There are nine **youth hostels**. The price of bed and breakfast includes linen and varies from 'standard' category to the slightly pricier 'comfort' category. Non-members pay a supplement. See www. youthhostels.lu for details.

FOOD AND DRINK

Cuisine has been pithily described as 'French quality, German quantity', but **eating out is pricey**. Keep costs down by making lunch your main meal and looking out for special deals: *plat du jour* (single course) or *menu* (two to three courses). Local specialities include: Ardennes ham, *träipen* (black pudding), *gromperekichelcher* (fried potato patties) and in September *quetschentaart* (a flan featuring dark plums).

Malta

Island archipelago (with three inhabited islands) in the Mediterranean. Explore the densely populated main island (Malta itself) and you'll find **old railway stations** in Mdina and Birkirkara. But the railway line that linked them was closed in 1931 and Malta is now a country without trains, although a 2017 government announcement hinted of a possible urban rail network. Malta has good ferry **links from Sicily**, so you can conclude **Route 44** with a sea voyage to Malta from the port of Pozzallo, south-west of Siracusa.

Essentials: Local name: Repubblika ta' Malta – Population: 5k – Capital: Valletta – Currency: Euro (EUR) – Languages: Maltese, English (Italian widely understood) – Accommodation costs: medium – Plug type: G – Time zone: winter GMT+1, summer GMT+2 – International dialling code: +356 – Public holidays: 1 Jan; 10 Feb; 19 Mar; Good Friday; 31 Mar; 1 May; 7, 29 June; 15 Aug; 8, 21 Sept; 8, 13, 25 Dec.

Moldova

The **landlocked country** of Moldova just touches the Danube and shares common borders with Ukraine and Romania. Moldova slipped quietly to independence as the Soviet Union was preoccupied with the August 1991 coup attempt in Moscow, and has been riven by strife ever since with the easternmost part of the country, called Transnistria, insisting that it is a separate state. Despite those difficulties, Moldova is an engagingly different place to visit with some beautiful wetlands, amazing old monasteries and **charmingly antiquated railways**. A paradise for those who appreciate slow travel!

Essentials: Local name: Republica Moldova – Population: 3.5m – Capital: Chişinău – Currency: Moldovan leu (MDL) – Language: Moldovan, Romanian, Russian – Accommodation costs: generally low – Plug types: C, F – Time zone: winter GMT+2, summer GMT+3 – International dialling code: +373 – Public holidays: 1 Jan; Orthodox Christmas; 8 Mar; 1 May; Orthodox Easter Monday; 9 May; 27, 31 Aug; 25 Dec.

Monaco

This tiny sovereign city state, a **constitutional monarchy** presided over by the Grimaldi family, is tucked away on a prime strip of real estate in the middle of the French Riviera. The main railway line from Nice to the Italian border at Ventimiglia (on **Route 40** in this book) cuts through Monaco or, more properly, under Monaco for most of this stretch is buried away in a tunnel. So not a lot of potential for sightseeing by train, but you can stop off at the sole station, called **Monaco-Monte Carlo** (in ERT 25, 360 and 361). All rail passes valid for France are deemed to include Monaco.

Essentials: Local name: Principauté de Monaco – Population: 38k – Capital: Monaco Ville – Currency: Euro (EUR) – Languages: French, Monégasque, Italian (English commonly understood) – Accommodation costs: generally high – Plug types: C, D, E, F – Time zone: winter GMT+1, summer GMT+2 – International dialling code: +377 – Public holidays: 1, 27 Jan; Easter Monday; 1 May; Ascension Day; Whit Monday; Corpus Christi; 15 Aug; 1, 19 Nov; 8, 25 Dec.

MONTENEGRO

The small **Adriatic republic** of Montenegro was part of socialist Yugoslavia. Upon the demise of the latter, it remained in a loose union with Serbia. Montenegro eventually split from Serbia in 2006 (without any of the problems associated with the later secession of Kosovo, for Montenegro was never politically integrated into Serbia). The left-leaning government in the capital **Podgorica** walks a political tightrope, maintaining good relations with both Moscow and the European Union. The country has fabulous coastal scenery, backed by the wild mountain landscapes of the Dinaric Alps. In the Bay of Kotor, Montenegro boasts the most spectacular fjord-like landscape of the entire Mediterranean region.

There has been some unflattering ribbon development in some of the coastal resorts, but even on the coast it's still possible to find unspoilt areas. One example is the **Luštica Peninsula** just by the entrance to the Bay of Kotor. In the far south of the country, Montenegro shares southern Europe's largest lake with neighbouring Albania. It's called *Skadarsko jezero* in Montenegrin (Lake Skadar).

A dash of **Venetian influence**, especially on the coast, along with the legacy of Habsburg and Ottoman adventurers, all combine to make Montenegro immensely appealing.

Essentials: Local name: Crna Gora/Црна Гора – Population: 7k – Capital: Podgorica – Currency: Euro (EUR) – Languages: Montenegrin, Serbian (English and Italian widely understood in coastal resorts) – Accommodation costs: generally low – Plug types: C, F – Time zone: winter GMT+1, summer GMT+2 – International dialling code: +382 – Public holidays: 1, 2 Jan; Orthodox Christmas; Orthodox Good Friday; 1 May; Orthodox Easter Monday; 21 May; 13, 14 July.

TRAVEL IN MONTENEGRO

Montenegro is one of Europe's last frontiers and is, for the first time, included in this edition of *Europe by Rail* with a journey from Belgrade to the port of Bar (**Route 45**). Since the country is served by direct trains from Belgrade (ERT 1370), a visit to Montenegro can also easily be combined with **Route 47**. The only other passenger railway within the country is from Podgorica to Montenegro's second city of Nikšić.

There are direct buses from Bar and Kotor to Dubrovnik to join **Route 46**. Passenger trains are operated by **Željeznički prevoz Crne Gore** (www.zcg-prevoz.me) and the only international rail link that exists is with Serbia.

Fares are extremely cheap, with the maximum one-way fare for any domestic journey being only €5.80 (with a €1 supplement if purchased on the train).

RAIL PASSES

Interrail and Eurail Global Passes are both valid, as is the Balkan Flexipass. With such a sparse rail network, it's no surprise that there is no Interrail and Eurail One-Country Pass for Montenegro.

OTHER PUBLIC TRANSPORT OPTIONS

There is a good network of **long-distance buses**, hubbed on the capital city of Podgorica. Air-conditioning is not always available, but the system is otherwise very reliable. You can see which carriers operate a route and buy tickets online at www.busticket4.me. Since Montenegro is not part of the European Union, chances are that border formalities will take a bit longer when crossing into neighbouring countries by bus. During the summer season, privately owned minibuses help tourists get around.

FURTHER INFORMATION

The website of the national tourist organisation is online at www.visit-montenegro.com.

ACCOMMODATION

Roll up on the Montenegrin coast in November or February (when temperatures may still be very mellow) and you can pick up well-appointed rooms for almost nothing. Hotel prices vary massively by season. For rooms in private houses, look for the sign SOBE. The accommodation scene has changed immensely in the last five years, with the emphasis on rather glitzy newly built hotels geared often to the Russian market. Upmarket spa treatments and casinos seem all the rage in Budva and Sveti Stefan.

FOOD AND DRINK

Expect a hefty dose of meat, mainly lamb and veal, plus plenty of fish. The latter may include sea catch, but there's also an ample supply of eel, carp and trout from Lake Skadar. Montenegrins are rightly proud of their dairy products and there's a **good range of locally cured meats**. But the real star, as in Albania, are the fresh salads, often a fabulous mix of tomatoes, cucumbers, peppers and onions topped with cubes of brined cheese. Try the **local wines**, both hefty reds and lighter whites, and the fiery *rakia*.

NETHERLANDS

Canals and 17th- and 18th-century gabled buildings are abiding memories of a visit to the Netherlands, whose numerous historic towns and cities have a strikingly uniform appearance. In between, the **bulb fields and windmills** lend the Dutch farmland a distinctive character. Amsterdam, laid-back and bustling at the same time, justifiably draws most visitors.

Essentials: Local name: Nederland – Population: 17m – Administrative Capital: Amsterdam, Legislative Capital: The Hague/Den Haag – Currency: Euro (EUR) – Language: Dutch (English

Haarlem, Netherlands (photo © Jan Kranendonk)

and German widely spoken) – Accommodation costs: generally high – Plug types: C, F – Time zone: winter GMT+1, summer GMT+2 – International dialling code: +31 – Public holidays: 1 Jan; Easter Monday; 27 Apr; Ascension Day; Whit Monday; 25, 26 Dec.

TRAVEL IN THE NETHERLANDS

The Netherlands are on **Route 17, 19** and **29** in this book. Frequent and modern electric trains, many of which are double-deckers, whizz around the country's dense rail network, linking well-kept stations, some completely modernised, others retaining traditional features such as Delft Blue tiles.

Domestic services fall into three categories: Intercity Direct, Intercity and local trains known as Sprinter or Stoptrein. Intercity Direct services are run on the **high-speed line** from Amsterdam to Schiphol, Rotterdam and Breda. A small supplement is compulsory if your route includes the stretch between Schiphol Airport and Rotterdam. Seat reservations are not necessary except on high-speed international services such as Thalys. A new direct Eurostar service to Amsterdam and Rotterdam from London started in April 2018. There are no international night trains serving the Netherlands. Most services are run by the national rail company **Nederlandse Spoorwegen** (NS), www.ns.nl. Tickets are mostly sold from machines, or online with e-tickets being printed at home. A contactless smartcard, OV-chipkaart, has been introduced for all public transport. Note that it is simply not allowed to board Dutch trains without having pre-purchased a ticket.

RAIL PASSES

Both Interrail and Eurail are valid. The barcode on your pass cover will open the gates at Dutch stations. The **Euregio Maas-Rhein pass** is valid for one day's travel by train and bus in the Maastricht area and over the border into nearby areas of Germany and Belgium (see www.ebrweb.eu/8). The **NS Dagkaart** allows unlimited travel for one day on all NS trains.

Other public transport options

Personalised and anonymous OV-chipkaarts are available for use on the entire public transport system. Chipkaart readers are located on railway platforms and in trams, buses etc. (swipe your card at the beginning and end of your journey).

Further information

A useful website is at www.holland.com. Tourist offices (VVV – *Vereniging voor Vreemde-lingenverkeer*) bear signs showing a triangle with three Vs.

Accommodation

Hotel standards are high and lower prices reflect limited facilities rather than poor quality. Booking is advisable. As a backpacker-magnet, **Amsterdam** has a wide range of independent hostels to choose from, although elsewhere in the country a better bet are the official **Stayokay youth hostels** (www.stayokay.com). Tourist offices (VVV) have listings of bed and breakfast accommodation in their area, where it exists.

Food and drink

Dutch cuisine is mainly **simple and substantial**: fish or meat, potatoes and vegetables. Many Indonesian restaurants offer spicy food and in cities a good variety of international cuisine is available. Most cheaper eating joints stay open all day. Some restaurants in smaller places take last orders by 21.30 or 22.00. Look for boards saying *dagschotel* (a very economical 'special'). 'Brown cafés' (traditional pubs) also serve good-value food.

Specialities include **apple pie** (heavy on cinnamon and sultanas), herring marinated in brine, smoked eels, *poffertjes* (tiny puff-pancakes with icing sugar) and *pannenkoeken* (pancakes: try bacon with syrup). **Street stalls** for snacks abound, options invariably including *frites/patates* (a cross between French fries and British chips) with mayonnaise or other sauces. **Excellent coffee** everywhere, often topped with whipped cream – *slagroom*.

Dutch beer is topped by two fingers of froth. Most local liqueurs are excellent. The main spirit is **Jenever**, a strong, slightly oily gin made from juniper berries.

North Macedonia

The Republic of North Macedonia is one of several countries that appeared on the political map of Europe following the break-up of Yugoslavia. The country has had an ongoing spat with neighbouring Greece over the use of the name Macedonia which was amicably resolved in 2019 when the country adopted the name North Macedonia. Too often overlooked by travellers, North Macedonia is a wonderful kaleidoscope of **Balkan life and culture**, and we hope that its inclusion in *Europe by Rail* in a new Sidetracks feature (see p405) helps it become better known.

There is an international rail link with **Kosovo** (Prishtinë) via Ferizaj/
Урошевац. Slow and infrequent **domestic services** link Skopje with Bitola
(Битола), Kočani (Кочани), Kičevo (Кичево), Tetovo (Тетово) and Prilep
(Прилеп). In late 2017, a funding package was agreed for a new line from
Skopje to the Bulgarian border. The North Macedonian national rail opera-
tor **Makedonski Železnici**, has a website at www.mzt.mk. Interrail, Eurail
and the Balkan Flexipass are all valid.

Essentials: Local name: Republika Severna Makedonija/Република Северна Македонија –
Population: 2m – Capital: Skopje/Скопје – Currency: Macedonian denar (MKD) – Languages:
Macedonian, Albanian – Accommodation costs: generally low – Plug types: C, F – Time zone:
winter GMT+1, summer GMT+2 – International dialling code: +389 – Public holidays: 1 Jan;
Orthodox Christmas; Orthodox Easter Monday; 1, 24 May; Ramazan Bajram; 2 Aug; 8 Sept;
11, 23 Oct; 8 Dec.

NORWAY

Stretching far **beyond the Arctic Circle** and as far east as a shared frontier
with Russia, Norway is one of Europe's great natural wonderlands. The
country's majestic fjords — massive watery corridors created scouring
glaciers — make up one of the finest coastlines in the world, backed by wild
mountainous terrain. The downside is the cost. Prices are higher than in
most of the rest of Europe, and even by camping or hostelling and living
frugally, you'll inevitably notice the difference. Be sure to stock up on the
essentials before you go.

Essentials: Local name: Norge – Population: 5.2m – Capital: Oslo – Currency: Norwegian
krone (NOK) – Language: Norwegian, i.e. Bokmål and Nynorsk (English widely spoken) –
Accommodation costs: generally high – Plug types: C, F – Time zone: winter GMT+1, summer
GMT+2 – International dialling code: +47 – Public holidays: 1 Jan; Maundy Thursday; Good
Friday; Easter Monday; 1, 17 May; Ascension Day; Whit Monday; 25, 26 Dec.

TRAVEL IN NORWAY

Norway is blessed with some of the most scenic railway lines in Europe. A
selection of those feature on **Route 29, 30, 31, 32 and 51** in this book.

In April 2019, the national rail operator NSB was renamed and rebrand-
ed as **Vy** (www.vy.no). Expect further big changes in mid-2020 when the
Swedish national operator SJ will take over a number of long-distance routes
in Norway. Seat reservations are recommended on long-distance trains. In
addition to standard class, many long- and medium-distance trains have
NSB Komfort areas (equivalent to first class) for a fixed supplement, which
includes complimentary tea and coffee. Reserved seats are not marked other
than on your confirmation. There's a good **night train network** and sleeping
cars have two-berth compartments, all available with a standard-class ticket
plus a supplement. Long-distance trains convey a bistro car serving hot and
cold meals, drinks and snacks.

Rail passes
Norway is covered by the Interrail and Eurail schemes. The **Flåm railway** is treated like a private line – Interrail and Eurail pass holders are however granted a 30% discount on the fare.

Other public transport options
Train, boat and bus **schedules are interlinked** to provide good connections. Often worth using buses or boats to connect two dead-end lines (e.g. Bergen and Stavanger), rather than retracing your route. Rail passes sometimes offer good discounts, even free travel, on linking services. **NOR-WAY Bussekspress** (www.nor-way.no) and **Nettbuss** (www.nettbuss.no), now also branded as **Vy**, are two big express bus operators. Long-distance buses: comfortable, with reclining seats, ample leg room. Tickets: buy on board or reserve.

Further information
Website: www.visitnorway.com. Tourist offices (*Turistinformasjon*) and tourist boards (*Reiselivslag*) can be found in virtually all towns; free maps, brochures etc available.

Accommodation

Because Norway is so expensive, the **youth hostel network** is a real asset if you don't want to break the bank. There are some 75 hostels (*vandrerhjem*), many of which are unfortunately only open between mid-June and mid-August. The standard of hostel accommodation is very high, with singles, doubles and dormitories, and there's a good geographical spread. Booking ahead is highly recommended, especially in summer (www.hihostels.no). Private houses can be quite good value, and in some cases almost the same price as hostels. More upscale are guesthouses and pensions.

Hotels are generally very pricey, but many cut rates at weekends and in summer. **Advance booking** is important, especially in Oslo, Bergen and Stavanger. Many of the more than 1,200 official **campsites** have cabins (*hytter*), sleeping two–four people and are equipped with a kitchen and maybe a bathroom. Rough camping is permitted as long as you don't intrude on residents (you must be 150 m from them) and leave no trace of your stay. Never light fires in summer.

Food and drink

Eating out is **very pricey** and you will save a lot by self-catering. Stock up at supermarkets and at *konditori* (bakeries), which often serve sandwiches and pastries cheaply. Restaurants sometimes have *dagens rett* (daily specials), relatively inexpensive full meals. Self-service cafeterias are also generally reasonable. Bigger towns have the usual array of fast food joints, plus hot dog and baked-potato stalls on the street; you may find *smørbrød*, the ubiquitous and diverse open sandwich, more appetising.

Lunch is normally 12.00–15.00, and sometimes features all-you-can-eat *koldtbord* at a fixed price, for a lot less than the equivalent evening meal. Dinner is 18.00–22.00 in towns, but may end earlier in rural areas.

Fresh fish is abundant, with numerous dishes based on salmon and trout. Meat is generally costlier, and includes *elg* (elk) and *reinsdyr* (reindeer), as well as hearty stews, sausages and *kjøttkaker* (meatballs). Anything above an alcohol content of 4.75% is sold at the state-run **Vinmonopolet** stores. Bottles of wines and spirits are quite reasonable when purchased there, while purchasing a glass of wine at a restaurant or bar is universally expensive.

POLAND

In the space of just a few years, Poland has established itself as one of Europe's **prime travel destinations**. Superb old city squares, many quite Italianate in character, and some dazzling Baltic beaches are just the start. There are stunning lake landscapes (especially in Masuria), memorably beautiful mountains (in the south of the country), tremendous nightlife and enough shrines to keep a shine on your rosary.

Essentials: Local name: Polska – Population: 38.5m – Capital: Warsaw/Warszawa – Currency: Złoty (PLN) – Language: Polish (English spoken by younger Poles, German by older ones) – Accommodation costs: medium – Plug types: C, E – Time zone: winter GMT+1, summer GMT+2 – International dialling code: +48 – Public holidays: 1, 6 Jan; Easter Monday; 1, 3 May; Corpus Christi; 15 Aug; 1, 11 Nov; 25–26 Dec.

TRAVEL IN POLAND

Poland features on **Route 48, 49** and **50** in *Europe by Rail*. The country has a **decent rail network** linking all major cities, though services in some rural areas can be infrequent. Timetables change with disconcerting frequency and the various rail operators lurch from one financial crisis to the next. There are two separate subsidiaries of the national railway: **PKP Intercity** (www. intercity.pl) operates Express Intercity (EIC), Express Intercity Premium (EIP), Intercity (IC) and TLK trains, in addition to international Eurocity (EC) and EuroNight (EN) services, whilst **Przewozy Regionalne** (www. polregio.pl) operates the slower and more local REGIO (R), InterREGIO (IR) and REGIO Ekspres (RE) trains, some of which nevertheless cover quite long distances. TLK trains are cheaper daytime and overnight services. Reservation is compulsory on EIC, EC and some TLK trains. Not all long-distance trains have refreshments. **Night trains** have first and second-class sleepers, second-class couchettes and seated accommodation.

RAIL PASSES
Both Interrail and Eurail are valid. PKP Intercity has a **weekend ticket** valid 19.00 Friday to 06.00 Monday, plus a similar **Bilet Podróżnika** (Traveller ticket) for TLK and IC trains only. Przewozy Regionalne has the **REGIOkarnet** valid for any 3 days out of 2 months, and **Bilet Turystyczny** valid 18.00 Friday to 06.00 Monday.

OTHER PUBLIC TRANSPORT OPTIONS
PKS Express buses are cheap and practical. Tickets normally include seat reservations (book at bus station). In rural areas, bus drivers often halt between official stops if you

wave them down. For longer-distance journeys, both within Poland and internationally, PolskiBus offers improbably cheap fares to those prepared to book a week or two in advance (www.PolskiBus.com).

FURTHER INFORMATION
The Polish Tourist Board has a website at www.poland.travel. Tourist offices can usually help with accommodation.

ACCOMMODATION

Expect **huge variations in prices**. A Kraków hotel in high season might charge several times more than a comparable place in a grim industrial city. There is a growing range of **pensions** (*pensjonaty*), which can be great value, but note that breakfast is often charged as an extra. Rooms in private houses (*kwatera prywatna*), often touted to young travellers at main railway stations, are a bit hit and miss. Check you won't be staying out in some distant estate before committing. Youth hostels are often lacklustre and spartan, but there are a growing number of **independent hostels**, especially in Kraków, Wrocław, Warsaw and Zakopane.

FOOD AND DRINK

Kiosks and cafés serve the ubiquitous pizzas, chips and unappealing burgers. A common Polish fast food is *zapiekanka* (cheese and mushrooms on toast). The **wholesome local food** is often excellent value. Look particularly for *pierogi* (tiny dumplings often filled with vegetables or meat), fried or grilled pork, and a great range of soups. *Barszcz* is one of the classics. Beer and vodka are very cheap, the latter coming in a thousand varieties. Try vodka flavoured with honey, juniper or lemon.

PORTUGAL

Portugal once prospered as a **great maritime power** and ruled a far-flung empire across Africa, the Far East and South America. Much of northern Portugal looks positively lush, with landscapes of rolling hills with orange, lemon and olive groves. Head inland to **explore hill country**, dotted with ancient fortified towns, and south to the Algarve for sun, sea and sand.

Essentials: Local name: República Portuguesa – Population: 10.5m – Capital: Lisbon/Lisboa – Currency: Euro (EUR) – Languages: Portuguese, Mirandese (English is a good bet, French or Spanish may be understood) – Accommodation costs: medium – Plug types: C, F – Time zone: winter GMT, summer GMT+1 – International dialling code: +351 – Public holidays: 1 Jan; Good Friday; 25 Apr; 1 May; 10 June; Corpus Christi; 15 Aug; 5 Oct; 1 Nov; 1, 8, 25 Dec. Many local saints' holidays.

TRAVEL IN PORTUGAL

Travel to Portugal by train, following **Route 16** in this book. Extensive modernisation in recent years has given Portugal a first-rate rail network, at least on the main lines, with tilting AP (**Alfa Pendular**) trains providing the fastest services on the core Porto-Lisbon-Faro route, alongside Intercity trains. AP and IC (Intercidades) trains all require compulsory reservation and a supplement is payable. Regional and semi-fast Inter Regional (IR) trains also run on many routes, including the picturesque **Douro Valley line** to Régua and Pocinho. National operator is **Comboios de Portugal** (CP), www.cp.pt.

RAIL PASSES

Apart from Interrail and Eurail, CP has its own **Intra-Rail pass**, for ages 12-30 with free nights at youth hostels, of which there are two different versions: *Xcape* is valid for three consecutive days and *Xplore* for seven consecutive days (not valid on AP trains). Note that you still need to get a physical ticket (which is free) before boarding your train (show your Intra-Rail and ID card at the ticket office). There is also a rail pass for non-residents valid on the entire Portuguese rail network (and also urban trains) for either three (€73) or seven (€129) days in a month. It is called the **Portugal Rail Pass**.

OTHER PUBLIC TRANSPORT OPTIONS

There is a good domestic express bus network run by **Rede expressos** (www.rede-expressos.pt). Buy long-distance bus tickets before boarding. Extend your arm to stop a bus.

FURTHER INFORMATION

Website of the Portuguese Tourist Board: www.visitportugal.com.

ACCOMMODATION

A good bet in most places is to find rooms (*quartos or dormidas*) in a private house, or in a **pension** (*pensão* – more of a business than a house, and graded from 1 to 3 stars). Other inexpensive places are boarding houses (*hospedarias/ casas de hóspedes*) and 1-star hotels. *Pousadas* are state-run places in four categories, with some of them being converted national historic monuments (*Pousadas Históricas*, Historic Pousadas) while others are, for example, in remote locations (*Pousadas Natureza*). More information at www.pousadas.pt.

Lisbon's distinctive yellow *elevadores* (funiculars) tackle steep gradients on their routes across the Portuguese capital. Here the Elevador da Bica (photo © Edyta Pawlowska)

To find out about **youth hostels** see www.pousadasjuventude.pt. For **campsites** contact the Federação de Campismo e Montanhismo de Portugal (www.fcmportugal.com).

Food and drink

The Portuguese pattern of eating is to have a fairly frugal breakfast and two big main meals: lunch (12.00–15.00) and dinner (19.30–22.30). Eating is not expensive but, if your budget is strained, go for the meal of the day, *prato do día or menú*. Eating is taken seriously, the cuisine flavoured with herbs rather than spices and rather heavy on olive oil. There is lots of **delicious seafood**, such as grilled sardines and several varieties of *caldeirada* (fish stew). Other local dishes are *bacalhau* (dried salted cod in various guises) and *leitão* (roasted suckling pig). The most popular pudding is a sweet egg custard. Portugal is, of course, the home of **port**, but there are also several excellent (and often inexpensive) **wines**, such as the *vinho verde* 'green' wines and the rich reds of the Dão and Bairrada regions. Do not be surprised if you are charged for pre-dinner bread, olives or other nibbles that are brought to your table unordered. If you don't want them, say so.

Romania

A member of the EU since 2007, and still hoping to be admitted to the Schengen area, Romania is a world apart from its neighbours. Its linguistic and cultural heritage is **more Romance than Slavic**, and many rural areas of the country are caught in a time warp. This is Europe as it used to be. Travel comes with a few inevitable frustrations, but stay cool and take time to interact with the warmly hospitable locals. The country covers a remarkable range of landscapes from the **rugged Carpathians** to the wetlands of the Danube delta.

Essentials: Local name: România – Population: 19.5m – Capital: Bucharest/București – Currency: Romanian Leu (RON) – Language: Romanian (English understood by younger people, plus some German, and Hungarian throughout Transylvania) – Accommodation costs: generally low – Plug types: C, F – Time zone: winter GMT+2, summer GMT+3 – International dialling code: +40 – Public holidays: 1, 2, 24 Jan; Orthodox Easter Monday; 1 May; Orthodox Pentecost Monday; 15 Aug; 30 Nov; 1, 25, 26 Dec.

Travel in Romania

The natural landscapes and historic cities of Romania are easily explored by rail, with 11,000 km of track to chose from. In this book we feature Romania in **Route 52**. With only a small number of Intercity trains, services can be quite slow, particularly on branch lines. Reservations are required for **long-distance trains**, either at the station or CFR agents. Fares for locally-purchased tickets depend on the type of train; there's a speed supplement for all but local trains. There are *trende persoane* (very slow services), *accelerat* (rather slow), *rapid* and IC services (that's the fastest and most expensive category). Food is only available on IC and some rapid trains, but drinks are occasionally available. **Night trains** offer sleepers and couchettes.

The national railway is **Societatea Naţională de Transport Feroviar de Călători** (CFR), www.cfrcalatori.ro, but some services are run by private operators, including some longer distance trains. Among them are **Regio Călători** (www.regiocalatori.ro) and **Astra Trans Carpatic** (www.astratranscarpatic.ro). Tickets are not interchangeable between companies.

RAIL PASSES
Interrail and Eurail are valid. Romania withdrew from the Balkan Flexipass scheme in 2017, but in 2019 passes were again being accepted but only on Regio Călători services.

OTHER PUBLIC TRANSPORT OPTIONS
There are a number of long-distance bus companies which provide inexpensive links between the country's main cities (see www.autogari.ro).

FURTHER INFORMATION
The Romanian National Tourism Authority has a website at www.romaniatourism.com.

ACCOMMODATION

At the bottom end, hotels can be basic and inexpensive, while some match the highest international standards and prices. **Private rooms** may be booked at tourist offices in some towns, and in a few tourist areas touts will meet trains at the station to offer their rooms — which may be centrally located in attractive old houses, or far out in grim suburban tower blocks, so make sure you know what you're agreeing to. Book in advance for hotels on the **Black Sea coast** in summer and in mountain ski resorts at winter weekends. There are a few decent hostels: see www.hostelz.com for an overview.

FOOD AND DRINK

A small piece of meat (*cotlet*) and chips is staple fare in many restaurants. You could do a lot better by samping *sarmale* which are tasty stuffed cabbage leaves, often without meat. Try the **local soup** (*ciorbă*), stews and rissoles. And if all else fails, there are plenty of takeaway stalls and pizzerias.

Cafés serve **excellent cakes** (*prăjitură*), soft drinks, beer and coffee; *turceasca* is Turkish-style ground coffee, while ness is instant coffee. Wines are superb and very cheap. Try the plum brandy known as *ţuică* (pronounced 'tswica'), or its double-distilled version *pálinca*.

RUSSIAN FEDERATION

That part of the Russian Federation which lies within Europe (viz. west of the Ural Mountains) is very much larger than the entire European Union. Russia is Europe's *terra incognita*, and deserves to be explored much more.

But a **strict visa regime** deters many visitors, although dispensations applicable to cruise ship passengers have now been extended to travellers arriving on scheduled ferry services. In 2019, a simplified e-visa scheme was introduced for Kaliningrad and St Petersburg. The e-visa is free. This new scheme applies to all Europeans except for holders of UK passports.

Even the European part of the country includes constituent republics that hardly figure in Europe's collective consciousness. When did you last hear of Komi, Mordovia or Chuvashia in the news? We dip a toe in the Russian pond with two routes to St Petersburg (see **Route 33** and **50**). Take that route, and travel more widely in the Russian Federation, and you'll inevitably discover that ordinary Russians have a very different view of the world from that which prevails in western Europe.

Essentials: Local name: Rossiya/Россия – Population: 144m – Capital: Moscow/Москва – Currency: Russian rouble (RUB) – Language: Russian. Several other languages are co-official in various regions (English or German are widely spoken by young people in larger cities) – Accommodation costs: medium – Plug types: C, F – Time zone (for the area covered in this book): GMT+3 (summer and winter) – International dialling code: +7 – Public holidays: 1–6 Jan; Orthodox Christmas; 23 Feb; 8 Mar; 1, 9 May; 12 June; 4 Nov.

Travel in Russia

The train was the making of the Russian Empire in tsarist times, and trains were a mainstay of Soviet life — hardly surprising given the essential roadlessness of much of the country in the first decades after the revolution. The **vast distances** covered have dictated that the traditional Russian train is one of sleeping cars of various grades (even including dormitory-style bunks in many cases), designed for daytime use as well as overnight.

A revolution has taken place, however, on the 650-km long Moscow to St Petersburg line with the introduction of **Sapsan high-speed trains** on daytime services, the fastest taking just four hours. A new fast link from **St Petersburg to Helsinki** has been very successful. Fast Swallow trains (called **Lastochka**) have also been introduced between St Petersburg and Veliky Novgorod, between Moscow and Nizhny Novgorod and between Moscow and Tver. New Talgo trains are being introduced and since 2017 have been running west from Moscow to Berlin. New double-deck sleeper trains have revolutionised domestic overnight services, although some travellers still hanker after the old-style communal carriages (see p431). Almost all Russian railway lines are of the Russian broad gauge.

Trains in Russia are operated by **RZD**, www.rzd.ru. All except suburban trains require advance reservation. Some long-distance services run only on alternate days. The ERT gives operating dates where appropriate. Most **sleeping cars** to western and central Europe (and especially on the premium routes from Moscow to Prague, Paris and Nice) are of the standard European type with single and double compartments in first class, 3- or 4-berth compartments in second class. Those trains are very comfortable and new carriages were introduced in 2015.

RAIL PASSES
Eurail and Interrail are not valid.

OTHER PUBLIC TRANSPORT OPTIONS
St Petersburg and Moscow both have the full range of public transport options: metro, trams, buses, trolleybuses and *marshrutkas*. **Lux Express buses** (www.luxexpress.eu) connect St Petersburg and Moscow with the Baltic States.

FURTHER INFORMATION
Website: www.visitrussia.com. Tourist offices exist in major cities.

ACCOMMODATION

There is a great advantage to staying in proper hotels, as they will handle the essential business of **local registration** for you. Your visa must be registered with the authorities in every city you stay. But in the main cities, the smarter hotels geared to western visitors are formidably expensive. There is a new breed of Mini hotels, some **independent hostels** and a lot of apartment rentals – the latter often very good value compared with hotels, but you will need then to handle your own visa registration.

FOOD AND DRINK

If you have travelled east to Russia across the vast North European Plain, enjoying along the way the local diet of meat and potatoes, then Russia comes as a pleasant surprise. The great Soviet experiment of the 20th century brought a wave of **new culinary influences** and you might run across an Azeri or Armenian restaurant in even a smallish Russian city. These exotic influences have tempered traditional Russian cooking too. Look for a wonderful **range of soups**, served both hot and cold, stuffed *pelmeni* or *pirozhki*, good grilled meat (especially *shashlik*) and all manner of spicy stews. According to season, try *kvass* or *sbiten*, the first a refreshing yeasty concoction sold ubiquitously from yellow barrels in summer, and the latter a mead-like hot winter drink. **First-class beer** and a flood of vodka compete with tea. The Russians are the most dedicated **tea** drinkers on the planet.

SAN MARINO

Serenissima Repubblica di San Marino. What a gracious name for a country! The Most Serene Republic of San Marino. Serene is not quite the word that springs to mind on a hot summer day when this little micro state is packed with tourists. This affluent territory, **enclaved within eastern Italy**, is not a member of the EU. Stunning scenery and its quirky political status pull the crowds, and it is well worth a visit. The railway from the Italian city of

Rimini to San Marino has long gone, so you'll have to take a bus nowadays. Although the territory is now train-less, you see **relics of the old railway** at several places in San Marino and some former railway tunnels have now been converted for pedestrian use.

Essentials: Local name: San Marino – Population: 32k – Capital: City of San Marino – Currency: Euro (EUR) – Language: Italian – Accommodation costs: medium – Plug types: C, F, L – Time zone: winter GMT+1, summer GMT+2 – International dialling code: +378 – Public holidays: 1, 6 Jan; 5 Feb; 25 Mar; Easter Monday; 1 Apr; 1 May; Corpus Christi; 28 July; 15 Aug; 3 Sept; 1 Oct; 1, 2 Nov; 8, 25, 26, 31 Dec.

SERBIA

Landlocked Serbia is a country that has reinvented itself. In 1999, NATO was pounding Serbia with aerial bombardment, and the Belgrade government was widely denigrated, at least in the West, for its renegade ways.

How times change! Now Serbia is hip, and angling to become a member of the EU. It may be short on beaches, but it offers other ingredients that make for great travel. The country has good affordable food, a famously vibrant nightlife, **mountain scenery aplenty** (with some decent skiing), some remarkable Orthodox churches and monasteries and bags of cultural history.

Essentials: Local name: Republika Srbija/Република Србија – Population: 7.7m – Capital: Belgrade/Београд – Currency: Serbian dinar (RSD) – Languages: Serbian (in the Vojvodina region also Hungarian, Slovak, Croatian, Rusyn and Romanian); note that Serbian is generally written in the Cyrillic alphabet (many younger Serbs know at least some English) – Accommodation costs: generally low – Plug types: C, F – Time zone: winter GMT+1, summer GMT+2 – International dialling code: +381 – Public holidays: 1, 2 Jan; Orthodox Christmas; 15, 16 Feb; 1, 2 May; Orthodox Good Friday and Easter Monday; 11 Nov.

TRAVEL IN SERBIA

Serbia is on **Route 45** and **47** of *Europe by Rail*. No one travels by train in this Balkan country if they are in a rush. The country's rail network is engagingly antiquated. New Russian rolling stock, introduced five years ago as part of a broader investment package, has brought improvements to some regional services across the country, but for now most **Serbian trains are slow but fun**. The national rail operator is **Železnice Srbije** (ZS), www.zeleznicesrbije.com. The country's timetable and booking site at www.srbvoz.rs. Neither site has much English content.

RAIL PASSES
Interrail and Eurail are valid as is the Balkan Flexipass.

OTHER PUBLIC TRANSPORT OPTIONS
Good network of buses connecting towns throughout the country with main hubs in Belgrade and Novi Sad. Buy tickets in advance at the bus station. Buses are usually comfortable though they might get very crowded on popular routes.

St Sava's Cathedral in Belgrade. The Serbian capital is on **Route 45** and **47** in this book (photo © Guruxox)

FURTHER INFORMATION
The official Tourist Board website is available at www.serbia.travel. The excellent *Bradt Guide* to Serbia by Laurence Mitchell is also a helpful travel companion.

ACCOMMODATION
If you don't mind staying in a charmless concrete block, you'll find **cheap rooms aplenty** in legacy state-run hotels constructed in the Yugoslav period. A growing private sector is bringing new standards with prices to match. There are hostels in Belgrade and Novi Sad, but elsewhere they are few and far between.

FOOD AND DRINK
Serbia is **a carnivore's dream** and you'll find excellent grilled-meat dishes at rock-bottom prices. Expect kebabs and *ćevapčići* aplenty, along with tasty tomatoes and peppers. A good range of snack food includes *burek* and *gibanica*. Serbs are notably restrained in their use of herbs and spices. Try the **decent local wines**, Serbian beer and the fiery plum brandy.

SLOVAKIA
Slovakia has progressed enormously since joining the EU in 2004, adopting the euro in advance of most of its neighbours. Easy to get around, tourist-friendly and still good value, Slovakia is beginning to cut a dash on the central European travel circuit. For real highlights, look to the **High Tatras**

for fabulous mountain scenery and **Carpatho-Ruthenia** for picture-perfect wooden churches and the remarkable Rusyn culture.

Essentials: Local name: Slovensko – Population: 5.4m – Capital: Bratislava – Currency: Euro (EUR) – Languages: Slovak (German, Hungarian in the south; some English and French is spoken) – Accommodation costs: medium – Plug types: C, E – Time zone: winter GMT+1, summer GMT+2 – International dialling code: +421 – Public holidays: 1, 6 Jan; Good Fri; Easter Mon; 1, 8 May; 5 July; 29 Aug; 1, 15 Sept; 1, 17 Nov; 24–26 Dec.

TRAVEL IN SLOVAKIA

The country is included in **Route 25** in this book. Slovakia's **main trunk route** from Bratislava to Košice through Žilina and the foothills of the impressive Tatra Mountains at Poprad-Tatry is well provided for, with fast trains every two hours. A good network covers the rest of the country. An excellent **narrow-gauge network** covers the Tatra Mountain resorts (ERT 1182). EU citizens aged 62 and above can register for free rail travel in Slovakia. Trains can be crowded, so reservation is recommended on express and **night trains** (at station counters marked R). Local services (*osobný*) are very slow. There are also faster Intercity (IC), *expresný* (Ex) and *rýchlik* (R) trains. Domestic night trains run from Bratislava to each of Humenné, Prešov and Košice. Night trains offer sleeping cars, couchettes and seated accommodation. **Železničná spoločnosť' Slovensko** (ŽSSK) is the national operator (www.slovakrail.sk), using the network of ŽSR. Private operators include **Regiojet** (www.regiojet.sk) and **Leo Express** (www.le.cz).

RAIL PASSES
Eurail and Interrail passes are both valid, plus the European East pass for non-European residents.

OTHER PUBLIC TRANSPORT OPTIONS
Comprehensive long-distance bus network, often more direct than rail in upland areas. You can buy tickets from driver, though priority might be given to those with bookings. For **international bus connections** see www.eurobus.sk and www.slovaklines.sk.

FURTHER INFORMATION
The website of the Slovakian Tourist Board is available at www.slovakia.travel.

ACCOMMODATION

There is a wide choice of hotels, private rooms and pensions, and, at a much more basic level, **hostels and inns** with a few spartan rooms, plus *chaty* (simple chalets) and *chalupy* (traditional cottages) in the countryside. Private rooms are often much better than similarly priced cheap hotels. Bratislava has an increasing number of stylish independent hostels.

FOOD AND DRINK

Slovak food has a lot in common with Hungarian food; a typical dish is *bryndzové halušky*, gnocchi with grated bryndza, a ewes' milk cheese that's only produced in Slovakia and Romania. You'll find *rezeň* (*schnitzel*, usually pork), fried chicken and goulash-style stews everywhere, the latter often accompanied by **steamed dumplings** (tasty, even though the habit of serving them in slices looks distinctly unappetising). Good local beers, and decent local wines, many of which are rarely seen outside Slovakia.

Slovenia

Slovenia, a pocket-sized land of beautiful **Alpine mountains and lakes**, undulating farmland and vineyards, blends Mediterranean style with central European efficiency. Not quite the first breakaway from the Yugoslav fold, for Croatia declared independence one day earlier, Slovenia was the first part of former Yugoslavia to join the EU and in 2007 the country also became party to the Schengen Agreement. The country has made fast progress economically, despite a blip in 2014 when a banking crisis cast a shadow over growth. The real surprise for many visitors is to discover a European country so **dedicated to the outdoors** and adventure.

Essentials: Local name: Republika Slovenija – Population: 2m – Capital: Ljubljana – Currency: Euro (EUR) – Language: Slovene (English, German and Italian often spoken in tourist areas) – Accommodation costs: medium – Plug types: C, F – Time zone: winter GMT+1, summer GMT+2 – International dialling code: +386 – Public holidays: 1 Jan; 8 Feb; Easter Mon; 27 Apr; 1–2 May; 25 June; 15 Aug; 31 Oct; 1 Nov; 25–26 Dec.

Travel in Slovenia

Slovenia features in **Route 27** in this book. The country's small and efficient rail network hubbed on Ljubljana mixes the traditional and charming aspects of this mountainous country with more modern features, such as the tilting ICS trains on the Maribor-Koper route.

The national operator is **Slovenske železnice** (SŽ), www.slo-zeleznice. si. ICS trains have compulsory reservation. Other train types include domestic and international long-distance services (IC and EC), international MV trains, EuroNight services (EN) and regional and other local trains (RG, LV). **Catering services** are available on most IC and EC trains and all ICSs. Tickets are available from stations or travel agents.

Rail passes
Interrail and Eurail passes are valid.

Other public transport options
A number of companies offer express bus connections from as far as Sweden and Denmark to Slovenia. **Long-distance bus services** are frequent and inexpensive; usually buy ticket on boarding.

Further information
The website of the Slovenian Tourist Board is at www.slovenia.info.

Accommodation

Refurbished hotels and high standards make for prices comparable to those of other EU countries. Private rooms are an option for the budget conscious, as are hostels.

The official **youth hostel organisation** can be found at www.youth-hostel.si, although the hostel network is concentrated on the alpine north, plus a few options – including independent hostels – in Ljubljana. There are numerous small but well-equipped **campsites**.

Food and drink

Places to eat go by many different names in Slovenia. A restaurant where you are served by a waitress is a *restvracija*, while a *gostilna* is an inn, which typically serves national dishes in a rustic setting. Both sometimes have a set menu (*dnevna kosila*) at lunch, which is usually the least expensive option. There are also a variety of self-service places (*samopostrežna restavracija*) where you can often eat standing. Slovenian cuisine reflects historic ties with Vienna. **Meat and dairy products** predominate: *Wiener schnitzel* (veal in breadcrumbs) is a speciality, as is *pohana piška* (breaded fried chicken), and French fries are served with almost everything. **Coffee shops** offer a wide range of pastries, cakes and ice creams. A *zavitek* is a light pastry filled with cream cheese, either sweet or savoury.

Spain

Inexpensive to travel in and blessed with a warm climate, Spain is **astonishingly varied**, ranging from the fashion-conscious sophistication and pulsing atmospheres of Madrid and Barcelona to rural scenes that look as if they might belong to another continent, or even another century.

It's not consistently beautiful – views from the train might take in ugly high-rise developments or monotonous cereal plains, while on much of the coast there are concrete resorts that sprang up in the 1950s and 1960s to provide cheap holidays. But the **classic Spanish elements** are there too: parched landscapes dotted with cypresses and cacti, backed by rugged sierras; lines of poplars receding to hazy horizons, and red-roofed fortified towns clustered around castles. Some scenes are peculiarly regional: the luxuriant greenness of Galicia; the snowy pinnacles of the Picos de Europa; the canyon-like badlands of Aragon on the southern fringes of the Pyrenees.

Essentials: Local name: España – Population: 46.5m – Capital: Madrid – Currency: Euro (EUR) – Languages: Castilian Spanish (most widely spoken), Catalan (east), Galego (north-west), Euskera (Basque country) (English widely spoken) – Accommodation costs: medium – Plug types: C, F – Time zone: winter GMT+1, summer GMT+2 – International dialling code: +34 – Public holidays: 1, 6 Jan; Good Friday; 1 May; 15 Aug; 12 Oct; 1 Nov; 6, 8, 25 Dec. Many other regional and local saints' holidays.

The Plaza de España in Seville was built for the 1928 Ibero-American Exposition. Seville is on **Route 13** in this book (photo © Zoom-zoom)

TRAVEL IN SPAIN

Spain has long had a prominent place in successive editions of *Europe by Rail*. In this edition, you'll find Spain featured principally on **Route 13 to 16** – and we have three journeys through France leading to Spain (viz. **Route 10 to 12**). Massive **investment in high-speed rail** has put Spain in the major league of European high-speed players, most notably with the Madrid to Barcelona line and the more established line to Seville, 26 years old in 2018. In 2015, new high-speed services were launched from Madrid to Léon, Salamanca and Zamora. An extension beyond Zamora to Galicia will open in 2020. In Spain 'high-speed' doesn't necessarily mean 'boring'. **Route 14**, a giant leap from Barcelona to Málaga, is unusual in being one of only two routes in *Europe by Rail* which rely entirely on high-speed trains (the other one being **Route 18**). There are high-speed trains linking Barcelona with Paris and a dozen other French cities. All major Spanish cities have good connections to Madrid and there are many useful cross-country and regional links. Train services to Granada, temporarily suspended during the construction of a new line, were reinstated in mid-2019.

The Spanish high-speed rail network uses the western standard gauge, while traditional lines run on the **Iberian broad gauge**. There are different train categories, AVE being the principal high-speed trains, along with Avant, Alvia and Altaria trains (the latter two can switch between both gauge types). Media Distancia (MD) trains provide regional services. Nowadays restricted to secondary routes are the slower long-distance Talgo services. *Regionales* are local stopping services and *Cercanías* suburban trains.

The highest-quality **night trains** are known as Trenhotel, which include compartments with en suite facilities. Reservation is essential on the majority of trains, including some regional services, whilst pass holders must purchase seat reservations (often pricey) on all high-speed and certain other long-distance trains. Note that at main stations you'll be required to check in and be on the platform a few minutes before the advertised departure time. The national railway company is **Renfe** (www.renfe.es). Of several **narrow-gauge railways** the largest network is that branded as **FEVE**, in the northern coastal provinces.

Rail passes
Interrail and Eurail passes are valid. Note that many trains require seat reservations.

Other public transport options
Numerous regional bus companies (*empresas*) provide fairly comprehensive and cheap service. Check routes and **book express buses** on www.movelia.es/en.

Further information
The website of the Spanish Tourist Board is at www.spain.info. *Oficinas de Turismo* (tourist offices) can provide maps and information on accommodation and sightseeing, and generally have English-speaking staff. Regional offices stock information on the whole region, municipal offices cover only that city; larger towns have both types of office.

Accommodation

There's generally no problem finding somewhere to stay, outside major festivals and other peak periods; however, some large cities (notably Madrid and Barcelona) can be problematic. By strolling around, you'll often find **budget places** congregated near the station and around the main square. Thanks to a useful hierarchy imposed by regional tourist authorities, **accommodation is graded** according to facilities, from *albergues juveniles* (youth hostels) via basic boarding houses, known variously as *fondas* (look for plaques marked F), *pensiones* (P), *posadas, ventas* and *casas de huéspedes*; then come *hostales* (HS) and *hostales residencias* (HR) up to *hoteles* (H), ranging from 1 to 5 stars.

    Private homes that offer rooms are known as *casas particulares*. They seldom have much by way of facilities, but are usually centrally located and almost invariably very cheap. *Casas rurales* are farmhouses and *refugios* are mountain huts. The **hostel scene** in Spain is developing fast. There are dozens of HI youth hostels around the country (www.reaj.com), as well as an increasing number of independent hostels. Barcelona, Madrid, Sevilla, San Sebastián and Granada all have a particularly good choice of hostel options. There are over 500 **campsites** (some open all year, others just in summer); the Spanish Tourist Office issues a list of the approved ones (*Guía de Campings*), which are classified as luxury, first, second and third class.

Food and drink

The locals take a light breakfast: coffee or hot chocolate with rolls or a *pan con tomate* (toasted bread rubbed with a ripe tomato, and sometimes garlic, and then drizzled with olive oil) or perhaps *churros* (deep-fried fritters dipped in hot chocolate). The main meal is lunch. Dinner is a little lighter, but can still consist of three courses, and is eaten later, around 22.00 in towns. *Platos combinados* and *menú del día* are both good value. If you want an **inexpensive light meal**, ask for raciones, a larger portion of tapas (little more than nibbles, intended as aperitifs). The best-known Spanish dish is *paella*, which originated in Alicante; it is at its best when made to order. Another famous summer dish is *gazpacho* (chilled tomato soup), which originated in Andalucía and is found mainly in the south. Choose your **drinking place** according to what you want to consume. For beer, you need a bar or *cervecería*, for wine a *taberna* or *bodega*. For cider (in the north), you need a *sidrería*. **Coffee** tends to be strong, and usually good. There are some excellent wines (notably, though by no means exclusively, from the Rioja and Ribera del Duero regions) and Jerez is, of course, the home of sherry.

SWEDEN

Scandinavia's largest country includes **huge tracts of forest** and thousands of lakes, with mildly rolling, fertile terrain to the south, and excitingly rugged uplands spilling over the Norwegian border and beyond the Arctic Circle into Lapland. The sheer amount of space is positively exhilarating, and it's the northern stretches that are easily the least populated.

Essentials: Local name: Sverige – Population: 9.8m – Capital: Stockholm – Currency: Swedish krona (SEK) – Languages: Swedish (English widely spoken); Sami and Finnish-speaking minorities – Accommodation costs: generally high – Plug types: C, F – Time zone: winter GMT+1, summer GMT+2 – International dialling code: +46 – Public holidays: 1, 6 Jan; Good Friday; Easter Monday; 1 May; Ascension Day; Whit Monday; 6 June; Midsummer's Eve Day; 25, 26 Dec.

TRAVEL IN SWEDEN

You will find Sweden included in **Route 28, 30, 32, 33** and **51** in this book. The fastest services are operated by **high-speed Snabbtåg** trains, whilst the new **Botniabanan** has begun to revolutionise services from Stockholm to the north. Services are efficient and frequent, though understandably sparse in the far north. Seat reservations are compulsory on night trains and Snabbtåg, the latter also requiring a supplement. Most long-distance trains have refreshments, some also have play areas for children. First-class sleeping cars have en suite facilities. Night trains carry sleeping cars and couchettes. The national rail company is **SJ AB** (www.sj.se). Several other operators are involved on certain routes, as for example **Inlandsbanan AB** (www.inlandsbanan.se), which run the route from Mora to Gällivare. Interrail and Eurail passes are generally valid whatever the operator. SJ fares are demand-driven, with best-value fares available to early bookers.

Rail passes

Interrail and Eurail passes are valid. The SJ Arctic Circle Pass offers a 3-day and 7-day hop-on, hop-off ticket for trains between Kiruna and Narvik.

Other public transport options

Transport system is highly efficient; ferries are covered (in whole or part) by rail passes and city transport cards. Sweden's biggest operator of long-distance buses is **Swebus Express** (www.swebus.se). Advance booking is required on some routes and always advisable in summer; bus terminals usually adjoin train stations.

Further information

Sweden's official tourism website is at www.visitsweden.com. Tourist offices are called *Turistbyrå*.

Accommodation

You can sleep in fair comfort at a reasonable price in Sweden. Tourist offices have listings of most places to stay and charge a small booking fee. Hotel standards are high and the cost usually includes breakfast. There are more than 300 **HI hostels** (*vandrarhem*), about half of which open only in summer; some are extremely characterful places and include castles and boats. Family rooms are available (www.swedishtouristassociation.com). There are also more than 190 **independent hostels** operated by **Sveriges Vandrarhem i Förening** (SVIF) (www.svif.se). Room-only accommodation in private houses is a good budget alternative (contact local tourist offices).

    Sveriges Campingvärdars Riksförbund (SCR), Swedish Camping Site Owners' Association (www.camping.se) lists more than 600 campsites. You can camp rough for one night if you keep more than 150 m from the nearest house and leave no litter.

Food and drink

Hearty buffet breakfasts are a good start to the day. Cafés and fast-food outlets are budget options for later on. *Pytt i panna* is a hefty fry-up; other traditional dishes are **pea soup** served with pancakes, and **Jansson's temptation** (potatoes, onions and anchovies).

    Systembolaget is the state-owned outlet for alcohol – shoppers must be over 20, but you can buy alcoholic beverages in some restaurants, pubs and bars at 18.

Switzerland

Even by European standards, Switzerland packs a lot into a small space, and, despite its **admirable transport system**, it can take a surprisingly long time to explore the country thoroughly, though it's predominantly scenery rather than cities that attracts the appreciable crowds. There are marked regional differences, and four separate official languages.

Zermatt with the Matterhorn in background (photo © Gerd Kohlmus)

Essentials: Local name: Schweiz/Suisse/Svizzera – Population: 8.2m – Capital: Berne/Bern – Currency: Swiss Franc (CHF) – Languages: German, French, Italian, Romansch (English is widespread) – Accommodation costs: generally high – Plug types: C, J – Time zone: winter GMT+1, summer GMT+2 – International dialling code: +41 – Public holidays: 1 Jan; Ascension Day; 1 Aug; 25 Dec. Various additional regional public holidays.

TRAVEL IN SWITZERLAND

Switzerland features principally on **Route 35 to 38** in this volume. **Route 19** and **20** lead south through the Rhine Valley to Switzerland. The country's reputation for being spotlessly clean, efficient, and above all punctual, certainly holds true on the **extensive Swiss rail system**, which covers every town and valley. Of course, if there's a mountain, there will often be a railway involved, with incredible views thrown in. But beware the long tunnels; there is not a lot of landscape to be seen in the new 57-km long Gotthard Base Tunnel. The principal operator is **Swiss Federal Railways** (SBB/CFF/FFS), www.sbb.ch. There are many small private or regionally run railways, particularly in mountainous areas. There is no compulsory reservation on domestic services, except for journeys on the popular *Glacier Express*, the *Bernina Express* and the new *Gotthard Panorama* tourist trains.

RAIL PASSES

Interrail and Eurail passes are valid, but do note that there are restrictions on their use on many mountain railways. The **Swiss Travel Pass** gives non-residents consecutive days on Swiss Railways, boats and buses, plus discounts on mountain railways; valid for 3, 4, 8 or 15 days. The **Swiss Travel Pass Flex** is similar but valid for 3, 4, 8 or 15 days within one month. The **Swiss Transfer Ticket**, for transfer from a Swiss border railway station or airport to one destination and back, was discontinued in 2019.

OTHER PUBLIC TRANSPORT OPTIONS

Swiss buses are famously punctual. Yellow **postbuses** (www.postauto.ch) stop at rail stations.

FURTHER INFORMATION
The official tourism website is at www.myswitzerland.com. Tourist offices in almost every town or village. The standard of information is excellent.

ACCOMMODATION

Swiss hotels have high standards but are expensive. In rural areas and Alpine resorts, it is often possible to get rooms in **private houses** (look for 'Zimmer frei' signs posted in windows and gardens), but these are few and far between in cities. Budget travellers (unless they are camping) rely heavily on **youth hostels** – so book these as far ahead as possible. Every major town and major station has a **hotel-finding service**, sometimes free and seldom expensive. The standard of hostel accommodation in Switzerland is excellent, and there are two organisations worth checking out. The **Swiss Hostels Association** (www.swisshostels.com) is an organisation of privately-run independent hostels, that have agreed to a set criteria of standards, whilst the official youth hostel organisation **Schweizer Jugendherbergen** has locations across the country (www.youthhostel.ch).

Mountain backpackers can stay at huts of the **Swiss Alpine Club (SAC)/ Schweizer Alpenclub** (www.sac-cas.ch); these are primarily climbing huts based at the start of climbing routes, but walkers are welcome. There are also (in more accessible locations) mountain inns known as *Berghotels* or *Auberges de Montagne*, with simple dormitory accommodation as well as private rooms ranging from basic to relatively luxurious. The country has about 450 **campsites** (most open summer only). They are graded on a 1- to 5-star system.

FOOD AND DRINK

Pork and veal are common menu items, but in the lake areas you'll also find fresh fish. **Swiss cheese** is often an ingredient in local dishes; the classic Swiss fondue, for instance, is bread dipped into a pot containing melted cheese, garlic, wine and kirsch. *Raclette*, a speciality of the canton of Valais, is simply melted cheese, served with boiled potatoes, gherkins and onions. The ubiquitous meal accompaniment in German-speaking areas is *Rösti*, fried potatoes and onions, while French Switzerland goes in for stronger tastes, such as smoked sausages. In the Grisons, *Bündnerfleisch* is a tasty raw smoked beef, sliced very thin. Don't miss the UNESCO-listed **Lavaux Vineyards** along the north shore of Lake Geneva (mentioned in **Route 19** and **38**) which produce some of the finest Swiss wines.

TURKEY

Europe meets Asia in Turkey. But before you write off Turkey as not being really European at all, bear it mind that it has in Istanbul the largest city anywhere in Europe. Even on the west side of the **Bosphorus**, you will find mosques, Islamic monuments and oriental-style bazaars and it is important to remember that Islam has been an important aspect of the cultural fabric of Europe for many centuries. Turkey has outstanding relics of Greek and Roman settlement, **superb mountain and coastal scenery** and a population that is ever welcoming to visitors.

Essentials: Local name: Türkiye – Population: 73m – Capital: Ankara – Currency: Turkish Lira (TL) – Language: Turkish (English and German often understood) – Accommodation costs: generally low – Plug types: C, F – Time zone: winter GMT+2, summer GMT+3 – International dialling code: +90 – Public holidays: 1 Jan; 23 Apr; 1, 19 May; Ramadan; 30 Aug; Bayram; 29 Oct.

TRAVEL IN TURKEY

Turkey does not feature in this edition of *Europe by Rail*. Many journeys by train are still tortuously slow, but new **high-speed lines** are transforming Turkish rail travel. When the new Ankara to Konya route opened in 2011, it slashed the journey time from over ten hours to less than two. A new rail tunnel for suburban services under the Bosphorus opened in 2013, linking the Asian and European parts of the country. The final sections of the Ankara to Istanbul high-speed line opened in 2019. Sirkeci as well as Istanbul's iconic Haydarpaşa station are currently closed to rail traffic as part of the rebuilding of exisiting lines in the aftermath of the **Marmaray tunnel project**. Services are operated by **Turkish State Railways** (TCDD). You'll find fares and timetables on www.tcdd.gov.tr.

RAIL PASSES
In addition to Interrail and Eurail passes, the Balkan Flexipass is valid.

OTHER PUBLIC TRANSPORT OPTIONS
Excellent long-distance bus system (generally quicker than rail), run by competing companies, for example **Kamil Koç** (www.kamilkoc.com.tr). Shorter rides are available via *dolmuş* (shared taxis) that pick up passengers like a taxi, but only along a specified route and much cheaper. IDO runs the **ferries** (www.ido.com.tr). Ankara and Istanbul have a modern metro line, Istanbul also has a light-rail and tram route.

FURTHER INFORMATION
The official website of the Turkish Ministry of Tourism is at www.goturkeytourism.com.

ACCOMMODATION

Turkey's accommodation spectrum is as varied and colourful as the country itself. You can hang your hat in converted Ottoman palaces (known as 'Special Licence Hotels') that aren't as expensive as you might think and almost define the word 'atmospheric'. Or try an international hotel that will deliver neither nice surprises nor hideous shocks, or go for a hostel. The **Turkish hostel scene** is particularly well developed and organised. *Pansiyons* (small guesthouses) are a good and affordable overnight option.

Food and drink

Turkish cuisine has many fans, and generally the fare is more varied than in Greece. Try **vegetable stews**, *shish* (lamb) kebabs, pizza and spicy meat dishes, or for a real blowout the all-encompassing meze, with a bit of everything. **Tea** is the national drink, but there are good-value wines and beers, and raki is the highly distinctive aniseed-flavoured brandy.

Ukraine

The former Soviet republic, now assertively independent for 25 years, is the largest country entirely within Europe. The **rich, fertile steppes** so often associated with Ukraine give way to the **Carpathian hills** in the west and wetlands on the Black Sea coast. Although sometimes hard work for travellers, Ukraine has a lot to offer and is remarkably good value. The country is sadly fractured, very oriented to the EU in the west, but with secessionist provinces in the far east. Many who live in the east of the country are deeply suspicious of the European Union. Those who live in the west of the country distrust Russia and have been quick to take advantage of new rules (in mid-2017) allowing Ukrainians to visit the EU without a visa. Read more in our **Sidetracks** feature on p251.

Essentials: Local name: Ukraina/Україна – Population: 44.5m – Capital: Kiev/Київ – Currency: Hryvnia (UAH) – Languages: Ukrainian, Russian; Hungarian-speaking minority (English spoken especially by younger people in major cities) – Accommodation costs: generally low – Plug types: C, F – Time zone: winter GMT+2, summer GMT+3 – International dialling code: +380 – Public holidays: 1 Jan; Orthodox Christmas; 8 Mar; Orthodox Easter Monday; 1, 2, 9 May; Orthodox Pentecost Monday; 28 June; 24 Aug; 14 Oct.

Travel in Ukraine

Ukraine is featured on **Route 26, 48** and **52** in this volume. Rail connections with the Russian Federation have been trimmed, but there are still good **overnight services** from Lviv and Kiev to Moscow. There are presently no rail services from Kiev into Ukraine's easternmost areas (abutting the Russian border) or to the Crimea region. The last two years have seen improvements in train services to the EU. There are new short-hop regional trains across the border into Slovakia, Hungary and Poland as well as longer-distance overnight trains. Vienna now has a direct overnight train to Lviv and Kiev. **Long-distance trains** in Ukraine are similar to Russian types with sleeping accommodation in various configurations designed for both night and daytime use. There are also a growing number of Intercity (IC) trains with seated accommodation. Advance reservation is essential. The operator is **Ukrainski Zaliznytsi** (UZ), www.uz.gov.ua. Tickets can be booked online at http://booking.uz.gov.ua/en. There is also a ticket booking site run by Kiev-based travel agent SoloEast Travel (www.trainticketsukraine.com).

Rail passes
Neither Interrail nor Eurail are valid.

Other public transport options
Extensive and cheap bus network with buses of varying comfort level. *Marshrutkas* (minibuses) are also used. Buy tickets at bus stations in advance or directly from the driver.

Accommodation

Inexpensive, but frankly uninspiring, hotels aplenty in the main cities, many of them concrete blocks that have had little maintenance since the day, long ago, when they first opened their doors to the public. Hot water may be a rarity in these old Soviet piles. The short-lived spate of new entrepreneurialism that followed the Orange Revolution of 2004/5 led to a rash of new small **privately owned hotels**, particularly in Kiev and western Ukraine, many of which are half empty and offer good value for money (with hot water too). There is a nascent independent hostel movement, most conspicuously in Kiev, Lviv and the Ukrainian Carpathian region. There are many **farmstay opportunities** in the Carpathians.

Food and drink

Fertile Ukraine produces a wealth of vegetables that find their way into **soups and stews** – of which the most celebrated is *borscht* (beetroot soup). Crescent-shaped dumplings called *vareniki* are a Ukrainian staple, usually served stuffed with cabbage, potato or cheese. Pork and chicken dishes aplenty, though many Ukrainians may eat meat only rarely. Drinkwise, vodka rules. But there are good local beers and some splendid hefty red wines from the Black Sea region. Try the sweet **kagor**, produced in southern Ukraine or imported from neighbouring Moldova.

Vatican City (Holy See)

Tiny theocratic state that survives as a political island within the Italian capital, and the sole remaining territory of the once much more extensive Stato Pontificio or Papal States. Churches, fabulous art collections and remarkable gardens characterise the planet's smallest country. And there is something for rail travellers too. The Vatican has a few hundred metres of **railway line** and its own train station – in days past generally used only by the Pope. But Pope Francis has brought a breath of fresh air to Vatican transport and now there is a regular Saturday morning train from Città del Vaticano to Castel Gandolfo.

Essentials: Local name: Stato della Città del Vaticano/Status Civitatis Vaticanae – Population: 690 – Capital: Vatican City – Currency: Euro (EUR) – Language: Latin, Italian (English and French spoken) – Plug types: C, F, L —Time zone: winter GMT+1, summer GMT+2 – International dialling code: +3906 – Public holidays: 1, 6 Jan; 11 Feb; 19 Mar; Easter Monday; 1 May; 29 June; 15 Aug; 1 Nov; 8, 25, 26 Dec.

Reference Section

The reference section that follows is packed with factual detail to assist in **journey planning**. You'll surely also want to refer back to this section while travelling. Top of the list are our city links tables, which start overleaf. Use them to check how long it will take to travel by direct train between key cities across Europe.

A WORD ON PLACE NAMES

To kick off this final section of the book, we throw in a thought on a topic which confounds many novice travellers. **Place names** are infinitely mutable. Even within a country you will find multiple renderings of the same place name. Luik, Lüttich and Liège are all the same place – the town in eastern Belgium that English speakers most commonly refer to as Liège.

The city you knew as Cologne when you were planning your journey turns out to be Köln when you reach it. The Viennese, it transpires, don't call their city Vienna, but favour Wien. And the Danish capital is København. Where a city has a very well established **English version** of its place name, then we have used that rather than the native version in this book: so Prague rather than Praha, Munich rather than München, Seville rather than Sevilla.

Before you throw up your hands in despair, rest assured that you'll quickly get used to these **various renderings**. With just a little practice, you'll master the knack of mapping one version onto the other, and by the time you get back home you'll be referring to Venezia and Firenze rather than Venice and Florence. In areas which use the **Cyrillic alphabet**, you'll pick up some interesting variations. Russia's second city (Санкт-Петербург to the locals) is commonly called St Petersburg by English speakers. A more accurate transliteration of the Cyrillic would be Sankt Peterburg.

While you are travelling, you'll almost certainly run across some **odd exonyms**, ie. names used by speakers of other languages to refer to a particular city. Italians often speak of a city called Monaco di Baviera (or sometimes just Monaco) which is in fact Munich. If you catch a train from Hungary to Bratislava, the chances are that it'll be signed as going to Pozsony – that's the Hungarian name for the Slovak capital.

City links

On these pages, you'll be able to see just how long it might take to travel by train between various European cities. The following list shows the **availability of direct trains** between 60 cities and rail hubs across a large part of Europe. We include for each city pair the fastest travel time by a direct train service. We also list direct journeys (where they exist) from any of our 60 cities to three capital cities in eastern Europe which lie beyond the area covered in this edition of *Europe by Rail*. Those three capitals are Moscow, Kiev and Chişinău.

The information we present here is based on timetables current as of October and November 2019. In a small number of cases we have anticipated likely changes to train services in 2020, usually qualifying these with an appropriate note – the key to the notes is on p515.

The numbers in brackets after the emboldened name of each departure city indicate on which **routes in this book** that city features. There are of course a handful of our 60 departure cities which don't feature on any route, but all are within easy reach of one or more of our 52 routes.

You can see here, for each departure city, a selection of places to which you can travel by direct **overnight train (N), daytime train (D)** or **ferry (F)**. These letters follow the destination name. We only include an overnight train if it has proper sleeping accommodation on board. That almost always means sleeping cars, but there are a handful of services which have only couchettes. We do not include overnight trains which only offer seats because, let's face it, that's not a very comfortable way of spending a night.

For each **city pair**, we list the **fastest travel time** by direct train (in hours and minutes), generally rounded up to the closest ten minutes. Note that faster travel times may occasionally be available by indirect services, requiring one or more changes of train along the way. We focus here only on direct trains, even if it's not necessarily the fastest connection. **Overnight trains** are generally slower than daytime trains – a device which nicely allows you to sleep longer. So for city pairs where there is a choice of daytime and overnight direct links, you can be pretty sure that the travel time we quote relates to the daytime service.

Of course, there is an infinite number of other daytime connections across Europe, but we limit this list to direct services only.

Abbreviations

N – Direct night train
D – Direct day train
F – Direct ferry (by day or by night)

For other notes used in the city links tables, see the boxed inset on p515.

Amsterdam (17, 19, 29)
Basel D (6h40)
Berlin D (6h30)
Brussels D (1h50)
Cologne D (2h40)
Frankfurt D (4h)
London DA (4h50)
Marseille D* (7h)
Paris D (3h20)

Athens
Thessaloniki D (4h10)

Barcelona (11, 12, 13, 14)
Lyon D (5h10)
Madrid D (2h30)
Marseille D (4h40)
Paris D (6h30)

Bari
Milan N D (6h50)
Rome N D (3h40)

Basel (19)
Amsterdam D (6h30)
Berlin N D (7h50)
Cologne D (4h)
Frankfurt D (2h50)
Hamburg N D (6h50)
Milan D (4h10)
Munich D (6h10)
Paris D (3h10)
Zurich D (1h)

Belgrade (45, 47)
Budapest NE DE (8h)
Ljubljana N D (10h20)
Sofia D* (10h20)
Vienna DE (11h50)
Zagreb N* D (7h30)

Berlin (21, 23, 25, 48)
Amsterdam D (6h30)
Basel N D (7h50)
Bratislava N D (8h40)
Budapest N D (11h10)
Cologne D (4h20)
Frankfurt D (4h)
Hamburg D (1h50)
Kraków N (10h40)
Minsk N* D* (14h50)
Moscow N* (22h50)

Munich D (4h)
Paris N* (12h40)
Prague D (4h10)
Przemyśl N (14h30)
Vienna N D (7h40)
Warsaw D (5h40)
Zurich N (12h)

Bordeaux (10)
Brussels D* (4h10)
Marseille D (6h)
Paris D (2h10)

Bratislava (25, 35)
Berlin N D (8h30)
Budapest D (2h30)
Hamburg D (11h10)
Kraków N (8h10)
Prague N D (4h)
Vienna D (1h)
Warsaw N D (8h)
Zurich D (9h10)

Brussels (18)
Amsterdam D (1h50)
Bordeaux D* (4h10)
Cologne D (1h50)
Frankfurt D (3h)
London D (2h)
Lyon D (3h30)
Marseille D (5h)
Paris D (1h30)

Bucharest
Budapest N D (14h30)
Chişinău N (13h30)
Kiev N* (25h50)
Sofia D (9h40)
Vienna N (19h20)

Budapest (25, 26, 45, 46)
Belgrade NE DE (7h50)
Berlin N D (11h)
Bratislava D (2h30)
Bucharest N D (15h10)
Hamburg D (13h40)
Kraków N (11h)
Ljubljana N* D (8h10)
Lviv N (13h30)
Munich N D (6h50)
Prague N D (6h30)

Salzburg D (5h20)
Split N* (13h50)
Vienna D (2h50)
Warsaw N D (10h30)
Zagreb D (5h40)
Zurich N D (10h40)

Cádiz (13)
Madrid D (4h)

Cherbourg (9)
Dublin F* (19h)
Paris D (3h)

Cologne (18, 20, 21)
Amsterdam D (2h50)
Basel D (4h)
Berlin D (4h20)
Brussels D (1h50)
Frankfurt D (1h)
Hamburg D (3h40)
Munich N D (4h30)
Paris D (3h20)
Salzburg D (7h40)
Vienna N D (9h)
Zurich D (6h10)

Copenhagen (28, 30)
Göteborg D (3h40)
Hamburg D (5h20)
Oslo F (17h20)
Stockholm D (5h20)

Cork
Dublin D (2h20)

Dublin (4, 5)
Cherbourg F* (19h)
Cork D (2h30)

Edinburgh (2, 3)
Fort William D (5h10)
London N D (4h)
Penzance D (10h30)
York D (2h30)

Florence (41, 42)
Milan D (1h40)
Munich N (10h30)
Rome D (1h30)
Venice D (2h10)
Vienna N (11h)

NOTES

The following notes are shown in **red** in our city links listings:

A – Although direct trains from London to Amsterdam were launched in 2018, the introduction of a direct service from Amsterdam back to London has been deferred until late 2020 or early 2021. Until then, passengers must change in Brussels.
B – During 2020, a short section of this route (about 15 km) may be on a bus.
E – Estimated travel time. Service will be reinstated in December 2019.
L – Passengers on this route are required to alight at **Lille Europe station** to satisfy UK immigration formalities before continuing on the same train to London.
P – Direct daytime services are likely to be introduced between Vienna and Przemyśl and between Prague and Przemyśl in 2020. The journey times are estimates.
Z – A much improved service will be introduced between Munich and Zurich in late 2020. Travel times will then be trimmed by over an hour.
* – Direct trains between these two cities operate **only seasonally** or run on **less than six days or six nights each week**. The asterisk is placed next to the D (for day train) or N (for night train) to indicate which is the irregular service.

Fort William (3)
Edinburgh D (5h30)
London N (12h)

Frankfurt
Amsterdam D (4h)
Basel D (2h50)
Berlin D (4h)
Brussels D (3h10)
Cologne D (1h)
Hamburg D (3h40)
Ljubljana D (10h20)
Lyon D (6h)
Marseille D (8h)
Milan D (7h40)
Munich D (3h10)
Paris D (3h40)
Salzburg D (5h40)
Vienna N D (6h30)
Zagreb D (12h40)
Zurich D (4h)

Göteborg (30)
Copenhagen D (3h40)
Oslo D (4h)
Stockholm D (3h)

Hamburg (25, 28, 29)
Basel N D (6h50)
Berlin D (1h50)
Bratislava D (11h10)
Budapest D (13h40)
Cologne D (3h40)
Copenhagen D (5h20)
Frankfurt D (3h40)
Munich N D (5h50)
Prague D (6h40)
Vienna N D (8h50)
Zurich N D (7h40)

Helsinki (33, 51)
Moscow N (14h40)
Rovaniemi N D (8h)
St Petersburg D F* (3h30)
Stockholm F (17h50)
Tallinn F (2h)

Kraków (48, 49)
Berlin N (11h)
Bratislava N (7h20)
Budapest N (10h)
Lviv N (8h40)
Prague N D (7h20)
Przemyśl D (3h20)
Vienna N D (6h10)
Warsaw D (2h30)

Lisbon (16)
Madrid N (10h20)

Ljubljana (27)
Belgrade N* D (9h)
Budapest N* D (8h20)

(Frankfurt continued)
Frankfurt D (10h20)
Munich N D (6h20)
Salzburg D (4h30)
Vienna D (6h20)
Zagreb D (2h20)
Zurich N (12h10)

London (1, 2, 5, 6)
Amsterdam D (4h)
Brussels D (2h)
Edinburgh N D (4h20)
Fort William N (12h40)
Lyon D* (4h40)
Marseille D* (6h30)
Paris D (2h20)
Penzance N D (5h10)
York D (2h)

Lviv (26, 48, 52)
Budapest N (12h20)
Kiev N D (5h10)
Kraków N (9h30)
Minsk N* (15h40)
Przemyśl D (2h10)
Vienna N (15h20)

Lyon (7)
Barcelona D (5h10)
Brussels D (3h20)
Frankfurt D (6h)
London D*L (5h50)

Marseille D (1h50)
Milan D (5h20)
Nice D (4h40)
Paris D (2h)

Madrid (14)
Barcelona D (2h30)
Cádiz D (4h)
Lisbon N (10h50)
Marseille D (8h)

Marseille (7, 8)
Amsterdam D* (7h30)
Barcelona D (4h40)
Bordeaux D (5h50)
Brussels D (5h10)
Frankfurt D (7h50)
London D*L (7h50)
Lyon D (1h40)
Madrid D (7h50)
Milan D* (7h30)
Nice D (2h40)
Paris D (3h10)

Milan (36, 43)
Bari N D (6h50)
Basel D (4h10)
Florence D (1h40)
Frankfurt D (7h40)
Lyon D (5h50)
Marseille D* (7h30)
Moscow N* (42h40)
Munich N (11h40)
Nice D (4h50)
Paris N D (7h20)
Rome N D (3h)
Venice D (2h30)
Vienna N (12h10)
Warsaw N* (23h40)
Zurich D (3h30)

Minsk (50)
Berlin N* D* (14h)
Kiev N (10h20)
Lviv N* (14h20)
Moscow D N (8h20)
Nice N* (40h20)
Paris N* (30h30)
Prague N* (19h30)
Riga N* (9h10)
St Petersburg N (13h10)

Vienna N* (19h10)
Vilnius D (2h30)

Munich (23, 39)
Basel D (6h)
Berlin D (4h)
Budapest N D (6h50)
Cologne N D (4h30)
Florence N (10h10)
Frankfurt D (3h20)
Hamburg N D (5h50)
Ljubljana N D (6h20)
Milan N (13h10)
Paris D (5h40)
Prague D (5h40)
Rome N (13h10)
Salzburg D (1h30)
Venice N D (6h30)
Vienna N D (4h)
Zagreb N D (8h40)
Zurich DZ (4h40)

Narvik (32)
Stockholm N (18h30)

Nice (8, 40)
Lyon D (4h30)
Marseille D (2h40)
Milan D (4h50)
Minsk N* (39h40)
Moscow N* (48h30)
Paris D (5h50)
Vienna N* (20h30)

Oslo (29, 30, 31, 51)
Bergen N D (6h40)
Copenhagen F (17h20)
Göteborg D (3h40)
Stockholm D (5h40)
Trondheim N D (6h30)

Paris (6, 7, 9, 10, 11)
Amsterdam D (3h20)
Barcelona D (6h20)
Basel D (3h10)
Berlin N* (12h30)
Bordeaux D (2h10)
Brussels D (1h30)
Cherbourg D (3h10)
Cologne D (3h20)
Frankfurt D (3h40)

London D (2h20)
Lyon D (2h)
Marseille D (3h10)
Milan N D (7h10)
Minsk N* (30h10)
Moscow N* (39h)
Munich D (5h40)
Nice D (5h50)
Venice N (14h20)
Warsaw N* (20h10)
Zurich D (4h10)

Penzance (1)
Edinburgh D (10h30)
London N D (5h)
York D (8h)

Prague (24, 25)
Berlin D (4h10)
Bratislava N D (4h)
Budapest N D (6h30)
Hamburg D (6h40)
Kraków N D (7h10)
Minsk N* (18h40)
Moscow N* (27h40)
Munich D (5h40)
Przemyśl DP (10h50)
Vienna D (4h)
Warsaw N D (8h10)
Zurich N (14h20)

Przemyśl (48)
Berlin N (14h40)
Kiev N D (7h10)
Kraków D (3h10)
Lviv D (2h)
Prague DP (10h50)
Vienna DP (10h)

Riga (51)
Kiev N* (20h40)
Minsk N* (9h10)
Moscow N (16h50)
St Petersburg N (16h)
Stockholm F (18h)
Vilnius D* (4h50)

Rome (41, 42, 44)
Bari N D (3h40)
Florence D (1h30)
Milan N D (3h)

Munich N (13h20)
Venice N D (3h40)
Vienna N (13h50)

Rovaniemi
Helsinki N D (8h30)

St Petersburg (33, 50)
Chişinău N* (36h20)
Helsinki D F* (3h30)
Minsk N (13h10)
Moscow N D (3h30)
Riga N (15h50)
Stockholm F* (38h)
Tallinn D F* (7h30)
Vilnius N* (21h)

Salzburg (23, 35)
Budapest D (5h10)
Cologne D (7h50)
Frankfurt D (5h40)
Ljubljana D (4h30)
Munich D (1h30)
Venice N (6h50)
Vienna D (2h30)
Zagreb N D (6h40)
Zurich D (5h30)

Sofia (47)
Belgrade D* (9h50)
Bucharest D (10h)
Thessaloniki DB (7h30)

Split (46)
Budapest N* (14h40)
Zagreb N D (6h10)

Stockholm (28, 32, 51)
Copenhagen D (5h10)
Göteborg D (3h)
Helsinki F (16h40)
Narvik N (18h50)
Oslo D (6h)
Riga F (17h)
St Petersburg F* (38h)

Tallinn (51)
Helsinki F (2h)
Moscow N (16h50)
St Petersburg D (7h10)

Thessaloniki (47)
Athens D (4h10)

Sofia DB (7h30)

Venice (27, 34, 43)
Florence D (2h10)
Milan D (2h30)
Munich N D (6h40)
Paris N (14h20)
Rome N D (3h40)
Salzburg N (7h)
Vienna N D (7h40)
Zurich D (6h30)

Vienna (34, 35)
Belgrade DE (11h40)
Berlin N D (7h50)
Bratislava D (1h)
Bucharest N (19h40)
Budapest D (2h40)
Cologne N D (8h50)
Florence N (11h)
Frankfurt N D (6h30)
Hamburg N D (8h40)
Kiev N (23h40)
Kraków N D (6h30)
Ljubljana D (6h20)
Lviv N (16h30)
Milan N (13h50)
Minsk N* (19h)
Moscow N* (28h)
Munich N D (4h)
Nice N* (21h10)
Prague D (4h)
Przemyśl DP (10h)
Rome N (14h)
Salzburg D (2h30)
Venice N D (7h40)
Warsaw N D (7h)
Zagreb D (6h50)
Zurich N D (7h50)

Vilnius
Kiev N* (15h50)
Minsk D (2h30)
Moscow N (13h10)
Riga D* (4h40)
St Petersburg N* (21h30)

Warsaw (48, 50)
Berlin D (5h40)
Bratislava N D (8h)
Budapest N D (10h20)

Kiev N (17h20)
Kraków D (2h30)
Milan N* (22h40)
Moscow N (15h30)
Paris N* (20h40)
Prague N D (8h10)
Vienna N D (7h10)

York (2, 3)
Edinburgh D (2h30)
London D (2h)
Penzance D (8h)

Zagreb (27, 46, 47)
Belgrade N* D (6h20)
Budapest D (5h50)
Frankfurt D (12h40)
Ljubljana D (2h20)
Munich N D (8h50)
Salzburg N D (7h)
Split N D (6h10)
Vienna D (6h40)
Zurich N (14h50)

Zurich (20, 35, 36, 38)
Basel D (1h)
Berlin N (12h)
Bratislava D (9h10)
Budapest N D (10h40)
Cologne D (6h10)
Frankfurt D (4h)
Hamburg N D (7h40)
Ljubljana N (11h40)
Milan D (3h30)
Munich DZ (4h50)
Paris D (4h10)
Prague N (13h20)
Salzburg D (5h30)
Venice D (6h30)
Vienna N D (7h50)
Zagreb N (14h10)

For an explanation of the annotations in **red** see the box on p515. Bear in mind that rail schedules may change from season to season and year to year.

Planning overnight stays

The question of how much money you might need to explore Europe by train is a tough one. So much depends on **length of journey**, your expectations, the **level of comfort** to which you aspire or the degree of discomfort you are prepared to tolerate. Train tickets booked three months in advance might cost only a quarter (or even less) of what you might pay if you buy tickets on the day of travel. We have made long journeys through Europe on just a pittance, taking advantage of special fare deals, opting for budget accommodation and surviving on a long litany of picnics. On other occasions, we have splashed out and enjoyed the comfort of crisp, clean sheets in air-conditioned sleeping cars and eaten in style in railway restaurant cars. We give more **advice on train fares and ticketing matters** in this book (on pp21–28 and pp525–28 respectively).

Here our focus is on **accommodation prices**. Hotel and hostel pricing policies vary considerably across Europe. In many countries dynamic pricing is the norm, which means that there is virtually no set price, and the rates paid for the same room may vary wildly according to season, day of the week, or even the weather. Britain follows this approach, and it means that travellers may encounter extraordinarily good low-season deals, while prices rocket at times of peak demand.

In many parts of Europe, the maximum price for which a room may be sold is clearly stipulated, and often subject to approval by the authorities. In some countries that may be the price that most travellers effectively pay. Elsewhere there is **regular discounting**, even to the extent that no one ever really pays the full list price.

Negotiating your way through the tariff jungle is not easy. Where deep discounts on room rates are available, they may be reserved for clients who book weeks (or even months) in advance and prepay the full cost of their stay. A growing range of online booking engines sometimes offer cheaper prices than those quoted by the hotel itself. But don't be too seduced by the power of the **online booking sites**. Many of our favourite hotels are small family-run places, which still simply cannot be booked through any of the major online agencies.

We realise that visitors to Europe sometimes place a certain premium on well-known hotel chains. But there are many areas of Europe where the international chains have no presence in the market. And in so far as Hilton or Marriott are there at all, perhaps in a capital city, their hotels are tailored to the international business market rather than to travellers eager to catch the pulse of local life. However, in **major commercial centres** – such as Brussels, Hamburg or Zurich – top-end business hotels may discount so heavily on Friday, Saturday and Sunday nights that travellers with only modest budgets can afford a weekend of rare luxury.

Throughout Europe, the most common way of pricing accommodation is by room. Although hostels sell beds in dorms on a per-bed basis, in most European countries hotels sell, in the main, **rooms for two people**. Where single rooms exist, they will generally cost much more than half the rate for a twin or double. Solo travel can be an expensive business.

Hotel accommodation in cities often costs more than in rural areas, though Europe's blossoming hostel sector, which offers discount accommodation in most cities, is less well represented in the rural regions of many countries. The new generation of **independent hostels** are not like the youth hostels of yesteryear. They attract clients of all ages and many offer private rooms, sometimes with en suite facilities.

Capital cities are often more expensive than elsewhere in the country, but this rule is not infallible. Hotels in Rome can often be better value than those in Florence or Venice. Berlin is often significantly cheaper than Munich or Cologne. We say a few words in the **gazetteer** (pp446–511) about accommodation issues in different countries.

Hotel rates do not always rise and fall in line with other costs. In Belarus and Russia rail travel is very cheap. Food, even in restaurants, can also be very affordable. But hotel prices are higher than you might expect. Folk flock to Andorra for cheap ciggies and alcohol, but that does not mean that hotels are any cheaper than in neighbouring Spain or France.

NOT ALL WHO WANDER ARE LOST

There are many journeys in this book, which can easily be taken without the need to book in advance. They follow routes where train tickets are economical. During low season, when few travellers are out and about, such journeys are well suited to travelling spontaneously. The **sense of freedom** that comes from travelling without knowing where you will rest that evening was a hallmark of travel in the early days of European railways. But it's not for everyone. The modern inclination is to plan every aspect of the journey to such a degree that every risk is minimised and every element of uncertainty banished.

But **some of our very best journeys** have been unstudied, unrehearsed and un-planned. We have set off with a map, the latest issue of the European Rail Timetable, a rail pass and a change of clothes. Not much more. And we have wandered. The point is not to plan, but to **savour the serendipity of chance**. To wander for its own sake. "Not all those who wander are lost," wrote Tolkien in The Lord of the Rings.

Our feeling is that many travellers have lost the capacity to wander. Travelling without knowing your precise destination or even your route is infinitely more exciting than following a well-mapped trail to a pre-booked hotel.

So, in the spirit of an earlier generation of travellers, we sometimes meander on the slowest of slow trains. We **pause at country stations** and eventually we stumble on a little pension, cheap but more than adequate, and there we stop overnight. The manner of the journey is more important than any specific destination. Without a guidebook and without expectation, we are led by a whim. It is a fine way of exploring Europe. Slow travel is fun. You might like to try it some time.

Night trains

It is very likely that, sooner or later on your explorations of Europe by train, you will end up taking an overnight service. Here we offer a few thoughts on what to expect. The first important distinction to make is between a **regular train** that just happens to run through the night and a proper **night train**. The first kind of train is, we feel, generally to be avoided. Yes, we have done it, but just take our word that the overnighter from Timişoara to Sighetu Marmaţiei is not a lot of fun. Following part of **Route 52** through northern Romania, this train has few creature comforts and even our considerable enthusiasm for slow trains waned after a dozen hours aboard. If you must travel by night, then make sure that the train you choose is equipped for overnight travel. Many Romanian overnight trains are. We just opted for the wrong one.

At their best, Europe's night trains are superb. They offer various **grades of sleeping accommodation**. Top of the range are luxury sleepers with en suite facilities. You'll only find these on a small number of trains, and they are not cheap. You will need a first-class ticket (or first-class rail pass) and in addition you'll have to pay a supplement. Second-class (or standard-class) ticket holders can opt for regular sleeping compartments designed for one or more passengers (but usually bookable as a single for an extra charge) or couchettes. The latter are a down-market version of a sleeper. A normal compartment by day converts to simple bunk beds by night. Some night trains also convey carriages with **reclining seats**, thus affording a little more comfort.

While only the most demanding travellers really need the luxury of the very poshest **sleeping compartments** (some of which may include minibars and flat screen TVs), it is worth trading up to a regular sleeper if you can possibly afford it. They are much more comfortable than **couchettes**. Remember you are saving a night's hotel or hostel accommodation and your appreciation of your destination in the morning will be vastly more positive if you have enjoyed a good night's sleep in crisp linen sheets.

Couchettes usually have four to six places per compartment. They are basic, but adequate. Bear in mind that a full six-berth couchette may be no fun in midsummer heat. Sleepers are usually air-conditioned and typically have one to four berths per compartment. **Sheets and towels** are provided, and generally beds are made up for you. Russia, Belarus and Ukraine are rare exceptions. In those countries, the carriage attendant (called a *provodnik*) gives you the sheets, and you make your own bed. Help is always available for the elderly or less agile. But on the excellent Russian trains on journeys to, from or within the EU, your bed will always be made for you.

A shared **two-berth** sleeper compartment usually provides a reasonable measure of comfort. Single travellers booking a berth in a multiple-berth compartment must expect to share with strangers (usually **segregated by gender**). This is a travel experience that, as you move east across the continent, becomes ever more convivial. In Russia, it often involves sharing salami, hard-boiled eggs and life stories with complete strangers. There is no requirement that the stories you tell be true. Some sleeper trains are ideal for **families**. Many Finnish overnight services and the *Caledonian Sleeper* trains from London to Scotland have interconnecting doors between compartments that can be opened to create a larger space for a family.

Especially in central and eastern Europe, a train may include sleeping cars from several different countries. For many night trains, you can check the provenance of sleeping cars and what facilities they have (eg. air conditioning, electric sockets, etc) on **vagonWEB** (www.vagonweb.cz). Choose the English-language version, then select 'composition' and find your service through its train number. Standards may vary widely between the carriages of the various railway administrations. Don't assume that 'east' is bad and 'west' is good. Some of the **most comfortable night trains** we have used are Russian ones, and they now ply many routes within the EU (eg. Paris to Berlin and Verona to Warsaw).

NIGHT TRAIN OPERATORS

Germany, so strategically positioned at the heart of Europe, once offered a fine network of night train services. That is less true nowadays as budget-conscious Germans seem happy to sit up all night in seats. The few remaining Deutsche Bahn CNL night trains disappeared in late 2016, with Austrian operator ÖBB stepping in to pick up many former CNL routes. These run under ÖBB's new *Nightjet* banner. It is thus still very easy to travel in the comfort of a sleeper on overnight trains to, from and within Germany. Trains leave Düsseldorf and Cologne every evening for Munich, Vienna and Innsbruck. *Nightjet* trains also link Munich and Vienna with Rome and Milan.

You will find **useful domestic night train links** within many European countries. It is always worth checking if a night train can usefully complement daytime travel on some of the journeys described in this book. There are excellent Spanish night trains, night trains across Austria, from Helsinki and Turku to the north of Finland, from northern Italy to Sicily and from one corner of Poland to the other. Overnight services leave Oslo and Stockholm each evening, all bound to far-flung corners of their respective countries.

France is a little unusual in that the few remaining overnight trains entirely within France have no sleeping cars, so a couchette is your best option. Conversely, night trains within Spain have no couchette option, instead favouring sleeping cars. Where Spanish night trains also have reclining seats, such carriages are reserved for first-class ticket holders (and on most of these trains there is no second-class seating).

Europe's most distinctive night trains run from Russia to central and western Europe. **Russian Railways** (RZD) offer through carriages from Moscow to far-flung destinations, among them a year-round service to the French Riviera. In 2015, RZD introduced brand-new carriages on its premium routes from Moscow to Helsinki, Paris, Nice and many cities in central Europe.

Check our **city links list** (on pp513–17) where the letter 'N' behind the destination in a city pair indicates that those two cities are linked by a direct night train.

LONDON CONNECTIONS

Britain **lost its proper night train** to the continent in 1980 with the demise of *The Night Ferry*, a train with comfortable *Wagons-Lits* sleeping cars that provided a direct overnight service from London to Paris and Brussels. Hardy souls who don't mind an overnight journey in an ordinary seat can still travel directly from London to the French Alps in winter using Eurostar's Friday evening departure from St Pancras station.

Travellers from Britain might consider using the convenient **night trains from Paris**. An afternoon journey from London to Paris with Eurostar and pre-dinner drinks in the French capital are the natural prelude to an overnight train journey. International night trains from Paris run directly to **Verona** and **Venice** (ERT 44). There is also a weekly direct train from Paris to Berlin, Warsaw and Moscow (ERT 24). In addition French night trains, all sadly without restaurant cars and with couchettes rather than sleeping cars, leave Paris for a number of destinations across France.

It also pays to know in advance if there will be a **restaurant car** on your train. Many menus on night trains nicely anticipate the destination. Thus on the journey from London to the Scottish Highlands you can enjoy haggis and neeps for supper and round off the evening with a good malt whisky in the lounge car.

And on the train from Stockholm to Narvik in northern Norway, a magnificent overnight journey that takes you beyond the Arctic Circle, meat patties made from elk are standard fare on the dinner menu. You can dine *à la russe* in the excellent restaurant car on the night train from Helsinki to Moscow. Some overnight trains may have no restaurant car. Go prepared! On most Russian trains, tea, coffee and a small selection of drinks and light snacks are available from the **carriage attendant**. In Germany and Austria, the train staff can usually provide drinks, soup and sandwiches on night trains with no restaurant car.

Night trains are of course the stuff of romance. They are a scriptwriter's delight – and a cameraman's nightmare, for the sleeping compartment offers few great panoramas when fixed on **celluloid**. That didn't stop Carol Reed in *Night Train to Munich* (1940) and Alfred Hitchcock in *North by Northwest* (1959) from both having a very good try. The mystery of the night train was forever sealed by *Murder on the Orient Express* (1974), where the accomplished music and superb cinematography that attend the train's departure from Istanbul's Sirkeci station more than compensate for the impish Belgian detective's subsequent difficulty in solving the murder that takes place at some unspecified but decidedly Balkan point along the route. Hercule Poirot will not be on your night train, so the chances are that you'll get a good night's sleep. Try it once, and you'll surely be hooked.

Night trains are in a **state of flux**, with fast daytime services trimming demand for overnight connections. We discuss this theme further in our **Sidetracks** feature on p146.

Cruise trains

The emphasis in this book is on independent travel. The rail journeys we recommend rely entirely on regular scheduled train services. We think that's a fine way to explore Europe by rail, but we understand that it is not for everyone. Some travellers prefer the feel of a specialist cruise train, so here we highlight just a couple of first-class ventures.

The most celebrated European cruise train is the **Venice Simplon-Orient-Express** (VSOE). Since 2019, it's been owned by LVMH Moët Hennessy — Louis Vuitton, adding a bit of retro style to that company's daunting portfolio of classy brands. London to Venice is VSOE's signature route, with about four trains per month from late March to mid-November 2020. The 30-hour journey from London includes a night aboard an **elegant heritage train** with beautiful Lalique glass panels and art deco marquetry. Such style does not come cheap. One-way from London to Venice for a couple sharing a double compartment costs over €5,000 (including meals) and over €20,000 for one of the posh grand suites (which are new for 2020). VSOE has a single showpiece trip from **Paris to Istanbul** in 2020, with grand suite fares for a couple running to over €100,000. You can check schedules and fares on www.vsoe.com. With VSOE commanding those sorts of prices, it is no surprise that many entrepreneurs have tried to emulate the VSOE model.

Golden Eagle Luxury Trains is a British company founded in 1989 by Tim Littler, who in the 1990s organised pioneering steam-hauled trains across the entire former Soviet Union. Golden Eagle is a very reliable operation which consistently offers the most adventurous cruise train itineraries in the European market (and beyond). The trains are the *Golden Eagle*, the recently acquired *Golden Eagle Danube Express* and the China-based *Shangri-La Express*.

The Golden Eagle itineraries offered by the two Europe-based trains are mouth-watering. If you want to ride the **Trans-Siberian Railway**, this is the way to do it in style. But take a look at some of their other offerings too: how about the June 2020 **Venice to Istanbul** cruise via Bosnia, North Macedonia and Greece? Golden Eagle here includes a border crossing from Volinja in Croatia to Dobrljin in Bosnia — a rail route which since December 2016 has simply not been used by any scheduled passenger trains. The prices naturally reflect the upmarket product. A couple will pay from €16,590 for that Venice to Istanbul run.

Golden Eagle also offer midwinter journeys from St Petersburg north through the Republic of Karelia to Russia's Kola coast. Now that would be the time to spot the Northern Lights! Read more at www.goldeneagleluxurytrains.com. See p166 for a note on the **El Transcantábrico** cruise trains exploring minor rail routes in northern Spain.

When a train is not a train

There may be times when your train turns out not to be a train at all. Sometimes this might be because of a **festival of track maintenance**, meaning that for a day or two buses replace trains on a particular stretch of line. At other times **buses permanently replace trains** on a 'rail' journey. For example, daytime services operated by Austrian Railways (ÖBB) from Venice to Klagenfurt (ERT 88) are not trains at all, but comfortable double-decker coaches. Similarly, the direct services between Munich or **Nuremberg and Prague** advertised by Deutsche Bahn (ERT 76) are in fact buses. Here at least there is a choice, and devotees of rail travel will much prefer to uses trains to travel from Nuremberg to the Czech Republic (see **Route 24**). The train follows deep wooded valleys and climbs over the hills that separate Bavaria from Bohemia. As so often in Europe, the rail route reveals a perspective on the landscape that is just not visible from the motorway.

RAIL FERRIES

On a few routes in Europe, rail travellers may be surprised to find themselves afloat on a ship. The night train from **Malmö to Berlin** is a fine example (ERT 50). Scarcely an hour into its journey, the train shudders to a halt on the quayside at Trelleborg. The entire train is then shunted onto a ship for a **nocturnal voyage across the Baltic** to Sassnitz in Germany. We have met sound sleepers who, when alighting from the train on arrival in Berlin, had no idea that they had spent four hours afloat during the night. There are routes where a daytime journey by train includes a stretch by ship. One is the **Hamburg to Copenhagen** part of **Route 28**, where until December 2019 the entire train is shipped on a ferry from Puttgarden to Rødby (ERT 720). Passengers can leave the train, stroll the decks of the ship, and enjoy the Baltic breeze on the 45-minute crossing. On **Route 44** trains are regularly loaded onto ships between the Italian mainland and Sicily.

MISSING LINKS

On journeys around Europe you will occasionally need to use a bus to bridge a gap in Europe's rail network. One **missing link in the continent's rail infrastructure** is plugged by the bus across the Tatra Mountains between Slovakia and Poland (ERT 1183).

Other gaps are between Split and Dubrovnik at the end of **Route 46**, on the stretch along the Norwegian coast between the railheads at Bodø and Narvik (ERT 787), on the border between Sweden and Finland on **Route 33** and between Poland and the Baltic States. The latter may (or may not) be ameliorated by the *Rail Baltica* project (read more on p439). Moving east from Trieste into Slovenia (**Route 27**) has long been an aggravating gap, but a new train service has run from Trieste to Ljubljana since late 2018.

Rail pass briefing

If you have just stumbled on this section of the book by chance, we strongly suggest you first read our **feature on tickets** at the start of this book (see pp21–28). In those pages we discuss whether or not a rail pass is even worth considering at all. You may find that individual tickets for the specific journeys you wish to make would together amount to less than the cost of a rail pass. But if you have considered those arguments and still judge that a pass is a plausible option, here are a few key facts.

INTERRAIL AND EURAIL

There were **big changes** in the Interrail and Eurail schemes in 2019, with the two pass programmes effectively converging. So there are now common conditions for both Eurail and Interrail, although promotional offers (eg. low-season discounts) are still geared to particular passes and target specific market segments.

Interrail passes can only be purchased by **residents of Europe** (this includes citizens of the Russian Federation, Turkey and Cyprus). So you need to be a European national, or have lived in Europe (as defined above) for at least six months, to be eligible for an Interrail pass. Eurail is the parallel scheme for those who don't meet the conditions to buy an Interrail pass.

Learn more about the two schemes at www.interrail.eu and www.eurail.com. You'll find up-to-date prices for passes on those two websites, where you can also **purchase passes**. All prices quoted below are valid in October 2019. There may be some price adjustments for 2020.

GLOBAL PASSES

The **classic Interrail product** is the Global Pass and from 2019 that's now effectively true also of Eurail. The Eurail Select Pass range (covering various regions of Europe) has been dropped. For both schemes, there are now **ten varieties** of Global Pass. Five are valid for a **fixed number of days** within a one-month period (3, 5 or 7 days), or a two month period (10 or 15 days respectively). With those variants of the Global Pass you choose exactly which days you want to use the pass. You don't need to decide in advance. You can enter the date in the relevant space on your pass, and head off, knowing that you can enjoy unlimited travel for the rest of that day.

Apart from the five types of passes valid for selected days within a defined period, there are five Global Passes valid for **continuous travel**. No one insists you actually use them every day, but these passes really do allow you to hop on and off trains at will for the entire period that the pass is valid. The periods on offer are 15 or 22 days, and then one, two or three months. We can only wonder if anyone really travels continuously for three months by train and still stays sane.

GLOBAL PASS AREA OF VALIDITY

The Global Passes – both Interrail and Eurail – are valid across much of Europe. Note that the area of validity was enlarged in 2019, with both passes becoming available in Lithuania, and Eurail now being accepted in Great Britain (where previously it was only Interrail that was valid).

The European countries with railways where the passes are **not valid** number just eight: Moldova, Albania, Kosovo, Latvia, Estonia, Belarus, Ukraine and the Russian Federation.

With a Global Pass you can roam from Finland to Portugal, from Scotland to Sicily, from Greece to Ireland. It covers in total **three dozen countries** – even including diminutive Monaco and lovely Liechtenstein. And Global Passes are also valid in Turkey, so you can use your pass all the way to Turkey's eastern border with Iran, though we do just wonder if the staff at Kapıköy – that's Turkey's easternmost railway station – have ever actually seen an Interrail or Eurail pass. The westernmost station in Europe where passes are accepted is Tralee in Ireland.

There's an **important caveat for Interrail**, namely that passes are not valid in the pass holder's country of residence, although a recent and very welcome concession is that Global Pass holders may make a one-day journey within their home country at the start of pass validity (which can be to an airport, seaport or border crossing), and a similar one-day trip to get home at the end of the pass validity.

Supplements are payable on many high-speed and premium-priced trains in a small number of countries, notably France, Spain, Sweden, Italy and Portugal and also on Thalys, Eurostar and Lyria services (see the box on p27 for further information on these supplements and reservation fees).

As well as the national rail operators, passes are often valid on **private or locally run railways**, or in some cases the latter may offer a discount to pass holders. Occasionally there is no discount at all, for example on some Swiss mountain railways. Many ferry companies also give **discounts**, and in fact the Global Pass gives free deck passage on the popular sailings between

SEDUCED BY FREEDOM

The seductive appeal of a **Eurail or Interrail Global Pass** lies in the chance to roam freely across Europe. Of course, as we have seen in our section on tickets at the front of this book (pp21–28), this freedom can be illusory as in some countries railway operators nowadays demand hefty supplements of pass holders.

But the very idea of being able to speed from Hamburg to Budapest on a mere whim is **quite tantalising**. We know of one young Irish traveller who had never once set foot outside his home country until he purchased a Interrail Global Pass. He set off from Cork by ferry for France and a month later was back, having visited 31 countries in 31 days. It was, he said, the worst month of his entire life. He has not once set foot on a train since.

Italy and Greece operated by Superfast Ferries, and Minoan Lines (you will, however, pay port taxes and there are high-season surcharges of €10 to €20 in summer). The pass may also give you discounts on **tourist attractions**, hostels, boat trips and even bike hire, so it's worth checking. There are good listings of these ancillary benefits on www.interrail.eu and www.eurail.com.

GLOBAL PASS PRICES

All passes come in **first and second-class variants**. Prices for Eurail and Interrail passes are the same. Expect to pay 30% more for first class; but there are sometimes special offers, usually in winter, where you can snap up a first-class pass for the price of a second-class one. For every pass there's a 10% discount for **seniors** (aged over 59) and 23% off for **youths** (under 28). Children under 12 travelling with an adult pass holder receive an equivalent kid's pass for free. Additional discounts may be available in special promotions – and for Interrail such promo sales seem pretty frequent.

A first-class Global Pass for three months of continuous travel for an adult costs €1,202. An **entry-level pass** valid for just three days in a month is €216 for an adult with the price for a five-day pass rising to €282. One long return journey across Europe can easily see you recouping the full cost of your pass, perhaps even leaving one or more free days on a three or five-day pass to enjoy an excursion by train from your destination.

A Global Pass valid for 15 days continuous travel in first class is €590 for an adult (€531 for seniors, €505 for youths). A brilliant deal, but before dashing to purchase it, just consider whether the Global Pass valid for 15 days' travel in a two-month period may not be a far better deal. The price for the latter is about 10% more than the 15 day continuous pass.

ONE COUNTRY PASSES (EURAIL & INTERRAIL)

Apart from the classic Global Pass products, both Interrail and Eurail offer passes **valid in just one country**. In addition, there are one-country passes offered by the national rail administrations of certain countries. Let's look at the Interrail and Eurail offer first, but bear in mind that there are rumours that their One Country Pass range may be revamped in 2020, so we give just the bare outlines here.

One Country Passes generally cover just one country, but there are exceptions. Belgium, the Netherlands and Luxembourg are combined together in the **BeNeLux Pass**. Eurail offer a **Scandinavia Pass** (covering Denmark, Norway, Sweden and Finland), but there's no equivalent for Interrail. There is no Eurail One Country Pass for Great Britain, Switzerland or Germany, but Interrail does offer One Country Passes for these territories. Visitors from outside Europe (who are not eligible to purchase Interrail) are nudged towards the one-country passes marketed by the respective national rail administrations (BritRail, Swiss Travel Pass and the German Rail Pass).

USING PASS DAYS WISELY

With Interrail and Eurail passes that are only valid for a certain number of days within a longer period, direct **overnight trains or ferries** are reckoned by their departure date. So if you are using a Global Pass, for example, to roam through Austria for a day, you can then join an overnight train from Vienna to, say, Rome or Berlin and your pass will be valid for the entirety of that journey (subject to any sleeper supplements), even though you don't disembark until the following morning. If on the day of arrival, you are only making a short onward connecting journey, it may be wiser just to buy a regular ticket for that short onward hop. **Pass days are valuable** so if you have a pass just valid for a certain number of days in one or two months, consider carefully whether the extent of your proposed travel warrants use of a pass day.

Eurail and Interrail One Country Passes are sold for a **fixed number of days** within one month (but of course nothing stops you from using your travel days consecutively). You can choose between 3, 4, 5, 6 or 8 travel days. The amount you'll pay depends on the size of the national rail network and the normal cost of rail travel in the country. Our view is that, for some of the cheaper countries, it may still be more economic to buy **point-to-point tickets** for the specific journeys you want to make. And for some of the top-tier countries, the price of a One Country Pass is only marginally below that of a Global Pass. For example, an Interrail One Country Pass for Britain for a youth (aged under 28), valid for three days, second-class travel in a month costs €166. That's not bad value for travel in a region where walk-up fares are pretty high. But the same traveller can pick up a Global Pass for just €168. When you take into account that the **off-season discount promos** for Interrail are usually applicable only to Global Passes, it does mean that a Global Pass price can sometimes undercut the One Country Pass price for the equivalent number of travel days.

OTHER USEFUL PASSES

There are many other passes covering more than one country. These include the **Balkan Flexipass** (covers Bosnia & Herzegovina, Bulgaria, Greece, North Macedonia, Montenegro, Serbia and Turkey) and the European East Pass (Austria, Czech Republic, Hungary and Slovakia).

Useful one-country passes include the **Renfe Spain Pass**, a fine range of **passes for Switzerland**, the **German Rail Pass** (which includes many routes way beyond Germany's borders) and of course BritRail. This latter is a long-established scheme with many variants. The classic **BritRail Pass** covers England, Wales and Scotland, but there are passes covering just Scotland, just England and also more limited areas. They can be excellent value if you are planning a lot of travel within the designated pass area, all the more so if you value spontaneity and don't want to commit to a specific itinerary by booking much cheaper train tickets (known in Britain as Advance tickets) weeks prior to travel. Find out more about BritRail at www.britrail.net.

A–Z of travel in Europe

BICYCLES

Before you start planning a comprehensive tour of Europe by train and bike, just be aware that many railway operators do not take an especially benign view of bicycles. Across much of Europe you can, usually for a small fee, take a bike on many local and regional trains, although restrictions may apply in many urban areas during peak travel times. Move to long-distance trains and the situation becomes much more varied.

For example, most German ICE trains simply have no allocated bike space, so the only way you can transport your bicycle on those trains is if it is folded and carried in a proper bike bag. There is **limited space** for pre-booked bicycles on many German IC trains. Spain is a problem area with bikes barred from all daytime long-distance services, even if they are folded and packed in a **bike bag**. In Finland and the Czech Republic, bicycles can be transported on Pendolino services, but only if pre-booked.

There is a limited amount of space for **pre-booked bicycles** on Eurostar. Some TGVs have bike space, others do not. On Thalys, a bicycle must be folded and packed. Okay, so you get the idea. This is a formidably complicated subject. In summary, many local trains are bike-friendly, but if you are planning stretches on fast trains, you will need to research carefully what trains are able to take your bike and at what price. You can see why many travellers decide to rent a bike at their destination.

BORDERS

Most travellers will need a **valid passport** to travel through Europe. A dispensation allows citizens of any of the 30 members of the **European Economic Area** (EEA), plus Switzerland too, to travel throughout the participating countries with just a National Identity Card.

In practice, passport checks are very low-key in much of Europe nowadays and the only occasions your documents are likely to be checked are at certain border pinch points, eg. entering Germany from Salzburg, crossing into Denmark from Flensburg or on the rail journey from Copenhagen to Malmö.

Such exceptions apart, it's only around the edges of the **Schengen area** and beyond that passports are scrutinised. Schengen consists of more than two dozen countries which are party to the Schengen Agreement, allowing freedom of movement across their mutual borders.

The UK and Ireland are conspicuously not members of Schengen and the UK in particular maintains strict **border controls**, even to the extent that you must pass through UK immigration in Brussels, Paris or Lille before joining Eurostar trains bound for London. The only instance in Europe of passengers being required to detrain to go through immigration formalities is on the direct Eurostar from Marseille to London (ERT 17) where pre-entry checks for the UK take place at Lille Europe.

So it is really only as you enter the UK, Russia, Belarus, Ukraine, Turkey and certain Balkan countries that you will encounter any significant **border bureaucracy**. See also **Visas** and **Customs checks** in this section.

CELLPHONES – SEE TELEPHONES

CHILDREN

Kids and trains just go together. Many children will tolerate a much longer journey on a train than in a car. But don't test their patience too much. Too packed an itinerary just won't wash with most youngsters. On some trains, such as Thalys and selected German ICE services, you'll even find **dedicated family space**. Some trains in Scandinavia and Switzerland have a children's play area. Almost without exception, European rail operators offer **discounted fares** for children.

CLIMATE – SEE SEASONS

CREDIT CARDS

If you come from a country with a strong credit card culture (such as the UK or USA), you may be surprised how little you can use your credit cards in some parts of Europe. Train ticket machines in many countries will not accept credit card payment and you may find that, especially once you get off the main tourist trails, hotels and restaurants will want payment in cash.

Of course in **major cities** payment with plastic is absolutely accepted, but just be aware that this may not apply to more **rural areas**. Where cards are accepted, VISA and MasterCard are your best bets. Some cards, such as AmEx and Diners Club, are quite unknown in many rural regions of Europe.

CYCLES – SEE BICYCLES

CURRENCY

With the uncertainties affecting some of the peripheral countries in the **eurozone**, currency remains a hot topic. At least for now, the euro remains by far the most useful currency for travellers exploring Europe by train. You can draw cash from ATMs across Europe.

Proffering UK pounds or US dollars in continental Europe on the assumption that these are valued currencies in foreign countries often simply invites derision. There's really no substitute for local currencies. In central and eastern Europe, as also in the Balkan region, you will find many more countries that use currencies other than the euro. Our country gazetteer (pp446–511) gives currency details for every territory in Europe.

Customs checks

With the development of the single European market, customs checks are becoming a thing of the past. Just be aware that there are still strict limits on **importing cigarettes and alcohol** from non-EU areas into the European Union. No-one will quibble over 200 cigarettes and a bottle of spirits, but that's about the limit. It goes without saying that narcotics, weapons and pornographic publications can all get you into serious trouble. See also **Borders** in this section.

Disabilities

Travellers with disabilities need to take special care in planning their journeys. The exemplary service provided by **Eurostar** (even with concessionary fares) is not emulated across the continent. On premium long-distance services (TGV, AVE, ICE, etc) there is designated space for wheelchairs and boarding assistance is available if pre-booked. Move to regional and local trains and accessibility is much more patchy. It pays to check carefully before booking.

Electricity

The invisible stuff that comes out of plugs isn't quite the same the world over. Most of the planet, including Europe, uses a 220 to 240 volt system (230 volts is standard across the EU). A small number of countries (including Japan, Taiwan, Mexico, Canada, USA and a handful of Caribbean and central American states) use 110 volts. If you are travelling with dual voltage appliances such as a hair dryer, check that they are correctly set.

Much more troublesome are **plugs which vary enormously**. A universal plug adaptor is a wise investment. And ponder on a continent that devotes enormous effort to standardising the size of strawberries but still has a bewildering variety of electrical sockets. See www.iec.ch/worldplugs for details.

Insurance

If you live in one of the 32 countries that are party to the EHIC scheme, make sure you get a **European Health Insurance Card** before leaving home. That will cover some (but by no means all) emergency medical expenses within the EHIC area. So best to take out **travel insurance** that covers additional medical expenses (including repatriation if necessary) as well as theft or loss of your belongings. Remember to take out insurance at an early stage, as most policies only provide cancellation cover for transport bookings and hotel reservations made *after* you have taken out the insurance.

Language

Use our **gazetteer** (pp446–511) to check which languages are spoken in each country. English will get you a long way across most of Europe, but it is presumptuous to assume that everyone you meet speaks English. Make sure you master at least a few words of the local lingo. And as you head east, it is important you are able to decipher the **Cyrillic alphabet**, if only to be able to transliterate place names.

Mobile phones – see Telephones

Passports – see Borders

Plugs – see Electricity

Rail passes – see pages 525–28

Seasons

As an area significantly larger than the continental United States, it'll be no surprise that Europe encompasses a great range of **climate zones**. Mainland Europe alone takes in 65° of longitude and 35° of latitude. Of course you really can follow the routes in this book at any time of year, but there can be a special pleasure in travelling to places at times when there are fewer folk on the move. Trains in many parts of Europe are significantly quieter in winter than in summer (provided of course you can avoid the Christmas and New Year rush and you are not bound for the main skiing areas). Our view is that **spring and autumn** are the best seasons for exploring Europe by rail. So April, May, September and October. But bear in mind that the timing of seasons varies greatly across the continent. The southern areas of Spain and Italy may have idyllic spring weather in late March, while at the same time northern Scandinavia and the Alps may still have deep snow.

Smoking bans

A smoking ban on all **public transport** and in some **public places** has prevailed in some European countries for over 25 years, augmented over the last ten years with more bans extended to cover cafés, bars and restaurants. Most of Europe now has such bans, with smoking rarely allowed on trains.

Telephones

If your mobile phone (**cellphone**) is enabled for roaming (ask your provider before leaving home if you're unsure), you'll be able to use it anywhere in Europe where your phone picks up an adequate signal and can log onto a network. It is no longer always the case that you incur a charge to receive calls when abroad. Thanks to an European Union initiative, the costs of receiving and making calls and sending texts have plummeted in recent years. End-user roaming charges were abolished in 2017. This benefits only those with EU SIM cards and applies only to communications within the EU.

If you plan on making a lot of calls from one country, you might consider the merits of buying a local SIM card. **Payphones** are still available in cities and at major rail stations. Increasingly they rely on **prepaid cards** (commonly available from newsstands and in some countries from post offices) rather than cash. Avoid making long calls from phones in hotel rooms. They are invariably expensive.

TIME ZONES

Europe's great longitudinal spread from west to east means that it extends over **seven time zones** (from the Azores to European Russia). Bear in mind that several routes in the book cross time zone boundaries. You can check the time zone for each country in the **gazetteer** section of this book (see pp446–511).

All but four countries mentioned in this book seasonally adjust their clocks, moving them forward an hour on the last Sunday in March and putting them back on the last Sunday in October. The four exceptions are Iceland, Belarus, Turkey and the Russian Federation.

TRAIN TICKETS – SEE PAGES 21–28

VISAS

EU passport holders can follow all but two of the routes in this book without having to worry about visas. The exception are **Route 33** and **50**, and you can read more about what's needed there by way of visas on p424. Much the same applies to citizens of EEA member states outside the EU, and passport holders from Switzerland, Japan, Australia, Canada and the United States. Yet even within these general precepts there are some intriguing exceptions. Australians need a visa to enter Ukraine (which features in **Route 26, 48** and **52** in this book). Note that citizens of many European countries (those outside the EEA or EU) require a visa to enter the United Kingdom.

We live in a divided world and citizens of most African countries, as well as those from Asia (except for Japan and one or two others), will need to secure one or more visas for almost every route described in this book. The same applies to holders of passports from the **Commonwealth of Independent States** (including the Russian Federation) and some Latin American countries. If in doubt, check out what visas might be necessary before purchasing tickets. The consular departments of the embassies of countries you propose to visit will always advise.

Index

In this index, we list the principal places and personalities mentioned in our 52 routes and elsewhere in the book. We also include some train names and selected thematic topics. See the **gazetteer** for country-by-country information. Country names are generally not included in this index.

Postscript

Rail travel has moved in and out of fashion. Today more people than ever before are **travelling by train across Europe**, whether for business or leisure. Over a quarter of a century, successive editions of *Europe by Rail* have helped shape the travel habits of a generation. Over 140,000 copies of the title have been purchased.

Of course, the book is just part of the story. More and more people these days incline towards rail rather than air travel, aware that part of the pleasure of a train trip is that the journey becomes part of the holiday.

On our travels around Europe, we have always valued good maps, be they online or paper ones. We've already mentioned the **Rail Map Europe** published by European Rail Timetable Ltd (see pages p10 and p15). Dedicated rail travellers may also enjoy Mike Ball's excellent **European Railway Atlas**. The comprehensive all-Europe edition really is the one to go for, but Mike also does concise and regional editions. Find out more at www.europeanrailwayatlas.com.

If you share our enthusiasm for maps, you can follow every route in this book in our **specially prepared online maps**. The weblinks shown at the start of each route (eg. www.ebrweb.eu/map1 for **Route 1**) will take you directly to the map for that route on the book's dedicated website at www.europebyrail.eu.

FEEDBACK REQUEST

We hope you've valued using this book as much as we've enjoyed creating it. If you identify errors, or if you'd like to give some feedback, **we'd love to hear from you**. Which routes did you follow? What did you find good about the book? What worked less well? Just send your comments to the authors, Nicky Gardner and Susanne Kries, at editors@europebyrail.eu.

★★★

ALSO FROM HIDDEN EUROPE PUBLICATIONS

Europe by Rail is a product of *hidden europe publications*, a Berlin-based publisher with a strong track record in promoting Slow Travel. If you like the style and approach of this book, then you will surely enjoy *hidden europe* magazine which is edited by the authors of *Europe by Rail*, Nicky Gardner and Susanne Kries.

With its focus on cultures and communities across Europe, *hidden europe* magazine has helped give a new edge to travel writing. No glitz, no gloss and definitely no infinity pools. But well-woven words about lesser-known places across Europe. The magazine is published thrice each year and mailed to subscribers across the world. Annual subscriptions are €23 (for destinations within Europe) or €26 (for destinations outside Europe), including postage. Find out more at www.hiddeneurope.co.uk.